EMPOWERED COLLEGE READING

MOTIVATION MATTERS

Linda A. Lee

San Diego Miramar College

Upper Saddle River, New Jersey 07458

Library of Congress Cataloging-in-Publication Data

Lee, Linda A.
Empowered college reading : motivation matters / Linda A. Lee.
p.m.
Includes index.
ISBN 0-13-183893-8
1. Reading (Higher education) 2. Reading comprehension. 3. Motivation in education 4. College readers. I. Title.
LB2395.3.L45 2008
428.40711--dc22 2006034374

Editorial Director: Leah Jewell
Executive Editor: Craig Campanella
Editorial Assistant: Deborah Doyle
Director of Operations/Associate Director Production: Barbara Kittle
Manufacturing Manager: Nick Sklitsis
Manufacturing Buyer: Benjamin Smith
Production Liaison: Joanne Hakim
Production Editor: Jessica Balch, Pine Tree Composition
Director of Marketing: Brandy Dawson
Marketing Manager: Kate Mitchell
Marketing Assistant: Kimberly Caldwell
Editor-in-Chief, Development: Rochelle Diogenes
Associate Director Development, English: Alexis Walker
Development Editor: Susan Messer
Senior Media Editor: Christian Lee
Creative Design Director: Leslie Osher
Art Director: Amy Rosen
Interior and Cover Design: Anne DeMarinis
Line Art Manager: Pine Tree Composition
Cover Photos: Back—Kay Blaschke/Stock 4B/Getty Images, Inc.; Spine—Soohn Matthieu/PhotoAlto/Getty Images, Inc.; Front—Kaoru Fujimoto/taxi/Getty Images, Inc.
Permissions Specialist: Mary Dalton Hoffman
Director, Image Resource Center: Melinda Patelli
Manager, Rights and Permissions: Zina Arabia
Manager, Visual Research: Beth Brenzel
Manager, Cover Visual Research & Permissions: Karen Sanatar
Photo Researcher: Beaura Kathy Ringrose
Image Permission Coordinator: Annette Linder
Composition/Full-Service Project Management: Pine Tree Composition
Printer/Binder: Quebecor Taunton
Cover Printer: Coral Graphics

Credits and acknowledgments borrowed from other sources and reproduced, with permission, in this textbook appear on pages 610–612.

Pearson Education LTD., London
Pearson Education Singapore, Pte. Ltd
Pearson Education, Canada, Ltd
Pearson Education–Japan
Pearson Education Australia PTY, Limited
Pearson Education North Asia Ltd
Pearson Educación de Mexico, S.A. de C.V.
Pearson Education Malaysia, Pte. Ltd
Pearson Education, Upper Saddle River, New Jersey

10 9 8 7 6 5 4 3 2 1
0-13-183893-8
978-0-13-183893-2

To Dana,

my inspiration

BRIEF CONTENTS

UNIT ONE: MOTIVATED READING

1 The Power of Motivation 1

2 Active Reading 31

10 Evaluating Arguments 469

The Reader 535

Reading for Learning Texts 535

The CD-ROM

The Motivation Measure

Reading for Learning Texts

Textbook Chapters

Subject Area Readings

The primary essays, articles, and textbook materials in *Empowered College Reading* are organized below by discipline, along with the type of text. Essays are texts that focus on the author's ideas and articles report on an event (see Chapter 9). The textbook materials are all excerpts from college textbooks, except for the two full chapters which are marked with asterisks (*). The Letters are Letters to the Editor.

A Note to Instructors

How Do You Motivate Your Students to Read?

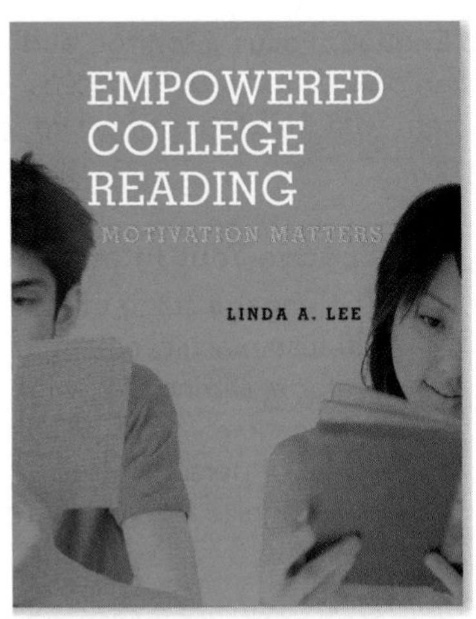

As with most activities, the key to successful reading is motivation. By combining the stages of motivation with active reading, author Linda Lee empowers students to become successful college readers.

Empowered College Reading: Motivation Matters provides:

- Motivating Content
- Motivating Features
- Motivating Software

Motivating Content

Unit One: Motivated Reading. This unit presents information about motivation and the way it applies to reading that is unique to this text. Chapter 1 introduces the concepts and stages of motivation. Chapter 2 presents specific reading processes that promote both motivation and comprehension. Chapter 3 adds information about reading at efficient speeds and Chapter 4 introduces vocabulary skills, two important ways to maintain motivation.

The Four Stages of Motivation: Engage, Focus, Monitor, and Reflect. Self-motivation for any activity can be broken down into these four steps. Linda Lee has taken these four steps and combined them with the stages of active reading to empower students to become better readers.

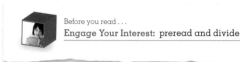

Before you read . . .
Engage Your Interest: preread and divide

Engage Your Interest

The **engage** stage of motivation generates interest in achievement, or the *"I want to"* attitude. During this stage, students increase their curiosity to know something, become aware of personal uses for the information, or recognize the benefits of completing the task.

As you read . . .
Focus Your Efforts: question and read

Focus Your Efforts

The **focus** stage of motivation is the working mode. Any technique or skill that keeps students thinking about the task, making progress, and increasing their *"I know how"* attitude will improve motivation at this stage.

Before you go on . . .
Monitor Your Progress: recite

Monitor Your Progress

Monitoring progress is the self-evaluation mode that keeps students on track. Monitoring means giving themselves feedback about how they are doing and making sure they identify problems that need to be resolved. This stage is directly related to students' self-confidence or the *"I believe I can do it"* attitude.

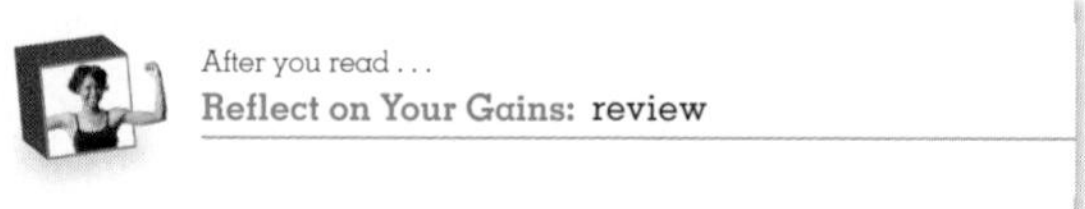

After you read . . .
Reflect on Your Gains: review

Reflect on Your Gains

The **reflection** stage of motivation promotes the *"I have achieved something"* attitude. It is the self-reward phase, which is essential for motivation.

Motivating Features

The Motivation Measure Survey

Knowing where you stand is a key first step to success. Available at the beginning of the text and on the CD-ROM, The Motivation Measure gives students direct information about their overall motivation for reading college material, as well as their levels for each of the four stages. These scores empower students to take further control of their reading. The Motivation Measure survey begins on page xxxi.

The Motivation Measure

OVERVIEW: This survey will give you information about your motivation for reading college materials. It includes questions about both your attitudes and your techniques. There are no right answers. To get the most accurate score, answer what is most true for you, even if you think there's a better answer.

DIRECTIONS: Read each statement and consider how it applies to the way you read course materials. Then on the line to the right, record the letter that matches how often it is true for you:

A = never B = sometimes C = usually D = always

	I	II	III	IV
Chapter 1				
1. I am interested in the reading assignments in my courses.	___			
2. I set goals or have a purpose when I read.	___			
3. I work where I can concentrate.		___		

Motivation Matters Readings

Sometimes we need to be inspired. Presented between the units of the text, the five Motivation Matters readings highlight issues of reading and motivation, giving students insight about how to take control of reading and inspiring them to strive for success. Motivation Matters readings are marked by red tabs, and begin on pages 177, 183, 381, 388, and 528.

Motivation Matters 1

Before you read . . .

Engage Your Interest: preread and divide

Think of people who you would call experts. How do you think they got to be so good in their field? Do you think talent is born or made?

After prereading, set a goal for your reading.

I want to _______________ about _______________.

My reward(s) will be _______________

_______________.

Right before you begin to read, record your START time in the Rate Box on page 182.

The Selections

Empowered College Reading has over 70 reading selections including essays, articles, letters to the editor, and textbook material. This variety of readings keeps the material fresh and engaging. Selections range from just a few paragraphs to many pages, and cover 19 different academic disciplines, including advertising, biology, business, health, history, music, psychology, sociology, and technology. The Subject Area Table of Contents on page xi lists all of the selections.

Subject Area Readings

The primary essays, articles, and textbook materials in *Empowered College Reading* are organized below by discipline, along with the type of text. Essays are texts that focus on the author's ideas and articles report on an event (see Chapter 9). The textbook materials are all excerpts from college textbooks, except for the two full chapters which are marked with asterisks (*). The Letters are Letters to the Editor.

Motivating Software

Prentice Hall is proud to offer **MyReadingLab,** where better reading is within reach.

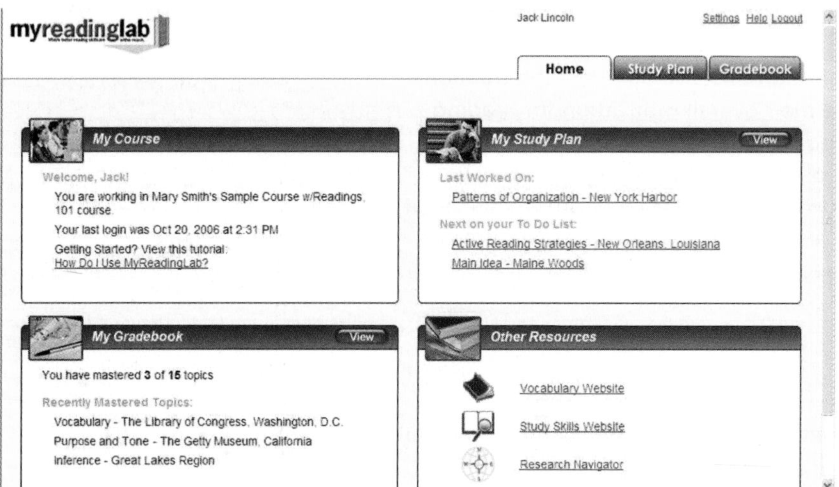

MyReadingLab is the first and only online learning system to diagnose both students' reading skills and their reading levels. This remarkable breakthrough utilizes diagnostic testing, personalized practice, and gradebook reports to allow instructors to measure student performance and help students gain control over their reading.

- **Diagnostic Testing:** MyReadingLab measures each student's reading ability in two ways: mastery of specific reading skills and overall reading level. Diagnostic tests conducted at the beginning and end of the course allow instructors to accurately measure student improvement during the course.
- **Personalized Practice:** Based on the diagnostic test results, each student receives a customized study plan. First, students are presented with instruction and practice from Reading Road Trip on the specific skills they need to master. Then they are assigned readings at their specific reading level. As students improve, they are assigned higher level readings.
- **Gradebook Reports:** MyReadingLab provides two ways to measure student improvement—by skill or by level. Gradebook reports enable instructors to analyze individual student performance as well as class performance.

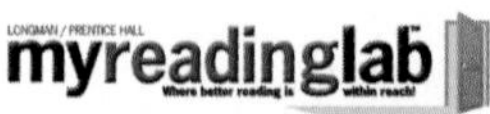

To learn more, please visit http://www.myreadinglab.com.

The Teaching and Learning Package

Instructor Resources

Instructor's Edition (ISBN: 0-13-183895-4). Written exclusively by Linda Lee, the Instructor's Edition contains the entire student text, complete with answers for instructors and a 35-page Instructor's Guide bound directly into the back. The Instructor's Guide features 10 Chapter Guides, which include a Lesson Plan in a Box and Challenging Ideas and Methods for each of the chapters in *Empowered College Reading.*

Instructor's Resource Manual (ISBN: 0-13-183896-2). The Instructor's Resource Manual for *Empowered College Reading* will help instructors reinforce the skills and methods presented in the text. Resources include chapter summaries, two 15-question multiple-choice quizzes, PowerPoint slides, and additional activities for each chapter. In addition, there are three 50-question diagnostic tests of reading skills and a 30-question multiple-choice quiz for each of the two complete textbook chapters on the CD-ROM.

BlackBoard and WebCT Content Cartridges for EMPOWERED COLLEGE READING. These downloadable content cartridges require no access code and include most of the material from the Instructor's Resource Manual in BlackBoard and WebCT formats.

The Prentice Hall Reading Skills Test Bank (ISBN: 0-13-041249-X). Available to college instructors at no additional charge upon adoption. Designed for use with any Prentice Hall text, this test bank contains 1,100 exercises, covering word analysis, context clues, stated main idea, implied main idea, tone and bias, details, major vs. minor details, style, study reading, reading rate, and visual aids. Questions are multiple-choice, matching, or true/false. Ask your local Prentice Hall representative for a copy of this wonderful book of quizzes.

Student Resources

Dictionary and Thesaurus. College instructors can choose to package *The New American Webster Handy College Dictionary* (ISBN: 0-13-032870-7) or *The New American Roget's College Thesaurus* (ISBN: 0-13-045258-0) with *Empowered College Reading.* By packaging these items together, students enjoy a significant discount over buying the items separately.

The Florida Exit Test Study Guide for Reading (ISBN: 0-13-184899-2). Designed specifically for students preparing for the Florida Exit Test, this study guide provides instruction and practice on the individual skills covered and also provides one complete sample test. The guide is available at a significant discount when packaged with *Empowered College Reading.*

The Prentice Hall THEA Study Guide for Reading (ISBN: 0-13-183643-9). Designed specifically for students preparing for Texas Higher Education Assessment, this study guide provides instruction and practice on the individual skills and also provides one complete sample test. The guide is available at a significant discount when packaged with *Empowered College Reading.*

TIME Special Editions. Prentice Hall and *TIME* Magazine are pleased to offer you and your students a chance to examine today's most current and compelling issues in an exciting new way. *TIME* Special Editions are available in Sociology, Psychology, Political Science, Philosophy, Religion, and International Business.

The New York Times Prentice Hall is pleased to offer students a discounted 10-week subscription to *The New York Times* at 50% off the regular subscription rate. (Subscription card ISBN: 0-13-112617-2). In addition, instructors ordering a Pearson/*NY Times* subscription package receive a complementary one-semester subscription.

The Prentice Hall Textbook Reader (ISBN: 0-13-184895-X). This supplementary reader includes eight complete college textbook chapters from a variety of disciplines. Each chapter includes a one-page introduction to the selection and various exercises after the selection.

Penguin Novels. We are delighted to offer Penguin Putnam titles at a substantial discount to your students when you request a special package of one or more Penguin titles with any Prentice Hall text. Please contact your local Prentice Hall representative for special ordering instructions to receive our special prices.

Contact your local Prentice Hall representative for information on all of these packaging options, ordering information, and ISBNs.

The Development Story—About the Author

Linda A. Lee, Ph.D., is a professor of developmental reading and writing, as well as transfer-level composition and literature courses at San Diego Miramar College. She brings her unique perspective to the pages of *Empowered College Reading: Motivation Matters.* After earning two Master's Degrees in English Literature from Georgetown University and in Curriculum and Instruction/Reading from San Diego State University, she went on to earn a Ph.D. in Education from San Diego State University and Claremont Graduate School.

She designed and developed the Oasis Reading and Study Skills Center at the University of California, San Diego. In her courses at Miramar, Lee uses computer-aided instruction and collaborative learning approaches that promote abstract and critical thinking skills, self-motivation, and metacognitive techniques. She designed, developed, and supervised the Miramar campus-wide learning center focusing on skills empowerment as well as content tutoring. She also developed linked classes that promote reading and learning skills in science courses.

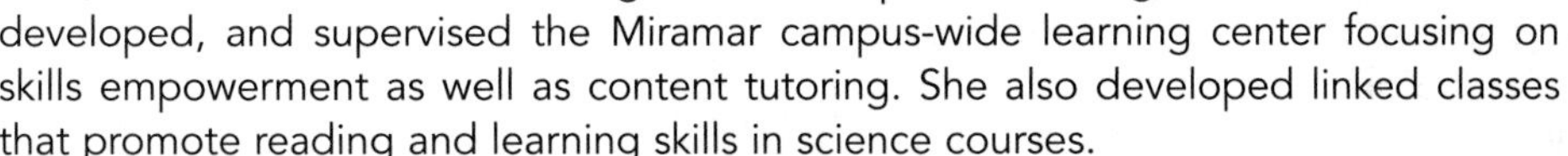

Among her many awards and achievements, Lee won the NISOD Excellence in Teaching Award, was an International Reading Association Dissertation of the Year finalist, and won the California Reading Association Constance McCullough Research Award for the dissertation of the year. She also was nominated to Who's Who Among American Teachers in 1996, 2004, 2005 and 2006.

Writing a first-edition college textbook is a team effort. *Empowered College Reading: Motivation Matters* is the product of over four years of development, incorporating insights and feedback from over 100 reading instructors. Before embarking on the project, Lee polled reading instructors nationwide, who told of their daily challenges to motivate students to read and who wholeheartedly applauded the concept of building a textbook around motivation. Lee's pedagogy—her answer to the problem of motivation in reading—was continually tested at both national reading conferences, The College Reading and Learning Association and The National Association for Developmental Education. In addition, Lee listened closely when instructors explained what they most valued in a book, in supplements, and in software.

Reviewers pored over the manuscript at every stage, providing invaluable feedback on all aspects of the textbook. They commented on the concept, the writing, the exercises, the selections, and more. They reviewed the table of contents, sample chapters, and multiple drafts of the manuscript.

In all, over 50 instructors contributed in-depth reviews at various stages of development, from proposal to final draft, helping to shape Linda Lee's ideas and classroom practice into *Empowered College Reading: Motivation Matters.* The list below includes the names of many of the instructors who so graciously contributed their time and expertise:

Karen Alderfer, *Miami Dade College*
Natalie Anagnos, *Southwest Missouri State University*
Anna Apple, *Cy-Fair College*
Karen Becker, *Youngstown State University*
Randy Beckham, *Germanna Community College*
Kathy Beggs, *Pikes Peak Community College*
Barbara Brown, *Olive Harvey College*
Chris Chapman, *Lewis and Clark Community College*
Dorothy Chase, *Community College of Southern Nevada*
Marlys Cordoba, *College of the Siskiyous*
Judy Davidson, *University of Texas-Pan Am*
Russell Davis, *Houston Community College Southwest*
Tom Dayton, *American River College*
Margaret Delapaz, *Broward Community College*
Carol Friend, *Mercer County Community College*
Polly Green, *Arkansas State University*
Virginia Guleff, *Miramar College*
Sue Hightower, *Tallahassee Community College*
Danica Hubbard, *College of DuPage*
Suzanne Hughes, *Florida Community College at Jacksonville*
Miriam Kinard, *Trident Technical College*
Adrienne King, *Sacramento City College*
Sharon Lagina, *Wayne County Community College*
Karen Lim, *San Diego City College*
Robert Mathews, *Miami Dade College*
Gladys Montalvo, *Palm Beach Community College*
Debbie Naquin, *Northern Virginia Community College*
Deborah O'Brien-Smith, *Nassau Community College*
Karen Patty-Graham, *Southern Illinois College*
Betty Perkinson, *Tidewater Community College*
Rick Richards, *St. Petersburg College*
Melinda Schomaker, *Georgia Perimeter College*
Elizabeth Schroeder, *Owens Community College*
Heather Severson, *Pima Community College*
Jeffery Siddall, *College of DuPage*
Holly Susi, *Community College of Rhode Island*
Sharon Taylor, *Western Wyoming Community College*
Margaret Triplett, *Central Oregon Community College*
Kristine Volpi, *Broward Community College*
Ted Walkup, *Clayton State University*
Jacquelyn Warmsley, *Tarrant County Community College*
Jim Wilkins-Luton, *Clark College*
Lynda Wolverton, *Polk Community College*

A Note to Students

**The more that you read, the more things you will know.
The more that you learn, the more places you'll go.**

—Dr. Seuss (1904–1991), American writer and cartoonist

What's in a title? For this book, it's everything I want to share with you.

Why *Empowered Reading*? *Empower* is one of my favorite words. It takes the noun *power,* meaning strength, and turns it into an action verb. *Empowered reading* is a personal and extremely effective way of reading that enables you to reap information, ideas, and inspiration from any text. But, more than just getting what the text offers, empowered reading is about how to use the text to gain academic success and enrich your knowledge. Thus, a single act of reading can greatly influence your life. As the French philosopher Jacques Maritain (1892–1973) said,

> **A single idea, if it is right, saves us
> the labor of an infinity of experiences.**

This is the kind of reading you may have already experienced with a book you couldn't put down, a text about something you really wanted to master, a very useful article, or a letter that was important to you. What do these experiences have to do with *college* reading? Consider for a moment what would happen if you were able to turn all of your course assignments into interesting reading tasks like that great book, article, or letter. Wouldn't you read without resistance, stress, and boredom? Possibly, you'd read faster; certainly you'd read better. And, logically, you'd remember more with less effort. While history and biology textbooks might not be written in the style of your favorite texts, you do have the power to transform your reading experience and read them for all they're worth.

Where does the power come from? That's the last part of the title: *Motivation Matters.* What this text will show you is that motivation is central to reading excellence. With it, all reading efforts and every reading experience will produce the best possible results. Moreover, as you will see throughout this book, motivation can change and you can control it.

So, the purpose of this book is to show you how to use the attitudes and techniques of motivation to get the most out of each reading process you use and every reading experience you have. The focus is on academic materials, because they are some of the most challenging and important texts you read. If ever there was a need for empowered reading, it's as you're mastering the complex knowledge that will support your future career efforts.

There are two ways to get the most from this textbook:

1. **Pay attention to the special features:** They will ensure that empowered reading becomes your approach.
2. ***Use* this information:** Make each idea and technique your own by using it on everything you read. Assignments in other courses are wonderful opportunities for you to practice, master, and use this approach. If you aren't taking any other classes, though, you can get the benefits on any text you read. Every empowered reading event you create makes you a more empowered reader.

The Organization of This Book

Empowered College Reading: Motivation Matters begins with **The Motivation Measure.** This survey will give you a way to identify your reading motivation levels and take control of your reading. (See pp. xxxi–xxxv or the CD-ROM.) Then, the text is divided into three units and The Reader.

Unit One, Motivated Reading, presents information about motivation and the general ways it applies to reading. Chapter 1 introduces the concepts and stages of motivation. Chapter 2 presents specific reading processes that promote both motivation and comprehension. Chapter 3 adds information about reading at efficient speeds, which promotes your motivation. Chapter 4 covers the skills of vocabulary mastery that make it easier to read college texts.

Unit Two, Textbook Reading, includes chapters 5 through 8. It covers ways to handle the challenges of textbooks, including reading for learning methods and comprehending the author's main ideas, details, logical patterns, and graphic aids.

Unit Three, Critical Reading, includes chapters 9 and 10. Chapter 9, "Drawing Conclusions," will show you how to analyze and evaluate the author's purpose, tone, facts and opinions, as well as judge the merits of essays and articles. Chapter 10, "Evaluating Arguments," describes methods for understanding and judging texts on controversial issues.

Between the units, you will find short essays called **Motivation Matters.** These texts provide inspiring ideas and effective methods for increasing your reading motivation for academic materials.

The last section of the book, **The Reader,** contains a variety of texts used in college courses, including essays, articles, and sections from freshman and sophomore textbooks. These readings are organized by academic discipline and introduced with specific reading tips for handling assignments in that field. Additional texts and two full-length textbook chapters are included on the accompanying CD-ROM.

Features of the Text

Empowered College Reading is meant to be read and used. It has a number of special features that will help you develop your motivation and comprehension while you are learning about them. Here's a preview of the special features and how to use each one.

The Motivation Measure

The Motivation Measure survey will give you information about your motivation for reading college materials, enabling you to take control of your reading. (See pp. xxxi–xxxv or the CD-ROM.)

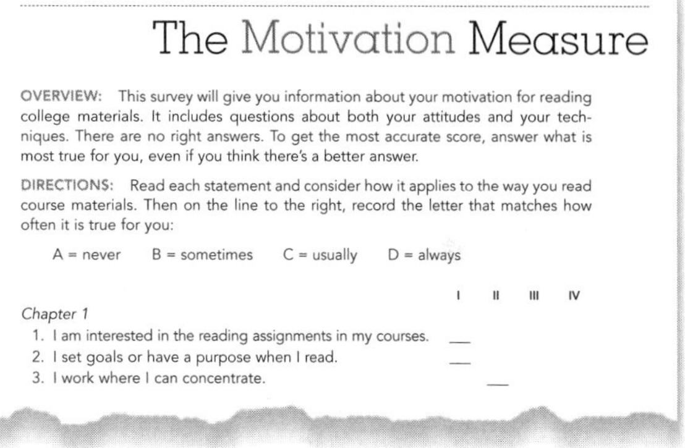

The Motivation Measure

OVERVIEW: This survey will give you information about your motivation for reading college materials. It includes questions about both your attitudes and your techniques. There are no right answers. To get the most accurate score, answer what is most true for you, even if you think there's a better answer.

DIRECTIONS: Read each statement and consider how it applies to the way you read course materials. Then on the line to the right, record the letter that matches how often it is true for you:

A = never B = sometimes C = usually D = always

	I	II	III	IV
Chapter 1				
1. I am interested in the reading assignments in my courses.	___			
2. I set goals or have a purpose when I read.	___			
3. I work where I can concentrate.		___		

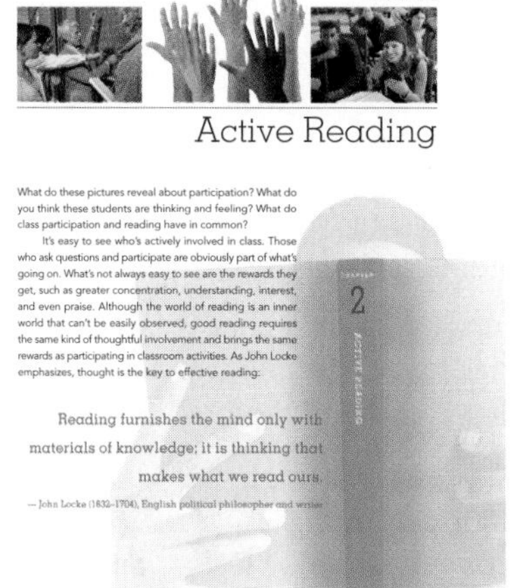

CHAPTER TWO

Active Reading

What do these pictures reveal about participation? What do you think these students are thinking and feeling? What do class participation and reading have in common?

It's easy to see who's actively involved in class. Those who ask questions and participate are obviously part of what's going on. What's not always easy to see are the rewards they get, such as greater concentration, understanding, interest, and even praise. Although the world of reading is an inner world that can't be easily observed, good reading requires the same kind of thoughtful involvement and brings the same rewards as participating in classroom activities. As John Locke emphasizes, thought is the key to effective reading.

Reading furnishes the mind only with materials of knowledge; it is thinking that makes what we read ours.

—John Locke (1632–1704), English political philosopher and writer

31

Chapter Openers

Each chapter begins with four features:

- *Images* that relate to the chapter theme
- *Questions* relating the pictures to your life
- A *paragraph* that links the pictures and your common experiences to the chapter topic
- A *quote* that states the chapter theme

USE: *Think about these. They will increase your motivation for the chapter topic.*

Chapter Overview

A *map or outline* identifies what the chapter will cover and lists the major section headings. In some chapters, you will be instructed to complete or create these visual aids.

USE: *Use these aids to get a big picture view of the chapter. They will increase your chapter comprehension.*

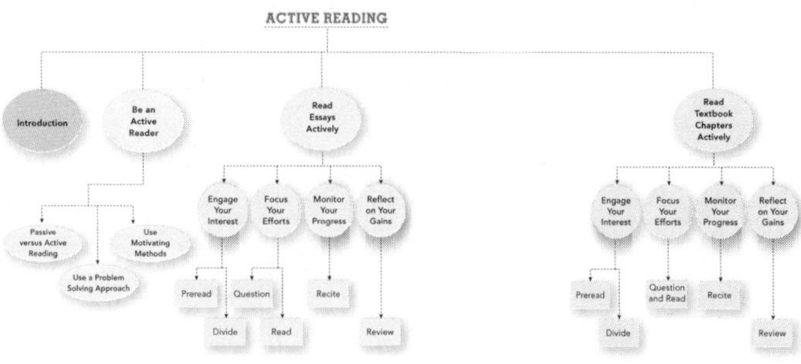

Goal Setting

In Chapters 2–10 and all of the readings, a space is provided where you can *set goals.*

USE: *Think about the topic and what you want to gain from your reading. Then, record your goal(s), including the reward(s) you'll get. Goals increase both motivation and comprehension.*

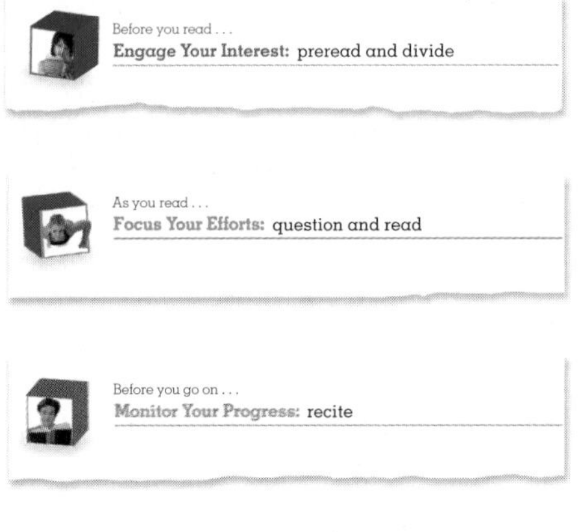

Banner Reminder Headings

After Chapter 2, you will find banners or *reminder headings* throughout the chapters and readings. They mark the places where the motivation methods described in Chapters 1 and 2 should be used.

USE: *Think about and use the methods at these points. These banners indicate when you should apply the empowered methods on the texts you are reading. They are a primary way to achieve empowered reading.*

A mind once stretched by a new idea never regains its original dimensions.

— Oliver Wendell Holmes (1809–1894) American author

Quotes

Quotes from famous thinkers are presented throughout each chapter. They relate to the text ideas and provide insights that can be applied to your life.

USE: *Think about the quotes as you come to them. They will emphasize key points, expand your knowledge, and inspire you.*

CHAPTER SUMMARY

Introduction

Textbook chapters often contain an overwhelming amount of new information. Readers can prevent a loss of concentration and improve comprehension by locating and using the main ideas to guide their reading.

Get the Most out of Main Ideas

Chapters are divided into discussion blocks that include major sections, subsections, minor sections, and paragraphs. Each block contains three structural elements: the **topic,** the **main idea,** and the **details.** An effective, active reading approach that aids comprehension is to use a **predict** and **verify** process. This process entails guessing what the topic and main idea sentence are as soon as possible and then reading on to see if the details verify the predictions. Marking captures the reader's understanding of the text and avoids unnecessary future rereading.

Chapter Summary

The *summary* highlights the major ideas and key terms in each chapter.

USE: *Skim the summary before reading to get an overview of the chapter. Use it after reading to review the key points. The summary will improve your chapter comprehension.*

Review Activities

At the end of each chapter and in The Reader, you will find a number of review activities.

- *Expand Your Vocabulary* checks your understanding of the terms.
- *Increase Your Knowledge* presents essay questions about the chapter information.
- *Develop Your Skills* provides materials for practicing the chapter skills and methods.
- *Check Your Comprehension* presents reading comprehension questions for the essays and articles.
- *Expand Your Thinking* presents discussion questions for the essays and articles.
- *Reading for Learning Questions* are actual exam questions for the textbook sections.

USE: *Complete these activities. They will alert you to information you should emphasize in your reading and help you develop your comprehension skills for college course materials.*

Check Your Motivation

1. Review your chapter goals. Did you achieve them? Explain.
2. Make a list of the new ideas and methods you've gained from this chapter. Think about how they will help you in the future.
3. Measure your motivation for this chapter topic. Think about each statement and how you will use it in the future. Mark it:

A = never B = sometimes C = usually D = always

	A	B	C	D
To engage my interest, I plan to . . .				
1. think about the benefits of developing my overall . vocabulary.	___	___	___	___
2. take an interested in knowing new terms.	___	___	___	___
To focus my efforts, I plan to . . .				
3. identify my level of knowledge before trying to learn a word.	___	___	___	___
4. pronounce a word as the first step to learning it.	___	___	___	___

Motivation Checks

Check Your Motivation activities are presented at the end of every chapter and reading.

USE: *Complete these activities. They will identify the motivation attitudes and techniques that are working, as well as those that need your attention.*

Motivation Matters Readings

Presented between the units of the text, the five Motivation Matters readings highlight issues of reading and motivation, giving you insights about how to take control your reading.

Motivation Matters 1

Before you read . . .

Engage Your Interest: preread and divide

Think of people who you would call experts. How do you think they got to be so good in their field? Do you think talent is born or made?

After prereading, set a goal for your reading.

I want to ______________ about ______________________.

My reward(s) will be ______________________

______________________________________.

Right before you begin to read, record your START time in the Rate Box on page 182.

As you read . . .

Focus Your Efforts: question and read

Strive to Become an Expert

Saul Kassin, *Psychology*

Very few people manage to climb to the very top of a skilled domain to become experts, among the best in the world. Those who do achieve these heights often dazzle us with their achievements. How do the great ones reach this level? Are they specially gifted, endowed at birth with brains and bodies uniquely suited to their talent? Are they, in other words, born, not made? Is the pursuit of excellence similar from one skill to another? How do people make it, as they say, to the top of their game? 1

The Reader

Beginning on page 535, The Reader includes the kind of textbook selections, essays, and articles that are assigned in freshman and sophomore courses. Four paired readings cover Psychology, Business Comunication, History, and Biology.

The Reader continues on the CD-ROM with two additional paired readings that cover Marketing and Business.

Reading for Learning from . . .

The Reading for Learning from . . . pages are guides presented in the Reader before each subject area. They include an overview of the topics covered in typical freshman courses, the kind of information to look for in the readings, and reading tips.

USE: *Read these pages before the texts that follow. They will increase your motivation and comprehension of the subject area texts.*

Rate Box

You will find a *Rate Box* with directions for computing your reading speed at the end of each essay and article.

USE: *Compute your rate and think about it along with your comprehension scores. Determine if your speed is effective, too slow, or too fast.*

Progress Charts

On the inside front and back covers of this book, you will find *progress charts* to record your motivation, vocabulary, comprehension, and rate scores.

USE: *Record your scores and track your progress. Use these charts to indicate where you are improving and areas that need more attention.*

PROGRESS CHARTS

Use the following charts to keep track of your motivation, rate, vocabulary, and comprehension scores. For each one, follow these steps:

1. Record the date you read it, the first page of the text, and put a check for the topics that interested you.
2. Put a dot on the middle of the box that matches your score.
3. Connect the dots to see how you are progressing.
4. Make mental notes about where you are improving and areas that need more attention.

Check Your Motivation Progress Charts

Use this chart for chapters 1–10. (15–43 = low; 44–60 = high)

DATE										
PAGE										
TOPIC										
55–60										
50–54										
44–49										
39–43										
33–38										
27–32										
15–26										

Two Complete Textbook Chapters

To further practice your skills, the CD-ROM includes two complete chapters from other college textbooks—one sociology text and one history text. A chapter each from *Marriages and Families* by Nijole J. Benokraitis and *The Heritage of World Civilizations* by Albert M. Craig are available in their entirety on the CD-ROM in the back of the book.

A Final Thought

This book is a journey. As you travel through it, you will undoubtedly encounter ideas you'll recognize, some that you've only heard of, and some that you never expected. It is my hope that at the end of your journey through these pages, you will be glad you took the trip and that you will take the knowledge and skills of empowered reading with you. As Aldous Huxley, the English novelist (1894–1963), said

> **Every man who knows how to read has it in his power to magnify himself, to multiply the ways in which he exists, to make his life full, significant and interesting.**

Huxley wrote in a time when the words "man" and "he" were used to refer to everyone. As you'll see from this text, however, no one is excluded from the benefits of reading!

Sincerely,
Linda A. Lee

Acknowledgments

This textbook could not have been written without the support and efforts of many others. I am very grateful for the time, work, and thoughts that so many gave so willingly.

My gratitude goes to all of the dedicated Pearson Prentice Hall professionals without whom this book would not have been published. Veronika Pasovska, Pearson Custom Solutions, helped to turn my interest in writing into this wonderful project. Thank you for your faith in these ideas and your tenacity until I "saw the light." Craig Campanella, Executive Editor English, shepherded the work from start to finish. Thank you for the many stimulating, creative, and problem-solving conversations, as well as your dedication to turning my vision into reality. Susan Messer worked tirelessly as the Development Editor. Thank you for all of your sensitive support, extraordinary efforts, marvelous insights, and overall dedication to perfecting the message on every page. Joan Polk was the Editorial Assistant throughout most of this project. Thank you for your extremely helpful and humorous "can do" aid and support. To Anne DeMarinis, Designer, thank you for creating an elegant visual canvas for the message of this book. To Kate Mitchell, Marketing Manager, thank you for your enthusiasm for this text and all of your creative ideas to let people know about it. To Jessica Balch, Production Editor, thank you for being a calm port within the final production phases. To Beaura Kathy Ringrose, Visual Research Manager, thank you for transforming my ideas into stunning visuals. My thanks and appreciation also go to Leah Jewell, Editorial Director; Rochelle Diogenes, Editor-in-Chief, Development; Alexis Walker, Associate Director of Development; Anne Marie McCarthy, Executive Managing Editor, Production; Amy Rosen, Art Director; Joanne Hakim, Production Liaison; and Debi Doyle, Editorial Assistant. Thank you all for your suggestions and untold efforts.

My deep appreciation goes to the many students who have used drafts of this text over the past years, overlooked the typos, and given me really valuable feedback. Your encouragement and excellent analyses were essential in the crafting of this book.

I am fortunate to have had colleagues who cheered me on and suggested resources. A special thanks to Kim Flachmann, Shirley Melcher, Dan Crocket, Gin Gee, Kevin Petti, and Mike McPherson. In addition, I very much appreciate all of the reviewers whose thoughtful comments helped me push deeper, get clearer, and improve every chapter.

Last, but by no means least, I with to thank the circle of friends and family who listened to endless updates and kept up my psychic energy. My heartfelt gratitude goes to Daphne Figueroa, Virginia Guleff, Leslie Klipper, Miriam Maneevone, Anjie Massey, Jo Ann Doherty, Annette Lee, Casey Stewart, and Dana Lee Stewart.

The Motivation Measure

OVERVIEW: This survey will give you information about your motivation for reading college materials. It includes questions about both your attitudes and your techniques. There are no right answers. To get the most accurate score, answer what is most true for you, even if you think there's a better answer.

DIRECTIONS: Read each statement and consider how it applies to the way you read course materials. Then on the line to the right, record the letter that matches how often it is true for you:

A = never B = sometimes C = usually D = always

Statement	I	II	III	IV
Chapter 1				
1. I am interested in the reading assignments in my courses.	C			
2. I set goals or have a purpose when I read.	C			
3. I work where I can concentrate.		B		
4. I try to manage my time and avoid working at the last minute.		B		
5. I believe that good grades depend mostly on a student's effort.			D	
6. I am confident about my reading methods and ability.			B	
7. I think about the information after finishing an assignment.				D
8. I reward myself for making a good effort and doing good work.				D
Chapter 2				
9. I preview assignments before I begin to read them.	B			
10. I divide long chapters into short reading tasks.	B			
11. I think about the author's points as I read.		B		
12. I underline or mark what's important in assigned texts.		C		
13. I realize when I have problems comprehending a text.			D	
14. I try to solve reading problems when they occur.			D	
15. I make notes or flashcards about what I need to learn.				B
16. I discuss the information in assignments with others.				A
Chapter 3				
17. I think about using the best speed for my purpose.	D			
18. I think about using the best speed for the text difficulty.	C			
19. I sit in a position that promotes reading speed.		A		
20. I hold or prop the text at an angle when I read.		D		
21. I make sure the lighting is very good when I read.		C		

I II III IV

22. I can comprehend most texts without stopping and rereading.
23. I read silently with expression and group words into phrases.
24. I change my speed during reading as needed.

Chapter 4

25. I think increasing the size of my vocabulary is important.
26. I find it interesting to learn about words I don't know.
27. I use word parts like prefixes and roots to figure out new words.
28. I look for context clues to help define new words.
29. I use a dictionary to define new words.
30. I try to pronounce new words when I'm learning them.
31. I try to paraphrase the meaning to check my understanding.
32. I try to use new terms that I've learned as I speak or write.

Chapter 5

33. I look over the preface or appendices before using a book.
34. I look at the beginning of a chapter to increase my motivation.
35. I write brief notes or comments in the margins of my texts.
36. I am confident about my ability to understand textbook chapters.
37. I paraphrase important points after reading them.
38. I create summaries of important parts after reading.
39. I use the chapter review questions after reading.
40. I use different formats when I take notes.

Chapter 6

41. I think the ideas in chapters are interesting, useful, or helpful.
42. I often think about what will come next as I read chapters.
43. I think about how the chapter sections are related as I read.
44. I look for the ideas in textbook chapters.
45. I know how to find the chapter topic.
46. I know how to find the topics in paragraphs.
47. I know how to find the ideas in paragraphs.
48. I can explain the paragraph idea when it is implied.

I II III IV

Chapter 7

49. The details in textbooks are interesting to me.
50. I understand why authors present details in textbooks.
51. I look for different types of details as I read.
52. I think about what details add to the author's points.
53. I look for the logical ways authors organize details.
54. I look for signal words or transitions to aid my comprehension.
55. I can organize numerous details without becoming stressed.
56. I create diagrams or charts to use as learning tools.

Chapter 8

57. I look at the graphics as a way to increase my interest.
58. I carefully read and think about a graphic when I come to it.
59. I understand the information in charts, tables, and diagrams.
60. I estimate actual numbers for the points on line graphs.
61. I relate each graphic aid to the text sentences about it.
62. I think about how the graphics apply to me and others I know.
63. I record anything I figure out next to the graphic.
64. I draw my own conclusions about the information in graphics.

Chapter 9

65. I think it's important to evaluate what I read.
66. I think about the author's purpose when I read.
67. I can recognize the author's attitude or tone when I read.
68. I pay attention to the underlying or implied meanings of words.
69. I can tell the difference between facts and opinions.
70. I know and think about the parts of an essay as I read.
71. I make inferences about points that are not directly stated.
72. I evaluate the merits of the essays and articles I read.

Chapter 10

73. I am skeptical about ideas that don't have good proof.
74. I can be fair and open-minded when I disagree with an author.
75. I recognize debatable issues in the texts that I read.

	I	II	III	IV
76. I look for the author's reasons as I read.		___		
77. I look for bias, stereotyping, and poor reasoning as I read.		___		
78. I look for excellent points and good reasoning as I read.		___		
79. I think about and evaluate how trustworthy an author is.				___
80. I form my own opinions about issues.				___

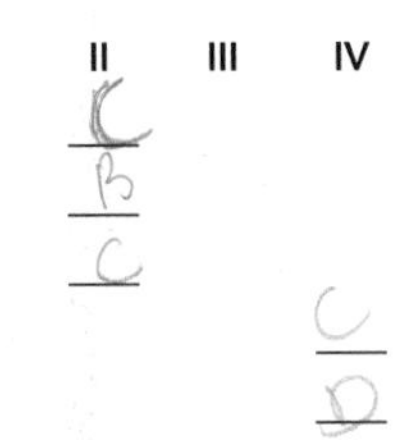

Scoring and Interpretation

SCORING: To compute your survey scores, follow these steps:

1. Look at one column at a time. Record the number of answers for each letter.
2. Multiply the number of answers for each letter by the points. Record the total.
3. Add up the letter points for each column. Write that number on the Column Points line.
4. Add up the four Column Points to get your Total Survey Score.

COLUMN I

\# of A's ___ × 1 pt. = ___
\# of B's ___ × 2 pt. = ___
\# of C's ___ × 3 pt. = ___
\# of D's ___ × 4 pt. = ___
(Total = 18 questions)

COLUMN I POINTS = ___

COLUMN II

\# of A's ___ × 1 pt. = ___
\# of B's ___ × 2 pt. = ___
\# of C's ___ × 3 pt. = ___
\# of D's ___ × 4 pt. = ___
(Total = 36 questions)

COLUMN II POINTS = ___

COLUMN III

\# of A's ___ × 1 pt. = ___
\# of B's ___ × 2 pt. = ___
\# of C's ___ × 3 pt. = ___
\# of D's ___ × 4 pt. = ___
(Total = 13 questions)

COLUMN III POINTS = ___

COLUMN IV

\# of A's ___ × 1 pt. = ___
\# of B's ___ × 2 pt. = ___
\# of C's ___ × 3 pt. = ___
\# of D's ___ × 4 pt. = ___
(Total = 13 questions)

COLUMN IV POINTS = ___

TOTAL SURVEY SCORE* = ___

INTERPRETATION: This survey provides three ways to look at your motivation.*

1. The Total Survey Score is a measure of your overall, reading motivation level.
2. The Column Points indicate your level for each of the four stages of motivation.
3. The Chapter answers indicate your familiarity with the concepts in each chapter.

*Note: For more information about motivation, the four stages, and the scores, see Chapter 1.

To interpret your scores, check off the levels that match your scores.*

Total Survey Score: ___ 80–229 = low ___ 230–320 = high

Column Points:

I. Engaging interest before reading:	___ 18–51 = low	___ 52–72 = high
II. Focusing during reading:	___ 36–103 = low	___ 104–144 = high
III. Monitoring during reading:	___ 13–36 = low	___ 37–52 = high
IV. Reflecting after reading:	___ 13–36 = low	___ 37–52 = high

Chapter Answers

CHAPTER 1	___ 0–5 C's or D's = low	___ 6–8 C's or D's = high
CHAPTER 2	___ 0–5 C's or D's = low	___ 6–8 C's or D's = high
CHAPTER 3	___ 0–5 C's or D's = low	___ 6–8 C's or D's = high
CHAPTER 4	___ 0–5 C's or D's = low	___ 6–8 C's or D's = high
CHAPTER 5	___ 0–5 C's or D's = low	___ 6–8 C's or D's = high
CHAPTER 6	___ 0–5 C's or D's = low	___ 6–8 C's or D's = high
CHAPTER 7	___ 0–5 C's or D's = low	___ 6–8 C's or D's = high
CHAPTER 8	___ 0–5 C's or D's = low	___ 6–8 C's or D's = high
CHAPTER 9	___ 0–5 C's or D's = low	___ 6–8 C's or D's = high
CHAPTER 10	___ 0–5 C's or D's = low	___ 6–8 C's or D's = high

The Power of Motivation

What do the pictures above show about motivated people? How does motivation affect achievement? How would you define motivation?

Every skill we try to learn or achievement we seek depends on motivation. The ability to motivate yourself, to become interested in tasks, and to generate ongoing energy is one of the most powerful success techniques there is. For students, motivation can make the difference between superior performance and just getting by, and between engaged, meaningful reading and understanding. Motivation is a psychological skill that everyone can develop. And, as the following quote by William James emphasizes, the power of motivation can truly be life-altering.

> The greatest discovery of my generation is that human beings can alter their lives by altering their attitudes of mind.
>
> — William James (1842–1910), American philosopher and psychologist

This chapter, mapped out below, will show you how to tap into the amazing power of self-motivation.

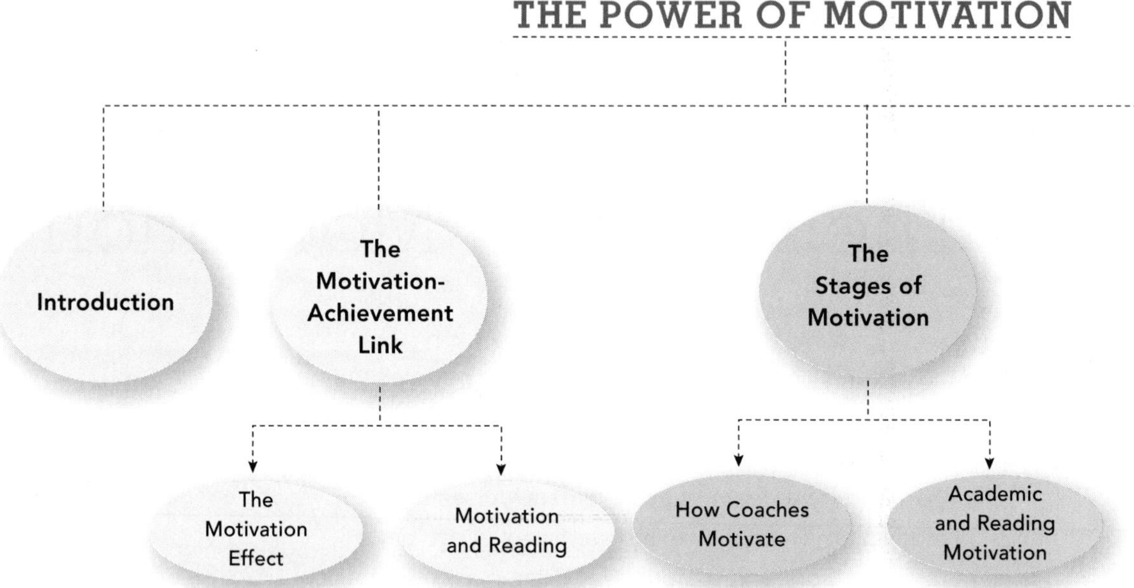

Note: This chapter will be more meaningful to you if you take and score the Motivation Measure (p. xxxi) before you continue reading. The information in this chapter will clarify what your scores mean. Look for the label *Motivation Measure* for specific explanations about it (pp. 5, 11, and 12).

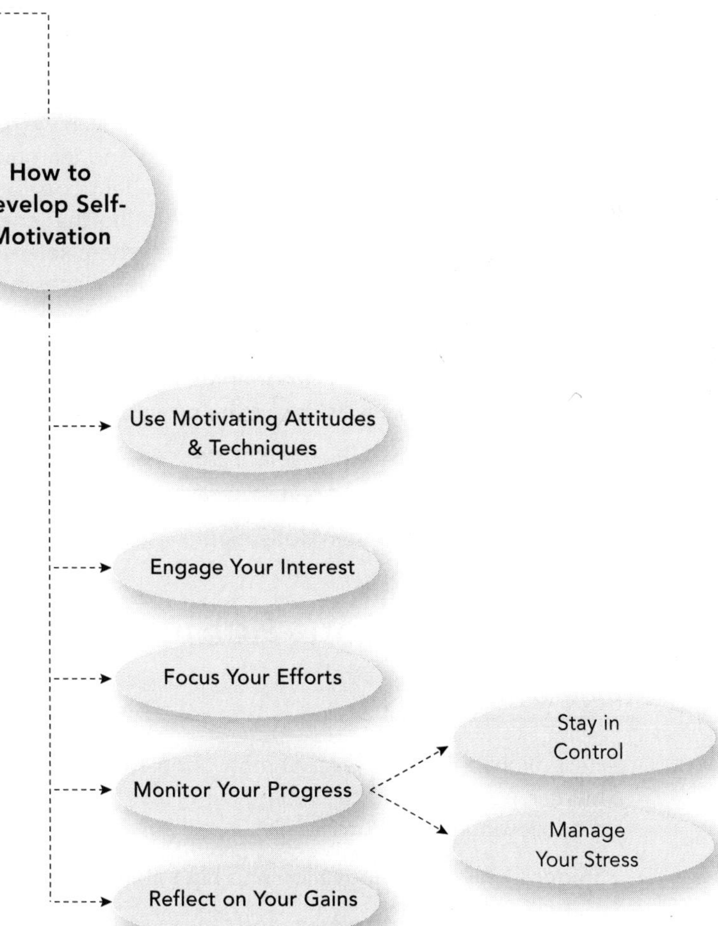
How to Develop Self-Motivation
Use Motivating Attitudes & Techniques
Engage Your Interest
Focus Your Efforts
Monitor Your Progress
Stay in Control
Manage Your Stress
Reflect on Your Gains

Motivation is behind some of the best of times in our lives. It creates enthusiasm, passion, focus, dedication, and achievement. With every skill we try to learn, every topic we need to master, and every gain we want to make, motivation is the driving force. It can come from others or from ourselves. However, while others can encourage and motivate us, the only lasting motivation comes from what we do for ourselves. This is where our "attitudes of mind" come in. By examining and changing the ways we use our minds, we can change everything, including the way we read and learn.

> Right now you are one choice away from a new beginning—one that leads you toward becoming the fullest human being you can be.
>
> —Oprah Winfrey (1954–), American talk show host and philanthropist

Motivation, or the desire and psychological energy to achieve and gain more than we have, is a critical component of academic reading and learning. Course assignments are meant to stretch students beyond their current knowledge and skill levels. Meeting that challenge requires effort, sustained energy, drive, and interest. And that's where self-motivation comes in. To handle the reading and learning tasks of college, successful students need **academic motivation,** which is the ability to create their own desire and energy to read, learn, and perform well in their courses.

This chapter introduces important concepts and techniques for developing your reading motivation and skills. It lays the groundwork by discussing three main topics:

- The Motivation–Achievement Link
- The Stages of Motivation
- How to Develop Self-Motivation

The Motivation–Achievement Link

THINK ABOUT THIS . . .

How might a person's level of motivation and ability affect his or her achievement in a college course? What final course grade would you expect each of the following students to receive?

Student 1 has high motivation and high ability: expected grade _____

Student 2 has low motivation and low ability: expected grade _____

Student 3 has low motivation and high ability: expected grade _____

Student 4 has high motivation and low ability: expected grade _____

You probably expected students with high motivation and high ability to get A's and those with low motivation and low ability to get D's and F's. And that is what generally happens. But, did you predict that Student 4, the one with high motivation and low ability, will get higher grades than Student 3, who has low motivation and high ability? This result is directly due to the motivation effect.

The Motivation Effect

As noted in the definition, motivation is both a desire and the energy to achieve. It is like fuel for an engine. Without it, the best machinery is useless; with it, the machine works as it should, and when it's enhanced, even more power can be created. So, the most obvious effect of motivation is that it works as a kind of mental fuel. And, like the amount of gas in your car, you can have a lot, use it up, need more, and even enhance it.

> *Motivation Measure.* Check your total survey score. This number indicates your current, overall motivation level for college courses. If it's high, you use many self-motivating methods. But do not worry or feel bad if it's low. You probably were never taught about motivation or the many self-motivating approaches available to you. And remember, motivation is mental fuel. Your score is like a gas gauge and simply indicates if you need to fill up. This text will provide numerous ways to do that.

How does motivation fuel the mind? Motivation affects how you use the ability you have, and the two together produce performance. If you're high on both, your desire and energy tap into your excellent abilities and high achievement results. If you're low on both, there's no energy or ability to tap into, which produces poor achievement. And the results are not much better when low motivation is combined with high ability, because there's not enough energy and drive to do demanding tasks well. So, in spite of ability, when a student's motivation is low, assignments are skipped or rushed and a high price is paid for skimpy work. Conversely, students with high motivation and low ability find ways to work through even the most difficult material. In fact, they often get B's or even higher because their energy and desire carries them through.

You may have noticed that only high or low ratings have been mentioned in this discussion. You could, of course, have moderate motivation or average ability levels. But for achievement purposes, that middle or "average" range is not very useful, as it doesn't offer any clearcut guidelines about what you need to do. High ratings are a direct message that you're on track and don't need to make changes; low ratings are an equally clear indicator that change is needed.

You can use the motivation effect to predict—and change—your performance in any course or on any task. How? Simply think about your motivation and ability levels for a class or assignment and determine whether they are high or low. With a little thought and honesty, you will know whether your motivation is high or low. **Ability,** which includes the knowledge and skills that you currently have, may be less obvious. To assess ability, think about your scores from a few recent assignments or tests. Rate yourself as high if you scored above average (B or above grades) or low if you scored at or below average (C or below). Once you have an idea about your motivation and ability levels, you can predict what your achievement level is likely to be and decide if you need to make any changes. Remember that motivation is the place to start: If it's high, use it; if it's low, work on it.

ACTIVITY 1: PREDICT YOUR ACHIEVEMENT LEVELS

DIRECTIONS: List your current courses. Then circle your general motivation and ability levels, and predict your achievement level, or grade, for each course.

COURSE	MOTIVATION LEVEL	ABILITY LEVEL	EXPECTED GRADE
Math	High/Low	High/Low	A
Eng	High/Low	High/Low	B
Read	High/Low	High/Low	C
ITSC	High/Low	High/Low	C
ITSE	High/Low	High/Low	B

Which course would benefit the most from a boost in your motivation? math.

Motivation and Reading

The motivation effect, or motivation-ability-achievement chain reaction, is a critical component of effective reading. For reading tasks, your motivation is your level of interest in the topic. And your ability involves the processes, skills, and methods you use to comprehend the text. When your motivation is high, it is usually easy to maintain your concentration, and you have the mental energy to use your best skills and work through any difficult parts. Low motivation, on the other hand, is characterized by mental drifting and feelings of boredom. Under these conditions, you may use poor methods such as skip-reading, or you may simply give up.

> Ability is what you're capable of doing. Motivation determines what you do. Attitude determines how well you do it.
>
> —Anonymous

Together, reading motivation and ability affect comprehension. As Table 1.1 shows, there are four expected combinations.

TABLE 1.1 **The Motivation Effect on Reading Comprehension**

MOTIVATION	ABILITY	COMPREHENSION
High	High	Superb
High	Low	Good
Low	High	Poor, uneven
Low	Low	Very poor

Once again, the motivation effect is a dynamic force that you can use to your advantage. Begin by assessing your motivation or interest level for the topic; rate it high or low. Then identify whether your ability level for the task is high or low. This will depend on the text difficulty as well as your reading skills. The newspaper is an easier text than a chemistry textbook, so your skill level for reading a newspaper is probably higher than for a difficult course text. Once you have assessed your levels, you can predict the likely comprehension level and make adjustments if needed. When motivation is high, you will automatically use your best skills and, if needed, find ways to work through difficult parts. When motivation is low, gaining interest will be your first reading task. Don't ignore low motivation. It will diminish your concentration as well as your skills, and the result will be a loss of comprehension.

ACTIVITY 2: ASSESS YOUR READING COMPREHENSION

DIRECTIONS: List your current courses and think about the reading assignments in each one. Circle your reading motivation and reading ability levels for each course. Then, predict your comprehension level for each course using this scale: extremely poor, poor, good, and superb.

COURSE	MOTIVATION	ABILITY	COMPREHENSION
____________	High/Low	High/Low	________
____________	High/Low	High/Low	________
____________	High/Low	High/Low	________
____________	High/Low	High/Low	________
____________	High/Low	High/Low	________

Which course would benefit the most from a boost in your reading motivation?

____

The Stages of Motivation

THINK ABOUT THIS . . .

Think about someone who has motivated you in the past. It might have been a teacher, coach, or relative. List what that person did that motivated you.

____

____

____

____

Good coaches work on their players' motivation almost all the time. Why? Why don't they just teach the skills of the sport and work on game plans? The answer is simple: motivated players play better and win more than unmotivated players. What good coaches do to produce winners provides excellent insights about motivation.

How Coaches Motivate

To coaches, the dream team is made up of engaged players. Those are the committed athletes who have the desire to achieve and participate wholeheartedly. To create this kind of desire, coaches talk enthusiastically about goals, achievement, and rewards. These motivating talks come frequently and cover both short-term objectives for training sessions and long-term goals for championships.

> The most important thing about motivation is goal setting. You should always have a goal.
>
> —Francie Larrieu Smith (1953–), American runner and coach

Once the players are engaged, coaches know that their effort has to be focused or channeled into productive practice sessions. Random effort and work will not turn desire into reality. So coaches train their players to use the best techniques and skills possible.

As the players practice, coaches monitor their progress. During this crucial skill-development time, they give feedback about what the players should continue to do and what changes they need to make. In addition, coaches are on the alert for attitudes that decrease motivation, such as a loss of confidence or high stress. Then they suggest solutions and encourage their players to fix the issues.

After a training session or a game, good coaches praise and celebrate achievements, including the small gains on the path to the major wins. They help players reflect and recognize what they've accomplished, which promotes feelings of satisfaction and pride, as well as the desire to strive for greater achievements in the future.

In conclusion: Coaches try to motivate their players at four stages: they engage their interest in achieving goals, focus their efforts on techniques and skills, monitor and guide their progress with feedback, and help them reflect on their gains. Their objective is to create the attitudes of "*I want to,*" "*I know how,*" "*I believe I can do it,*" and "*I've achieved something!*" Figure 1.1 illustrates these stages.

> A good coach will make his players see what they can be rather than what they are.
>
> —Ara Parasheghian (1923–), American football coach at Notre Dame University and Northwestern University

These four stages usually occur before, during, and after a task. That is, as you would expect, engaging interest comes before you begin, focusing and monitoring occur during the task, and reflection happens at the end. But motivation is not rigid, so the sequence can change. For example, after a mistake or a lost game, a focused training session may be needed, and to counteract a loss of desire, the coach may need to re-engage the players as well.

Academic and Reading Motivation

In life, sports, and classes, we don't always have the benefit of someone who works to motivate us. So the key to motivation is to be your own best coach and help yourself maintain high levels of drive at all four stages of motivation. Being your own best coach means that you

- **Engage** your own interest in goals and achievement;
- **Focus** your efforts by using effective techniques and methods;
- **Monitor** your progress to identify and solve problems;
- **Reflect** on your gains to get the benefits of your work.

FIGURE 1.1 **The Stages of Motivation**

These motivation stages are essential for reading academic assignments. By using them, you can achieve thorough comprehension and get the most out of your reading time. In Chapter 2, you will learn how to Engage, Focus, Monitor, and Reflect before, during, and after reading. You will find reminders of these stages and methods in each chapter starting with Chapter 3, and in all the essays, articles, and textbook excerpts in this book.

> **Believe and act as if it were impossible to fail.**
>
> —Charles F. Kettering (1876–1958), American engineer

Being reminded of the stages will not guarantee success, however. To get the benefits of motivation, you need to approach your work with positive attitudes and use the techniques that promote each stage. The rest of this chapter will introduce you to the attitudes and techniques that contribute most to academic motivation. Adopting them may seem cumbersome at first. But be patient. The more you use them, the more automatic they will become. In addition, as you work on the materials in this textbook, you will develop skills that will serve you well in all your lifelong reading and learning activities.

How to Develop Self-Motivation

THINK ABOUT THIS . . .

Think of two activities in your life where your motivation level is very different. That is, pick one where you're very motivated and another where you're not. With these activities in mind, complete each of the following statements with words and phrases, and write them in the appropriate box.

STATEMENT	THE ACTIVITY WHERE I'M MOTIVATED	THE ACTIVITY WHERE I'M NOT MOTIVATED
In terms of this activity . . . 1. My interest level is _____.		
2. My goals are _____.		
3. The techniques I use are _____.		
4. My skills are _____.		
5. My confidence is _____.		
6. My level of stress is _____.		
7. The rewards I get are _____.		
8. I feel _____ when I finish.		

As you did this exercise, you probably noticed that when your motivation is low, you list negative attitudes and ineffective approaches, and when it's high, you have positive thoughts and successful methods. Your answers point to a very important principle about motivation. *The activity does not produce motivation; your attitudes and techniques do.* Look at the *Zits* cartoon and notice how it emphasizes this idea.

The principle that attitudes and techniques produce motivation is the key to empowering yourself. It means that you can control and change your own motivation. And that is precisely what self-motivation is.

Motivation Measure. You may have been surprised to find questions about attitudes and reading methods in the Motivation Measure. Both were included because research shows that those who use effective techniques generally have high motivation, and vice versa. Poor techniques produce frustration and low motivation; successful techniques produce the ingredients of high motivation: a sense of power, confidence, and eagerness to see results. The lesson? One sure way to change your motivation for reading is to learn the techniques that make it easier to do.

Use Motivating Attitudes and Techniques

To increase your motivation, identify and change demotivating attitudes and techniques. **Attitudes** are your reactions to a task, person, place, or idea. They tend to be negative or positive. **Techniques** are the methods you use to complete tasks. They're usually effective or ineffective.

To unlock and change your attitudes, identify the thoughts or comments you make to yourself. Those thoughts are called **self-talk.** Low motivation comes from negative thinking. So a statement such as "This is boring" is demotivating. You will become more motivated as soon as you find something that is interesting or useful in the text.

There's one caution about changing your self-talk. You can't just replace a negative thought ("I'm going to fail the test") with its opposite. You have to find a new thought that is both reasonable and helpful. For example, it doesn't do any good to say "I'm going to get an 'A'" when you really believe that you're going to fail. In this situation, the positive thought could be "If I learn the information (or work with a friend, or put in extra time, or take notes), I will do better on the test." This example also illustrates the role of techniques. Poor methods—in this case fantasizing either disaster or out-of-the-blue success—lead to negative attitudes

> We all have voices in our heads which talk to us on an almost constant basis. Our voices give us messages continually, and what they say to us affects us.
>
> —Juliene Berk (contemporary), American author and psychologist

and poor results. If you substitute a better method, your attitude will improve and, almost certainly, so will your results.

ACTIVITY 3: CHANGE NEGATIVE SELF-TALK

DIRECTIONS: The following negative thoughts are ones that most students have at one time or another. Rephrase each one into a more positive statement and write it on the lines.

1. "I'm not smart in math (or English, or science)."

   ____

   ____

2. "Instructors give too much homework."

   ____

   ____

3. "This assignment is boring."

   ____

   ____

4. "Why should I try? I've failed in the past, so I'll probably just fail again."

   ____

   ____

5. "When the text is difficult, I just want to quit."

   ____

   ____

Attitudes and techniques affect each stage of motivation. The following sections describe successful approaches that you can learn and use for each stage.

> *Motivation Measure.* Before you read each of the following sections, look at your column score for each stage. If it is high, note the attitudes and techniques that you already use and continue to use them. If your score is low, note where you can change your self-talk or use better techniques. Again, remember that your score is just an indication of your current level. You can increase it.

Engage Your Interest

The **engage** stage of motivation generates interest in a task, text, or achievement. It is the *"I want to"* attitude. During this stage, you increase your curiosity to know something, your awareness of personal uses for the information, or your recognition of the benefits that task completion will bring. For example, if your biology assignment is to read a chapter about human circulation, you might engage your own interest by wondering how the heart works, thinking that the information will help you stay healthy, or wanting to perform well on the chapter quiz.

To engage your own interest, be on the alert for negative thoughts, which label tasks and information as boring, worthless, useless, or impossible to do. Change such statements to reasonable, positive versions such as these:

EXAMPLES

NEGATIVE SELF-TALK	REPHRASED STATEMENTS
This is boring.	This part is interesting.
This is not important; I don't want to do this.	Learning about this will help me to . . .
This task is too much; I don't even want to start it.	I can break this into short, easy tasks and do a little at a time.

To become engaged, use techniques that get you intellectually involved, such as the following.

1. *Talk to those who appear engaged.*

   If you find a task irrelevant and boring, ask others what they find useful in it. Your professors and tutors are excellent resource people to help you see benefits that aren't obvious.

2. *Preview the task.*

   Before beginning any task, quickly look it over. Try to identify interesting, useful, or relevant parts that increase your motivation. Notice what the task entails so that you can plan your time, gather resources, and choose successful methods before you begin. Think about what you already know. Accessing your background knowledge will make it easier to take in new information.

Before everything else, getting ready is the secret to success.

—Henry Ford (1863–1947), American car manufacturer

3. *Divide long tasks.*

   College courses are designed to have an average of six to nine hours of outside class work per week. Doing all of that in one sitting is a marathon that will lower your motivation and interest. Instead, divide the weekly assignment into 60- to 90-minute tasks that you can easily do in one sitting. Then, spread the tasks out over the course of several days. This approach is called **spaced learning,** and research shows that it creates higher motivation, comprehension, and memory.

4. *Create motivating goals.*

   A motivating **goal** is a positive statement that describes what you want and the rewards you'll get once you achieve it. Goals are critical to self-motivation, because they establish a personal reason for doing the work, a focus to minimize wasted effort, and a way to gauge progress.

   To create a motivating goal, follow these steps:

   a. Make your goal personal; start it with the words *I want.*
   b. Add a specific *task* or *topic* that you will focus on.

c. End with the *reward* you'll get; emphasize the *reasons* why the work is personally important. You can also add a *bonus* you'll give yourself when you're finished.

Here are examples of demotivating statements that have been reworded into effective goals. The parts of each motivating goal are labeled.

EXAMPLES

1. Demotivating statement: The next section looks boring.
   Motivating goal:
   personal | *specific task* | *specific topic*
   I want to read the next section of this chapter, called Focus Your Efforts, and identify the best ways to work. Then I'll take a break.
   reward–reason | *reward–bonus*
2. Demotivating statement: I'll be glad when this essay is done.
   Motivating goal:
   personal | *specific task* | *specific topic*
   I want to write this psychology essay about siblings. My reward will be a better understanding of my brother and how we interact.
   reward–reason

These examples bring up a few more points about goals. First, focused goals are more motivating than general ones. So, for a lengthy task, create a number of goals—for example, one for each part of a textbook chapter. Second, in terms of rewards, the reason why the work is personally important to you is generally more motivating than a bonus. So, either have both a reason and a bonus or just a reason. Third, don't include any negative words or statements in your goals, such as "If I don't do this, I'll fail." Negativity is demotivating. Finally, don't name a specific grade in your goal, such as "I want to study so that I can get an A." Focusing on grades raises stress and lowers motivation.

Give yourself something to work toward—constantly.
—Mary Kay Ash (1918–2001), American businesswoman, founder of Mary Kay Cosmetics

ACTIVITY 4: ENGAGE YOUR INTEREST

DIRECTIONS: Apply the techniques for engaging your interest as you complete the following tasks.

1. Think about a course or task where you are demotivated. Whom can you talk to about what's useful or what the benefits are?

____

____

2. Preview the next section of this chapter entitled Focus Your Efforts.
   a. What will it cover?

      ____

      ____

   b. List five terms that you already know something about.

      ____

      ____

   c. What looks interesting, useful, or relevant in this section?

      ____

      ____

3. Look at the next chapter. Assume that it's your assignment for the coming week. Apply the principle of spaced learning by dividing the chapter into short tasks and planning to do them over a number of days.

TASKS	DUE DAYS AND TIMES
______________________________	__________
______________________________	__________
______________________________	__________

4. Use the characteristics of motivating goals to complete the following items.
   a. If I don't understand my chemistry text. I'm going to fail the quiz about atoms and molecules.

      I want to ______________ about ________________ because (or so that) ______________________________

      ____.

   b. This psychology assignment about learning theory is too long and too hard to read.

      I want to ______________________ about ____________________.

      My reward(s) will be ______________________________

      ____.

   c. Think of two course assignments from your current class(es). Form a goal for each one.

      I want to ______________________ about ____________________.

      My reward(s) will be ______________________________

      ____.

      I want to ______________________ about ____________________.

      My reward(s) will be ______________________________

      ____.

> Life takes on meaning when you become motivated; set goals and charge after them in an unstoppable manner.
>
> —Les Brown (1945–), American speaker, author, and lecturer

Focus Your Efforts

The **focus** stage of motivation is the working mode. Any technique or skill that keeps you thinking about the task, making progress, and increasing your *"I know how"* attitude will improve your motivation at this stage. Your methods, standards, concentration level, and time management techniques all affect your focus.

To become more focused, recognize and change negative thoughts about the task, your methods, or your concentration and time management to reasonable, positive versions like these:

EXAMPLES

NEGATIVE SELF-TALK	REPHRASED STATEMENTS
I don't know how to do this.	I can ask others to show me how or give me suggestions about where to start.
I can just hand in anything and do this at the last minute.	I'll get more information and understand more if I take my time. The more I know about this, the easier the rest of the course will be.
I can't concentrate on this.	What's distracting me? I can eliminate most distractions and control my attention.
I'm going to cram for the test because I don't have time to study.	I'll reduce my stress if I don't work in a rush. I can also rearrange some activities, find short blocks, and do a little at a time.

Use techniques that promote quality work, improve your concentration, and allow time to do your best.

1. *Set high standards.*

> Striving for excellence motivates you; striving for perfection is demoralizing.
>
> —Harriet Braiker (1949–2004), American psychologist and management consultant

Poor quality work is embarrassing, and even more important, it creates poor comprehension and memory, confusion, loss of interest, and low motivation. Before beginning a task, think about what an excellent result would be. Perhaps it's an essay that's edited and typed or text information that's captured in organized notes. Making a deliberate choice to give every task your best effort produces better results and also increases your sense of pride, self-esteem, and motivation.

2. *Concentrate.*

Pay attention to your attention. When it wanders, refocus yourself. Also, identify what's distracting you and try to eliminate it. Make a note of any distracting thoughts you have and plan to think about them later; turn off the TV and phone;

move to where it's quiet. Avoid working in the living room, bedroom, or kitchen. These places invite interruptions and distractions. Finally, invest in your college career by creating a comfortable and functional workspace that's outfitted with all the supplies, equipment, and resources you need.

3. *Manage your time so that you can do quality work.*

   College is not a hobby that you can do whenever you have time. To succeed and gain the benefits for your future, make your courses a priority: allow time to read and learn, time to handle the problems that inevitably come up, and time to do well. If you're in the habit of reading the text right before the exam, you're not going to do well in college, because tests usually cover four or more chapters, and no one can read and learn all of that in one night. Plan to read the assignments and review them during the week the material is covered in class. This approach reduces stress and produces much higher comprehension and motivation than last-minute or rushed work.

One of the secrets of getting more done is to make a To Do list every day, keep it visible, and use it as a guide to action as you go through the day.

—Alan Lakein (contemporary), American time management expert

ACTIVITY 5: FOCUS YOUR EFFORTS

DIRECTIONS: Pretend that you are taking courses in biology, chemistry, and English, and you have the following assignments for the week. Pick one assignment and put a checkmark next to it. Then think about how you could focus your efforts by answering the questions that follow.

A. Read a 30-page biology chapter on the immune system. It will be the topic for a lecture this coming week, and it will be on the midterm in two weeks.

B. Complete 20 practice problems in chemistry. They'll be part of the in-class midterm test review session, but they won't be collected.

C. Write a 1,000-word essay for English. The essay must present a common interpersonal problem and a solution. The first draft is due in four days; the final typed draft is due next week.

1. Set high standards.

   a. What would "doing your best" be on this assignment?

   ____

   ____

   b. What techniques could you use to promote your success?

   ____

   ____

2. Think about your concentration.

   a. What would be the best place and time to do this task?

   ____

   ____

b. What might distract you?

____

____

c. How could you fix these problems?

____

____

d. What special supplies, equipment, or resources would you need to do this task?

____

____

3. Think about your time management.

a. How could you divide this assignment up into easy to complete tasks? List them.

____

____

b. About how much time would you need for each task?

____

____

c. How would you space out these tasks over the week?

____

____

Monitor Your Progress

Monitoring your progress is the self-evaluation mode that keeps you on track. Monitoring means giving yourself feedback about how you're doing and also identifying problems that need to be resolved. This stage is directly related to your self-confidence or "*I believe I can do it*" attitude. Two general issues that affect your motivation at this stage are your sense of control and your stress management methods.

Stay in Control If you feel that you have no control over an outcome, you will have little reason to work or strive to achieve. If you believe that your efforts matter a great deal, you will be motivated even if the task is difficult. **Locus of control,** which literally means the "place of power," is the psychological term that covers these two viewpoints. It can be either external or internal.

Students with an **external locus of control** believe that others have more power than they do, particularly in terms of their motivation and success. So they depend on others, such as professors and family, to stimulate their interest and encourage them. And they believe that success comes from forces that they often cannot control. These students blame poor grades on a lack of intelligence, poor luck, interference and demands of others, poor instruction, or personality clashes with their professors. In general, those with an external locus of control have a pessimistic attitude, believe that they have little to do with the course of their lives, and are convinced that their efforts don't matter very much.

Students with an **internal locus of control** believe that they have the power to determine most outcomes. These students believe that effort and learning contribute more to college success than natural ability or luck. When problems arise, they try to identify what they can do to correct them. These students remind themselves of past successes and of their own strengths. Overall, students with an internal locus of control are optimists who believe they have a great deal of control over most parts of their life and that their efforts matter a great deal. Research shows that students with an internal locus of control get higher grades than those with an external locus of control.

A pessimist sees the difficulty in every opportunity; an optimist sees the opportunity in every difficulty.

—Winston Churchill (1874–1965), British politician; prime minister during World War II

To create and maintain an internal locus of control, recognize and change negative thoughts about your skills, intelligence, and poor performance. Examples of external locus of control comments and positive rephrased statements are:

EXAMPLES

NEGATIVE SELF-TALK	REPHRASED STATEMENTS
I'm not smart.	I am intelligent, and I can learn what I don't know.
It doesn't matter what I do; I always get low grades.	The methods I've used in the past didn't work well; I can change them.
I'm not very lucky; test questions are always on the parts I didn't study.	Luck is not the issue. Test questions are on what's important. I can identify that and learn the information.
If others didn't bother me, I could do better in my courses.	I need to ask others not to interrupt me, or I need to schedule better places and times to work.
The grades I get are unfair.	Grades are feedback from the instructor. If I don't understand them, s/he will explain how I can improve if I ask.
The instructor doesn't like me and always gives me low grades.	The instructor grades my work; it's not personal. I can ask for ways to improve.

To increase your sense of control, use techniques that focus on the positive.

If you believe you can, you probably can. If you believe you won't, you most assuredly won't. Belief is the ignition switch that gets you off the launching pad.

—Denis Waitley (contemporary), American author and consultant on human achievement

1. *Use a positive, self-fulfilling prophecy.*

   If you believe that you will succeed and can do a task, you will work to succeed, and your motivation will be high; if you believe that you will fail, you won't work hard, and your motivation will be low. This is called the **self-fulfilling prophecy.** A sense of control comes from the view that you will succeed.

2. *Use positive visualizations.*

   Visualization means imagining yourself going through an experience. On every task, but particularly on those that are challenging, visualize yourself working productively, feeling confident, succeeding, and feeling proud of yourself. Create, play, and replay this inner movie. Visualization is a mental rehearsal that motivates you to do your best.

ACTIVITY 6: MONITOR YOUR LOCUS OF CONTROL

DIRECTIONS

A. Check off the amount of control you think you have in each of the following situations.

B. Then, anywhere you marked "very little" or "none," come up with positive actions you could take—even if they seem extreme or unlikely (like quitting a job). The point here is to create a mindset that says "I do have the power to act."

A.

	AMOUNT OF CONTROL			
SITUATION	Complete	A great deal	Very little	None
Health	______	______	______	______
Relationships	______	______	______	______
Money matters	______	______	______	______
Job requirements	______	______	______	______
Job performance	______	______	______	______
Having to work late	______	______	______	______
Motivation	______	______	______	______
Difficult textbooks	______	______	______	______
Reading comprehension	______	______	______	______
Many tests in one week	______	______	______	______
Grades	______	______	______	______

B. List possible actions for the "very little" or "none" items.

____

____

____

____

Manage Your Stress Stress directly affects motivation. It creates tension and breeds external locus of control thoughts, which dramatically reduce performance in reading and learning activities. Many students "just live with stress" or complain about it. The self-motivating approach is to identify the stress-producing issues and resolve them.

To manage stress, watch for the negativity that stress creates. Then, change de-motivating self-talk to motivating statements such as:

EXAMPLES

NEGATIVE SELF-TALK	REPHRASED STATEMENTS
I don't get enough sleep, relaxation, or fun.	I need to delay some things, get to bed a little earlier, and plan an activity that's fun.
This is confusing and hard; I'm frustrated; I can't do this.	I'm going to look for resources, people, and methods that will make this easier.
I'm worried about failing and showing how little I know.	I'm going to do my best. The grade will show me if I need to use different approaches.

There are many ways to cope with stress. The following are some successful approaches that are particularly geared to student life.

1. *Balance your life.*

   Balance means creating a healthy daily routine that takes care of your physical and psychological needs. For example, we need to work, but we also need to rest. We need others, but we also need time alone. Don't discount the importance of rest and leisure activities. Plan rest, relaxation, exercise, and quality social activities every week.

2. *Set limits on non-school activities.*

   To gain the future that college learning can bring, you may have to reduce the time you spend on something else. For most of us, responsibilities like family and work can't be easily changed. So you may need to set limits with the people in your life or take fewer courses in a term.

3. *Develop support groups.*

   Seek out friends and family who will encourage you when the work is difficult and you doubt your abilities. Find tutors and professors who will explain confusing material and teach you successful methods. Find classmates you can work with and form study groups to comprehend and learn the material more easily.

4. *Prioritize.*

   Much of the stress that students feel about coursework comes from trying to do too much with too little time. The problem is trying to work with no system of priorities, as if everything is of equal importance. One solution is to spend a little time planning. Decide what subject or assignment is the priority for each day, and work on that.

5. *Take a problem-solving approach.*

   When you're learning something new, you're stretching beyond your current levels, and that can be uncomfortable. In addition, course information is sometimes confusing and difficult. When you're feeling overwhelmed or confused, look for solutions. For example, try rereading, doing a web search, finding other information resources, or seeking out the aid of friends, tutors, and professors.

6. *Change your attitude about grades.*

   Recognize that a grade is not about you; it's about the piece of work you produced. Many factors contribute to the quality of the work you do: background knowledge, following directions, reading, comprehension, learning, memory, and time on task. In turn, many elements affect those factors, such as health, self-confidence, stress management, concentration, and vocabulary. View grades as helpful feedback about the work. Once you get the feedback, you can decide if you need to change or improve your methods.

ACTIVITY 7: MONITOR YOUR STRESS MANAGEMENT TECHNIQUES

DIRECTIONS: What causes stress in your life? List your general and course-related stressors in the first column. Then in the second column, record a possible way to eliminate each one or reduce the tension it creates.

STRESSORS	MANAGEMENT METHODS
General	
Course-related	

Reflect on Your Gains

The **reflection** stage of motivation promotes the "*I've achieved something!*" attitude. It's the self-reward phase, which is essential for motivation. Many students don't reward themselves. They wait for others to give them praise, good grades, and compliments. But, those are not enough to keep a student motivated during the many hours of reading and learning. Self-motivated students, on the other hand, reflect on their work and recognize that they've gained useful ideas, skills, or practice. They feel a sense of accomplishment and they reward themselves.

> It is not the horse that draws the cart, but the oats.
>
> —Russian proverb

To reflect, spend a moment at the end of a task and look over your work. Think about what you've gained. Recognize and stop negative thoughts such as:

EXAMPLES

NEGATIVE SELF-TALK	REPHRASED STATEMENTS
I take courses, but I never seem to accomplish much.	I learned _____ in the _____ course.
Every time I finish an assignment, there's just more to read.	When I finish an assignment, there's one less to do.
I'm tired of working so hard in school and not getting anything for all of my effort.	I've worked hard and gained knowledge and skills. I am getting closer to my degree and meeting people who might help me find a great job.

Use techniques such as the following to solidify your accomplishments and reward yourself.

1. *Review the information.*

   After a task, work with the text: sum it up, take notes on it, discuss it with others, or answer chapter review questions. Looking over what you just worked on is the best way to set it in your mind and feel that you are gaining knowledge.

2. *Recognize what's useful.*

   Think about how you can use the information in your class or in other areas of your life. Recognize that each small addition to your knowledge makes you more intellectually powerful.

3. *Reward yourself often.*

   Rewards can come from others, but those rarely come when we want or need them. True motivation comes from the rewards we give ourselves. As mentioned in the discussion about goals, rewards can be bonuses or reasons, and as psychologists put it, they can be extrinsic or intrinsic.

   Extrinsic rewards are tangible. Grades and certificates are examples of extrinsic rewards that others may give you. You can also give yourself extrinsic rewards, such as a TV show, snack, or leisure activity at the end of every task, project, and course. Extrinsic rewards are most motivating if you plan them before you start to work and make them part of your goals.

   Intrinsic rewards are the feelings of pleasure and pride that come from accomplishments. The praise of others creates these feelings, but you can also create your own intrinsic rewards in three ways. First, approach tasks in an enjoyable, creative way. For example, you could create pictures or diagrams to help you understand complex texts, or use color and computer programs to make your work look professional. Second, compliment yourself as you work with statements such as "I am doing

"Knowledge is power." Rather, knowledge is happiness, because to have knowledge—broad, deep knowledge—is to know true ends from false, and lofty things from low.

—Helen Keller (1880–1968), American blind and deaf author, lecturer

The reward of a thing well done is to have done it.

—Ralph Waldo Emerson (1803–1882), American poet and essayist a good job of reading and understanding this" or "That looks good." Third, when you're finished with a task, recognize and praise your achievements.

ACTIVITY 8: REFLECT ON YOUR GAINS

DIRECTIONS: Think about how you can use the reflect stage of motivation in your work by completing these activities.

1. Think of an assignment that you've completed recently. Then answer these questions.
   a. What useful information did you get from the task?

   ____

   ____

   b. Did you reward yourself? If so, how?

   ____

   ____

   c. If you were planning to do the task now, what would be a good extrinsic reward?

   ____

   d. If you were planning to do the task now, what would be a good intrinsic reward?

   ____

2. Reread the two goals that you formed in Activity 3. What additional extrinsic and intrinsic rewards could you give yourself for each one?

   Goal #1: Extrinsic: ______________________________

   Intrinsic: ______________________________

   Goal #2: Extrinsic: ______________________________

   Intrinsic: ______________________________

You are what you think. You are what you go for. You are what you do!

—Bob Richards (1926–),
American Olympic pole vaulting champion

CHAPTER SUMMARY

Introduction

Motivation is the driving force that creates success. It provides the desire and psychological energy to achieve. While others can stimulate it, lasting motivation comes from what you do for yourself. College students need to develop high **academic motivation** that creates the desire to read, learn, and perform well in courses meant to challenge and stretch their knowledge.

The Motivation–Achievement Link

Motivation affects how you use the ability you have, and the two together produce performance. It is a dynamic, changing force that can be controlled and used to enhance effort and achievement. Students can improve their achievement and their reading comprehension by thinking about their motivation and **ability** levels, predicting the likely outcome, and making changes where needed.

The Stages of Motivation

Athletic coaches provide a useful model of how motivation works. They engage their players' interest, focus their efforts, monitor their progress, and encourage them to reflect on their gains. Students can greatly improve their academic and reading motivation by being their own best coach and using the approaches that best enhance each stage.

How to Develop Self-Motivation

High motivation is the result of positive **attitudes** and effective **techniques.** To increase motivation, change negative **self-talk,** or demotivating statements made to yourself, to positive and encouraging thoughts. Also, replace haphazard methods with more thoughtful approaches that **engage** your interest, **focus** your efforts, **monitor** your progress, and **reflect** on your gains.

REVIEW ACTIVITIES

Use the following activities to check your understanding and aid your learning of the information in this chapter.

Expand Your Vocabulary

Match each term with the correct definition or characteristic.

_____ **1.** motivation
_____ **2.** academic motivation
_____ **3.** ability
_____ **4.** attitude
_____ **5.** technique
_____ **6.** self-talk
_____ **7.** engage
_____ **8.** spaced learning
_____ **9.** goal
_____ **10.** focus
_____ **11.** monitor
_____ **12.** locus of control
_____ **13.** external locus of control
_____ **14.** internal locus of control
_____ **15.** self-fulfilling prophecy
_____ **16.** visualization
_____ **17.** balance
_____ **18.** reflect
_____ **19.** extrinsic rewards
_____ **20.** intrinsic rewards

a. the knowledge and skills you currently have
b. thoughts or comments you make to yourself
c. responses from others for good work
d. desire and psychological energy to achieve
e. imagining yourself going through an experience
f. the methods you use to complete tasks
g. the self-evaluation stage of motivation
h. a healthy daily routine that takes care of your needs
i. what you want to achieve and the benefits of it
j. the belief that success comes from outside, uncontrollable forces
k. the working mode, or stage, of motivation
l. the ability to create your own desire to read and do well in courses
m. your reactions to a task, person, place, or idea
n. the stage that generates interest, curiosity, or relevance
o. the place of power
p. feelings of pleasure and pride about good work
q. doing short tasks over a number of study sessions
r. the stage in which you get the rewards of working
s. beliefs about task outcomes that create your future
t. the belief that success comes from personal effort

Increase Your Knowledge

These tasks will help you identify the important ideas in this chapter. They will also help you prepare for quizzes and exams on this material.

1. The following questions focus on the major chapter topics. Discuss them with others or form your own detailed answers.
   a. What are the four combinations of motivation and ability? What task or course grade is likely to result from each one?
   b. What are the four combinations of reading motivation and ability? What level of comprehension is likely to result from each one?
   c. List the four stages of motivation. Explain how coaches use the four stages of motivation. How do these stages apply to academic motivation?
   d. How do attitudes and techniques affect motivation?
   e. For each stage of motivation, give examples of negative self-talk that need to be changed. Then list the effective techniques that promote each stage.
2. Take detailed and organized notes on the information in this chapter.

Develop Your Skills

The following review tasks will give you an opportunity to practice the methods presented in this chapter.

REVIEW 1: IDENTIFY THE STAGES OF MOTIVATION Match the stage of motivation to each of the descriptive statements.

a. Engage your interest **b.** Focus your effort
c. Monitor your progress **d.** Reflect on your gains

Motivated students . . .

______ **1.** set high standards for their own work.
______ **2.** want to achieve.
______ **3.** think and plan what they'll do before they start to work.
______ **4.** pay attention to their own learning and progress.
______ **5.** set goals.
______ **6.** praise themselves for their achievements.
______ **7.** manage their time to allow for quality work.
______ **8.** review frequently.
______ **9.** identify what's interesting and relevant before beginning a task.
______**10.** think about how the information is useful after working on a task.
______**11.** do their best to manage the stress in their lives.
______**12.** have curiosity, interest, and enthusiasm for their reading assignments.
______**13.** pay attention to their concentration as they work.
______**14.** visualize and believe they will succeed.
______**15.** think of grades as useful feedback.

REVIEW 2: USING THE STAGES OF MOTIVATION Read the following situation, which describes an imaginary student named Jonathan who is having trouble with a reading assignment. Then, answer the questions under "Your Task."

The Situation

Jonathan plans to be an elementary school teacher. He is taking a biology class to satisfy the science requirement for his degree. He has been assigned to read a chapter entitled "The Defenses against Disease." This material will be part of the upcoming midterm exam. Jonathan has started and stopped reading this chapter twice. Both times he was trying to read in the kitchen after dinner. He was tired, and his family came into the room several times, so he felt he had to stop to talk to them. Jonathan is worried about the midterm, because he's always found science courses difficult, doesn't think he has any natural ability in science, and predicts that he won't do any better than his past "C" performances.

Your Task: Create self-motivating approaches and advice for Jonathan by answering the following questions. Refer to the chapter sections as you work.

1. How could Jonathan engage his interest in the biology chapter?
   a. Suggest specific techniques he could use.
   b. Form one goal that Jonathan could use.
2. Present some guidelines about how Jonathan could focus his efforts.
   a. How could he improve his concentration?
   b. How would time management help him?
3. How could monitoring his progress help Jonathan?
   a. What aspect of external locus of control is Jonathan using? How could he change it?
   b. What stress management techniques would you recommend?
4. How could Jonathan reflect on the gains he's made after he works?
   a. How could he review the information?
   b. How could the information in the chapter help him in his career?
   c. What rewards could he give himself?

Check Your Motivation

1. List the new ideas and methods you've gained from this chapter. Think about how they will help you in the future.
2. Measure your motivation for this chapter topic. Think about each statement and how you will use it in the future. Mark it:

   A = never B = sometimes C = usually D = always

	A	B	C	D
To engage my interest, I plan to . . .				
1. initiate an *"I want to"* attitude about reading topics and tasks.	___	___	___	___
2. preview tasks and look for interesting parts.	___	___	___	___
3. divide long assignments into short tasks and spread them out.	___	___	___	___
4. set motivating goals.	___	___	___	___
To focus my effort, I plan to . . .				
5. develop my techniques and *"I know how"* attitude.	___	___	___	___
6. set high standards for myself.	___	___	___	___
7. work where I can concentrate.	___	___	___	___
8. manage my time and avoid working at the last minute.	___	___	___	___
To monitor my progress, I plan to . . .				
9. promote my self-confidence and *"I believe I can do it"* attitude.	___	___	___	___
10. remind myself that good grades depend mostly on my efforts.	___	___	___	___
11. use stress management techniques, when needed.	___	___	___	___
To reflect on my gains, I plan to . . .				
12. promote an *"I've achieved something!"* attitude.	___	___	___	___
13. use review activities like note taking and discussions.	___	___	___	___
14. think about the useful information I've acquired.	___	___	___	___
15. give myself extrinsic and/or intrinsic rewards.	___	___	___	___

SCORING: In the following spaces, record the number of answers for each column. Compute the column scores, and then add them up to determine your total score.

# of A's ______ × 1 pt. = ______
# of B's ______ × 2 pt. = ______
# of C's ______ × 3 pt. = ______
# of D's ______ × 4 pt. = ______

Total points = ______

INTERPRETATION: 15–43 points = low motivation; 44–60 points = high motivation

SUGGESTIONS

1. Compare your current chapter score to the one from The Motivation Measure (see p. xxxi). If they're both low, review the list above and find approaches you'd be willing try. If you've improved or have a high score, reward yourself for your empowered approaches.
2. Record the methods you wish to use on a card and use it as a bookmark. Look it over before you begin reading the next assignment. Apply those approaches.

CHAPTER TWO

Active Reading

What do these pictures reveal about participation? What do you think these students are thinking and feeling? What do class participation and reading have in common?

It's easy to see who's actively involved in class. Those who ask questions and participate are obviously part of what's going on. What's not always easy to see are the rewards they get, such as greater concentration, understanding, interest, and even praise. Although the world of reading is an inner world that can't be easily observed, good reading requires the same kind of thoughtful involvement and brings the same rewards as participating in classroom activities. As John Locke emphasizes, thought is the key to effective reading:

> Reading furnishes the mind only with materials of knowledge; it is thinking that makes what we read ours.
>
> — John Locke (1632–1704), English political philosopher and writer

This chapter, mapped out below, deals with the kind of deliberate, mental activity that increases both motivation and comprehension. It covers:

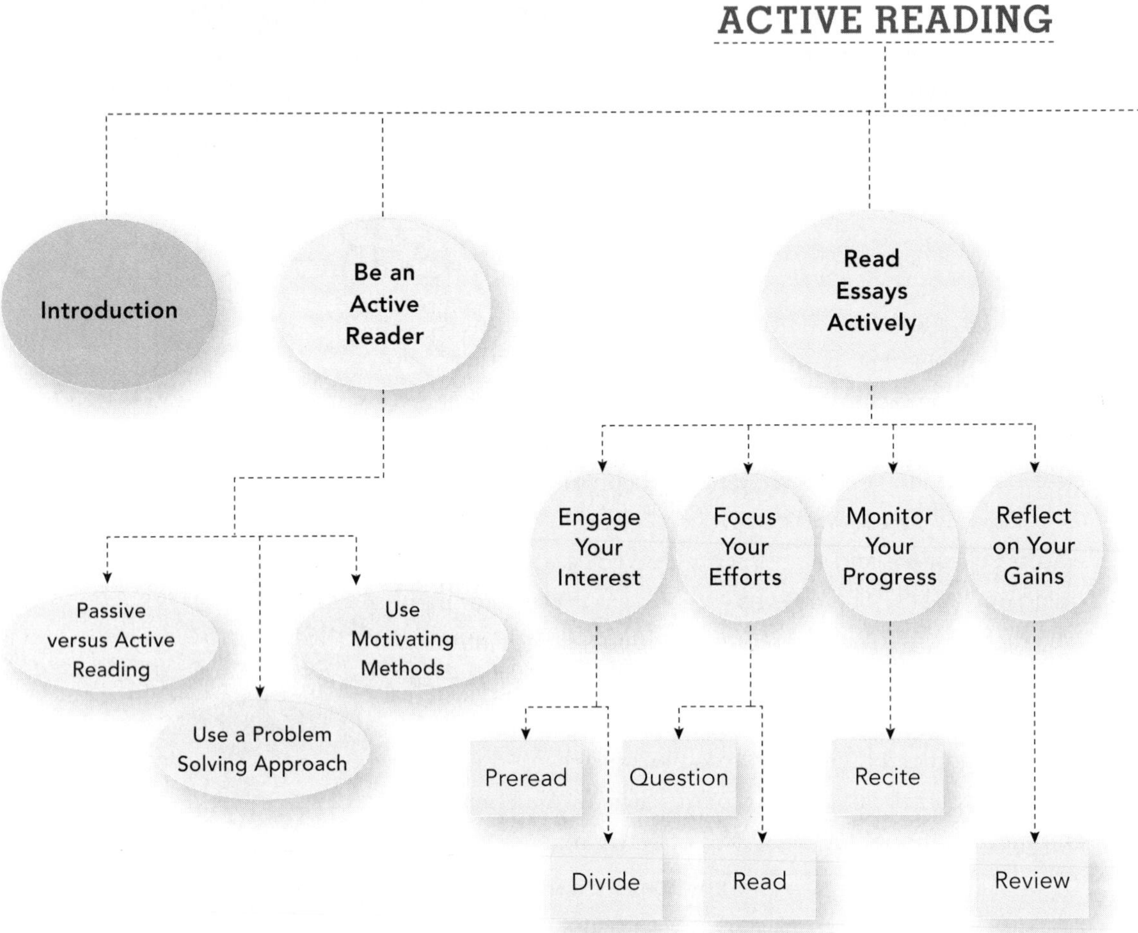

From the map you can see what the chapter covers. Now make those topics personal by listing three reading goals. Include a specific task, topic, and reward for each one. (See Chapter 1, p. 13, for more guidelines about setting reading goals.)

1. I want to ________________ about ______________________________.
   My reward(s) will be ______________________________________
   ____.

2. I want to ________________ about ______________________________.
   My reward(s) will be ______________________________________
   ____.

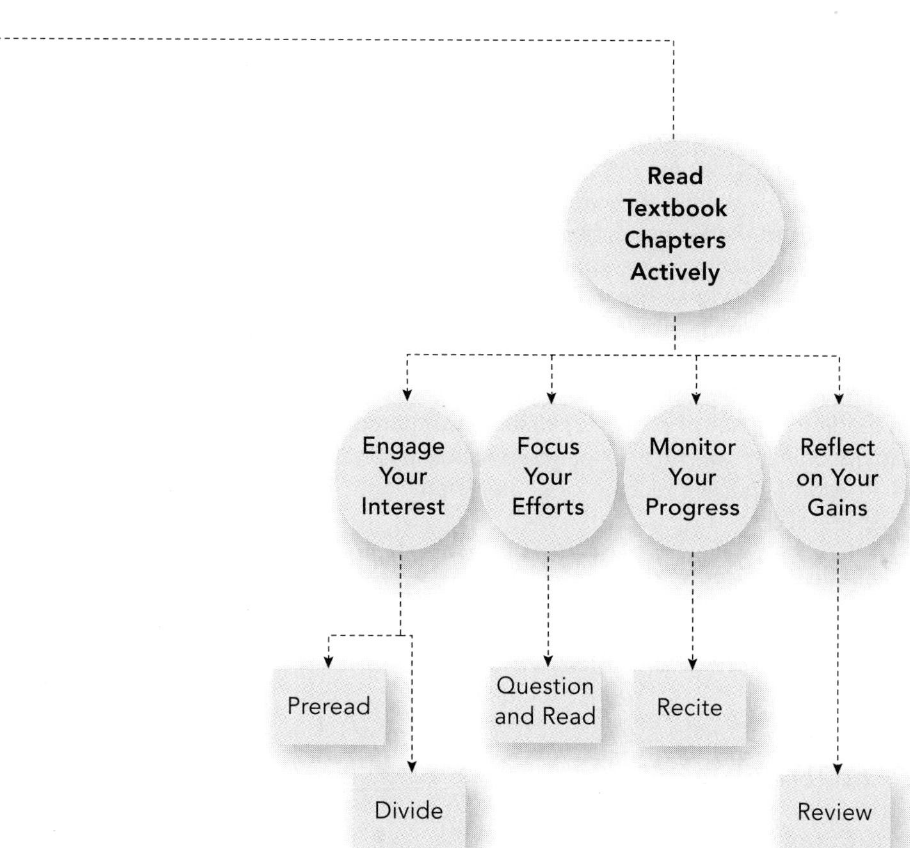

3. I want to ________________ about ______________________________________.
My reward(s) will be ____
____.

College reading is more challenging than any other kind of reading for two reasons. First, it involves **reading for learning.** That is, your reading leads directly to other writing, studying, and exam activities for the course. Think of reading as the beginning of a pipeline that sends information into a mental tube to be used for various tasks at the other end. So, in addition to understanding the text, you must also figure out what you will need in the future. And anything you miss or misunderstand will affect the tasks that follow, the products you produce, and the grades you receive. To start the content moving properly through the pipeline, then, accurate and thorough reading is essential.

Thinking is like loving and dying—each of us must do it for himself.
—Josiah Royce (1855–1916), American philosopher

Comprehending college reading assignments is also challenging because you are at a different level from the text. The texts are usually very complex and filled with a great deal of technical vocabulary and information. Most students, on the other hand, have very limited vocabulary and background knowledge about the field. And those two aspects of knowledge—vocabulary and background—are the major tools of comprehension. Put another way, **comprehension** is a process of thinking in which readers combine text information with their vocabulary and background knowledge to build units of meaning. The less you know, the more difficult the process is.

Active reading is a set of processes that create thorough comprehension when you are reading for learning and/or when your vocabulary and background knowledge are limited. In addition, active reading promotes motivation. This chapter focuses on the processes needed to

- Be an Active Reader
- Read Essays Actively
- Read Textbook Chapters Actively

Be an Active Reader

THINK ABOUT THIS . . .

Think about a TV program that you watched even though you didn't care about it. Then, think about a program that you were extremely interested in, such as a sporting event or a good movie. Describe each of these experiences by writing brief answers to the following questions.

	LOW-INTEREST PROGRAM	HIGH-INTEREST PROGRAM
What was your attitude about the program?		
What did you do, say, or think as you watched the program?		

	LOW-INTEREST PROGRAM	HIGH-INTEREST PROGRAM
How well did you understand the program? How much did you remember when it was over?		

Your descriptions about low- and high-interest programs undoubtedly revealed opposite attitudes, methods, and outcomes. When people are not interested in a program, they experience boredom, think about other things, stare blankly at the screen, comprehend little, and recall even less. When they are interested, they watch intently, think about what they're seeing and hearing, and respond. They may comment to themselves and others, criticize or applaud, recall similar programs or information, and feel emotions about what they see. As a direct result of all that intellectual and emotional involvement, these viewers understand and remember a great deal.

As with TV viewing, students get better comprehension when they're interested in the topic. But when they start to read something they're not already interested in—like many course assignments—reading is like watching a boring program: it's difficult and time-consuming, with few positive results. Students who feel this way do not know that they can dramatically change their experience. How? By using the attitudes and methods of active reading.

Passive versus Active Reading

Reading is, of course, an intellectual act. It involves the mind and learned skills for making sense of print. But it is much more than that. Two aspects are critical. First, reading is also an emotional experience. In fact, current research emphasizes that emotions directly affect whether or not the mind comprehends a subject, as well as how well it recalls those thoughts. Disinterest and high stress interfere with understanding and recall. Interest and low stress promote comprehension and memory.

Second, reading involves the selection and use of methods for accessing background knowledge, grouping units of print, and linking the two into something meaningful. Readers can, for example, choose to preview, skim, read slowly, use a dictionary, mark the text, and/or take notes. Even if you're not conscious of making these choices, what you do affects every reading experience. Ineffective methods interfere with comprehension; effective approaches aid understanding.

Like TV viewing, reading can be done with low or high emotional and intellectual involvement. When the involvement is low, it's called **passive reading,** and when it's high, it's called **active reading.** Figure 2.1 illustrates these two approaches.

Passive readers move their eyes across the text and see words, but fail to comprehend the points because they aren't thinking about the information. They expect the author to stimulate their interest and believe that the writing determines their comprehension, so they do not try to get interested in the topic or choose methods that aid comprehension. As a

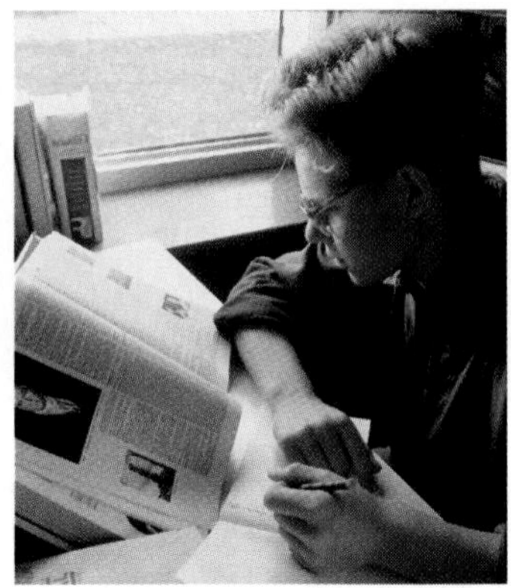

FIGURE 2.1 **Passive and active reading**

result, they experience boredom, poor concentration, confusion, and low comprehension. This is actually a very common situation, as the *Peanuts* cartoon illustrates.

But there is an alternative. Active reading is a mindset of personal control. It begins with a desire to find and think about interesting, useful, and relevant information. Active readers make choices about what is important, try to figure out the confusing parts, and use dictionaries, marking, and note taking to gain the highest possible comprehension. Afterwards, they recall quite a bit and often replay the points in their mind or share them with others.

Are you an active or passive reader? You probably already have a pretty good idea, but complete Activity 1 to see exactly how you read.

ACTIVITY 1: IDENTIFY YOUR PASSIVE AND ACTIVE APPROACHES

DIRECTIONS: Think about how you typically read course assignments. Then, for each question, circle one answer that reflects what you usually think or do. If you feel that both answers fit the way you read, pick the one that occurs slightly more often. When you are through, score your answers.

1. When I get a reading assignment, I generally
   - **a.** dread doing it.
   - **b.** have a positive or neutral attitude about it.

2. I assume that course textbooks are
   a. difficult and confusing.
   b. written to help me understand and learn information.
3. I generally think most textbook topics
   a. are boring.
   b. have some interesting points or parts.
4. I read to
   a. get through the assignment.
   b. understand information.
5. While I'm reading,
   a. I lose interest easily.
   b. I maintain my interest in most parts.
6. While I'm reading, I
   a. have no feelings or reactions to the author's points.
   b. react to the information with feelings and/or thoughts about my own beliefs and experiences.
7. While I'm reading, I generally think that the information
   a. is unrelated to real life.
   b. applies to some of my personal experiences.
8. As I read, I
   a. experience frequent frustration and want to quit reading.
   b. work through confusing parts and reading problems.
9. If the text is difficult or confusing, I
   a. do not want to look for more information or ask for help.
   b. try to find resources, information, or others to help me understand it.
10. After reading, I
    a. give no thought to the information.
    b. think about some of the information.
11. I usually read assignments
    a. at the last minute.
    b. during times I've set aside to do homework.
12. I start reading by
    a. trying to comprehend the first sentence.
    b. looking over the text before I start.
13. I tend to
    a. skip words and sentences that are new and complex so I can get through faster.
    b. read carefully and skip information only when I've decided it's not important.

14. I read
  a. where there's noise, poor lighting, or distractions.
  b. in an environment that promotes concentration.

15. I read
  a. word by word.
  b. for the meaning of the phrases, sentences, and paragraphs.

16. As I read, I usually
  a. find nothing or everything important.
  b. separate important points from unimportant ones.

17. When I come across new words, I
  a. skip over them.
  b. try to figure out what they mean.

18. When I read, I
  a. do not use a dictionary.
  b. have a dictionary and use it at times to figure out what an important word means.

19. In terms of text marking, I
  a. do not mark anything or tend to highlight almost every line.
  b. try to mark just the important information.

20. After reading, I
  a. do not look at the end of chapter questions or take notes.
  b. think about the end of chapter questions and/or take notes.

SCORING: Questions 1–10 assess your attitude. Count up the number of *b* answers and put a check next to the description that matches your responses.

8–10 *b* answers	_____ Very active reading
6–7	_____ Fairly active
5	_____ Active about half the time
3–4	_____ Fairly passive
0–2	_____ Very passive

Questions 11–20 assess your methods. Count up the number of *b* answers and put a check next to the description that matches your responses.

8–10 *b* answers	_____ Very active reading
6–7	_____ Fairly active
5	_____ Active about half the time
3–4	_____ Fairly passive
0–2	_____ Very passive

After scoring Activity 1, you probably found that you use both active and passive approaches. That's normal. In truth, we all engage in some passive approaches from time to time. But the key to effective reading is to emphasize the active approaches that you do use and change the passive ones as soon as they occur.

ACTIVITY 2: CHANGE YOUR PASSIVE APPROACHES

DIRECTIONS: Use your answers in Activity 1 to answer the following questions.

1. List the four active approaches (*b* answers) that you use the most often. (If you have fewer than four *b* answers, select the items you use the most, even if you answered *a* to the item.)

   ____

   ____

   ____

   ____

2. List the four passive approaches that you use the most often and that you think would be the easiest to change.

   ____

   ____

   ____

   ____

Thought is the strongest thing we have. Work done by true and profound thought—that is a real force.

—Albert Schweitzer (1875–1965),
German philosopher, physician, winner of the Nobel Peace prize

Use a Problem-Solving Approach

College reading assignments create comprehension problems for everyone at one time or another. Why shouldn't they? After all, the content is new, the information is technical, some vocabulary is unfamiliar, and the writing is directed at a sophisticated rather than a general audience. At some point, your mind may wander or your background knowledge won't match the level of the text writing. That's when reading problems will occur.

There are seven common reading problems. Look at Table 2.1. It lists them along with the 16 reasons that could cause any one of these problems.

We all have the ability to detect reading problems, to hear the little voice that lets us know we aren't comprehending as well as we could. Active readers respond to problems by giving a little thought to the cause(s) and figuring out logical ways to improve their reading. Sometimes rereading, using the dictionary, or re-engaging interest is needed. At other times, a Web search or the help of friends, family, tutors, or professors is needed. Whatever the method, action is the solution.

When solving problems, dig at the roots instead of just hacking at the leaves.

—Anthony J. D'Angelo (1972–),
American motivational speaker

TABLE 2.1 **Common Reading Problems**

PROBLEMS	
1. Poor concentration	5. Frequent rereading
2. Confusion	6. Stress, frustration, desire to quit
3. Vague, unclear points	7. Boredom
4. All or nothing seems to be important	
POSSIBLE CAUSES	
1. Distractions	9. Reading without a break
2. Fatigue	10. Not understanding the author's organization
3. Lack of reading goals	11. Not linking the ideas with the details
4. Low motivation	12. Not relating the ideas to real world examples
5. Skip reading and skimming	13. Lack of background knowledge
6. Reading too quickly or too slowly	14. Unknown vocabulary terms
7. Cramming	15. Stress about the course or upcoming exam
8. Taking in too much new information at one time	16. Worry about personal problems

ACTIVITY 3: SOLVE YOUR READING PROBLEMS

DIRECTIONS: Think about the following reading problems. Note a situation when you experienced each one. Then identify the cause(s) and a solution that you think would have worked for you.

1. Poor concentration
   A past experience: ______________________________
   The cause(s): ______________________________
   A possible solution: ______________________________
2. Confusion
   A past experience: ______________________________
   The cause(s): ______________________________
   A possible solution: ______________________________
3. All or nothing seems important
   A past experience: ______________________________
   The cause(s): ______________________________
   A possible solution: ______________________________

4. Stress, frustration, desire to quit
A past experience: ____________________
The cause(s): ____________________
A possible solution: ____________________

5. Boredom
A past experience: ____________________
The cause(s): ____________________
A possible solution: ____________________

If things go wrong, don't go with them.
—Roger Babson (1875–1967),
American statistician and author

Use Motivating Methods

Active reading is the deliberate use of processes. That is, active readers choose steps, strategies, or mental actions that promote thought. These processes have the added advantage of raising motivation, because they focus readers' efforts, put them in control, and produce results. Six core processes are used during reading for learning tasks: preread, divide, question, read, recite, and review. A quick way to remember these methods is the acronym PDQ3R.

As described below, each PDQ3R process is designed to replace passive attitudes and methods.

1. *Preread*

   In an effort to finish reading assignments quickly, passive readers just "jump right in," often without even looking at the title. Soon they are lost and bored. Active readers **preread,** or ease into the text by looking it over before they start reading in order to identify the topic, start thinking, and initiate motivation.

2. *Divide*

   Passive readers just read. They don't think about how the information is organized or what they want to accomplish during their reading time. They also tend to read entire assignments in one sitting no matter how long they are. Active readers **divide** texts by looking for organizing clues, setting goals, and splitting long assignments into easy reading tasks.

3. *Question*

   Passive readers wait for the text to make sense. Often they get overly focused on the separate words or sentences. Active readers seek out the important information by anticipating what will come next. They do this by turning important words and points into **questions** that they hope the author will answer.

4. *Read*

   Passive readers read with their eyes only. They do not make a record of what is important by marking their texts. As a result, they are forced to relocate, reread, and re-comprehend the information at a later time. Active readers **read** and mark their texts. They see reading as the time to identify, understand, and underline what they will need to return to later.

5. *Recite*

   Passive readers read one sentence after another, even when the information does not make sense. They don't stop to think how the pieces of information fit together. Active readers pause from time to time to **recite** or look over what they've marked, to check their understanding, and to link points together.

6. *Review*

   Passive readers close the book as soon as they read the last page, so they read without getting any benefits. Active readers **review** after reading and, as a result, gain something every time they read. They may simply think about the new information, reward their own efforts, or prepare for future learning tasks.

Most college readers have heard about and used some of these processes. Use the following activity to identify the ones that you already know something about.

ACTIVITY 4: ASSESS YOUR PDQ3R KNOWLEDGE

DIRECTIONS: Think about your knowledge of the PDQ3R processes. Which of them have you heard about? Which ones have you tried? Have you found them to be helpful?

____

____

____

____

____

____

The PDQ3R processes also promote the stages of motivation. That is, active readers

- **Preread** and **divide** assignments to **engage** their interest.
- **Question** and **read** for answers to **focus** their efforts.
- **Recite** what they've read to **monitor** their progress.
- **Review** the text to **reflect** on their gains.

Figure 2.2 shows how the motivation stages and the PDQ3R processes work together. The following sections describe how to use these processes when you are reading essays and textbooks chapters. Each section also presents a banner/reminder heading about the process that you will see throughout this text. Learn the active reading

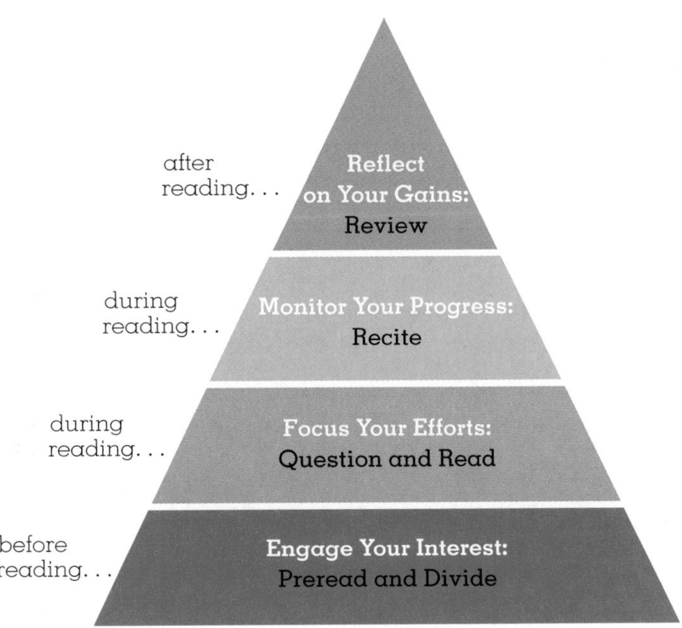

FIGURE 2.2. **Motivated Reading for Learning**

processes that go with each heading. Then, when you come to a reminder heading throughout the book, use the PDQ3R processes that promote that stage of motivation. Refer back to this chapter if you're ever unsure about what to do.

> **Without ambition one starts nothing.**
> **Without work one finishes nothing.**
> —Ralph Waldo Emerson (1803–1882),
> American lecturer, poet, and essayist

Read Essays Actively

THINK ABOUT THIS . . .

Think about what you already know about the PDQ3R processes and how they might be used to read essays assigned in your courses.

1. What would you look at to preread?

____

____

2. How could you use the divide methods for reading the essay?

____

____

3. What would be the easiest way to form questions?

____

____

4. What kind of information would you underline and mark?

____

____

5. When would you pause to recite?

____

____

6. What review techniques would be the most useful for your later learning tasks?

____

____

Professors assign essays to add current information to the course or to stimulate discussions. You may also read essays as resources for your papers and projects. While they tend to be short, these texts are challenging whenever they deal with complex issues, numerous ideas, or expert opinions. For example, look at just the first paragraph of the following sample essay. Identify any phrases that might be challenging.

EXAMPLE

School, Girls, and the Information Age

Maggie Ford

As the information age rapidly envelops every facet of our society, it is imperative that our schools not only integrate technology into the classroom but also ensure that girls and young women don't become bystanders in the computer-driven twenty-first century.

According to the report, "Gender Gaps: Where Schools Still Fail Our Children" by the American Association of University Women Educational Foundation, while girls have gained ground in math and science, they are falling behind in technology. For example, more girls enrolled in Algebra I and II, geometry, precalculus, trigonometry and calculus in 1994 than in 1990. On the other hand, girls make up only a small percentage of students in computer science classes. And, as recently as 1996, only 17 percent of Advanced Placement test-takers in computer science were girls.

Outside of school, boys enter the classroom with more prior experience with computers and other technology than girls. Girls are less interested and comfortable with computers than boys, consistently rating themselves lower on computer ability. Girls encounter fewer powerful, active female role models in computer games and software. Thus, it comes as no surprise that girls of all ethnicities consistently rate themselves lower than boys on computer ability.

So what's keeping girls from computer science? Computer labs certainly aren't locked or have signs on them that say, "No Girls Allowed." Geoff Jones, principal of one of the nation's top public science and technology magnet high schools in Fairfax County, Va., says that even in a school like his where all students are required to take basic computer science, many girls steer clear of advanced courses in computer technology. According to Jones, the widespread perception that computer programming is a "boys' thing" starts at a very early age.

That is why Gender Gaps recommends that our schools take strong steps to prepare girls and young women for the Information Age. States should make Algebra I and geometry—the gatekeeper classes for college admissions and advanced study in math, science, engineering and computer science—mandatory for all students.

Schools should make sure that their software programs and classroom experiences do not send girls and young women subtle signals that computer technology is not really for them. Teacher training, too, should be improved. Teachers need to integrate technology into the curriculum in a challenging and equitable way to encourage both girls and boys to be "power users" of technology. Moreover, School-to-Work programs need to encourage girls to explore fields such as engineering so that they can compete in fields traditionally not open to them.

Since the AAUW Educational Foundation's landmark 1992 report "How Schools Shortchange Girls," public schools have made remarkable progress in targeted programs to help girls and young women improve in math and science. As a result, the gender gaps in math and science are narrowing. Now, our schools need to make similar efforts to prepare girls and young women to compete and succeed in the highly technical fields that will define the twenty-first century. What's at stake is not only the future of our daughters and granddaughters but our nation itself. (517 words)

As you can see, the first paragraph includes at least four complex issues: the term *information age,* how it envelops society, how to integrate technology into classrooms, and what schools can do to prevent girls from becoming bystanders. Issues like these, which are mentioned but not explained, can start a chain reaction of poor motivation and comprehension that continues throughout the task. But PDQ3R is a way to maintain your interest and make sense of abstract, unexplained points like these.

Engage Your Interest

Essays have a standard, three-part structure, which includes an introduction of the topic, a body of main points and supporting information, and a conclusion. Introductions and conclusions can be one or more paragraphs long; body sections have two or more paragraphs. Before you do a close reading of any of these parts, however, you need to initiate your motivation. The preread and divide processes engage interest by calling attention to the parts, the topic, and your purpose(s). The banner you'll see throughout this text reminding you to use these processes looks like this:

Before you read . . .

Engage Your Interest: preread and divide

Preread Prereading should accomplish three objectives: (1) identify the topic, (2) start your thinking, and (3) initiate your motivation. To preread an essay, quickly look over or skim the following:

1. Title
2. Introduction
3. Conclusion
4. First sentences of the major, or longest, paragraphs in the body, if needed.

You may think that the order of these steps—beginning, end, middle—is odd, but it works quite well. Introductions and conclusions provide overviews and summaries, so together, they tell you what the topic is and give you something interesting to think about. After that, the middle will be more meaningful.

Since introductions and conclusions can be longer than one paragraph, you may be wondering how you will identify them. In addition, you may also be curious about how you will determine whether you need to look at the body paragraphs. The answer to both of these is to simply look at enough to accomplish the three prereading objectives. Sometimes the first and last paragraphs are all you need; in other texts, that's not enough to get you started. In short, prereading means that you will skim parts, skip others, and look for the topic, points to think about, and something to motivate you to read more. Here's an example of good prereading on the sample essay on page 44.

EXAMPLE

PREREAD OR SKIM THIS PART		REACTIONS AND THINKING
School, Girls, and the Information Age Maggie Ford	→	*The essay seems to be about schools and girls. I wonder what the information age is.*
First paragraph		
As the information age rapidly envelops every facet of our society, it is imperative that our schools not only integrate technology into the classroom	→	*I agree. Technology needs to be part of every classroom.*
but also ensure that girls and young women don't become bystanders in the computer-driven twenty-first century.	→	*How can girls become bystanders?* *There seem to be two issues here. Which is the topic?*

Last paragraph

Since the AAUW Educational Foundation's landmark 1992 report "How Schools Shortchange Girls," public schools have made remarkable progress in targeted programs to help girls and young women improve in math and science. As a result, the gender gaps in math and science are narrowing. Now, our schools need to make similar efforts to prepare girls and young women to compete and succeed in the highly technical fields that will define the twenty-first century. What's at stake is not only the future of our daughters and granddaughters, but our nation itself.

→ *Why are schools doing a better job of teaching math and science than technology?*

→ *The topic is preparing girls to succeed in technical fields.*

→ *This is an interesting idea. How do women in technical fields affect our nation?*

I want to read more. I hope the author talks about what schools can do.

Notice how prereading includes asking questions and reacting to the author's point. These thoughts stimulate the motivation that leads to careful reading. Also notice that only the first and last paragraphs were needed to identify the topic, stimulate thinking, and initiate interest.

The beginning is the most important part of the work.
–Plato (427–347 B.C.), Greek philosopher

ACTIVITY 5: PREREAD AN ESSAY

DIRECTIONS: Preread the following essay by completing these steps and answering the questions.

1. Look over the title and the first four introductory paragraphs.
   a. The title: Record any reactions and questions you have.

   ____
   ____
   ____
   ____

   b. The introduction: Record any reactions and questions you have.

   ____
   ____
   ____

   c. The topic seems to be ______________________________

2. Look over the last paragraph.
   Record any reactions and questions you have.

   ____

   ____

   ____

3. Optional: Look over some of the body paragraphs.
   Record any reactions and questions you have.

   ____

   ____

   ____

   ____

"Going Thin" in Fiji Now that Television Has Arrived

Ellen Goodman

First of all, imagine a place women greet one another at the market with open arms, loving smiles, and a cheerful exchange of ritual compliments.

"You look wonderful! You've put on weight!"

Does that sound like dialogue from Fat Fantasyland? Or a skit from fat-is-a-feminist-issue satire? Well, this Western fantasy was a South Pacific fact of life. In Fiji, before 1995, big was beautiful and bigger was more beautiful—and people really did flatter one another with exclamations about weight gain.

In this island paradise, food was not only love, it was a cultural imperative. Eating and overeating were rites of mutual hospitality. Everyone worried about losing weight—but not the way we do. "Going thin" was considered to be a sign of some social problem, a worrisome indication the person wasn't getting enough to eat. The Fijians were, to be sure, a bit obsessed with food; they prescribed herbs to stimulate the appetite. They were a reverse image of our culture. And that turns out to be the point.

Something happened in 1995. A Western mirror was shoved into the face of the Fijians. Television came to the island. Suddenly, the girls of rural coastal villages were watching the girls of *Melrose Place* and *Beverly Hills 90210.* Within 38 months, the number of teenagers at risk for eating disorders more than doubled to 29 percent. The number of high school girls who vomited for weight control went up five times, to 15 percent. Worse yet, 74 percent of the Fiji teens in the study said they felt "too big or fat" at least some of the time and 62 percent said they had dieted in the past month.

This before-and-after television portrait of a body image takeover was drawn by Anne Becker, an anthropologist and psychiatrist who directs research at the Harvard Eating Disorders Center. She presented her research at the American Psychiatric Association last week with all the usual caveats. No, you cannot prove a direct causal link between television and eating disorders. Heather Locklear doesn't cause anorexia.

Fiji is not just a Fat Paradise Lost. It's an economy in transition from subsistence agriculture to tourism and its entry into the global economy has threatened many old values.

Nevertheless, you don't get a much better lab experiment than this. In just 38 months, and with only one channel, a television-free culture that defined a fat person as robust has become a television culture that sees robust as, well, repulsive. "Going thin" is no longer a social disease but the perceived requirement for getting a good job, nice clothes, and fancy cars. As Becker says carefully, "The acute and constant bombardment of certain images in the media are apparently quite influential in how teens experience their bodies."

Speaking of Fiji teenagers in a way that sounds all-too familiar, she adds, "We have a set of vulnerable teens consuming television. There's a huge disparity between what they see on television and what they look like themselves—that goes not only to clothing, hairstyles, and skin color, but size of bodies."

In short, the sum of Western culture, the big success story of our entertainment industry, is our ability to export insecurity: We can make any woman anywhere feel perfectly rotten about her shape. I'm not surprised by research showing that eating disorders are a cultural byproduct. We've watched the female image shrink down to Calista Flockhart at the same time we've seen eating problems grow. But Hollywood hasn't been exactly eager to acknowledge the connection between image and illness. Since the Columbine High massacre, we've broken through some denial about violence as a teaching tool. It's pretty clear that boys are literally learning how to hate and harm others. Maybe we ought to worry a little more about what girls learn: To hate and harm themselves. (Adapted; 645 words)

Divide The purpose of the divide process is to get a general idea of the author's organization and to identify your personal reason(s) for reading the text. So, to divide an essay, do the following:

1. Identify the obvious parts of the discussion.
2. Form your own reading goals.

Your comprehension will be faster and more accurate if you start your reading with a mental road map of the text. From prereading, you will already have an idea of what's in the introduction and conclusion. Now, look at the body and simply count the number of major—or long—body paragraphs. That number is a good estimate of the number of major points that will be presented. For example, in the sample essay on page 44, you might determine that either the first paragraph or the first and second paragraphs are the introduction and the last paragraph is the conclusion. That leaves either five or six body paragraphs, which indicates that the author will probably present five or six points about the topic.

What would you do if an essay has quite a few short paragraphs? Simply skim them and look for common key words that indicate a connection between them. Then count connected paragraphs as one point. Don't worry about accuracy; just guess and get a starter idea of how many points to look for during close reading.

The second part of divide turns your attention from the number of points to your specific reading purpose(s). This is the time to think about the topic, consider why your instructor assigned the reading, and identify what you personally can gain from it. If the sample essay was assigned in an education class, for instance, you might assume that the professor wants you to think about what schools can do to educate girls about technology. Personally, the essay might stimulate reflection about your own school experiences or what you would want your children to learn. Complete the divide step by forming goals that start with "I want" and end with rewards, such as the following examples.

EXAMPLES

I want to read about "Schools, Girls, and the Information Age," because I want to understand what schools can do to educate girls about technology. My rewards will be a greater awareness of what schools can accomplish.

I want to read about "Schools, Girls, and the Information Age," because I'm concerned about the technical programs in my children's schools. My reward will be knowledge that I can use to evaluate school programs.

Notice that these goals include the essay title. Using the title in your goal ensures that you don't skip over it and that your goals are specifically related to the text.

> **You can do anything if you have enthusiasm.**
>
> —Henry Ford (1863–1947), American industrialist, founder of Ford Motor Company

ACTIVITY 6: DIVIDE AN ESSAY

DIRECTIONS: Divide the essay in Activity 5 by answering the following questions.

1. Look at what you think is the body. How many major points does the author seem to present? ______
2. Assume that the professor in your health class assigned this essay.
   a. What might the professor want you to gain from this reading?

   ____

   ____

   b. What could you personally gain from this reading?

   ____

   ____

   c. Form a reading goal for this essay.

   I want to ____________________ about ____________________.

   My reward(s) will be ____

   ____.

One final point about prereading and dividing: these quick overview steps can be combined. That is, you can look over the introduction and conclusion (and body if needed), count the body paragraphs, and form your goal(s) all in one step.

Focus Your Efforts

Good reading produces understanding and achieves your goals with a minimum of wasted time. The more you direct your mind, the more efficiently it works. Two very effective methods to focus your efforts during reading are asking questions and reading to find the answers. Like prereading and dividing, these two processes can be combined. The reminder banner for focus looks like this:

As you read . . .

Focus Your Efforts: question and read

Question The purpose of the question method is to direct your attention to what the author is saying. Good questions help you anticipate what is coming. You might wonder how you can come up with questions that relate to what you haven't yet read. It's not hard. To question, do the following:

1. Turn the title, headings if there are any, and key words or phrases into questions.
2. Start the questions with What, How, or Why.

Look at these examples created from the sample essay on page 44.

EXAMPLES

Questions from the title:

How do schools affect girls in the Information Age?

What is the Information Age?

Questions from the first two paragraphs:

How should schools integrate technology in the classroom?

Why are girls bystanders?

How can schools ensure that girls don't become bystanders?

Notice the emphasis on "what," "how," or "why" questions. While you could ask "who," "where," or "when" questions, they lead to factual information, not to sentence and paragraph comprehension. So, if you use those more limited questioning terms, make sure you also ask the broader, reading comprehension questions.

ACTIVITY 7: FORM QUESTIONS

DIRECTIONS: Practice forming questions by completing these activities.

1. On the lines provided, record at least one question for each of the following headings, titles, and sentences. Use What, How, or Why to begin each question.
   a. Sociology as a Science

   ____

   ____

   b. Debunking

   ____

   ____

   c. Sociology is among the newest of the sciences, having arisen in Europe during the latter half of the nineteenth century. (Lindsey and Beach 9)

   ____

   ____

   d. Types of Defenses to a Criminal Charge

   ____

   ____

2. Read the following sentences from the sample essay on page 44, and create questions about them.
   a. Outside of school, boys enter the classroom with more prior experience with computers and other technology than girls.

   ____

   ____

   ____

   ____

   b. That is why Gender Gaps recommends that our schools take strong steps to prepare girls and young women for the Information Age.

   ____

   ____

   ____

Read The purpose of reading for learning is to locate, comprehend, and identify the important information that you will need for future tasks. It takes careful reading and thinking to accomplish this kind of "close" reading. To read this way, do the following:

1. Think about your questions.
2. Read to find the answers.
3. Mark the important information with underlining and margin notes.

Effective marking is a major part of active reading. The simple act of deciding what to mark gets you involved with the text message and, as a result, improves both your concentration and your comprehension. Later, being able to refer to what you've marked speeds up all of your recite, review, and learning activities and prevents needless rereading.

The most effective marking starts with underlining, which visually emphasizes what's important. This does not mean that you should underline whole sentences. Instead, mark the key words and phrases that capture the important information.

Here's an example of effective underlining from the first beginning of the sample essay on page 44.

EXAMPLE

As the information age rapidly envelops every facet of our society, it is imperative that our schools not only integrate technology into the classroom but also ensure that girls and young women don't become bystanders in the computer-driven twenty-first century.

Notice that the amount of underlining is not the same in every line. Underlining emphasizes what is important, and that will vary from sentence to sentence. How will you know the right amount to underline? To test your underlining, use the marked terms and your own words to form sentences that capture the original meaning the previous example, you might look at the underlined terms and create the following sentence:

The Underlined Terms

imperative	schools	integrate	technology	classroom
also ensure	girls	don't	bystanders	computer-driven

"*It's* imperative *for* schools *to integrate* technology *into the* classroom *and* also ensure *that* girls don't *end up as* bystanders *in the* computer-driven *world.*"

The italicized words are the terms that were added to make a complete sentence. Notice that they are different from the original but they don't change the meaning. When it's easy to turn the underlined words into your own sentences, you've underlined the right amount. If it's hard or you have to reread the unmarked text, underline more. On the other hand, if you find yourself just rereading the author's words and not putting in any of your own, underline less.

ACTIVITY 8: IDENTIFY THE RIGHT AMOUNT OF UNDERLINING

DIRECTIONS: Read the following underlined versions of a paragraph from the sample essay and evaluate the underlining. Then complete these tasks:

A. Label each paragraph as "too much," "too little," or "right amount" of underlining.
B. Under the paragraph with too much, list the words that were unnecessary to underline.

C. Under the one with too little underlining, note what should have been underlined.

D. For the paragraph with the right amount of underlining, combine the underlined words in the first sentence with your own terms and form a sentence.

Version A: __________

Outside of school, boys enter the classroom with more prior experience with computers and other technology than girls. Girls are less interested and comfortable with computers than boys, consistently rating themselves lower on computer ability. Girls encounter fewer powerful, active female role models in computer games and software. Thus, it comes as no surprise that girls of all ethnicities consistently rate themselves lower than boys on computer ability.

____

____

Version B: __________

Outside of school, boys enter the classroom with more prior experience with computers and other technology than girls. Girls are less interested and comfortable with computers than boys, consistently rating themselves lower on computer ability. Girls encounter fewer powerful, active female role models in computer games and software. Thus, it comes as no surprise that girls of all ethnicities consistently rate themselves lower than boys on computer ability.

____

____

Version C: __________

Outside of school, boys enter the classroom with more prior experience with computers and other technology than girls. Girls are less interested and comfortable with computers than boys, consistently rating themselves lower on computer ability. Girls encounter fewer powerful, active female role models in computer games and software. Thus, it comes as no surprise that girls of all ethnicities consistently rate themselves lower than boys on computer ability.

____

____

In addition to underlining, marking also includes margin notes, which are written right beside the text they refer to. Writing is, of course, an active technique; so margin notes ensure active reading, excellent comprehension, and productive time on task.

These brief notes capture your understanding, reactions, and good reading questions. They can include any or all of the following:

1. The paragraph topic
2. Labels about important types of information (definitions, facts, examples)
3. Your reading questions
4. Very brief notes about the complex or important points
5. Your personal comments, ideas, and reactions to the author's points
6. Symbols that note special parts (such as a question mark for a confusing part, T for a possible test item, a star for something important)

Here's an example of underlining and margin notes on the first two paragraphs of the sample essay.

EXAMPLE

Margin notes	Text
Schools must *- technology in classes* *- girls not left out of computer world*	As the information age rapidly envelops every facet our society, it is imperative that our schools not only integrate technology into the classroom but also ensure that girls and young women don't become bystanders in the computer-driven twenty-first century.
How have girls gained in math & science, but fallen behind in technology? *Facts*	According to the report, "Gender Gaps: Where Schools Still Fail Our Children" by the American Association of University Women Educational Foundation, while girls have gained ground in math and science, they are falling behind in technology. For example, more girls enrolled in Algebra I and II, geometry, precalculus, trigonometry and calculus in 1994 than in 1990. On the other hand, girls make up only a small percentage of students in computer science classes. And, as recently as 1996,
Only 17% take the Advanced Placement.	only 17 percent of Advanced Placement test-takers in computer science were girls.

Notice how these margin notes emphasize what's important, record good questions, and capture the reader's thinking. They will make future learning activities easier and make the information more memorable.

This is a good place to mention highlighting. Highlighters are convenient and easy to use, but they can lead to passive reading in two ways. First, when you're highlighting, it's tempting to simply color whole sentences without really reading or comprehending them. Second, when you highlight, you have to make a special effort to stop and switch tools in order to write anything in the margin. So pencils and pens are the recommended marking tools because you can do both without extra effort. But if you do use highlighters, make sure to mark just the key words, avoid full line coloring, switch tools, and write margin notes for every important paragraph.

ACTIVITY 9: QUESTION, READ, AND MARK AN ESSAY

DIRECTIONS: Use the essay in Activity 5 to complete these tasks.

1. As you read, mentally create questions for the key words and points.
2. Read to find the answers and important information.
3. Mark the text as follows:
   a. Underline the key words and phrases.
   b. Create margin notes that include your reactions, useful questions, and/or brief notes on the important points.

Monitor Your Progress

Monitoring is the feedback part of motivation where you check that you are making progress. The recite method is a quick and accurate way to give yourself feedback about your reading comprehension. Recite, which literally means "say again," involves talking to yourself about the message as you're looking at the text. This quick check identifies problems that need attention and, even more importantly, links the points in several paragraphs together to produce greater comprehension. The monitor banner looks like this:

Before you go on . . .

Monitor Your Progress: recite

You will find this banner at the end of each essay and article, but you should feel free to recite at any time and as often as needed.

Recite The purpose of reciting is to check and improve your comprehension. There are two ways to recite. First as you read, recognize when you don't comprehend the text. Stop and try to explain the text or take action to correct the problem. This kind of reciting takes care of the moment to moment comprehension. Second, as you finish reading a group of related paragraphs, stop, look them over, and explain how they work together. To find a group of paragraphs, just look at paragraphs in order that are about the same point. There's no one way to group paragraphs; link up what makes sense to you.

For both types of reciting, look at what you've marked and do the following:

1. Note the key points.
2. Mentally combine the underlined terms with your own words to form sentences.
3. Form sentences from your margin notes.

Reciting has a number of immediate benefits. First, it identifies what you do and don't understand. Second, as you recite, you can check your marking and change it, if needed. Third, reciting provides an immediate review, which initiates long-term memory and reduces study time. Finally, reciting provides new comprehension of multiple sentences or paragraphs, as well as how they work together.

New recite insights should be added to your margin notes. Here's the previous example of marked text with added insights from reciting noted in bold-faced font.

EXAMPLE

Margin notes	Text
*Schools must **do 2 things:*** *- technology in classes* *- girls not left out of computer world*	As the information age rapidly envelops every facet of our society, it is imperative that our schools not only integrate technology into the classroom but also ensure that girls and young women don't become bystanders in the computer-driven twenty-first century.
AAUW report – 2 findings: *Why have girls gained in math & science, but fallen behind in technology?* *Facts* *Only 17% take the Advanced Placement. **That is a very small number!*** ***Falling behind = girls don't enroll or take Adv. Placem't. test***	According to the report, "Gender Gaps: Where Schools Still Fail Our Children" by the American Association of University Women Educational Foundation, while girls have gained ground in math and science, they are falling behind in technology. For example, more girls enrolled in Algebra I and II, geometry, precalculus, trigonometry and calculus in 1994 than in 1990. On the other hand, girls make up only a small percentage of students in computer science classes. And, as recently as 1996, only 17 percent of Advanced Placement test-takers in computer science were girls.

**A man is not idle because he is absorbed in thought.
There is a visible labour and there is an invisible labour.**

—Victor Hugo (1802–1885), French poet, dramatist, novelist

ACTIVITY 10: RECITE AN ESSAY

DIRECTIONS: Recite the essay that you marked in Activity 5. Add to your underlining if needed. Briefly jot down your additional thoughts and insights here.

____

____

____

____

Reflect on Your Gains

The first five steps of PDQ3R directly improve your comprehension of the author's ideas. The last R, review, is much more personal. Here's where you'll reflect and get the rewards for your efforts. The reflect banner looks like this:

After you read . . .

Reflect on Your Gains: review

This banner is placed before each chapter summary and the essay comprehension questions, because those are standard review elements that should be used after you finish reading the text.

Review The purpose of review is to get the benefits of your reading efforts and create something that you take away from the task. You might simply reward yourself for a job well done, have a new thought or idea, gain knowledge, or create an extensive product such as notes or a summary. What you create is a function of what you will need in the future. Without this step, reading is just a task to do. With review, reading is a way to create a useful outcome.

To review, do the following:

1. Reward yourself.
2. Think about the information and/or discuss it with others.
3. Engage in pre-learning tasks, such as answering review questions and/or creating notes, flashcards, and other learning tools (see Chapter 5).

ACTIVITY 11: REVIEW AN ESSAY

DIRECTIONS: Practice reviewing the essay in Activity 5 by answering the following questions.

1. List the new and useful ideas you gained from this essay.

____

____

____

2. Review the goals you created in Activity 6. Did you accomplish your goals? Briefly explain.

____

____

3. Answer these review questions using the information in this essay:

a. Why do female students often avoid computer science courses? How do boys have advantages over girls in this area?

____

____

____

b. What does the AAUW Educational Foundation report recommend that schools do to prepare female students for the Information Age?

____

____

____

____

____

c. Why is it imperative to narrow the gender gaps in highly technical fields? Who will benefit if we succeed?

____

____

____

(Questions adapted from Mims and Nollen 44)

To read without reflecting is like eating without digesting.
–Edmund Burke (1729–1797),
British political writer

Read Textbook Chapters Actively

THINK ABOUT THIS . . .

Think about how you could apply PDQ3R to textbook assignments by answering these questions.

1. What parts of a chapter would be most helpful to inspire your interest as you preread?

____

____

2. How could the divide methods make reading textbook chapters easier?

____

____

3. What would be the easiest way to form questions?

____

____

4. What kind of information would you underline and mark?

____

____

5. How often would you pause to recite?

____

____

6. What review techniques would be the most useful for your later learning tasks?

____

____

Textbooks are designed to present the knowledge of experts in an organized format that promotes learning. But they often present a number of challenges. The chapters are often lengthy. The writing is usually technical, filled with specialized vocabulary, abstract ideas, and complex explanations. Finally, the sheer amount of new information in a chapter is, simply, overwhelming. But textbooks also have a number of features that can be used to stimulate your interest and understanding of the information. The PDQ3R processes work well with these features to promote effective and efficient reading.

Engage Your Interest

Before you read . . .

Engage Your Interest: preread and divide

Due to the length and technical nature of textbook chapters, the preread and divide processes are absolutely essential for engaging your interest. And they are virtually the only way to avoid boredom and high stress. So they are well worth your time. As with essay reading, you can preread and divide in one, combined process.

Preread Textbook prereading includes the same beginning, end, and middle approach used on essays. It also focuses on the same objectives: identify the topic, start your thinking, and initiate your interest. However, a textbook has far more pages and features than an essay does. So you will need a little more time for this step.

Table 2.2 lists what to look at as you preread a chapter, as well as what each part will show you.

TABLE 2.2 **Prereading a Chapter**

	WHAT TO LOOK AT	WHAT IT SHOWS YOU
The beginning	Chapter title	A label for the chapter topic
	The introduction, including everything between the title and the first major heading	Motivating information about the topic, including pictures, questions, a chapter outline or map, human-interest stories, background information, key terms, an overview of the chapter, and/or a statement of the chapter purpose
The end	The chapter summary or conclusion	A condensed version of the most important main ideas in each section What to look for as you read
	End of chapter learning tools	Activities that highlight the most important information, including a vocabulary list, review questions, or practice tasks What to look for as you read What to learn
The middle	Boldfaced headings	The organization of the information
	Graphics, including pictures, cartoons, graphs, tables, charts, and diagrams	Important points and information

Practice prereading by completing the following activity.

ACTIVITY 12: PREREAD A CHAPTER TEXT

DIRECTIONS: The following material is part of a sociology chapter entitled "Culture." It includes the chapter introduction, part of the first major section, and the relevant concluding parts. Preread the text and answer these questions.

1. What is the chapter topic? ___________
2. Skim the introduction.
   Record any reactions and questions you have:
   ____
   ____
   ____
3. Skim the summary and learning tools.
   Record any reactions and questions you have:
   ____
   ____
   ____
4. Skim the middle.
   Record any reactions and questions you have:
   ____
   ____
   ____

Culture

Initiating a Masai Warrior

"Circumcision will have to take place even if it means holding you down," my father explained to the teenage initiates. "The pain you feel is symbolic. There is deeper meaning because circumcision means a break between childhood and adulthood. For the first time you will be regarded as a grown-up. You will be expected to give and not just receive and no family affairs will be discussed without your being consulted. Coming into manhood is a heavy load. If you are ready for these responsibilities tell us now." After a prolonged silence, one of my half-brothers said awkwardly, "Face it . . . it's painful. I won't lie about it. We all went through it. Only blood will flow, not milk." There was laughter and my father left. Among the Masai of East Africa, the rite of circumcision swiftly transforms an adolescent boy to an adult man. (Adapted from Saitoti, 1994:159)

You Don't Love Me: The Disappointed Chinese Child

"My parents do not love me. They are cold, distant, and remote." This feeling is commonly voiced among children of Chinese immigrants to the United States. Many Chinese children long for the affection they see in American movies and television and read about in magazines. Their expe-

riences with their parents and other members of their extended family are formal and distant, so they conclude that love is lacking. In China, where such behavior is the norm, children do not question it. The lack of open affection extends to spouse and friends. To the Chinese, physical intimacy and love are private matters. Even when it comes to handshaking, the traditional Chinese way is to clasp one's own hands in greeting. Kissing and hugging a friend is most inappropriate, and kissing a spouse in public is shameless and ill-mannered. In fact, until recently any kissing in China was considered so vulgar it was thought to suggest cannibalism! In America, Chinese children feel deprived because they see affection all around them but receive no outward expression of it themselves. It is an important example of bicultural conflict that confronts newcomers to America and several succeeding generations. (Hsu, 1981; Sung, 1994)

Human behavior is immensely varied, and the variations are fundamentally determined by culture. **Culture** is a human society's total way of life; it is learned and shared and includes the society's values, customs, material objects, and symbols. Our culture provides our social heritage and tells us which behaviors are appropriate and which are not. Unlike the Masai, most Americans would regard circumcision at adolescence as cruel. Unlike the Chinese, Americans regard kissing as a typical and accepted pattern of showing affection. As these vignettes suggest, culture both unites and divides people—a theme we will explore in this chapter as we examine culture's powerful role in determining human social behavior.

Culture and Society

Culture encompasses all that we have developed and acquired as human beings. Culture guides our choices of food and clothing, our reading material and art, and our dating partners and friends. Stop reading for a moment and quickly survey the area around you. If you are in your dorm, the library, sitting on a bench in the quad, or reading at the beach, everything that encircles you is culturally produced. Culture can be subdivided into two major segments: **material culture,** which includes tangible artifacts, physical objects, and items that are found in a society; and **nonmaterial culture,** which includes a society's intangible and abstract components such as values, beliefs, and traditions. The two are inextricably bound.

Each person is a unique individual with his or her own hopes and dreams, likes and dislikes, attitudes and opinions, habits and routines. Yet many of our feelings, beliefs, and customs are reflections of our culture. For example, selecting a marriage partner on the basis of romantic love seems like the natural thing to do in the United States. Yet in most of the world's cultures, selection of a spouse is in the hands of marriage brokers, parents, other relatives, or matchmakers. Culture is so much taken for granted that we rarely think about alternatives to what we usually think and do. Only when we compare our cultural beliefs and customs with those of other cultures do we discover what we take for granted in our own culture.

Ethnocentrism and Cultural Relativism

In the study of culture, the essential element that sociology shares with all other sciences is a neutral and unbiased approach to the subject. The scientific method gives some protection against inaccurate reporting, but it does not tell us how to remain emotionally aloof from attitudes and behavior that we may find personally disturbing. Culture exerts such a powerful influence that most people exhibit **ethnocentrism,** the tendency to evaluate their own culture as superior to others. Being a citizen of a particular culture instills a sense of group loyalty and pride that is useful when cultural unity is necessary, such as when facing a common enemy in war. But for social scientists or those who simply want to study or understand another culture, ethnocentrism is inappropriate.

The opposite of ethnocentrism is **cultural relativism,** the view that all cultures have intrinsic worth and that each culture must be evaluated and understood according to its own standards. On one level, cultural relativism is an ethical principle: You should not judge another people's customs, especially until you understand them. On another level it is pragmatic: You cannot do business with members of a different culture if you unknowingly behave in ways that offend them and if you misinterpret their polite behavior for stubbornness or backwardness. Equally important, cultural relativism is a scientific principle. In studying other cultures, as in all scientific endeavors, anthropologists and sociologists strive to be objective.

Cultural relativism is easier said than done. Scientists, tourists, students, or businesspeople who first encounter cultures vastly different from their own will likely experience a feeling of **culture shock**—they will tend to experience feelings of alienation, depression, and loneliness until they become acclimated to the new culture. Anthropologist Conrad Kottak describes his own culture shock on his first encounter with Bahia, Brazil:

> I could not know just how naked I would feel without the cloak of my own language and culture.... My first impressions of Bahia were of smells—alien odors of ripe and decaying mangoes ... and of swatting ubiquitous fruit flies.... There were strange concoctions of rice, black beans, and gelatinous globs of meats and floating pieces of skin. I remember ... a slimy stew of beef tongue in tomatoes. At one meal a disintegrating fish head, eyes still attached, but barely, stared up at me as the rest of its body floated in a bowl of bright orange palm oil. (Kottak, 1987:4)

Kottak eventually grew accustomed to this world. He not only learned to accept what he saw, he began to appreciate and enjoy its new wonders. Culture shock and ethnocentrism gave way to cultural relativism.

Values and Beliefs

Values are cultural ideals about what is considered moral and immoral, good and bad, or proper and improper. As shared beliefs about ideal goals and behavior, they serve as standards for social life. Values also serve as criteria for assessing your own behavior as well as that of others.

In small, traditional, relatively isolated societies, agreement on values may be close to universal. However, even larger, ethnically diverse cultures that experience ongoing and rapid social change have identifiable core values. These core values are embraced by most members of the culture and help distinguish it from other cultures. Over a half century of research continues to document a consistently held core value set that defines

A college education in the United States represents an important cultural value related to achievement. Women and racial minorities now attend college in the highest numbers since the founding of the United States.

America's national character (Mead, 1942; Williams, 1951; Devine, 1972; Harris, 1981). The following list, although not inclusive, identifies some of the most important U.S. values. Some of these values are not only taken for granted, but may be viewed negatively by people from other cultures.

1. *Individualism.* The United States is a highly individualistic culture emphasizing personal independence and self-reliance. Individual self-interest rather than group goals is an acceptable guide to behavior.
2. *Achievement.* Talent, motivation, and work are the ingredients for success. Rewards are based on merit. Individuals whose hard work transforms their rags to riches are idealized models for Americans. A related value is competition, which maximizes both the merit and the reward. May the best person win.
3. *Material comfort.* The fruits of hard work and achievement are the financial rewards that can buy a desired lifestyle—what is wanted as well as what is needed.
4. *Democracy and equality of opportunity.* These values can be accomplished only in a political, educational, and economic climate that maximizes freedom of choice and equality of opportunity at all institutional levels. If the playing fields are equal—in school, the political system, and the economy—then the best person should succeed.
5. *Nationalism.* America is the world's role model for democracy, and Americans are proud of their political system and economic accomplishments. Regardless of their ethnic background, most people see themselves as Americans first.
6. *Group superiority.* Americans believe that their culture is superior to other cultures. Beliefs about superiority also extend to how Americans rank groups within their culture. Although Americans believe that all individuals are equal, they view

some as "more equal"—more deserving of respect—than others because of their race, ethnicity, gender, age, wealth, achievements, or other social markers.

7. *Science and efficiency.* Americans use scientific principles as a basis for action. They favor logical ways of doing things that save time and money. Emotion and intuition are out; practicality and rationality are in.
8. *Humanitarianism.* Despite their highly individualistic culture, Americans are concerned for the welfare of others. They believe assistance should be offered to people who both need it and deserve it.

Some of these core values (for example, individualism and achievement) are functionally integrated: They support and reinforce one another. But the list also contains obvious contradictions. For example, only about one-fourth of Americans think that science will solve environmental problems, yet science is considered a core American value (Fig. 2.1). The core values are not disappearing, but their rank shifts or emphasis on one or the other changes over time.

At the same time, other values are emerging that may eventually become part of this core set. For example, the pursuit of material comfort and financial success has increased sharply (Astin et al., 1989). People expect to work hard to succeed, but they want to work less, retire earlier, and have more leisure time. Leisure itself is becoming so important to Americans that it is emerging as another core value. In other cultures, such as Germany, leisure has long been a priority (Glouchevitch, 1992). Americans "take" vacations; Germans feel entitled to time off for recreation.

In some cases, contradictions in values are so obvious that open and contentious public debate revolves around moral dilemmas they create. For example, most Americans now disdain public expressions about the superiority of certain groups, especially regarding race and ethnicity. In fact, condemnations of racism are routine. However, many Americans are also uncomfortable with programs that mandate equal opportunity for people of color, such as affirmative action. Ethnocentrism is a fact of group life, and one that can translate into feelings of superiority, both between and within cultures. The value of maintaining cultural identity in a diverse society is rapidly increasing, and as we shall see, has produced much social tension.

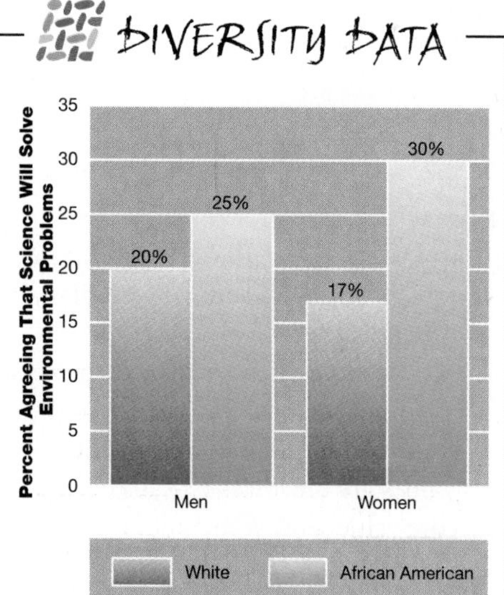

FIGURE 2.1 Will Science Solve Environmental Problems? For both men and women, and for whites and African Americans, only about one-fourth tend to agree science will solve environmental problems. Yet Americans also highly value science as a basis of action. What explains this apparent cultural contradiction? Why is the largest difference in level of agreement between African American and white women?

Source: NORC General Social Surveys, 1972–1996. Chicago: National Opinion Research Center, 1996.

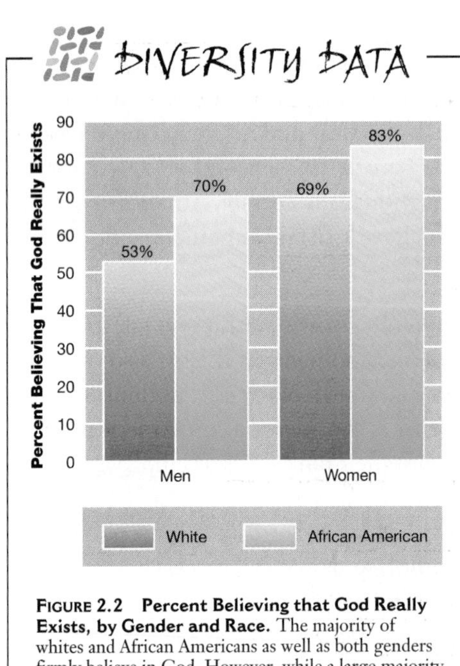

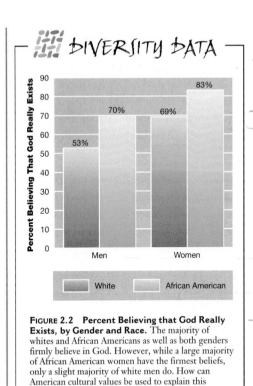

FIGURE 2.2 Percent Believing that God Really Exists, by Gender and Race. The majority of whites and African Americans as well as both genders firmly believe in God. However, while a large majority of African American women have the firmest beliefs, only a slight majority of white men do. How can American cultural values be used to explain this difference?

Source: NORC General Social Surveys, 1972–1996. Chicago: National Opinion Research Center, 1996.

Another example is the American reliance on science as the key to social progress. Science is, by definition, secular. Science demands that assertions be questioned, tested, and proved or disproved. But Americans also express very high degrees of faith, as indicated by religious affiliation, beliefs, and practices. Regardless of the particular religion with which they may identify, almost all Americans believe in the existence of God or a universal spirit (Fig. 2.2), and the majority attend religious services on a regular basis. Faith and science represent opposite viewpoints in debates related to teaching evolution in the schools, scientific experimentation on animals and humans, euthanasia and prolonging life, and research on fertility and cloning, to name a few issues. (Adapted from Lindsey and Beach 42–47)

The following parts are from the end of the chapter:

Summary

1. Culture is a shared way of life that includes everything from material objects—food, clothing, furniture—to intangibles like values, customs, and symbols. Culture is learned.
2. Most people consider their own culture superior to other cultures, a view known as ethnocentrism. But as a science, sociology is based on cultural relativism, the principle that all cultures must be understood and respected on their own terms.
3. Values are the ideals that underlie a culture's moral standards. Americans have a core value set that includes individualism, achievement, equality of opportunity, and humanitarianism. It is possible for core values to be contradictory.

Key Terms

cultural relativism	culture shock	material culture	values
culture	ethnocentrism	nonmaterial culture	

Critical Thinking Question

Based on your understanding of the role of culture in attitudes, language, and behavior, argue for or against the idea that "we are all prisoners of our own culture." (Adapted from Lindsey and Beach 62–63)

Divide Textbook dividing includes three objectives. First, like essay dividing, one purpose is to understand how the author has organized the information. In textbooks, authors use a system of headings, and readers can scan these headings to get a quick understanding of how the topic is presented. Second, unlike essays, textbook chapters tend to be long. So dividing textbook chapters involves one new purpose: to split long assignments up into easy reading tasks. Again, the headings can be used to accomplish this objective. The final part of textbook dividing involves creating goals for each reading task.

To understand what the headings and subheadings reveal, you need to understand how authors create them. Headings are not just extra lines in the text. Each one names or labels the central topic in the section that follows. And, together, the headings make up the author's outline. Here's how they are created:

1. Chapters are divided into major sections.
   a. Each major section is labeled with a major heading.
   b. Major headings correspond to the Roman numeral level (I, II, III) in an outline.
   c. In the text, they are printed in large bold-faced print that is above the paragraphs that follow. Frequently, they are in all capital letters.
2. Major sections may be subdivided into subsections.
   a. Each subsection is labeled with a subheading.
   b. Subheadings correspond to the capital letter level (A, B, C) of an outline.
   c. These bold-faced headings are smaller in size than the major headings and usually above the paragraphs that follow. Often they are in upper and lower case letters.
3. Subsections may, in turn, be divided into minor sections.
   a. Each minor section has a minor heading.
   b. Minor headings correspond to the Arabic number level (1, 2, 3) of an outline.
   c. These bold-faced headings are smaller than the subheadings. They are often placed on the first line of the minor section.

Here's an example of the headings in a major section about parenting from a sociology chapter, followed by an outline of them. The major section has two subsections, and the first subsection has two minor sections. Notice how the font sizes change and how the minor headings are part of the first line in the paragraph.

EXAMPLE

The Text

Parenting, Ethnicity, and Social Class

Parenting across Racial-ethnic Families

Spending Time with Children One important characteristic of a child's well-being is . . .

Monitoring Children's Activities African American and Latino fathers typically supervise . . .

Parenting Biracial Children

In 1997, professional golfer Tiger Woods sparked a controversy when he told talk show host Oprah Winfrey that he objected to being called an African American. He said he was "Cablinasian," a word he'd made up as a boy. . . . (Adapted from Benokraitis 338)

The Outline

I. Parenting, Ethnicity, and Social Class
  A. Parenting across Racial-Ethnic Families
    1. Spending Time with Children
    2. Monitoring Children's Activities
  B. Parenting Biracial Children

This example illustrates a general rule of textbook organization and outlining: when a section is divided, the parts are equally important. Once you know that, you can look ahead whenever you come to a heading and see if other, equally important parts are included.

What else can you do with these headings? First, use them to guide your reading by doing one of the following:

1. Put outline numbers and letters next to the headings; notice them as you read.
2. Record just the headings on paper in an outline format; refer to it as you read.
3. Make up a map of the headings (like the one at the beginning of this chapter); refer to it as you read.

One note about using outline numbers on textbook headings: In the author's outline, Roman numeral I generally refers to the chapter introduction. The introduction, which includes everything between the chapter title and the first major heading, usually does not have a heading. But because it may have very important information in it, it's useful to label the introduction with a Roman numeral I. Then use Roman numeral II for the first major heading, and so on.

It doesn't matter where you are coming from. All that matters is where you are going.
—Brian Tracy (contemporary), American speaker and businessman

In addition to using the headings to understand the chapter organization, you can also use them to divide the chapter into reading tasks. The length of each task depends on your background knowledge and concentration span for the subject. If you are familiar with a subject, you may take on a major section. If your prior knowledge is limited or the section is very long, a subsection or two might be more manageable. In either case, make sure that each task starts and ends at a heading, not in the middle of a discussion. Then treat it as a unit. That is, create a reading goal, question, read, and recite those pages together.

ACTIVITY 13: DIVIDE A CHAPTER TEXT

DIRECTIONS: Divide the text in Activity 12 by completing these tasks and answering the questions.

1. Outline number and letter the headings. Start by putting "I. INTRO." next to the first sentence.
2. Would you read these pages as one task or would you divide them up? Explain.

   ____

   ____

   ____

3. Assume that your sociology professor assigned this text.
   a. What might the professor want you to gain from this reading?

      ____

      ____

   b. What could you personally gain from this reading?

      ____

      ____

   c. Form two reading goals for this text.

      I want to ____________ about ____________.
      My reward(s) will be ____________
      ____________________.

      I want to ____________ about ____________.
      My reward(s) will be ____________
      ____________________.

Focus Your Efforts

As you read . . .

Focus Your Efforts: question and read

It is easy to waste time and gain little as you read textbook chapters. Asking questions and reading to find the answers is an effective way to stay focused and gain information. Once again, these processes work together as you read.

Question and Read The question, read, and mark methods are basically the same for essays and textbooks. The only difference is that in textbooks, the headings are a central part of the author's thinking. Thus, they are direct guides for readers. To make the most of these headings, create what, how, and/or why questions for every one you come to. Then, read to find and mark the answers, as well as anything else that seems important. Record your questions, comments, and any brief notes you think of next to the paragraphs. Those margin notes will provide good aids during the recite and review processes.

ACTIVITY 14: QUESTION, READ, AND MARK A CHAPTER TEXT

DIRECTIONS: Use the text in Activity 12 to complete these tasks.

1. Create questions for each heading.
2. Read to find the answers and important information.
3. Mark the text as follows:
   a. Underline the key words and phrases.
   b. Create margin notes that include your reactions and/or useful questions.

Read, mark, learn, and inwardly digest.

—Book of Common Prayer

Monitor Your Progress

Before you go on . . .

Monitor Your Progress: recite

Textbook sections are integrated paragraphs that work together to present major concepts or ideas on the topic. Monitoring your comprehension by reciting each section is an essential way to comprehend these textbook units.

Recite As with essays, when you recite a section, quickly look at what you've marked, assess your comprehension, and check your marking. In addition, pay particular attention to what each paragraph contributes to the topic in the heading and how it relates to the other paragraphs. As you consider the way the paragraphs are linked, you will gain additional insights about the topic. Make sure to add these thoughts to your margin notes.

ACTIVITY 15: RECITE A TEXTBOOK SECTION

DIRECTIONS: Recite the textbook section that you marked in Activity 14. Add to your underlining and margin notes if they're not complete. Then, briefly jot down your additional thoughts and insights here.

____

____

____

____

Reflect on Your Gains

After you read . . .

Reflect on Your Gains: review

Reflecting on the information is a critical part of reading chapters for learning. The review methods suggested for essay reading are even more important on textbook reading tasks.

Review Review includes much more than just studying for an exam. Before that time, review is an essential way to promote your motivation and ensure your comprehension.

It is very important that you feel good about what you've accomplished from your textbook reading efforts. Without rewards, you will find it difficult to get motivated to complete the next textbook reading assignment. So give yourself the rewards you listed in your goals, and make sure to use self-talk that recognizes the new and useful information you've acquired, your increased knowledge, or your increased intellectual abilities. With those in mind, it's much easier to start another chapter.

Review is also essential for comprehension. Without some form of review, even good textbook understanding will be diminished, and you will need to waste time rereading and rethinking the same information later. So when you finish reading a chapter, choose the review methods that will best support your comprehension as well as your future learning tasks. You might complete chapter review questions, take notes, create learning tools (see Chapter 5), or discuss the interesting points with others. For maximum benefit, complete these activities before going on to a new chapter in the course. And, after working on these review tasks, reward yourself again. Work attached to rewards is the secret to ongoing motivation.

> The major reason for setting a goal is what it makes of you to accomplish it. What it makes of you will always be the far greater value than what you get.
> —Jim Rohn (contemporary), American speaker and businessman

ACTIVITY 16: REVIEW A CHAPTER TEXT

DIRECTIONS: Practice reviewing the text that you marked in Activity 14 by completing these activities.

1. Review the goals you created in Activity 13. Did you accomplish your goals? Explain.

____

____

____

2. List the new and useful ideas you gained from this text.

____

____

____

____

____

3. Answer this Critical Thinking and Review question: Based on your understanding of the role of culture, argue for or against the idea that "we are all prisoners of our own culture."

 ____

 ____

 ____

 ____

 ____

He who learns but does not think, is lost!
He who thinks but does not learn is in great danger.
—Confucius (551–479 B.C.), Chinese teacher and philosopher

CHAPTER SUMMARY

Introduction

Reading academic materials is challenging. First, it involves **reading for learning,** which requires that you not only comprehend the material, but also identify what you will need for future tasks. It is also difficult because you are not at the same level as the text. Texts are complex and technical; students have only a basic knowledge of the subject. Active reading is the way to overcome these issues and achieve accurate and thorough **comprehension.**

Be an Active Reader

Reading is an intellectual act that also involves emotions and methods. **Passive reading** is characterized by disinterest and ineffective methods. **Active reading,** on the other hand, is a mindset in which the reader chooses ways to control the task and read effectively. Since a high level of comprehension is essential for effective reading, active readers recognize and solve reading problems when they occur. They also use six reading processes to promote the motivation stages and to produce high comprehension: **preread, divide, question, read, recite,** and **review** (PDQ3R for short).

Read Essays Actively

Students may find essay assignments boring and difficult to comprehend when they deal with complex subjects, ideas, or expert opinions. PDQ3R processes overcome these problems and increase motivation. To engage interest, preread and divide by looking over the essay, identifying obvious parts of the discussion, and creating motivating goals. To focus your efforts, question and read. Good reading questions combine the author's key words and points with the terms *what, how,* or *why.* With those questions in mind, read to find and mark the important information. To monitor your progress, recite or periodically look over what you've marked. Finally, to reflect on your gains, recognize the new information you've acquired, reward yourself, and prepare for future learning activities.

Read Textbook Chapters Actively

The challenges in reading textbook chapters have to do with the length of the chapters and the amount of new information they contain. The PDQ3R processes are particularly effective ways to generate motivation and comprehension during textbook reading. With only a few additions, the methods used for reading essays can be applied to textbook chapters as well.

REVIEW ACTIVITIES

Use the following activities to check your understanding and aid your learning of the information in this chapter.

Expand Your Vocabulary

Match each term with the correct definition or characteristic.

______ **1.** reading for learning
______ **2.** comprehension
______ **3.** passive reading
______ **4.** active reading
______ **5.** preread
______ **6.** divide
______ **7.** question
______ **8.** read
______ **9.** recite
______ **10.** review

a. processes that identify the author's organization and create goals
b. reading when you are not involved or thinking about the text
c. the processes designed to gain the benefits of reading
d. a preview process used to initiate motivation
e. combining text and background knowledge to create meaning
f. a feedback process for checking and improving comprehension
g. a process of using important terms and points to form questions
h. the experience of reading with thought and reacting to the text
i. reading to identify what's needed for future tasks
j. processes for understanding important information

Increase Your Knowledge

These tasks will help you identify the important ideas in this chapter. They will also help you prepare for quizzes and exams on this material.

1. The following questions focus on the major chapter topics. Discuss them with others or form your own detailed answers.
   a. Contrast the attitudes and methods of passive and active readers.
   b. What is the problem-solving approach to reading? List the common problems and discuss possible causes for each one.

c. How do the steps of PDQ3R promote motivation?
d. Explain the purpose of each PDQ3R process.
e. Explain the PDQ3R methods used to read essays actively.
f. Explain the PDQ3R methods used to read textbook chapters actively.

2. Take notes on the information in this chapter.

Develop Your Skills

The following review tasks will give you an opportunity to practice the methods presented in this chapter.

REVIEW 1: USE PDQ3R TO READ AN ESSAY Apply the PDQ3R processes to the essay "Illusions Are Forever" by completing the following tasks.

Before you read . . .

Engage Your Interest: preread and divide

1. Preread the essay and then answer these questions.
   a. List the interesting points and the questions you thought of.

   ____

   ____

   ____

   ____

   ____

   b. The topic seems to be ______________________

2. Divide the essay by answering these questions.
   a. How many points does the author seem to present? ______
   b. Assume that your marketing professor assigned this essay. What might the professor want you to gain from this reading?

   ____

   ____

   ____

   c. What could you personally gain from this reading?

   ____

   ____

   ____

   d. Form a reading goal for this essay.

   I want to ________________ about ______________________.

   My reward(s) will be ______________________

   ______________________________.

As you read . . .

Focus Your Efforts: question and read

Question, read, and mark the essay by doing the following:

A. Create questions for the key words and points.
B. Read to find the answers and important points. Underline the key words and phrases.
C. Create margin notes as you read.

Illusions Are Forever

Jay Chiat

I know what you're thinking: That's rich, asking an adman to define truth. Advertising people aren't known either for their wisdom or their morals, so it's hard to see why an adman is the right person for this assignment. Well, it's just common sense—like asking an alcoholic about sobriety, or a sinner about piety. Who is likely to be more obsessively attentive to a subject than the transgressor?

Everyone thinks that advertising is full of lies, but it's not what you think. The facts presented in advertising are almost always accurate, not because advertising people are sticklers but because their ads are very closely regulated. If you make a false claim in a commercial on network television, the FTC will catch it. Someone always blows the whistle.

The real lie in advertising—some would call it the "art" of advertising—is harder to detect. What's false in advertising lies in the presentation of situations, values, beliefs, and cultural norms that form a backdrop for the selling message.

Advertising—including movies, TV, and music videos—presents to us a world that is not our world but rather a collection of images and ideas created for the purpose of selling. These images paint a picture of the ideal family life, the perfect home. What a beautiful woman is, and is not. A prescription for being a good parent and a good citizen.

The power of these messages lies in their unrelenting pervasiveness, the twenty-four-hour-a-day drumbeat that leaves no room for an alternative view. We've become acculturated to the way advertisers and other media-makers look at things, so much so that we have trouble seeing things in our own natural way. Advertising robs us of the most intimate moments in our lives because it substitutes an advertiser's idea of what ought to be—What should a romantic moment be like?

You know the De Beers diamond advertising campaign? A clever strategy, persuading insecure young men that two months' salary is the appropriate sum to pay for an engagement ring. The arbitrary algorithm is preposterous, of course, but imagine the fiancée who receives a ring costing only half a month's salary? The advertising-induced insult is grounds for calling off the engagement, I imagine. That's marketing telling the fiancée what to feel and what's real.

Unmediated is a great word: It means "without media," without the in-between layer that makes direct experience almost impossible. Media interferes with our capacity to experience naturally, spontaneously, and genuinely, and thereby spoils our capacity for some important kinds of personal "truth." Although media opens our horizons infinitely, it costs us. We have very little direct personal knowledge of anything in the world that is not filtered by media.

Truth seems to be in a particular state of crisis now. When what we watch is patently fictional, like most movies and commercials, it's worrisome enough. But it's absolutely pernicious when it's packaged as reality. Nothing represents a bigger threat to truth than reality-based television, in both its lowbrow and highbrow versions—from *Survivor* to A & E's *Biography.* The lies are sometimes intentional, sometimes errors, often innocent, but in all cases they are the "truth" of a media-maker who claims to be representing reality.

The Internet is also a culprit, obscuring the author, the figure behind the curtain, even more completely. Chat rooms, which sponsor intimate conversation, also allow the participants to misrepresent themselves in every way possible. The creation of authoritative-looking Web sites is within the grasp of any reasonably talented twelve-year-old, creating the appearance of professionalism and expertise where no expert is present. And any mischief-maker can write a totally plausible-looking, totally fake stock analyst's report and post it on the Internet. When the traditional signals of authority are so misleading, how can we know what's for real?

But I believe technology, for all its weaknesses, will be our savior. The Internet is our only hope for true democratization, a truly populist publishing form, a mass communication tool completely accessible to individuals. The Internet puts CNN on the same plane with the freelance journalist and the lady down the street with a conspiracy theory, allowing cultural and ideological pluralism that never previously existed.

This is good for the cause of truth, because it underscores what is otherwise often forgotten—truth's instability. Truth is not absolute: It is presented, represented, and re-presented by the individuals who have the floor, whether they're powerful or powerless. The more we hear from powerless ones, the less we are in the grasp of powerful ones—and the less we believe that "truth" is inviolable, given, and closed to interpretation. We also come closer to seeking our own truth.

That's the choice we're given every day. We can accept the very compelling, very seductive version of "truth" offered to us daily by media-makers, or we can tune out its influence for a shot at finding our own individual, confusing, messy version of it. After all, isn't personal truth the ultimate truth? (842 words)

Before you go on . . .

Monitor Your Progress: recite

Recite the essay. Add to your underlining and margin notes if needed. Then, briefly jot down your additional thoughts and insights here.

____

____

____

____

After you read . . .

Reflect on Your Gains: review

Review the essay by answering the following questions.

1. Review the goals you created above. Did you accomplish them? Briefly explain.

2. Answer the following review questions. (Questions from Mims and Nollen 227)

   a. According to Chiat, what is the "real lie" in advertising? What "truth" does advertising represent?

   b. According to Chiat, why is advertising so effective? In what ways is this beneficial or harmful for consumers?

   c. According to Chiat, what will be "our savior"? What will it save us from? How will this be accomplished?

3. List the new and useful ideas you gained from this essay.

REVIEW 2: USE PDQ3R TO READ A TEXTBOOK SECTION Apply the PDQ3R processes to the textbook excerpt "Pricing the Product" by completing the following tasks.

Before you read . . .

Engage Your Interest: preread and divide

1. Preread the text and then answer these questions.
   a. The topic seems to be ______________________________.
   b. Record any reactions and questions you have.
   ____
   ____
   ____
   ____
2. Divide the text by answering these questions.
   a. Use outline numbers and letters to label the headings.
   b. What could you personally gain from this reading?
   ____
   ____
   c. Form two goals.
   I want to ______________ about ______________________.
   My reward(s) will be ______________________________
   ______________________________.
   I want to ______________ about ______________________.
   My reward(s) will be ______________________________
   ______________________________.

As you read . . .

Focus Your Efforts: question and read

Question, read, and mark the text by doing the following:

A. Create questions for the headings, key words, and points.
B. Read to find the answers and important information. Underline the key words and phrases.
C. Create margin notes as you read.

Pricing the Product

Meet John Chillingworth, a Decision Maker at Aithent, Inc.

Current Position: Senior Sales Consultant

Career Path: 1999–2000 Lexmark International. Account Executive responsible for General Electric. 1990–1999 Prentice Hall, Sales Representative, Regional Marketing Specialist, Southwest Region, Senior Marketing Manager, Senior Acquistions Editor, Sociology

John Chillingworth is a Senior Sales Consultant for Aithent, Inc., a software developer located in New York City. His job is to identify and pursue business opportunities for the company. In September 2000, John learned of a need at Chase Manhattan Bank. Its fraud prevention and investigation department needed to update the software that tracked the incidents of fraud. John smelled an opportunity. He knew that the pricing strategy he chose would play a major role in determining if he could bring home a prize contract for his company. He decided that he had three options. First, he could build the full software system and then present it to Chase for approval. Second, he could wait. Eventually Chase would send out a request for a proposal and he could respond then. Or, finally, he could share his vision of the software with Chase and hope that they would buy it.

As John's case illustrates, the question of what to charge for a product—or even for an idea—is a central part of marketing decision making. In this chapter we'll tackle the basic question "What is price?"

Monetary and Nonmonetary Prices

"If you have to ask how much it is, you can't afford it!" We've all heard that, but how often do you buy something without asking the price? If the price wasn't an issue, we'd all drive dream cars, take trips to exotic places, and live like royalty. Wake up! In the real world, most of us need to consider a product's price before buying.

Price is the value that customers give up or exchange to obtain a desired product. Payment may be in the form of money, goods, services, favors, votes, or anything else that has *value* to the other party. Let's examine the concept of price from various perspectives and discuss how pricing strategies are important to the success of an organization. Then we'll see how price works with the other Ps of the marketing mix.

As we explained in Chapter 1, marketing is the process that creates exchanges of things of value. We usually think of this exchange as people trading money for a good or a service. Sometimes the monetary value of a product has a different name than price, perhaps to assume an air of greater respectability. For example, universities charge *tuition* for an education, a lawyer or accountant charges a *professional fee,* and students who join a chapter of the American Marketing Association pay *dues.* No matter what it is called, it's still a price.

But in some marketplace practices, price can mean exchanges of nonmonetary value as well. Long before societies minted coins, people exchanged one good or service

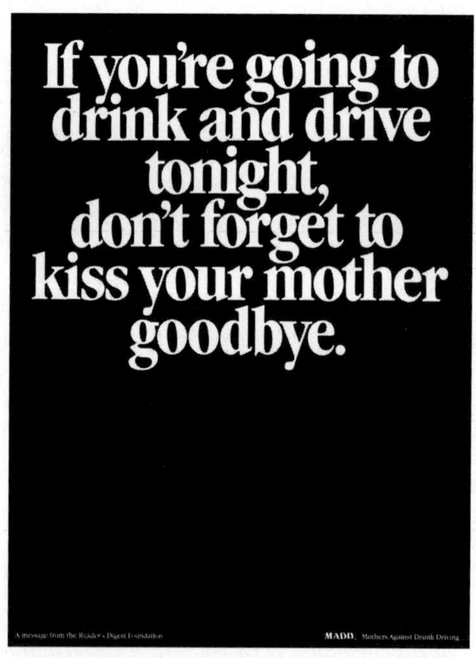

Selling sobriety behind the wheel: Sometimes intangible costs are too high.

for another. This practice still occurs today. As we saw in Chapter 4, international countertrade is quite common. But even in our own country these noncash exchanges occur frequently. Someone who owns a home at a mountain ski resort may exchange a weekend stay for car repair or dental work. No money changes hands but there is an exchange of value. The U.S. Internal Revenue Service understands this kind of deal: It requires taxpayers to report as income the value of goods or services received in exchange for other goods or services. Oh, well . . .

Other nonmonetary costs are often important to marketers. What is the cost of wearing seat belts? What is it worth to people to camp out in a clean national park? It is also important to consider *opportunity cost,* or the value of something that is given up to obtain something else. For example, the cost of going to college includes more than tuition—it also includes the income that the student could have earned by working instead of going to classes (no, we're not trying to make you feel guilty . . .).

One of the difficulties in the marketing of people or ideas is the perceived *cost–value relationship.* Sometimes, as one author put it, it's a lot more difficult to sell "brotherhood than soap." Take, for example, public service campaigns intended to reduce alcohol-related accidents. The cost is a designated driver, a taxi fare—or simply not drinking. The value is reducing the risk of having a serious or possibly fatal accident. Unfortunately, too many people feel the chance of having an accident is so slim that the cost of abstaining from drinking is just too high.

The Importance of Pricing Decisions

How important are good pricing decisions? Pricing is probably the least understood and least appreciated element of the marketing mix. Marketers like to talk about advertising and other promotional elements. It's fun to think about changing technology and how firms invest in new-product development. Even decisions about channels of distribution seem to be more exciting than setting the right price. But price issues can be hugely important.

The plight of U.S. airlines is a good example of how bad pricing decisions can hurt an entire industry. From about 1982 to 1992, the airline industry engaged in a fierce price war, lowering the per mile fare nearly 25 percent (accounting for inflation of the dollar) while costs such as labor and fuel more than doubled. As a result, from 1990 to

1992 the airlines lost over $10 billion—more than they had earned since the start of commercial air travel. Sometimes it's not advantageous for a firm to cut its prices.

Even during the best of economic times, most consumers rank "reasonable price," a price that makes the product affordable and that appears to be fair, as the most important consideration in a purchase and one that counts the most when consumers decide where to shop. Price is even more important during recessions, when consumers have less to spend and count their pennies carefully. Marketers try to come as close to "reasonable" as possible when deciding on a price.

Individual consumers aren't the only buyers who focus on price. As we saw in Chapter 7, purchasing agents for firms often put a high priority on getting the best price. At least one study has found that price may be second only to quality in these decisions. Buying professionals know that, when all else is equal, getting a low price keeps costs down and helps make their firm's product competitive.

Pricing and the Marketing Mix

Pricing decisions, like product decisions, are intertwined with all other marketing mix (four Ps) decisions. Let's take a look at each relationship.

Price and Place

We must study pricing decisions from the viewpoint of not only the manufacturer but also from the perspectives of the other members of the channel of distribution—wholesalers and retailers—that help get the product to consumers. Will the pricing plan allow each channel member to be successful in reselling the product to end customers? Is the **margin** (the difference between the cost of the product and the selling price) that a wholesaler or retailer earns too low to cover its costs?

Channel members normally perform a number of marketing, selling, and physical distribution tasks that add to their costs of doing business. By taking these costs into account, channel members can figure out the margin they need to operate at a profit—a margin that covers their shipping costs, inventory costs, customer credit, overhead, and marketing and selling costs. Manufacturers that often set a suggested retail or final selling price must take these margins into consideration in deciding on a price for their product. In the United States, manufacturers are legally restricted from forcing channel partners to resell a product at a given price because this would hamper competition and hurt consumers. Thus, a pricing plan must appeal to channel partners on its own merits.

Let's say a supermarket needs a margin of 20 percent on goods to cover costs and required level of profit. If a manufacturer offers the supermarket a new potato chip brand at a price that, based on the suggested retail price printed on the package, will give the retailer a 30 percent markup, will the retailer be willing to add the product to its stock? Sure it will. The new product will give the retailer a margin that will cover its costs and profit goals with an extra 10 percent to spare.

Price and Product

Obviously, the price of the product must cover the costs of doing business but price also sends a *signal* about product quality. The relationship between place and price also means that marketers select retail channels that match their product's price and image.

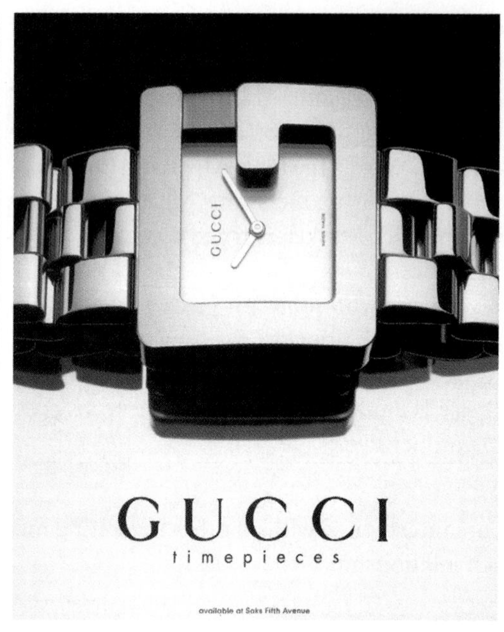

Gucci knows that its high price is a signal of quality for many consumers.

For example, a shopper would not expect to find a Rolex watch in Sears or Wal-Mart, or expect to see Timex watches on display at Tiffany's.

The sky-high price of a Rolex watch tells consumers a lot about the timepiece, and it also signals that those who can afford one are probably in an upper-income class (or they have gone deeply into debt to make it look like they are). And although experts and the media often try to tell women that most makeup and skin care products have identical ingredients and are pretty much the same, the premium prices charged for certain brands continue to convince consumers that higher price means a better product.

The stage of the product's life cycle also affects pricing. Early in the life cycle, a single firm may be the only producer of a highly desirable product. At this point the firm is a *monopoly supplier,* so it's able to charge a premium price. Later, as competitors enter the market and costs of production decrease, prices often go down. For example, when small handheld calculators were introduced into the market in the late 1960s, the price tag was about $200. Around 1970, the price was cut in half and thousands of consumers were thrilled to be able to buy a great little handheld calculator that added, subtracted, multiplied, and divided for $89.99. Today a calculator that also calculates a variety of statistical and trigonometric functions is sold for less than $20.

Price and Promotion

Pricing is strongly related to promotional activities, if for no other reason than the firm needs to be sure it has enough revenue to pay for the promotion.

It is just as important that the advertising strategies justify the cost of the product. For example, an ad for an expensive fragrance should project luxury, quality, and status imagery to convince shoppers that they are getting "quality" for their money. Even ads for high-end building materials such as countertops can create a luxury appeal through advertising. (Adapted from Solomon and Stuart 341–346)

The following parts are from the end of the chapter:

Chapter Summary

Explain the importance of pricing and how prices can take both monetary and nonmonetary forms.

monetary = monetary

Price, the amount of outlay of money, goods, services or deeds given in exchange for a product, may be monetary or nonmonetary. Bartering occurs when consumers or businesses exchange one product for another. Pricing is important to firms because it creates profits and influences customers to purchase or not. Pricing decisions are tied to decisions about the rest of the marketing mix. Prices must allow channel members to cover their costs and make a profit. For the product, price is an indicator of quality. Prices vary during stages in the product life cycle. Prices must cover the cost of promotions, and promotions must justify the product price.

Chapter Review

Marketing Concepts: Testing Your Knowledge

1. What is price and why is it important to a firm? What are some examples of monetary and nonmonetary prices?
2. How are pricing decisions interrelated with other elements of the marketing mix?

Key Terms

margin
price

(Adapted from Solomon and Stuart 365–368)

Before you go on . . .

Monitor Your Progress: recite

Recite the text. Add to your underlining and margin notes if needed. Then, briefly jot down your additional thoughts and insights here.

___

___

___

___

After reading . . .

Reflect on Your Gains: review

Review the text by completing these activities.

1. Review the goals you created above. Did you accomplish them? Explain.

___

___

___

2. List the new and useful ideas that you gained from this text.

____

____

____

____

3. Answer the following questions:

   a. What is price and why is it important to a firm? What are some examples of monetary and nonmonetary prices?

   ____

   ____

   ____

   ____

   ____

   b. How are pricing decisions interrelated with other elements of the marketing mix?

   ____

   ____

Check Your Motivation

1. Review your chapter goals. Did you achieve them? Explain.
2. Make a list of the new ideas and methods you've gained from this chapter. Think about how they will help you in the future.
3. Measure your motivation for this chapter topic. Think about each statement and how you will use it in the future. Mark it:

A = never B = sometimes C = usually D = always

	A	B	C	D
To engage my interest, I plan to . . .				
1. preread assignments before I do a close reading.	___	___	___	___
2. look for the introduction, conclusion, and body points in essays	___	___	___	___
3. number or outline the headings in textbooks.	___	___	___	___
4. divide long chapters into short reading tasks.	___	___	___	___
5. form reading goals.	___	___	___	___
To focus my efforts, I plan to . . .				
6. turn titles, headings, and key words into questions.	___	___	___	___
7. underline or highlight the important information.	___	___	___	___
8. record my thoughts in margin notes.	___	___	___	___
To monitor my progress, I plan to . . .				
9. be on the alert for reading problems.	___	___	___	___
10. solve reading problems as soon as they occur.	___	___	___	___
11. recite what I've read and marked in the text.	___	___	___	___
12. add any additional insights I get to my margin notes.	___	___	___	___
To reflect on my gains, I plan to . . .				
13. think about the new ideas and information I've gained.	___	___	___	___
14. reward myself for my reading efforts.	___	___	___	___
15. complete pre-learning activities.	___	___	___	___

SCORING: Write the number of answers you marked in each column in the following spaces. Compute the column scores, and then add them up to determine your total score.

\# of A's _____ × 1 pt. = _____
\# of B's _____ × 2 pt. = _____
\# of C's _____ × 3 pt. = _____
\# of D's _____ × 4 pt. = _____

Total points = _____

INTERPRETATION: 15–43 points = low motivation; 44–60 points = high motivation

SUGGESTION

1. Compare your current chapter score to the one from The Motivation Measure. If they're both low, review the list above and find approaches you'd be willing to try. If you've improved or have a high score, reward yourself for your empowered approaches.
2. Record the methods you wish to use on a card and use it as a bookmark. Look it over before you begin reading the next assignment. Apply those approaches.

CHAPTER THREE

Reading Efficiently

What does a speeding cyclist miss? How is that related to reading too fast? What happens when you read too slowly? What would it mean to read efficiently?

While readers are physically still, their minds can be racing through the text or barely moving from one point to the next. When we race, we overlook much of what's there, just like the scenery that's a blur to the racing cyclist. When we move too slowly, we lose focus and momentum. Using the right speed is part of good reading. As the quote from Blaise Pascal suggests, you sacrifice comprehension when it's not right.

> When we read too fast or too slowly, we understand nothing.
>
> — Blaise Pascal (1623–1662), French scientist and religious philosopher

Before you read . . .

Engage Your Interest: preread and divide

This chapter focuses on choosing your reading speed and improving your rate as needed. Each of the two major sections has a number of subheadings and minor headings. Find the headings and complete the map.

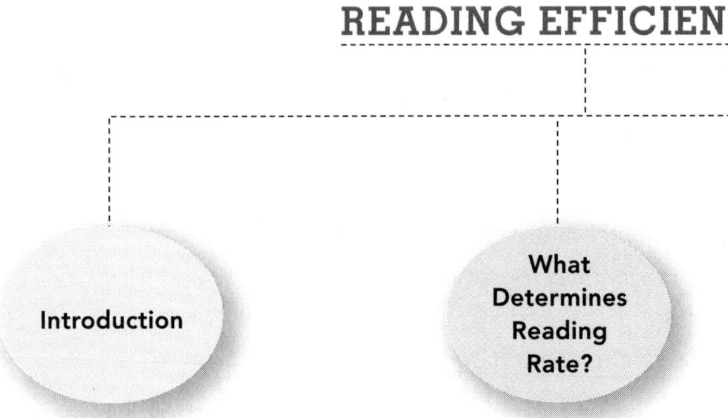

After you preread and divide the chapter into reading tasks, set a goal for each one. Be specific about the task, topic, and reward(s).

1. I want to ________________ about ______________________________________.
   My reward(s) will be ____
   ____.

2. I want to ________________ about ______________________________________.
   My reward(s) will be ____
   ____.

How Can I Improve My Speed?

As you read . . .

Focus Your Efforts: question and read

In reading, speed is not just a matter of getting through tasks in the shortest time possible. That is what many people mean by "speed reading." Fast reading is not good reading if you miss important information. Slow reading, on the other hand, is not good reading if you lose your focus on the text or if you can't recall the beginning of the paragraph when you get to the end.

> **I found out that if you are going to win games, you had better be ready to adapt.**
>
> —Scotty Bowman (1933–), American hockey coach

Reading efficiently, on the other hand, means reading at a pace that keeps the mind focused on the topic and allows you to comprehend the message. When you read with speed and efficiency, your reading is flexible, so you speed up and slow down as needed. Flexible reading is essential when you're reading for learning. It promotes complete comprehension and mastery of the 50 to 100 pages of weekly assignments you'll get in most courses.

To help you gain efficient and flexible rates, this chapter answers two main questions:

- What Determines Reading Rate?
- How Can I Improve My Speed?

What Determines Reading Rate?

THINK ABOUT THIS . . .

To determine your normal reading speed and comprehension for various types of texts, follow these directions:

1. Read each text without marking it.
2. Time yourself in minutes and seconds by following these steps:
   a. Just before you start, record your start time on the second line.
   b. As soon as you finish reading, record your end time on the first line.
   c. Subtract the start time from the end time. Look at the Rate Chart at the end of the text. Circle the speed that is closest to your total reading time.
3. Answer the questions that follow without looking back at the passage. After you finish all three texts, score your answers using the key at the end of the chapter.

Text A

	MINUTES : SECONDS
Record your END time here:	______ : ______
Record your START time here:	–______ : ______
Subtract and record your TOTAL reading time here:	______ : ______

Even a New Yorker can tell you how to treat a snake bite in the middle of the woods. Apply a tourniquet, suck out the poison and spit it out. Wrong, experts say. Putting your mouth on a venomous wound is the last thing you should do.

A study in *The New England Journal of Medicine* two years ago found that cutting, sucking or cutting off the blood supply to a bite could damage nerves and blood vessels and lead to infection. A poisonous bite requires antivenin and emergency treatment. Victims should be taken to a medical center as soon as possible.

More than 7,000 Americans a year are bitten by venomous snakes. Most attacks occur when people go after the animals or try to handle them. Dr. Barry S. Gold, an author of the 2002 report, said he has seen many people use stun guns, electrical wires and even car batteries to try to deactivate the venom in a bite. "The only thing that's effective is taking people to the hospital," he said.

Nausea, weakness and other symptoms of a poisonous bite usually set in after 30 minutes. But experts say the chances of survival are excellent as long as the victim reaches a medical center within a few hours. After a bite, victims should stay warm and keep the wounded body part below the level of the heart. (Adapted from O'Connor) (229 words)

Text A Rate Chart: Circle your rate.

:30 seconds	458 wpm
:45	305
1:00	229
1:15	183
1:30	153
1:45	131

1. Sucking out snake poison can lead to an infection. T F
2. Just 7,000 Americans are bitten by snakes each year. T F
3. Car batteries are an effective way to deactivate snake venom. T F
4. Symptoms of poison usually set in before 30 minutes. T F
5. After a bite, keep the wounded body part below heart level. T F

\# Right: _____

Text B

MINUTES : SECONDS

Record your END time here: _____ : _____

Record your START time here: –_____ : _____

Subtract and record your TOTAL reading time here: _____ : _____

In 1954, the U.S. Supreme Court, in *Brown* v. *Board of Education of Topeka,* declared racial segregation unconstitutional. Shortly thereafter, the Court ordered the desegregation of schools. For the next 10 years, the struggle over school integration and civil rights for black Americans stirred the nation. Southern states attempted to resist desegregation. American blacks began to protest it. In 1955, Reverend Martin Luther King, Jr. (1929–1968) organized a boycott in Montgomery, Alabama, against segregated buses. This marked the beginning of the use of civil disobedience to fight racial discrimination in the United States. The civil rights struggle continued well into the 1960s. The greatest achievements of the movement were the Civil Rights Act of 1967, which desegregated public accommodations, and the Voting Rights Act of 1965, which cleared the way for blacks to vote. Black citizens were brought nearer to the mainstream of American life than they had ever been.

However much remained undone. In 1967, race riots occurred in American cities. Those riots, followed by the assassination of Martin Luther King, Jr., in 1968, weakened the civil rights movement. Furthermore, as other groups, particularly Latino Americans, began to raise issues on behalf of their own communities, racial relations became more complicated. Black Americans and other minorities continue to lag behind white Americans economically. (Craig 740) (213 words)

Text B Rate Chart: Circle your rate.

:30 seconds	426 wpm
:45	284
1:00	213
1:15	170
1:30	142
1:45	121

1. Civil rights was a major national issue for 10 years after 1954. T F
2. The Supreme Court ordered desegregation in the court case of *Brown* v. *Board of Education of Topeka.* T F
3. Reverend Martin Luther King used civil disobedience to fight discrimination. T F
4. The Civil Rights Act of 1967 desegregated the public schools. T F
5. Many blacks were barred from voting before 1965. T F

\# Right: _____

Text C

	MINUTES : SECONDS
Record your END time here:	_____ : _____
Record your START time here:	–_____ : _____
Subtract and record your TOTAL reading time here:	_____ : _____

I remember the first time I cursed in front of my grandmother. She's an old farm wife, straight midwest and God-fearing. She looked at me, still dishing out home-made fried chicken and said "Only stupid people cuss. It's because they can't think of any way else to say what they want to say."

This was my introduction to the large group of people who don't like the way I talk. But it really wasn't my fault. I was raised in a baseball dugout crowd. My dad coached a team of semi-pro players who were to vulgarity what Jimi Hendrix was to the guitar.

Most of them were young, early twenties, and would string together a profanity-laced sentence better than Michelangelo could paint ceilings. Then they would look down at my skinny, six-year-old face, take a short breath, and say, "Don't ever say that."

Telling me not to repeat the new words I was picking up weekly was like giving a sixteen-year-old a new car and saying, "Hey, don't drive that."

So I grew up into who I am. I speak English adequately, Spanish horribly, and Profanity fluently. I thrive on it. I live through it. I'm only comfortable in class if the professor lets some curse words slip. Vulgar language is my home. (Weaver) (213 words)

Text C Rate Chart: Circle your rate.

:30 seconds	426 wpm
:45	284
1:00	213
1:15	170
1:30	142
1:45	121

1. The first time the author cursed was in front of his grandmother. T F
2. The grandmother thinks cursing is a sign of low intelligence. T F
3. The author's father coached professional athletes. T F
4. The players did not want the author to curse. T F
5. Profanity makes the author feel more comfortable. T F

\# Right: _____

Scoring: Use the Answer Key at the end of the chapter to score the comprehension questions.

Did your speeds change from one text to the next? Did you answer the questions with 80 to 100 percent accuracy? If you read efficiently, you answered "yes" to both questions. But most students who have not been trained to read with variable rates read all three texts at nearly the same speed and find that their comprehension depends on their interest level or the difficulty of the text. Before you can develop a more efficient style, you need to know how to choose efficient rates and become aware of your personal speed blocks.

Efficient Rates

Have you ever felt overwhelmed by the amount of reading that your instructors assign? If so, you are not alone. Many students complain that professors assign too much work and, as the cartoon suggests, wish that their professors would give them a lighter load.

"I don't like to give a lot of homework over the weekend, so just read every other word."

To turn this desire into reality, some students skim or skip read their assignments or fail to read them at all. Obviously, these approaches produce very poor comprehension, which in turn, affects future learning tasks and grades. A far better approach is to use efficient rates. **Efficient rates** are optimum speed choices determined by your reading purpose and text difficulty.

Your **reading purpose** has to do with how important the information is, what you will do with it in the future, and how much you already know. When you are reading for learning, you will usually have one of three general purposes: to learn, to supplement, or to survey. The learning purpose requires close reading of new information and thorough understanding to prepare for accurate learning in the future. Most textbook assignments fall into this category. A supplemental purpose is at work when you are adding to what you already know. Most assigned essays and articles fall into this category. You will survey when you already know a lot of the information, you're just interested in getting a few ideas, or you're prereading texts before close reading. Surveying uses the techniques of skimming and scanning that are covered at the end of this chapter.

> If you want to reach a goal, you must "see the reaching" in your own mind before you actually arrive at your goal.
>
> —Zig Ziglar (contemporary), American motivational speaker and author

Text difficulty is something you generally recognize as soon as you begin reading. It depends on sentence length, the difficulty of the vocabulary, and the author's writing style. You can categorize texts as difficult, moderate, or easy.

Efficient reading rates match your purpose with the text difficulty. If your purpose is learning and the text is difficult, slow speeds are called for. Within that range, an easier sociology textbook will be faster to read than a complex biology book. Similarly, a survey purpose on easy materials should be read very quickly. But fast speeds also have a range: surveying an article written by a scientist will require a slower speed than one written by a newspaper reporter. Figure 3.1 shows how these relationships work.

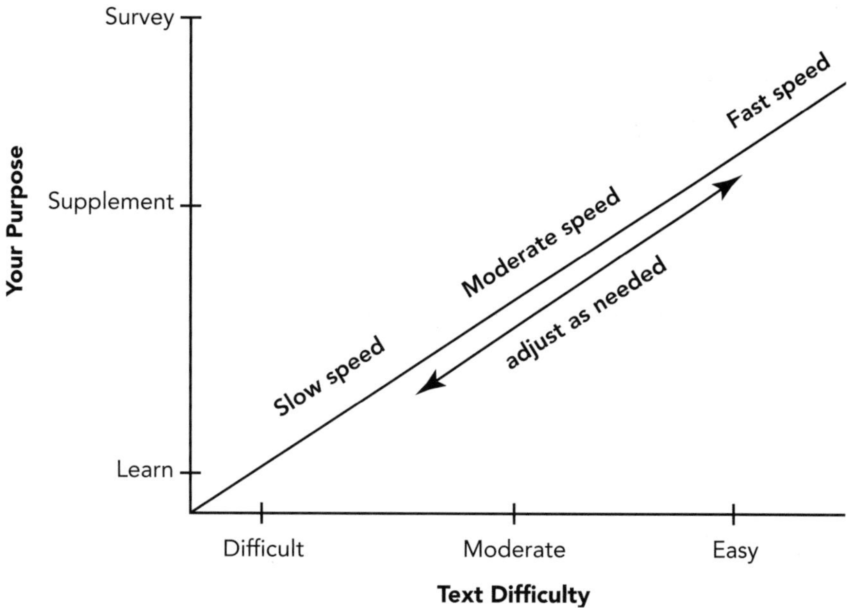

FIGURE 3.1 **Determining Efficient Rates**

You may be wondering how to set the right speed. Efficient readers don't pick a specific speed. Instead, they choose a slow, moderate, or fast range depending on the task. Slow rates range from 100 to 300 words per minute (wpm), moderate rates from 300 to 500 wpm, and fast speeds start at 500 wpm and go up from there. Notice that the speed ranges do not include speeds under 100 wpm. It is certainly possible and even necessary to read some texts slower than 100 wpm. For example, you would use a very slow rate with a math book or a poem where you have to stop often, think, and even backtrack. But, in general, 100 wpm is the lower limit for comprehension of college texts, because with slower speeds, it is very difficult to recall the beginning of a paragraph by the time you reach the end.

ACTIVITY 1: ASSESS YOUR READING SPEEDS

DIRECTIONS: Think about your reading speeds by completing the following tasks.

1. If the passages in the previous ***Think about this*** . . . activity were course assignments, how would you read them? Identify a purpose (learning, supplement, survey) and text difficulty (difficult, moderate, easy) for each one. Then record the speed range (slow, moderate, fast) that you actually used to read that selection.

   Text A: Purpose: ___________ Difficulty: ___________ My speed: ___________

   Text B: Purpose: ___________ Difficulty: ___________ My speed: ___________

   Text C: Purpose: ___________ Difficulty: ___________ My speed: ___________

2. Look at your answers to question 1 and analyze your reading style.
   a. Did you recognize the different purposes or levels of difficulty for the texts you read? Explain.

   ____

   ____

   b. Do you have three speed ranges? If not, which one(s) do you need to develop?

   ____

   ____

3. List four texts that you'll be reading this semester. Include some non-course materials in your list. For each text, identify a purpose, the text difficulty, and the best speed range (slow, moderate, or fast) to use.

	TEXT	PURPOSE	DIFFICULTY LEVEL	SPEED RANGE
1.	________	________	________	________
2.	________	________	________	________
3.	________	________	________	________
4.	________	________	________	________

When should you decide about your purpose, the text difficulty, and the optimum speed? These decisions are very quick assessments that you will make during prereading. But you will also need to remain flexible and change them as needed during the reading task.

Personal Speed Blocks

Personal blocks are self-restricting ideas and habits that promote inefficient rates. They are the reasons for reading too fast without comprehension or too slowly without concentration. Personal blocks result from psychological, physical, or skills aspects of your reading style.

Psychological Blocks Psychological blocks are the thoughts, attitudes, and beliefs that you have about reading speed. They include all aspects of low motivation mentioned in Chapter 1.

Efficient reading requires high motivation at each stage. If you are not *engaged,* you won't have any desire to read and you'll dread the task or find the text boring. If you aren't *focused,* you won't set standards for your comprehension, concentrate, or leave enough quality time for the task. Without *monitoring,* you won't identify and resolve reading problems or adjust your rate as needed. Since efficient reading does require some effort, you will need to *reflect* to provide the rewards, self-praise, and gains necessary to maintain this more attentive approach.

Belief also controls the mind. Many readers wrongly believe that good readers are fast readers. So they read fast even if they don't understand the material. Other readers think that every word must be read in order to comprehend, that they will not understand the text if they speed up, and that everything in print is supremely important. So they read very slowly and pay too much attention to individual words. These misconceptions will govern your reading rate until you dismiss them.

Use Activity 2 to determine how much of your reading rate is due to psychological causes.

It's amazing what ordinary people can do if they set out without preconceived notions.

—Charles F. Kettering (1876–1958), American engineer

ACTIVITY 2: ASSESS YOUR PSYCHOLOGICAL BLOCKS

DIRECTIONS: Think about the way you generally read course assignments. For each item below, check off the answer that most closely describes what you think and do. Then answer the questions that follow the survey.

	USUALLY	SOMETIMES	NEVER
1. I find the topic boring.	_____	_____	_____
2. The information is not important to me.	_____	_____	_____
3. My mind wanders as I read.	_____	_____	_____
4. I daydream as I read.	_____	_____	_____
5. I read in front of the TV.	_____	_____	_____
6. I read where noise or music distracts me.	_____	_____	_____
7. I read where other people can distract me.	_____	_____	_____
8. I'm very busy and don't have time for reading.	_____	_____	_____
9. I read when I'm tired.	_____	_____	_____
10. I don't expect to get much out of my reading.	_____	_____	_____
11. I don't think I read well or efficiently.	_____	_____	_____
12. I read when I'm stressed.	_____	_____	_____
13. I feel discouraged or frustrated when I read.	_____	_____	_____
14. I don't reward or praise myself for reading well.	_____	_____	_____
15. I think good readers read fast.	_____	_____	_____
16. I worry that I'll miss something important if I read fast.	_____	_____	_____

Interpretation

Each *Usually* answer is a block that will create inefficient rates.
Each *Sometimes* answer signals an occasional block that needs attention.
Each *Never* answer indicates a helpful approach that you should continue to use.

1. Review your answers. List the number of items you checked for each answer.

   Usually: _____ *Sometimes:* _____ *Never:* _____

2. Look at the items where you answered *Usually*. What can you do to change these areas?

____

____

3. Look at the items where you answered *Sometimes*. What can you do to improve these areas?

____

____

4. Look at the items where you answered *Never*. What helpful approaches should you continue to use?

____

____

Physical Blocks Part of reading is obviously physical. It has to do with the way you move your eyes and focus on the page. Over the years and without training, many readers unknowingly put up with eyestrain and use eye movements that hamper reading speed.

Eyestrain makes reading very difficult. If you can't read comfortably for an hour, if your eyes water or become red, if you get headaches, if you become fatigued when you read, or if you have trouble focusing, your eyes are straining. Quite logically, eye discomfort makes it very difficult to read efficiently.

Eyestrain typically comes from one (or more) of three causes. The first possible cause is body position. If you read lying on a bed or lounging on a sofa, or if the text is parallel to your face, your eyes will become fatigued and uncomfortable. Body position also comes into play when you're sitting at a desk or a table. If the height of the table or the distance and angle of the book to your eyes is not right, if the book is flat on the table top, and if there's a glare from glossy paper, your eyes will be strained. The second cause of eyestrain is inadequate lighting. Without enough illumination, the eyes very quickly become strained and tired. The last cause has to do with your eyesight. Eyesight does change over time, and even subtle vision shifts can have dramatic effects on reading. If you have problems focusing or symptoms of eyestrain, you may need professional attention.

Three kinds of eye movements interfere with reading speed. The first is **line tracking.** Your eyes should move across a line of text, and then move back to the next line quickly and accurately. Unnecessary, slow reading occurs when the eyes don't stay on the right line, when the return sweep is slow, or when the return sweep misses the next line.

The second eye movement that affects speed has to do with the way the eyes actually "see" the print. Your eyes don't read while they're moving. To see print, they stop and focus on a small section of a line. That focal point is called a **fixation.** Only a fraction of a second is needed to transmit the text information to the brain. But many readers get in the habit of **over-fixating,** or staring at the text much longer than necessary.

The third eye movement related to reading speed is called a regression. A **regression,** or the act of looking back at what you've already read, can be something you choose to do, because you want or need to think more about a point. Regressions of choice are not a problem, unless they occur very often. But regressions that are a habitual part of your reading style, that occur in the middle of sentences, or that occur often are a serious problem. They slow you down. They also interfere with comprehension because they stop the flow of information and lead you to take in information out of order. All of that contributes to confusion.

Use Activity 3 to determine how your physical reading style affects your speed.

ACTIVITY 3: ASSESS YOUR PHYSICAL BLOCKS

DIRECTIONS: Think about the way you generally read course assignments. For each item below, check off the answer that most closely describes what you think and do. Then answer the questions that follow the survey.

	USUALLY	SOMETIMES	NEVER
1. I read lying down.	_____	_____	_____
2. The chair I use is uncomfortable.	_____	_____	_____
3. The furniture I use promotes relaxation.	_____	_____	_____
4. My desk or table is not at a comfortable height.	_____	_____	_____
5. I place texts flat on a tabletop or in my lap.	_____	_____	_____
6. I read where the lighting is poor.	_____	_____	_____
7. I have vision problems that I ignore.	_____	_____	_____
8. My eyes water and get red when I read.	_____	_____	_____
9. I experience headaches or fatigue when I read.	_____	_____	_____
10. I can't read comfortably for more than 20 minutes.	_____	_____	_____
11. I lose my place when I'm reading a line.	_____	_____	_____
12. I lose my place when I sweep my eyes to the next line.	_____	_____	_____
13. I stare at the print.	_____	_____	_____
14. I make a conscious effort to see each word.	_____	_____	_____
15. I regress in the middle of sentences.	_____	_____	_____
16. I reread parts of every paragraph.	_____	_____	_____

Interpretation

Each *Usually* answer is a block that will create inefficient rates.
Each *Sometimes* answer signals an occasional block that needs attention.
Each *Never* answer indicates a helpful approach that you should continue to use.

1. Review your answers. List the number of items you checked for each answer.

   Usually: _____ *Sometimes:* _____ *Never:* _____

2. Look at the items where you answered *Usually*. What can you do to change these areas?

   ____

   ____

3. Look at the items where you answered *Sometimes*. What can you do to improve these areas?

   ____

   ____

4. Look at the items where you answered *Never*. What helpful approaches should you continue to use?

   ____

   ____

Skills Blocks Reading involves numerous comprehension skills, along with the methods that access them. Think of skills as knowledge and methods as tools. You may know how to use a dictionary, for instance, but you sometimes choose to skip over unknown words. What you know is your skill; skip reading is your method of choice. Poor reading skills and methods hinder efficient reading.

Reading skills include how you make sense of the vocabulary, ideas, details, and relationships in texts. Reading comprehension always starts with vocabulary. Just as you can't read in a language you don't know, you can't read a text efficiently if many of the words are foreign, or unknown, to you. But even when the words are easy, poor comprehension skills can interfere with reading efficiency. For example, comprehension suffers whenever a reader fails to combine words and phrases into meaningful sentences and paragraphs, identify major and minor points, or recognize how the ideas and details work together.

Methods, especially passive reading methods, also affect your reading experience. Some of the most counterproductive reading for learning methods include not prereading, not accessing background knowledge, not thinking about the message, and not marking what's important. The result of these approaches is poor concentration, confusion, frustration, and very poor comprehension. To compensate for these problems, passive readers often use very fast or very slow speeds. But these rate changes can't solve the problems created by passive methods.

Use Activity 4 to determine how your skills and methods affect your rate.

ACTIVITY 4: ASSESS YOUR SKILLS AND METHODS

DIRECTIONS: Think about the way you generally read course assignments. For each item below, check off the answer that most closely describes what you think and do. Then answer the questions that follow the survey.

	USUALLY	SOMETIMES	NEVER
1. I encounter a lot of words that I don't know.	_____	_____	_____
2. My background knowledge is limited.	_____	_____	_____
3. I start reading without looking over the text.	_____	_____	_____
4. I try to read long assignments in one sitting.	_____	_____	_____
5. I read without a goal or purpose.	_____	_____	_____
6. I read without thinking of questions about the subject.	_____	_____	_____
7. I read without thinking about how the text is organized.	_____	_____	_____
8. I find it hard to identify what's most important in the text.	_____	_____	_____
9. I find it hard to understand the message of the text.	_____	_____	_____
10. It's hard to see how sentences relate to each other.	_____	_____	_____
11. It's hard to see how paragraphs relate to each other.	_____	_____	_____
12. When I lose my concentration, I just continue reading.	_____	_____	_____
13. When I'm confused, I just continue reading.	_____	_____	_____
14. When I don't comprehend, I just continue reading.	_____	_____	_____

Interpretation

Each *Usually* answer is a block that will create inefficient rates.
Each *Sometimes* answer signals an occasional block that needs attention.
Each *Never* answer indicates a helpful approach that you should continue to use.

1. Review your answers. List the number of items you checked for each answer.

   Usually: _____ *Sometimes:* _____ *Never:* _____

2. Look at the items where you answered *Usually*. What can you do to change these areas?

 ____

 ____

3. Look at the items where you answered *Sometimes*. What can you do to improve these areas?

 ____

 ____

4. Look at the items where you answered *Never*. What helpful approaches should you continue to use?

 ____

 ____

If you always put a limit on everything you do, physical or anything else, it will spread into your work and into your life. There are no limits. There are only plateaus, and you must not stay there. You must go beyond them.

—Bruce Lee (1940–1973), Chinese-American actor, director, martial artist

Before you go on . . .

Monitor Your Progress: recite

As you read . . .

Focus Your Efforts: question and read

How Can I Improve My Reading Speed?

THINK ABOUT THIS . . .

1. Think about how you motivate yourself to read. Put a checkmark next to the stage(s) where you use some motivating approaches (even if it's only occasionally or only since reading this textbook). Put an *x* next to the stage(s) where you don't use any motivating methods at all.

 ______ Engage my interest ______ Focus my efforts

 ______ Monitor my progress ______ Reflect on my gains

2. Look at the following two lines. The letters in the following two lines are not fully formed. Put a checkmark next to the line that is easier to read and understand.

_____ **a.** It was warm in Los Angeles

_____ **b.** We were working the day watch out of burglary.

3. Have you ever used a ruler, card, or your finger to aid your reading speed? If so, did it help?

____

____

4. How do you normally read? Read each of the following sentences with a very brief pause at each slash mark. Then, put a check mark next to the one that matches the way you normally read.

_____ **a.** Most / adults / read / slowly / because / their / early / reading / patterns / became / their / only / reading / strategies.

_____ **b.** Most adults / read slowly / because their / early reading / patterns became / their only / reading strategies.

_____ **c.** Most adults / read slowly because / their early reading patterns / became their only / reading strategies.

The ***Think about this*** . . . items highlight your psychological, physical, and skills reading styles. The following sections provide techniques for improving those areas, as well as using the techniques of skimming and scanning.

Eliminate Psychological Blocks

Inefficient reading rates are often caused by a lack of control. Many readers do not know that they can and should control the way they read. They have an external locus of control (see Chapter 1, p. 18), which means that their motivation and even their methods are determined by the author's style or the look of the text. Efficient reading means that you have internal control over your reading attitudes, processes, and outcomes. How do you do this? You will find that adopting positive self-talk (see Chapter 1, p. 11) at each stage of motivation will change your locus of control and promote efficient reading.

Thoughts have power; thoughts are energy. And you can make your world or break it by your own thinking.

—Susan Taylor (1946–), Editor-in-Chief, *Essence* magazine

In addition to taking control of your motivation, recognize and change any reading misconceptions that you might have. To do this, state the belief, identify where it came from, and replace it with better information. For example, you might think that good readers read fast right before exams so that they can recall more. You got this idea by watching your sister, who did well in high school with this approach. But if you think about it, you'll realize that your sister learned a lot in class and used the book only as a quick review, that her high school texts were much less demanding than your college textbooks, that reading before a test won't work if there are a lot of chapters, and that trying to do that is very stressful. A more logical approach is to read when the professor covers the material and use techniques such as dividing a chapter up and choosing the most efficient rate for your purpose.

ACTIVITY 5: ELIMINATE YOUR PSYCHOLOGICAL BLOCKS

DIRECTIONS: Focus on eliminating psychological blocks by completing the following tasks.

1. Look at your responses to Activity 2 and item 1 in the ***Think about this*** . . . box on page 102. Review the preceding suggestions and list what you can do to take more control of your reading motivation.

   ____

   ____

   ____

   ____

   ____

   ____

2. Identify one reading misconception that you have (or had in the past). Describe how you acquired this idea and new information that could replace it.

   The misbelief: ____

   ____

   How I got this idea: ____

   ____

   New information: ____

   ____

The man who believes he can do something is probably right, and so is the man who believes he can't.

—Oprah Winfrey (1954–), American talk show host and philanthropist

Eliminate Physical Blocks

A person's reading methods are often habitual. But bad habits can be changed, and inefficient ones can be improved. To get the most out of your eyes, check your body position, pay attention to line focusing, and use pacing.

Body Position To get in the best position for reading with speed, make sure that the lighting is very good and that there is no glare or reflection from the page. Then use a

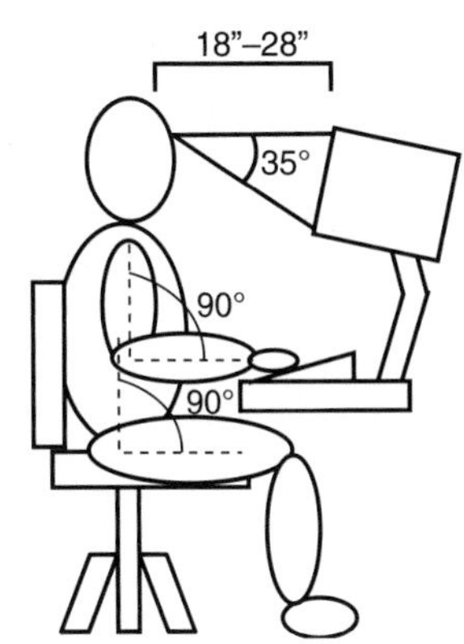

FIGURE 3.2 **The Best Eye-Print Positions**

chair that allows you to sit up straight and possibly a table or desk to hold the text. Make sure that the chair is padded and adjusted for your height so that your body is comfortable for at least 45 minutes. Then adjust the text so that it's in the best eye-to-page relationship: 12–18 inches from your eyes and somewhat lower than eye level. The distance and how much lower the page should be will depend on the print size and your eyesight. In addition, the text should be at a 45-degree angle to your body. This would be the natural place that you would hold a page for reading out loud if you were standing up. To create the most comfortable eye-to-page relationship, also consider using a bookstand, or prop something behind the text so that it's at the right angle. Figure 3.2 illustrates the best positions for holding a book, reading at a desk, or reading a computer screen.

Line Focusing Did the second task in the ***Think about this*** . . . box (p. 102) surprise you? It illustrates an important point about English: the top half of English letters are more distinctive than the bottom half. So, as you read line 2.a in that exercise, your eyes probably moved over the line in an easy, flowing motion. Many people remark that it's as if their eyes were suddenly set free. But most people don't read this way. Instead, they focus on the bottom of the lines, so it's harder to figure out the words. Reading with texts that are flat on a tabletop encourages you to read the bottom of the lines. When your book is propped up or held lower than your eyes, you can more easily look down at the top of the letters.

In addition to positioning the text properly, you may need to change your habit of focusing on the bottom line. To do this, first think about looking at the top of the letters and then practice focusing there by using Activity 6, which is a training tool for this purpose. To break the old habit, use this tool every day or so for several weeks until top line reading becomes a part of your reading style.

ACTIVITY 6: TOP LINE FOCUSING

DIRECTIONS: Read through the following text and think about what it says.

To develop the habit of looking at the tops of the lines, first make sure that your text is propped and held at a height that is lower than your eyes. Then think about the fact that in English the top part of the letters has more distinctive information than the lower part of the letters. Remind yourself that you will be able to move your eyes better if you focus on the upper parts of he letters. In fact, with this technique your eyes will feel as if they have been set free.

If you have trouble doing this, do not worry about it or get stressed. That will only make it harder to do. You may find that using the pacing card (see page 107) will help you to focus. Or you may find that you can only use this technique on very simple material that you know a lot about. That makes sense. Reading speed is linked to how much you know, and you will be able to use the techniques the best on material that you are already familiar with. Finally, some people find that specific techniques just don't work for them. If this technique gets in the way of your good reading on easy material, then definitely don't use it. There are plenty of other techniques that will work for you.

Continue to practice with this tool. Even though you may have read it in the past, read it again. The repetition of the message will help to change your habit.

A couple of hours of practice is worth ten sloppy rounds.

—Babe Didrikson Zaharias (1924–1956),
American sportswoman in basketball, golf, track and field

Eye Swings Inaccurate eye tracking across the lines, over-fixating, and regressing are habits that can be changed. Those eye movements often come from years of stop-and-go reading. If your eyes move in this halting way, you first need to realize that this approach does not create good comprehension. When you lose your place, stop frequently, or regress, you interrupt the message. You also add information from the wrong line into your thinking, which creates confusion. Reading is a process of comprehending whole units of sentences and paragraphs together and in order. To do this, you have to keep going forward. (Of course, if you know you have missed something, you can always choose to go back. But make that decision at a logical point, such as the end of a paragraph.)

To counteract stop-and-go or regressive eye movements, be aware of what your eyes are doing. Move them to the right across the lines. Then quickly swing them back to the next line. Activity 7 is a training device to help you get the feeling of this kind of eye movement. Like the top line tool, use this every day or so for several weeks until good eye swings become an automatic part of your reading style.

ACTIVITY 7: EYE SWINGS

DIRECTIONS: Use the eye swings training device like this:

A. Move your eyes over the following "lines" as if you were reading them. Focus on the dot above each bar as if it were a word.

B. Make your eyes swing faster on the return sweep. Also move them faster and faster as you move from line 3 to the end.

C. Go from the beginning to the end of the chart three to five times in a session, with brief rests in between each one. (Adapted from Baldridge 32)

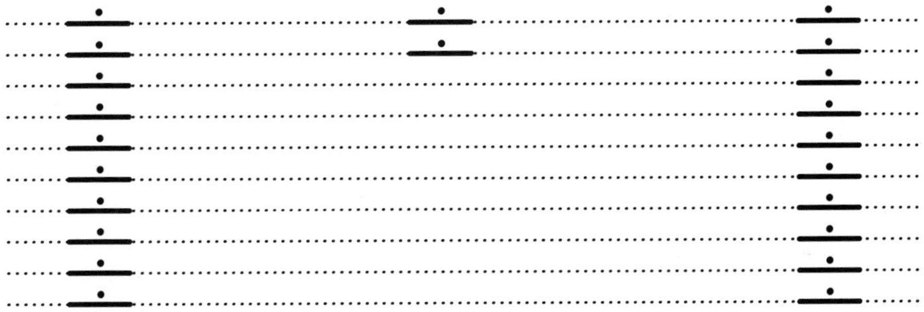

Practice only makes for improvement.

—Les Brown (1945–), American motivational speaker and author

Pacing **Pacing** is a proven technique for increasing speed in any physical or mental activity. It involves pushing yourself slightly faster than your comfort zone for brief periods of time, until the new speed becomes comfortable. There are a number of ways to use this method.

1. *Direct yourself to read faster.*

   Simply telling yourself to read the next paragraph or page a little faster will improve your rate for that session. Don't go so fast that you can't comprehend the material. Simply go a little faster than your most comfortable speed.

2. *Use a pacing card or ruler.*

   Slide a white 3 × 5 or 4 × 6 card down the page so that you read the line under the bottom edge of the card. You can use a ruler the same way; just make sure that you slide it down the page and don't put it under the line you're reading. The card has the added advantage that it helps to break the regression habit, because it blocks out what you've already read and reminds the mind that reading is a go-forward process. With either the card or the ruler, move it only a little faster than your current speed, not at a speed that causes poor comprehension.

3. *Use a timer.*

   Time how long it takes you to read one page of a text. Then reduce that time by 10 to 15 percent. Set a timer for the shorter time period and try to read the next page before the timer dings. Adjust the timer if needed to allow more or less time, so that you push yourself but are not reading too fast or too slowly. Then use the timer on your best setting for the rest of the pages in the task.

You may have seen or heard about speed reading courses that encourage readers to use their hand, a finger, or a pencil as a pacer. While those tools can help you track very small fonts or difficult texts, they are not good tools to use all the time. It's hard to be accurate with your hand or a pencil, and after a few minutes you'll find that it either covers or misses a line. In the end, these tools often encourage the stop-and-go habit you're trying to break.

ACTIVITY 8: USE THE PHYSICAL TECHNIQUES TOGETHER

DIRECTIONS: Practice using the physical techniques by following these steps.

A. Record your start time just before you begin to read.
B. As you read, sit up, prop the text, swing your eyes, and use a pacing method.
C. Record your end reading time, subtract the times, and circle your speed on the Rate Chart.
D. Answer and score the comprehension questions using the key at the end of the chapter.

	MINUTES : SECONDS
Record your END time here:	______ : ______
Record your START time here:	–______ : ______
Subtract and record your TOTAL reading time here:	______ : ______

At this time of year, dermatologists are wringing their hands in dismay and frustration. Why don't people listen to the warnings about the risks of sunlight? Vanity and the recklessness of the young usually get the blame. But maybe there's more to the urge to bake than looks and youthful abandon. A small study seems to say so. It links the ultraviolet rays to the release of pleasure-inducing endorphins in the brain.

A group of researchers reported that they sought out volunteers who regularly went to tanning salons and invited them to lounge in tanning beds at no charge over a period of six weeks. The 14 volunteers—13 women and a man—came in twice a week. Each one was directed to one of two seemingly identical tanning beds. But one of the beds was equipped with a UV filter and the other wasn't. When the volunteers were given mood assessments afterwards, those who had not been shielded from the ultraviolet light were more content and more relaxed. And when the group was given the opportunity to come in on a third day and choose one bed or the other, 11 of the 12 people headed straight for the bed that provided ultraviolet light.

The researchers liken that response to the persistence of other risky behaviors, like smoking and drug use. They note that tanning salons are increasingly popular. And college-age tanning-bed users often say that sunbathing enhances their sense of well being. The lead author of the study was Dr. Steven R. Feldman, professor of dermatology, pathology and public health sciences at Wake Forest University Baptist Medical Center in Winston-Salem, NC. He said: "They're lying out on their backs and they're saying, 'Ah, this feels so good.' These people are getting their little hit of UV." (Adapted from Eric Nagourney) (298 words)

Rate Chart: Circle your rate.

:30 seconds	594 wpm
:45	396
1:00	298
1:15	238
1:30	198
1:45	170

1. Ultraviolet rays may increase the levels of endorphins in the brain. T F
2. The volunteers were all women. T F
3. The volunteers who received the ultraviolet light were less relaxed. T F
4. Ultraviolet rays appear to increase a sense of well-being. T F
5. Doctors claim that UV light is addictive. T F

Right: ______

Scoring: Use the Answer Key at the end of the chapter to score the comprehension questions.

To give yourself the best possible chance of playing to your potential, you must prepare for every eventuality. That means practice.

—Seve Ballesteros (1957–   ), Spanish golfer

Improve Your Skills and Methods

Improving your reading skills will directly affect your rates. If your rates are habitually slow, better skills will increase them. If they're too fast, more knowledge about comprehension will indicate where to slow down and pay more attention to the text. These skills are the focus of chapters 4 through 7, and you can expect your rate to improve as you work on each of them. Two other ways to improve your skills and methods are covered here: active reading and phrase reading.

Active Reading The active reading approaches described in Chapter 2 put you in charge of the reading process, which means that you can control and change your rate. In particular, the preread, divide, and question methods directly affect rate. Prereading gives the mind two things that it needs. First, looking over even the most unfamiliar text gives the mind a chance to think about the words and information that are familiar and to access your background knowledge. With this in mind, it's much easier and faster to take in new information. Second, prereading provides a mental map of the author's organization. Like using any map, knowing where you're going makes it easier to proceed at an optimum speed.

The divide and question methods also aid efficiency. If the assignment is long, dividing it into short tasks ensures that you stop reading before fatigue sets in. And the goal setting step puts you in control of your purpose. A moment's thought as to whether you want to learn, supplement, or survey a topic and whether the writing is easy, moderate, or difficult creates efficient reading. Forming questions and reading to find the answers will also promote reading efficiency, because you will be looking for something specific and have a way to judge when to shift your rate.

When you're prepared, you're more confident. When you have a strategy, you're more comfortable.

—Fred Couples (1959–), American golfer

Finally, knowing that you will recite and review will lower your stress about "getting everything," and make it more comfortable to push your rate up a little. In addition, the recite step gives you an opportunity to identify and fix any reading problems, including portions of the text you missed. And review allows you to reinforce your comprehension and realize the benefits of your efficient reading.

Phrase Reading Look back at item 4 in the ***Think about this*** . . . box (p. 103). Are you most comfortable reading one word at a time, two-word groups, or phrases? Word-by-word reading interferes with comprehension because it chops up sentences and makes each word equally important. Reading two words at a time is a transition phase between word-by-word reading and reading in phrases. Both word-by-word and two-word reading interfere with understanding and promote regressions.

Phrase reading is a solid technique to use at all speeds. When you read in phrases, you group words and use emphasis to form meaningful units. As a result, you usually reduce or eliminate unnecessary regressions. Phrase reading is the skill used by those who read well out loud. They separate pieces of information with pauses and use tone of voice to stress the important parts. They may even read at different rates—moving fast over nonessential material and slowing down to emphasize important points. When readers read this way silently, they get three benefits: increased reading speed, comprehension, and motivation.

To phrase read, think in meaningful word groups. On average, these groups will be three to five words long, with an occasional word left by itself. But the number of words is not as important as grouping the words meaningfully. How do you do this? Use the guidelines out-loud readers use:

1. Group adjectives and nouns together.
2. Group adverbs and verbs together.
3. Group the words in prepositional phrases together.

4. Pay attention to punctuation. Give a short pause to commas; use a slightly longer pause for colons, dashes, and semicolons; stop at periods and question marks.
5. Read with expression: Vary the emphasis and rate according to the meaning of the text.

Here's an example of a phrased version of two sentences about how technology helps a blind man see. Read each group of words with expression and pause slightly between the phrases.

EXAMPLE

A blind man   can read large letters   and navigate around big objects   by using a tiny camera   wired directly to his brain.   This device   is the first artificial eye to provide useful vision   a researcher reports.

Two additional points need to be made about phrasing. First, notice that a group of words can run from the end of one line to the beginning of the next line, as it does in the example with "by using a tiny camera." Second, be assured that there's room for variations in grouping. In the second sentence of the example, the verb "is" could go with the first phrase or the second one. The key is to group words in a way that best promotes your comprehension.

Practice phrasing by completing the following activity. It presents the rest of the article about this blind man.

ACTIVITY 9: PHRASE READING

DIRECTIONS: Read this article by doing the following:

A. Read the first sentence with expression and phrase each group of words as written.
B. As you read the remaining sentences, place slash marks (/) after each meaningful group of words.
C. Reread the article by grouping the words that you have phrased together. Change any marks that are not in the best place.

The 62-year-old man   doesn't see an image.   He perceives up to 100 specks of light   that appear and disappear,   like stars   that come and go behind passing clouds,   as his field   of vision shifts.

But as he showed a reporter last week, that's enough to let him find a mannequin in a room, walk to a black stocking cap hanging on a white wall, and then return to the mannequin to plop the cap on its head. He also can recognize a 2-inch-tall letter from five feet away, said researcher William Dobelle.

"He can do remarkably well" with the limited visual signal, said Dobelle, who is developing the artificial vision system.

The man who asked to be identified only as Jerry, has been blind since the age of 36. He volunteered for the study and got the brain implant in 1978; scientists have been working since then to improve the software.

Richard Normann, who studies artificial vision at the University of Utah, said he's encouraged by how much Jerry can do. He said Dobelle's report suggests that, someday, even limited signals to the brain will let blind people do relatively complicated visual tasks.

It's the first demonstration of useful artificial vision, he said, but he stressed the device is "a very limited navigational aid, and it's a far cry from the visual experience that normal people enjoy." (Adapted from Ritter) (231 words)

To train yourself to phrase read, practice on easy materials such as newspaper articles, and follow these steps: read, mark the phrases with slashes, reread with expression, and move the marks as needed.

Learn by practice.
—Martha Graham (1894–1991), American dancer, teacher, and choreographer

---

ACTIVITY 10: USE THE METHODS TOGETHER

DIRECTIONS: Practice using active reading and phrasing by following these steps.

A. Preread. Then set a goal by circling your purpose, identifying the topic, circling your rate, and listing your reward(s).
B. Record your start time just before you begin to read. Then form mental questions and phrase read with expression.
C. Record your end time, subtract the times, and circle your speed on the Rate Chart.
D. Answer and score the comprehension questions.

I want to read to (learn / supplement / survey) the information about ____________ at a (slow / moderate / fast) rate. My reward(s) will be ____________________ ____.

	MINUTES : SECONDS
Record your END time here:	____ : ____
Record your START time here:	− ____ : ____
Subtract and record your TOTAL reading time here:	____ : ____

More than a century ago, Freud proposed that dreams concealed subconscious wishes and desires. This theory has in recent decades fallen from scientific favor. A new study, however, may add weight to the idea that what people suppress during the day returns when they close their eyes at night.

Deliberately blocking thoughts about someone before going to sleep, the researchers found, made it more likely that the person would appear in a dream that night. In the study, by scientists at Harvard and the University of Texas at San Antonio, college students were asked to choose someone they knew. Then, some students were told to concentrate on that person. Others were told to suppress thoughts about that person for five minutes before bedtime. A final group of students was told simply to pick a person and then to think about anything at all.

"Not surprisingly, any kind of thinking about something increases the likelihood that it will show up in a dream," said Dr. Daniel M. Wegner, a professor of psychology at Harvard and the lead author of the study. "But trying to suppress something increases the chances even more, indicating that the meanings of our dreams involve things we've tried to sweep under the rug."

During sleep, Dr. Wegner said, the cortex loosens its grip on distractions tuned out earlier in the day. As a result, studies show, people who try to quit smoking have dreams about cigarettes, and an actor who is gearing up for a big show has nightmares about going blank on stage. Going to bed lifts the lid on all the thoughts that the mind keeps under wraps. "A lot of the things we dream about tend to be negative, because they're the things we're most likely to deliberately keep out of our minds," Dr. Wegner said. "It's often the most awful things we can think about that we crowd into our dreams."

Concerted efforts to block things, experts say, give them special value and can have the unintended effect of making them more memorable. In a study several years ago, for example, Dr. Wegner showed that telling people not to think about a white bear made them obsessed with that very thought. In the courtroom, other researchers have found, telling a jury to disregard a witness's testimony can actually increase its influence. (O'Connor) (388 words)

Rate Chart: Circle your rate.

:45 seconds	517 wpm
1:00	388
1:15	310
1:30	259
1:45	222
2:00	194
2:15	172

1. Freud's theory is well accepted. T F
2. New research suggests that we dream about what we think about. T F
3. The thing you think about will not show up in a dream unless you suppress it. T F

4. We dream about negative things because we are worried about them. T F

5. Efforts to block things make them more valuable and memorable. T F

Right: ______

Scoring: Use the Answer Key at the end of the chapter to score the comprehension questions.

Use Skimming and Scanning

Skimming and scanning are super-fast reading techniques that you can use when your purpose is to survey a text. Since they involve a lot of skipping, they are not effective speeds for learning, although they can be part of an multitasked reading and learning approach. For example, you will skim a biology assignment as part of prereading and might scan during studying to locate topics that need to be learned. In short, skimming and scanning are good techniques for prereading, for locating information, and for some personal reading.

The purpose of **skimming** is to find the main ideas in a text or get an overview of what it includes. As noted above, you already use this technique when you preread. You probably also skim when you're looking for information on the Internet or have only a few minutes to read the newspaper.

To skim, very quickly read only the parts that are most likely to present the topic and the ideas: the title, introduction, headings (if there are any), first sentences of major paragraphs, and the conclusion. During skimming, as soon as you "get" the point, skip the rest, including parts of and whole sentences, as well as paragraphs.

Here's an example of skimming. The highlighted parts are what a reader might actually take in.

EXAMPLE

U.S. Border Patrol

Typical Positions

Border patrol agent, detention enforcement officer, immigration inspector, immigration officer, and deportation officer. The primary mission of the U.S. Border Patrol is to detect and prevent the smuggling and unlawful entry of undocumented aliens into the United States and to apprehend anyone found in the United States in violation of federal immigration laws. Currently, border patrol agent positions are available in Texas, New Mexico, Arizona, and California along the U.S.–Mexico border. Immigration inspector positions are available nationwide.

Employment Requirements

Applicants for the position of border patrol agent must meet the general requirements for a federal law enforcement officer and must (1) be a U.S. citizen; (2) hold a bachelor's degree or have three years of responsible experience or have an equivalent combination of education and experience; (3) be in excellent physical condition, with good eyesight and hearing; (4) submit to urinalysis screening prior to employment; (5) possess emotional and mental stability; (6) be 21 to 34 years of age at the time of employment; and (7) have no felony convictions or records of improper or criminal conduct.

Other Requirements
Border patrol agents must demonstrate proficiency in the Spanish language.

Salary
A bachelor's degree in any field qualifies applicants for appointment at the GS-5 level, while individuals with exceptional experience or education may be appointed at the GS-7 level or higher.

Benefits
Benefits include paid annual vacation, sick leave, life and health insurance, and a liberal retirement plan.

Direct Inquiries to:
U.S. Border Patrol
425 I Street, N.W.
Washington, DC 20536
Phone: (800) 238-1945
Website: **http://www.immigration.gov**

Source: U.S. Office of Personnel Management.

For additional career information in the criminal justice field visit **http://cjbrief.com/careers.** (Schmalleger 214)

As the example shows, skimming gives you the "gist," or a sense of the author's main points. It may not give you a full understanding of the main points, and it doesn't focus on the detailed information. This technique only works when an overview of the topic is needed and when the text is easy and well organized with clearly stated ideas. If you need complete understanding or if the ideas are difficult, the vocabulary is new, or the main points are not clearly stated, you will get very little out of skimming. If you can't get what you need from skimming, switch to a slower speed and a more thorough method.

ACTIVITY 11: SKIMMING

DIRECTIONS: Assume that you came across the following text in a magazine and that you are curious about what GPS is, how it works, and how it's used. Skim the following text and then answer the questions at the end.

The Power of GPS

Where in the world is Carmen San Diego? Or, more importantly, where in the world is the nearest gas station? Many people aren't whizzes at geography, but knowing your current location and the location of your destination can often come in handy. Luckily for those who are "directionally" impaired, **Global Positioning System (GPS)** technology enables you to carry a powerful navigational aid in your pocket.

You've probably heard of GPS, but what is it exactly and how does it work? The Global Positioning System is a system of 21 satellites (plus three working spares), built and operated by the U.S. military, that constantly orbit the earth. GPS devices use an antenna to pick up the signals from these satellites and special software to transform those signals into latitude and longitude. Using the information obtained from the satellites, GPS devices can tell you what your geographical location is anywhere on the planet to within 10 feet. Because they provide such detailed positioning information, GPS units are now used as navigational aids for aircraft, recreational boats, and automobiles, and they even come in handheld models for hikers.

While this precise positioning information clearly redefines the fields of surveying and of search and rescue operations, it has also changed other fields. Wildlife researchers now tag select animals and watch their migration patterns and how the population is distributed. Meanwhile, GPS was important to the two teams that created the Chunnel, the tunnel under the English Channel that connects England to France. One team worked from France toward England and the other from England toward France. They used GPS information along the way to make sure they were on target, and in 1990, the two sections joined to become the first physical link between England and the continent of Europe since the Ice Age.

Although it sounds easy enough to find a geosite with a GPS device, reaching these sites can be another matter—some lie underwater, on the side of a cliff, or inside the basement of a city building. Once participants arrive at the geosite, they find the "cache," which usually consists of a logbook in which other geocachers have left notes. Sometimes caches also contain trinkets, which geocachers can take as long as they leave one behind. When they get back home, geocachers e-mail the person who created the cache, reporting on the cache. The game can be expanded into multicaches—a treasure hunt leading players from one site to another—or a virtual cache, where the cache is a landmark and players have to answer a question from that spot to prove to the "cache owner" they were there.

However, having the ability to locate and track an object anywhere on earth does bring with it societal implications. For example, GPS units could potentially help criminals as easily as they could law enforcement officials. And what about the privacy risks of GPS-like tracking devices? Currently, devices like the VeriChip are being used to identify animals. The miniature implant contains identification information and is inserted under the skin of the animal. If VeriChip-like implants are developed to include a GPS receiver, parents could track their children. Would the benefits of decreasing the number of missing children outweigh the possible privacy risks? In what ways could the tracking information provided by GPS devices be used unethically? As GPS becomes more popular, expect to see such debates in the media. (Adapted from Evans et. al 328) (574 words)

For items 1–4, do not look back as you record your answers.

1. How does GPS work?

____

____

2. What technical fields has GPS changed?

3. Why is it difficult to reach some geosites?

4. What are the societal implications of GPS?

5. Look back at the text and check the accuracy and completeness of your answers. Was skimming useful? Did it produce good comprehension? Explain.

Scanning is a technique for locating specific information. It is used mainly on reference materials or texts that have details. When you use the dictionary, you scan to find a word. When you're looking up the answer to an end-of-chapter question in a textbook, you scan the pages to locate the information.

To scan, think of a question you want answered or an item you want to find. Then identify a specific key word or phrase that you think will be listed in the text near the information you are seeking. With the word(s) in mind, move your eyes from the top of the text and from side to side until the term "pops out." You will not read anything during scanning; you're simply looking for the word(s) you have in mind. Once you locate that word or phrase, stop and read the information.

Here's an example of scanning.

EXAMPLE

Question: What do people use to deactivate the venom in a snake bite?
Focus words: deactivate and venom

Even a New Yorker can tell you how to treat a snakebite in the middle of the woods. Apply a tourniquet, suck out the poison and spit it out. Wrong, experts say. Putting your mouth on a venomous wound is the last thing you should do.

A study in The New England Journal of Medicine two years ago found that cutting, sucking or cutting off the blood supply to a bite could damage nerves and blood vessels and lead to infection. A poisonous bite requires antivenin and emergency treatment. Victims should be taken to a medical center as soon as possible.

More than 7,000 Americans a year are bitten by venomous snakes. Most attacks occur when people go after the animals or try to handle them. Dr. Barry S. Gold, an author of the 2002 report, said he has seen many people use stun guns, electrical wires and even car batteries to try to deactivate the venom in a bite. "The only thing that's effective is taking people to the hospital," he said.

Nausea, weakness and other symptoms of a poisonous bite usually set in after 30 minutes. But experts say the chances of survival are excellent as long as the victim reaches a medical center within a few hours. After a bite, victims should stay warm and keep the wounded body part below the level of the heart. (O'connor) (228 words)

Notice that scanning only helps you find the focus words. To answer the question, you have to go back to the beginning of the sentence that has those words in it and read the entire thought. Also notice that when you scan, you skip many words and lines. Scanning even encourages you to look backwards, or from right to left, across the text. Although these are not good methods for close reading, they offer an efficient means to locate specific information. The key is, of course, thinking about the right term.

ACTIVITY 12: SCANNING

DIRECTIONS: Do not read the following text. For each question, circle the word(s) that you think will help you locate the answer in the text. Then, with the word(s) in mind, scan the text, locate the information, read it, and then record your answer. If you can't find the information easily, go back to the question and circle a different focusing term.

1. What are American teenagers cutting back on?

   ____

2. How much has illegal drug use dropped?

   ____

3. Has the use of any drugs increased?

   ____

4. Has there been any other survey or poll? If so, what did it show?

   ____

   ____

5. What is the most widely used illegal drug?

   ____

American teenagers are cutting back on their use of illicit drugs and cigarettes, but alcohol consumption is holding steady, the government says.

An annual survey of eighth, 10th, and 12th graders done for the Department of Health and Human Services found declines in many kinds of drugs used by high school students, especially Ecstasy and LSD.

Overall, the Bush administration said the annual survey, funded by the National Institute on Drug Abuse, showed an 11 percent drop in illegal drug use in the last two years, slightly surpassing President Bush's goal of a 10 percent reduction during that period.

The survey, known as Monitoring the Future, tracked drug use and attitudes among 48,500 students from 392 schools.

There was one troubling sign: slowing declines in the use of certain drugs by eighth-graders—and a slight increase in their use of inhalants, said Lloyd D. Johnston, who directed the study by the University of Michigan's Institute for Social Research.

"We should take this as a little warning, because eighth-graders have been indicative of things to come in the past," Johnston said.

In addition there was an overall increase in the illicit use of the synthetic painkillers OxyContin and vicodin, reflective of patterns seen in the general population.

The survey showed a different picture of drug use from another poll of teens that also is used to measure the effectiveness of White House drug-control policy. A private study by Pride Surveys in September showed illegal drug use and cigarette smoking among sixth through 12th graders increased slightly during the last school year compared with the years before. But both surveys agreed that marijuana remains by far the most widely used illegal drug. Monitoring the Future reported that it had been tried at least once by 46 percent of 12th graders and used by more than a third in the last year. Both numbers showed a decrease over last year. (Sherman) (316 words)

I was thinking that I might fly today.
Just to disprove all the things you say . . .
please be careful with me,
I'm sensitive, and I'd like to stay that way.

—Jewel Kilcher (1974–   ), American singer

Before you go on . . .

Monitor Your Progress: recite

After you read . . .

Reflect on Your Gains: review

CHAPTER SUMMARY

Introduction

Reading with speed and efficiency means reading at a pace that keeps the mind focused, comprehending the information, and moving forward. Efficient reading depends on using variable speeds. It's particularly useful for handling lengthy college assignments and gaining the degree of comprehension needed for each task.

What Determines Reading Rate?

To develop an efficient style of reading, you need to know how to choose efficient rates and identify personal speed blocks. To choose the best speed, first think about your **reading purpose** and assess the **text difficulty.** Then use slow speeds when your purpose requires learning and/or the text is difficult; use faster speeds when your purpose is to supplement or survey or the material is easy to read. Second, in order to use efficient rates, you have to recognize the self-restricting ideas and habits, or blocks, that promote speeds that are too fast or too slow. These blocks may be psychological, physical, or skills based. Psychological blocks include low motivation and misconceptions about reading. Physical blocks come from anything that creates eye strain and inefficient eye movements, such as poor **line tracking, over-fixating,** and **regressions.** Skills blocks are the result of vocabulary and comprehension skill weaknesses and the use of passive reading methods.

How Can I Improve My Reading Speed?

Techniques that counteract the blocks can greatly improve reading efficiency. You can eliminate psychological blocks by taking control of your reading with motivation techniques and new ideas that replace your misconceptions. To address the physical blocks, improve your body position and overcome inefficient eye movements with line focusing training, the eye swing exercise, and **pacing** methods. To address skills issues, use active reading techniques and **phrase reading.** Finally, use the very fast speeds of skimming and scanning whenever your purpose is to review or locate information.

REVIEW ACTIVITIES

Use the following activities to check your understanding and aid your learning of the information in this chapter.

Expand Your Vocabulary

Match each term with the correct definition or characteristic.

_____ **1.** efficient rates
_____ **2.** reading purpose
_____ **3.** text difficulty
_____ **4.** line tracking
_____ **5.** fixation
_____ **6.** over-fixating
_____ **7.** regression
_____ **8.** pacing
_____ **9.** phrase reading

a. staring at a word longer than needed
b. the focal point when the eyes are reading
c. determined by sentence length, vocabulary, and the author's style
d. moving your eyes to the next line and staying on it as you read
e. looking back at what you've already read
f. pushing yourself slightly faster than your comfort zone
g. grouping words to form meaningful units
h. optimum speed choices for purpose and text difficulty
i. determined by text importance and background knowledge

Increase Your Knowledge

These tasks will help you identify the important ideas in this chapter. They will also help you prepare for quizzes and exams on this material.

1. The following questions focus on the major chapter topics. Discuss them with others or form your own detailed answers.
   a. Explain how to use efficient rates. Include the guidelines for the three reading purposes, levels of text difficulty, and speed ranges.
   b. Explain what psychological, physical, and skills blocks are.
   c. What can you do to overcome the psychological blocks to efficient reading?
   d. What can you do to overcome the physical blocks to efficient reading?
   e. What can you do to overcome the skills blocks to efficient reading?
   f. What is the difference between skimming and scanning? How can they be used in course reading tasks?
2. Take notes on the information in this chapter.

Develop Your Skills

The following review tasks will give you an opportunity to practice the methods presented in this chapter.

REVIEW 1: PHRASE READING As you read the following article, place slash marks (/) after each meaningful group of words. Then, reread the article with expression and slight pauses at your slash marks. Change any marks that are not in the best place.

Dolphins Using Tools to Help in Hunting for Food

A group of dolphins living off the coast of Australia apparently teach their offspring to protect their snouts with sponges while foraging for food in the sea floor.

Researchers say it appears to be a cultural behavior passed on from mother to daughter, a first for animals of this type, although such learning has been seen in other species.

The dolphins, living in Shark Bay, Western Australia, use conically shaped whole sponges that they tear off the bottom, said Michael Kruetzen, lead author of a report on the dolphins in today's issue of *Proceedings of the National Academy of Science.*

"Cultural evolution, including tool use, is not only found in humans and our closest relatives, the primates, but also in animals that are evolutionally quite distant from us. This convergent evolution is what is so fascinating," said Kruetzen.

Researchers suspect the sponges help the foraging dolphins avoid getting stung by stonefish and other critters that hide in the sandy sea bottom, just as a gardener might wear gloves to protect the hands.

Kruetzen and colleagues analyzed 13 "spongers" and 172 "non-spongers" and concluded that the practice seems to be passed along family lines, primarily from mothers to daughters.(Associated Press, *North County Times*) (207 words)

REVIEW 2: USING EFFICIENT RATES The following three short passages all come from a section in a business communication textbook (Thill and Bovee 478). For each passage, do the following:

A. Preread. Then set a goal by circling your purpose, identifying the topic, circling your rate, and listing your reward(s).
B. Record your start time just before you begin to read. Read with efficient techniques: use the best body position, prop the text, top line focus, phrase read, question, and read to find the answers.
C. Record your end reading time, subtract the times, and circle your rate on the chart.
D. Answer the comprehension questions and score them using the end of chapter key.
E. Decide whether to adjust your rate on the next passage.

Passage A

I want to read to (learn / supplement / survey) the information about ____________ at a (slow / moderate / fast) rate. My reward(s) will be ________________________

____.

	MINUTES : SECONDS
Record your END time here:	______ : ______
Record your START time here:	– ______ : ______
Subtract and record your TOTAL reading time here:	______ : ______

Adapting to the Changing Workplace

Before you limit your employment search to a particular industry or job, do some preparation. Analyze what you have to offer and what you hope to get from your work. This preliminary analysis will help you identify employers who are likely to want you and vice versa.

Analyze What You Have to Offer

When seeking employment, you'll be asked to tell people about yourself, about who you are. So knowing what talents and skills you have is essential. And to be most effective, be sure you can explain how these skills will benefit potential employers. Here are some suggestions to help your self-analysis:

- **Jot down 10 achievements you're proud of.** Did you learn to ski, take a prizewinning photo, tutor a child, edit your school paper? Think about what skills these achievements demanded (leadership skills, speaking ability, and artistic talent may have helped you coordinate a winning presentation to your school's administration). You'll begin to recognize a pattern of skills, many of which might be valuable to potential employers.

- **Look at your educational preparation, work experience, and extracurricular activities.** What do your knowledge and experience qualify you to do? What have you learned from volunteer work or class projects that could benefit you on the job? Have you held any offices, won any awards or scholarships, mastered a second language?
- **Take stock of your personal characteristics.** Are you aggressive, a born leader? Or would you rather follow? Are you outgoing, articulate, great with people? Or do you prefer working alone? Make a list of what you believe are your four or five most important qualities. Ask a relative or friend to rate your traits as well.

Your college placement office may be able to administer a variety of tests to help you identify interests, aptitudes, and personality traits. These tests won't reveal your "perfect" job, but they'll help you focus on the types of work best suited to your personality. (325 words)

Passage A Rate Chart: Circle your rate.

:30 seconds	650 wpm
:45	433
1:00	325
1:15	260
1:30	217
1:45	186

1. It's recommended that you identify your talents and skills. T F

2. Listing personal achievements and awards is not useful. T F

3. Volunteer work and class projects are parts of your achievements. T F

4. Friends and family can help you rate your personal qualities. T F

\# Right: _____

Passage B

I want to read to _(learn / supplement / survey)_ the information about ____________ at a _(slow / moderate / fast)_ rate. My reward(s) will be ______________________

____.

	MINUTES : SECONDS
Record your END time here:	______ : ______
Record your START time here:	– ______ : ______
Subtract and record your TOTAL reading time here:	______ : ______

Decide What You Want to Do

Knowing what you *can* do is one thing. Knowing what you *want* to do is another. Don't lose sight of your own values. Discover the things that will bring you satisfaction and happiness on the job. Ask yourself some questions:

- **What would you like to do every day?** Talk to people in various occupations about their typical workday. You might consult relatives, local businesses, or former graduates (through your school's alumni relations office). Read about various occupations. Start with your college library or placement office.
- **How would you like to work?** Consider how much independence you want on the job, how much variety you like, and whether you prefer to work with products, machines, people, ideas, figures, or some combination thereof. Do you like physical work, mental work, or a mix? Constant change or a predictable role?
- **What specific compensation do you expect?** What do you hope to earn in your first year? What kind of pay increase do you expect each year? What's your ultimate earnings goal? Would you be comfortable getting paid on commission, or do you prefer a steady paycheck? Are you willing to settle for less money in order to do something you really love?
- **Can you establish some general career goals?** Consider where you'd like to start, where you'd like to go from there, and the ultimate position you'd like to attain. How soon after joining the company would you like to receive your first promotion? Your next one? What additional training or preparation will you need to achieve them? (261 words)

Passage B Rate Chart: Circle your rate.

:30 seconds	522 wpm
:45	348
1:00	261
1:15	209
1:30	174
1:45	149

1. Reading about occupations is not recommended; talk to people instead. T F
2. How you like to work shouldn't be considered; that's up to the employer. T F
3. Knowing the salary you want is part of determining what you want to do. T F
4. Career goals can't really be set until you find a job. T F

\# Right: _____

Passage C

I want to read to _(learn / supplement / survey)_ the information about ___________ at a _(slow / moderate / fast)_ rate. My reward(s) will be _____________________

____.

	MINUTES : SECONDS
Record your END time here:	_____ : _____
Record your START time here:	− _____ : _____
Subtract and record your TOTAL reading time here:	_____ : _____

- **What size company would you prefer?** Do you like the idea of working for a small entrepreneurial operation? Or would you prefer a large corporation?
- **What type of operation is appealing to you?** Would you prefer to work for a profit-making company or a nonprofit organization? Are you attracted to service businesses or manufacturing operations? Do you want regular, predictable hours, or do you thrive on flexible, varied hours? Would you enjoy a seasonally varied job such as education (which may give you summers off) or retailing (with its selling cycles)?
- **What location would you like?** Would you like to work in a city, a suburb, a small town, an industrial area, or an uptown setting? Do you favor a particular part of the country? A country abroad? Do you like working indoors or outdoors?
- **What facilities do you envision?** Is it important to you to work in an attractive place, or will simple, functional quarters suffice? Do you need a quiet office to work effectively, or can you concentrate in a noisy, open setting? Is access to public transportation or freeways important?
- **What sort of corporate culture are you most comfortable with?** Would you be happy in a formal hierarchy with clear reporting relationships? Or do you prefer less structure? Are you looking for a paternalistic firm or one that fosters individualism? Do you like a competitive environment? One that rewards teamwork? What qualities do you want in a boss? (241 words)

Passage C Rate Chart: Circle your rate.

:30 seconds	482 wpm
:45	321
1:00	241
1:15	193
1:30	161

1. The type of operation includes the work schedule you want to have. T F
2. The location of the business should also be considered. T F
3. Facilities include the corporate culture and who you report to. T F
4. Thinking about the kind of boss you'd like is part of the corporate culture. T F

Right: ______

REVIEW 3: SKIMMING Skim the following text and answer the questions at the end. For items 1–5, do not look back as you record your answers.

Can I Borrow Software That I Don't Own?

Most people don't understand that unlike other items they purchase, software applications they buy don't belong to them. The only thing they're actually purchasing is a license that gives them the right to use the software for their own purposes as the *only* user of that copy. The application is not theirs to lend or copy for installation on other computers, even if it's another one of their own.

Software licenses are agreements between you, the user, and the software developer that you "accept" prior to installing the software to your machine. It is a legal contract that outlines the acceptable uses of the program and any actions that violate the agreement. Generally, the agreement will state who the ultimate owner of the software is, under what circumstances copies of the software can be made, or whether the software can be installed on any other machine. Finally, the license agreements will state what, if any, warranty comes with the software.

A computer user who copies an application onto more than one computer, if the license agreement does not permit this, is participating in software piracy. Historically, the most common way software has been pirated among computer users has been when they supplement each other's software library by borrowing CDs and installing the borrowed software on their own computers. Larger-scale illegal duplication and distribution by counterfeiters is also quite common. The Internet also provides a means of illegally copying and distributing pirated software.

Is it really a big deal to copy a program or two? As reported by the Business Software Alliance, 40 percent of all software is pirated. Not only is pirating software unethical and illegal, the practice also has financial impacts on all software application consumers. The reduced dollars from pirated software lessens the amount of money available for further software research and development while increasing the up-front cost to legitimate consumers.

To tell if you have a pirated copy of software installed on your computer at work or at home, you can download a free copy of GASP (a suite of programs designed to help identify and track licensed and unlicensed software and other files) from the Business Software Alliance Web site **(www.bsa.org/usa/freetools).** There is a similar program available at Microsoft's Web site **(www.microsoft.com/piracy/).** These programs check the serial numbers for the software installed on your computer against software manufacturer databases of official licensed copies and known fraudulent copies. Any suspicious software installations are flagged for your attention.

As of yet, there's no such thing as an official "software police," but software piracy is so rampant that the U.S. government is taking steps to stop piracy worldwide. Efforts to stop groups that reproduce, modify, and distribute counterfeit software over the Internet are in full force. Software manufacturers also are becoming more aggressive in programming mechanisms into software to prevent repeated installations. For instance, with the launch of Microsoft Office 2003, installation requires the registration of the serial number of your software with a database maintained at Microsoft. Failure to register your serial number in this database or attempting to register a serial number that has been used previously results in the software failing to operate after the 50th time you use it. (Evans et al. 139) (545 words)

1. What do you really own when you buy software?

 ____

 ____

2. What is a software license?

 ____

 ____

3. What is software piracy?

 ____

 ____

4. How can you tell if you have pirated any software?

 ____

 ____

5. What steps are being taken to prevent software piracy?

 ____

 ____

6. Check your answers for accuracy and completeness by referring to the text. Was skimming useful? Did it produce good comprehension? Explain

____

____

REVIEW 4: SCANNING Do not read the following texts. Instead, for each question, circle the word(s) you think will help you locate the information. Then scan the text, find the information, read it, and record your answers.

Passage A

1. What does "North American" refer to?

____

____

2. What does the term North American continent commonly include?

____

____

3. What might be a better dividing line?

____

____

The United States and Canada are commonly referred to as "North America," but that regional terminology can sometimes be confusing. In some geography textbooks the realm is called "Anglo America" because of its close connections with Britain and its Anglo-Saxon cultural traditions. The increasingly visible cultural diversity of the realm, however, has discouraged the widespread use of the term in more recent years. While more culturally neutral, the term "North America" also has its problems. As a physical feature, the North American continent commonly includes Mexico, Central America, and, often, the Caribbean. Culturally, however, the United States–Mexico border seems a better dividing line. However, the growing Hispanic presence in the southwest United States, as well as ever-closer economic links across the border, make even that regional division problematic. (Rowntree et al. 45) (139 words)

Passage B

1. What does sub-Saharan Africa include?

____

____

2. What do many scholars suggest about this region?

____

____

3. What does the Organization of African Unity show?

___

___

4. What are the dominant language and religion of North Africa?

___

___

5. How large is Sudan?

___

___

6. Do the people in southern Sudan have a lot in common with those in the North?

___

___

Sub-Saharan Africa includes 43 mainland states plus the island nations of Madagascar, Cape Verde, São Tome and Principe, Seychelles, Mauritius, and the French territory of Réunion. When setting this particular regional boundary, the major question one faces is how to treat North Africa.

Many scholars argue for keeping the African continent intact as a culture region. The Sahara has never formed a complete barrier between the Mediterranean north and the remainder of the African landmass. Moreover, the Nile River forms a corridor several thousand miles long of continuous settlement linking North Africa directly to the center of the continent. There is no obvious place to divide the watershed between northern and sub-Saharan Africa. Political units, such as the Organization of African Unity, are modern examples of the continent's unity.

The lack of a clear divide across Africa does not mean it cannot be divided into two world regions. North Africa is generally considered more closely linked, both culturally and physically, to Southwest Asia. Arabic is the dominant language and Islam the dominant religion of North Africa. Consequently, North Africans feel more closely connected to the Arab hearth in Southwest Asia than to the sub-Saharan world.

Sudan is Africa's largest state in terms of area; it is one-fourth the size of the United States. In the more populous and powerful north, Muslim leaders have crafted an Islamic state that is culturally and politically oriented toward North Africa and Southwest Asia. Southern Sudan, however, has more in common with the animist and Christian groups of the sub-Saharan region. Moreover, peoples in the south continue to fight for their independence from central authority in the northern capital of Khartoum. (Rowntree et al. 134) (276 words)

Check Your Motivation

1. Review your chapter goals. Did you achieve them? Explain.
2. Make a list of the new ideas and methods that you've gained from this chapter. Think about how they will help you in the future.
3. Measure your motivation for this chapter topic. Think about each statement and how you will use it in the future. Mark it:

   A = never B = sometimes C = usually D = always

	A	B	C	D
To engage my interest, I plan to . . .				
1. think about my purpose before I start reading.	___	___	___	___
2. identify the level of text difficulty before I start reading.	___	___	___	___
3. choose an appropriate speed range before I start reading.	___	___	___	___
4. develop an interest in a topic before I start reading.	___	___	___	___
5. preread the text.	___	___	___	___
6. set reading goals.	___	___	___	___
To focus my efforts, I plan to . . .				
7. use a body position that promotes efficient reading.	___	___	___	___
8. prop or hold the text at a 45 degree angle.	___	___	___	___
9. use good lighting.	___	___	___	___
10. use top line reading.	___	___	___	___
11. practice eye swings to reduce regressions.	___	___	___	___
12. use pacing techniques.	___	___	___	___
13. read in meaningful phrases.	___	___	___	___
To monitor my progress, I plan to . . .				
14. change my reading speed as needed during reading.	___	___	___	___
To reflect on my gains, I plan to . . .				
15. praise myself for using efficient rates.	___	___	___	___

SCORING: Write the number of answers you marked in each column in the following spaces. Compute the column scores, and then add them up to determine your total score.

# of A's _____ × 1 pt. = _____
# of B's _____ × 2 pt. = _____
# of C's _____ × 3 pt. = _____
# of D's _____ × 4 pt. = _____

Total points = _____

INTERPRETATION: 15–43 points = low motivation; 44–60 points = high motivation

SUGGESTION

1. Compare your current Chapter score to the one from The Motivation Measure. If they're both low, review the list above and find approaches you'd be willing try. If you've improved or have a high score, reward yourself for your empowered approaches.
2. Record the methods you wish to use on a card and use it as a bookmark. Look it over before you begin reading the next assignment.

Answer Key for Self-Scoring Comprehension Questions

Think about this . . .

Text A:	1. T	2. F	3. F	4. F	5. T
Text B:	1. T	2. F	3. T	4. T	5. T
Text C:	1. F	2. T	3. F	4. T	5. T

Activity 8	1. T	2. F	3. F	4. T	5. F

Activity 10	1. F	2. T	3. F	4. T	5. T

Review 2

Passage A:	1. T	2. F	3. F	4. T
Passage B:	1. F	2. F	3. T	4. F
Passage C:	1. T	2. T	3. F	4. T

Vocabulary Expansion

What part does vocabulary play in mental activities like reading, writing, listening, and speaking? What part does vocabulary play in college success?

Vocabulary is the medium of the mind. Through words, you convey what you know, want, and feel. Your vocabulary also determines what you understand as you read and listen, and it determines how easily you learn. The quote below from Ludwig Wittgenstein emphasizes the importance of vocabulary.

> The limits of my language are the limits of my mind. All I know is what I have words for.
>
> — Ludwig Wittgenstein (1889–1951), Austrian philosopher

Anyone can push beyond their current limits by expanding their knowledge of words.

Before you read . . .

Engage Your Interest: preread and divide

This chapter presents methods for building a powerful and useful vocabulary. Use this space to create a map of the chapter headings like the ones presented in Chapters 1 and 2.

After you preread and divide the chapter into reading tasks, set a goal for each one. Be specific about the task, topic, and reward(s).

1. I want to ________________ about ______________________________.
   My reward(s) will be ______________________________________
   ____.

2. I want to ________________ about ______________________________.
   My reward(s) will be ______________________________________
   ____.

3. I want to ________________ about ______________________________.
   My reward(s) will be ______________________________________
   ____.

As you read . . .

Focus Your Efforts: question and read

Vocabulary learning is not new to you. You have undoubtedly studied for vocabulary tests, and outside school, you have acquired new words from other people, including family and friends. But exactly what do we mean by "vocabulary"? It's a broad term, and many people describe it according to size. But an effective vocabulary is one that includes the skills of comprehension and learning as well. Each of these aspects affects your college reading and learning. The sheer number of words you know and how well you know them determines your initial ability to understand course materials, presentations, and resources. The skills you use when you encounter new words affects your ability to comprehend new information and avoid reading problems. Finally, the methods you use to learn new words influence future comprehension tasks, as well as how easily you learn course information.

If your vocabulary is not helping you comprehend and learn, you will want to expand it. But even if you currently have a good vocabulary, you will need to add to it with every course you take, because college courses place a heavy emphasis on learning the terms of the field. This chapter focuses on three aspects of vocabulary that will directly affect your studies:

- Develop Your Vocabulary
- Understand New Terms
- Learn New Terms

Developing Your Vocabulary

THINK ABOUT THIS . . .

Think about how extensive your vocabulary is by answering these questions.

1. Do you use all the words you know? Explain.

____

____

2. What do you think you could do to expand your vocabulary?

____

____

Vocabulary varies with experience. When you participate in an activity, read about it, or study it, you learn new words. But often, your word knowledge is only partial: you might understand a word, but struggle to define it precisely, for example. So, as you develop your vocabulary, you perfect your knowledge about words as well as your way of learning them.

Levels of Knowledge

Words can be divided into two useful categories: general vocabulary and technical terms. **General vocabulary** terms are words that are used in similar ways by almost all writers and that are not tied to any field by specialized meanings. These words can be common or unusual, such as *home* or *hearth* and *accidental* or *serendipitous.* **Technical terms,** on the other hand, are the words experts in the field use to discuss information in their discipline. *Homeostasis* in biology, *metaphor* in English, and *Electoral College* in political science are good examples of technical words.

Expanding your vocabulary means gaining words in each category. Your general vocabulary is the foundation of your thinking abilities, and it is absolutely fundamental to your reading ability. Simply put, the more words you know, the easier it is to read. In addition, the more you understand about how these words are used and any multiple meanings they have, the more useful they are. In contrast, your knowledge of technical terms is generally related to the courses and technical areas that you study. These terms tend to have one specific meaning that may be complex, but does not change.

Knowing a word is not just a simple "I know it" or "don't know it" situation. There are four levels of word knowledge: unknown, recognized, understood, and well known. *Unknown* words are the ones you've never heard or seen before. *Recognized* words are the ones you've heard or read, but don't comprehend without help from the speaker, writer, or other resources. *Understood* terms are the ones you comprehend and may even use, but your definition—and your knowledge—is memorized, imprecise, or incomplete. The last category, *well known* words, includes the terms you understand, can readily define, and are able to accurately explain.

Note that these four levels work like stairs: As you learn more about a word, you move it up to the next step, which is higher in terms of the amount of knowledge you have. Table 4.1 shows the differences between these levels.

TABLE 4.1 **Vocabulary Levels of Knowledge**

	UNKNOWN	RECOGNIZED	UNDERSTOOD	WELL KNOWN
Have heard or read	No	Yes	Yes	Yes
Can understand with help	No	Yes	Yes	Yes
Can define	No	No	Yes, but not well	Yes
Can explain	No	No	No	Yes

It might seem ideal to move all the words in your vocabulary to the well known level, but that's unrealistic. For good reading comprehension, most general terms need to be at the understood level, although you can certainly handle terms in the recognized group if the author provides explanations. For technical terms, the understood level is the minimum for reading comprehension, but you will need the well known level to correctly answer multiple choice questions and to use the terms as you speak or write about them.

ACTIVITY 1: IDENTIFY YOUR LEVELS OF KNOWLEDGE

DIRECTIONS: Practice identifying your level of knowledge for words. Check off the highest level you have for each of the following words. Then answer the questions that follow.

	UNKNOWN	RECOGNIZED	UNDERSTOOD	WELL KNOWN
a. worldwide				
b. dominance				
c. critical				
d. area				
e. inert				
f. terrorism				
g. preprocessed				
h. prosopagnosia				

Choose one term from the recognized column and one from the understood group. Then answer the following questions.

1. Recognized term: ____________________

   What would you need to do to move it into your well known level?

   ____

   ____

2. Understood term: ____________________

   What would you need to do to move it into your well known level?

   ____

   ____

Active Learning

Some students think that developing their vocabulary is a boring school task that requires a great deal of effort and achieves small gains. These students have had the experience of memorizing vocabulary terms and definitions, only to find that they soon forget what they learned. No wonder they think of vocabulary development as boring and useless. The memorization approach is guaranteed to be time-consuming and unsatisfying.

A much better alternative exists, and you already know it. It's the natural process you've employed from early childhood. Think about small children that you know or how you learned language. Children all over the world watch, listen, pronounce words, guess meanings, and use new terms eagerly and without worrying about being right. That process probably changed for you when you started memorizing words and worrying about quizzes.

You can recapture your early enthusiasm and methods for learning words by simply following these steps:

1. Be interested in new words.
2. Say the word.
3. Think about the meaning.
4. Apply a memory aid.
5. Use the term.

> **Language is not an abstract construction of the learned, or of dictionary makers, but is something arising out of the work, needs, ties, joys, affections, tastes, of long generations of humanity, and has its bases broad and low, close to the ground.**
>
> —Noah Webster (1859–1843), American lexicographer

Notice that step 4—apply a memory aid—has been added to the natural process. Children use repetition and the feedback of others to remember words. As a college student, it's much more efficient to choose a memory strategy and use it deliberately.

This natural five-step process works for general as well as technical terms, and it promotes all four levels of knowledge. One reason it works so well is that it employs the four stages of motivation.

Engage

Step 1: Be interested in new words.

Vocabulary expansion begins with desire. Whether you're working to expand your overall vocabulary or learning just one word, recapture that eagerness for words that you had as a child. Why are children so eager? Because intuitively they know what the cartoon suggests: the primary function of vocabulary is to communicate with others. New words give you new ways to share your thoughts.

"ALTHOUGH HUMANS MAKE SOUNDS WITH THEIR MOUTHS AND OCCASIONALLY LOOK AT EACH OTHER, THERE IS NO SOLID EVIDENCE THAT THEY ACTUALLY COMMUNICATE WITH EACH OTHER."

In addition, your vocabulary affects how well you learn, read, and write. And it will serve you equally well in the job market: high-paying jobs generally require the good communication and intellectual skills that a larger vocabulary brings. A moment's thought about these benefits will initiate the motivation needed to focus and learn.

> **Language is not only the vehicle of thought; it is a great and efficient instrument in thinking.**
> —Humphry Davy (1778–1829), British chemist

Focus

Step 2: Say the word.

Step 3: Think about the meaning.

As you focus your efforts on a new term, make sure you can pronounce it. When you say a new word out loud, you are initiating the auditory and verbal memory parts of your brain. If you can't automatically pronounce a word, break it into syllables and make your best guess, use the phonetic markings in the dictionary, or use an online dictionary with an audio feature (such as Merriam Webster Online at *http://www.m-w.com*).

> **Words are the most powerful drug used by mankind.**
> —Rudyard Kipling (1865–1936), British author and poet

Then give a little thought to the meaning. Begin by guessing what the meaning is and then gaining more knowledge by looking at the word parts, context, or other sources (see the next section of this chapter).

Monitor and Reflect

Step 4: Apply a memory aid.

Step 5: Use the term.

As you work with new words, monitor your progress by testing yourself to see how well you recall the definition and whether or not you can explain it. Then, reflect by applying memory aids as needed to ensure long-term recall (see the last section in this chapter.)

> **Understanding is nothing else than conception caused by speech.**
> —Thomas Hobbes (1588–1679), British philosopher

Finally, use the term. This is where you get the benefits of your efforts. Mention and talk about it with others; use it in your thinking; include it in your assignments. Then, reward and praise yourself for even the smallest efforts and gains in order to promote continued motivation for future vocabulary activities.

ACTIVITY 2: MOTIVATE YOURSELF FOR VOCABULARY LEARNING

DIRECTIONS: Think about your motivation for expanding your vocabulary by answering the following questions.

1. *Engage*
   a. What would be the general or long-term benefits of improving your vocabulary?

      ____

      ____

   b. Think of a specific class you're taking. What would be the benefits of improving your course vocabulary?

      The class: ______________

      ____

      ____

2. *Focus*

   How do you generally learn words? Do you say them, think about the meaning, and/or apply a learning strategy?

   ____

   ____

   ____

   ____

3. *Monitor and reflect*

   Do you test your knowledge of the words you learn? Do you use new terms? Do you reward and praise your efforts?

   ____

   ____

   ____

   ____

A word after a word after a word is power.

—Margaret Atwood (1939–   ), Canadian novelist, poet, and critic

Before you go on . . .

Monitor Your Progress: recite

As you read . . .

Focus Your Efforts: question and read

Understand New Terms

THINK ABOUT THIS . . .

1. Define these terms based on what you know.

   Displacement: ______________________________

   Reminisce: ______________________________

   Abstract: ______________________________

2. These terms were used in the following sentences:

   A property of language is displacement. *Displacement* refers to the fact that language can be used to communicate about things that are not in our immediate surroundings, matters that extend beyond the limits of the here-and-now. Thus, we *reminisce* about the good old days, we talk about our hopes and dreams for the future, we gossip about others behind their backs, and we discuss *abstract* ideas concerning God, politics, social justice, and love. (Adapted from Kassin 282)

After reading this passage, what would you add to your definitions?

Displacement: ______________________________

Reminisce: ______________________________

Abstract: ______________________________

The more information you have about a word, the easier it is to make sense of it. The primary ways to gain information about new terms are to use word parts, context clues, or a dictionary.

Use Word Parts

English words are formed from structural **word parts** called prefixes, roots, and suffixes. Every word must have at least a **root,** or base element. Other parts can be added in front of the root, called **prefixes,** or behind it, called **suffixes.** In general, prefixes change the meaning of the root, while suffixes show the part of speech and very general categories of meaning. Look at this example.

EXAMPLE

root	*prefix + root*	*root + suffix*	*prefix + root + suffix*
judge	prejudge	judgment	prejudgment

The verb *judge* means "to make an opinion." With the prefix *pre* meaning "before," a new verb is formed, which means "to form an opinion before hand." With the suffix *ment* added, meaning "act of," a noun has been formed, which means "the act of judging or forming an opinion." With both those parts added, we get *prejudgment,* another noun, which means "the act of forming an opinion before hand."

In addition to adding to your understanding of terms, learning word parts is the single most efficient way to expand the overall size of your vocabulary. For example, since the prefix *pre* is used in over 700 words listed in the dictionary, knowing that it means *before* gives you a piece of the definition for all those words. So each word part you learn leads to at least a partial understanding of many words. In fact, one vocabulary expert claims that learning the meaning of just 34 words parts, including the 20 most common prefixes and 14 most common roots, will give you insight into 100,000 words (Brown, 1971)! This is certainly a faster way to learn vocabulary than memorizing terms one at a time. Those prefixes and roots are listed Table 4.2 and used in Activity 3.

TABLE 4.2 **The 34 Most Common Word Parts**

PREFIX	MEANING	EXAMPLE
Prefix that refer to a number		
mono	one, alone	monogram
Prefixes with a negative meaning		
dis	not, opposite	disbelieve
ex (e, ec, ef)	out	eject
in (im, il, ir)	not	insensitive
mis	wrong	misbelieve
non	not	nonsense
ob (of, oc)	against	obscene
un	not	unaccepted
Prefixes dealing with position		
ad (ab, ac)	away from, to, toward	admit
com (con, col)	together, with	communication
de	away	depart
epi	upon	epidermis
in	into	import
inter	between	interstate
over	above	overdraw
pro	forward	projection
sub	under	submarine
trans	across, beyond	transportation

PREFIX	MEANING	EXAMPLE
Prefixes dealing with time		
pre	before	preview
re	again, back	review

ROOT	MEANING	EXAMPLE
Roots about communication		
graph (gram)	write	graphics
log (logue, logo)	word, speech, science, study of	dialogue
scrib (script)	write	scribble
Roots about actions		
cap (cep)	take, seize	capable
duc	lead	educate
fac	make	factory
fer	bear, carry	transfer
mitt (miss)	send	mission
plic (pli, ply)	fold	pliable
pon (pos)	place, set	position
spec	watch, see	spectator
sta	stand	station
ten (tain)	hold, have	tenant
tend (tens, tent)	stretch	tension

Adapted from Brown, James I. (1971). *Programmed vocabulary* (2nd ed.). Englewood Cliffs, NJ: Prentice Hall.

Notice that some word parts have alternate spellings, which are listed in parentheses. These variations are used to make them easier to pronounce when they are used before certain letters. A good example is the prefix *ad* which is used in *admit* and changed when it is used in *accept.*

ACTIVITY 3: USE THE MOST COMMON WORD PARTS

DIRECTIONS: Listed below are some of the most common word parts along with a sample word. Use Table 4.2 and define each word part. Then use that meaning as you define the sample term. Last, come up with another word for that part. The first one is done for you.

Part A: Common Prefixes

	PART	PART DEFINITION	SAMPLE WORD	WORD DEFINITION	YOUR SAMPLE WORD
1.	mono	one	monologue	speech by one person	monochrome
2.	dis	not/opposite	disbelieve	not believe	discharge
3.	ex	out	eject	throw out	exhale
4.	mis	wrong	misbelieve	wrong believe	misunderstand
5.	ob	against	obscene	against what is decent	obstacle
6.	ad	away from	admit	to enter	admition
7.	com	with	communication	converse together	community
8.	de	away	depart	go away	defrost
9.	pro	forward	projection	look in to the future	protest
10.	trans	across	transportation	away to move across distance	transition

Part B: Common Roots

	PART	PART DEFINITION	SAMPLE WORD	WORD DEFINITION	YOUR SAMPLE WORD
1.	spec	watch/see	spectator	who sees	spectator
2.	graph	write	graphic		photograph
3.	log	word/speach	dialogue	Communication	monologue →?
4.	scrib	write	scribble		discribe
5.	cap	take	capable	able to take	capture
6.	duc	lead	educate		conduct
7.	fac	make	factory		manufactor
8.	fer	bear/carry	transfer		chofer
9.	mitt	send	mission		transmit ?
10.	plic	fold	pliable		apply

Other common, useful word parts are listed in Tables 4.3–4.5.

TABLE 4.3 **Other Common Prefixes**

PREFIX	MEANING	EXAMPLE	PREFIX	MEANING	EXAMPLE
Prefixes that refer to numbers			**Prefixes with a negative meaning**		
bi	two	bicycle	a (an)	not, without	asexual
cent	1 hundred	century	anti	against, opposite	antiwar
dec	ten	decimal			
di (du)	two	diameter	**Prefixes dealing with position**		
equ	equal	equality	circ	around	circle
hemi	half	hemisphere	dis	apart	disjointed
kilo	1 thousand	kilometer	hyper	over	hypertension
magni	great	magnify	hypo	under	hypodermic
milli	1/1000	millimeter	intra	within	intrastate
pan	all	panacea	med (mid)	middle	median
poly	many	polygon	peri	around	perimeter
quadr	four	quadrangle	super	above	supernatural
semi	half	semicircle	syn (sym)	together	sympathy
sol	one, alone	solitary			
uni	one	universe			

TABLE 4.4 **Other Common Roots**

ROOT	MEANING	EXAMPLE	ROOT	MEANING	EXAMPLE
Roots about the body			**Roots about science**		
aud	hear	auditory	anthro	man	anthropology
corp	body	corpse	aqua	water	aquatic
derm	skim	dermatitis	auto	self	autobiography
hema, hemo	blood	hemoglobin	astro, aster	star	astronomy
ped, pad	foot	anthropod	bio	living	biology
psych	mind, spirit	psychic	geo	earth	geography
scope	see	microscope	hetero	different	heterosexual
son	sound	sonata	homo	same	homosexual
			hydra	water	hydrate
Roots about communication			macro	large	macrosystem
dict	speak, tell	diction	meter	measure	thermometer
leg, lect	read	legible	micro	small	microscope
			mot (mov)	move	motion
Roots about time			path	feeling	sympathy
ann, enn	year	annual	photo	light	photograph
neo	new	neolithic	socius (soc)	companion	society
chrono	time	chronological			
temp	time	temporary			

TABLE 4.5 **Common Suffixes**

SUFFIX	MEANING	EXAMPLE	SUFFIX	MEANING	EXAMPLE
Noun suffixes			**Adjective suffixes**		
ician, ist, or	one who is a doer	physician	able, ive, ible, ate	have the quality of	capable
ism	belief	patriotism	full, ous	full of	stressful
it, ty, hood, ance, ence	quality, state of	personality	less	without	hopeless
tion, ation, ion	act of	discussion			
Verb suffixes			**Adverb suffixes**		
ate	to make, do	negotiate	ly	like, in the manner of	hourly
fy	to make or become	magnify	ward	in the direction of	forward
ize	to engage in	sterilize			

While word parts don't give a complete definition, they help you quickly guess what a new word means. And, as you will see in Activity 4, they can help you figure out technical terms as well.

ACTIVITY 4: USE WORD PARTS WITH TECHNICAL TERMS

DIRECTIONS: Listed below are terms used in a variety of college textbooks. Complete the following tasks on each word:

A. Circle each word part that's listed in the tables above.

B. Define the word; include the word part meaning in your definition.

1. retirement the state of cutting back on work
2. anti-social ______
3. binomial ______
4. biotechnology ______
5. capitalism ______
6. detain ______
7. elongation ______
8. imperceptible ______
9. inanimate ______
10. interaction ______

Syllables govern the world.

—George Bernard Shaw (1856–1950), Irish-born British dramatist

Use Context Clues

Using context clues is a primary skill for understanding words as you read. **Context clues** are the words and information that surround a term and provide hints about its meaning. Look at this example about what happened to several American Indian tribes of the Ohio and Mississippi river valleys. As you read the text, try to figure out what a "population sink" is before you read the explanation under *Using the hints.*

EXAMPLE

Although these tribes were aggressive, their collapse does not seem to have been caused by warfare. Instead, pre-industrial cities were probably "population sinks" in which densely packed populations without effective sanitation systems served as breeding grounds for lethal diseases. (Boydston et al., 14)

Using the hints: From your background knowledge and the text, you could figure out that the cities were like kitchen sinks—a small basin or area of land surrounded by higher "sides" or hills. From the reference to sanitation and diseases, you could conclude that they didn't have a good system for draining away waste. So these cities trapped unhealthy germs and caused serious diseases that killed many people.

Notice that using context clues relies on more than just what is in the text. You also use background information, word knowledge, and logical thinking. To put all these pieces together, you **infer,** or figure out, a logical meaning that is not directly stated. Inferring from context clues does not create a precise definition; instead, it produces a general understanding. But often, that is all you need to comprehend the text.

You can perfect your use of context clues by becoming aware of four common types: definition, explanation, comparison, and contrast, along with the signals authors use to alert you to these clues.

Definition Clues When introducing a new term, authors provide either a direct definition or synonym. A **direct definition** is a statement of the exact meaning. This is the method textbook authors use most frequently for technical terms. To signal the clue, authors usually present the term in bold-faced or italics, along with the definition. Occasionally, they also use words such as *means* or *is* to connect the term to its definition. Here is an example.

EXAMPLE

A primary ingredient of human cognition is **language,** the ability to combine elements that are themselves meaningless into an infinite number of utterances that convey meaning. (Wade and Tavris 241)

Authors can also define a word with a synonym. A **synonym** is a good substitute word or phrase for the term. It is not an exact definition. To signal the use of synonyms, authors often use the term *or* to connect the word to its substitute, as well as punctuation marks such as commas and parentheses. Look at this example.

EXAMPLE

Mohammad fled Mecca in July 622 for Yathrib. Some dozen years later, this "emigration," or *Hegira,* became the starting point for the Islamic calendar, the event marking the creation of a distinctive Islamic community, or *Umma.* (Adapted from Craig et al., 225)

You do not need to make an inference with a direct definition or synonym clue. You need only recognize that a definition is being presented and then determine how much of the sentence is the definition. Synonym definitions are generally just a word or a short phrase. But in a direct definition, the meaning is usually all of the words that follow the term up to the period. You won't understand the full definition if you just pay attention to a short phrase in a direct definition clue. So, in the example above, the technical definition for language is not just "the ability to combine elements." According to the definition, it's combining elements "that are themselves meaningless" and making them "into an infinite number of utterances that convey meaning."

A single word often betrays a great design.
—Jean Baptiste Racine (1639–1699), French dramatist

ACTIVITY 5: USE DEFINITION CLUES

DIRECTIONS: For each of the following texts, use definition clues to identify the meaning of the italicized words. For items 1 and 2, circle the correct answer; for items 3 and 4, record the definition given in the clues.

1. *Cellulose* is a rigid, complex carbohydrate contained in the cell walls of many organisms. (Krogh 48)

   Cellulose is

   a. A rigid, complex carbohydrate.
   b. Contained in the cell walls of many organisms.
   c. A carbohydrate contained in the cell walls of many organisms.
   d. A rigid, complex carbohydrate contained in the cell walls of many organisms.

2. *Ethology* is the study of animal behavior, especially in natural environments. (Wade and Tavris 240)

   Ethology is

   a. The study of animal behavior, especially in natural environments.
   b. Animal behavior.
   c. In natural environments.
   d. The study of animal behavior.

3. The tendency among Muslims was to define Islam in terms of what Muslims do—namely by *orthopraxy* (practice) rather than by *orthodoxy* (beliefs). (Craig et al. 261)
   Orthopraxy is ____.
   Orthodoxy is ____.

4. *Goals* are well defined stepping-stones that help you progress from where you are now to where you eventually want to be. (Makely 90)
   Goals are ____
   ____.

Explanation Clues When authors want to ensure that readers have a general understanding rather than a precise definition, they use **explanation clues.** These clues clarify the term by providing details and/or examples. Look at this example and how the details help you understand the term *water frame.*

EXAMPLE

The invention that took cotton textile manufacture from the home to the factory was Richard Arkwright's (1732–1792) *water frame,* patented in 1769. It was a water-powered device to produce a purely cotton fabric rather than one containing linen for durability. (Craig et al., 470)

Using the hints: Here, the term *water frame* is not defined, but the details help you understand that it was a machine, powered by water, which produced cotton fabric.

Examples provide real-world instances or samples that illustrate the new term. You will have to infer a common element among the samples to understand the term. Examples may be introduced with signal words like *such as, for example, for instance, include(s),* and *that is.* Look at the following sentence and explanation.

EXAMPLE

In the Islamic penal code, *qisas* crimes include murder, manslaughter, battery, and mutilation. (Adapted from Lindsey and Beach 181)

Using the hints: Here, considerable inferencing is required. You need to think about the common elements in the four types of crime named. Once you realize that all of them are violent crimes against people, you understand exactly what *qisas* are.

ACTIVITY 6: USE EXPLANATION CLUES

DIRECTIONS: For each of the following texts, use explanation clues to infer the meaning of the italicized words. For items 1 and 2, circle the correct answer; for items 3 and 4, record the definition suggested by the clues.

1. Broad concern for public health first *manifested* itself as a result of the great cholera epidemics of the 1830s and 1840s. (Craig et al., 571)

   Manifested means

   a. Showed concern.
   b. Was attacked.
   c. Was plainly shown.
   d. Was discussed.

2. *Infectious waste* includes laboratory cultures, blood and blood products from blood banks, operating rooms, and patient rooms, as well as used needles and syringes. It must be placed in specially designed waste containers to prevent the spread of dangerous micro-organisms such as the hepatitis A and B viruses. (Adapted from Fremgen 157)

   Infectious waste is

   a. Byproducts from laboratory cultures.
   b. Byproducts from laboratory cultures, blood and blood products, and needles.
   c. Blood products that could create infection.
   d. Products and tools that could create infections or diseases.

3. One grandparenting style is the *surrogate* parent, where grandmothers usually care for grandchildren and exert a great deal of control. (Adapted from Lindsey and Beach 116)

   A *surrogate* parent is ______________________________.

4. Dating fulfills a number of *manifest* functions. It signals maturation; provides fun, recreation, and companionship; and provides a socially accepted way of pursuing love and affection. (Adapted from Benokraitis 205)

   A *manifest* function is ______________________________.

Comparison Clues **Comparison clues** link a term to another word or situation that is familiar to most people. This is called an analogy. For example, you could describe the idea of using *efficient reading rates* by comparing it to driving a stick-shift car, because they both require deliberate actions to move from slow to fast speeds. To use comparison clues, you will need to infer how the terms are logically similar. These clues are usually signaled with the words *like* or *as*. Here is an example of a comparison clue.

EXAMPLE

In the computer we call the human mind, *short-term memory* (STM) is a mental workspace, like the screen. On a computer, material displayed on the monitor may be entered on a keyboard or retrieved from previously saved files. Similarly, STM contains both new sensory input and material that is pulled from long-term storage. (adapted from Kassin 218)

Using the hints: Using what you know about computers, you can infer that STM is a present-time part of the mind where you can work on information that you get from current experience or from memory.

ACTIVITY 7: USE COMPARISON CLUES

DIRECTIONS: For each of the following texts, use comparison clues to infer the meaning of the italicized words. For items 1 and 2, circle the correct answer; for items 3 and 4, record the definition suggested by the clues.

1. Another important development in language occurs when children begin to form two- and three-word phrases. These early word combinations illustrate what is called *telegraphic speech* because—as in telegrams, kept short for cost reasons—they include only nouns, verbs, and essential modifiers. (Adapted from Kassin 39)

   Telegraphic speech is

   a. Two- or three-word phrases.
   b. The language used by children.
   c. The kind of sentences used in telegrams.
   d. Short phrases made up of only essential words.

2. Does language have the power to shape the way people think? As a result of many years of research, nobody believes that language *determines* thought the way genes determine a person's height. But most psychologists do agree with a less radical claim: that language *influences* thinking. (Kassin 288)

   Determines means

   a. Shapes.
   b. Interferes with.
   c. Limits.
   d. Encourages.

   Influences means

   a. Controls.
   b. Affects.
   c. Creates.
   d. Limits.

3. Like maps, *economic models* are abstractions that strip away detail to expose only those aspects of behavior that are important to the question being asked. (Case 9)
   Economic models are ____
   ____.

4. Hackers often use *Trojan horses* to install other programs on computers. The term Trojan horse derives from Greek mythology and refers to a siege of Troy by the Greeks. Unable to break through the Trojan defenses, the Greeks left behind a large wooden horse, which the Trojans thought was a gift from the gods and brought into the city. Later that night, a group of Greek soldiers who were hiding in the belly of the horse, snuck out, and opened the city gates so that the Greek army could march in and destroy Troy. (Adapted from Evans et al. 272)
   A *Trojan horse* is ____
   ____.

Contrast Clues **Contrast clues** provide information and details. However, these clues point to what the term *does not* mean. To use contrast clues, then, you must understand the information that is given and then infer its opposite. The most common signals are *although, in contrast, on the other hand, except, but, the opposite,* and *however.* Here is an example.

EXAMPLE

Although born helpless, human infants are equipped at birth with *reflexes* that orient them toward people. They are responsive to faces, turn their head toward voices, and are prepared to mimic certain facial gestures on cue. (Kassin 315)

Using the hints: The text suggests that reflexes contrast with helplessness; that is, they help infants. The examples illustrate natural actions that occur without thought. So reflexes are helpful, natural or inborn reactions.

This example also illustrates an important point about context clues: authors can and do combine various kinds. So, it's not uncommon to get explanation, comparison, and contrast clues in the same paragraph. When presented with multiple clues, use all the available information.

Language is to the mind more than light is to the eye.
—William Gibson (1948–),
American author and playwright

ACTIVITY 8: USE CONTRAST CLUES

DIRECTIONS: For each of the following texts, use contrast clues to infer the meaning of the italicized words. For items 1 and 2, circle the correct answer; for items 3 and 4, record the definition suggested by the clues.

1. Adolescents say they can be themselves only when with their friends; they do not have to show *deference* to adults and can use the peer group to mock adult authority. (Lindsey and Beach 112)

   Deference is

   a. Mocking adult authority.
   b. Not mocking adult authority.
   c. Showing respect and esteem.
   d. Saying what's expected of them.

2. Behavioral psychologists believe that motivation can be changed by using rewards and punishments. But *cognitive* psychologists focus more on what people think about these reinforcements. (Adapted from Kassin 320)

   Cognitive refers to

   a. What people believe.
   b. Reinforcements.
   c. The mind and what people think.
   d. Counseling.

3. *Positive economics* attempts to understand behavior and economic systems without making judgments. (Adapted from Case 7)

   Positive economics is ______________________________

   ______________________________.

4. Immigration, the movement of individuals into an area, can cause a population to grow. *Emigration* is just the opposite. (Adapted from Miller 120)

   Emigration is ______________________________

   ______________________________.

One final note: As you work with context clues, it's less important to identify the type of clue than it is to use the hints effectively and understand new words within the texts you're reading.

Use Parts and Clues Together

As stated at the beginning of this part of the chapter, the more you know about a word, the easier it is to determine its meaning. So, whenever possible, good readers use both their word-part knowledge and context clues to gain the best comprehension of new or unfamiliar terms. Look at this example.

EXAMPLE

When sociologists examine social interaction from a *microlevel perspective,* they concentrate on the details of interaction that usually occur between two people or in other small groups. (Lindsey and Beach 118)

Using the word parts and the hints: Since *micro* means small and the context clues refer to two people or a small group, you could infer that the *microlevel perspective* is one where the sociologist focuses on a few people at a time.

ACTIVITY 9: USE WORD PARTS AND CONTEXT CLUES TOGETHER

DIRECTIONS: Use your knowledge of word parts and context clues to infer the meanings of the italicized words as they are used in the following texts. Record your definitions in the space provided.

1. During the early nineteenth century virtually all European women faced social and legal *disabilities* in property rights, family law, and education. Women remained, generally speaking, economically *dependent* and legally inferior, whatever their social class. Their position thus resembled that of women around the world in that all women found their lives *circumscribed* by traditional social customs and *expectations.* (Craig et al. 575) (58 words)
   a. Disabilities means ______________________________.
   b. Dependent means ______________________________.
   c. Circumscribed means ______________________________.
   d. Expectations means ______________________________.

2. Age-segregated housing offers both *psychosocial* benefits and costs. It can be attractive to those of the same birth *cohort* who share similar interests and lifestyles. Residences designed specifically for the elderly are usually safer, *accessible* to public transportation, and offer a range of services and recreational activities. After the move, residents report higher levels of social participation, an improved sense of well-being, and satisfaction with housing. On the down side, the elderly may be more subject to isolation because they are separated from the larger society, caught in a narrow corridor where they interact only with other age peers. When younger people are deprived of contact with elders, *ageism* and negative stereotypes are heightened between both groups. (Lindsey and Beach 115) (117 words)
   a. Psychosocial means ______________________________.
   b. Cohort means ______________________________.
   c. Accessible means ______________________________.
   d. Ageism means ______________________________.

Use Dictionaries

Dictionaries are reference tools. They are a good aid when word parts and context clues don't help you out enough, when precise definitions are needed, or when you're trying to figure out the differences between closely related terms. Dictionaries are generally the last resource to use during reading, because looking up a word interrupts the flow of the author's message. So, if you need to consult a dictionary, try to read to the end of a paragraph or section before you do so.

There are two categories of dictionaries: general English dictionaries and technical dictionaries. It's important to know the differences and to select the right one for your needs.

General English Dictionaries General English dictionaries provide information about terms that are not specific to any one field. But as you probably know, dictionaries vary greatly in size. Unabridged, or complete, dictionaries present extensive information about each word. Look at Figure 4.1 and notice all the information listed for the word *prepare*. An abridged, or shortened, dictionary, which may come in hardcover or paperback, provides fewer terms, definitions, and information.

As the figure shows, an unabridged dictionary is a wealth of information about words. They provide nine basic types of information which are listed below, along with line number references to the figure.

1. *Phonetic markings* provide directions for correct pronunciation. (line 1)
2. The *part of speech* indicates how the word is used in a sentence and whether it's a noun, verb, or adjective, for example. (line 1)
3. *Alternate forms* list grammatical and spelling variations for that part of speech. (lines 1–2)
4. *Etymology* indicates the history of the word and is a good way to learn more about word parts. (lines 2–4)
5. *Definitions* list the meaning(s) of the entry word. (lines 5–19)
6. *Examples* use the word in a phrase or sentence, making it easier to understand the definition. (lines 9, 11, 15, 23, 29, 38)
7. *Restricted definitions* present a meaning that is used only in a particular professional field. (line 18)

prē·pâre′, *v.t.*; prepared, *pt.*, *pp.*; preparing, *ppr.* [Fr. *préparer*; L. *præparare*, *præparatus*; *præ*, before, and *parare*, to set or place in order, to get ready.]

1. to make ready, usually for a specific purpose; to make suitable; to fit; to adapt; to train.

2. to make receptive; to dispose; to accustom; as, he *prepared* them for the bad news.

3. to equip or furnish with necessary provisions, accessories, etc.; to fit out; as, they *prepared* an expedition.

4. to put together or make out of materials, ingredients, parts, etc., or according to a plan or formula; to construct; to compound; as, they *prepared* dinner, he *prepared* the medicine.

5. in music, to use (a dissonant tone) in preparation (sense 5).

Syn.—fit, adjust, adapt, qualify, equip, provide, procure, form, make.

prē·pâre′, *v.i.* 1. to make all things ready; to put things in suitable order; as, *prepare* for dinner.

2. to make oneself ready; to hold oneself in readiness.

prē·pâre′, *n.* preparation. [Rare.]

prē·pâred′, *a.* fitted; made ready; provided; holding oneself in readiness.

As to being *prepared* for defeat, I certainly am not. —Farragut.

prē·pâr′ed·ly, *adv.* **1.** in a manner showing preparation.

2. in such a way as to be prepared.

prē·pâr′ed·ness, *n.* the state of being prepared; specifically, possession of sufficient armed forces, matériel, etc. for waging war.

prē·pâr′ẽr, *n.* one who or that which prepares, fits, or makes ready; as, a *preparer* of textbooks; a *preparer* of copy for the press.

FIGURE 4.1 **Information in dictionary entries**
(Webster's *New Twentieth Century Dictionary*, 1421)

8. *Synonyms,* or substitute terms, extend your understanding of the definitions and provide alternatives you can use when you speak and write. (line 20)
9. *Other parts of speech* indicate additional grammatical forms for the word. (lines 22–39)

In addition, good dictionaries also define idioms or words and phrases that have a special, nonliteral meaning in a language, such as *all thumbs,* which means *clumsy.* They also generally list and define common prefixes, roots, and suffixes, as well as slang and foreign terms used in English. Finally, good dictionaries include geographical and biographical information as well. In short, the dictionary is a specialized type of encyclopedia for anything that can be reduced to a term or well known phrase.

> **Dictionaries are like watches; the worst is better than none, and the best cannot be expected to be quite true.**
>
> —Samuel Johnson (1709–1784), British author

When using a dictionary, however, finding the right definition for a term requires a little thought. You cannot just use the first one listed or scan to find a familiar one. Instead, to accurately define a term, you must substitute the key word(s) from each relevant entry for the unfamiliar word in the sentence. The substitution that makes the most sense is the correct definition. Here's an example and brief exercise that illustrates this kind of thinking.

EXAMPLE

The word *floor* has the following definitions. The key word is underlined.

1. The <u>surface</u> of a room on which one stands
2. A <u>story</u> or level of a building
3. The part of a legislative <u>chamber</u> where members are seated
4. The <u>right</u> to address an assembly

Which definition is correct for each of these sentences? Substitute the key words.

A. The senator from California is not in her office; she's on the floor.
Is that the surface, story, chamber, or right?

B. Her office is on the third floor.
Is that the surface, story, chamber, or right?

C. The senator said "I have the floor" to those who tried to interrupt her.
Is that the surface, story, chamber, or right?

D. The floor needs to be repaired.
Is that the surface, story, chamber, or right?

With the substitution method, you probably easily determined that the right definitions for these sentences are chamber, story, right, and surface.

I was reading the dictionary.
I thought it was a poem about everything.
—Steven Wright, (contemporary),
American humorist

ACTIVITY 10: USE A GENERAL DICTIONARY

DIRECTIONS: Read this short text and use a general English dictionary to answer the following questions.

The United States has started to lose its worldwide *dominance* in *critical* areas of science and innovation. Foreign advances in basic science now often *rival* or even exceed America's, *apparently* with little public awareness of the *trend* or its *implications* for jobs, industry, national security or the *vigor* of the nations' intellectual and cultural life. (Broad, *New York Times Learning Connections*) (57 words)

1. Dominance is a
   - a. Noun.
   - b. Verb.
   - c. Adjective.
   - d. Adverb.
2. Dominance means
   - a. The most important.
   - b. The most obvious or easiest to see.
   - c. To govern or rule.
   - d. Control.
3. Critical is a(n)
   - a. Noun.
   - b. Verb.
   - c. Adjective.
   - d. Adverb.
4. Critical means
   - a. Inclined to judge severely.
   - b. Careful evaluation.
   - c. Forming a crisis.
   - d. Crucial.

5. Rival is a(n)
   a. Noun.
   b. Verb.
   c. Adjective.
   d. Adverb.

6. Rival means ____
____.

7. What is the author suggesting with the phrase *apparently with little public awareness?*

____
____
____

8. What does the whole quote mean?

____
____
____
____

> "When I use a word," Humpty Dumpty said in rather a scornful tone, "it means just what I choose it to mean—neither more nor less."
> "The question is," said Alice, "whether you can make words mean so many different things."
> "The question is," said Humpty Dumpty, "which is to be master—that's all."
> —Lewis Carrol (1832–1898), British author

One word of caution about general dictionaries: they do not provide complete or accurate definitions for technical terms. For example, the general dictionary definition for the biological term *diffusion* is "spreading" or "the intermingling of molecules from two or more substances" (*Webster's New Twentieth Century Dictionary Unabridged*, 2nd edition). But in the field of biology, *diffusion* involves "the net movement of molecules from regions of high concentration to regions of low concentration" (Audesirk 60). To define technical terms, you will need a technical dictionary.

Technical Dictionaries Technical dictionaries list and define the technical words for an entire discipline. Dictionaries exist for literature, medicine, economics, and so on. Your library is a good place to locate these reference books. Glossaries, which appear at the end of textbooks, provide definitions for the technical terms presented in the book. Unlike general terms, the terms in a technical discipline do not have numerous definitions or alternative forms. So you will not have to try out various definitions to find the right one.

Your knowledge of word parts and context clues can supplement the glossary definitions and help you fully comprehend them. Look at this example from a marketing textbook. Try to define *service intangibility* before you look at the explanation under *Using all of the information.*

EXAMPLE

Service intangibility means that customers can't see, touch, or smell good service. Unlike the purchase of a good, services cannot be inspected or handled before the purchase is made. Although it may be easy to evaluate your new hair cut, it is far less easy to determine if the dental hygienist has done a great job cleaning your teeth.

From the glossary:

> *Intangibles:* Experience-based products that cannot be touched.
>
> *Services:* Intangible products that are exchanged directly from the producer to the customer. (Adapted from Solomon and Stuart 319, 596, 602)

Using all of the information: From the glossary, it's clear that services and intangibles have to do with personal products that are experienced rather than touched. But the term means more if you note the prefix meaning *not* in *intangible,* think about what *inspected* or *handled* means, and consider the example about dentists. Then, it's clear that *service intangibility* refers to personal experiences that customers cannot easily evaluate with their senses.

ACTIVITY 11: USE THE GLOSSARY

DIRECTIONS: Practice using a glossary along with word parts and context clues to help you understand the technical terms in the following passages. Record your explanations in the space provided. For item 2, use your own words; do not just copy the glossary definition.

1. One operation required for problem solving is *metacognition.* Metacognitive skills help you learn. Students who are weak in metacognition fail to notice when a passage in a textbook is difficult, and they do not always realize that they haven't understood what they've been reading. As a result, they spend too little time on difficult material and too much time on material they already know. (64 words)

   From the glossary:

   > *Metacognition:* The knowledge or awareness of one's own cognitive processes. (Adapted from Wade and Tavris 232, 499)

   Metacognition is best explained as

   a. A mental operation used for problem solving.
   b. A skill that only helps you learn new information.
   c. Mental awareness of the way the mind is working.
   d. Knowing when a passage is difficult.

2. Some psychologists have identified *emotional intelligence* as an aspect of cognitive ability. Emotional intelligence is the ability to identify your own and other people's emotions accurately, express your emotions clearly, and regulate emotions in yourself and others. People with high emotional intelligence—popularly known as EQ—use their emotions to motivate themselves, to spur creative thinking, and to deal

empathically with others. People who are low in emotional intelligence are often unable to identify their own emotions; they express emotions inappropriately, and they misread nonverbal signals from others. (88 words)

From the glossary:

Emotion: A state of arousal involving facial and bodily changes, brain activation, cognitive appraisals, subjective feelings, and tendencies toward action.

Intelligence: The ability to profit from experience, acquire knowledge, think abstractly, act purposefully, or adapt to changes in the environment. (Adapted from Wade and Tavris 233, 496, 498)

Emotional intelligence is ____

____.

Before you go on . . .

Monitor Your Progress: recite

As you read . . .

Focus Your Efforts: question and read

Learn New Terms

THINK ABOUT THIS . . .

Think about how you learn new words by answering these questions.

1. Which of the following types of words would be the easiest for you to learn and which would be the hardest?

   general terms   technical words   slang   terms about things I do

   The easiest would be ____________________.

   The hardest would be ____________________.

2. What makes terms easy to learn? What makes terms hard to learn?

   ____

   ____

3. What are the worst and the best methods for you to use when you're trying to learn new terms?

   ____

   ____

You can ensure long-term memory of both general and technical vocabulary by using active learning methods and avoiding memorization. Three particularly effective techniques are paraphrasing, creating memory aids, and using the new words.

Paraphrase the Definition

A meaning, we know, depends on the key of interpretation.
—George Eliot (1819–1880), British novelist

Paraphrasing, or defining and explaining a term in your own words, is a skill that is often overlooked. But, it shouldn't be, because it is the only way to check that you really understand what a word means. Furthermore, it is also the only way to move a word to the understood and well known levels. Finally, paraphrasing is an extremely powerful active learning technique that automatically increases motivation, engages your thinking, and creates memory pathways. When you use it as a comprehension check, it promotes the monitoring stage of motivation; used as a way to create memory, it's a method of reflection.

There are two ways to paraphrase—one for general terms and one for technical words. To paraphrase the definition of a general term, identify a synonym or short phrase that you can substitute for the term. You could, for example, use *control* or *act in an all-powerful manner* in place of *dominate* to identify synonyms. Think of words you already know or refer to a dictionary or a thesaurus (a book that lists only synonyms).

When you are dealing with technical terms, paraphrasing requires more thought. The definitions for these terms are generally longer, more complex, and more precise. Thus, your paraphrase will read like an explanation and it may be several sentences long. In addition, it may include a number of terms from the original definition that are specific to that topic and don't have accurate synonyms. To paraphrase technical definitions, follow these steps:

1. Start your definition with the term.
2. Use topic-specific terms from the definition that don't have accurate synonyms.
3. Use synonyms for the other words.
4. Break the original definition up into a number of sentences, if possible.
5. Change the order of the information, if possible.
6. Form your own sentence(s) that completely convey the meaning of the original.

Here's the definition of *marketing* from a business textbook and a paraphrase of it. The topic-specific words that were used in the paraphrased definition are underlined.

EXAMPLE

Marketing is the process of planning and executing the conception, pricing, promotion, and <u>distribution</u> of <u>ideas</u>, <u>goods</u>, and <u>services</u> to create exchanges that satisfy individual and <u>organizational</u> goals. (Griffin and Ebert 280)

Paraphrased version: Marketing involves all of the procedures used to deliver <u>ideas</u>, <u>goods</u>, and <u>services</u>. It emphasizes meeting personal and <u>organizational</u> objectives. It includes creating and carrying out an overall idea, as well as determining price, publicity, and distribution.

This kind of paraphrase is what professors expect you to do when they ask for an explanation of a concept.

ACTIVITY 12: PARAPHRASE DEFINITIONS

DIRECTIONS: Paraphrase the definition for each of the following bold-faced words. For the general terms, think of a synonym or substitute phrase. For the technical words, write a complete paraphrase of the original definition.

1. General terms
   a. Very few people manage to become an expert in any field. People often assume that's because you have to be born with special **attributes** to become an expert. But usually, it's not genetics but training and effort that make the difference.

   ____

   ____

   b. Several **misconceptions** about reading prevent many readers from assuming greater control over their reading and thereby affect how efficiently they read and how well they learn.

   ____

   ____

2. Technical terms and definitions
   a. To **infer,** or figure out, is to create a logical meaning that is not directly stated in the text.

   ____

   ____

   b. **Cellulose** is a rigid, complex carbohydrate contained in the cell walls of many organisms.

   ____

   ____

Create Memory Aids

Memory aids promote motivation, active thinking, and recall. But you don't have to focus on these mental actions to get the benefits. Simply devise associations and graphic aids.

Associations **Associations** are powerful memory aids that connect the information you're trying to learn with something you already know. They can be verbal, visual, or both. And they can be created while you paraphrase or as a separate reflection activity.

You probably already use associations for many memory tasks. For example, many people use associations to learn people's names. So, if you're introduced to a person named Tom Swingle, you might make mental associations like these: "Tom is the same name as my uncle. Swingle makes me think of a swing plus the letter *L.*" When you talk to yourself this way, you make a verbal association. Here are two examples using a technical term.

EXAMPLES

Hindsight bias is the "I knew it all along" phenomenon, where people overestimate their ability to have predicted an event once the outcome is known. (Adapted from Wade and Tavris 224)

Association: "My aunt always uses hindsight bias. Whenever a couple she knows breaks up, she claims to have always known they wouldn't make it, although she never says that before it happens."

Photosynthetic organisms, from mighty oaks to the zucchini plants in your garden to single-celled diatoms in the ocean, are called **autotrophs** (Greek, "self-feeders") or **producers,** because they produce food for themselves using nonliving nutrients and sunlight. (Audesirk et al., 837)

Association: "My fern is a self-centered autotroph; it produces its own food from nutrients and sunlight."

Associations do not have to be logical or true. Maybe your aunt doesn't always use hindsight bias, and plants aren't thought of as being self-centered. But simply making these statements makes the term and the definition memorable.

Visual aids are a form of association where you mentally visualize or physically draw images and pictures that remind you of the new information. If you can make these images odd, exaggerated, or funny, so much the better. Using the previous examples, you could picture Tom Swingle swinging on a huge L-shaped swing, your aunt talking to you wearing a silly hat, or your fern puffing out its leaves as it says "I'm an autotroph." If you draw these images, by the way, artistic ability is not important. Stick figures, doodles, cartoon figures, and even geometric forms can be very effective aids for remembering a new word.

ACTIVITY 13: USE ASSOCIATIONS

DIRECTIONS: Practice using verbal and visual associations on the terms from Activity 10.

1. Dominance.
   a. Record a personal association for this term.

   ____

   ____

   b. Draw a visual aid for this term.

2. Critical
   a. Record a personal association for this term.

   ____

   ____

   ____

   b. Draw a visual aid for this term.

3. Rival
   a. Record a personal association for this term.

   ____

   ____

   ____

   b. Draw a visual aid for this term.

Graphic Aids Many students believe that studying one small piece of information at a time is the best way to learn. Actually, it's easier to remember a word if you group related pieces of information together. Maps and charts are **graphic aids** that organize separate pieces of information on paper into a logical unit.

You have probably already used maps in writing classes, where they are called cluster or brainstorming diagrams. To create a map for learning vocabulary, write the term in the middle of a page. Then add lines like spokes on a wheel that link to pieces of information about the word. Helpful pieces of information might include the word parts, phonetic pronunciation, part of speech, definition, your personal associations, synonyms, antonyms, or a sentence using the word. You don't have to use all of these when you map a word; just use more than the definition, and choose additional pieces of information that are useful and interesting to you. Here's an example of a text and map about the biological term *heterotroph*.

EXAMPLE

Organisms that cannot photosynthesize, called heterotrophs (Greek, "other feeders") or consumers, must acquire energy and many other nutrients prepackaged in the molecules that compose the bodies of other organisms. (Audesirk et al., 837)

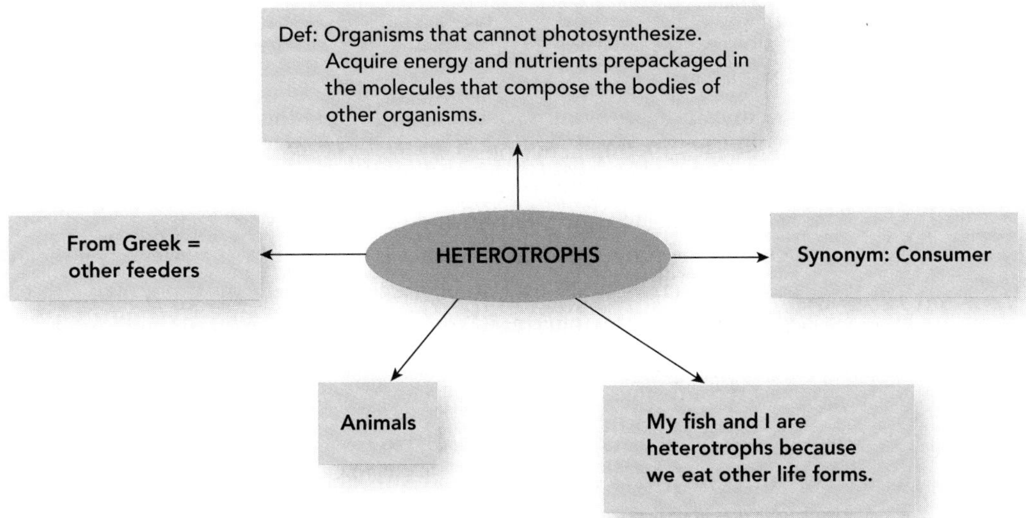

Maps work well for an individual word. But, when you need to learn a group of related terms, a chart is a better memory aid. Use rows and columns to present the terms, definitions, and other useful information about the words in an organized way. Here's an example of a chart about word parts.

EXAMPLE

Word Parts

TERM	DEFINITION	FUNCTION	EXAMPLES
Prefix	Parts added before a root	Add to / change the root meaning	*Bi* means two *Pre* means before
Root	The base element of every word	Every word has one	*Aud* means hear *Dict* means speak or tell
Suffix	Parts added after a root	Shows the part of speech and general meanings	*Ion* is a noun ending meaning state of *Ate* is a verb ending meaning to make or do

Notice the column headings in the previous example. You can use any headings that make sense to you, but these are standard ones that you might want to use if nothing else occurs to you.

ACTIVITY 14: USE GRAPHIC AIDS

DIRECTIONS: Practice using graphic aids by completing the following tasks.

1. Read the following text. Then, on your own paper, create a map for the term *edutainment.*

   Many educational programs for children disguise the learning process by combining it with interactive puzzles, games, and other fun activities. Because it combines education and entertainment, this software is referred to as *edutainment.* Often these programs include a theme or story that is carried throughout the program and the learner is rewarded with prizes when they've correctly answered questions. Edutainment software is most popular with preschool and early elementary-aged students, but adult edutainment programs exist to assist older learners in mastering certain skills such as typing or English as a second language. (Evans et al., 130) (92 words)

2. Read the text and fill in the chart that follows.

   Edward Tylor (1871), a founder of the anthropology of religion, argues that religion evolves through stages. The first stage is *animism,* the belief that supernatural beings or spirits capable of helping or hurting people inhabit living things (plants and animals) and inanimate objects (rocks and houses). The next stage of religious evolution is characterized by *theism,* the belief in one or more independent supernatural beings (gods), who do not exist on earth and who are more powerful than people. *Polytheism* is the belief in many gods. When an all-powerful, all-knowing god replaced a hierarchy of gods, polytheism was replaced by *monotheism* in Tylor's evolutionary scheme. (Adapted from Lindsey and Beach, 307) (105 words)

Stages of Religion

STAGE	TERM	BELIEF	WHERE SUPERNATURAL BEINGS EXIST

Use the Word

Recall that the final step in learning vocabulary the way children do is to use the new word. This is the reward for your efforts; now is the time to talk and write about your expanded knowledge. And it is the time to feel good about the efforts and gains you've made.

One forgets words as one forgets names. One's vocabulary needs constant fertilizing or it will die.

—Evelyn Waugh (1903–1966)
British novelist

One word of caution: **Usage** involves creating a sentence that correctly employs the term to communicate a thought. It is not a restatement of the definition. For example, the sentence "My aunt uses hindsight, because she claims to know people will break up after they do" is a good use of the term. But "hindsight is where people overestimate their ability to have predicted an event once the outcome is known" is not usage; it's just repeating the definition.

Language most shows a man; speak that I may see thee.

—Ben Jonson (1573–1637)
British dramatist and poet

ACTIVITY 15: USE NEW TERMS

DIRECTIONS: Write your own sentences for the terms in Activity 14.

1. Attributes

____

____

2. Misconceptions

____

____

3. Infer

____

____

4. Cellulose

____

____

In the end we retain from our studies only that which we practically apply.

—Johann Wolfgang Von Goethe (1749–1832),
German poet, dramatist, and novelist

Before you go on . . .

Monitor Your Progress: recite

After you read . . .

Reflect on Your Gains: review

CHAPTER SUMMARY

Introduction

Vocabulary is a broad term that includes the size or number of words you know, the skills you use to understand new terms, and the methods you employ to learn new words. Each aspect affects your comprehension and learning of college materials.

Developing Your Vocabulary

To effectively develop your vocabulary, add both **general vocabulary** and **technical terms** to it. While learning, move the new terms up the levels of knowledge—from "unknown" or just "recognized" to the "understood" and, "well known" categories. The natural way you learned words as a child provides an effective way to expand your vocabulary. It works because it's active and promotes the stages of motivation.

Understanding New Terms

Knowing word parts, using context clues, and using dictionaries are the three major ways to understand new terms when you encounter them. English words are made from standard **word parts,** including **prefixes, roots,** and **suffixes.** Learning these parts is a very efficient way to expand your vocabulary, because once you know the meaning of a part, you have a key to the definition of numerous words. **Context clues** are hints provided by the author to help you understand terms as you read. To figure out the meaning of a term from context, you will **infer** it from the **definition, explanation, comparison,** or **contrast clues.** The final method for understanding new terms is to use dictionaries, which include both general English and technical dictionaries. With dictionaries, you can locate precise definitions and information about the various ways words are used.

Learning New Terms

Active learning methods ensure long-term memory of new terms and their definitions. Three effective techniques are **paraphrasing, creating memory aids,** and **using new words.** Paraphrasing is the only way to check your comprehension and move a term up the levels of knowledge. Memory aids, including **associations** and **graphic aids,** are powerful alternatives to memorizing. Using new words is the way to reflect on the knowledge you've gained and reward your efforts.

REVIEW ACTIVITIES

Use the following activities to check your understanding and aid your learning of the information in this chapter.

Expand Your Vocabulary

Match each term with the correct definition or characteristic.

_____ **1.** general vocabulary
_____ **2.** technical terms
_____ **3.** word parts
_____ **4.** prefix
_____ **5.** root
_____ **6.** suffix
_____ **7.** context clues
_____ **8.** infer
_____ **9.** definition clue
_____ **10.** explanation clue
_____ **11.** comparison clue
_____ **12.** contrast clue
_____ **13.** paraphrasing
_____ **14.** associations
_____ **15.** visual aids
_____ **16.** graphic aids
_____ **17.** usage

a. an image or picture that you use to remember a definition
b. to define and explain a term in your own words
c. a hint that gives the exact meaning or a synonym
d. information that shows the opposite of what a word means
e. terms with a meaning that is not specific to any one field
f. creating a sentence that includes the term to communicate a thought
g. words used by experts in a field
h. the base element of a word
i. clues provided by the author about the meaning of a word
j. maps and charts used to organize information
k. details and examples given to clarify the meaning of a term
l. a syllable at the end of a word that indicates the part of speech
m. syllables that function as roots, prefixes, or suffixes
n. to figure out what is logically meant but not stated
o. a syllable added before the base element of a word
p. hints that compare one word to another or to a situation
q. personal information used to remember a definition

Increase Your Knowledge

These tasks will help you identify the important ideas in this chapter. They will also help you prepare for quizzes and exams on this material.

1. The following questions focus on the major chapter topics. Discuss them with others or form your own detailed answers.
   a. Explain the difference between general and technical terms.
   b. What does it mean to know a word? What are the levels of vocabulary knowledge?
   c. What is the natural vocabulary-learning process? Relate each step to the stages of motivation.

d. What are the three word parts used in English? How can they help you to expand your vocabulary?
e. Explain what context clues are. What types of clues do authors use? What kind of information does each clue provide?
f. Identify and describe the two types of dictionaries. When do you use each one?
g. Explain how to paraphrase. What benefits does it provide?
h. What are memory aids? Explain how to create them.
i. How and why should you use the new words you learn?

2. Take notes on the information in this chapter.

Develop Your Skills

The following review tasks will give you an opportunity to practice the methods presented in this chapter.

REVIEW 1: USE WORD PARTS For each of the following words, circle the common word parts that are listed in Tables 4.2–4.5. Then use the word part definitions to form your best definition. You may use the word part tables, but do not refer to a dictionary.

1. Intermittent
word part meanings: ______________________________
word definition: ______________________________

2. Microlevel
word part meaning: ______________________________
word definition: ______________________________

3. Reinforce
word part meanings: ______________________________
word definition: ______________________________

4. Resolution
word part meanings: ______________________________
word definition: ______________________________

5. Subordinate
word part meanings: ______________________________
word definition: ______________________________

REVIEW 2: USE WORD PARTS AND CONTEXT TOGETHER Use your knowledge of word parts and context clues to infer the meaning of the italicized words in the following text. Do not use the dictionary while you work.

A survey released on Thursday reports that reading for pleasure is way down in America among every group—old and young, wealthy and poor, educated and *uneducated*, men and women, Hispanic, black and white. The survey, by the National Endowment for the Arts, also *indicates* that people who read for pleasure are many times more likely than those who don't to visit museums and attend musical performances, almost three times as likely to perform volunteer and charity work, and almost twice as likely to attend sporting events. Readers, in other words, are active, while nonreaders—more than half of the population—have settled into *apathy.* There is a basic *social divide* between those for whom life is an *accrual* of fresh experience and knowledge, and those for whom *maturity* is a process of mental *atrophy.* The shift toward the latter category is frightening. (Solomon, *The New York Times*) (143 words)

1. Uneducated ______________________
2. Indicates ______________________
3. Apathy ______________________
4. Social divide ______________________
5. Accrual ______________________
6. Maturity ______________________
7. Atrophy ______________________

REVIEW 3: USE THE DICTIONARY Use a dictionary to find precise meanings for each of the italicized words in the following text.

The electronic media tend to be *torpid.* Despite the existence of good television, fine writing on the Internet, and video games that test logic, the electronic media by and large invite *inert reception.* One selects channels, but then the information comes out *preprocessed.* Most people use television as a means of turning their minds off, not on. Many readers watch television without *peril;* but for those for whom television replaces reading, the consequences are far-reaching. (Solomon, *The New York Times*) (75 words)

1. Torpid slow and apathetic
2. Inert powerless to move
3. Reception The act of receiving
4. Preprocessed to do prelimimary processing of
5. Peril danger

REVIEW 4: USE A GLOSSARY Read each of the following texts along with the glossary entry that follows it. Then use that information along with word parts and context clues to write your own paraphrased definition. Do not just copy the glossary definition.

1. *Androgyny* might be especially beneficial for men. Many men might stop being workaholics, relax on weekends, refrain from engaging in risky sexual behavior (to demonstrate their sexual prowess), live longer, and stop worrying about being

"real men." If we were more comfortable when children display nontraditional traits, assertive girls and nonaggressive boys would be happier and emotionally healthier. (58 words)

From the glossary:

Androgny: A blend of culturally defined male and female characteristics. (Benokraitis 135, 546)

Androgyny is ____
____.

2. Do you understand how a virus spreads from one computer to another? Can you describe how an engine works? What about the economy? Do you know how the inflation and unemployment rates interact? At times, the problems that confront us can be best represented in the form of *mental models.* When accurate, these theories can be powerful tools for reasoning. (60 words)

   From the glossary:

   Mental model: Intuitive theories about the way things work. (Adapted from Kassin 262)

   Mental models are ____
   ____.

REVIEW 5: LEARN NEW TERMS Practice using the active learning methods by completing these activities.

A. Paraphrase. Write a paraphrase for each of the following technical definitions.

1. *Trait:* A characteristic of an individual, a habitual way of behaving, thinking or feeling.

   ____
   ____

2. *Animism* is the belief that supernatural beings or spirits capable of helping or hurting people inhabit living things (plants and animals) and inanimate objects (rocks and houses).

   ____
   ____

3. *Theism* is the belief in one or more independent supernatural beings (gods) who do not exist on earth and who are more powerful than people.

   ____
   ____

4. *Polytheism* is the belief in many gods.

   ____
   ____

B. Associations: First, complete Review Activity 3. Then, write down a personal association and a visual aid for each of the following terms.

1. Torpid

a. Record a personal association for this term.

He was a torpid worker

b. Draw a visual aid for this term.

2. Inert

a. Record a personal association for this term.

She stay inert after the discussion with her sister

b. Draw a visual aid for this term.

3. Reception

a. Record a personal association for this term.

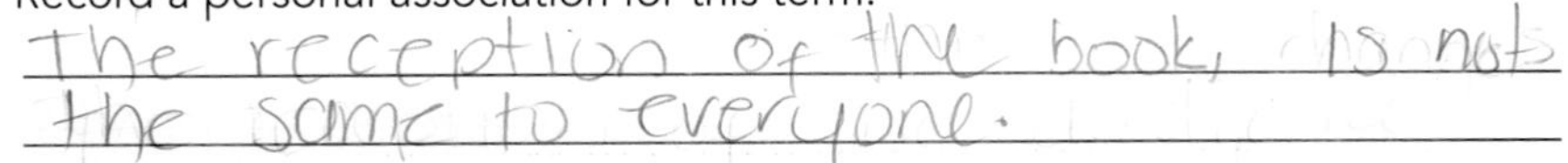
The reception of the book, is not
the same to everyone.

b. Draw a visual aid for this term.

C. Graphic aid. Read the following text. Then, on your own paper, create a map or chart for the italicized terms about brain waves.

When you first climb into bed, close your eyes, and relax, your brain emits bursts of alpha waves. On an EEG recording, *alpha waves* have a regular, slow rhythm and a high amplitude (height). Gradually, these waves slow down even further, and you drift off into slumber, passing through four stages:

- Stage 1. Your brain waves become small and irregular, and you feel yourself drifting on the edge of consciousness, in a state of light sleep. If awakened, you may recall fantasies or a few visual images.
- Stage 2. Your brain emits occasional short bursts of rapid, high-peaking waves called *sleep spindles.* Minor noises probably won't disturb you.
- Stage 3. In addition to the waves characteristic of stage 2, your brain occasionally emits *delta waves,* very slow waves with very high peaks. Your breathing and pulse have slowed down, your muscles are relaxed, and you are hard to rouse.
- Stage 4. Delta waves have now largely taken over, and you are in deep sleep. It will probably take vigorous shaking or a loud noise to awaken you. Oddly, though, if you talk or walk in your sleep, this is when you are likely to do so.

This sequence of stages takes about 30 to 45 minutes. Then you move back up the ladder from stage 4 to 3 to 2 to 1. At that point, stage 1 does not turn into drowsy wakefulness, as one might expect. Instead, your brain begins to emit long bursts of very rapid, somewhat irregular waves, and most skeletal muscles go limp. You have entered the realm of REM (rapid eye movement), when you are most likely to dream. (Wade and Tavris 152–153) (274 words)

D. Usage. Create a sentence that correctly uses each of the following terms from Review 2 and 4.

1. Accrual

____

____

2. Atrophy

____

____

3. Androgyny

____

____

4. Mental models

____

____

Check Your Motivation

1. Review your chapter goals. Did you achieve them? Explain.
2. Make a list of the new ideas and methods you've gained from this chapter. Think about how they will help you in the future.
3. Measure your motivation for this chapter topic. Think about each statement and how you will use it in the future. Mark it:

A = never B = sometimes C = usually D = always

	A	B	C	D
To engage my interest, I plan to . . .				
1. think about the benefits of developing my overall vocabulary.	___	___	___	___
2. take an interest in knowing new terms.	___	___	___	___
To focus my efforts, I plan to . . .				
3. identify my level of knowledge before trying to learn a word.	___	___	___	___
4. pronounce a word as the first step to learning it.	___	___	___	___
5. think about the meaning of words I'm learning.	___	___	___	___
6. look for word parts and context clues to help define new words.	___	___	___	___
7. use dictionaries, when appropriate.	___	___	___	___
To monitor my progress, I plan to . . .				
8. use paraphrasing to check my comprehension and level of knowledge.	___	___	___	___
9. think about and test my level of knowledge as I learn.	___	___	___	___
To reflect on my gains, I plan to . . .				
10. use paraphrasing as a review technique.	___	___	___	___
11. use associations to learn new words.	___	___	___	___
12. use maps and charts to learn terms, where appropriate.	___	___	___	___
13. use the new words I learn as I speak or write.	___	___	___	___
14. think about the knowledge I've gained.	___	___	___	___
15. praise and reward myself for my vocabulary expansion efforts.	___	___	___	___

SCORING: Write the number of answers you marked in each column in the following spaces. Compute the column scores, and then add them up to determine your total score.

# of A's ______ × 1 pt. = ______
# of B's ______ × 2 pt. = ______
# of C's ______ × 3 pt. = ______
# of D's ______ × 4 pt. = ______
Total points = ______

INTERPRETATION: 15–43 points = low motivation; 44–60 points = high motivation

SUGGESTION

1. Compare your current Chapter score to the one from The Motivation Measure. If they're both low, review the list above and find approaches you'd be willing to try. If you've improved or have a high score, reward yourself for your empowered approaches.
2. Record the methods you want to use on your bookmark. Look it over before you begin reading the next assignment. Apply those approaches.

Motivation Matters 1

Before you read . . .

Engage Your Interest: preread and divide

Think of people who you would call experts. How do you think they got to be so good in their field? Do you think talent is born or made?

After prereading, set a goal for your reading.

I want to ________________ about ______________________________.

My reward(s) will be ______________________________________

____.

Right before you begin to read, record your START time in the Rate Box on page 182.

As you read . . .

Focus Your Efforts: question and read

Strive to Become an Expert

Saul Kassin, *Psychology*

1 Very few people manage to climb to the very top of a skilled domain to become experts, among the best in the world. Those who do achieve these heights often dazzle us with their achievements. How do the great ones reach this level? Are they specially gifted, endowed at birth with brains and bodies uniquely suited to their talent? Are they, in other words, born, not made? Is the pursuit of excellence similar from one skill to another? How do people make it, as they say, to the top of their game?

2 To answer these questions, psychologists have looked at expertise across a broad range of domains. In *The Road to Excellence,* K. Anders Ericsson (1996) brought together researchers who have studied great musicians, visual artists, medical doctors, memory experts, inventors, chess masters, bridge players, and typists, as well as golfers, tennis players, and gymnasts. Together, these studies have converged on some core principles that are surprising.

3 To begin with, you don't have to be born with special attributes to become an expert. When people see a brilliant performer—as when watching Tiger Woods play golf—they are quick to assume that he or she was born specially endowed. Thus, Ericsson noted that when people watch someone memorize a string of over fifty rapidly presented digits, they assume that this person has a photographic memory. In fact, this person was most likely to have spent hundreds of hours practicing digit-recalling techniques. Ask highly gifted children about their achievements, and they'll be the first to attribute what they've done to "hard work and effort, not luck and genes" (Winner, 1996, p. 213).

4 So what does it take to become among the best? First, to become an expert at anything one must make a long-term commitment. The great ones do not emerge all at once. Studying chess masters, Simon and Chase (1973) proposed that it takes at least ten years of playing to reach the international level in chess. Ericsson and his colleagues (1993) concluded that no matter how much talent someone has, this same ten-year rule applies to attaining expertise in music composition, science, arts, and sports.

5 Time spent on a task is necessary for greatness, but it's not enough. There are plenty of weekend golfers who enjoy hours on driving ranges, putting greens, and fairways, who quickly become good but never great. The reason is that time must be used for concentrated, intense, purposeful activities specifically designed to improve performance. This is what Ericsson and others have called *deliberate practice* (as opposed to mere mindless repetition). Major league baseball hitters study videotapes of pitchers. Hockey goalies study the tendencies of shooters. One can only imagine the number of hours Michael Jordan spent shooting hoops.

6 Like time spent, deliberate practice may be necessary, but it too is not enough. No one makes it to the top alone. Case studies show that great achievers received guidance from highly skilled teachers. These teachers instructed them, set goals for them, designed practices and programs, and set their competitive schedules.

7 To sum up, great talents are made, not born. To be sure, some people are more innately talented in some ways than others. But the real key is tireless if not obsessive motivation, hard work, and assistance from an expert. Practice may not make you perfect, but you can't become perfect without it. (558 words)

As soon as you finish reading, record your END time in the Rate Box on page 182.

Before you go on . . .

Monitor Your Progress: recite

After you read . . .

Reflect on Your Gains: review

REVIEW ACTIVITIES

Use the following activities to check your understanding of this reading.

Expand Your Vocabulary

Define the underlined terms as they are used in the essay by circling the correct response. The numbers after each item indicate the paragraph where the term appears.

1. the very top of a skilled domain (1)
   a. land   b. territory   c. sport   d. field

2. endowed at birth (1)
   a. bestowed b. equipped c. awarded d. given
3. uniquely suited to their talent (1)
   a. fitted b. clothed c. courted d. appealed
4. pursuit of excellence (1)
   a. hunting b. trying c. striving d. hoping
5. core principles (2)
   a. central b. important c. inner d. hidden
6. to attribute what they've done (3)
   a. characterize b. credit c. explain d. justify
7. applies to attaining expertise (4)
   a. attending to b. achieving c. acquiring d. winning
8. concentrated, intense, purposeful activities (5)
   a. clustered b. spread out c. focused d. concentration
9. are more innately talented (7)
   a. intelligently b. inbred c. inner d. genetically
10. tireless if not obsessive motivation (7)
   a. overwhelming c. neurotic
   b. all-encompassing d. preoccupied

Check Your Comprehension

Use the following questions to determine how well you understand the ideas, details, and inferences in this article. Circle the best response to each question.

1. The main idea of this essay is best stated as
   a. People need talent to become an expert.
   b. Experts perfect their talents.
   c. People can create their own talent and expertise.
   d. No one becomes an expert without natural talent.
2. Becoming an expert
   a. Requires more natural talent in the arts than in sports.
   b. In medicine is not the same as becoming an artist.
   c. Requires some inner talent, dedication, and hard work.
   d. In any field requires similar levels of effort.
3. Anders Ericsson
   a. Researched musicians, visual artists, and other experts.
   b. Brought together researchers who had studied various types of excellence.
   c. Believed that core principles explain excellence.
   d. Studied the research of many psychologists in order to write a book.
4. People assume that brilliant performers
   a. Have natural talent.
   b. Have a photographic memory.

   c. Don't have to practice.
   d. Are more intelligent than the average person.

5. Gifted children
   a. Recognize their special talents.
   b. Take their success for granted.
   c. Believe their efforts lead to their success.
   d. Believe that luck and genes are needed to succeed.

6. Long-term commitment
   a. Involves 10 or more years of practice and performing or producing works.
   b. Involves 10 years to master mental activities such as chess.
   c. Requires planning to allow for enough practice time.
   d. Is not needed if the person is very talented.

7. It is implied that the reason weekend golfers don't become great is that
   a. They do not practice enough.
   b. They do not spend enough time playing the game.
   c. They care more about enjoyment than high scores.
   d. Their practice sessions and games are not designed to develop perfection.

8. Deliberate practice involves ___________ activities.
   a. concentrated
   b. intense
   c. purposeful
   d. all of the above

9. True or false? Long-term commitment and deliberate practice are enough to produce excellence in most fields.

10. Highly skilled teachers
    a. Can be helpful, but are not absolutely necessary for achievement.
    b. Who instruct and guide are essential for great achievement.
    c. Are needed to provide motivation for great achievement.
    d. Are very helpful if they instruct and set up a good practice schedule.

Expand Your Thinking

Use these activities to expand your understanding of the ideas in this article.

1. The following discussion questions will help you comprehend the major text points and develop your own thoughts about the topic.
   a. What do gifted children generally say is the source of their success?
   b. What are the core principles for greatness and high achievement?
   c. Why is time not enough to gain greatness? What kind of practice is needed?
   d. What do skilled teachers provide that helps people become high achievers?
   e. Think of something you've learned to do very well. How did time commitment, deliberate practice, and expert help contribute to your success?
   f. How does this information relate to high achievement in college courses?

2. Take notes on this reading.

Check Your Motivation

1. Review your reading goal. Did you achieve it? Explain.
2. Make a list of the new ideas that you've gained from this text. Think about how they will be useful to you in the future.
3. Assess your current motivation. Think about how you read this text. Then mark each statement:

   A = not at all B = a little C = fairly well D = very well

	A	B	C	D
To engage my interest, I . . .				
1. initiated an "I want to read about this" attitude.	___	___	___	___
2. preread the text.	___	___	___	___
3. identified the topic and/or thought about relevant or interesting points before reading.	___	___	___	___
4. looked for the author's organization before reading.	___	___	___	___
5. set a reading goal before reading.	___	___	___	___
To focus my efforts, I . . .				
6. chose my methods and had an "I know how to read this" attitude.	___	___	___	___
7. read where I was able to concentrate.	___	___	___	___
8. formed questions and read to find answers and other important points.	___	___	___	___
To monitor my progress, I . . .				
9. felt confident and had an "I believe I can read this well" attitude.	___	___	___	___
10. solved any reading problems during reading. (Mark D if there were none.)	___	___	___	___
11. marked the text as I read.	___	___	___	___
12. recited parts or all of the text.	___	___	___	___
To reflect on my gains, I . . .				
13. had an "I've accomplished something" attitude once I finished.	___	___	___	___
14. recognized the new or useful information I gained.	___	___	___	___
15. rewarded myself.	___	___	___	___

SCORING: Write the number of answers you marked in each column in the following spaces. Compute the column scores, and then add them up to determine your total score.

# of A's ______ × 1 pt. = ______
# of B's ______ × 2 pt. = ______
# of C's ______ × 3 pt. = ______
# of D's ______ × 4 pt. = ______
Total points = ______

INTERPRETATION: 15–43 points = low motivation; 44–60 points = high motivation

4. Compute your reading rate by following these steps:

Rate Box

1. **RECORD** your END time here: ____________
2. **RECORD** your START time here: ____________
3. **DETERMINE** your TOTAL reading time here: ____________
4. **ROUND OFF** the seconds to the nearest ¼ minute. For example, 4 minutes, 15 seconds would be 4.25. Write this on the **** line.
5. **DIVIDE** the number of words by your rounded off time:

558 words / ______ = ______ WPM
****

5. Record your rate, comprehension, vocabulary, and motivation scores on the Progress Charts that are on the inside front and back covers of this text.

Motivation Matters 2

Before you read . . .

Engage Your Interest: preread and divide

Do you read efficiently? Do your ideas about reading match any of those listed in bold face in this essay?

After prereading, set a goal for your reading.

I want to ________________ about ______________________________.
My reward(s) will be ____
____.

Right before you begin to read, record your START time in the Rate Box on page 188.

As you read . . .

Focus Your Efforts: question and read

Misconceptions About Reading

Joan Rasool, Caroline Banks, and Mary-Jane McCarthy

From *Critical Thinking: Reading and Writing in a Diverse World*

Unfortunately, several misconceptions about reading prevent many readers from assuming greater control over their reading and thereby affect how efficiently they read and how well they learn. Which of the following misconceptions might be "getting in your way"? 1

Misconception 1: Done correctly, reading is easy *and/or* fun

Belief in this misconception may be due to students' early reading experiences with teachers who, eager for them to be successful readers, steered them away from materials they couldn't read aloud without 90 percent accuracy. Thus, for instance, if Trevia stumbled over too many words, it was assumed she needed an "easier" book. As a consequence, she developed a very low reading frustration level. Now when Trevia struggles to read difficult material, she quickly gives up. Of course we would like you to find reading easy and fun, but when it is not, it does not necessarily mean that you aren't reading "correctly." Some reading material is just difficult, either because the topic is unfamiliar, the material is complex, or the selection is badly written. Some reading material is not inherently entertaining, but the information within it is important. When the reading seems difficult you need to stop and assess the situation: Why are you read- 2 ing this—what is your purpose? What is causing the difficulty? How can you minimize frustration and maximize comprehension?

Misconception 2: Readers should understand everything they read

3 Here is a situation where you must take more responsibility for the reading. How much you should comprehend from a reading depends on your purpose: Are you looking for an answer to a particular question? Do you just want to know the author's position? Will you be required to take a test on the material? As a reader you need to decide what your purpose is before reading and let that guide you in how much you need to comprehend. If you are assigned material to read in a course and the instructor hasn't set forth any purpose, you should ask about it.

Misconception 3: Good readers should read quickly

4 Speed should not be confused with flexibility. Good readers are flexible readers and vary their reading rate depending on their purpose. Some students bemoan the time it takes to read ten pages in their history texts, but the unhappy truth is that some material does take considerable time to read well. It may, indeed, take you an hour to read and remember the important ideas in ten pages of history. If you need to acquire only a general understanding of the author's viewpoint, then you can go more quickly. Your reading rate also depends upon the writer's style, the complexity of the material, and your background knowledge. Does this sound familiar? It should; reading is an interaction between the reader and the writer. When the reader and the writer use the same language (vocabulary and style) and share similar interests, knowledge, and experiences, then comprehension will come more easily and the reading will go more quickly. When any of the variables clash, then comprehension will take you more time.

Misconception 4: Reading is done with the eyes

5 At this point misconception 4 should not come as any shock to you. Reading is only incidentally visual; in fact, were you to lose your eyesight you could learn to read with your fingertips. Although your eyes receive the print stimuli, it is your brain that processes and understands the data. Reading is a cognitive or mental process. It is the reconstruction of the writer's meaning. Thus you can understand why speed reading courses that rely on eye movement exercises may not be very effective. Simply learning how to move your eyes more quickly will not guarantee that you understand what passes before them. (Sometimes these courses offer additional exercises that do increase your flexibility as a reader or help you develop more reading concentration; however, eye movement exercises alone will have little impact on your comprehension.) (657 words)

As soon as you finish reading, record your END time in the Rate Box on page 188.

Before you go on . . .

Monitor Your Progress: recite

After you read . . .

Reflect on Your Gains: review

REVIEW ACTIVITIES

Use the following activities to check your understanding of this reading.

Expand Your Vocabulary

Define the underlined terms as they are used in the essay by circling the correct response. The numbers after each item indicate the paragraph where the term appears.

1. several misconceptions about reading (1)
   a. mistakes **b.** errors **c.** misjudgments **d.** erroneous ideas
2. assuming greater control (1)
   a. adopting **b.** undertaking **c.** taking **d.** inferring
3. steered them away from materials (2)
   a. drove **b.** directed **c.** aimed **d.** took
4. assess the situation (2)
   a. evaluate **c.** analyze
   b. identify the value of **d.** look over
5. the instructor hasn't set forth any purpose (3)
   a. conveyed **b.** developed **c.** fixed **d.** decided upon
6. students bemoan the time it takes (4)
   a. grieve over **b.** complain about **c.** consider **d.** regret
7. reading is only incidentally visual (5)
   a. randomly **b.** haphazardly **c.** occasionally **d.** casually
8. your eyes receive the print stimuli (5)
   a. message **b.** incentive **c.** activator **d.** words
9. reading is a cognitive process (5)
   a. thoughtful **b.** mental **c.** comprehension **d.** complex
10. it is the reconstruction of the writer's meaning (5)
    a. reassembling **b.** remodeling **c.** remaking **d.** reshaping

Check Your Comprehension

Use the following questions to determine how well you understand the ideas, details, and inferences in this article. Circle the best response to each question.

1. The main idea of this essay is best stated as
   a. Many readers don't know how to read.
   b. Many readers have bad habits.
   c. Erroneous ideas get in the way of or prevent good reading.
   d. Readers don't assume control over their reading.

2. The authors imply that
   a. Reading out loud without mistakes is uncommon.
   b. People should be able to read out loud with a high degree of accuracy.
   c. Children can read out loud with a high degree of accuracy.
   d. Easier books are not always the best solution to reading problems.

3. If children are always given easier books to read, they
   a. Don't learn to read.
   b. Develop a low reading frustration level.
   c. Learn to read out loud with 90 percent accuracy.
   d. Enjoy reading.

4. Material might be difficult to read because it is
   a. An unfamiliar topic
   b. Complex
   c. Poor writing
   d. All of these

5. When the reading seems difficult, you should
   a. Determine why the material is hard and how to get the best comprehension.
   b. Stop reading and find an easier text.
   c. Change your reading purpose to one that matches the text difficulty.
   d. Just get whatever information you can from the text.

6. True or false? Good readers always understand everything they read.

7. The authors imply that
   a. Good readers ignore frustrations.
   b. Good readers can comprehend every text.
   c. Accomplishing your purpose is the measure of good reading.
   d. Good readers usually read quickly.

8. Reading with speed depends on
   a. Your vocabulary.
   b. A smooth interaction between the reader and writer.
   c. Similar interests between the reader and the writer.
   d. A set of reader-writer variables.

9. Reading is ______.
   a. Primarily visual
   b. Just mental
   c. A difficult task
   d. A cognitive process

10. The phrase "reconstruct the writer's meaning" implies that readers
   a. Change the author's meaning to match their personal experiences.
   b. Interpret what the author meant.
   c. Put the author's original thought back together.
   d. Must read quickly enough to take in the author's meaning.

Expand Your Thinking

Use these activities to expand your understanding of the ideas in this article.

1. The following discussion questions will help you comprehend the major text points and develop your own thoughts about the topic.
   a. What is the authors' main point in this essay?
   b. What three questions should you ask when the reading seems difficult?
   c. What are the four common misconceptions about reading?
   d. Did you have any of the four misconceptions about reading before you read this essay? How did you acquire these false ideas?
   e. How do you think the misconceptions affect readers' attitudes about reading? How do you think they affect the way people read?
   f. If you could speak to teachers, what would you tell them about how to teach reading?
2. Take notes on this reading.

Check Your Motivation

1. Review your reading goal. Did you achieve it? Explain.
2. Make a list of the new ideas that you've gained from this text. Think about how they will be useful to you in the future.
3. Assess your current motivation. Think about how you read this text. Then mark each statement:

A = not at all B = a little C = fairly well D = very well

	A	B	C	D
To engage my interest, I . . .				
1. initiated an "I want to read about this" attitude.	___	___	___	___
2. preread the text.	___	___	___	___
3. identified the topic and/or thought about relevant or interesting points before reading.	___	___	___	___
4. looked for the author's organization before reading.	___	___	___	___
5. set a reading goal before reading.	___	___	___	___
To focus my efforts, I . . .				
6. chose my methods and had an "I know how to read this" attitude.	___	___	___	___
7. read where I was able to concentrate.	___	___	___	___
8. formed questions and read to find answers and other important points.	___	___	___	___

To monitor my progress, I . . .

9. felt confident and had an "I believe I can read this well" attitude. ___ ___ ___ ___
10. solved any reading problems during reading. (Mark D if there were none.) ___ ___ ___ ___
11. marked the text as I read. ___ ___ ___ ___
12. recited parts or all of the text. ___ ___ ___ ___

To reflect on my gains, I . . .

13. had an "I've accomplished something" attitude once I finished. ___ ___ ___ ___
14. recognized the new or useful information I gained. ___ ___ ___ ___
15. rewarded myself. ___ ___ ___ ___

SCORING: Write the number of answers you marked in each column in the following spaces. Compute the column scores, and then add them up to determine your total score.

# of A's ______ × 1 pt. = ______
# of B's ______ × 2 pt. = ______
# of C's ______ × 3 pt. = ______
# of D's ______ × 4 pt. = ______
Total points = ______

INTERPRETATION: 15–43 points = low motivation; 44–60 points = high motivation

4. Compute your reading rate by following these steps:

Rate Box

1. **RECORD** your END time here: ____________
2. **RECORD** your START time here: ____________
3. **DETERMINE** your TOTAL reading time here: ____________
4. **ROUND OFF** the seconds to the nearest ¼ minute. For example, 4 minutes, 15 seconds would be 4.25. Write this on the **** line.
5. **DIVIDE** the number of words by your rounded off time:

657 words / ______ (****) = ______ WPM

5. Record your rate, comprehension, vocabulary, and motivation scores on the Progress Charts that are on the inside front and back covers of this text.

Reading for Learning Methods

Why do textbooks require more effort than other types of reading materials? What's mentally involved when you're reading a textbook? What techniques have you found that help you comprehend textbook chapters?

Reading and learning from textbooks is a major task in almost every college course. This kind of reading can take twice as much time (or more) as in-class activities. In addition to time, college reading assignments require considerable thinking to understand the concepts, recognize what you do and don't know, and identify what you will need to learn. How you approach this multitask job has everything to do with how much you get out of the time you spend. As the following quote suggests, your own intellectual efforts dramatically affect your understanding and ability to handle textbook reading challenges.

CHAPTER 5 READING FOR LEARNING METHODS

> To pass from understanding less to understanding more by your own intellectual effort in reading is something like pulling yourself up by your bootstraps.
>
> — Adler and Van Doren, *How to Read a Book* (8)

Before you read . . .

Engage Your Interest: preread and divide

This chapter presents the intellectual approaches that create in-depth understanding of textbooks. Here's an outline of the chapter.

I. Introduction
II. Preread and Divide for Organization
   A. Preread the Textbook
   B. Preread and Divide the Chapter
   C. Preread and Divide the Section
III. Question and Read for In-depth Comprehension
   A. Vary Your Level of Thinking
   B. Extend Your Margin Notes
IV. Recite and Review for Future Learning
   A. Compose
      1. Paraphrase
      2. Summarize
      3. Answer Review Questions
   B. Take Notes
      1. Guidelines
      2. Formats

After you preread and divide the chapter into reading tasks, set a goal for each one. Be specific about the task, topic, and reward(s).

1. I want to ________________ about ____.
My reward(s) will be ____
____.

2. I want to ________________ about ____.
My reward(s) will be ____
____.

3. I want to ________________ about ____.
My reward(s) will be ____
____.

As you read . . .

Focus Your Efforts: question and read

Textbooks are demanding. Just from a visual standpoint, they often look complicated: they may use multiple-colored headings of different sizes, paragraphs with different font styles, graphics, articles inserted in the middle of chapters, margin notes, practice exercises, and review questions. Further, because they focus on **technical informa-**

tion—the knowledge that experts in the field use—the discussions are often long, complex, and loaded with new terms and information. Finally, you need to both understand the text and prepare for later learning sessions, which adds to an already challenging task. Successfully handling all of the textbook aspects and your own needs is what reading for learning entails. How can it be done?

> **Everyone has to learn to think differently, bigger, to open to possibilities.**
>
> —Oprah Winfrey (1954–), American producer and author

The active reading PDQ3R processes (see Chapter 2) are the fundamental approach, because they promote your motivation. But to unravel complex concepts and master textbook information, you will need to expand those steps, as well as your reading skills. The next three chapters are devoted to perfecting your comprehension skills for ideas, details, and graphics. This chapter presents expanded PDQ3R techniques for handling the challenges of textbooks, and enhancing your ability to

- Preread and Divide for Organization
- Question and Read for In-depth Comprehension
- Recite and Review for Future Learning

Preread and Divide for Organization

THINK ABOUT THIS . . .

How do you use these textbook features? Check off what you usually do when you come to each one of the following.

WHEN I SEE THIS FEATURE, I . . .	SKIP IT	SKIM IT	READ IT	THINK ABOUT IT
Preface				
Table of Contents				
Glossary				
Answer Key				
Chapter Title				
Headings				
Bold-faced words				

(continued)

WHEN I SEE THIS FEATURE, I . . .	SKIP IT	SKIM IT	READ IT	THINK ABOUT IT
Tables, figures, and graphics				
Inserted articles				
Chapter summary				
End-of-chapter study questions				

Understanding complex textbook concepts depends on your recognition of how the information is organized. More specifically, you must be able to identify the way the chapter topic is broken down into concepts, the pieces of information that contribute to each concept, how all the pieces relate to each other, and what's important. The ***Think about this*** . . . task lists common **textbook aids,** which are features designed to present the organization of the information, increase motivation, and aid your reading-for-learning efforts. Many students overlook these aids, thinking that they are unnecessary and a waste of time. Nothing could be further from the truth. Using these aids as you preread and divide can transform the chapter from busyness to order and from endless pages to meaningful content. But to get the most out of them, you have to use them at different times and for different purposes.

Preread the Textbook

Prereading the book is a one-time insurance task. Some students only read what's assigned and fail to discover the author's explanation of how the information is organized, helpful supplemental information in the appendices, or answer keys for the exercises. Prereading the text ensures that you won't waste time struggling to comprehend information that is directly provided by the author. The aids that address this kind of information are called **general aids.** They organize the entire book, provide tools to locate information, and present useful, supplementary information. Think of them as the blueprint and the chapters as the rooms in a building you are constructing. Looking at the blueprint obviously makes the construction much easier.

The most common general aids and the function of each one are listed in Table 5.1. Two of the most useful general aids for quickly understanding the organization of the text are the Brief Table of Contents and the Preface.

The Brief Table of Contents is the most useful tool for quickly seeing what's in the entire book. It lists what comes before the chapters, the chapter titles, and the aids that come at the end of the text. As you identify the aids that come before and after the chapters, turn to them and determine what they contain. Later, when you need the information, you'll know it's there.

TABLE 5.1 **Common General Aids**

AID	FUNCTION
Brief Table of Contents	Lists all of the general aids and chapters
Alternate Table of Contents	Lists the features or special types of content that are common to more than one chapter
Preface	Identifies the purpose and organization of the book
Glossary	Lists the technical terms and definitions presented in the book
Answer Key	Provides answers for selected exercises and questions
Appendices	Gives background or reference information to make it easier to understand some of the topics
Index	Lists each concept, topic, or key term and all the pages where it's mentioned in alphabetical order
CDs and Web sites	Provides supplementary resources and learning aids

The Preface presents the author's organizational scheme for the book. It can transform your initial view that the book is confusing, uninteresting, and complex. It may include any of these:

- The purpose of the book.
- The organizational framework for the book, units, and chapters.
- The organizational layout for each chapter.
- A list of the chapter aids.
- Expert tips about how to read and learn the information in the text.

The second item, the framework for the book, is particularly useful. The chapters will be more meaningful if you recognize how they are arranged. Most texts cover the subject for one college course, which is indicated in the title. The subject is usually divided into major parts called units, which present large issues in the field. Each chapter presents one part of the issue, and all of the chapters are generally arranged in a basic-to-complex order. Recognizing the issues and their parts ensures that you understand the scope of the book and the importance of each chapter.

What is the perspective of the author of this text and how does that shape my perceived meaning?

—Jim Burke (contemporary),
American teacher and author

ACTIVITY 1: PREREAD THE BOOK

DIRECTIONS: Use the general aids in this book to complete the following tasks.

1. Look at the Brief Table of Contents to answer these questions.
   a. What aids come before Chapter 1? What do you think is the purpose of each one?

   b. What aids come after the last chapter? What is the purpose of each one?

2. Review the preface to this book, A Note to Students (p. xxiii). Then answer these questions:
   a. Why is this text called *Empowered College Reading: Motivation Matters*?

   b. What is the purpose of this textbook? How does that relate to you?

   c. How is the book organized into units?

   d. From the suggestions for how to use the chapter aids, select two that seem to be very useful. How will these aids help you to develop your reading?

Preread and Divide the Chapter

General methods for prereading and dividing textbook chapters were already covered in Chapter 2. The emphasis here is on improving your understanding of the chapter organization by placing more emphasis on the **chapter aids.** These aids are tailored to the chapter information, provide motivational tools, highlight what's important, and guide your reading for learning processes. Chapter aids include the Detailed Table of Contents, aids in the introduction (anything that comes between the chapter title and the first major heading) and aids in the conclusion (anything that comes after the last paragraph in the last section).

The most common chapter aids are listed in Table 5.2.

TABLE 5.2 **Common Chapter Aids**

AID	FUNCTION
Detailed Table of Contents	List the primary headings and end of chapter aids
Introductory Aids	
Objectives	Lists what you should gain from the chapter
Outlines or maps	Presents the author's outline and chapter headings
Pictures, human-interest stories, quotes	Motivate and engage interest in the topic
Background information	Reminds readers what they know or presents basic information needed to understand the chapter
Sentences about the chapter, its main idea, or purpose	Explain the underlying main point of the chapter
Concluding Aids	
Summary	Provides a condensed version of the major ideas
Vocabulary list	Lists the technical terms introduced in the chapter
Review questions	Activities to test comprehension and memory of the content
Practice exercises	Provide skill development materials

> **If you want to understand today, you have to search yesterday.**
>
> —Pearl S. Buck (1892–1973), American novelist

Here's what to cover and look for as you Preread and Divide the chapter:

1. The Detailed Table of Contents
   a. Look at the unit; recognize how the chapter fits into it.
   b. Look at the title; identify the chapter topic.

   c. Look at the chapter headings; outline number and letter them. (As mentioned in Chapter 2, page 68, it's useful to insert "I. Intro." before the first heading.)
   d. Look at the page numbers and size of each section; divide the assignment into easy tasks.
   e. Form a goal for each task.
2. The Introductory Aids
   a. Look for statements about how the chapter is organized.
   b. Look for statements about the main idea or purpose of the chapter.
   c. Look for background information and other points or aids to engage your interest.
3. The Concluding Aids
   a. Skim the conclusion; identify the major chapter points.
   b. Skim the vocabulary list; notice the technical terms to read about.
   c. Skim the questions and practice tasks; think of them as a guide to your reading.

Notice that in this expanded version of Prereading, you don't need to look at the aids in the middle of the chapter. You still can, of course, look at anything that's helpful or interesting to you. But those aids will be more useful when you turn your attention to reading each of the major sections.

> **No one can become really educated without having pursued some study in which he took no interest. For it is part of education to interest ourselves in subjects for which we have no aptitude.**
>
> —T. S. Eliot (1888–1965), British poet and critic

ACTIVITY 2: PREREAD AND DIVIDE THE CHAPTER

DIRECTIONS: Use the Detailed Table of Contents and Chapter 6 of this textbook to complete these tasks.

1. Using the Detailed Table of Contents, answer these questions:
   a. What is the topic of Chapter 6? ____________________
   b. How does Chapter 6 fit into Unit 2? Why do you think it comes after this one?

   ____

   ____

   ____

   ____

   c. Number the headings in outline style. Insert "I. Intro." before the first heading.

d. How many major sections or concepts are covered in Chapter 6? ______

e. How might you divide this chapter up into reading tasks?

____

____

f. Form a goal for your first task:

I want to ____________________ about ______________________________.

My reward(s) will be ____

____.

2. Look over the introduction to Chapter 6. List three of the aids. How could each one increase your motivation? How could it aid your reading?

   a. ____________________

   Motivation aid: ______________________________

   Comprehension aid: ______________________________

   b. ____________________

   Motivation aid: ______________________________

   Comprehension aid: ______________________________

   c. ____________________

   Motivation aid: ______________________________

   Comprehension aid: ______________________________

3. Look over the conclusion to Chapter 6. List three of the aids. How could each one increase your motivation? How could it aid your reading?

   a. ____________________

   Motivation aid: ______________________________

   Comprehension aid: ______________________________

   b. ____________________

   Motivation aid: ______________________________

   Comprehension aid: ______________________________

   c. ____________________

   Motivation aid: ______________________________

   Comprehension aid: ______________________________

Preread and Divide the Section

To read new and complex technical information well, you need a high level of motivation, an initial understanding of the topic's organization, and advance notice of what to emphasize. A chapter prereading can get you interested in the overall topic, but it won't satisfy these section-specific needs. That's why you will want to preread and divide each major section before you begin to read.

I read part of it all the way through.

—Sam Goldwyn (1882–1974), American film producer, founder of MGM

TABLE 5.3 **Common Section Aids**

AID	FUNCTION
Bold-faced headings	Label each section of information with a heading from the chapter outline
Bold-faced terms	Highlight the technical terms presented in the chapter
Graphics	Provide visual aids to explain or support the information
Inserted articles	Present human interest stories and real life applications of the information to make it more relevant
Margin notes	Highlight key points or vocabulary in a paragraph
Questions	Give readers a way to check their understanding or promote thinking about a key point
Activities	Provide surveys and reflection questions to help readers recognize what they already know or how to relate to the information
Exercises	Provide practice and skill development materials

The aids within the major sections are designed to increase your interest in and comprehension of the topic. Table 5.3 lists the most common ones.

Most of these aids are probably familiar to you. One new one might be the inserted article. This textbook does not use that aid, but many texts do. To see an example, look at the article "Courting Throughout U.S. History" in the chapter *Choosing Others,* which you will find on the CD-ROM. Notice how this article is separated from the chapter paragraphs by a special heading and a colored background. Generally, all section aids will use boxes, special fonts, or background colors to make them stand out so that you'll notice and use them.

When you preread and divide a section, there may be a lot to look at. So choose what's most interesting and useful to you. Here's a list of what you might cover:

1. The headings
   a. Look at the major heading; it usually states the section topic.
   b. Number and letter the subheadings and minor headings; notice the topic parts.
2. The first paragraph

   Look for an introduction that states the main idea, purpose, or organization of the section.
3. The graphics and inserted articles

   Skim over any graphics, articles, margin notes, questions, and activities; recognize which ones will aid your motivation and which will aid your comprehension.
4. The summary and concluding aids

   Skim the relevant parts of the summary, keywords, questions, and exercises at the end of the chapter; pay special attention to the main ideas and important information emphasized during reading.

Notice that the summary and concluding aids are used in both the chapter and section prereading. For the chapter prereading, look over the entire aid; it will give you an overview of the assignment. During a section prereading, look at only what's relevant to the section and identify what to emphasize as you read. How will you find the right concluding parts quickly? Sometimes they will be labeled with headings. But even without those labels, the concluding aids are always presented in chapter order. So, keep the section heading in mind as you look through the concluding aids, and you'll easily find the parts that go with it.

ACTIVITY 3: PREREAD AND DIVIDE A SECTION

DIRECTIONS: Assume that the following text section is an assigned reading in a sociology course. Do a section preread and answer these questions.

1. The headings:
   a. What is the section topic? ______________________________
   b. How many parts does this section have? ______
   c. Outline number and letter all the headings. (Assume there was "I. Intro" before this. So start with II.)
2. Based on the first paragraph, what idea will the section emphasize?

   ____

   ____
3. Look at the graphics. What interesting points do they cover?

   ____

   ____
4. What kind of margin notes, questions, or activities are there?

   ____

   ____

   ____
5. Look at the section summary and concluding aids.
   a. What major points does the summary emphasize?

   ____

   ____

   b. From the other aids, what else should you focus on during reading?

   ____

   ____

Alternative Family Forms

Most families in the United States are still composed of a married couple who, at some point, raise children. But in recent decades, our society has displayed greater diversity in family life.

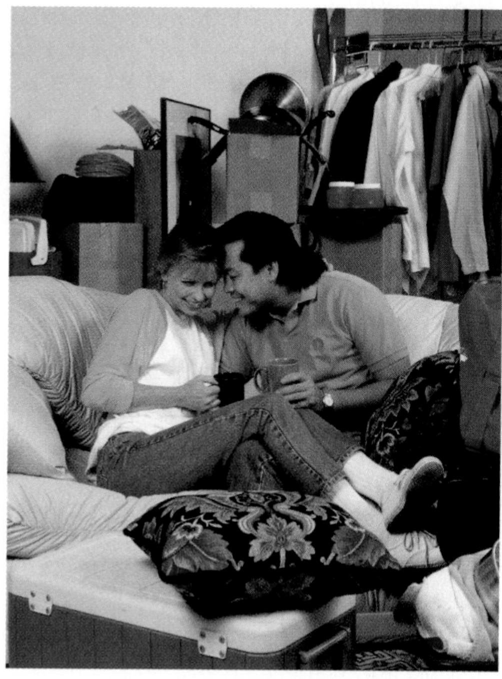

In recent years, the proportion of young people who cohabit—that is, live together without being married—has risen sharply. This trend contributes to the debate over what is and is not a family: Do you consider a cohabiting couple a family? Why or why not?

One-Parent Families

Twenty-nine percent of U.S. families with children under eighteen have only one parent in the household, a proportion that more than doubled during the last generation. Put another way, 27 percent of U.S. children now live with only one parent, and about half will do so before reaching eighteen. One-parent families—80 percent of which are headed by a single mother—result from divorce, death, or an unmarried woman's decision to have a child.

Single parenthood increases a woman's risk of poverty because it limits her ability to work and to further her education. The converse is also true: Poverty raises the odds that a young woman will become a single mother (Trent, 1994). But single parenthood goes well beyond the poor, since at least one-third of women in the United States become pregnant as unmarried teenagers, and many decide to raise their children whether they marry or not. . . . Note that 52 percent of African American families are headed by a single parent. Single parenting is less common among Hispanics (32 percent), Asian Americans (20 percent), and non-Hispanic whites (18 percent). In many single-parent families, mothers turn to their own mothers for support. In the United States, then, the rise in single parenting is tied to a declining role for fathers and the growing importance of grandparenting.

Research shows that growing up in a one-parent family usually disadvantages children. Some studies claim that because a father and a mother each make distinctive contributions to a child's social development, it is unrealistic to expect one parent alone to do as good a job. But the most serious problem for one-parent families, especially if that parent is a woman, is poverty. On average, children growing up in a single-parent family start out poorer, get less schooling, and end up with lower incomes as adults. Such children are also more likely to be single parents themselves (Astone & McLanahan, 1991; Li & Wojtkiewicz, 1992; Biblarz & Raftery, 1993; Popenoe, 1993; Blankenhorn, 1995; Shapiro & Schrof, 1995; Webster, Orbuch, & House, 1995; Wu, 1996; Duncan et al., 1998; Kantrowitz & Wingert, 2001; McLanahan, 2002).

Cohabitation

Cohabitation is *the sharing of a household by an unmarried couple.* The number of cohabiting couples in the United States increased from about 500,000 in 1970 to about 5.5 million today (almost 5 million heterosexual couples and 0.6 million homosexual couples), or about 9 percent of all couples (Miller, 1997; U.S. Census Bureau, 2003).

In global perspective, cohabitation as a long-term form of family life, with or without children, is common in Sweden and other Scandinavian nations. But it is rare in more traditional (and Roman Catholic) nations such as Italy. Cohabitation is gaining in popularity in the United States, with almost half of people between ages twenty-five and forty-four having cohabited at some point.

Cohabiting tends to appeal to more independent-minded individuals as well as those who favor gender equality (Brines & Joyner, 1999). Most couples cohabit for no more than a few years, about half then deciding to marry and half ending the relationship. Mounting evidence suggests that living together may actually discourage marriage because partners (some research points especially to men) become used to low-commitment relationships. For this reason, cohabiting couples who have children—currently representing about one in eight births—may not always be long-term parents. Figure 18–5 shows that just 5 percent of children born to cohabiting couples will

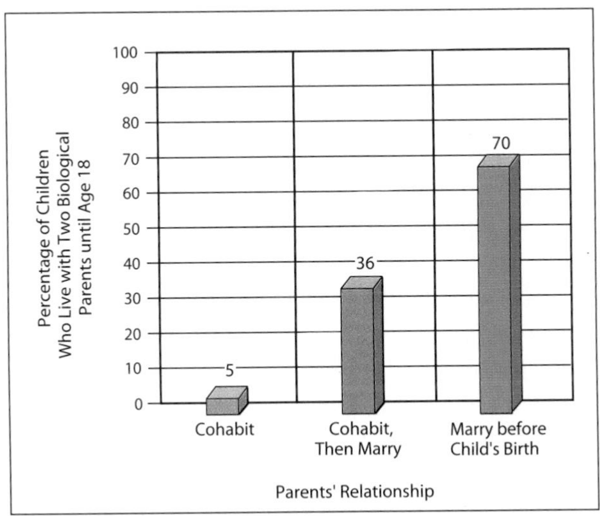

FIGURE 18–5 Parental Involvement in Children's Lives: Cohabiting and Married Parents

Source: Phillips (2001).

live until age eighteen with both biological parents who remain unmarried. The share rises to 36 percent among children whose parents marry at some point, but even this is half of the 70 percent figure among children whose parents married before they were born. When cohabiting couples with children separate, the involvement of both parents, including financial support, is far from certain (Popenoe & Whitehead, 1999; Smock, 2000; Phillips, 2001; Zimmer, 2001; Scommegna, 2002).

Gay and Lesbian Couples

In 1989, Denmark became the first country to lift its legal ban on same-sex marriages. This change offered social legitimacy to gay and lesbian couples and equalized advantages in inheritance, taxation, and joint property ownership. Norway (in 1993), Sweden (1995), the Netherlands (2001), and Canada (2003) have followed suit. In 1996, however, the U.S. Congress passed a law banning gay marriage. Homosexual marriage is also illegal in all fifty states, although Vermont and Hawaii, as well as a number of major cities, including San Francisco and New York, confer limited marital benefits on gay and lesbian couples. Whereas about one-third of U.S. adults support gay marriage, half support civil unions providing the rights enjoyed by married couples (Gallup, 2002). Among U.S. college students, as Figure 18–6 shows, opposition to homosexual relationships fell from almost half in the 1970s to about one-fourth in 2001 (Astin et al., 2002).

Most gay couples with children in the United States are raising the offspring of previous heterosexual unions; some couples have adopted children. But many gay parents are quiet about their sexual orientation, not wishing to draw unwelcome attention to their children. Moreover, in several widely publicized cases, courts have removed children from homosexual couples, citing the best interests of the children.

Gay parenting challenges many traditional ideas. But it also shows that many gay people want to form families just as heterosexuals do (Gross, 1991; Pressley & Andrews, 1992; Henry, 1993).

Singlehood

Because nine out of ten people in the United States marry, we tend to see singlehood as a passing stage of life. In recent decades, however, more people are deliberately choosing to live alone. In 1950, just one household in ten contained a single person; by 2002, this share had risen to one in four: a total of 51 million single adults (U.S. Census Bureau, 2003).

Most striking is the rising number of single young women. In 1960, 28 percent of U.S. women aged twenty to twenty-four were single; by 2002, the proportion had soared to 74 percent. Underlying this trend is women's greater participation in the labor force. Women who are economically secure view a husband as a matter of choice rather than a financial necessity (Edwards, 2000).

By midlife, many unmarried women sense a lack of available men. Because we expect a woman to "marry up," the older a woman is, the more education she has, and the better her job, the more difficulty she has finding a suitable husband.

The following parts are from the end of the chapter.

Summary
Our society's family life is becoming more varied. One-parent families, cohabitation, gay and lesbian couples and singlehood have proliferated in recent years. While the law does not recognize homosexual marriages, many gay men and lesbians form long-lasting relationships and, increasingly, are becoming parents.

Key Concepts
cohabitation: the sharing of a household by an unmarried couple.

Critical Thinking Question
On balance, are families in the United States becoming weaker or simply different? What evidence can you cite? (Adapted from Macionis 479–481, 484–485)

Before you go on . . .
Monitor Your Progress: recite

As you read . . .
Focus Your Efforts: question and read

Question and Read for In-depth Comprehension

THINK ABOUT THIS . . .

Consider these two questions:

A. What do you need to shop for this week?
B. Is it better to shop for electronics at a discount store, an electronics dealer, or online?

1. How do these questions differ?

____

____

2. What would you have to do to prepare a good answer for question *a*?

____

____

3. What would you have to do to prepare a good answer for question *b*?

____

____

____

____

4. Before reading this section, preread and divide it. Look at the introductory paragraphs, the subheadings, the graphics, as well as the summary and questions about this section that appear at the end of the chapter. Outline number the headings.

The ***Think about this*** . . . questions illustrate that all questions and intellectual tasks are not the same. Question *a* is simple, based on personal experience, and just requires a moment of time to record a list. Question *b*, on the other hand, is complicated. It has three options, and to choose the best, you would first have to decide what's most important to you: price, service, delivery speed, or selection. Then you'd have to investigate the various options to determine which one offers you the most.

Similarly, reading tasks also vary in terms of what you need to do and how much thinking is required. Some need only a basic reading approach to locate and list important information. Other tasks require more in-depth comprehension to figure out what the pieces of information are and how they work together. Two effective ways to handle this variety and ensure that you achieve in-depth understanding when needed are using various levels of thinking and extending your margin notes.

Vary Your Level of Thinking

What are the various levels of thinking? In general, **levels of thinking** refer to the degree of understanding a reader has about a topic. It can range from very simple to very complex. More specifically, the levels refer to the complexity of questions that readers form about a text or comments they make about it. Once you know the levels, you can easily change your thinking at will and dramatically improve your comprehension.

For reading and thinking purposes, six levels are relevant. Starting with the lowest level, they are knowledge, comprehension, application, analysis, synthesis, and evaluation. The first level, knowledge, may seem out of place to you, because you think of knowledge as all of the results of reading and learning. But in this system, it refers to the most basic understanding—just the start of thinking.

While the system is not rigid, the six types of thinking are more or less sequential: That is, you will usually have to understand something at one level before you can work at the next, and at each level you comprehend more and can do more with the information than you did at the lower level. Examples of the types of thinking for each of the levels are presented in Table 5.4. Read the information carefully; the tables include the specific characteristics of each level of thinking.

Notice that the levels are divided into two groups. The first group of three levels is called *lower-level thinking*, because readers at these levels rely only on the text

TABLE 5.4 **Levels of Thinking for Comprehension**

LEVEL *Characteristics and what you can do*	SAMPLE QUESTIONS AND COMMENTS *(Note: The last item for each level is a template that you can use with any text to get to that level.)*
Lower-level thinking ***Knowledge*** Locate and repeat information or ideas from the text.	1. What are the six levels of thinking? The six levels are knowledge, comprehension, application, analysis, synthesis, and evaluation. They label different degrees of understanding. 2. What does the text say about ______? The text states that . . .
Comprehension Understand, explain, and paraphrase text information.	1. Explain what the comprehension level is. The comprehension level means that you understand the text and can clarify and interpret the information in your own words and sentences. 2. What is the main point of this text? The main point is . . .
Application Relate the text information to real world situations; solve hypothetical problems that are similar to those presented in the text.	1. How do the levels of thinking apply to the way I read? I usually read at the first three levels: I locate important information, understand it, and think about how it applies to me or situations I know about. 2. How can a reader test his/her understanding of a technical term in a course? To ensure understanding, the reader should paraphrase the definition using his/her own vocabulary and sentences. 3. How does this relate to my life? How could this problem be handled? I often . . . To solve this problem . . .
Higher-level thinking ***Analysis*** Figure out logical relationships that are not stated in the text; break the text down into sequences, advantages, disadvantages, comparisons, contrasts, categories, causes, or effects.	1. What are the advantages of using the levels of thinking? This system gives the reader guidelines for getting varying degrees of comprehension from texts. 2. How are ______ and ______ similar? Different? Both ______ and ______ are . . . The differences are . . . What categories can ______ be divided into? ______ can be divided into . . . What caused ______? What are the results of ______? The causes of ______ are . . . The effects are . . .

(continued)

TABLE 5.4 **Levels of Thinking for Comprehension *(continued)***

LEVEL *Characteristics and what you can do*	SAMPLE QUESTIONS AND COMMENTS *(Note: The last item for each level is a template that you can use with any text to get to that level.)*
Higher-level thinking ***Synthesis*** Combine separate pieces of information and explain how they can be combined; predict trends and outcomes; determine problems along with their causes and effects; propose solutions that the author did not cover.	1. How can the levels of thinking be used with PDQ3R? The levels of thinking can be used during the question step. They can also be used during reading, reciting, and review. 2. What are the long-term trends/outcomes of _____? Over time, _____ will . . . What problems are there in _____? Explain them. The problems are . . . Their causes/effects are . . .
Evaluation Develop appropriate criteria for judging the value of some-thing and use them to make and explain a judgment.	1. How could a reader judge the effect of using the levels of thinking? If successful, each level should provide more in-depth understanding and more to say about the text. So, as the levels are used, the reader should be able to add more explanations about the information. 2. What characteristics should be to used when judging _____? The criteria for judging _____ are . . . Using those criteria, what is the value of _____? _____ ranks high (or low), because . . .

"What you can do" adapted from Carin, Arthur A. & Sund, Robert B. (1971). *Developing questioning techniques.* Columbus, OH: Merrill, pp.56–72.

information to form their thoughts. The second group of three levels is called *higher level thinking,* because readers go beyond the text and use independent thinking to draw logical conclusions.

Take special note of the application level of thinking; it's particularly useful for two reasons. First, application thinking serves as a bridge between the two levels. It doesn't require a lot of time, but thinking about how the information applies to you or to real-life situations makes it much easier to come up with insights that were not covered in the text. Second, this level is particularly motivating. When information is relevant to you, it's automatically more interesting.

Here's an example of a paragraph from a sociology textbook about the importance of groups and how the levels of thinking can be applied to it.

EXAMPLE

Groups are essential to human life. They shape our goals, our values, our behavior, and our self-concepts. In a very real sense, we are different people in different groups. Compare what you are like at home with how you behave as a member of a team or among your close friends. The differences result from the fact that we occupy different statuses and play different roles in different groups. (Lindsey and Beach, 69)

Lower level questions and statements

Knowledge: What is the paragraph about?

Groups are essential to human life.

Comprehension: How are groups essential to human life?

Group membership affects our goals, values, self-concept, and behavior.

Application: How am I different in different groups?

I tend to be a leader in my writing group but a follower in my family.

Higher level questions and statements

Analysis: What are the different roles that people can play in groups?

In groups, I think people can be leaders, followers, helpers, critics, or bystanders.

Synthesis: How could the groups that teenagers belong to affect their adult life?

It could diminish career choices. A football player, for example, might not think about becoming an artist because competition would be emphasized more than creativity.

Evaluation: What criteria would you use to judge whether a group is successful?

Successful groups should promote the individual's self-confidence and goals. They should be comfortable and safe places to think. Finally, they should have successful ways of resolving conflicts.

Every thought we think is creating our future.

—Louise L. Hay (contemporary), American metaphysical lecturer and author

ACTIVITY 4: USE THE LEVELS OF THINKING

DIRECTIONS: Read the following paragraph about the benefits of chocolate. Then form a question or a comment at each level of thinking.

Health Food?

When 35 million people in the United States got their loved ones boxes of chocolates last Valentine's Day, they knew they were giving sweet comfort—but health food? Sometimes described as "sinfully delicious," chocolate has often been a source of guilt for those who indulge (or overindulge) in it. Chocolate candy is certainly a significant source of fat and sugar calories, but recent research suggests that chocolate itself—the dark, bitter powder made from the seeds within cacao pods—may also be a significant source of protective molecules. Medical scientists have known for some time that many things that go wrong with our bodies can be traced to destructive molecules called free radicals. Many free radicals contain oxygen in a form that reacts strongly with, and damages, various biological molecules and their cellular structures. This process is called oxidative stress and it is a fact of life, because as our cells use energy, they naturally produce free radicals. So what's a person to do? Well, maybe eat chocolate! (Adapted from Audesirk et al. 21) (168 words)

1. Knowledge: ______________________________

2. Comprehension: ______________________________

3. Application: ______________________________

4. Analysis: ______________________________

5. Synthesis: ______________________________

6. Evaluation: ______________________________

In addition to forming their own questions, students often have to answer those that authors and instructors create. These questions usually span the levels of thinking. One, for example, may require a basic, knowledge response, and another, a much more complex synthesis of several pieces of information. Here's an example of some textbook questions from a chapter entitled "Networking and Security" in a computer science textbook.

EXAMPLE

Knowledge:	What are the two types of computer hackers?
Comprehension:	Explain how a hacker gains access to a computer.
Application:	Can your next door neighbor use his wireless-equipped notebook to surf off your Internet connection?
Analysis:	What do you think are the advantages and disadvantages of wireless computer technology?
Synthesis:	What precautions should the U.S. military take to ensure that networks involving national defense remain secure from terrorist attacks?
Evaluation:	Hackers often argue that hacking is for the good of all people since it points out flaws in computer systems. Do you agree with this? Why or why not? (Adapted from Evans et al. 291)

Identifying the level that is needed for a quality answer is part of reading and understanding these questions. When you will be graded on your responses, answering at the wrong level usually lowers your score. Low-level answers to high-level questions are generally marked down because they're incomplete. And high-level answers on low-level questions are often marked down because they drift off the topic.

To identify the level of thinking, look at a question and determine what you would have to do to answer it. If you're asked to copy or simply name items using the text information, the level is knowledge. If you have to explain the text information, it's comprehension. Applying the information to the real world or yourself, or solving problems, requires application thinking. If you're asked to figure out information like causes or effects that weren't given in the text, that's the analysis level. If you're asked to combine information from different sources, predict trends, or discuss problems and solutions not mentioned in the text, that's synthesis. And, finally, if you're asked to judge the merits of an idea, object, or plan, you're being asked to evaluate it.

ACTIVITY 5: IDENTIFY THE LEVELS OF THINKING

DIRECTIONS: Match the level of thinking that would be required to answer each of these textbook questions.

a. knowledge
b. comprehension
c. application
d. analysis
e. synthesis
f. evaluation

The following questions come from a chapter about software programming in an introductory computer science textbook that explains how databases, like online purchasing tools or bank account information, are created and the common languages used to develop them.

______ **1.** What do you think the computer programming languages of the future should be able to do?

______ **2.** Identify the most common computer applications used in small businesses.

______ **3.** Explain what machine languages are.

______ **4.** Companies use beta testing to detect problems before releasing the final version to the retail market. What programs would you be interested in beta testing?

______ **5.** What do you think are the risks involved in beta testing a software program?

______ **6.** Some companies make their programmers sign agreements to prevent them from using code developed for one company with a new employer or competitor. Do you think that this is an appropriate requirement? (Adapted from Evans et al. 422–424)

The following questions come from a chapter about religion in a sociology textbook. The chapter covers basic concepts of religion, historical information, the effects of religion on social change, and facts about religion in the United States.

_____ **1.** Some colleges are decidedly religious; other are passionately secular. What place does religion hold on your campus?

_____ **2.** What evidence can you cite that suggests that religion is declining in importance in the United States? In what ways does religion seem to be getting stronger?

_____ **3.** Go to the library or local newspaper office. Obtain an issue of your local newspaper published 50 years ago and one published within the past month. Compare the amount of attention to religious issues then and now.

_____ **4.** Explain the difference between the sacred and the profane as outlined in this chapter.

_____ **5.** How did Karl Marx view the effect of religion on society? (Adapted from Macionis 514)

You don't understand anything until you learn it more than one way.

—Marvin Minsky (1929–),
American professor and scientist

Extend Your Margin Notes

Marking, including underlining key words and making margin notes, was introduced in Chapter 2. Those basic techniques capture what you comprehend during reading, and they are usually at the lower levels of thinking. So students with similar educational backgrounds would probably have very similar basic marking on the same assignment: They would distinguish what's important from what is not, label the topic or definitions for later review, and include lower level questions created from the headings and key words.

In contrast, extended margin notes capture higher level thinking and, as the cartoon emphasizes, are a very personal matter.

Table 5.5 provides a quick guide to basic and extended marking techniques.

TABLE 5.5 **Guide to Basic and Extended Marking**

LEVEL OF THINKING	UNDERLINING	MARGIN NOTES
Basic		
Knowledge and Comprehension	The topic Main ideas Details	1. The paragraph topic 2. Labels about important types of information (definitions, facts, examples) 3. Your reading questions 4. Very brief notes that sum up complex ideas 5. Your personal ideas about the topic 6. Symbols to note special parts (a question mark for a confusing part, T for a possible test item, a star for something important)
Application		7. References to personal situations 8. Reference to real-life situations
Extended		
Analysis		9. Steps, causes, effects, parts, similarities, differences, advantages that you think of
Synthesis		10. Trends, problems, solutions that you think of 11. Insights that link separate parts of the text, the text to other sources, the text to other things you know
Evaluation		12. Your judgments about the author's points

Underlining can be used at any level.

Here's an example of basic and extended marking on a paragraph about radio advertising from a marketing textbook. Note the terms *advantages* and *disadvantages*. They are not in the paragraph and, thus, reflect analysis level thinking. The level of thinking for each margin note is listed in parentheses.

EXAMPLE

Radio advertising can be very effective. About eight percent of all advertising outlays goes to radio advertising. Over 227 million people—or 96 percent of all persons aged 12 and older in the United States—listen to the radio each day. Radio ads are inexpensive. A small business in a Midwestern town of 100,000 people pays about $20 for a 30-second local radio spot. (A television spot

Radio ad—why effective? (Knowledge/Comprehension)

Advantages (Analysis)

1. 96% of people 12+ (Knowledge)

2. cheap (Comprehension)

costs over $250.) In addition, because stations are usually segmented into categories such as rock 'n' roll, news, and jazz, audiences are largely segmented. Unfortunately, radio ads, like TV ads, go by quickly, and people tend to use the radio as background while doing other things. (Griffin and Ebert, 369)

3. categories (Knowledge)
Me: jazz & news (Application)
Disadvantages (Analysis)
1. quick (Knowledge)
2. poor attention (Comprehension)

I think ads are cheap & good for small businesses. (Evaluation)

Would you mark every paragraph this way? Probably not. Most textbook paragraphs contain important information that requires basic underlining and margin notes. But on the most complex and important parts where in-depth understanding is needed, do apply multiple levels of thinking and extended margin notes. One note of caution, however: Marking too little is usually a more serious problem than recording too much. It may be a symptom of superficial comprehension that can lead to learning errors and omissions. So, when in doubt, think and record more.

I have no riches but my thoughts. Yet these are wealth enough for me.
—Sara Teasdale (1884–1933), American poet

ACTIVITY 6: USE BASIC AND EXTENDED MARKING

DIRECTIONS: Practice using marking techniques by completing these tasks.

1. Read and mark the topic, idea, and important details in the following paragraph. Then also create margin notes at both the lower and higher levels of thinking.

Too Loud

Notes

Our sense of hearing can easily be damaged. Eighty percent of the hearing loss in the United States—affecting 22 million people—involves damage to either the auditory hair cells or to the large nerve into which these cells feed. This type of hearing loss often comes as a consequence of old age, but it can come as a consequence *of young* age, which is to say the tendency of young people to listen to loud music. Damage caused by loud noise may be limited only to the hair cell's cilia—their roots may break off or the links between them may be destroyed—and in most of these instances, the hair cells can recover. When noise is loud or long-lasting enough, however, it can kill hair cells outright and once this happens, they are gone. There is no way to grow new ones (though scientists are trying awfully hard to figure out how to coax the body into doing this). The lack of hearing that results from this damage is bad enough, but some people also get a so-called tinnitus, meaning a permanent ringing in the ears.

So, how loud is too loud? The rule of thumb is, if you have to shout to be heard, you're in the danger zone. The amount of time a person is exposed to loud noise matters, however. You could be around a typical lawn mower for several hours without harm, but after 15 minutes at a loud rock concert, you are damaging your hair cells. (Krogh 575) (255 words)

Notes

2. Look at your margin notes. Label the level of thinking for each one. (You can use the following abbreviations: K, C, Ap, An, S, E.)
3. Use the following spaces and note the level(s) of thinking that you did not use. Then create a question or comment at that level.
   a. Level: ______________

   ____

   ____

   b. Level: ______________

   ____

   ____

   c. Level: ______________

   ____

   ____

4. Using the textbook section in Activity 3 (p. 199), question, read, underline, and create margin notes at three or more levels of thinking.

Before you go on . . .

Monitor Your Progress: recite

As you read . . .

Focus Your Efforts: question and read

Recite and Review for Future Learning

THINK ABOUT THIS . . .

1. Look at the following list of review methods. Check off how often you use each one and how useful it is to you. If you're not familiar with the technique, leave the row blank.

	HOW OFTEN DO YOU USE THIS METHOD?			HOW USEFUL IS IT TO YOU?		
	NEVER	OCCASIONALLY	OFTEN	NOT USEFUL	SOMEWHAT	VERY USEFUL
Paraphrasing						
Summarizing						
Answering chapter review questions						
Making outline notes						
Making double column notes						
Mapping						
Flash cards						
Time lines						
Flow charts						
Diagrams						
Comparison charts						

2. Before reading this section, preread it by looking at the introductory paragraph, the subheadings, the graphics, and the summary and questions about this section that appear at the end of the chapter. Outline number the headings.

You are probably familiar with many of the methods listed in the ***Think about this*** . . . activity. Most students use some of these as studying techniques. But they are also excellent Recite and Review methods, because they capture your best comprehension, lead to additional insights, and prepare for future learning. Think of these methods as finishing tasks for reading. Like a builder's framework, reading the assignment is only the first part of the job. Reading for learning tasks needs additional steps to ensure that your future learning time will be spent on learning, not rereading. Two general ways to ensure your future productivity are to compose and take notes.

To keep a lamp burning we have to keep putting oil in it.

—Mother Teresa (1910–1997), Albanian-born Roman Catholic missionary

Compose

You probably associate composing with writing essays, letters, and reports, or even with creating musical arrangements. But to **compose** also means to frame or shape a topic. And that is what you do as you use your own words and sentences to explain text information.

Composing can be done in a number of ways. You can compose silently and mentally as you recite a section that you've just read or during the review step, when you reflect on all of the information in the chapter. And you can compose on paper or in discussions with others. Regardless of how you do it, there are three methods of composing: paraphrasing, summarizing, and answering review questions.

Words are the small change of thought.

—Jules Renard (1864–1910), French writer

Paraphrase Paraphrasing, as discussed in Chapter 4, is one way to learn new vocabulary terms and their definitions. It is an equally effective way to promote text comprehension, because it requires you to explain and think about new information. You use this method when you recite what you've read, because you're combining what you marked with your own words and sentences. You can also paraphrase during review, as a way to learn the information and as a way to study with others.

To paraphrase any text, avoid copying the author's writing. Instead, form your own sentences that completely convey the meaning of the original by following these steps:

1. Start with the topic.
2. Use the technical terms and any topic-specific words from the original that don't have accurate synonyms.
3. Use synonyms for the other words.

4. Divide up long sentences, if possible.
5. Change the order of the information, if possible.
6. Combine points and/or short sentences, if possible.

Here's an example showing a paraphrased version of the radio advertising text presented earlier.

EXAMPLE

ORIGINAL TEXT	PARAPHRASED VERSION
Radio advertising can be very effective.	*Advertising on the radio can be a very successful approach.*
About eight percent of all advertising outlays goes to radio advertising.	*Radio advertisements account for about 8 percent of all the money spent on advertising.*
Over 227 million people—or 96 percent of all persons aged 12 and older in the United States—listen to the radio each day. Radio ads are inexpensive. A small business in a Midwestern town of 100,000 people pays about $20 for a 30-second local radio spot. (A television spot costs over $250.) In addition, because stations are usually segmented into categories such as rock 'n' roll, news, audiences are largely segmented.	*Radio advertising has three advantages. First, a lot of people will hear it, because about 96% of those who are 12 or older listen to the radio. That's over 227 million people. Second, these ads are cheaper than TV ads. Third, ads can target specific groups, because the stations focus on target groups, such as those interested in news or rock 'n' roll music.*
Unfortunately, radio ads, like TV ads, go by quickly, and people tend to use the radio as background while doing other things.	*But there are also two disadvantages. The ads are over very quickly, and listeners may not pay attention to them, because the radio is often on for background sounds.*

Notice that paragraph 3 starts with a sentence that was not in the original. When you paraphrase, you can add clarifying sentences like this as long as you don't change the original meaning.

ACTIVITY 7: PARAPHRASE

DIRECTIONS: Paraphrase the paragraph in Activity 6 (p. 212).

Summarize Summarizing is a way to reduce a text to only the most important points. A **summary** is a condensed version of the main ideas in a text. But a good summary does more than restate the important points. It also paraphrases them and, in some cases, synthesizes or blends them. The difference between a paraphrase and a summary has to do with emphasis and length. In a paraphrase, you change the original words and sentences to your own, but don't leave anything out. The final version is often a little longer than the original. But in a summary, you emphasize and paraphrase the ideas, leave out all or most of the details, and end up with a condensed version that is shorter than the original.

You're already familiar with summaries in textbooks. Reading them focuses your attention on what the writer thinks are the main points. While those summaries are very useful, they have some limitations. First, they may leave out points that are important to you, such as new information that you didn't know or information that's important in the course. In addition, they don't create the depth of comprehension that you get when you create your own summary.

Here are two sample summaries of the text about families that was part of Activity 3. One is an author's summary and the other is a reader's summary. Notice how the reader's version is longer and a bit more detailed, but both are a condensed version of the original pages of text.

EXAMPLE

AUTHOR'S SUMMARY

Our society's family life is becoming more varied. One-parent families, cohabitation, gay and lesbian couples and singlehood have proliferated in recent years. While the law does not recognize homosexual marriages, many gay men and lesbians form long-lasting relationships and, increasingly, are becoming parents.

READER'S SUMMARY

In the U.S., four alternative family forms have increased the variety of family living. One-parent families are very common. Almost half of the children will live in one-parent families at some point. Cohabitation is gaining popularity, but the relationships tend to have low commitment and only last a few years. Gay and lesbian couples face legal issues because their unions are not recognized in the U.S. Singlehood is a style that is gaining popularity, especially among women.

To summarize a text, follow these steps.

1. Start with the author's topic and a paraphrase of the overall idea or main point.
2. Include the other main ideas in order, unless changing the order adds clarity.
3. Combine points that go together logically.
4. Leave out the details unless they are very important and needed to make the ideas understandable.

ACTIVITY 8: SUMMARIZE

DIRECTIONS: Read, underline, and create margin notes for the following text. Then, choose the most important points and write a summary of it.

Purring Predators: Housecats and Their Prey

Notes

Housecats are famous for bringing home animals they've killed or captured, of course; intrigued by the carnage brought into their own homes in the 1980s, Peter Churcher and John Lawton decided to make a scientific study of the predatory behavior of the domestic cat. To do so, they enlisted the help of 172 households in the small English village of Bedfordshire, where Churcher lived. The two researchers asked the locals to "bag the remains of any animal the cat caught" and turn the evidence over to them once a week. This process went on for a year, with a high degree of cooperation from the cat owners.

Some of the results were not surprising. Young cats hunt more than older cats; small mammals, such as mice, are the favored prey; and cat hunting is not based purely on hunger—all the cats were fed by their owners and yet hunting was widespread.

What was remarkable, however, was the *scale* of the killing. Concentrating on the village's house sparrow population, Churcher and Lawton found that cats were responsible for between one-third and one-half of all sparrow deaths in the village, a figure they believed no other single predator could match. When they looked at all animals killed, and projected the village figures onto the whole of Great Britain, the researchers calculated that cats were responsible for about 70 million deaths a year.

Given that birds account for somewhere between 30 and 50 percent of these kills, this means that cats kill at least 20 million birds a year in Britain. The "at least" here may be an important qualifier. An American biologist, the researchers note, found that cats bring home only about half of the food they catch. (Krogh 695) (293 words)

Answer Review Questions The questions you find at the end of textbook chapters are useful to check your comprehension after reading or to assess your memory after studying. The best ones, from a comprehension standpoint, require sentence or paragraph-length answers. As with paraphrasing and summarizing, you can answer these questions mentally, on paper, or in a discussion with others. If you use paper, you can either write complete sentences or use key words and phrases, along with any form of note taking and shorthand you know.

> **The prize will not be sent to you. You have to win it.**
> —Ralph Waldo Emerson (1803–1882), American lecturer and author

When you use review questions as a comprehension review activity, make sure to look back at the original text as you answer each question. Then decide how much information to include. If your purpose is to get a general sense of your comprehension, use the summary form and emphasize the most important ideas. But if you'll need to know the details, be thorough and paraphrase all the information.

ACTIVITY 9: ANSWER REVIEW QUESTIONS

DIRECTIONS: Assume that you will be having a detailed test on this chapter. Practice answering review questions by completing these tasks.

1. Compose a detailed answer to question 1a on page 228. You may answer with a paragraph, list, or any note taking format you like.
2. Mentally answer question 1b on page 228. You may refer to the text as you form your answer.
3. Discuss question 1d, page 229, with someone else. You may refer to the text as you talk about it.

Take Notes

Notetaking promotes in-depth thinking and comprehension. Good textbook notes capture rather than copy the information. If you organize the information and group-related ideas together as you take them, you will be working at the analysis and synthesis levels and adding to your insights about the information. In addition, notetaking is the bridge between reading and learning. Your notes will be an essential tool for later learning when your goal is to transfer information to long-term memory.

> **All thought is a feat of association.**
> —Robert Frost (1874–1963), American poet

While successful students create notes for virtually every assignment, they approach the task with flexibility. For example, they don't automatically take notes on every paragraph, and they use a variety of formats. As the following sections stress, careful analysis of when and how to take notes, as well as what format to use, will ensure that you not only create effective study tools, but enhance comprehension as well.

Guidelines To take the best notes, consider when to take them, what to record, and how to write them. Here are some guidelines.

1. *Take notes after you mark a section or an assignment.*

   Reading and notetaking are different mental tasks. If you try to do them together, your comprehension will be low, and you may end up copying whole sentences that you don't need. So, read and mark first; then take notes. There are two options here: You can take notes after a section or after completing the whole chapter. When you take notes after a section, you benefit from immediate review and short tasks. If you take notes after finishing the entire chapter, the task will be longer, but you will be able to connect the sections.

2. *Take notes when your comprehension is highest.*

   If you take notes when your comprehension is high, the task will go much faster and your notes will be clearer and better organized than those taken at any other time. For each course and for each text, you will need to decide whether your comprehension is best right after reading or after the professor's lecture.

3. *Take notes on the topics, ideas, and details.*

   Even if you know some of the information, record complete units of information, including the topic, idea, and details. The details will be very hard to learn if you do not link them with the ideas. And ideas without a topic and details are too brief to be meaningful once a little time has elapsed. Take brief notes about what you know, and more detailed ones on new information.

4. *Include your margin notes if they're useful.*

   Your questions and comments can add clarity as well as make the information more memorable.

5. *Use a shorthand system.*

   Writing complete words and sentences wastes time, slows down your thinking, and can even lead to mindless copying, which interferes with comprehension. Use key words and phrases that capture information rather than whole sentences. Also use abbreviations and symbols instead of whole words wherever possible to speed up the process. You will see some examples of this kind of shorthand in Figure 5.1.

6. *Use a variety of note-taking formats.*

   Be flexible. Use formats that match the organization of the information and that work as good learning tools for you. Look for opportunities to use several formats together. You might insert a map, chart, or diagram into outline notes, or put details and vocabulary on flashcards.

Learning without thought is labor lost.

—Confucius (551–479 BC), Chinese teacher and philosopher

Formats Outline notes, double-column notes, and maps are some of the most common and useful formats to promote comprehension. But as you will see at the end of this section, there are other effective formats that you can also incorporate into your notes.

Outline Notes Outlining is probably the most frequently used note-taking format, because it captures relationships, follows the author's organization, and creates a good learning tool. It is also a quick and efficient way to take notes, especially if you have outline numbers and letters next to the rest of the headings in the text. (See Chapter 2, page 68.) Then you simply copy those numbers, letters, and headings to organize your notes.

THE POWER OF MOTIVATION—CH. 1

I. Intro.
   A. Motiv.
      1. driving force 4 all lrnng & achvmt
      2. fr. others or self
         -only lasts when fr. self
      3. can chge attitudes of mind
   B. Acad. rdg & lrng
      1. def. motiv.: desire & psycholog. energy to achieve & gain more
      2. courses stretch knowldg & skills
         a. req's self-motiv
         b. successful studs have acad. motiv.
         c. def. acad motiv: ability to create own desire & energy to rd, lrn, & perfrm well in crses
II. The Motivation-Achievement Link
   Sect. Intro:
      1. studs w/hi motiv & abil = A's
      2. studs w/lo motiv & abil = D/F
      3. stud w/ hi motiv & lo abil higher grades than lo motiv & hi abil
         -due to motiv effect
   A. The Motivation Effect
      1. motiv = mental fuel
      2. how does motiv fuel mind?
         a. affects how you use your abil
         b. motiv + abil = perfrmnce
         c. lo motiv w/ lo or hi abil =
            i. not enuf energy to do work well
            ii. skip & rush assignments
         d. hi motiv w/lo abil
            i. usually B's
            ii. motiv energy/desire to go thru difficlt material

FIGURE 5.1 **Sample Outline Notes**

Be flexible when you outline. Since the system of headings varies from book to book and from section to section, the numbers and letters won't always be used the same way. Here are some general guidelines for taking outline notes:

1. Always list the chapter title and number at the top of your notes.
2. Include important information from the introduction as "I. Intro."
3. When there are three levels of headings
   a. Use Roman numerals for the major headings starting with II.
   b. Use capital letters for the subheadings (A, B, C . . .).
   c. Use Arabic numbers for the minor headings (1, 2, 3 . . .).

   d. Use small letters for the paragraph topics or details (a, b, c).
   e. Use small Roman numerals for additional details (i, ii, iii . . .).
4. For information between a major heading and subheading
   a. Use a Roman numeral for the major heading.
   b. Use a label, such as "Section Intro."
   c. Indent, list, and number the details with Arabic numbers.
   d. Use a capital letter for the subheading.

Throughout your outline, vertically align numbers and letters that are on the same level. So all the Roman numerals should line up in a column down the page, and the capital letters should have their own column, and so on.

Figure 5.1 illustrates this method with notes from the beginning of Chapter 1.

ACTIVITY 10: OUTLINE NOTE TAKING

DIRECTIONS: Use this chapter. Take detailed outline notes on the introduction and the major section entitled "Preread and Divide for Organization." Use these guidelines:

A. Start with "I. Intro." and take notes from the introduction.

B. Continue with "II. Preread and Divide for Organization."

C. Use capital letters for the subheadings.

D. Use Arabic numbers for the paragraph topic labels.

E. Use small letters for the details.

F. Use key words, phrases, and any shorthand techniques you know.

Double-column Notes Some information does not fit into the strict categorizing system of outlines. And some students prefer a less restrictive format. Double-column notes can satisfy those needs.

For double-column notes, you draw a vertical line down the page, but the columns do not have to be even. The left-hand column is used for labels, a topic word, a vocabulary term, or a question; the right-hand column provides the information, definition, or answer. Figure 5.2 shows samples of double-column notes and a vocabulary list.

ACTIVITY 11: DOUBLE-COLUMN NOTES

DIRECTIONS: Develop a set of double-column notes for the second major section in this chapter entitled "Question and Read for In-depth Comprehension."

Sample Notes:

	THE POWER OF MOTIVATION–CHAPTER 1
Intro	
Motivation	1. driving force 4 all lrning & achmt 2. fr. others or self -only last when fr. self 3. can chge attitudes of mind
Aca. Rdg & lrng	1. def. motiv.: desire & psycholog. energy to achieve & gain more 2. courses stretch knowldg & skills a. req's self-motiv b. successful studs have adad. Motiv.

Sample Vocabulary List:

	CHAPTER 1 VOCABULARY
Motivation	desire & psycholog. energy to achieve & gain more
Academic motivation	ability to create own desire & energy to rd, lrn, & perfrm well in cases

FIGURE 5.2 **Examples of Double-Column Notes**

Maps As you learned in Chapter 4, maps are a good way to learn vocabulary. They can work equally well as a note-taking format for some information. A note-taking map can be drawn with the topic placed in a central hub, with spokes of information extending from it (see Chapter 4, p. 164), or it can be created with boxes organized into a tree diagram like the one in Figure 5.3.

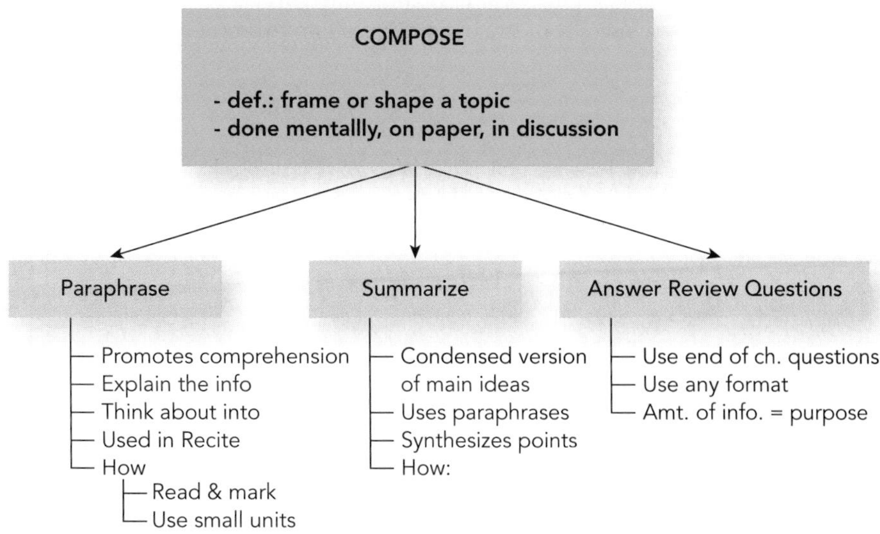

FIGURE 5.3 **A Tree Diagram**

ACTIVITY 12: MAPPING

DIRECTIONS: Create one or more maps for the information in the sections entitled "Paraphrase," "Summarize," and "Answer Review Questions."

When I write down my thoughts, they do not escape me.
This action makes me remember my strength
which I forget at all times.
I educate myself proportionately to my captured thought.
—Isidore Ducasse Lautreamont (1846–1870), French author and poet

Other Note-taking Formats In addition to the three formats already mentioned, five others work well for certain types of information.

The first is the old-fashioned but very effective flash card. Flash cards are useful for learning specific details and vocabulary. Simply put a question or term on one side of the card and the answer or definition on the other.

The remaining four formats use various diagrams to organize information. They are undoubtedly familiar to you, because they're standard ways to present details in textbooks. They are also easy and interesting to draw, so they promote motivation and in-depth comprehension. The function of each format and a sample are presented below.

Timelines A timeline is an excellent way to comprehend the order of events. To construct one, simply draw a horizontal line with important dates on top and events on the bottom. Leave spaces between the events to indicate a shorter or longer time span. Add a title to indicate the subject of the events. Here's an example.

EXAMPLE

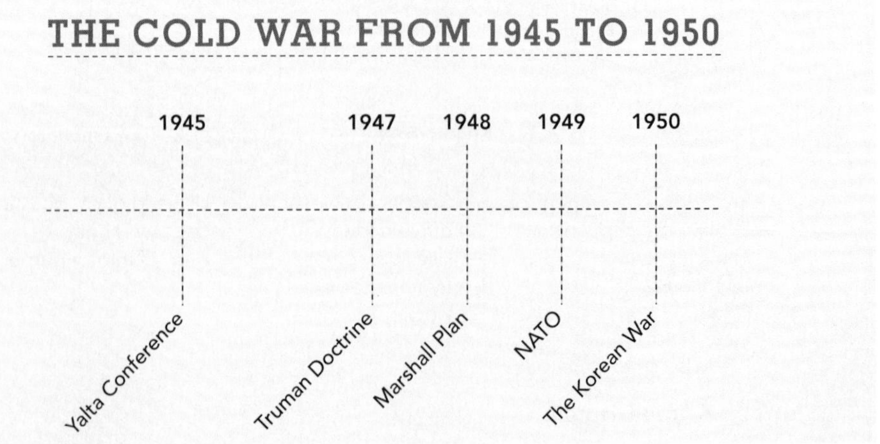

Process Diagrams These diagrams generally use boxes, arrows, and/or circles to represent procedures, processes, and cause-and-effect relationships. Use a circle for a continuous process, or cycle; use a left-to-right lineup for a noncyclical process. Look at the examples below.

EXAMPLES

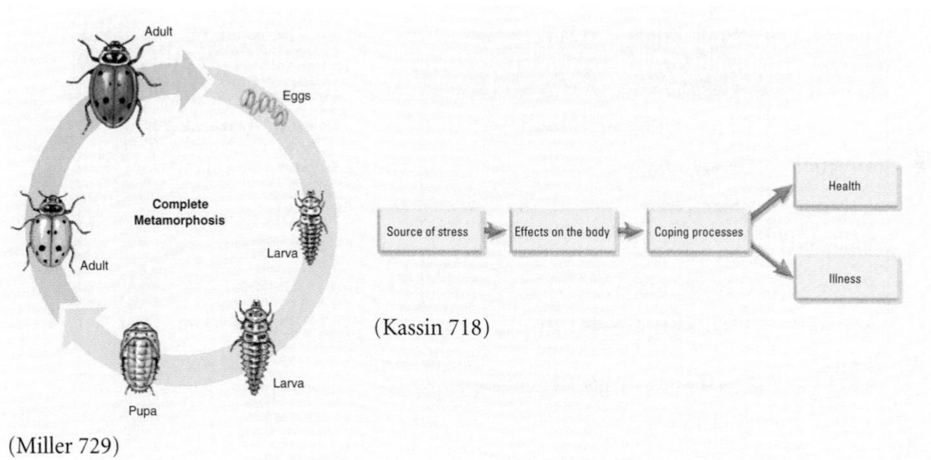

(Miller 729)

(Kassin 718)

Hierarchy Diagrams Pyramid, layer-cake, and step diagrams emphasize the stages and phases of a topic. They can present information in a hierarchy that moves from simple to complex or basic to advanced. They also show a progression from one step or stage to another.

EXAMPLES

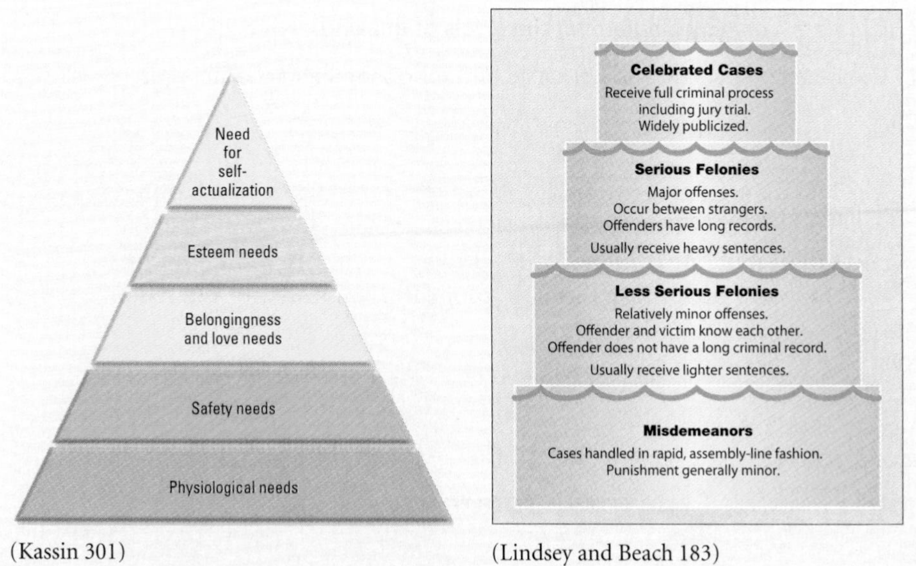

(Kassin 301)

(Lindsey and Beach 183)

Comparison and Contrast Charts In charts, you can use rows and columns to compare and contrast categories of information (see Chapter 4, p. 165). In the example, the first five rows display contrasting characteristics. The bottom row displays a characteristic that the two processes have in common.

EXAMPLE

Comparing Photosynthesis and Cellular Respiration

	Photosynthesis	Cellular Respiration
Function	Energy storage	Energy release
Location	Chloroplasts	Mitochondria
Reactants	CO_2 and H_2O	$C_6H_{12}O_6$ and O_2
Products	$C_6H_{12}O_6$ and O_2	CO_2 and H_2O
Equation	$6CO_2 + 6H_2O \rightarrow C_6H_{12}O_6 + 6O_2$	$6O_2 + C_6H_{12}O_6 \rightarrow 6CO_2 + 6H_2O$
Process	biochemical	

(Adapted from Miller 232)

ACTIVITY 13: OTHER NOTE-TAKING FORMATS

DIRECTIONS: Practice using other note-taking formats by completing the following tasks.

1. Create flash cards for the first five bold-faced terms in this chapter.
2. Create a process diagram for the steps for paraphrasing.
3. Create a hierarchy diagram for the levels of thinking.
4. Create a comparison and contrast chart for general and chapter aids.

Just as the largest library, badly arranged, is not so useful as a very moderate one that is well arranged, so the greatest amount of knowledge, if not elaborated by our own thoughts, is worth much less than a far smaller volume that has been abundantly and repeatedly thought over.

—Arthur Schopenhauer (1788–1860), German philosopher

Before you go on . . .

Monitor Your Progress: recite

After you read . . .

Reflect on Your Gains: review

CHAPTER SUMMARY

Introduction

Textbooks can be demanding because they are visually complex, focus on **technical information,** and involve a complex set of reading for learning objectives. The PDQ3R processes provide a basic, motivated approach for reading textbook assignments. These methods need to be expanded to ensure mastery of the complex concepts presented in college textbooks.

Preread and Divide for Organization

Understanding depends on your recognition of how the textbook information is organized into topics, concepts, and parts, the relationships among them, and what's most important. To gain this kind of understanding, focus on the **textbook aids** as you Preread and Divide the book, chapter, and each major section. Use the **general aids** during a one-time textbook prereading. These aids reveal the organization of all the chapters and also provide supplemental tools to support your comprehension efforts. During chapter and section prereading, use the **chapter aids** to identify the most important information and guide your reading.

Question and Read for In-depth Comprehension

To gain in-depth comprehension of complex texts, vary your **levels of thinking.** The levels, which range from very simple to very complex, include **knowledge, comprehension, application, analysis, synthesis,** and **evaluation.** The first three levels are called lower level thinking, because readers at these levels rely on the text information to form questions and statements about the text information. The last three levels are called higher level thinking, because readers go beyond the text and draw their own logical conclusions. To capture your comprehension, use basic marking techniques for the lower levels of thinking and extended margin notes to record higher level insights.

Recite and Review for Future Learning

After you finish reading, use the PDQ3R Recite and Review steps to compose and take notes. These processes capture your comprehension, lead to additional insights, and prepare for future learning. To **compose,** frame or shape a topic by paraphrasing, **summarizing,** or answering the chapter review questions. You can also use these methods right after reading as you recite what you've just marked or during the review step, when you reflect on the entire chapter. In addition to composing, you can take notes after marking a section or finishing a chapter. Choosing the best time to take notes and using a variety of formats will ensure that your notes aid your understanding and are a useful tool for later learning.

REVIEW ACTIVITIES

Use the following activities to check your understanding and aid your learning of the information in this chapter.

Expand Your Vocabulary

Match each term with the correct definition or characteristic.

_____ 1. technical information
_____ 2. textbook aids
_____ 3. general aids
_____ 4. chapter aids
_____ 5. levels of thinking
_____ 6. knowledge
_____ 7. comprehension
_____ 8. application
_____ 9. analysis
_____ 10. synthesis
_____ 11. evaluation
_____ 12. compose
_____ 13. summary

a. the level at which a reader can explain what the text information means
b. the level at which a reader can locate and repeat text information
c. to frame or shape a topic by using methods such as paraphrasing and summarizing
d. degrees of understanding or explanation about a topic
e. aids that organize the book and supplement your knowledge
f. the level at which a reader can identify parts and explain connections not stated in the text
g. a condensed version of the main ideas in a text
h. knowledge used by experts in the field
i. the level at which a reader judges the merits of a work or idea
j. aids that are tailored to the chapter information
k. the level at which a reader uses the information to explain real-world situations
l. features that reveal organization, increase motivation, and aid reading and learning
m. the level at which a reader can combine information and propose solutions not stated in the text

Increase Your Knowledge

The following tasks will help you assess how well you understand the ideas presented in this chapter. They will also help you prepare for quizzes and exams on this material.

1. The following questions focus on the major chapter topics. Discuss them with others or form your own detailed answers.
   a. What makes textbooks so demanding to read?
   b. How and why would you preread a textbook? A chapter? A major section?

c. Explain the differences between general and chapter aids. Give two examples of each one. Describe the kind of information found in the examples you cite.
d. Name and define the six levels of thinking. What can readers do at each level?
e. Explain what extended margin notes are. Give examples of the kind of questions or comments that a reader might make at each level of thinking.
f. Explain how to use the three composing techniques.
g. What options do you have for note-taking formats?

2. Take notes on the information in this chapter if you have not already completed activities 10–13.

Develop Your Skills

The following review tasks will give you an opportunity to practice the methods presented in this chapter.

REVIEW 1: LEVELS OF THINKING The following textbook questions come from a chapter entitled "Motivating, Satisfying, and Leading Employees" in a business textbook. The chapter covers psychological aspects of the workplace, job satisfaction and employee morale, theories of employee motivation, and leadership styles. Match the level of thinking that would be required to answer each of the questions.

a. knowledge
b. comprehension
c. application
d. analysis
e. synthesis
f. evaluation

______ 1. Do you think that most people are relatively satisfied or dissatisfied with their work?

______ 2. Compare and contrast the information about Maslow's hierarchy of needs with the two-factor theory of motivation.

______ 3. How can participation in management programs enhance employee satisfaction and motivation?

______ 4. Identify three U.S. managers who you think would qualify as great leaders. Why would you put them in that category?

______ 5. Some evidence suggests that recent college graduates show high levels of job satisfaction. Levels then drop dramatically as they reach their late twenties, only to increase gradually once they get older. What might explain this pattern?

______ 6. What are the three major leadership styles? (Adapted from Griffin and Ebert 273)

REVIEW 2: LEVELS OF THINKING Read and mark the following text. Then form a question or a comment at each level of thinking.

The Psychology of Drug Effects

Notes

People often assume that the effects of a drug are automatic, the inevitable result of the drug's chemistry. But reactions to a psychoactive drug involve more than the drug's chemical properties. They also depend on a person's physical condition and experience with the drug.

Physical factors include body weight, metabolism, initial state of emotional arousal, and physical tolerance of the drug. For example, women generally get drunker than men on the same amount of alcohol because women are smaller, on average, and their bodies metabolize alcohol differently. Similarly, many Asians have a genetically determined adverse reaction to even small amounts of alcohol, which can cause severe headaches, facial flushing, and diarrhea. For individuals, a drug may have one effect after a tiring day and a different one after a rousing quarrel, or the effect may vary with the time of day because of the body's circadian rhythms.

Experience with the drug refers to the number of times a person has used the drug. Trying a drug—a cigarette, an alcoholic drink, a stimulant—for the first time is often a neutral or unpleasant experience. But reactions typically change once a person has become familiar with the drug's effects. (Wade and Tavris 166) (198 words)

1. Knowledge:

____

____

2. Comprehension:

____

____

3. Application:

____

____

4. Analysis:

____

____

5. Synthesis:

____

____

6. Evaluation:

____

____

REVIEW 3: EXTENDED MARGIN NOTES Read, underline, and create margin notes for the following text. Focus on creating extended margin notes. Then complete the tasks that follow.

Keeping Cut Flowers Fresh

Notes

Xylem is the plant tissue through which water moves *up*, from roots through leaves. The flowers we put in vases in our homes have lost their roots, of course, but they haven't lost their xylem, which continues to function long after the flower has been picked. Given this, many flowers can last a long time indoors; but we can maximize their stay if we follow a few simple rules.

First, realize that the liquid in the xylem is under negative pressure—its natural tendency is to move up *into* the stem, not to flow out of it. As such, if the stems are cut when they are out of water, *air* gets sucked up into the cut ends, creating air bubbles that can then get trapped in the xylem and keep water from rising up through it. When this happens, flowers can wilt, even when their stems are submerged in clean water. Recutting the stem under water (or under a steady stream from the faucet) can remove this blockage. Better yet, cut the stems under water the first time.

Beyond this, acidic sugar-water, such as can be found in citrus-flavored soft drinks, will prolong the life of some flowers by keeping bacterial growth down; changing water frequently is a good idea, particularly when it starts to look gummy or discolored. Keep your arrangement out of direct light or heat, and remove dead and dying flowers in the arrangement, because the hormone ethylene is given off by dying flowers and in many cases will hasten the demise of the healthy ones in the bunch. (Krogh 492) (267 words)

Notes

1. Look at your margin notes. Label the level of thinking for each one. (You can use the following lettering system: K, C, Ap, An, S, E.)
2. Use the following spaces and note the level(s) of thinking you did not use. Then create a question or comment at that level.
   a. Level: ______________
   ____
   ____
   b. Level: ______________
   ____
   ____
   c. Level: ______________
   ____
   ____

REVIEW 4: PARAPHRASE Read and mark the following text. Then paraphrase it, using your own paper.

You might be someone who thinks that if food is nutritious, then it probably doesn't taste very good! In fact, all foods, whether they fall in the "broccoli" or the "chocolate" category, contain nutrients that you need to survive. **Nutrition** is the process of acquiring and processing nutrients into a usable form. Animal **nutrients** are substances that must be supplied in the diet. Nutrients fall into five major categories: (1) lipids, (2) carbohydrates, (3) proteins, (4) minerals, and (5) vitamins. These substances provide the body with its basic needs:

Notes

- Energy to fuel cellular metabolism and activities, provided by lipids, carbohydrates, and proteins;
- The chemical building blocks, such as amino acids, to construct complex molecules unique to each animal; and

- Minerals and vitamins that participate in a variety of metabolic reactions. (Audesirk et al. 584) (130 words)

Notes

REVIEW 5: SUMMARIZE Read and mark the following text. Then summarize it, using your own paper.

Free Radicals

Notes

Their name makes them sound like a group of sixties activists set loose after years in jail, but **free radicals** aren't people at all; they are atoms or molecules. They *have* been set loose, however—to damage human bodies in illnesses that may range from cancer to coronary heart disease.

The way the public normally hears about these culprits is through the recommended means of limiting their harm: a diet rich in vitamins C, E, and the substance beta carotene. Looking at free radicals from another angle, however, we can see how they represent a damaging exception to the rules of chemical bonding.

You know that atoms "seek" to have a full outer energy shell, which in most cases means eight electrons. In covalent bonding, atoms achieve this state by sharing *pairs* of electrons with one another, one electron of each pair coming from each of the atoms involved. Occasionally in nature, however, atoms come together to create a molecule in which one of the component atoms has an *unpaired electron* in its outer shell. Nitrogen can come together with oxygen, for example, to form nitric oxide (NO). Recall that oxygen has six outer electrons (and thus needs two for stability), while nitrogen has five outer electrons (and thus needs three). When oxygen and nitrogen hook up, they can share only two electrons with one another before oxygen's outer shell is filled. This, however, leaves nitrogen with an unpaired electron.

Unstable molecules like this usually exist only briefly, as intermediate molecules in chemical reactions. And in people, that's just the problem.

Notes

Human beings are among the many species that use a terrific amount of oxygen to extract energy from food. In this process, oxygen is constantly picking up electrons. Through the many steps in metabolism, oxygen may come together with other substances to create a type of free radical called reactive oxygen. Though any one reactive oxygen molecule is short-lived, the damage comes by way of a destructive chain reaction: Seeking partners, one free radical begets more, which beget more.

Where's the harm? Well, for one thing, free radicals may irritate or scar artery walls, which invites artery-clogging fatty deposits around the damage. They also may have a mutation-causing or "mutagenic" effect on human DNA, which can be a factor leading to cancer. Some primary sites of free-radical generation and damage are the "powerhouses" in cells—structures called mitochondria—which are primary sites at which energy is extracted from food. Indeed, a growing body of evidence supports a long-standing theory of human aging, which holds that many of the things we associate with getting older—memory loss, hearing impairment—can be traced to the cumulative effects of free radicals damaging DNA in the mitochondria, thus diminishing the body's energy supply. (Krogh 30) (462 words)

REVIEW 6: READING FOR LEARNING METHODS Assume that the following textbook section has been assigned in your psychology class. Use all the reading for learning methods to complete the following tasks.

Task 1: Preread and divide for organization

1. What is the topic? ____________________
   a. How many parts does this section have? _____
   b. Assume that this is the first major section in the chapter after the introduction. Number and letter the headings using the outline method.
2. Look at the first paragraph, which is the section introduction. What ideas will the section emphasize?

   ____

   ____

3. Skim the concluding aids.
   a. What major points does the summary emphasize?
   b. From the other concluding aids, what else should you focus on during reading?
4. Skim the middle.
   a. What did you find that's interesting?
   b. List any useful aids you found. How and when will you use each one?

Task 2: Question and read for in-depth comprehension

1. Question, read, and mark the text.
   Create both basic and extended margin notes.
2. Choose four levels of thinking. Record your most useful questions or comments for each level.
   a. Level: ____________
   b. Level: ____________
   c. Level: ____________
   d. Level: ____________

Task 3: Recite and review for future learning

1. Recite what you marked. Add your new insights to your margin notes.
2. Paraphrase the definitions for each of the seven Key Terms.

3. Write a summary answer to the first Looking Back question.
4. Use any form of note taking to answer the second "Looking Back" question.

The Rhythms of Sleep

Perhaps the most perplexing of all our biological rhythms is the one governing sleep and wakefulness. Sleep, after all, puts us at risk: Muscles that are usually ready to respond to danger relax, and senses grow dull. As the late British psychologist Christopher Evans (1984) once noted, "The behavior patterns involved in sleep are glaringly, almost insanely, at odds with common sense." Then why is sleep such a profound necessity?

Why We Sleep

Surprisingly, the exact functions of sleep are still uncertain (Maquet, 2001). However, generally speaking, sleep appears to provide a time-out period, so that the body can eliminate waste products from muscles, repair cells, strengthen the immunc system, and recover abilities lost during the day. When we do not get enough sleep, our bodies operate abnormally. For example, levels of hormones that are necessary for normal muscle development and proper immune-system functioning decline (Leproult, Van Reeth, et al., 1997).

Although most people can still get along reasonably well after a day or two of sleeplessness, sleep deprivation that lasts for four days or longer becomes uncomfortable, and soon unbearable. In animals, forced sleeplessness leads to infections and eventually death, and the same seems to be true for people. In one tragic case, a 51-year-old man abruptly began to lose sleep. After sinking deeper and deeper into an exhausted stupor, he developed a lung infection and died. An autopsy showed that he had lost almost all the large neurons in two areas of the thalamus that have been linked to sleep and hormonal circadian rhythms (Lugaresi et al., 1986).

Sleep is also necessary for normal *mental* functioning. After the loss of even a single night's sleep, mental flexibility, attention, and creativity all suffer. In chronic sleep deprivation, high levels of cortisol may damage or impair the brain cells that are necessary for learning and memory (Leproult, Copinschi, et al., 1997). After several days of staying awake, people may even begin to have hallucinations and delusions (Dement, 1978).

Of course, sleep deprivation rarely reaches that point, but people frequently suffer from milder versions. Many people are plagued by insomnia—difficulty in falling or staying asleep. Insomnia can result from worry and anxiety, psychological problems, hot flashes during menopause, physical problems such as arthritis, and irregular or overly demanding work and study schedules. (For advice on how to get a better night's sleep, see "Taking Psychology With You.")

Another cause of daytime sleepiness is **sleep apnea,** a disorder in which breathing periodically stops for a few moments, causing the person to choke and gasp. Sleep apnea has several causes, from blockage of air passages to failure of the brain to control respiration correctly, and, if chronic, it can cause high blood pressure and irregular heart beat. In **narcolepsy,** another serious disorder, an individual is subject to irresistible and unpredictable daytime attacks of sleepiness or actual sleep, lasting from 5 to 30 minutes. A quarter of a million people in the United States alone suffer from this condition, many without knowing it. Genetic factors seem to be involved (Overeem et al., 2001).

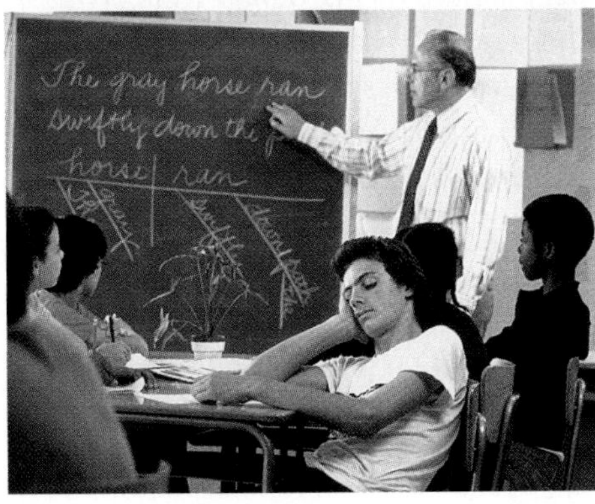

Whatever your age, sometimes the urge to sleep is irresistible—especially because in fast-paced modern societies, many people do not get as much sleep as they need.

The most common cause of sleepiness is probably the most obvious one—staying up late and not allowing yourself to get enough sleep at night. Because sleep is so vital to physical and mental well-being, many researchers are worried about the growing numbers of sleep-deprived people in modern societies. When people are sleepy, traffic and work accidents become far more likely (Coren, 1996; Maas, 1998). The National Transportation Safety Board has reported that tired truck drivers who fall asleep at the wheel are responsible for up to 1,500 road deaths a year; driver fatigue is a greater safety problem than use of alcohol or other drugs.

Two-thirds of all Americans get fewer than the recommended eight hours. American students get only about six hours of sleep a night on average, even though most people need at least eight or nine hours for optimal performance and adolescents typically need ten. Not surprisingly, lack of sleep has been linked to lower grades (Wolfson & Carskadon, 1998). According to sleep researcher James Maas (1998), many students "drag themselves through high school and college like walking zombies . . . moody, lethargic, and unprepared or unable to learn."

The Realms of Sleep

Until the early 1950s, little was known about the physiology of sleep. Then a breakthrough occurred in the laboratory of physiologist Nathaniel Kleitman, who at the time was the only person in the world who had spent his entire career studying sleep.

Kleitman had given one of his graduate students, Eugene Aserinsky, the tedious task of finding out whether the slow, rolling eye movements that characterize the onset of sleep continue throughout the night. To both men's surprise, eye movements did indeed occur, but they were rapid, not slow (Aserlinsky & Kleitman, 1955). Using the electroencephalograph (EEG) to measure the brain's electrical activity (see Chapter 4), these researchers, along with another of Kleitman's students, William Dement, were able to correlate the rapid eye movements with changes in sleepers' brain-wave patterns (Dement, 1992). Adult volunteers were soon spending their nights sleeping in laboratories while scientists measured changes in their brain activity, muscle tension, breathing, and other physiological responses.

As a result of this research, today we know that during sleep, periods of **rapid eye movement (REM)** alternate with periods of fewer eye movements, or *non-REM (NREM) sleep,* in a cycle that recurs about every 90 minutes or so. The REM periods last from a few minutes to as long as an hour, averaging about 20 minutes in length. Whenever they begin, the pattern of electrical activity from the sleeper's brain changes to resemble that of alert wakefulness. Non-REM periods are themselves divided into shorter, distinct stages, each associated with a particular brain-wave pattern (see Figure 5.2).

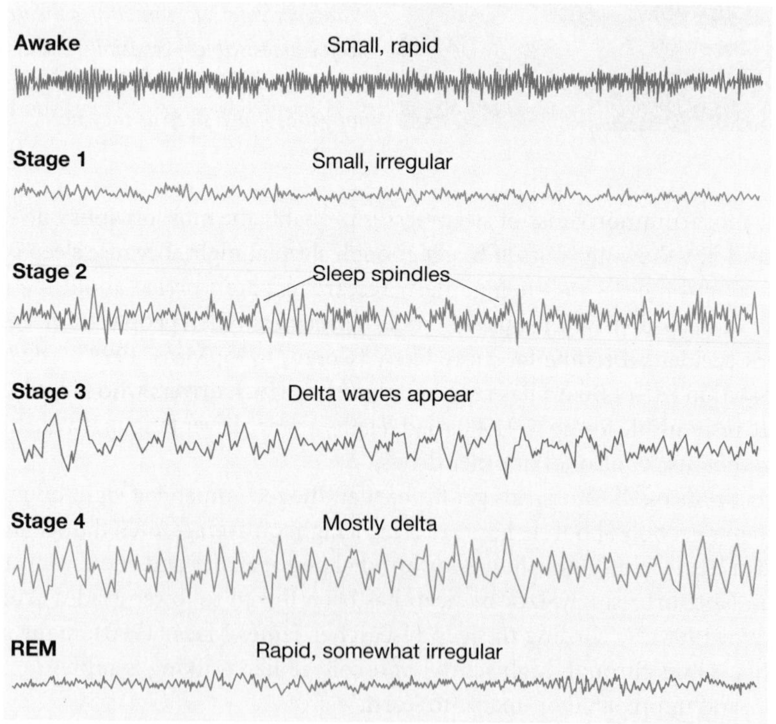

FIGURE 5.2
Brain-Wave Patterns During Wakefulness and Sleep
Most types of brain waves are present throughout sleep, but different ones predominate at different stages.

When you first climb into bed, close your eyes, and relax, your brain emits bursts of *alpha waves.* On an EEG recording, alpha waves have a regular, slow rhythm and a high amplitude (height). Gradually, these waves slow down even further, and you drift off into slumber, passing through four stages:

- *Stage 1.* Your brain waves become small and irregular, and you feel yourself drifting on the edge of consciousness, in a state of light sleep. If awakened, you may recall fantasies or a few visual images.
- *Stage 2.* Your brain emits occasional short bursts of rapid, high-peaking waves called *sleep spindles.* Minor noises probably won't disturb you.
- *Stage 3.* In addition to the waves characteristic of Stage 2, your brain occasionally emits *delta waves,* very slow waves with very high peaks. Your breathing and pulse have slowed down, your muscles are relaxed, and you are hard to rouse.
- *Stage 4.* Delta waves have now largely taken over, and you are in deep sleep. It will probably take vigorous shaking or a loud noise to awaken you. Oddly, though, if you talk or walk in your sleep, this is when you are likely to do so. The causes of sleepwalking, which occurs more often in children than adults, are still unknown, but they may involve unusual patterns of brain activity (Bassetti et al., 2000).

This sequence of stages takes about 30 to 45 minutes. Then you move back up the ladder from Stage 4 to 3 to 2 to 1. At that point, about 70 to 90 minutes after the onset of sleep, something peculiar happens. Stage 1 does not turn into drowsy wakefulness, as one might expect. Instead, your brain begins to emit long bursts of very rapid, somewhat irregular waves. Your heart rate increases, your blood pressure rises, and your breathing becomes faster and more irregular. Small twitches in your face and fingers may occur. In men, the penis becomes somewhat erect as vascular tissue relaxes and blood fills the genital area faster than it exits. In women, the clitoris enlarges and vaginal lubrication increases. At the same time, most skeletal muscles go limp, preventing your aroused brain from producing physical movement. You have entered the realm of REM.

Because cats sleep up to 80 percent of the time, it's easy to catch them in the various stages of slumber. A cat in non-REM sleep (left) remains upright, but during the REM phase (right), its muscles go limp and it flops onto its side.

Because the brain is extremely active while the body is entirely inactive, REM sleep has also been called "paradoxical sleep." It is during these periods that you are most likely to dream. Even people who claim they never dream at all will report dreams if awakened in a sleep laboratory during REM sleep. But dreaming is also often reported during non-REM sleep, though the dreams tend to be shorter, less vivid, and more realistic. In one study, for example, dream reports occurred 82 percent of the time when sleepers were awakened during REM sleep, but they also occurred 51 percent of the time when people were awakened during non-REM sleep (Foulkes, 1962).

REM and non-REM sleep continue to alternate throughout the night, with Stages 3 and 4 tending to become shorter or even to disappear, and REM periods tending to get longer and closer together as the hours pass. This pattern explains why you are likely to be dreaming when the alarm clock goes off in the morning. But the cycles are far from regular. An individual may bounce directly from Stage 4 back to Stage 2, or go from REM to Stage 2 and then back to REM. Also, the time between REM and non-REM is highly variable, differing from person to person and also within any given individual.

The purpose of REM sleep is still a matter of debate, but clearly it does have a purpose. If you wake people up every time they lapse into REM sleep, nothing dramatic will happen. When finally allowed to sleep normally, however, they will spend a much longer time than usual in the REM phase, and it will be hard to rouse them. Electrical brain activity associated with REM may burst through into quiet sleep and even into wakefulness, as if the participants are making up for something they were deprived of. Many people think that in adults, at least, this "something" is connected with dreaming, to which we now turn.

Quick Quiz

Wake up and take this quiz!

A. Match each term with the appropriate phrase.

1. REM periods	**a.** delta waves and talking in one's sleep
2. alpha	**b.** irregular brain waves and light sleep
3. Stage 4 sleep	**c.** relaxed but awake
4. Stage 1 sleep	**d.** active brain but inactive muscles

B. Sleep is necessary for normal (a) physical and mental functioning, (b) mental functioning but not physical functioning, (c) physical functioning but not mental functioning.

C. *True or false:* Most people can get by fine with six hours of sleep a night.

Answers: A. 1. d 2. c 3. a 4. b B. a C. false

The following parts are from the end of the chapter.

Summary

The Rhythms of Sleep

- Sleep, which recurs on a circadian rhythm, is necessary not only for bodily restoration but also for normal mental functioning. Many people get less than the optimal amount of sleep. Some suffer from insomnia, *sleep apnea,* or *narcolepsy.*
- During sleep, periods of *rapid eye movement,* or *REM,* alternate with non-REM sleep in approximately a 90-minute rhythm. *Non-REM sleep* is divided into four stages on the basis of characteristic brain-wave patterns. During REM sleep, the brain is active, and there are other signs of arousal, yet most of the skeletal muscles are limp; vivid dreams are reported most often during REM sleep.

Key Terms

Sleep apnea
Narcolepsy
Rapid eye movement (REM) sleep
Non-REM sleep
Alpha waves
Delta waves
Sleep spindles

Looking Back

1. Why do we sleep?
2. What happens when we go too long without enough sleep?
3. Why are you likely to be dreaming when the alarm goes off in the morning? (Wade and Tavris 150–153, 171–173)

Check Your Motivation

1. Review your chapter goals. Did you achieve them? Explain.
2. List the new ideas and methods you've gained from this chapter. Think about how they will help you in the future.
3. Measure your motivation for this topic. Think about each statement and how you will use it in the future. Mark it:

   A = never B = sometimes C = usually D = always

To engage my interest, I plan to . . .	A	B	C	D
1. preread the general aids and see how the book is organized.	___	___	___	___
2. preread the chapter to gain interest in the topic.	___	___	___	___
3. preread sections to get motivated and see what's important.	___	___	___	___
4. outline number the headings to see the topic organization.	___	___	___	___

	A	B	C	D
To focus my efforts, I plan to . . .				
5. form questions and comments at various levels of thinking during reading.	___	___	___	___
6. think about how important points relate to myself and others.	___	___	___	___
7. identify the levels of thinking in the author's or professor's questions.	___	___	___	___
8. add extended margin notes to my marking.	___	___	___	___
To monitor my progress, I plan to . . .				
9. use paraphrasing as I recite.	___	___	___	___
10. use summarizing as I recite.	___	___	___	___
11. use the chapter review questions as I recite.	___	___	___	___
To reflect on my gains, I plan to . . .				
12. use paraphrasing or summarizing during review.	___	___	___	___
13. use the chapter questions as part of my review process.	___	___	___	___
14. take textbook notes when my comprehension is highest.	___	___	___	___
15. use a variety of note taking formats whenever possible.	___	___	___	___

SCORING: Write the number of answers you marked in each column in the following spaces. Compute the column scores, and then add them up to determine your total score.

# of A's ______ × 1 pt. = ______
# of B's ______ × 2 pt. = ______
# of C's ______ × 3 pt. = ______
# of D's ______ × 4 pt. = ______

Total points = ______

INTERPRETATION: 15–43 points = low motivation; 44–60 points = high motivation

SUGGESTION: Evaluate your scores. Reward yourself for your gains. Make a plan to improve anything that needs more attention.

Main Ideas

How do you comprehend the many sections and paragraphs of new information in textbooks? How can you tell if your understanding is accurate?

While instructors and others can provide valuable insights about a text, comprehension is, ultimately, an individual task. But that does not mean that readers work alone or without support. The author provides paths and roads called ideas that lead through the countryside of information. Finding and following the paths is a way to avoid getting lost and a way to ensure that you don't miss the sights. In short, ideas lead to comprehension. And, even more than that, what they provide can truly expand your world. As Oliver Wendell Holmes, Jr. said,

CHAPTER 6 MAIN IDEAS

A mind once stretched by a new idea never regains its original dimensions.

— Oliver Wendell Holmes, Jr. (1841–1935), American judge

Before you read . . .

Engage Your Interest: preread and divide

This chapter is devoted to teaching you how to find and use the path of ideas that authors present in textbook chapters. Here's a partial outline, which includes the subheadings and the minor headings. Add the major section headings to this outline, and think about how the subheadings and minor headings relate to each major heading.

I. ______________________________

II. ______________________________

- A. The Structural Elements
- B. The Predict and Verify Process

III. ______________________________

- A. Chapter Main Ideas
  1. Stated Ideas
  2. Implied Ideas
- B. Section Main Ideas
  1. Stated Ideas
  2. Implied Ideas

IV. ______________________________

- A. The Paragraph Elements
  1. Topics
  2. Main Ideas
  3. Marking the Elements
- B. Paragraph Formats
  1. Topic Sentence First
  2. Topic Sentence in the Middle
  3. Topic Sentence Last
  4. No Topic Sentence
- C. Analyzing as You Read

After you preread and divide the chapter into reading tasks, set a goal for each one. Be specific about the task, topic, and reward(s).

1. I want to ____________ about ______________________.
My reward(s) will be ______________________
______________________________________.

2. I want to ____________ about ______________________.
My reward(s) will be ______________________
______________________________________.

3. I want to ____________ about ______________________.
My reward(s) will be ______________________
______________________________________.

As you read . . .

Focus Your Efforts: question and read

Textbooks often appear to be endless pages of information. And in part, they are, and that is what they are meant to be. Along with encyclopedias, technical reports, and even some magazines, textbooks are a form of **expository writing,** which is meant to expose or explain information, ideas, or scientific theories. Without a way to make sense of expository texts, many readers lose track of the information, become lost in endless sentences, find it hard to concentrate, and finish with little comprehension.

Fortunately, there is a way to focus your efforts, attention, and understanding as you read textbooks. The key is to find the main ideas in the chapter, sections, and paragraphs. These ideas are called the main ideas because, while they may not be the only ones presented, they are the most important ones. Finding them provides direct benefits. First, grasping main ideas improves your comprehension, because you "get" the point. Second, with the main idea in mind, you can take in whole units of information rather than slogging through isolated sentences or data bits. Third, the sentences that contain the main ideas can easily be turned into valuable questions that guide your thinking during reading and learning. And fourth, as already mentioned, the ideas are often valuable insights that you'll take away with you.

> Write to be understood, speak to be heard, read to grow.
>
> —Lawrence Clark Powell (1906–2001), American librarian and writer

The purpose of this chapter is to present guidelines and skills to help you:

- Get the Most Out of Main Ideas
- Find Main Ideas in Chapters and Sections
- Find Main Ideas in Paragraphs

Get the Most Out of Main Ideas

THINK ABOUT THIS . . .

1. Look at each of the following sentences. The first one might come from a novel; the second one could come from a newspaper article. Briefly record what you would expect the rest of the text to cover.
   a. "When she looked into the room, she screamed."

   ____

   ____

   ____

   b. "The School Board passed a new policy last night about student cheating."

   ____

   ____

   ____

2. Reminder: Preread this section.

When you read the first sentence, you probably wondered why the woman screamed, came up with your own possibilities, or expected the next part of the story to explain what she saw. For the second sentence, you probably assumed that the rest of the article would describe the policy and maybe even explain why it was voted on at this time. In both cases, after anticipating what might come, you would want to read on to get more information. This is a natural and very effective way to read. It's called *predict and verify.* Once you know what to look for, this same approach works very well for reading textbooks.

There is an art of reading, as well as an art of thinking, and an art of writing.
—Isaac D'Israeli (1766–1848), British critic and historian

The Structural Elements

Most students think of information as data and facts. Thus, they focus on separate sentences. This view leads to a lack of interest and the belief that textbooks are boring. But writers see information very differently. To them, what's important are the interesting ideas. These cartoons illustrate the two perspectives.

How do authors decide which ideas to include? Some of them are the accepted and most important ideas in their field. Others are created in a top-down method of writing where authors describe what's in their sections or paragraphs. For the top-down method, authors start with a general chapter topic and divide it into major sections. Each major section is then labeled and divided into subsections, minor sections if needed, and paragraphs. With each division, the smaller parts support the larger unit. Working within this organizational structure, authors have main ideas in mind about what's in each part. You can think of this top-down structure as a pyramid, like the one in Figure 6.1.

Imagine that each level of the pyramid is made up of blocks. The blocks differ in size, but all are necessary to make the whole pyramid. In addition, no matter how big or small the blocks, they all have the same composition. Similarly, in a textbook, each part—the chapter, each section, each paragraph—is a discussion block that may vary in size but is important to the whole chapter. And all discussion blocks have similar el-

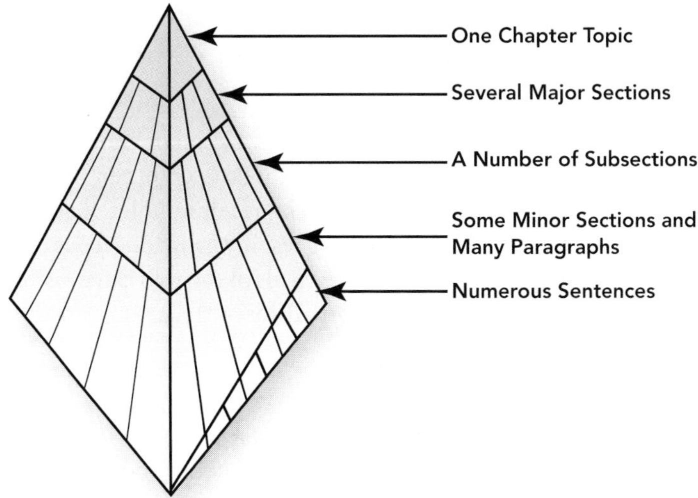

FIGURE 6.1 **Top-Down Structure**

ements: each one has a topic, main idea, and details. The definitions and major characteristics for each of these elements are as follows.

The Topic

1. The **topic** is the subject of the discussion.
2. It is a word or phrase, not a whole sentence.
3. The key topic word is a noun that names a person, place, or thing.

The Main Idea

1. The **main idea** is the author's dominant message or opinion about the topic.
2. It can be stated in the text or implied.
   a. A stated main idea is
      i. a declarative sentence (or occasionally sentences), not a question.
      ii. general and includes other points or applies to many instances.
   b. An **implied main idea** is not directly stated; it is only suggested by what is presented. Readers must infer or figure it out from clues in the writing.

Where an opinion is general, it is usually correct.

—Jane Austen (1775–1817), British novelist

The Details

1. The **details** are pieces of information that describe the topic or support the idea.
2. A detail is specific. It
   a. applies to one or just a few instances.
   b. is a piece of information, such as a definition, a fact, a description, or an example.

Here is an example of the parts in just one paragraph. Notice the differences.

EXAMPLE

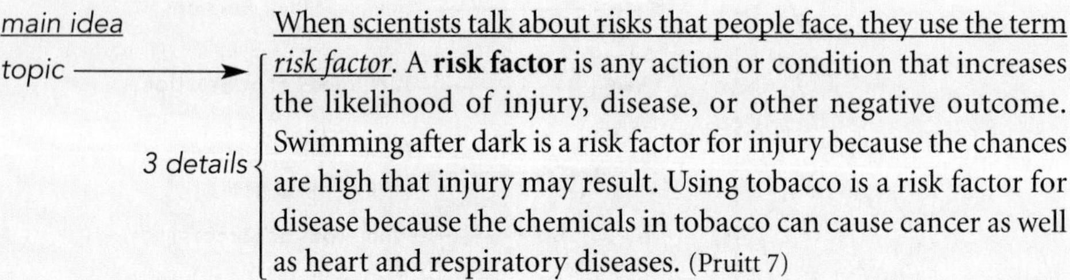

<u>When scientists talk about risks that people face, they use the term</u> *<u>risk factor</u>*. A **risk factor** is any action or condition that increases the likelihood of injury, disease, or other negative outcome. Swimming after dark is a risk factor for injury because the chances are high that injury may result. Using tobacco is a risk factor for disease because the chemicals in tobacco can cause cancer as well as heart and respiratory diseases. (Pruitt 7)

The paragraph topic, risk factors, is easy to spot because of the italics and bold-faced words. But authors do not always use font styles to emphasize the topic. A more important indicator is that every sentence in the paragraph is about risk factors. The first sentence is the main idea, because the scientific view of risk factors is the author's focus and dominant message. The other sentences offer a definition and examples; they are details that give more information about the topic and main idea.

ACTIVITY 1: IDENTIFY THE STRUCTURAL PARTS

DIRECTIONS: Each of the following lists contains one topic, one main idea, and a number of details. Label each part with the following letters: T for topic, MI for main idea, and D for detail.

1. __MI__ People need to realize that the earth has a very limited supply of fossil fuels.
   __D__ In just a century we will have used up more than half the fossil fuels that were formed over the ages.
   __D__ Ninety percent of all the fuels that ever existed will have been used in a period of 300 years.
   __D__ Coal reserves should last 300 years at the present rate of use.
   __T__ Fossil fuels (Adapted from Hill and Kolb 399)

2. __T__ The endocrine and nervous systems
   __MI__ The **endocrine system** is a communication system that works more slowly than the nervous system.
   ______ It works through chemical messengers called hormones.
   ______ Many of these hormones are produced in specialized glands.
   ______ Both the endocrine and nervous systems send signals throughout the body. (Adapted from Krogh 541)

3. ______ Once babies are emotionally attached to the mother or other caregiver, separation can be a wrenching experience.

______ Between 6 and 8 months of age, babies become wary or fearful of strangers.

______ They wail if they are put in an unfamiliar setting or are left with an unfamiliar person.

______ And they show **separation anxiety** if the primary caregiver temporarily leaves them.

______ This reaction usually continues until the middle of the second year.

______ Separation anxiety

______ Some children show signs of distress at parental separation until they are about 3 years old. (Adapted from Wade and Tavris 76)

4. ______ From the honky-tonk women of Memphis to the fear-no-SARS partiers of Toronto, over four decades of touring has taught the Rolling Stones all about how to rock the crowd.

______ And their fans have learned all about the crowds of scalpers that grab up the best seats!

______ Scalpers at Rolling Stones concerts

______ One ticket reseller paid $20 each to the brothers of a college fraternity just for standing in the ticket line.

______ That reseller hired over 150 stand-ins for a single Rolling Stones concert. (Ayers and Collinge 99)

There is a great difference between knowing and understanding: You can know a lot about something and not really understand it.

—Charles F. Kettering (1876–1958), American engineer

The Predict and Verify Process

As you saw in the ***Think about this*** . . . activity (p. 245), predict and verify is a logical way to think about a text. When you use this approach, you read a small amount of information, **predict,** or guess what will come next, and then read on to **verify** or check your predictions. If the information is what you expected, you continue reading with those predictions in mind. If the text doesn't match what you anticipated, or when the author brings up a new point, you change your focus and predict that the text will go in a different direction.

Predictions . . . are never anything but projections of present automatic processes and procedures, that is, of occurrences that are likely to come to pass . . .

—Hannah Arendt (1906–1975), German-born American political philosopher

Obviously, the best and fastest comprehension occurs when your predictions are accurate. How can you be accurate when you are reading for learning on topics that you know little about? Simply focus on the three elements of expository writing. That is, predict a possible topic and main idea as soon as you can; then, expect that the details will give more information about them. So, if a paragraph begins with "There are three problems with email," you'd predict that the topic is email and the idea is that there are three problems. If you're right, the details will be about those problems; if you're wrong, the mismatch will be obvious. Recognizing the match between your predictions and the text is the first way to verify your predictions.

Two additional methods of verification are to:

1. Check that the predicted topic and main idea match the general characteristics listed above (p. 247).
2. Turn your predictions into what, how, or why questions. If they're correct, the details will answer one or more of those questions.

The second method is particularly powerful because it requires active thinking to create questions and search for answers. Thus, it automatically engages interest, focuses your attention, and provides a way to monitor your comprehension. Because it is so motivating, this method will be stressed throughout the rest of the chapter.

Here's an example of this approach using a paragraph about culture and health. Notice that the questions start as soon as a possible topic and main idea are identified.

> **Tell me and I'll forget.**
> **Show me, and I may not remember.**
> **Involve me, and I'll understand.**
> —Native American saying

EXAMPLE

PREDICT: *This is the topic.* → *Is sent. 1 the MI?* *How enormous is the impact?* *How serious is the impact?*	The impact of culture on health is enormous. Worldwide, people have symptoms that are classified as disease within their culture. Among Aboriginal Australians, "fear of sorcery syndrome" is linked to voodoo and causes a range of ailments. Death can occur by "bone-pointing," in which a sharp stick is ritually cast into the victim's body. In Japan, men who are otherwise healthy drop dead from karoshi, the disease of overwork. (Adapted from Lindsey and Beach 55)

VERIFY:

-The predicted topic is correct, because every sentence talks about the impact of culture on health.

-Sentence 1 is the main idea, because the details answer the questions by showing how widespread it is, and why it's serious.

Once you have verified your predictions, mark the topic, idea, and important details in the text and record your insights in the margin. This step will capture your thinking so that you don't have to reread the material in the future.

In brief, the predict and verify process is as follows:

Step 1: Predict

A. Predict a likely topic and main idea.

B. Form what, how, or why questions about them.

Step 2: Verify and mark

A. Read to verify your predictions and find answers to your questions. If they're correct, continue; if not or if the focus shifts, change them.

B. Mark the text with underlining and margin notes for future use.

With the exception of marking, these steps generally occur in this order. Good marking is done as soon as you comprehend the text. On easy materials, you can often mark as you read; when the topic is complex or new to you, it may be necessary to read a little and then go back to mark what you've understood.

ACTIVITY 2: USE THE PREDICT AND VERIFY PROCESS

DIRECTIONS: Use the predict, verify, and mark process as you read the following texts.

Passage 1

1. From the beginning of the text, predict:
   a. The topic is: ______________________________.
   b. The main idea states that ______________________________
   ______________________________.
   c. Form questions:
   ____
   ____
   ____
2. Read on, verify and mark:
   Explain how your predictions are verified. If needed, revise them.
   ____
   ____

Notes

Supercomputers are the biggest and most powerful type of computer. Scientists and engineers use these computers to solve complex problems or to perform massive computations. Some supercomputers are single computers with multiple processors, while others consist of multiple computers that work together. The fastest supercomputer today is the Japanese-developed NEC Earth Simulator, which is used for climate modeling. It operates at nearly 40 teraflops (or 40 trillion operations per second). That's almost 40,000 times faster than the average personal computer! The supercomputer ASCI Q operates at 30 teraflops and is the fourth supercomputer in the U.S. Department of Energy's five-stage Advanced Simulation and Computing

Initiative (ASCI). The final objective for the DOE is development of a supercomputer that will achieve 100-teraflop speed by 2004. These ASCI supercomputers are designed to maintain the safety and reliability of the U.S. nuclear supply and to avoid underground testing. (Evans 365) (145 words)

Passage 2

1. From the beginning of the text, predict:
   a. The topic is: ____________________.
   b. The main idea states that ____________________
   ____________________.
   c. Form questions:
   ____
   ____
   ____
2. Read on; verify and mark:
   Explain how your predictions are verified. If needed, revise them.
   ____
   ____

The Trumps' American Dream

Notes

In the 1980s Donald and Ivana Trump were one of the most famous couples in the United States. Rich, glamorous, and powerful, the Trumps appeared to prove that the American Dream could still come true. Donald, the son of a prosperous real estate developer, seemed unaffected by recent history. As a young man, he ignored the rebellions of the 1960s and the economic troubles of the 1970s. At boarding school in the 1960s, he was "something of an alien," a writer explained. "His mind was on business when the minds of most of his peers were on pot, permissiveness, and hard rock music." Going into business in New York in the 1970s, Trump refused to be pessimistic about the city's depressed real estate market and uncertain finances. While the nation learned to live with less in a time of economic decline, Trump bought more and more. He aggressively acquired land and buildings at low prices. "I like beating my enemies to the ground," he boasted.

Trump's strategy paid off in the 1980s. By the time he turned 40 in 1986, Trump had accumulated one of the largest fortunes in America. He owned apartment houses and hotels. He built the posh Trump Tower on Fifth Avenue, complete with a five-story glass atrium and condominiums with price tags as high as 10 million dollars each. He had a glitzy gambling casino, Trump's Castle, in Atlantic City, New Jersey. He owned an airline, the Trump Shuttle. He owned a football team, the New Jersey Generals. He even had his own best-selling book, naturally titled *Trump*. Along with his three-story penthouse in the Trump Tower, he acquired a forty-seven-room hideaway in Connecticut and a seventeen-and-one-half-acre, 118-room estate in Palm Beach, Florida. He traveled in his own jet and his own helicopters. His twenty-nine-million-dollar yacht, the *Trump Princess,* had gold and onyx bathroom fixtures. "Who has done as much as I have?" he asked.

Trump's wife, Ivana, was a success story as well. She lived both an old dream for immigrants and a new dream for women. Born in Austria and raised in Czechoslovakia, she found riches and happiness in the United States. A modestly successful skier and model, Ivana married the man she called "The Donald" in New York in 1977 and became "a stunning prototype of the truly fashionable world-class billionairess." (Boydston et al. 865) (393 words)

Notes

When the mind is thinking, it is talking to itself.

—Plato (427–347 BC), Greek philosopher

Before you go on . . .

Monitor Your Progress: recite

As you read . . .

Focus Your Efforts: question and read

Find Main Ideas in Chapters and Sections

THINK ABOUT THIS . . .

1. How do these statements differ?
   a. Technology has changed how we do business.
   b. New technology allows you to record and play almost anything anywhere.
   c. You can now give up your big, bulky briefcase and carry a presentation or record an entire meeting on the same small device.

   ____

   ____

   ____

2. Reminder: Preread this section.

Ideas can be either broad or restricted. In the ***Think about this . . .*** activity, the thought that technology has changed business is a very broad idea, because it could cover all kinds of technology. The second sentence about new recording devices refers to just one type of technology, so it's more restricted. And recording presentations and meetings is just one application of the new technology, so the final sentence is even more restricted than the other two.

Ideas are the roots of creation.
—Ernest Dimnet (1866–1954), French clergyman

The broader the idea, the bigger the discussion block needs to be. A very broad idea, such as the first one about technology, would probably require an entire chapter. Others, such as the second idea about new technology, are restricted enough to be covered in a section. In either case, the predict and verify approach can be used to aid your understanding.

Chapter Main Ideas

Each chapter is focused on a topic or issue within the discipline, which is divided into major sections of information about it. The chapter main idea unifies the major sections. When it is stated, the author tells you how the sections relate to the topic and to each other; when it's implied, you will need to figure out those relationships.

Stated Ideas Using the predict and verify process, you can locate the chapter topic and idea, recognize the details that will be presented, and improve your understanding of the chapter discussion.

To find the chapter elements, use these characteristics in addition to the general ones presented earlier (p. 247).

The Chapter Topic
The chapter topic is usually stated in the chapter title.

The Main Idea

1. The stated main idea of the chapter is called the **thesis.**
2. The thesis has these characteristics:
   a. It's generally stated in one sentence, although it can be in two or three sentences that follow one another.
   b. It's usually located at the end of the chapter introduction.
   c. It's often introduced by a phrase such as "In this chapter . . . ," "The purpose of this discussion . . . ," or "We will consider . . ."

The Details

1. The major details are named in the major headings.
2. The information related to those major details is contained in the major sections.

To predict and verify, start looking for the topic and thesis as soon as you begin prereading. When you find elements that match the characteristics, form what, how, or why questions about them. Verify your predictions with information in the introduction and by checking the major headings. If you're right, the introduction should talk about your predicted topic and the headings should identify the kind of details that will answer your main idea questions. Here's an example of this approach using the chapter title, introduction, and major headings from a psychology chapter.

EXAMPLE

PREDICT:	**Learning**
-This is the topic. → *(points to "Learning")*	Implicit learning, which occurs without our awareness, is a primitive but powerful form of adaptation. Without really trying, subjects learn the grammar in their native tongue, figure out how to behave properly, or "calculate" the trajectory of a ball in order to catch it. To learn from experience, people must be attuned to associations between the stimuli in their environment and between behavior and its consequences. As we'll see in this chapter, association is the basic building block for all learning.
-How do we learn?	
-The last sentence is the thesis.	
-How does association promote learning?	
VERIFY:	
Look at the major headings:	Classical Conditioning Operant Conditioning Observational Learning (Adapted from Kassin 172–174)

-The topic is verified because the introduction focuses on it and the three headings appear to answer the question "How do we learn?"

-The thesis will be verified if each section shows how association is basic to each way of learning.

ACTIVITY 3: PREDICT AND VERIFY CHAPTER ELEMENTS

DIRECTIONS: Use the predict, verify, and mark process as you read the following excerpts.

Excerpt 1

1. From the beginning, predict:

a. The chapter topic is: ____________________.

b. The thesis states that ____________________

____________________.

c. Form questions:

____

____

____

2. Read on; verify and mark:

Explain how your predictions are verified. If needed, revise them.

____

____

____

Chapter Title:	**Memory**	*Notes*
Introduction:	Psychologists often liken human memory to a computer that faithfully records information for later use. Studies reveal, however, that there is much more to the story. As we'll see in this chapter, remembering is an active process, and we sometimes construct memories in light of our own beliefs, wishes, needs, contextual factors, and information received from outside sources.	
Major Headings:	An Information-Processing Model The Sensory Register Short-Term Memory Long-Term Memory Autobiographical Memory (Adapted from Kassin 208–210)	

Excerpt 2

1. From the beginning, predict:

a. The chapter topic is: ______________________________.

b. The thesis states that ______________________________

______________________________.

c. Form questions:

____

____

____

2. Read on; verify and mark:

Explain how your predictions are verified. If needed, revise them.

____

____

____

Chapter Title: **Family Violence and Other Crises** *Notes*

Introduction: Families can be warm, loving, and nurturing, but they can also be cruel and abusive. Family members are more likely than outsiders to assault or kill other family members. This chapter examines the different forms of domestic violence and discusses why people who say they love each other are so abusive. We then turn to other family crises such as drug abuse and depression, as well as some successful intervention strategies.

Major Headings: Marital and Intimate Partner Violence
Violence against Infants and Children
Hidden Victims: Siblings and Adolescents
Violence against Elderly Family Members
Explaining Family Violence
Other Family Crises
Intervening in Domestic Violence (Adapted from Benokraitis 393)

The most important thing in science is not so much to obtain new facts as to discover new ways of thinking about them.

—Sir William Bragg (1862–1942), Australian physicist, 1915 Nobel Prize Laureate

Implied Ideas If the author doesn't directly state the chapter thesis, it is implied. Since you need to understand the chapter's main idea in order to recognize how the major sections relate to the topic, you will need to state the chapter's main idea yourself as part of the verification step.

How do you form a chapter main idea? There are three ways. First, you can simply restate the chapter title and headings in a sentence. Second, you can state the chapter title and the number of sections in the chapter. Third, you can identify a simple insight that you infer from looking at the title, introduction, and major headings. Once you have a main idea, turn it into questions. Here's an example from a sociology chapter that has an implied main idea, along with three possible main idea statements and questions that could be created.

EXAMPLE

Chapter Title: **The Family and Religion**

Introduction: The family is not only a cultural universal, it is the oldest and most conservative social institution. Diversity within it may be viewed as either a threat to social stability or an opportunity for growth. Religion is a social institution that is almost as old as the family. All religions search for ways to reconcile faith within modern life. Clearly there are major disagreements regarding how best to do this.

Major Headings:
What Is a Family?
Emerging Lifestyles
Theoretical Perspectives on Religion
World Religions and Social Change (Adapted from Lindsey and Beach xiii)

Possible main idea statements

1. The topic family and religion includes what is a family, emerging lifestyles, theoretical perspectives on religion, and world religions and social change. How do family and religion affect lifestyles, religious theories, world religions, and social change?
2. The topic, family and religion, includes four issues. What are the four issues?
3. Family and religion affect everything from what we mean by family to social change. How do family and religion affect us?

Get your ideas on paper and study them. Do not let them go to waste!
—Les Brown (1945–), American speaker and author

How does forming your own main idea fit into the predict and verify process? It's simply another step that you'll perform as you verify the topic. In other words, predict the topic from the title and form questions about it. Look over the introduction to verify the topic. Recognize that there's no thesis. Read the headings and form a main idea sentence.

ACTIVITY 4: CREATE A CHAPTER MAIN IDEA

DIRECTIONS: The following excerpt does not have a thesis. Use the predict, verify, and mark process as you read it.

1. From the beginning, predict:
   a. The chapter topic is: ______________________________.
   b. Form questions:
      ____
      ____
      ____
2. Read on; verify and mark:
   a. Form a main idea statement:
      ____
      ____
      ____
   b. Form questions:
      ____
      ____
      ____
   c. Explain how your predictions are verified. If needed, revise them.
      ____
      ____

Chapter Title:	**Prison Life**	*Notes*
Introduction:	For many years, prisons and prison life could be described by the phrase "out of sight, out of mind." Very few citizens cared about prison conditions. By the mid-twentieth century, however, this attitude started to change. Concerned citizens began to offer their services, neighborhoods began accepting work-release prisoners, and social scientists initiated a serious study of prison life.	
Major Headings:	The Male Inmate's World The Female Inmate's World The Staff World Prison Riots Prisoners' Rights (Adapted from Schmalleger 506–507)	

Section Main Ideas

In a chapter, you will have several major sections and some of those will have subsections, which might also have minor sections. Each of these sections has a topic, a main idea, and details that explain it. Understanding the section idea is critical to your comprehension of the whole unit. Like chapter main ideas, section ideas can be stated or implied.

Stated Ideas If the section topic is brief and straightforward, the heading will be followed by the paragraphs of information. If the topic is lengthy or more complex, the section will be broken up into subsections or minor sections, each with its own heading, idea, and set of details.

Finding section topics and main ideas is the primary way to comprehend these units. To locate them, use these guidelines in addition to the general ones (p. 247).

The Section Topic

The section topic is usually stated in the section heading.

The Section Main Idea

1. The main idea of a section is called the **central idea.**

   It is rarely more than one sentence long.

2. The central idea has these characteristics:
   a. It may be introduced by a phrase such as "In this section . . . ,".
   b. In a section that only has paragraphs, it is usually located at the beginning of the first paragraph.
   c. In a section with subheadings, there is a major section idea, as well as a central idea for each subsection.

      -The major idea is generally presented right before the first subheading.

      -Each subsection idea is usually presented in the first paragraph of that section.

The Details

1. In a section with just paragraphs, the details are contained in the sentences.
2. In a section with subheadings, the details are named in the subheadings. The specific information is then provided in the actual paragraphs.

The following examples show how the predict and verify process would be applied to a major section with paragraphs and one with subsections. The predicted central ideas are italicized in the left column, which presents the original text. The predicted topics are underlined in the right column, which shows the reader's thoughts.

EXAMPLES

MAJOR SECTION WITH PARAGRAPHS

Why Are Drug Rates So High?

Although there are many reasons, parents play an important role in their children's drug use. Many middle-class parents, especially, rely on Ritalin and other drugs to control young children's behavior. And children who experience domestic violence are more likely to use drugs and alcohol in adolescence and adulthood than their nonabused counterparts.

Although even the best parents can't prevent their children from trying drugs, many parents don't discuss drug use with their children or do not do so adequately. According to one national survey, for example, 35 percent of parents but only 14 percent of teenagers age 14 to 17 said that parents talk to teenagers about drugs "a lot."

What's more, in a study of drug addicts in drug treatment centers in four states, 20 percent of the respondents said that their parents had introduced them to drugs. (Adapted from Benokraitis 417)

PREDICT AND VERIFY

PREDICT: Drug rates is the section topic.
Why are the rates so high?

VERIFY: The question is answered.

PREDICT: Sentence 1 is the central idea.
How do parents influence children's drug use?

VERIFY: Here's one answer.

Here's a second answer.

Here's a third answer.

MAJOR SECTION WITH SUBSECTIONS

Long-Term Memory

Like the hard drive on a PC, long-term memory is a relatively enduring storage system that has the capacity to retain vast amounts of information for long periods of time. *This section examines long-term memories of the recent and remote past—how they are encoded, stored, and retrieved.*

Encoding

Information can be kept alive in short-term memory by rote repetition, or maintenance rehearsal. *But, as the following discussion shows, to transfer something into long-term memory, you would find it much more effective to use elaborative rehearsal.*

Storage

Cognitive psychologists have long been interested in the format, the content, and the neural bases of memory storage as it is represented in the brain. (Adapted from Kassin 221–236)

PREDICT: Long-term memory is the section topic.
What is it? How does it work?

VERIFY: Long-term memory is the topic of the text.

PREDICT: Sentence 2 is the central idea CI.
How are long-term memories encoded, stored, and retrieved?

VERIFY: The subheadings match the 3 CI terms.

PREDICT: Encoding is the subsection topic.
How does encoding work?

PREDICT: Sentence 2 is the subsection CI.
Why is elaborative rehearsal more effective?

VERIFY: Reading needed to answer the questions.

PREDICT: Storage is the subsection topic.
How does storage work?

PREDICT: Sentence 1 is the subsection's CI.
What are the format, content, and neural bases of storage?

VERIFY: Reading needed to answer questions.

ACTIVITY 5: PREDICT AND VERIFY SECTION ELEMENTS

DIRECTIONS: Use the predict, verify, and mark process as you read the following excerpts.

Section 1 Excerpt

1. From the beginning, predict:
   a. The section topic is: ______________________________.
   b. The central idea states that ______________________________
   ______________________________.
   c. Form questions:
   ____
   ____
   ____
2. Read on; verify and mark:
   Explain how your predictions are verified. If needed, revise them.
   ____
   ____

New Women, New Ideas

Notes

By the early 1900s, the woman question had grown to include a number of issues. One was the question of lifestyle. How should women dress and behave? As more women entered the work force or went to college, they took this matter into their own hands. Because they valued convenience, they began to wear shorter hairstyles, raise their hemlines, and wear skirts and blouses that were more suited to their new activities.

Courting and marriage customs also changed. For example, instead of being limited to entertaining a man at home under the watchful eyes of their parents, many young women now went out on dates without supervision. "New women," as they were sometimes called, still hoped to marry. Yet they seemed to have higher expectations of fulfillment in marriage than earlier generations of women did. As a result, the divorce rate rose from one in twelve in 1900 to one in nine by 1916. Many "new women" who married began to push for the legalized spread of information about birth control, a campaign led by New York nurse Margaret

Sanger. Such developments were shocking to more traditional Americans.

What was the consensus among women on the woman question? Although the majority wanted "their rights," most women still saw domestic fulfillment as their chief goal. But the right to vote was another matter. The issue of the vote prompted huge numbers of women to support the suffrage movement in some way. Soon the vote would be the one issue on which women from many walks of life would unite. (Adapted from Cayton et al. 573) (262 words)

Notes

Section 2 Excerpt

1. From the beginning of the major section, predict:
   a. The major section topic is: ______________________________.
   b. The major central idea states that ______________________________
   ______________________________.
   c. Form questions:
   ____
   ____
   ____

   Read on; verify and mark:
   d. Explain how your predictions are verified. If needed, revise them.
   ____
   ____

2. From the beginning of the first subsection, predict:
   a. The subsection topic is: ______________________________.
   b. The subsection central idea states that ______________________________
   ______________________________.
   c. Form questions:
   ____
   ____
   ____

   Read on; verify and mark:
   d. Explain how your predictions are verified. If needed, revise them.
   ____
   ____

3. From the beginning of the second subsection, predict:
   a. The subsection topic is: ______________________________
   b. The subsection central idea states that ______________________________
   ______________________________.
   c. Form questions:
   ____
   ____
   ____

   Read on; verify and mark:
   d. Explain how your predictions are verified. If needed, revise them.
   ____
   ____

The Early Years of Marriage

Notes

The bridal media bombard women with merchandise. Many people spend more on a wedding than the cost of a four-year degree at an average-priced state college. Because most couples don't attend premarital classes, what happens after the romantic wedding ceremonies are over? Two kinds of adjustments occur.

After the Vows For every generation, the first year involves basic adjustments. After a tumultuous and exciting wedding, the groom takes on the new and unfamiliar role of husband. Brides, especially, often encounter a "marriage shock." Unlike their husbands, many women must take on such "wifely" roles as pleasing the husband's family and friends and being the "emotional guardians" of the marriage (Heyn, 1997). Many experience a "wedding postpartum":

> When . . . you find that your new husband blows his nose in the shower, few brides escape feeling some degree of disillusionment. You know then you're not at the champagne fountain anymore. Even though you weren't expecting perpetual bubbly from your marriage, the reality can be startling (Stark, 1998: 88).

It takes some women up to a year to feel comfortable with their new married name and the new identity of "wife" that it brings (Nissinen, 2000).

Notes

A second adjustment involves putting a mutual relationship before ties with others. Couples must strike a balance between their relationships with their in-laws and their own marital bond. Parents (especially mothers) who fear losing contact with their married children sometimes create conflict by calling and visiting frequently and "meddling" in the couple's life (Chadiha et al., 1998; Greider, 2000).

Settling In Many twenty-first-century newlyweds must adjust to three other changes after the marriage that their parents and grandparents rarely experienced. First, because many couples have lived together before saying "I do" (see Chapter 9), they must now address issues like where to spend the holidays.

Second, two-paycheck newlyweds—especially those who marry after a long period of independence—must make a transition from "my" money to "our" money. Adjusting to a joint bank account isn't always easy, because individuals aren't used to pooling their money. In addition, the couple will have to reach consensus about paying off college loans, credit card debts, mortgage payments (if she just bought a house and he hasn't, for example) and saving for the future. And what if he's a spender and she's a saver?

Third, and as you saw earlier, many contemporary newlyweds are from divorced homes. They are simultaneously wary of marriage and more determined to make their marriage succeed. Because these couples haven't had role models for a successful marriage, they have to work especially hard at being married. (Adapted from Benokraitis 277) (434 words)

Implied Ideas When the central idea for a section is implied, form your own main idea sentence. This process is very similar to forming a chapter main idea. If there are subheadings or minor headings in the section, thread them together into a logical sentence. Here's an example from a biology book; the major heading is followed by two subheadings, but the section has no stated central idea.

EXAMPLE

WHAT IS SCIENCE?

Science as a Body of Knowledge

Science as a Process

Main Idea: Science is a body of knowledge and a process.

When you have no smaller section headings to work with, you will need to read the paragraphs before you can form a main idea. Then follow these steps:

1. Predict the section topic. Form a question.
2. Read and note what each paragraph is about.
3. Infer an idea that is common to all the paragraphs.
4. Create a main idea sentence using the topic and your inference. Form a question.
5. Verify your topic and main idea by looking for answers to your questions.

Here's an example of this process using a section that has three paragraphs but no central idea. The main point in each paragraph is underlined.

EXAMPLE

Parenting Teenagers

Adolescence is a time of tremendous change. Like younger children, teenagers are active agents in the family. Adolescents are establishing their own identity and are testing their autonomy as they mature and break away from parental supervision, a healthy process in human development. Teenagers often complain that parents treat them like little children: "Have you done your homework?" "Did you brush your teeth?"

A good parent–child relationship may change suddenly during adolescence. As children enter the seventh and eighth grades, there may be conflict over such issues as relationships, money, and spending time with friends.

As teenagers become more independent, parents may feel rejected and suspicious. The most difficult part of parenting adolescents, according to some mothers, is dealing with adolescents' changing moods and behavior. (Adapted from Benokraitis 343)

Creating a section main idea:

1. The topic is Parenting Teenagers. How do you parent teenagers?
2. The paragraphs state that:
   Adolescent reactions change.
   Parent–child relationships change.
   Parents may be feeling differently.
3. Each paragraph shows a change that occurs.
4. The main idea: Parenting teenagers involves dealing with three major changes. What three changes do parents have to deal with?
5. The topic and main idea are verified because the questions are answered.

ACTIVITY 6: CREATE SECTION MAIN IDEAS

DIRECTIONS: Practice creating section main ideas by completing the following tasks. *Part 1.* Form a main idea statement for each of the following lists of major headings and subheadings.

A. Why Have Abortion Rates Decreased?
   Attitudes about Abortion
   Contraceptives
   Abortion Services
   Laws and Policies (Benokraitis 320)

Main idea: ______________________________

____

B. Types of Retailers
   Amount of Service
   Product Line
   Relative Prices
   Retail Organizations (Armstrong 435)

Main idea: ______________________________

____

Part 2. The following section does not have a stated central idea. Use the predict, verify, and mark process as you read it. Form your own main idea.

1. From the beginning, predict:
   a. The section topic is: ______________________________.
   b. Form questions:

____

____

____

2. Read on; verify and mark:
   a. Form a main idea statement:

____

____

____

   b. Form questions:

____

____

____

   c. Explain how your predictions are verified. If needed, revise them.

____

____

____

What Causes Mutations?

Notes

A critical question, of course, is what causes DNA to mutate? One answer is so-called environmental insults. The chemicals in cigarette smoke are powerful *mutagens,* meaning substances that can mutate DNA. So is the ultraviolet light that comes from the sun. To look at the latter example in a little more detail, ultraviolet light is a form of radiation that can link adjacent T's together in a single strand of DNA; sometimes it even causes both strands of the DNA helix to break. When this latter damage takes place in a cell, one of three things can happen. First, enzymes can successfully repair the damage. Second, the cell will recognize that this damage *cannot* be repaired, in which case the cell will commit suicide in the process known as apoptosis. Third, the enzymes will not repair the damage, but the cell will fail to initiate apoptosis. In this instance, the *failed* repair action may mean permanent change in base sequence—a mutation, in short.

Not all mutations are caused by environmental influences. Mutations happen simply as random, spontaneous events. Molecules collide in a cell, for example, causing DNA damage. The very process of eating and breathing produces so-called free radicals that can damage DNA. And the DNA replication machinery itself may introduce errors, irrespective of any outside influences.

Once such errors occur, it is understandable that some of them will go uncorrected. When a human cell divides, billions of DNA base pairs have to be copied. And some 25 million cells are dividing each second in human beings. The surprise, therefore, is not that mistakes happen, but that so *few* of them happen, and that fewer still become permanent. (Krogh 258) (282 words)

Before you go on . . .

Monitor Your Progress: recite

Reading is to the mind what exercise is to the body.

—Joseph Addison (1672–1719), British writer of essays, poems, and dramas

As you read . . .

Focus Your Efforts: question and read

Find Main Ideas in Paragraphs

THINK ABOUT THIS . . .

1. Assume that you want to ask your boss for a raise. You have a meeting with him today and you're thinking about a number of ways to bring up the subject. Look at each of these options and then describe the benefits of leading the conversation that way.
   a. You could begin with a request for a raise followed by a list of your accomplishments on the job.

   ____

   ____

   b. You could begin with a list of your accomplishments and then end with a request for a raise.

   ____

   ____

   c. You could begin with one or two accomplishments, ask for the raise, and then present more of your achievements.

   ____

   ____

   ____

   d. You could simply list your accomplishments and data about the salaries people in your position generally make and not specifically ask for a raise.

   ____

   ____

2. Reminder: Preread this section.

Like speakers, authors must decide how to arrange the important ideas and details. And, as the ***Think about this*** . . . activity demonstrates, communicators can present their message in four very different formats. Placing the main idea first is a way to "get down to business." Putting it last makes it a logical conclusion or summary of the details. If it's presented in the middle, details that spark interest are generally presented before the idea, and additional explanations or proof are given after it. And, finally, the idea may be implied rather than directly stated, which allows the facts to "speak for themselves."

Like listeners, readers have to work with the order of presentation to comprehend the message. To do this, they predict and verify topics, main ideas, and details, but they shift their thinking as the format changes.

The Paragraph Elements

In textbooks, introductory and concluding paragraphs make up a very small part of a chapter. The majority of paragraphs are body paragraphs. Like chapters and sections, they also have topics, main ideas, and details with some unique characteristics. Once you locate them, using a special marking system that separates the three elements will enhance your focus and eliminate unnecessary rereading.

Topics The term **body paragraphs** refers to a group of related sentences that focus on one major point. The sentences are related because they are all about the same, focused topic. Finding a paragraph topic is one of the most useful steps in understanding a paragraph, because it makes it easier to find the main idea. How do you identify the topic?

1. The topic is the best label for the entire paragraph.
   If it focuses on only one detail, it will be too narrow; if it goes beyond what's in the paragraph, it's too broad.
2. The topic noun may be emphasized by one of these writing techniques:
   a. Repetition
   b. Use of synonym(s) that refer to the topic noun
   c. Use of pronoun(s) that refer to the topic noun
   d. Stating the topic in both the beginning and end of the paragraph

Look at following paragraph. Which of the author's terms would be too narrow, too broad, and the best label for the entire paragraph? Which writing techniques helped you find your answer?

EXAMPLE

The status of colonial women was determined by the men in their lives. Most women were legally the dependents of men and had no legal or political standing. Married women could not own property. Laws prevented women from voting or holding office or serving on a jury. Even a widowed woman did not have any political rights, although she could inherit her husband's property and conduct business. (Adapted from Cayton et al. 80)

"Married women" would be too narrow, because the details also cover widows. "Colonial women" would be too broad, because the paragraph is not about everything in their lives, such as children or education. The best label would be "the status of colonial women," because each of the following sentences is about just that. The writing techniques include repetition of the term "women," which is part of the topic phrase, as well as the pronouns "she" and "her" that refer to it.

ACTIVITY 7: FIND THE BEST TOPIC LABEL

DIRECTIONS: Practice finding the best label by completing the following tasks.

1. Read each of the following list of details. Then mark the possible topics as follows:

   A. Too narrow **B.** Too broad **C.** Best label

DETAILS	TOPICS
a. BMW	______ cars
Mercedes Benz	______ luxury car manufacturers
Cadillac	______ European auto manufacturers
b. family	______ social groups
friends	______ relatives
those you spend time with	______ people
c. love	______ three reactions
anger	______ feelings we all want
guilt	______ emotions
d. physician	______ care givers
folk healer	______ doctors
shaman	______ healers
witch doctor	

2. Read each of the following paragraphs. Then, mark the possible topics as follows:

   A. Too narrow **B.** Too broad **C.** Best label

   a. Although a pleasant appearance is desirable in both women and men, it may not always increase one's chances of finding a suitable partner. In a study of black women, for example, some of the respondents felt that being attractive sometimes had negative consequences. A good-looking woman might make a man feel so insecure that he will not approach her: "People assume you already have enough candidates." Many of the women also felt that "the guys want to show off because an attractive woman increases a man's status in his friends' eyes" (Sterk-Elifson, 1994: 108). If some men treat attractive women as trophies instead of serious marriage candidates, the women may have a large pool of dating partners but few serious suitors. (Benokraitis 214)

   Possible topics:

   ______ Pleasant appearance ______ Black women

   ______ Attractive women ______ A good-looking woman

   b. The "family values" agenda of social conservatives supports traditional gender roles and opposes gay marriage, affirmative action, and other "special programs" that take account of people's group membership rather than their individual abilities and efforts. Social conservatives condemn abortion as morally wrong and support the death penalty as a just response to heinous crime. (Macionis 442)

Possible topics:

______ "Family values"

______ Traditional gender roles

______ "Family values" agenda of social conservatives

______ Social conservatives

You can verify your topic prediction in a number of ways. First, you can look for a match between it and what the sentences focus on. Second, you can check whether your predicted topic has the characteristics of a topic listed above. Third, you can look for the writing techniques that emphasize it. Finally, you can form what, how, or why questions about the topic; if you're accurate, the details will answer one or more of them.

ACTIVITY 8: FIND PARAGRAPH TOPICS

DIRECTIONS: Use the predict, verify, and mark process to locate the topic of the following paragraphs.

Paragraph 1

1. From the beginning, predict:
   a. The paragraph topic is: ______________________________.
   b. Form questions:

      ____

      ____

      ____

2. Read on; verify and mark: *Notes*

   Video teleconferencing allows doctors to consult with each other and with patients in real time, at a distance. A patient may be in his or her primary physician's office with a camera and a telecommunications link to a specialist's office. Everyone can be seen and heard in real-time. Only a videophone and a connection to the Internet might be required. However, the most sophisticated systems involve microphones, scanners, cameras, medical instruments, and dedicated phone lines. One form of video teleconferencing is the remote house call, involving only one medical practitioner and a patient in another location. (Adapted from Burke and Weill 61)

Notes

Verify: Check off all the verification reasons that apply.

_____ Matches what the text focuses on

_____ Repetition _____ Synonym(s) _____ Pronoun(s)

_____ Topic is stated in both the beginning and end of the paragraph

_____ Answers my question(s)

Paragraph 2

1. From the beginning, predict:
   a. The paragraph topic is: ______________________________.
   b. Form questions:

____

____

____

2. Read on; verify and mark:

Notes

Just how safe are online transactions? When you buy something over the Web, you most likely use a credit card; therefore, the exchange of money is done directly between you and a bank. Because online shopping eliminates a sales clerk or other human intermediary from the transaction, it can actually be safer than traditional retail shopping. Still, businesses must have some form of security certification to give their customers a level of comfort. Businesses hire security companies such as VeriSign to certify that their online transactions are secure. Thus, if a Web site displays the VeriSign seal, you can trust that the information you submit to the site is protected. (Adapted from Evans et al. 91)

Verify: Check off all the verification reasons that apply.

_____ Matches what the text focuses on

_____ Repetition _____ Synonym(s) _____ Pronoun(s)

_____ Topic is stated in both the beginning and end of the paragraph

_____ Answers my question(s)

Main Ideas A paragraph's main idea is the author's opinion or dominant point about the topic. The main idea works with the topic to unite all the sentences into a single unit. In addition to the general characteristics (p. 247), paragraph main ideas have these characteristics:

1. When the main idea is stated, it is called the **topic sentence.**
   It is rarely more than one sentence long.
2. The topic sentence has these characteristics:
   a. It can be located anywhere in the paragraph.
   b. Since it is the author's own idea or opinion, it will *not* be
      1) a quote or reference from another source.
      2) a saying.
      3) a detail.
      4) a question.

So, to predict which sentence is the topic sentence, look for one that is the author's opinion, that's broad enough to cover the rest of the sentences, and that isn't on the "will not be" list. To verify it, check that it matches the text and the above characteristics. Also, turn it into what, how, or why questions; as always, your thinking is on track when the details answer your questions. Look at this example from a paragraph in Activity 7. Which sentence do you think is the topic sentence?

EXAMPLE

Although a pleasant appearance is desirable in both women and men, it may not always increase one's chances of finding a suitable partner. In a study of black women, for example, some of the respondents felt that being attractive sometimes had negative consequences. A good-looking woman might make a man feel so insecure that he will not approach her: "People assume you already have enough candidates." Many of the women also felt that "the guys want to show off because an attractive woman increases a man's status in his friends' eyes" (Sterk-Elifson, 1994: 108). If some men treat attractive women as trophies instead of serious marriage candidates, the women may have a large pool of dating partners but few serious suitors.

If you chose the first sentence, you are correct. It can be verified because it's the author's opinion about a pleasant appearance, and the rest of the sentences are details about a specific study of black women. And, it's not a quote or reference, saying, detail, or question. Also, if you ask the question "How can a pleasant appearance decrease the chances of finding a suitable partner?" the details provide answers.

ACTIVITY 9: FIND TOPIC SENTENCES

DIRECTIONS: Use the predict and verify approach to identify the topic sentence for each of the paragraphs in Activity 8.

Paragraph 1

1. Predict:
   a. The topic sentence states that ______________________________
   ______________________________.
   b. Form questions:
   ____
   ____
   ____
2. Verify: Check off all the verification reasons that apply.
   ______ Presents an opinion ______ Broad and covers other sentences
   ______ Not a quote or reference
   ______ Not a saying ______ Not a detail ______ Not a question
   ______ Answers my question(s)

Paragraph 2

1. Predict:
   a. The topic sentence states that ______________________________
   ______________________________.
   b. Form questions:
   ____
   ____
   ____
2. Verify: Check off all the verification reasons that apply.
   ______ Presents an opinion ______ Broad and covers other sentences
   ______ Not a quote or reference
   ______ Not a saying ______ Not a detail ______ Not a question
   ______ Answers my question(s)

The third ingredient of body paragraphs—details—are all the sentences except for the topic sentence. They form the bulk of each paragraph. Details support the topic and main idea with specific pieces of information, such as a definition, a fact, a description, or an example. They are so important in reading for learning that this book devotes a whole chapter to them (Chapter 7). For now, simply remember that a detail cannot be either the paragraph topic or main idea.

Marking the Elements Distinguishing the topic from the main idea and details as you read adds significantly to your comprehension. And you will gain the most from your efforts if you develop an underlining system that visually separates these elements so that you won't have to reread or figure them out again in the future.

You can devise your own method or use one of the following. Some students use three colors of highlighters or pens to identify the elements. But a simpler system is to just use different underlining styles. Here's an effective method:

1. Circle the paragraph topic.
2. Completely underline the topic sentence.
3. Underline only the key words or short phrases in the details.

Here's an example of how this method looks on the risk-taking paragraph.

EXAMPLE

When scientists talk about risks that people face, they use the term *risk factor*. A **risk factor** is any action or condition that increases the likelihood of injury, disease, or other negative outcome. Swimming after dark is a risk factor for injury because the chances are high that injury may result. Using tobacco is a risk factor for disease because the chemicals in tobacco can cause cancer as well as heart and respiratory diseases.

ACTIVITY 10: USE A MARKING SYSTEM

DIRECTIONS: Use the three underlining styles to mark the following paragraphs.

1. The status of colonial women was determined by the men in their lives. Most women were legally the dependents of men and had no legal or political standing. Married women could not own property. Laws prevented women from voting or holding office or serving on a jury. Even a widowed woman did not have any political rights, although she could inherit her husband's property and conduct business. (Adapted from Cayton et al. 80)

2. Supercomputers are the biggest and most powerful type of computer. Scientists and engineers use these computers to solve complex problems or to perform massive computations. Some supercomputers are single computers with multiple processors, while others consist of multiple computers that work together. The fastest supercomputer today is the Japanese-developed NEC Earth Simulator, which is used for climate modeling. It operates at nearly 40 teraflops (or 40 trillion operations per second). That's almost 40,000 times faster than the average personal computer! The supercomputer ASCI Q operates at 30 teraflops and is the fourth supercomputer in the U.S. Department of Energy's five-stage Advanced Simulation

and Computing Initiative (ASCI). The final objective for the DOE is development of a supercomputer that will achieve 100-teraflop speed by 2004. These ASCI supercomputers are designed to maintain the safety and reliability of the U.S. nuclear supply and to avoid underground testing. (Evans 365)

Practice this kind of differential marking system, along with annotating, on the rest of the activities in this chapter.

Reading is always at once the effort to comprehend and the effort to incorporate.

—Robert Scholes (contemporary), *Textual Power: Literary Theory and the Teaching of English*

Paragraph Formats

The predict and verify approach works well on paragraphs. However, since the author's thinking and the order of the parts may differ from paragraph to paragraph, the reader's thinking must change as well. The following sections will help you recognize and get comfortable with these shifts.

Topic Sentence First In some paragraphs, the topic and topic sentence appear in the very first sentence of the paragraph. All the supporting details come after it. This format is the easiest for readers to comprehend, because the reader can locate the topic, topic sentence, and details in that order. The predict and verify approach works without any modifications, and you can usually mark as you read.

Here's how the predict and verify process works on a paragraph from a sociology textbook about traditional women's jobs. The topic sentence (TS) is the first sentence.

EXAMPLE

PREDICT:
-This is the topic
-Sent. 1 is the TS.
-What is gender stratification?
-How is it easy to see?

Gender stratification in the workplace is easy to see. Female nurses assist male physicians, female secretaries serve male executives, and female flight attendants are under the command of male airplane pilots. And, in education, for example, women represent 98 percent of kindergarten teachers, 83 percent of elementary school teachers, 58 percent of secondary school teachers, 43 percent of college and university professors, and 19 percent of college and university presidents. (Adapted from Macionis 333)

VERIFY:
The topic is verified, because every sentence is about gender stratification.
The topic sentence is verified, because the details answer the "how" question.

ACTIVITY 11: RECOGNIZE PARAGRAPHS WITH THE TOPIC SENTENCE FIRST

DIRECTIONS: The topic sentence is the first sentence in each of the following paragraphs. Use the predict, verify, and mark approach as you read each one.

Paragraph 1

1. From the beginning, predict:
   a. The paragraph topic is: ______________________________.
   b. The topic sentence states that ______________________________
   ______________________________.
   c. Form questions:
   ____
   ____
   ____
2. Read on; verify and mark:
   Explain how your predictions are verified. If needed, revise them.
   ____
   ____

Cultural practices can help to transmit disease. Malaria in Nigeria occurs when water in clay pots is left at shrines that then become breeding grounds for mosquitoes. Cement footbaths in mosques in Muslim countries produce skin fungus. Resistance to using condoms is found throughout Africa and Asia because of strong cultural beliefs that they compromise a man's sexual potency, surely hastening the spread of AIDS. (Adapted from Lindsey and Beach 55)

Notes

Paragraph 2

1. From the beginning, predict:
   a. The paragraph topic is: ______________________________.
   b. The topic sentence states that ______________________________
   ______________________________.
   c. Form questions:
   ____
   ____
   ____

2. Read on; verify and mark:

Explain how your predictions are verified. If needed, revise them.

___

___

___

Most people aren't very good listeners. We face so many distractions that we often give speakers less than our full attention. We listen at or below a 25 percent efficiency rate, remember only about half of what's said during a 20-minute conversation, and forget half of that within 48 hours. Furthermore, when questioned about material we've just heard, we are likely to get the facts mixed up. That's because although we tend to listen to words, we don't necessarily listen to the message. (Thill and Bovee 47)

Notes

Topic Sentence in the Middle When the topic sentence is in the middle, it may be any sentence except the very first or the very last one. In this format, introductory information is given first, followed by the topic sentence, with more support ending the paragraph. The introduction may include details, a question, or background information, and it may not specifically name the paragraph topic. So, when you encounter questions or general information, read on and continue looking for the topic and topic sentence. Once you've found them, you can form questions. Use your detail marking method until you verify the topic and topic sentence; then, mark those elements.

Here are some guidelines for finding topic sentences in the middle:

1. *Recognize the paragraph introduction.*

   When a paragraph beings with details, a question, or background information, look elsewhere for the topic and topic sentence.

2. *Look for signal words.*

   Authors often start middle topic sentences with signal words like these: *in other words, as a result, therefore, and so,* or *thus.* In addition, if the paragraph is about two contrasting issues, the topic sentence might be introduced by signals such as *yet, however, but, in contrast,* or *on the other hand.*

Here is an example of how the predict and verify strategy works on a revised version of the paragraph about women's jobs.

EXAMPLE

PREDICT:
-Sent. 1–3 are an introduction.
-This is the topic.
-Sent. 4 is the TS.
-What is gender stratification?
-How is it easy to see?

Do men and women have the same responsibility in the workplace? No. Female nurses assist male physicians, female secretaries serve male executives, and female flight attendants are under the command of male airplane pilots. **In other words, gender stratification in the workplace is easy to see.** In education, for example, women represent 98 percent of kindergarten teachers, 83 percent of elementary school teachers, 58 percent of secondary school teachers, 43 percent of college and university professors, and 19 percent of college and university presidents.

VERIFY:
Sentences 1–3 are not the topic sentence, because those sentences present a question and detailed examples. They're the paragraph introduction.
The topic is verified, because every sentence is about gender stratification.
The topic sentence is verified, because the phrase "in other words" signals it and the details answer the "how" question.

ACTIVITY 12: RECOGNIZE PARAGRAPHS WITH A TOPIC SENTENCE IN THE MIDDLE

DIRECTIONS: The topic sentence is in the middle in each of the following paragraphs. Use the predict, verify, and mark approach as you read each one.

Paragraph 1

1. As soon as you can, predict:
   a. The paragraph topic is: ______________________________.
   b. The topic sentence states that ______________________________
   ______________________________.
   c. Form questions:
   ____
   ____
   ____
2. Read on; verify and mark:
   Explain how your predictions are verified. If needed, revise them.
   ____
   ____

During the colonial period, attendance at school was not required by law, and most children received very little formal education. The New England Colonies, however, became early leaders in

Notes

the development of public education. This was due to the fact that the Puritan settlers believed everyone should be able to read the Bible and that was the responsibility of the public system. As a result, literacy rates were higher in New England than anywhere else in British North America. (Cayton et al. 82)

Notes

Paragraph 2

1. As soon as you can, predict:
   a. The paragraph topic is: ______________________________.
   b. The topic sentence states that ______________________________
   ______________________________.
   c. Form questions:
   ____
   ____
   ____
2. Read on; verify and mark:
   Explain how your predictions are verified. If needed, revise them.
   ____
   ____

Is there any way that people can help maintain the health of the biosphere without drastically changing their lifestyles? The answer is yes. People can make wise choices in the use of resources and in the disposal of recycling materials. Energy conservation is probably the most important shift that a society can make. Most people, without seriously affecting their quality of life, could better insulate their homes and offices, purchase cars that are more fuel-efficient, and recycle. (Adapted from Miller and Levine 160)

Notes

Topic Sentence Last When the topic sentence comes last, all the sentences that precede it are details. Like the topic sentence in the middle format, the topic may not be clearly stated in the beginning. So you'll need to use the detail marking method as you read until you find the author's topic sentence. Then, form questions. To find answers to your questions and verify the topic and topic sentence, you will need to look back at the details. Once you have done that, you can mark the topic and topic sentence.

Here are some guidelines for how to read this kind of paragraph and identify the topic sentence:

1. *Recognize the opening details.*

   Take note of facts, examples, definitions, and descriptions. They are details, because they do not state an opinion about the whole topic.

2. *Look for signal words.*

   To emphasize the importance of the last sentence, authors often start it with signals such as *in other words, in summary, to summarize, in conclusion, as a result, therefore, and so,* or *thus.*

The predict and verify strategy works like this on a topic sentence last paragraph.

EXAMPLE

PREDICT:

-Sent. 1 presents examples.

-Sent. 2 presents facts.

-This is the topic.

-Sent. 3 is the TS.

-What is gender stratification?

-How is it easy to see?

Female nurses assist male physicians, female secretaries serve male executives, and female flight attendants are under the command of male airplane pilots. And, in education, women represent 98 percent of kindergarten teachers, 83 percent of elementary school teachers, 58 percent of secondary school teachers, 43 percent of college and university professors, and 19 percent of college and university presidents. **In conclusion, gender stratification in the workplace is easy to see.**

VERIFY:

-The topic sentence is not the first or second one, because those present examples and facts.

-The topic is verified, because every sentence is about gender stratification.

-The topic sentence is verified, because the phrase "in conclusion" signals it; in addition, the details about it answer the "how" question.

ACTIVITY 13: RECOGNIZE PARAGRAPHS WITH THE TOPIC SENTENCE LAST

DIRECTIONS: The topic sentence is last in each of the following paragraphs. Use the predict, verify, and mark approach as you read each one.

Paragraph 1

1. As soon as you can, predict:

   a. The paragraph topic is: ______________________________

   b. The topic sentence states that ______________________________

   ____.

c. Form questions:

____

____

____

2. Look back at the details; verify and mark:
Explain how your predictions are verified. If needed, revise them.

____

____

Notes

Between 20 and 50 kilometers above Earth's surface, the atmosphere contains a concentration of ozone gas—the **ozone layer.** Molecules of ozone consist of three oxygen atoms. Although ozone at ground level is a pollutant, the naturally occurring ozone layer serves an important function. It absorbs a good deal of harmful ultraviolet, or UV, radiation from sunlight before it reaches Earth's surface. You may know that overexposure to UV radiation is the principal cause of sunburn. You may not know that exposure to UV can also cause cancer, damage eyes, and decrease organisms' resistance to disease. Intense UV radiation can also damage tissue in plant leaves and even phytoplankton in the oceans. Thus, by shielding the biosphere from UV light, the ozone layer serves as a global sunscreen. (Miller and Levine 157)

Paragraph 2

1. As soon as you can, predict:
   a. The paragraph topic is: ______________________________.
   b. The topic sentence states that ______________________________
   ____.
   c. Form questions:

   ____

   ____

   ____

2. Look back at the details; verify and mark:
Explain how your predictions are verified. If needed, revise them.

____

____

It's important to be cautious in diagnosing ADHD (Attention-Deficit Hyperactivity Disorder)—and not identify as disordered children who are merely active and somewhat rambunctious. It's also important, if Ritalin is prescribed, to combine its use with psychologically oriented therapy and classroom teaching strategies aimed at modifying the child's behavior and problem-solving skills. When she talks to children about Ritalin, teacher Sally Smith likes to hold up a ruler, point to the one-inch mark, and say, "This is how much Ritalin does for you. It makes you available to learn. You and your parents and teachers have to work on all the rest" (Hancock, 1996, 56). In this intersection of clinical psychology and education, it's clear, therefore, that parents, teachers, psychologists, and physicians must collaborate in their efforts. (Adapted from Kassin 627)

Notes

No Topic Sentence When the main idea is implied, none of the sentences state the author's idea. Instead, only details are presented. The paragraph will read like one that has the topic sentence at the end. However, once you reach the end, you will realize that there is no stated idea. You will need to create a main idea statement as part of the verification step. After that, form questions about your main idea. You have understood and formed a correct main idea if the details answer at least one of your questions. Mark the details during reading and the topic as soon as you've verified it; record your main idea in the margin.

Use these guidelines when reading paragraphs without stated main ideas.

1. *Recognize that the paragraph contains only details.*
2. *Create your own statement of the main idea.*

   To form a main idea statement, follow these steps:

   a. Use the paragraph topic.
   b. Note what each detail is about.
   c. Infer an idea that is common to all the details.
   d. Form a sentence using the topic and your inference.
3. *Form questions.*

   Form what, how, or why questions about your main idea. Look back at the details and make sure they answer at least one of your questions. If they don't, revise your main idea.

The predict and verify strategy works like this on a paragraph with no topic sentence.

EXAMPLE

PREDICT:
Sent. 1 presents examples.
Sent. 2 presents facts.
This is the topic.
There is no TS.

Female nurses assist male physicians, female secretaries serve male executives, and female flight attendants are under the command of male airplane pilots. And, there is also gender stratification in education. Women represent 98 percent of kindergarten teachers, 83 percent of elementary school teachers, 58 percent of secondary school teachers, 43 percent of college and university professors, and 19 percent of college and university presidents.

VERIFY:
-There is no topic sentence, because the sentences present only details.
-The topic is verified, because every sentence is about gender stratification.
-Create a main idea:

1. *Gender stratification is the topic.*
2. *The details state that*
    a. *in many professions, women assist men*
    b. *in education, more women at the lower levels; more men at the higher ones*
3. *The details show that women have less important or less powerful jobs than men.*
4. *Main idea: Gender stratification occurs when women have less important and less powerful jobs than men.*

-Questions can now be formed:
What is gender stratification?
How do we know that women tend to have less important jobs than men?
-A review of the paragraph shows that the details answer the how question.

Creating a good main idea sentence requires analysis of the details. If you try to do this mentally, you may find that you have only copied the author's terms. That won't be the implied idea because it will be what the author said rather than what the author suggested. To avoid this error, it's often useful to list the details as part of your margin notes. Then look for an unstated similarity among them. That is the heart of the implied main idea.

ACTIVITY 14: RECOGNIZE PARAGRAPHS WITH NO TOPIC SENTENCE

DIRECTIONS: None of the following paragraphs have topic sentences. Use the predict, verify, and mark approach as you read each one.

Paragraph 1

1. As soon as you can, predict:
   - a. The paragraph topic is: ______________________________.
   - b. Form questions:

     ____

     ____

     ____

2. Look back at the details; verify and mark:
   - a. Form a main idea statement:

     ____

     ____

     ____

   - b. Form questions:

     ____

     ____

     ____

   - c. Explain how your predictions are verified. If needed, revise them.

     ____

     ____

At the time Congress banned literacy tests, 18 states had some form of a literacy requirement. Some required potential voters to prove they had the ability to read; other states required the ability to read and write. Still others required the ability to read, write, and "understand" some printed material—usually a passage taken from the state or federal constitution. Often whites were asked simple questions; African Americans were asked questions so complex they would stump even a judge who was familiar with the passage. (McClenaghan 135)

Notes

Paragraph 2

1. As soon as you can, predict:
   - a. The paragraph topic is: ______________________________.
   - b. Form questions:

     ____

     ____

     ____

2. Look back at the details; verify and mark:

a. Form a main idea statement:

____

____

____

b. Form questions:

____

____

____

c. Explain how your predictions are verified. If needed, revise them.

____

____

Nutrients are elements essential to normal life; they differ for different organisms. Plants require relatively large quantities of the following nutrients: carbon, hydrogen, oxygen, phosphorus, nitrogen, magnesium, calcium, and potassium. Plants also require very small quantities of nutrients such as iron, chlorine, copper, manganese, zinc, boron, and molybdenum. Carbon dioxide and oxygen usually enter a plant by diffusion from the air into leaves, stem, and roots. Roots extract water and all other nutrients, collectively called **minerals,** from the soil. (Adapted from Audesirk 481)

Notes

Analyzing As You Read Obviously, you will not have directions, guide questions, or lines on which to record your thinking when you read texts. All the previous activities have been designed to demonstrate how to predict and verify topics, ideas, and details. The results of your mental efforts should be captured in your underlining and margin notes. Using different markings for each of the elements will capture your basic comprehension; recording your verified questions and the main ideas you create in the margin will be part of your extended notes (see Chapter 5).

One last point about finding main ideas: Even when authors state their ideas and you locate them, you may have a better idea in mind. That is, sometimes authors don't write the clearest idea sentence. And sometimes, they don't present the idea in the way that best supports your learning. In the end, finding stated ideas can guide your thinking, but it should not restrict it.

Here's an example of a paragraph analysis and rephrased main idea.

EXAMPLE

Realizing that people can be pressured by others is only the first step in understanding the process of social influence. The next step is to identify the situational factors that make us more or less likely to conform. One obvious factor is the size of a group. Common sense suggests that as a majority increases in size, so does its impact. (Adapted from Kassin 502)

Analysis: Sentence 1 is not the topic sentence, because the whole paragraph is not about it. The author's focus is situational factors that make us conform. Sentence 2 seems to be the topic sentence since the rest of the paragraph gives details about that. But a better idea is that there are two steps needed for understanding social influence. And good questions are: What are the steps for understanding social influence? Why do situational factors promote conformity? Both questions are answered, which verifies my version of the main idea.

> **Ideas are powerful things, requiring not a studious contemplation but an action, even if it is only an inner action.**
>
> —Midge Decter (1927–), American author, editor, social critic

Thinking beyond the stated main idea is a form of reflection, and it's highly motivating. Add those thoughts to your margin notes.

ACTIVITY 15: ANALYZE PARAGRAPHS

DIRECTIONS: In the following paragraphs, the topic sentences may be implied or stated anywhere in the paragraph. Complete these tasks:

1. Use the predict and verify approach as you read each paragraph.
   a. Predict the topic and main idea. Form questions.
   b. Verify and mark the text. Revise as needed.
2. Write your own main idea sentence or paraphrase of the author's topic sentence on the lines following the paragraph.

1. Like the populations of many other living organisms, the size of the human population tended to grow slowly. For most of human existence, life was harsh, and limiting factors kept population numbers low. Food was scarce. Incurable diseases were rampant. Until fairly recently, only half the children in the world survived to adulthood. Because death rates were so high, families had many children, just to make sure that some would survive. (Miller and Levine 129)

Notes

Main idea: ______________________________

____

____

2. Identity theft, which involves obtaining credit, merchandise, or services by fraudulent personal representation, is a special kind of larceny. It affects as many as 500,000 victims annually, although most do not report the crime. Identity theft became a federal crime in 1998, with the passage of the Identify Theft and Assumption Deterrence Act. The law makes it a crime whenever anyone "knowingly transfers or uses, without lawful authority, a means of identification of another person with intent to commit, or to aid or abet, any unlawful activity that constitutes a violation of federal law, or that constitutes a felony under any applicable state or local laws." (Schmalleger 56)

Notes

Main idea: ______________________________

____

____

3. As industrialization took hold in the United States, people asked "how should women spend their time and their energy?" Most people believed that women should remain in the home. Middle-class women were expected to raise and educate their children, entertain guests, and serve their husbands. They were also expected to do community service and engage in at-home activities such as needlework and quilting. (Cayton et al. 326)

Notes

Main idea: The role of women during the industralization

4. The coastal ocean extends from the low-tide mark to the outer edge of the continental shelf, the relatively shallow border that surrounds the continents. The continental shelf is often shallow enough to fall mostly or entirely within the photic zone, so photosynthesis can usually occur throughout its depth. As a result, the coastal ocean is often rich in plankton and many other organisms. (Miller and Levine 110)

Notes

Main idea: ____

____

____

Authors write the way they think. So they generally use a variety of paragraph formats within the same section. As a result, you will need to shift your thinking as you move from one paragraph to another.

ACTIVITY 16: ANALYZE AS YOU READ

DIRECTIONS: In the following passages, the paragraphs may have implied or stated main ideas. Use the predict, verify, and mark approach as you read each passage.

Passage 1

Notes

The term **debunking** refers to a habit of looking beyond the obvious or surface-level explanations that people provide for social behavior and of seeking out less obvious and deeper explanations (Berger, 1963). Durkheim was debunking when he showed that suicide stems not only from psychological problems but also from low levels of social integration. Debunking is not limited to sociology—it is a theme in all the social sciences—but sociologists put a particularly strong emphasis on it.

As sociology has become more popular, debunking has become increasingly common among the general public. For example, when the United States waged the Gulf War against Iraq in the early 1990s, almost everyone recognized that the government's motive was not just to free Kuwait from Iraqi domination but also to keep cheap oil flowing to the developed world. Similarly, when neighborhood residents band together to fight the establishment of a halfway house for recovering drug addicts on their block, claiming that they are worried about the safety of their children, most people realize that, while the residents may indeed be genuinely concerned about their children, they are also motivated by fear that their property values might decline if a halfway house is built.

The individuals who are most likely to question the established truths and thus to be naturally most inclined to debunk are those who are not members of the more powerful groups in society. Such people display the quality of **social marginality;** they are to some extent excluded, through no fault of their own, from the mainstream of society. It is not a coincidence that most of the European founders of the discipline of sociology were Jewish, or that a great deal of the most important work now being conducted in sociology is being done by racial and ethnic minorities and women. As partial outsiders, marginalized people are especially well situated to realize that the emperor may indeed be wearing no clothes. (Lindsey and Beach 7) (321 words)

Notes

Passage 2

Notes

The media are filled with reports of "toxic chemicals." You might think that chemicals are a leading cause of death and injury. Some chemicals are quite toxic. Misused, they can make you sick or even kill you. However, when you look at the leading causes of death, it is difficult to associate any of them directly with chemicals. In developed countries, most of the causes of premature death are related to lifestyle. Nearly half are due to cardiovascular diseases, and another 20% or so are due to cancer. In these countries, it is, therefore, "sociologicals," not "chemicals," that kill us.

Accidents and suicides often involve automobile crashes and guns. More than 20,000 people are murdered each year in the United States, most with guns, knives, or clubs of some sort. The physical force of a moving projectile, not its chemical nature, does the damage. These "physicals" kill us.

Worldwide, the main causes of premature death are infectious and parasite diseases, "biologicals" that account for nearly one-third of the total. Three million children under the age of 5 die each year of diarrhea caused by drinking water contaminated with microorganisms, and 2,700,000 people die each year of tuberculosis, 1,200,000 of measles, and 2,000,000 of malaria. Even in the United States, pneumonia, influenza, and AIDS—caused by bacteria and viruses—are major causes of death. Food poisoning, caused by *E. coli, Cyclospora, Listeria, Salmonella,* and other microorganisms sicken thousands each year. Chicken meat and eggs are frequently contaminated with *Salmonella. Eschericia coli* is a common inhabitant of cow intestines; people who eat beef that is carelessly slaughtered or foods exposed to water contaminated with cow manure are often infected.

Notes

In all these cases, of course, chemistry is involved at some level. We can identify the toxins produced by bacteria and work out the molecular mechanisms by which viruses invade and destroy cells. Nicotine is the chemical—a natural one, but a chemical nonetheless—that makes tobacco addictive. Perfectly natural ethanol is the most dangerous chemical in alcoholic beverages.

Chemicals can be dangerous, but with care we can use them to our advantage. As far as being threats to our lives and health, though, chemicals are far down the list. We are even more likely to die of "geologicals"—earthquakes, floods, storms, and extremely hot or cold weather. (Adapted from Hill and Kolb 662) (386 words)

Reading is a means of thinking with another person's mind: it forces you to stretch your own.

—Charles Scribner, Jr. (1921–),
American publisher

Before you go on . . .

Monitor Your Progress: recite

After you read . . .

Reflect on Your Gains: review

CHAPTER SUMMARY

Introduction

Textbook chapters often contain an overwhelming amount of new information. Readers can prevent a loss of concentration and improve comprehension by locating and using the main ideas to guide their reading.

Get the Most out of Main Ideas

Chapters are divided into discussion blocks that include major sections, subsections, minor sections, and paragraphs. Each block contains three structural elements: the **topic,** the **main idea,** and the **details.** An effective, active reading approach that aids comprehension is to use a **predict** and **verify** process. This process entails guessing what the topic and main idea sentence are as soon as possible and then reading on to see if the details verify the predictions. Marking captures the reader's understanding of the text and avoids unnecessary future rereading.

Find Main Ideas in Chapters and Sections

Ideas can be broad, requiring an entire chapter to cover them, or more limited, requiring only a section. Ideas can also be stated in the text or implied by it. When a chapter idea is stated, it is called the **thesis;** when a section idea is stated, it is called the **central idea.** Finding these ideas along with the topics they relate to and the details they organize simplifies the comprehension process. With slight modifications, the predict and verify process is an effective approach for finding both stated and implied ideas in chapters and sections.

Find Main Ideas in Paragraphs

Body paragraphs are a group of related sentences that focus on one major point. These paragraphs have a topic, main idea, and details. When stated, the paragraph idea is called the **topic sentence.** It can be located in the first sentence of the paragraph, in the middle, or at the end. Each of these patterns changes the order of the ideas and details and creates a shift in the reader's thinking, as well as the predict and verify approach.

REVIEW ACTIVITIES

Use the following activities to check your understanding and aid your learning of the information in this chapter.

Expand Your Vocabulary

Match each item with the correct definition or characteristic.

_____ **1.** expository writing
_____ **2.** topic
_____ **3.** main idea
_____ **4.** details
_____ **5.** predict
_____ **6.** verify
_____ **7.** thesis
_____ **8.** central idea
_____ **9.** body paragraph
_____ **10.** topic sentence

a. to make an educated guess about what's coming next
b. to check your expectations against the text
c. a group of related sentences about one topic
d. the stated dominant message about the section topic
e. the stated main idea for a chapter
f. the author's stated main idea for a paragraph
g. writing that exposes information, ideas, or theories
h. the author's dominant message about the topic
i. the subject of a discussion
j. specific pieces of information that describe the topic or support the main idea

Increase Your Knowledge

The following tasks will help you assess how well you understand the ideas presented in this chapter. They will also help you prepare for quizzes and exams on this material.

1. The following questions focus on the major chapter topics. Discuss them with others or form your own detailed answers.

a. Explain the difference between readers' and authors' views of textbook information. How do the two views affect motivation?

b. Name, define, and describe the characteristics of the three structural elements of discussion blocks.

c. Describe the elements in each discussion block by filling in the following chart.

	TOPIC LOCATION	MAIN IDEA NAME	MAIN IDEA LOCATION	LOCATION OF THE DETAILS
Chapter				
Major section				
Subsection				

d. Explain the predict and verify process. How does it work on chapters and sections with stated ideas?

e. How do you create a main idea statement in chapters, sections, and paragraphs when they are implied?

f. What are the four paragraph formats? How does the predict and verify process work with each format?

2. Take notes on the information in this chapter.

Develop Your Skills

The following review tasks will give you an opportunity to practice the methods presented in this chapter.

REVIEW 1: PREDICT AND VERIFY CHAPTER ELEMENTS Look at the following excerpted sentences from a chapter in a sociology textbook. They include the title, thesis, two major section headings, subsection headings, and the section central ideas. Complete the following tasks:

A. Number the headings in outline style, put a T next to the thesis, and put CI next to each of the central ideas.

B. Use the predict, verify, and mark process as you read.

1. From the beginning, predict:

a. The chapter topic is: ______________________________.

b. The thesis states that ______________________________

____

______________________________.

c. Form questions:

____

____

____

2. Read on; verify and mark:

Explain how your predictions are verified. If needed, revise them.

____

____

____

Racial and Ethnic Minorities

We begin this chapter by discussing the key concepts of race, ethnicity, and minority groups, prejudice, discrimination, and racism. Next we consider the various ways that dominant and minority groups interact. The chapter concludes with a discussion of the emergence of multiracialism and the policy of affirmative action.

Race, Ethnicity, and Minority Groups
The people whom sociologists have traditionally regarded as minorities may be somewhat arbitrarily divided into races and ethnic groups.

Race: A Social Concept
Although nineteenth-century scientists devoted a great deal of time to investigating what they believed to be the inherent characteristics of different races, we now know that what most people call races are nothing more than the result of historic geographic isolation of human populations in very different environments.

Ethnic Groups
If race is—or, at least, is believed to be—about biology, ethnicity is a matter of culture.

Minority Groups
A minority group, whether based on race, ethnicity, or gender is defined by its lack of power.

Prejudice, Discrimination, and Racism
Both race and ethnicity are frequently master statuses—the primary determinants of how people are thought of and treated. Accordingly we turn now to the dynamics of prejudice and discrimination. (Adapted from Lindsey and Beach 234–237)

REVIEW 2: CREATE A SECTION MAIN IDEA The following section has no central ideas. Read and mark it, and create a main idea statement.

1. From the beginning, predict:
   a. The section topic is: ____.
   b. Form questions:

   ____

   ____

   ____

2. Read on; verify and mark:
   a. Form a main idea statement:

   ____

   ____

   ____

   b. Form questions:

   ____

   ____

   ____

   c. Explain how your predictions are verified. If needed, revise them.

   ____

   ____

Notes

Computer Threats: Hackers

Although there is a great deal of dissension (especially among hackers themselves) as to what a hacker actually is, a **hacker** (also called a cracker) is defined as anyone who breaks into a computer system (whether an individual computer or a network) unlawfully.

Are there different kinds of hackers? Some hackers are offended by being labeled criminals and therefore attempt to divide hackers into classes. Many hackers who break into systems just for the challenge of it (and who don't wish to steal or wreak havoc on the systems) refer to themselves as white-hat hackers. They tout themselves as experts who are performing a needed service for society by helping companies realize the vulnerabilities that exist in their systems.

These white-hat hackers look down on those hackers who use their knowledge to destroy information or for illegal gain. White-hat hackers refer to these other hackers as black-hat hackers. The terms *white hat* and *black hat* are references to old Western movies in which the heroes wore white hats and the outlaws wore black hats. Irrespective of the opinions of the hackers themselves, the laws in the United States (and in many foreign countries) consider any unauthorized access to computer systems a crime.

What about the teenage hackers who get caught every so often? Although some of these teenagers are brilliant hackers, the majority are amateurs without sophisticated computer skills. These amateur hackers are referred to as **script kiddies.** Script kiddies don't create programs used to hack into computer systems; instead, they use tools created by skilled hackers that enable unskilled novices to wreak the same havoc as professional hackers. Unfortunately, a search on any search engine will produce links to Web sites that feature hacking tools, complete with instructions, allowing anyone to become an amateur hacker.

Fortunately, since the users of these programs are amateurs, they're usually not proficient at covering their electronic tracks. Therefore, it's relatively easy for law enforcement officials to track them down and prosecute them. Still, script kiddies can cause a lot of disruption and damage to computers, networks, and Web sites before they're caught.

Notes

Why would a hacker be interested in breaking into my home computer? Some hackers just like to snoop. They enjoy the challenge of breaking into systems and seeing what information they can find. Other hackers are hobbyists seeking information about a particular topic wherever they can find it. Since many people keep proprietary business information on their home computers, hackers may break into home computers bent on industrial espionage. For other hackers, hacking is a way to pass time. (Evans et al. 270–273) (431 words)

REVIEW 3: ANALYZE PARAGRAPHS In the following paragraphs, the topic sentences may be implied or stated anywhere in the paragraph. Complete these tasks:

1. Use the predict and verify approach as you read each paragraph.
   a. Predict the topic and main idea. Form questions.
   b. Verify and mark the text. Revise as needed.
2. Write your own main idea sentence or paraphrase of the author's topic sentence on the lines following the paragraph.

1. Products that are successful in one country may be useless in another. Snowmobiles, for example, are popular for transportation and recreation in Canada and the northern United States, and they actually revolutionized reindeer herding in Lapland. However, there is no demand for snowmobiles in Central America. Although this is an extreme example, the point is basic to the decision to go international: Foreign demand for a company's product may be greater than, the same as, or weaker than domestic demand. (Adapted from Griffin and Griffin 78)

Notes

Main idea: ____

____

____

2. Research shows that people with high scores on the Social Readjustment Rating Scale are more likely to come down with physical illnesses (Dohrenwend & Dohrenwend, 1978).

Notes

Since this scale deals with life changes, it raises the question "is change *per se* necessarily harmful?" There are two problems with this notion. First, although there is a statistical link between negative events and illness, positive change—a vacation, graduating, starting a new career—does not seem to have the same harmful results. The second complicating factor is that the impact of any change depends on how the person interprets it. (Adapted from Kassin 720)

Notes

Main idea: ____

____

____

3. Boys and girls alike crawl, walk, and smile at about the same age, and both become curious about sex in adolescence. Similarly, both men and women see better in daylight than in the dark and fall prey to optical illusions. In their social behavior, both men and women are biased by their first impressions, are attracted to others who are similar, and are more likely to help others when they're alone than in a group of bystanders. In other words, as human beings, men and women are more alike than different in many "invisible" ways. (Adapted from Kassin 561)

Notes

Main idea: ____

____

____

4. Horses changed much about Native American life, from the nature of warfare to the division of labor between men and women. Many Native Americans, however, took advantage of the horse without allowing it to transform their cultures. The Pawnee, Mandan, and other Native American nations continued to live primarily as farmers, hunters, and gatherers. As in most Native American societies, the women in those villages did most of the farming, while the men took charge of the hunting. (Cayton et al. 259)

Notes

Main idea: ______________________________

____

____

5. By 1970, the median age at first marriage was 21 for women and 23 for men. By 2000, these ages had risen to 25 for women and 27 for men, the oldest ages at first marriage ever recorded by the U.S. Census Bureau. (Remember that the median represents the midpoint of cases. Thus, half of all men were 27 or older and half of all women were 25 or older the first time they got married.) (Benokraitis 237)

Notes

Main idea: ______________________________

____

____

REVIEW 4: ANALYZE AS YOU READ In the following passages, both the section and paragraph ideas may be stated or implied. Use the predict, verify, and mark process as you read them.

Passage 1

Biological Rhythms and Sports

Notes

We human beings have our own internal clock that functions much as internal clocks do in the rest of the animal world. The circadian rhythms this clock controls can have some surprising effects on our functioning.

Scientists have known for decades that a human internal clock exists, but they have made great strides in recent years in figuring out its detailed workings. The primary governor of the human master clock is a small group of cells, called the suprachiasmatic nucleus or SCN, located in an area of the brain called the hypothalamus. In the complete absence of external cues, cells in the SCN will take an average of 24.2 hours to complete one full cycle of activity. As with the circadian clocks of other animals, however, this human clock is entrained by an external cue—the presence or absence of sunlight.

Here's how one part of this system works. The presence of sunlight is signaled to the SCN through pathways coming from the eyes. When sunlight is not present, the SCN sends a signal to the pineal gland, located in the brain, to raise its production of the hormone melatonin. This hormone acts to lower body temperature and bring on sleepiness. When sunlight reaches our eyes the next day, it entrains a signal to the pineal gland that essentially says, "Day is here again; time to be alert; shut down melatonin production."

This system, the product of millions of years of evolution, runs into problems when humans undertake the very modern practice of travel by jet airplane. Getting off a plane, a traveler is in a different location, where daylight may begin, say, three hours earlier than in the old locale. The critical thing is that it takes several days for the timing of sunlight in a new locale to reset our internal clock. Thus, a person whose alarm clock is saying, "get up" may have an internal clock that is saying, "still time for sleep." This is what it means to be jet-lagged.

We normally think of jet lag as some minor annoyance that makes us feel "off" for a few days in a new location. But it can have practical effects as well. Research has shown that athletic performance tends to peak in late afternoon, as measured by such things as reflex speed and quick muscular bursts. In line with this, athletes tend to report that they perform best from about 3 to 6 p.m. and worst before 9 in the morning or after 9 at night. So what happens when an athlete *travels?* Researchers looked at the results from the National Football League's "Monday Night Football" and found that the outcome of the games was significantly skewed in favor of West Coast teams, who won 71 percent of their home games, while the East Coast teams won only 44 percent of theirs. These results held up even when Las Vegas point spreads were taken into account. Why should this be? Monday night games begin at 6 p.m. Pacific Coast time, which means 9 p.m. East Coast time. The East Coast athletes, then, are starting to perform at one of the worst times of the day in terms of their circadian rhythms. (Krogh 758) (538 words)

Notes

Passage 2

Notes

Foster Care

The growth of poverty, child abuse, and parental neglect has increased children's out-of-home placements. The most common out-of-home placement for children is the foster home, where parents raise children who are not on their own for a period of time but do not formally adopt them.

Prevalence and Characteristics of Foster Homes Currently, more than 580,000 children are in foster care in the United States, twice as many as in 1987. In contrast, there are only 144,000 foster families. This means that hundreds of thousands of children end up in group homes, temporary detention, and psychiatric wards awaiting placement, a wait that can last months or even years (Marks, 2003).

An estimated 40 to 80 percent of the families who become child protective service cases have problems with alcohol or drugs. Of the children in foster care, two-thirds are African American or Latino, nearly 45 percent enter care as babies or toddlers, and nearly all have been neglected rather than abused (Pascual, 1999/2000). About 72,000 to 125,000 of the children are in foster homes because they have lost their parents to AIDS (Children's Defense Fund, 2000*a*).

Recent years have seen a dramatic growth in kinship care, sometimes called relative foster care. In 1986, 18 percent of the children in foster care lived with relatives—the number had increased to 25 percent by 2000. Some states limit kinship care to biological relatives; others extend the definition of kin to include neighbors, godparents, and other adults with a close relationship but no biological ties to the child (Barbell and Freundlich, 2001).

Problems of Foster Homes In theory, foster homes are supposed to provide short-term care until the children can be adopted or returned to their biological parents. In reality, there are many problems associated with foster homes. Many children go through multiple placements and remain in foster care until late adolescence. Approximately 25 to 30 percent of the children returned to their biological parents are soon back in foster care. Children who are older or have behavioral or emotional problems are the most likely to bounce from home to home. In this sense, the foster care system may sometimes worsen children's already significant physical and mental health problems (Barbell and Freundlich, 2001).

The typical foster parent, usually a woman, is paid little to care for a child (about $400 a month for a child age 2). Although this might sound like a hefty sum to some people, foster parents typically use their own income to pay for many expenses (Barbell and Freundlich, 2001).

Some children are closer to their foster families than their biological parents and prefer to live with their foster parents (Gardner, 1996). Others never adjust to a foster home (Fanshel et al., 1989). The children are often confused about why they were taken from their homes and don't know what will happen in the future. Many experience fear, anger, and a sense of loss about not seeing their family and relatives (Whiting and Lee, 2003).

If children have gone through more than two placements and have been in foster care for more than a few years, their self-esteem, self-confidence, and ability to forge satisfying relationships with peers may erode (Kools, 1997). The solution, some propose, is to move children as quickly as possible from foster care to adoption (Bartholet, 1999). (Benokraitis 354) (554 words)

Notes

Check Your Motivation

1. Review your chapter goals. Did you achieve them? Explain.
2. Make a list of the new ideas and methods you've gained from this chapter. Think about how they will help you in the future.

3. Measure your motivation for this chapter topic. Think about each statement and how you will use it in the future. Mark it:

A = never B = sometimes C = usually D = always

	A	B	C	D
To inspire my interest, I plan to . . .				
1. remember that chapters are organized around the ideas.	___	___	___	___
2. use predictions to increase my interest in the text.	___	___	___	___
3. predict the chapter topic and thesis as I preread chapters.	___	___	___	___
4. predict the section topic and idea as I preread each section.	___	___	___	___
5. predict paragraph topics and ideas as I read paragraphs.	___	___	___	___
To focus my efforts, I plan to . . .				
6. use the verify step to increase my comprehension.	___	___	___	___
7. look for the characteristics of topics and ideas to locate them.	___	___	___	___
8. form questions about topics and ideas.	___	___	___	___
9. underline topics, ideas, and details differently.	___	___	___	___
10. record my thoughts in margin notes.	___	___	___	___
To monitor my progress, I plan to . . .				
11. form main ideas when they are unstated in chapters.	___	___	___	___
12. form main ideas when they are unstated in sections.	___	___	___	___
13. shift my thinking as the paragraph formats change.	___	___	___	___
14. create main ideas when they are unstated in paragraphs.	___	___	___	___
To reflect on my gains, I plan to . . .				
15. think beyond the text and improve on stated ideas as needed.	___	___	___	___

SCORING: Write the number of answers you marked in each column in the following spaces. Compute the column scores, and then add them up to determine your total score.

# of A's ______ × 1 pt. = ______
# of B's ______ × 2 pt. = ______
# of C's ______ × 3 pt. = ______
# of D's ______ × 4 pt. = ______
Total points = ______

INTERPRETATION: 15–43 points = low motivation; 44–60 points = high motivation

SUGGESTION: Evaluate your scores. Reward yourself for your gains and empowered approaches. Make a plan to improve anything that needs more attention.

Details and Logical Patterns

What do these pictures illustrate about textbooks? Do the details in textbooks make the topics clear to you? Or do they confuse you, slow you down, or even overwhelm you?

Some textbooks seem to have nothing but details. And, as most students know, those specifics usually appear on tests. Is there any way to overcome the feeling that there's just too much to understand and know? Yes. The secret is to organize the details while you're reading. In short, as Henri Frederic Amiel put it,

> Order is power.
>
> —Henri Frederic Amiel (1821–1881), Swiss philosopher, poet, and critic

Before you read . . .

Engage Your Interest: preread and divide

This chapter presents two ways to organize details: by type and by pattern. Here's a partial outline, which includes only the major headings. Add the subheadings and minor headings to this outline, and think about how they relate to each major heading.

I. Introduction

II. Details

III. Logical Patterns

After you preread and divide the chapter into reading tasks, set a goal for each one. Be specific about the task, topic, and reward(s).

1. I want to ________________ about ________________________________.
My reward(s) will be ____
____.

2. I want to ________________ about ________________________________.
My reward(s) will be ____
____.

3. I want to ________________ about ________________________________.
My reward(s) will be ____
____.

As you read . . .

Focus Your Efforts: question and read

Why do college texts have so many details? First, modern science and the work of professionals in each field have produced a great deal of knowledge, and the purpose of college courses is to present the "state of the art" in the field. Second, as mentioned in Chapter 6, details are essential in expository writing as support for each main idea. By themselves, ideas can be imprecise, vague, questionable, and ambiguous. Specific information, or details, clarify and prove them.

These are good reasons for including so many details in textbooks, but they don't help readers, who are often overwhelmed by the sheer amount of information. What does help readers is to analyze what the information contributes to the message. So, instead of juggling endless individual sentences, active readers recognize the type of information that's presented and the logic that links the pieces. This approach transforms endless details into orderly units of information.

To help you achieve this kind of comprehension, the sections in this chapter will show you how to recognize, comprehend, and use

- Details
- Logical Patterns

I have always wanted to be somebody, but I see now I should have been more specific.

—Lily Tomlin (1939–),
American comedienne

Details

THINK ABOUT THIS . . .

1. Imagine that you just returned from a wonderful two-week vacation, where everything went just as you planned. You're now talking to some friends and they're asking the following questions. What type of information would you use to answer each question?
   a. Why did you choose the hotel where you stayed?

      ____

   b. How were the restaurants and food?

      ____

   c. What interesting things did you do during the day?

      ____

2. Reminder: Preread this section.

To answer the ***Think about this*** . . . questions, you would probably give reasons for your choice of hotels, descriptions of the food, and examples of your daily activities. In other words, you would pick different types of details to answer different questions. Authors do the same thing. They use the kind of information that best supports each idea. Part of good reading comprehension, then, is recognizing the types of information presented by the author and whether each piece is a major or minor part of the discussion.

Men who wish to know about the world must learn about it in its particular details.

—Heraclitus (535–475 B.C.), Greek philosopher

Types of Information

Textbook authors use five basic types of information: facts, descriptions, examples, definitions, and references. Each accomplishes a different purpose. Looking for the type of detail will increase both your interest and your comprehension.

Facts A **fact** is information that can be verified, or proven to be either true or false. Facts include events, dates, numbers, percentages, and observable data. Facts generally answer questions such as "when," "where," "what happened," or "how many?" Authors use facts to demonstrate that a point is accurate.

Look at these examples from textbook paragraphs. In the first paragraph, numbers and dates prove the author's opinion that a popular rebellion was brewing. In the second paragraph, observations that could be made from experience show how boys and girls are treated differently. (*TS* stands for Topic Sentence.)

EXAMPLES

TS	By the 1990s there were signs of a brewing popular rebellion against politics as usual. As late as 1964, 76 percent of Americans had believed they could trust the government to do what was right always or most of the time. Then Lyndon Johnson's "credibility gap" and Richard Nixon's lies and cover-ups had shaken Americans' faith in presidents and politicians in the 1960s and 1970s. By 1994 only 19 percent of the people felt they could trust government. (Adapted from Boydston et al., 904)
Dates and percentages	
TS	Teachers often treat boys and girls differently in the classroom. Even when their behavior is disruptive, "problem girls" often receive less attention than do either boys or "problem boys." Moreover, teachers tend to emphasize "motherwork" skills for girls, such as nurturance and emotional support. Although both girls and boys are evaluated on academic criteria, such as work habits and knowledge, teachers are more likely also to evaluate girls on such nonacademic criteria as grooming, personal qualities such as politeness, and appearance. (Benokraitis 122)
Observations	

The ultimate umpire of all things in life is—fact.

—Agnes C. Laut (1871–1936), Canadian journalist and author

Descriptions A **description** presents either sensory information—that is, information that can be determined by one of the five senses—or emotional reactions. It includes what you would see, hear, taste, and smell as well as feel through touch or emotions if you were experiencing the object or situation being described. In expository writing, descriptive details are usually used to explain the characteristics of an object, group, experience, or situation.

In the following example, both visual and emotional details illustrate the feedback that come from body posture.

EXAMPLE

TS	Body posture can provide us with sensory feedback and influence how we feel.
Visual and emotional information	When people feel proud, they stand erect with their shoulders raised, chest expanded, and head held high. When people feel sad and dejected, however, they slump over with their shoulders drooping and head bowed. (Adapted from Kassin 341)

Examples An **example** is a representative sample of objects, situations, or ideas that could occur in the real world. The example can be real or imaginary, but its purpose is to clarify an idea by making it concrete and realistic. So by way of example, an author of a business textbook could describe an imaginary business owner faced with striking workers or use scenarios from real companies.

> **Example is a bright looking-glass,**
> **Universal and for all shapes to look into.**
> —Michel Evquem De Montaigne (1533–1592), French philosopher, essayist

Finding examples as you read is not hard. Signal words like *such as, for example,* and *for instance* are often included to alert readers that an example will follow. When these signals are not stated, the reader can insert them mentally.

In the following paragraph, the examples make the idea about barriers more concrete and understandable. Also, notice how you can insert the words "for example" in the second sentence to emphasize the illustrations.

EXAMPLE

TS	Despite considerable progress, female athletes still face numerous institutional barriers in college athletics.
Examples	They play in inferior facilities, stay in lower-caliber hotels on the road, eat in cheaper restaurants, get smaller promotional budgets, and have fewer assistant coaches. (Benokraitis 121)

Definitions A **definition** includes both the term and the precise, authoritative meaning given to it. The definition detail is used so that all readers will have access to one, specific meaning of a word as they read. In expository texts and particularly in textbooks, the technical terms and precise definitions are easy to spot, because they are usually presented in italics or bold-face with the definition following. Authors may also use signal words such as *is, means, refers to, is called,* or *can be defined* to highlight the definition detail.

Look at these examples and notice how exact each definition is. (The terms are in boldface; the signal words are in italics.)

EXAMPLES

Sociologists use the term **socialization** to *refer to* the lifelong social experience by which individuals develop their human potential and learn culture. (Macionis 115)

Culture *is* the values, beliefs, behavior, and material objects that together form a people's way of life. (Macionis 59)

References A **reference** is information that comes from another author or source. References are used either to show that the author's points have merit or to convey the ideas and facts that experts have discovered. Textbook authors usually use experts who have conducted research as their sources. They indicate these references by using signal words such as *study, investigation, research, subjects, concluded,* or *found* in their sentences. They also include source information, such as the expert's name and the date the findings were published. This information may be part of the sentences, in parentheses within the paragraph, or at the end of the chapter or book in a reference list. If it's part of the text, the source information in parentheses functions as a signal.

Notice how references are included in the following examples and how they add to the importance of each idea. (The signal words are in italics.)

EXAMPLES

Source	*Research* shows that punishment has mixed effects *(Axelrod and Apsche, 1983).* (Kassin 193)
TS *Source* *Research*	Clearly, punishment can be an effective deterrent. In a *research article* entitled "Taking the sting out of the whip," *Rebecca Bennett (1998)* had 263 college students play the role of a corporate executive faced with an ethical dilemma. Those who selected an unethical path in order to maximize profits were then assessed a large or small fine and told that a competitor who had made the same choice was or was not similarly fined. Indicating the benefits of punishment, *Bennet found* that the large fine deterred *subjects* from later making another unethical choice. (Kassin 193)

What is research, but a blind date with knowledge.

—William Henry (1774–1836), British chemist

While the example paragraphs presented so far in this section emphasize a single type of detail, authors often use a variety of details in their paragraphs, because one type is usually not enough to support an idea. In a discussion about how crime is increasing, for instance, an author might define the term crime, present examples of specific crimes, include factual and historical data, and even mention research that has been done in this area. Review Table 7.1 so that you can become familiar with the five types of details and recognize them whenever they are presented.

TABLE 7.1 **Types of Details**

TYPE / BRIEF DEFINITION	PURPOSE	WHAT TO NOTE	HOW TO LOCATE
Fact Provable information	Explain a point / prove that it is accurate	Events, dates, numbers, percentages, observable data	Use questions such as: When? Where? What? What happened? How many?
Description Sensory information or emotional reactions	Present characteristics of an object, group, experience, or situation	What you could see, hear, taste, smell, or feel through touch or emotions	Pretend that you are there and imagine what your senses would reveal.
Example A real-world sample	Make a point concrete and realistic	Real or imagined illustrations of objects, situations, or ideas in the world	Look for signal words: *such as, for example,* and *for instance.*
Definition A term plus its authoritative meaning	Present one precise meaning for a term for all readers to use	The exact meaning of the term	Look for signal words: *is, means, refers to, is called,* or *can be defined as.* Look for bold-faced or italicized words.
Reference Information from another source	Show that a point has merit because it's supported by others	Sayings, quotes, and information from other authors	Look for signal words: *study, investigation,* or *research.* Look for source information.

ACTIVITY 1: IDENTIFY THE TYPE OF INFORMATION

DIRECTIONS: Identify which of the following kinds of details are used in each item: facts, descriptions, examples, definitions, and references. Refer to Table 7.1 as you work.

1. Identify the primary type of detail used in items a–e. Record it on the line.
   a. The Census Bureau reports that there is at least one television set in 90 percent of the nation's 103 million homes. (McClenghan 189)

      Type of detail: ____________________

   b. Perhaps the most interesting example of stigmatization is the concern over smoking. (Adapted from Lindsey and Beach 171)

      Type of detail: ____________________

c. **Conformity** is the tendency for people to bring their behavior in line with group norms. (Kassin 500)

Type of detail: ______________________________

d. Labradors have short coats, poodles have curly fur, wolfhounds have long noses, and bulldogs have pug noses. (Adapted from Miller and Levine 319)

Type of detail: ______________________________

e. Cataloging more than 10,000 dream reports, Calvin Hall and Robert Van de Castle (1966) found that 65 percent were associated with sadness, fear, or anger. (Kassin 147)

Type of detail: ______________________________

2. More than one type of detail is used in each of the following paragraphs. For each paragraph, do the following:

   Put brackets around each detail.

   Label each detail by type in the margin next to the line where it begins.

   Describe the purpose of each detail.

a. We are currently in the midst of a worldwide AIDS epidemic that has killed about 22 million people. UNAIDS, the United Nations organization responsible for tracking AIDS cases, estimates that 36 million people (including 1.4 million children) are infected with HIV and that more than 14,500 new infections and nearly 7,000 deaths from AIDS occur daily. (Audesirk et al. 637)

Purpose: ______________________________

____

____

b. Whatever we may think of them, the activities of supremacist groups may be constitutionally protected, at least in some instances. Some authors suggest that statutes intended to control hate crimes may run afoul of constitutional considerations insofar as they (1) are too vague, (2) criminalize thought rather than action, (3) attempt to control what would otherwise be free speech, and (4) deny equal protection of the laws to those who wish to express their personal biases. The U.S. Supreme Court seems to agree. In the 1992 case of *R.A.V.* v. *City of St. Paul*, which involved a burning cross on the front lawn of a black family, the court struck down a city ordinance designed to prevent the bias-motivated display of symbols or objects such as Nazi swastikas or burning crosses. In 1995, in the case of *Capitol Square Review and Advisory Board* v. *Pinette*, the Court reiterated its position, saying that KKK organizers in Ohio could legitimately erect an unattended cross on the Statehouse Plaza in Columbus's Capitol Square. (Schmalleger 75)

Purpose: ______________________________

____

____

Major and Minor Details

Details take on the most meaning when you see what they relate to. Details can support either the main idea or another detail. The details that clarify or prove ideas are called **major details.** They answer the what, how, or why questions you form about the paragraph main idea. Details that clarify or prove other details are called **minor details.** These details usually answer questions like when, where, and who or they provide examples of a previous, broader detail.

Here's a paragraph that has both types of details.

EXAMPLE

Sent. 1—TS *Sent. 2—major* *Sent. 3—minor* *Sent. 4—major* *Sent. 5—minor* *Sent. 6—major* *Sent. 7—minor* *Sent. 8—minor*	At the microscopic level, there are three different types of cells involved in the growth and maintenance of bone. **Osteoblasts** are immature bone cells that are responsible for the production of new bone. They secrete the material that becomes the bone ground substance. **Osteocytes** are mature bone cells. They maintain the structure and density of normal bone by continually recycling the calcium compounds around themselves. The third type of bone cell, the **osteoclasts,** could be thought of as the demolition team of bone tissue. Osteoclasts are cells that move along the outside of bones, releasing enzymes that eat away at bone tissue. These cells liberate minerals stored in the bone. (Adapted from Krogh 548)

Notice that the definition details directly answer the question "What are the three types of cells involved in growth and maintenance of bones?" The remaining sentences give descriptive information about each of those types of cells. The very clear topic sentence and the bold-faced words in this paragraph make it easy to spot the major and minor details. However, not every paragraph has such clear indicators, so you will often have to identify these relationships without the author's clues.

A place for everything, and everything in its place.
—Isabella Mary Beeton (1836–1865), British author

ACTIVITY 2: IDENTIFY MAJOR AND MINOR DETAILS

DIRECTIONS: In the following items, the topic sentence is presented first and the details are listed below it. Number the major details in order (1, 2, 3 . . .). Leave the minor details blank. Then record a what, how, or why question that is answered by the major details.

1. When the glaciers disappeared, three major environmental changes occurred.

_______ **a.** The melting of the glacial ice caused the oceans to rise.

_______ **b.** As the seas moved inland, the waters inundated some of the coastal plains.

_______ **c.** Islands, inlets, and bays were created.

_______ **d.** The warmer temperatures changed the treeless plains and tundras.

______ **e.** Eventually, the plains and grasslands gave way to dense mixed forests, mostly birch, oak, and pine.

______ **f.** The warming waterways spawned new life.

______ **g.** They filled with fish and other aquatic resources. (Adapted from Ember and Ember 137)

Question: ____

____

2. Middle-income parents devote a good deal of their resources (time, money, education) to enhancing their children's development.

______ **a.** They are able to support their children's emotional well-being.

______ **b.** Generally, they have time to listen to their children and talk to them about how to handle problems.

______ **c.** They also can afford counseling in times of crisis.

______ **d.** Middle-income parents devote a good deal of resources to the social well-being of their children.

______ **e.** They enroll their children in extracurricular activities from an early age.

______ **f.** They also support athletic involvement with sports equipment, driving to practices and games, volunteer coaching, and attending games.

______ **g.** Middle-income families tend to encourage house parties and sleepovers, and often pay for entertainment during those occasions.

______ **h.** Finally, middle-income families often support educational advancement with special schooling, tutoring, encouragement, and even tuition. (Adapted from Benokraitis 339)

Question: ____

____

3. Humor stems from the contrast between two different realities.

______ **a.** Generally, one reality is *conventional.*

______ **b.** Conventional reality is what people expect in a specific situation.

______ **c.** The other reality is *unconventional.*

______ **d.** That is what is unexpected.

______ **e.** It is a violation of cultural patterns.

______ **f.** Humor, therefore, arises from contradiction, ambiguity, and double meanings found in differing definitions of the same situation.

______ **g.** It is a form of reality play.

______ **h.** In other words, humor is a product of reality construction. (Macionis 157)

Question: ____

____

Once you find the major details, it's useful to mark and visually separate them from the minor ones so that you don't have to repeat this thought process at a later time. One easy way to do this is to simply number the major details in the margin next to the line where they begin. It will then be obvious that any sentences without numbers are either the topic sentence or minor details. If you use this method along with the marking system presented in Chapter 6, you will circle the paragraph topic, underline the topic sentence, and underline the key words of the detail sentences. Here's an example of this marking system.

EXAMPLE

1 The sensation of touch is vital for survival. Without it, you would not
know that you're in danger. Without touch, you would not realize that
you are becoming frostbitten or burned; you would not know if you've
2, 3 been stung by a bee. You would be unable to swallow food. When other
sensory systems fail, touch takes on even more importance. All of us can
feel the differences between leather, sandpaper, brick, cork, velvet, and
other textures. Indeed, most of us react with disgust to substances that
are scabby, slimy, gooey, oily, clammy, and sticky. But for Virgil, the blind
man, shapes and textures are particularly important for recognizing objects. When passed a bowl of fruit, he could easily distinguish among a
slick plum, a soft fuzzy peach, a smooth nectarine, and a rough dimpled
orange. He was even able to "see" through the disguise of an artificial wax
pear that had fooled everyone else. "It's a candle," he said, "shaped like a
bell or a pear." (Adapted from Kassin 105)

This entire paragraph is made up of descriptive details, and it would be easy to overlook the ones that are the most important. The major details answer the question "How is touch vital to survival?" Notice that line 4 has two numbers. That's because two major details begin in that line. Also notice that most of the paragraph is taken up with minor details that show how touch takes on more importance when other systems fail. Without the main idea question and attention to what the major details are, it would be easy to over-emphasize the last part of the paragraph as being the most important, when in fact it is not.

A fact in itself is nothing. It is valuable only for the idea attached to it, or for the proof which it furnishes.

—Claude Bernard (1813–1878), French physiologist

The predict and verify process (see Chapter 6) will help you find the major and minor details in paragraphs. The questions you form about the predicted topic sentence will direct you to the major details. As you find the answers and major details, the minor points will be obvious because they don't answer your questions.

ACTIVITY 3: MARK THE MAJOR AND MINOR DETAILS

DIRECTIONS: Read and mark the following paragraphs using these steps.

A. Predict the topic and topic sentence. Form questions.
B. Verify and mark the text.
-Circle the topic.
-Underline the complete topic sentence.
-Underline key words in the detail sentences.
-Number the major details in the margin.
C. Record a what, how, or why question that is answered by the major details.

1. What does the unemployment rate fail to tell us about the labor market? The unemployment rate, while useful, does not tell us all we would like to know about the labor market. Some workers who have part-time jobs would like to have full-time jobs. Those workers are underemployed. Other workers would like to have a job, but have tried unsuccessfully to find one in the past and have given up looking. Because they have stopped looking, they are not counted in the unemployment statistics. Such would-be workers are called discouraged workers. Government estimates put the number of discouraged workers at about 480,000 people toward the end of 2003. The presence of discouraged workers would cause the reported unemployment rate to understate true unemployment because discouraged workers are not in the labor force. (Adapted from Ayers and Collinge 150)

Notes

Question: ____

____

2. Although the male Christian clergy depicted women as the physical, mental and moral inferiors of men, most medieval women worked as equals with the men. Evidence suggests that they were respected and loved by their husbands, perhaps because they worked shoulder to shoulder and hour by hour with them in fields, trades, and businesses. Between the ages of 10 and 15, girls were apprenticed in a trade, much like boys, and they learned a marketable skill. Women appeared in virtually every "blue-collar" trade, but were especially prominent in the food and clothing industries. They belonged to guilds and they could become

Notes

craft masters. In the late Middle Ages, townswomen often went to school and gained vernacular literacy, although they were excluded from universities and the professions of scholarship, law, and medicine.
(Adapted from Craig et al., 307)

Notes

Question: ____________________

____

You might be wondering if all paragraphs have major and minor details. The answer is no. A short paragraph can have just a topic sentence and major details. But a paragraph can't have a minor detail without first presenting a major one. You also might wonder if you are supposed to number the major details in every paragraph in a text. That's up to you and what best serves your reading needs. You certainly want to number major details in paragraphs that you will need to return to. Those numbers will greatly aid your note taking and learning efforts. Number other paragraphs to aid your comprehension. But remember: it's better to underline too much than to do too little.

Before you go on . . .

Monitor Your Progress: recite

As you read . . .

Focus Your Efforts: question and read

Logical Patterns

THINK ABOUT THIS . . .

1. How would you organize the information in each of these situations?
   a. Your friend asks you to show her how to change a tire.

      ____

   b. You're studying for an exam about the differences between small and large businesses.

      ____

   c. You have to write a political science essay about why John Kerry lost the 2004 presidential election.

      ____

2. Reminder: Preread this section.

> Logic is the anatomy of thought.
>
> —John Locke (1632–1704), British philosopher

When we have to deal with a lot of information, we try to organize it. In the ***Think about this*** . . . situations, you would probably break the tire job down to steps, list or chart the differences between the business types, and write paragraphs about the causes of the election outcome. Each task indicates a logical way to present the information. Similarly, authors use appropriate **logical patterns,** or orderly, valid, and reasoned relationships that link pieces of information. An author may use a logical pattern to connect parts of a sentence, sentences in a paragraph, or even a number of paragraphs.

Recognizing the logical patterns used by authors increases your engagement with the text. It also adds to your comprehension in two ways. First, when you recognize a pattern, you can predict what's coming and thus follow the author's train of thought. Second, patterns help you group unrelated bits of information into larger, simpler, and more manageable pieces. Even if you find the details very interesting, a flood of unrelated bits like those in the cartoon will overwhelm you eventually.

It's far easier to understand and remember two groups with five related parts in each one than it is to work with ten unrelated pieces of information. To get these benefits, you will need to recognize and use the thinking and writing patterns that authors provide.

Thinking Patterns

Textbook authors use six common thinking patterns: list, definition, sequence, classification, comparison and contrast, and cause and effect. Each of these patterns is a standard way of thinking that you will probably recognize, because you use it in your courses and daily activities. When authors use them, they often include signal words to indicate the thinking pattern. Good reading involves recognizing the patterns with or without these helpful indicators.

How will you use these patterns during PDQ3R? Once you know the signal words, you will find that you quickly recognize them as you read and use them to form questions and understand the author's points. But when signal words are not used, you will need to figure out the logic as soon as you can. Ideally, that will occur as you read, but in very difficult texts, you may not recognize the pattern until you have finished the section and recite what you've marked. Once you understand the text through the pattern, you can use a helpful diagram or map as part of your note taking or composing activities during review. These visual aids will capture the information and display the way it's organized in a memorable format.

List In the **list pattern,** the author presents a number of items that are equally important; the order of the items does not matter. This pattern is like your shopping list: it's important to have everything on the list, but it doesn't matter if the dairy items come before or after the fruits and vegetables. The listed items in a text are used to support a main idea or generalization, which is usually presented in the beginning of the paragraph or section. The items themselves could be any form of detail: facts, examples, descriptive information, research studies, or even definitions.

Authors often signal that a list is coming with either punctuation or specific signal words. Commas are used within a sentence to separate a series of three or more items. A colon can also be used within a sentence to introduce a list of details. Numbered items or a list of bulleted items can be used in a paragraph. Finally, in both sentences and paragraphs, authors may also use signal words like the following to alert readers to the pattern:

also	*another*	*besides*	*equally important is*
finally	*further*	*furthermore*	*first, second, etc.*
in addition	*last*	*moreover*	*several*

Here are examples of a sentence and a paragraph using the list pattern. The signals are in italics and bold font to emphasize their importance.

EXAMPLES

5 Examples

During early adulthood—until about age forty—young adults learn to manage day-to-day affairs for themselves, often juggling conflicting priorities***:*** parents, partner, children, schooling, and work. (Macionis 130)

TS

5 Facts

The Industrial Revolution added a new dimension to our water pollution problems. ***First,*** factories were often built on the banks of streams, and wastes were dumped into the water to be carried away. ***Second,*** the rise of modern agriculture has led to increased contamination as fertilizers and pesticides have found their way into the water system. ***Third,*** transportation of petroleum results in oil spills in oceans, estuaries, and rivers. ***Fourth,*** acids enter waterways from mines and factories and from acid precipitation. *And **finally,*** household chemicals *also* contribute to water pollution when detergents, solvents, and other chemicals are dumped down drains. (Adapted from Hill and Kolb 370)

The outline format, using headings and indented items, is an easy way to record listed information. Figure 7.1 shows an outline for the sample paragraph.

Industrial Revolution added to water pollution.

1. Factories dumped wastes into streams.
2. Agricultural fertilizers and pesticides got into the water.
3. Transportation resulted in oil spills in oceans, estuaries, and rivers.
4. Mines, factories, and acid rain added acids.
5. Household chemicals dumped down drains.

FIGURE 7.1 **An Outline List**

ACTIVITY 4: THE LISTING PATTERN

DIRECTIONS: Practice marking and recording listed information by completing the following tasks.

1. In each of these sentences, highlight the signal word(s) or punctuation that indicate the list pattern. Then answer the questions that follow.
   a. Marketing must identify, evaluate, and select market opportunities and lay down strategies for capturing them. (Armstrong and Kotler 53)

      The topic is: ____.

      How many details are there? ________________________________

   b. Short-term approaches to crime tend to be "hard-line" strategies, using the criminal justice system to incapacitate and (perhaps) deter: more cops, more prisons, and also longer sentences. (Lindsey and Beach 186)

      The topic is: ____.

      How many details are there? ________________________________

2. For each of the following paragraphs, complete these steps.
   a. Highlight the signal word(s) and/or punctuation that indicate the list.
   b. Predict, verify, and mark the text. (See Activity 3, p. 316.)
   c. Outline the information on your own paper.

Text A

Misdemeanors are relatively minor crimes, consisting of offenses such as petty theft (the theft of items of little worth), simple assault (in which the victim suffers no serious injury and in which none was intended), breaking and entering, the possession of burglary tools, disorderly conduct, disturbing the peace, filing a false crime report, and writing bad checks (although the amount for which the check is written may determine the classification of the offense). (Schmalleger 108)

Text B

In general, misdemeanors are any crime punishable by a year or less in prison. In fact, most misdemeanants receive suspended sentences involving a fine and supervised probation. If an "active sentence" is given for a misdemeanor violation of the law, it will probably involve time to be spent in a local jail, perhaps on weekends, rather than imprisonment in a long-term confinement facility. In addition, some misdemeanants are sentenced to perform community service activities, such as washing school buses, painting local government buildings, and cleaning parks and other public areas. (Schmalleger 108)

Text C

Concussions vary a great deal in their severity. Mild "Grade 1" concussions tend to cause headaches, dizziness, disorientation, blurred speech, and a ringing in the ears. In sports, this type of concussion is difficult to diagnose and is commonly referred to as a "dinger" (athletes like to describe the state as "having their bell rung"). At the other extreme are severe "Grade 3" concussions, which are easy to spot because they cause unconsciousness for a brief or prolonged time. This type of injury can damage the brainstem and disrupt such autonomic functions as heart rate and breathing. Over time, it may also result in such symptoms as persistent headaches, vision problems, memory loss, sleep loss, an inability to concentrate, a lack of tolerance for loud noises and bright lights, fatigue and, finally, anxiety or depressed mood. (Kassin 74)

Definition As you learned earlier, a definition is a type of detail. Sometimes, however, a term cannot be explained in one sentence, because it is complex or includes variations. In this case, authors present an extended definition that takes up an entire paragraph or more. The **definition pattern** is an extended definition that often includes a one-sentence meaning plus descriptions, examples, and/or references.

Since the definition pattern can use a variety of details, a variety of signals may also be used, including those that signal definitions, description, example, or reference details, as well as those that indicate the list pattern. So you may encounter words such as *means, is,* or *refers to* that introduce the one-sentence definition; *for example* or *for instance* before examples; *study* or *research* before references, and *also* or *in addition* to emphasize that a list will follow.

In the animal kingdom, the rule is, eat or be eaten; in the human kingdom, define or be defined.

—Thomas Szasz (1920–), American psychiatrist

In the following example the term is discussed, and a great deal more information than just the one sentence technical definition is given. The term is in bold-faced type; the signal words are in italics and bold font.

EXAMPLE

Definition	**Discrimination** ***is*** the unequal and unjust treatment of individuals on the basis of their group memberships (***Feagin and Feagin, 1996***). <u>In</u>
TS	<u>modern societies, widespread norms mandate equal treatment of all</u>
Examples	<u>people</u>. Teachers and employers, ***for example,*** must not let ascribed factors ***such as*** race, ethnicity, and gender influence how they treat their students and employees. Anyone who violates these norms is guilty of discrimination. (Lindsey and Beach 238)

Notice that the first sentence, the technical definition, is not the topic sentence. Remember that a topic sentence cannot be a detail. The second sentence is the author's idea. The question "how do norms mandate equal treatment?" is answered by the definition, examples, and the final sentence, which connects the two.

A vertical tree diagram is a good way to capture the information in an extended definition. Figure 7.2 shows how this form would work on the previous example.

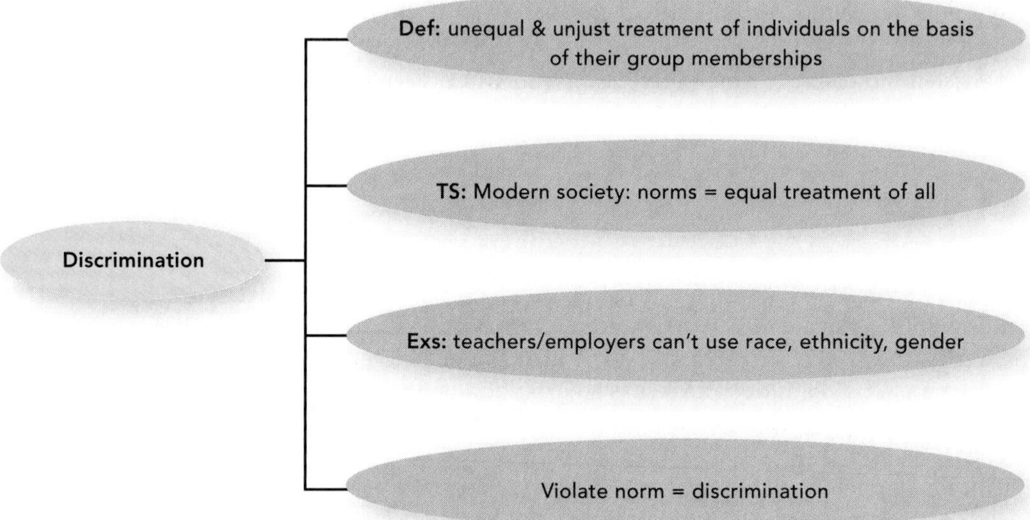

FIGURE 7.2 **A Definition Diagram**

ACTIVITY 5: THE DEFINITION PATTERN

DIRECTIONS: For each of the following paragraphs, complete these steps.

A. Highlight the signal word(s) and/or punctuation that indicates the definition pattern.
B. Predict, verify, and mark the text. (See activity 3, p. 316.)
C. Diagram the information on your own paper.

1. **Positivism** is an approach to understanding human behavior based on the scientific method. Positivistic theories are research-based, concentrate on measurable aspects of empirical reality, and aim to identify the precise causes of behavior. They are also strongly oriented toward reducing deviance: If we can identify the cause of a behavior pattern, we can use that knowledge to change the behavior. Finally, positivistic theories explore the reasons for our choices, therefore allowing us to develop more effective techniques of social control. (Adapted from Lindsey and Beach 161)

2. Torn between the need to fit in and a desire to retain their own heritage, ethnic group members differ in how they manage **acculturation**—the process by which persons are changed by their immersion in a new culture. John Berry and his colleagues (1989) noted that there are four types of coping strategies. At one extreme is *assimilation*, in which the person abandons the old for the new and completely

embraces his or her host culture. At the opposite extreme is *separation*, a pattern characterized by a desire to maintain one's ethnic traditions and not become part of the host culture. Native American Indians who live on reservations and the Amish who live in Lancaster, Pennsylvania, are good examples. A third strategy is *integration*, a bicultural pattern in which the person tries to make the best of both worlds by retaining old traditions while, at the same time, adapting to the new way of life. The fourth strategy is *marginalization*, in which the person has no desire to maintain traditional ties or adopt the new host culture, perhaps due to prejudice and discrimination. (Kassin 548)

Sequence The **sequence pattern** is an organized presentation of information that must go in a certain order. There are two types of sequences: chronological and process order. **Chronological order** is used when events are presented according to time, day, or date of occurrence. This is the pattern you generally find in history texts. **Process order** is a series of steps or stages that, once they begin, must continue in a specified order. Directions for a lab experiment or the stages of falling asleep would follow this pattern.

Chronological signals often have to do with time, such as *today, tomorrow, morning, evening, now,* and *later.* Dates are also a signal for this pattern. Except for words like those, the transition words used to signal either chronological or process order are terms like:

after	*afterward*	*as*	*finally*	*first, second, etc.*
last	*next*	*then*	*when*	*while*

Like lists, sequences can be presented within a sentence, series of sentences, paragraph, or even a number of paragraphs. But, as the following examples illustrate, no matter how long or short the text is, unlike a list, the details in a sequence are arranged in an order that cannot be changed. The signals are in italics and bold font.

EXAMPLES

Chronological Order

TS While old battles for rights continued throughout the 1990s, the decade also saw new and unsettling demands for rights. Some Americans insisted on the right to die—that is, the right of people dying or suffering great pain to end their lives. ***In 1990*** a retired Michigan pathologist, Jack Kevorkian, helped a fifty-two-year-old woman in the early stages of Alzheimer's disease to commit suicide. ***In 1997*** Congress banned the use of federal funds to support assisted suicide, but Oregon voters affirmed the right of doctors to prescribe lethal doses of drugs for terminally ill patients. ***In 1999*** a Michigan court convicted Kevorkian of second degree murder for assisting in the death of a man suffering from Lou Gehrig's disease. (Boydston et al. 924)

Facts and dates in order

Process Order

TS George Herbert Mead (1863–1931) proposed that the self develops not out of biological urges but out of social interactions. For

Descriptive steps in order Mead, the infant was a blank slate with no predisposition to behave in any particular way. The child learns ***first*** by imitating the behavior of specific people, such as parents, sisters, and brothers. ***As*** the child matures, he or she learns to identify with the generalized roles that these people and many others fulfill. (Adapted from Benokraitis 331)

Time lines are a traditional way to represent chronological information, and flow charts work well for processes with steps or stages. Figure 7.3 shows how the previous paragraphs could be diagrammed. Notice that each one is titled. The title is essential to identify the common element among sequenced details.

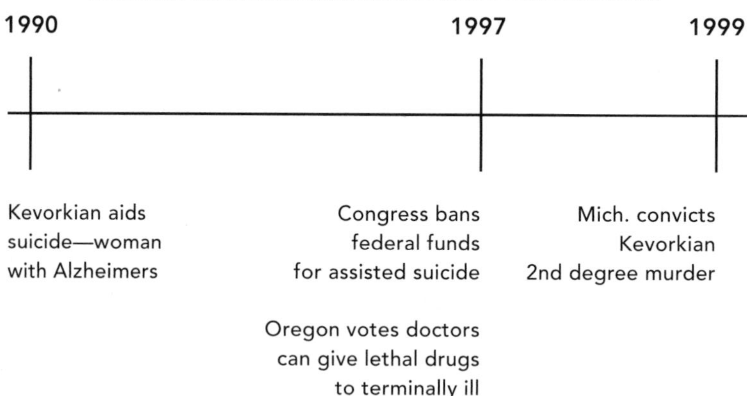

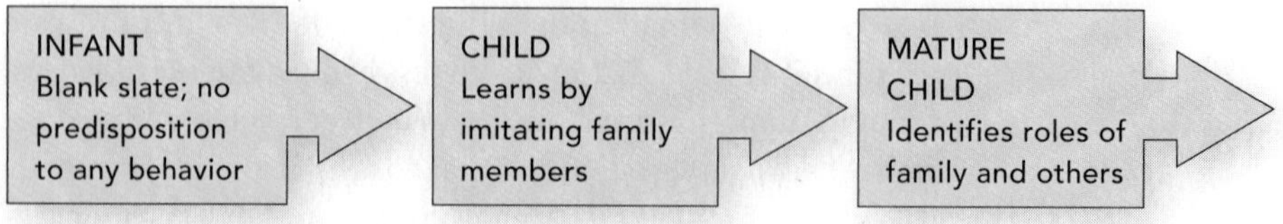

FIGURE 7.3 **Sequence Diagrams**

ACTIVITY 6: THE SEQUENCE PATTERN

DIRECTIONS: Practice marking and recording information in a sequence by completing the following tasks.

1. In each of these sentences, highlight the signal word(s) that indicate sequence. Then answer the questions that follow.
   a. **Igneous rocks** form when molten rock, called **magma,** cools and solidifies. (Tarbuck and Lutgens 26)

      The topic is: ______________________________.

      How many steps are there? ______________________________

   b. In 1700 there were just over 250,000 people living in all of the American colonies, but by 1750 the population had grown more than 300 percent, to more than 1 million. (Adapted from Boydston et al. 125)

      The topic is: ______________________________

      How many events are there? ______________________________

2. For each of the following paragraphs, complete these steps.
   a. Highlight the signal words that indicate the sequence pattern.
   b. Predict, verify, and mark the text. (See activity 3, p. 316.)
   c. Create a time line or flow chart of the information on your own paper.

Text A

In 1529 Parliament convened for what would be a seven-year session that passed a flood of legislation that harassed and finally placed royal reins on the clergy. In January 1531 the clergy publicly recognized Henry as head of the church in England; in 1533 Parliament passed the Submission of the Clergy, effectively placing canon law under royal control; in 1534 Parliament ended all payments by the English clergy to Rome and also passed the Act of Succession, which made Anne Boleyn's children legitimate heirs to the throne. (Adapted from Craig et al. 344)

Text B

Developing a good package for a new product requires making many decisions. First, the company must establish the *packaging concept*, which states what the package should *be* or *do* for the product. Should it mainly offer product protection, introduce a new dispensing method, suggest certain qualities about the product, or do something else? Decisions then must be made on specific elements of the package, such as size, shape, materials, color, text, and brand mark. These elements must work together to support the product's position and marketing strategy. The package must be consistent with the product's advertising, pricing, and distribution. (Armstrong and Kotler 300)

Good order is the foundation of all great things.
—Edmund Burke (1729–1797), British political writer, statesman

Classification The **classification pattern** divides a group into categories of equal importance. When authors use this pattern, they name, define, provide examples, and/or describe each category so that a member will belong in only one group. For example, most people are familiar with the classification system for nutrients: carbohydrates, fats, proteins, vitamins, minerals, and so on. Within this system, sugar is an example of a carbohydrate, and cooking oil is an example of a fat.

The classification signal words announce that groups will be presented, and they are often preceded by a number. These signals are generally placed in a topic sentence that begins a paragraph, such as "There are three types, groups, parts . . ." Classification signals include terms such as these:

class	*classified*	*category*	*divided into*
group	*kind*	*parts*	*type*

In the following example, definitions help to identify the groups, and descriptive details help to explain the definitions. The signal words are in italics and bold font; the category labels are in bold only.

EXAMPLE

TS + signal *1st kind + def.* *Description* *2nd kind + def.* *Description*	Groups typically benefit from two ***kinds*** of leadership. **Instrumental leadership** refers to group leadership that emphasizes the completion of tasks. Members look to instrumental leaders to make plans, give orders, and "get things done." **Expressive leadership,** on the other hand, focuses on collective well-being. Expressive leaders take less of an interest in achieving goals than in promoting the well-being of members, raising group morale, and minimizing tension and conflict among members. (Macionis 165)

A horizontal tree diagram or organizational chart, as it is sometimes called, is an excellent way to represent a classification system. Figure 7.4 shows how the tree diagram would organize the information from the preceding paragraph.

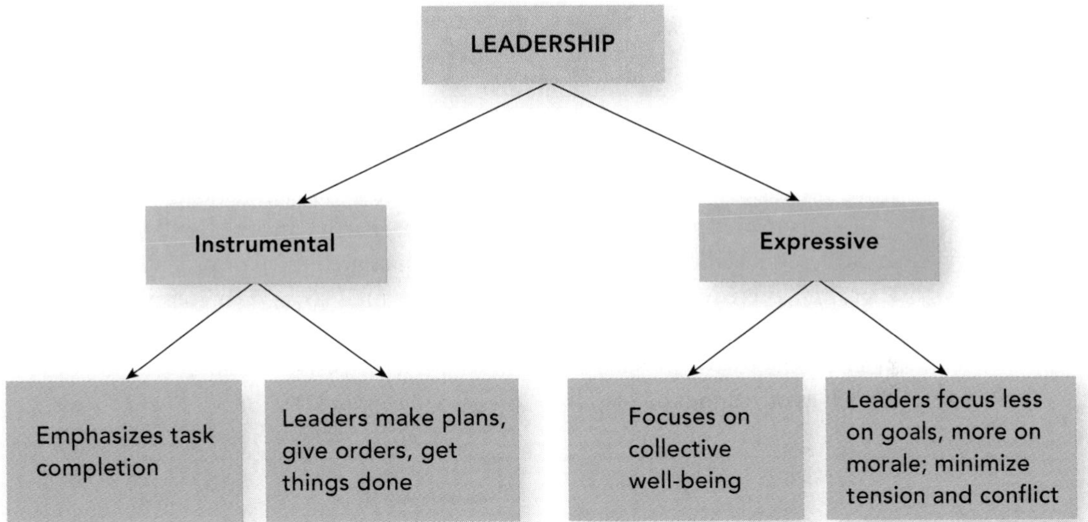

FIGURE 7.4 **Classification Tree Diagram**

ACTIVITY 7: THE CLASSIFICATION PATTERN

DIRECTIONS: Complete these tasks on each of the following texts.

A. Highlight the signal words that indicate the sequence pattern.
B. Predict, verify, and mark the text. (See activity 3, p. 316.)
C. Create a tree diagram of the information on your own paper.

1. Even among adults, individuals differ in the number of taste buds they have—and in their sensitivity to taste. Indeed, recent studies have shown that people can be divided into three groups: nontasters, medium tasters, and supertasters. At one extreme, nontasters (25 percent of the population) react strongly to certain sweet and bitter compounds. Compared to most, supertasters use only half as much sugar or saccharin in their coffee or tea. They also suffer more oral burn from eating the active ingredient in chili peppers. These differences in taste sensitivity correspond nicely to our physiological makeup. Using videomicroscopy to count the number of taste buds on the tongue, researchers have found that nontasters have an average of 96 taste buds per square centimeter, medium tasters have 184, and supertasters have 425. (Kassin 104)

2. Resources are commonly divided into two broad categories—renewable and non-renewable. **Renewable resources** can be replenished over relatively short time spans such as months, years, or decades. Common examples are plants and animals for food, natural fibers for clothing, and trees for lumber and paper. Energy from flowing water, wind, and the sun are also considered renewable.

   By contrast, **nonrenewable resources** continue to be formed in Earth, but the processes that create them are so slow that significant deposits take millions of years to accumulate. For human purposes, Earth contains fixed quantities of these substances. When the present supplies are mined or pumped from the ground, there will be no more. Examples are fuels (coal, oil, natural gas) and many important metals (iron, copper, uranium, gold). Some of these non-renewable resources, such as aluminum, can be used over and over again; others, such as oil, cannot be recycled. (Tarbuck and Lutgens 624)

Comparison and Contrast The comparison and contrast pattern actually has three variations. Authors can **compare** two or more items by describing how they are similar. Second, they can **contrast** two or more items by explaining their differences. Or last, they can provide both the similarities and the differences for a number of items. For comparisons, authors use signal words like the following:

alike	*analogous to*	*as well as*	*both*	*similarly*
comparison	*correspondingly*	*equivalent*	*identical*	
in comparison	*in the same way*	*like*	*likewise*	

For contrasts, authors use terms like these:

alternatively	*although*	*but*	*contrast*
conversely	*despite*	*differences*	*differs from*
however	*in contrast*	*less*	*more*
on the contrary	*on the other hand*	*still*	*unlike*
-er suffix (e.g., higher, better, newer)			

The rose and the thorn, and sorrow and gladness are linked together.
—Saadi (c. 1210–1290), Persian poet

The following examples show the common variations of this pattern. The signal terms are in italics and bold font; the items that are compared or contrasted are in bold only.

EXAMPLES

Comparison

TS *Descriptive similarities*	Indus culture was remarkably constant over time. Because the main **cities** and **towns** lay in river lowlands subject to periodic flooding, they were rebuilt often, each new level of construction closely following its precursor's pattern. ***Similarly,*** the **Indus script** shows no evidence of change over time. (Craig et al. 13)

Contrast

TS *Descriptive differences*	The environments in which coal, petroleum, and natural gas are formed are very ***different,*** as are the organisms. **Coal** is formed mostly from plant material that accumulated in a swampy environment above sea level. **Oil** and **gas** are derived from the remains of both plants and animals having a marine origin. (Adapted from Tarbuck and Lutgens 627)

Comparison and contrast

TS *Similar examples*	Most women and men, especially working parents, share the ***same*** concerns and want the ***same*** things in life. ***Both*** sexes worry about health care and retirement security, a lack of fairness and respect in the workplace, and limited family medical leave and child care.
TS *Differences from a reference*	*Despite* these ***similarities,*** there are still a number of ***differences*** in gender roles. Employed **mothers,** especially, consistently report ***more*** stress than **men** in their everyday lives. Mothers who work full time report being exhausted by juggling jobs and family responsibilities. **Men, *on the other hand,*** complain that their wives' housecleaning standards are too high. And they may feel unappreciated or inadequate. (Adapted from Benokraitis 133)

Charts and diagrams are useful to capture the comparison and contrast variations. For comparisons, a double-arrow diagram works well; for contrasts, a chart with columns for the categories and rows for the characteristics (or vice versa) works well. When a text has both comparisons and contrasts, you can use a chart and simply delete the column line that separates similar items. Figure 7.5 illustrates these types of charts and diagrams using the example paragraphs. Notice that each one is given a title.

Comparison

Indus Culture Constant

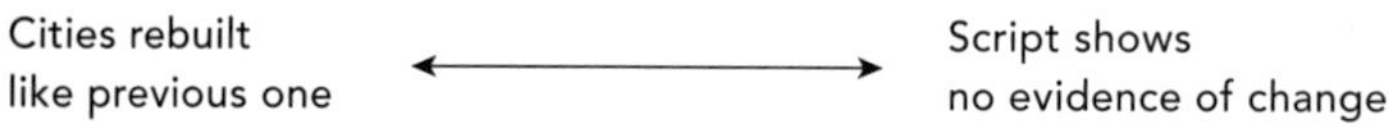

Contrast

How Three Natural Resources Formed

	Coal	*Petroleum/natural gas*
Environments	Swampy, above sea level	Marine
Organisms	Plant material	Remains of both plants and animals

Comparison and Contrast

Roles for Women and Men

	Women	*Men*
Similar Concerns	Health care, retirement security, fairness and respect at work, family medical leave, child care	
Differences reported	More everyday stress	Complain wives' standards to high
	Exhausted by juggling jobs and family responsibilityes	Feel unappreciated or inadequate

FIGURE 7.5 **Comparison and Contrast Charts and Diagrams**

ACTIVITY 8: THE COMPARISON AND CONTRAST PATTERN

DIRECTIONS: Practice marking and recording comparison and contrast information by completing the following tasks.

1. In each of these sentences, highlight the signal word(s) that indicate the comparison or contrast. Then answer the questions that follow.
   a. In contrast to the migration of the seventeenth century, an increasing proportion of the eighteenth-century migrants were skilled but relatively impoverished artisans. (Boydston et al. 127)

      The topic is: ______________________________.

      The pattern is: ______________________________.

List all the similarities or differences:

____

____

____

____

b. Seeing and hearing are similar processes. Just as we do not see a jumbled collection of lines and colors, so we do not hear a chaotic collection of disconnected pitches and timbres. With both senses, we use our perceptual powers to organize patterns of light or sound and to construct a meaningful world. (Adapted from Wade and Tavis 195)

The topic is: ____.

The pattern is: ____.

List all the similarities or differences:

____

____

____

____

2. For each of the following paragraphs, complete these steps.

a. Highlight the signal word(s) that indicate the comparison or contrast.

b. Predict, verify, and mark the text. (See activity 3, p. 316.)

c. Chart the information on your own paper.

Text A

The three main forms of treatment are (1) surgery, (2) radiation, and (3) chemotherapy. Like surgery, however, radiation cannot be used to treat widespread cancers, because to irradiate the whole body would damage a great deal of healthy tissue. Both surgery and radiation therapy can be traumatic and dangerous. (Audesirk et al. 638)

Text B

Are there sex differences in emotion, or is this perception a mere illusion? There is little support for the conclusion that the sexes differ in their feelings. Both men and women become happy when they achieve something that they have strived for. Similarly, both sexes become saddened by the loss of a loved one, angry when frustrated, fearful when in danger, and embarrassed when they slip up in front of others. Men and women also exhibit similar facial expressions and autonomic reactions to emotion-triggering events. People surely differ in their propensity for certain types of feelings, but these differences say more about us as individuals than as men or women. (Adapted from Kassin 351)

Text C

Psychologists have been eager to understand the nature and extent of gender differences. At this point, this is what we know. On average, girls are better spellers. They also score slightly higher than boys on tests of reading comprehension, writing, and foreign language. Girls are better at arithmetic in grade school, but males surpass females early in junior high school—a difference that continues to college and beyond and is found in other countries as well. Consistently, males outperform females on spatial tasks such as mentally rotating objects to determine what they look like from another perspective. (Adapted from Kassin 473)

Cause and Effect The **cause and effect pattern** is used to explain both events and ideas. The **cause** is the stimulus or reason for an event or idea. The **effect** is the result or consequence of the event or idea. A cause comes before the event or idea that is being discussed, and the effect follows it. Finally, causes answer the question "why?" and effects answer the question "what happened afterwards?"

Like comparison and contrast, the cause and effect pattern has three variations. Authors can present only the causes, only the effects, or both. In addition, any situation or idea can have one or more causes and one or more effects. For example, the causes of a wildfire could have been dry brush and children playing with matches. The effects could include property damage, harm to wildlife, and the cost of putting the fire out. The words that generally signal causes are:

so	*because*	*cause*	*comes from*	*due to*
if	*on account of*	*reasons*	*since*	*stems from*

The words that generally signal effects are:

accordingly	*according to*	*affect*	*as a result*	*consequence*
consequently	*creates*	*effect*	*hence*	*leads to*
result	*then*	*therefore*	*thus*	

The following texts show examples of the variations of this pattern. The signals are in italics and bold font; the causes and effects are in bold only.

EXAMPLES

Cause

TS

Factual causes

Many factors ***affect*** the rate at which photosynthesis occurs. ***Because*** **water** is one of the raw materials of photosynthesis, a shortage of water can slow or even stop photosynthesis. **Temperature** is also a factor. Photosynthesis depends on enzymes that function best between 0° C and 35° C. Temperatures above or below this range may damage the enzymes, slowing down the rate of photosynthesis or even stopping it entirely. (Adapted from Miller and Levine 214)

Effect

TS

Descriptive effects

Some writers describe marriage as having "medical power." Overall, married people are generally **healthier** and **happier** than those who are single, divorced, or widowed. ***As a result,*** they **attempt suicide** less frequently and have fewer **automobile accidents** than singles. They are less likely to suffer from depression, anxiety, and other forms of **psychological distress.** (Adapted from Benokraitis 271)

Cause and Effect

TS

Factual effects and a cause

Every winter, a wave of influenza, or flu, sweeps across the world. Thousands of the elderly, the newborn, and those already suffering from illness **perish,** while hundreds of millions more **suffer** the respiratory distress, fever, and muscle aches of milder cases. Flu is ***caused by*** several **viruses** that invade the cells of the respiratory tract, turning each cell into a factory for manufacturing new viruses. (Audesirk et al., 632)

Diagramming cause and effect relationships is easiest if you use brackets, arrows, and labels to emphasize the before and after relationships. Figure 7.6 illustrates the previous examples. Notice that each one is given a title.

Notice in the last example how flu is both an effect and a cause for new effects. Cause-and-effect relationships often go on in a chain like this. If you look at only a small segment, you will see a single cause and effect relationship. But once you add three or more elements, the effects will also be the cause of new consequences.

Take away the cause, and the effect ceases.

—Miguel de Cervantes (1547–1616),
Spanish novelist, dramatist, poet

Causes

Rate of Photosynthesis

Causes
Shortage of water
Temperature out of range
} Slows or stops photosynthesis

Effects

Medical Power of Marriage

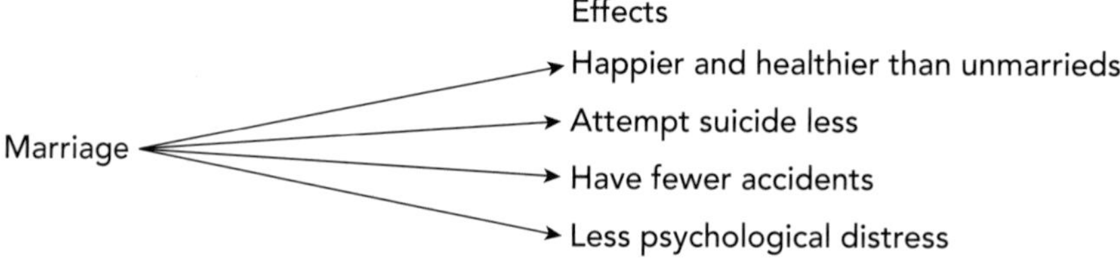

Cause and Effect

Influenza (flu)

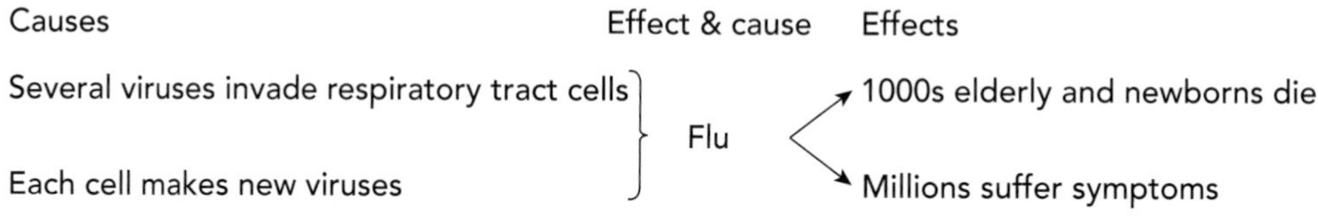

FIGURE 7.6 **Cause and Effect Diagrams**

ACTIVITY 9: THE CAUSE AND EFFECT PATTERN

DIRECTIONS: Practice marking and recording cause and effect information by completing the following tasks.

1. In each of these sentences, highlight the signal word(s) that indicates the cause or effect pattern. Then answer the questions that follow.
   a. What are the results of glycolysis? It accomplishes three valuable things in energy harvesting: It yields two ATP molecules, it yields two energized molecules of NADH, and it results in two molecules of pyruvic acid. (Adapted from Krogh 138)
   The topic is: ______________________________.
   Do these sentences present causes, effects, or both? Explain.
   ____
   ____

b. Because AIDS is deadly and the incidences of other sexually transmitted diseases are on the rise, "safer sex" practices are important for everyone. (Audesirk et al., 637)

The topic is: ______________________________.

Do these sentences present causes, effects, or both? Explain.

____

____

____

2. For each of the following paragraphs, complete these steps.

a. Highlight the signal word(s) that indicate the cause-and-effect pattern.

b. Predict, verify, and mark the text. (See activity 3, p. 316.)

c. Diagram the information on your own paper.

Text A

The use of marijuana, the hallucinogen LSD, and other drugs increased during the 1960s. Drugs appealed to the countercultures for a number of reasons. First, because most drugs were illegal, using them was a way of flouting adult convention. Second, drugs were a way of escaping everyday reality and finding some higher, more liberated consciousness. Sex offered a similar combination of pleasure and defiance. By celebrating and enjoying sexual intercourse outside marriage, young people could shock adults. And, many young people hoped that the counterculture would weave sex, drugs, and rock into a new lifestyle. (Adapted from Boydston et al., 824)

Text B

Two centuries of contact with European settlers affected the Cherokee way of life. Some Cherokees embraced racial slavery. Most grew more dependent on farming. Trying to accommodate white practices, Cherokees adopted a written alphabet. Then, in 1836 a small splinter group (claiming to speak for the whole nation) agreed to removal. The Treaty of New Echota was ratified in the spring of 1836. The pro-treaty Cherokees began to leave almost immediately. The overwhelming majority of Cherokees, who considered the treaty fraudulent, remained in the East. (Adapted from Boydston et al. 328)

Multiple Patterns Just like details, authors often use a variety of thinking patterns in one paragraph or section. The variety is needed to fully cover the topic. As a thoughtful reader, you will need to look out for all of the patterns, identify each one as you come to it, and shift your thinking from one to another. Then, as you recite the text or use review methods, you will decide if the text has a primary pattern or if several are equally important.

Here's an example of a paragraph that presents a list, causes and effects, and contrasts. The signal words are in italics and bold font.

EXAMPLE

Whether we define deviance as a moral or a medical issue has several ***consequences. First,*** it ***affects*** who responds to deviance. An offense against common morality usually brings about a reaction from members of the community or the police. A medical label, ***however,*** places the situation under the control of clinical specialists, including counselors, psychiatrists, and physicians. A ***second difference*** is how people respond to deviance. A moral approach defines deviants as "offenders" subject to punishment. Medically, ***however,*** they are patients who need treatment. ***Third,*** and most important, the two labels ***differ*** on the personal competence of the deviant person. Morally speaking, whether we are right or wrong, at least we take responsibility for our behavior. Once defined as sick, ***however,*** we are seen as lacking the capacity to control our actions. (Adapted from Macionis 198)

The paragraph clearly discusses the consequences of how deviance is viewed. However, the contrasts between the moral and medical approaches seem to be emphasized even more because the paragraph has five contrast signal words versus two for effects. Still, most students reading this information would probably need to understand both the effects and the differences between them.

> Logic takes care of itself: all we have to do is to look and see how it does it.
>
> —Ludwig Wittgenstein (1889–1951), Austrian philosopher

Table 7.2 summarizes the definitions and signal words for the most common types of patterns. Review it before you complete the following activity.

TABLE 7.2 **Thinking Patterns**

DEFINITION/ DESCRIPTION	SIGNAL WORDS
List Presents a number of items that are equally important, but the order of the items does not matter	*also, another, besides, equally important is, finally, further, furthermore, first, second, etc., in addition, last, moreover, several*
Definition An extended definition that may include a one-sentence meaning, descriptions, references, and/or examples.	Uses signals for definition, example, or reference details, as well as those from the list pattern

(continued)

TABLE 7.2 **Thinking Patterns *(continued)***

DEFINITION / DESCRIPTION	SIGNAL WORDS
Sequence **Chronological order:** Presents events according to time, day, or date of occurrence. **Process order:** Presents a series of steps or stages that, once begun, must continue in a specified order	*after, afterward, as, finally, first, second, etc., last, next, then, when, while*
Classification Divides a group into categories of equal importance.	*class, classified, category, divided into, group, kind, parts, type*
Comparison and contrast **Comparison:** Describes how two or more items are similar. **Contrast:** Describes how two or more items are different.	*alike, analogous to, as well as, both, comparison, correspondingly, equivalent, identical, in comparison, in the same way, like, likewise, similarly* *alternatively, although, but, contrast, conversely, despite, differences, differs from, however, in contrast, less, more, on the contrary, on the other hand, still, unlike, -er suffix*
Cause and effect **Cause:** The stimulus or reason(s) for an event or idea **Effect:** The result(s) or consequence(s) of an event or idea.	*so, because, cause, comes from, due to, if, on account of, reasons, since, stems from* *accordingly, according to, affect, as a result, consequence, consequently, creates, effect, hence, leads to, result, then, therefore, thus*

ACTIVITY 10: IDENTIFY MULTIPLE RELATIONSHIPS

DIRECTIONS: For each of the following texts, complete these steps.

A. Highlight any signal word(s) and punctuation that indicate the pattern(s).
B. Predict, verify, and mark the text. (See activity 3, p. 316.)
C. Identify which of the following patterns are used: list, definition, sequence, classification, comparison and contrast, and/or cause and effect.
D. Answer the question that follows.

1. A divided Supreme Court ruled Tuesday that people stopped for minor traffic offenses can be subject to a full-scale police arrest including handcuffs, booking, and jail. (Schmalleger 210)

   The patterns are: ____.

   Is there a primary pattern? Explain your answer:

   ____

   ____

   ____

2. Participants in a criminal trial can be divided into two categories: professionals and outsiders. The professionals are the official courtroom actors, well versed in criminal trial practice. In contrast, "outsiders" are generally unfamiliar with courtroom organization and trial procedure. (Schmalleger 338)

   The patterns are: ____.

   Is there a primary pattern? Explain your answer:

   ____

   ____

   ____

3. Identity thieves use several common techniques. Some engage in "Dumpster diving," which is going through trash bags, cans, or Dumpsters to get copies of checks, credit card and bank statements; credit card applications; or other records that typically bear identifying information. Others use a technique called "shoulder surfing." It involves simply looking over the victim's shoulder as he or she enters personal information into a computer or on a written form. Eavesdropping is another simple, yet effective technique that identity thieves often use. (Schmalleger 56)

   The patterns are: ____.

   Is there a primary pattern? Explain your answer:

   ____

   ____

   ____

4. The body normally regulates blood pressure in two ways. Sensory neurons at several places in the body detect the level of blood pressure, sending impulses to the medulla oblongata region of the brain stem. When blood pressure is too high, the autonomic nervous system releases neurotransmitters that cause the smooth muscles around blood vessels to relax, lowering blood pressure. When blood pressure is too low, neurotransmitters are released that elevate blood pressure by causing these smooth muscles to contract. (Miller and Levine 948)

   The patterns are: ____.

   Is there a primary pattern? Explain your answer:

   ____

   ____

   ____

5. Earth is surrounded by a life-giving gaseous envelope called the **atmosphere**. Compared with the solid Earth, the atmosphere is thin and tenuous. One half lies below an altitude of 5.6 kilometers (3.5 miles), and 90 percent occurs within just 16 kilometers (10 miles) of earth's surface. By comparison, the radius of the solid Earth (distance from the surface to the center) is about 6400 kilometers (nearly 4000 miles)! (Tarbuck and Lutgens 14)

   The patterns are: ______________________________.

   Is there a primary pattern? Explain your answer:

   ____

   ____

   ____

6. When sunlight excites electrons in chlorophyll, the electrons gain a great deal of energy. These high-energy electrons require a special carrier. Think of a high-energy electron as being similar to a red-hot coal from a fireplace or campfire. If you wanted to move the coal from one place to another, you wouldn't pick it up in your hands. You would use a pan or bucket—a carrier—to transport it. Cells treat high-energy electrons in the same way. Instead of a pan or bucket, they use electron carriers to transfer high-energy electrons from chlorophyll to other molecules. A carrier molecule is a compound that can accept a pair of high-energy electrons and transfer them along with most of the energy to another molecule. (Miller and Levine 209)

   The patterns are: ______________________________.

   Is there a primary pattern? Explain your answer:

   ____

   ____

   ____

Writing Patterns

In addition to the six common thinking patterns, writers may also use four additional writing patterns to link information. While none of these patterns is associated with specific diagrams, each has its own set of signal words. Recognizing these patterns with or without the signals will aid your comprehension.

> **Writing is thinking on paper.**
> —William Zinsser (1922–), American author, teacher

Statement and Clarification The **statement and clarification** pattern begins with an idea that needs to be explained, because it's complex, unusual, ambiguous, or open to interpretation. The details clarify what the author means. Typical signal words for this pattern are:

clearly	*in other words*	*obviously*	*put another way*
simply	*that is*	*to clarify*	

Here's an example of this pattern. Notice that the first sentence benefits from further explanation. The signal words are in italics and bold font.

EXAMPLE

The condition called aneuploidy is one in which an organism has either more or fewer chromosomes than normally exist in its species' full set. ***Put another way,*** aneuploidy is a condition in which an organism has one chromosome too many, or one too few. Among human genetic malfunctions, aneuploidy is unusual in that it occurs quite commonly and yet goes largely unrecognized. This is so because it most often occurs not in fully formed human beings, but in embryos. A would-be mother may know only that she is having a hard time getting pregnant. What she may not know is that she actually has been pregnant—perhaps several times—but that aneuploidy has doomed the embryo in each case. (Krogh 237)

Spatial Order **Spatial order** is used to describe the position or physical location of an object or part of an environment. In this pattern, the author picks a starting point and then presents the details in an orderly way, such as top to bottom, left to right, North to South, and so on. With the spatial pattern, authors often include pairs of signal words such as the following:

above, below	*east, west*	*front, back*	*left, right*
near, far	*north, south*	*over, under*	*top, bottom*

In addition, you might also see terms like these:

adjacent to	*behind*	*between*	*beyond*
in the distance	*in the middle*	*nearby*	*next*
on top opposite to	*straight ahead*	*where*	

The following paragraph shows how spatial order is used in descriptive, academic writing. The signal words are in italics and bold font.

EXAMPLE

Where is the San Andreas fault system located? It trends in a ***northwesterly*** direction for nearly 1,300 kilometers (780 miles) through much of ***western*** California. At its ***southern*** end, the San Andreas connects with a spreading center located in the gulf of California. In the ***north,*** the fault enter the Pacific Ocean at Point Arena. (Tarbuck and Lutgens 323)

Order of Importance The **order of importance** pattern presents information from least to most important, from most to least important, or from the base to the top of a hierarchy. For example, in the U.S. court system, which includes city, state and federal courts, the highest court in the land, the one with the most far-reaching powers, is the U.S. Supreme Court. Information about the judicial system could begin with the city courts and move up to the most powerful court or start with the Supreme Court and move down to the local level. In the hierarchy form, each stage after the base is more complex or more important than the one(s) before or "below" it. The levels of thinking (see Chapter 5) are a good example of a hierarchy. Hierarchies are described from the base up to the highest stage. Typical signal words for order of importance are:

base	*biggest*	*chief*	*critical*
essential	*first*	*hierarchy*	*highest*
key major	*importance*	*more important*	*most important*
next step/stage up	*primary*	*principal*	*second, secondary*

The following paragraphs are examples of the most important and hierarchy versions of this pattern. The signal words are in italics and bold font.

EXAMPLES

How do adult children and parents get along, especially when they're living under the same roof? Some parents report that they are tolerant of but unhappy with the return of their children. There is often conflict about clothes, helping out, the use of the family car, and the adult child's lifestyle. The ***biggest*** problems arise if the adult children are unemployed or if grandchildren live in the home. (Adapted from Benokraitis 346)

Psychologist Abraham Maslow's ***hierarchy*** of human needs model proposed that people have several kinds of needs that they attempt to satisfy in their work. He classified them into five basic categories and suggested that they be arranged in a ***hierarchy of importance,*** where the ***lower*** level needs (physical and security) must be met before a person will try to satisfy the ***higher*** needs (social, esteem, and self-actualization). (Adapted from Griffin and Ebert 255)

Summary As noted in Chapter 5, a **summary** is a condensed version of the main points in a text. You're already familiar with summaries as chapter aids. But authors also use them to provide a concise version of a discussion they have just presented, and these appear within the text rather than at the end of the chapter. Authors also use the summary pattern to present essential points of someone else's research, books, or articles. Summaries may include signals such as these:

article	*book*	*concluded*	*found*	*in conclusion*
in short	*investigation*	*then*	*therefore*	*to review*
to summarize	*research*	*study*	*subjects*	

The following examples illustrate a summary of a discussion and of an expert's research, respectively. The signal words are in italics and bold font.

EXAMPLES

When parents fight about children, or when children blame themselves for the conflict, children as young as fifth-graders have problems in school and experience stress. Children who grow up in households where parents fight and are cold, unsupportive, and neglectful are more likely as teenagers and adults to engage in drug and alcohol abuse or smoking, and to suffer lifelong health problems such as cancer, heart disease, obesity, and depression. Parenting, ***then,*** can be harmful to many children's health. (Adapted from Benokraitis 350)

Can glucose treatments be used to enhance memory? ***Research*** suggests that it can. In one ***study,*** Paul Gold (1993) had twenty-two healthy senior citizens listen to a taped passage and then drink lemonade sweetened with glucose or saccharine, the sugar substitute. When tested the next day, those who had ingested the glucose recalled 53 percent more information from the passage. (Kassin 228)

ACTIVITY 11: IDENTIFY WRITING PATTERNS

DIRECTIONS: Read each of the following texts and identify the writing pattern as you complete these steps.

A. Highlight any signal word(s) that indicate the pattern.
B. Predict, verify, and mark the text. (See activity 3, p. 316.)
C. Identify which pattern is used: statement and clarification, spatial order, order of importance (or a hierarchy), and summary of a discussion or another work.
D. Answer the question that follows.

1. Many companies now distribute information on CD-ROM or computer disk rather than on paper. CD-ROMs hold a large amount of information, they're inexpensive, and their small size saves money in postage and shipping. Of course, one of the most popular methods for distributing documents is the Internet. (Adapted from Thill and Bovee 182)

   The pattern is: ______________________________.

   How does the pattern organize the information?

   ____

   ____

2. Ironically, Pavlov's most important contribution was the result of an incidental discovery. In studying the digestive system, he strapped dogs in a harness, placed different types of food in their mouths, and measured the flow of saliva through a tube in their mouths. But there was a "problem": After repeated sessions, the dogs would salivate before the food was put in their mouths. That is, they would drool at the mere sight of food, the dish, or the footsteps of the assistant. Pavlov saw these "psychic secretions" as a nuisance, but later realized that he had stumbled on a very basic form of learning. (Adapted from Kassin 177)

The pattern is: ____.
How does the pattern organize the information?

____

____

3. In 1957, behaviorist B. F. Skinner wrote a book entitled *Verbal Behavior*, in which he argued that children learn to speak the way animals learn to run mazes. They associate objects and words, imitate adults, and repeat phrases that are met by social reinforcement. (Kassin 393)

The pattern is: ____.
How does the pattern organize the information?

____

____

4. The eyes sense light, which enters through the cornea, a tough transparent layer of cells. The cornea helps to focus the light, which then passes through a small chamber called the anterior chamber. At the back of the chamber is a disklike structure called the iris. The iris is the colored part of the eye. In the middle of the iris is a small opening called the pupil, which regulates the amount of light that enters the eye. Just behind the iris is the lens, where small muscles attached to the lens change its shape to help you adjust your eyes' focus to see near or distant objects. (Adapted from Miller and Levine 906)

The pattern is: ____.
How does the pattern organize the information?

____

____

5. To summarize, the "plumbing" and "wiring" that turn sound waves into meaningful input—or hearing— are fairly intricate. Air collected in the outer ear is transformed first into a salt-watery fluid and then into electrical impulses in the inner ear. From the auditory nerve, signals then cross to the other side of the brain, where they get routed to the thalamus and then relayed to areas of the auditory cortex. (Adapted from Kassin 96)

The pattern is: ____.
How does the pattern organize the information?

____

____

6. The building blocks of matter, called atoms, lie at the base of life's organizational structure. Atoms come together to form molecules which, in turn, form what are called organelles, meaning "tiny organs." At the next step up the organizational chain are entities that are actually living, as opposed to entities that are components of life. These start with cells, which collect into tissue. Several kinds of tissues come together to form an organ. An assemblage of cells, tissues, and organs can then form a multicelled organism. (Adapted from Krogh 12)

   The pattern is: ______________________________.

   How does the pattern organize the information?

   ____

   ____

Just as the largest library, badly arranged, is not so useful as a very moderate one that is well arranged, so the greatest amount of knowledge, if not elaborated by our own thoughts, is worth much less than a far smaller volume that has been abundantly and repeatedly thought over.

—Arthur Schopenhauer (1788–1860), German philosopher

Before you go on . . .

Monitor Your Progress: recite

After you read . . .

Reflect on Your Gains: review

CHAPTER SUMMARY

Introduction

Textbook chapters rely on numerous details to represent the knowledge in the field and adequately support the ideas. To handle these complex texts, effective readers analyze the type of information that's being presented and the logic used to group the details together.

Types of Details

Textbook authors use five basic types of details: facts, descriptions, examples, definitions, and references. **Facts** are provable pieces of information, **descriptions** present sensory information, **examples** provide specific illustrations, **definitions** give precise meanings to terms, and **references** introduce information from other sources. Details that are used to support the main idea are called **major details;** those that expand on other details are called **minor details.**

Logical Patterns

Logical patterns include the thinking and writing patterns that authors use to link pieces of information. These patterns are orderly and reasoned relationships that help readers predict what's coming, see how the details work together, and comprehend as well as remember numerous bits of information. Thinking patterns include six standard methods of organizing information: **list, definition, sequence, classification, comparison and contrast,** and **cause and effect.** In addition, authors can also use four writing patterns: **statement and clarification, spatial order, order of importance,** and **summary.** Each of these can be used within a single sentence, among several sentences, or over a number of paragraphs. Signal words used by the author can help readers recognize the patterns.

REVIEW ACTIVITIES

Use the following activities to check your understanding and aid your learning of the information in this chapter.

Expand Your Vocabulary

Match each term with the correct definition or characteristic.

_____ 1. fact
_____ 2. description
_____ 3. examples
_____ 4. definition detail
_____ 5. references
_____ 6. major details
_____ 7. minor details
_____ 8. logical patterns
_____ 9. list pattern
_____ 10. definition pattern
_____ 11. sequence pattern
_____ 12. chronological order
_____ 13. process order
_____ 14. classification
_____ 15. comparison
_____ 16. contrast
_____ 17. cause
_____ 18. effect
_____ 19. statement and clarification
_____ 20. spatial order
_____ 21. order of importance
_____ 22. summary

a. shows the similarities of two or more items
b. information that supports or clarifies other details
c. the results or consequences of an event or idea
d. the reason for an event or idea
e. a pattern that starts with an idea followed by explanations
f. has items of equal importance but the order does not matter
g. divides a group into equally important categories
h. a condensed version of the main points
i. events presented according to time, day, or date
j. shows the differences of two or more items
k. orderly relationships that link pieces of information together
l. samples or illustrations of an object, situation, or idea
m. a pattern presenting information in a most to least important way
n. information from other authors or sources
o. a pattern used to describe position or physical location
p. organization of details that must go in a certain order
q. an extended definition with explanations and examples
r. a provable piece of information
s. a term and authoritative meaning
t. information that supports or clarifies parts of the main idea
u. information presented in order of steps or stages
v. presents sensory information or emotional reactions

Increase Your Knowledge

The following tasks will help you assess how well you understand the ideas presented in this chapter. They will also help you prepare for quizzes and exams on this material.

1. The following questions focus on the major chapter topics. Discuss them with others or form your own detailed answers.
   a. Why do authors present numerous details?
   b. Name and define the five types of details. Then explain the purpose of each one and how readers can recognize it.
   c. What is the difference between major and minor details?
   d. Name and explain what the six common thinking patterns are. Include examples of the signal words that can be used to indicate each one.
   e. Name and explain what the four common writing patterns are. Include examples of the signal words that can be used to indicate each one.
2. Take notes on the information in this chapter.

Develop Your Skills

The following review tasks will give you an opportunity to practice the methods presented in this chapter.

REVIEW 1: IDENTIFY DETAILS Read and mark the following texts. Label the type(s) of detail in the margin: facts, descriptions, examples, definitions, and references.

Notes

1. Between 6 and 8 months of age, babies become wary or fearful of strangers. They wail if they are put in an unfamiliar setting or are left with an unfamiliar person. (Wade and Tavris 76)
2. In 2001, international terrorist attacks totaled 864 worldwide—down from the 1,106 reported a year earlier. (Adapted from Schmalleger 86)
3. Many shoe manufacturers including Nike, Reebok, and Adidas vigorously compete with one another to offer consumers some unique benefit. (Adapted from Solomon and Stuart 79)
4. Janis (1972) and other researchers have identified group-think as a key factor in a number of disastrous governmental decisions. (Adapted from Lindsey and Beach 73)
5. The substance in a part that hardens to form a continuous surface coating is called a *binder*. (Hill and Kolb 288)

Notes

6. Child-training practices might well be relived in dealings with the supernatural. For example, if a child was nurtured immediately by her parents when she cried or waved her arms about or kicked, she might grow up expecting to be nurtured by the gods when she attracted their attention by performing a ritual. On the other hand, if her parents often punished her, she would grow up expecting the gods to punish her if she disobeyed them. (Ember and Ember 398)

7. The U.S. educational system is shaped by both affluence and our democratic principles. Thomas Jefferson thought the new nation could become democratic only if people "read and understand what is going on in the world" (quoted in Honeywell, 1931:3). The United States has an outstanding record of higher education for its people: No other country has as large a share of adults with a university degree (U.S. Census Bureau, 2002). Schooling in the United States also tries to promote equal opportunity. National surveys show that most people think school is crucial to personal success, and a majority also believe that everyone has the chance to get an education consistent with personal ability and talent (NORC, 2003). In truth, this opinion expresses our aspirations better than our achievement. Earlier in this century, for example, women were all but excluded from high education, and even today, most people who attend college come from families with above-average incomes. (Adapted from Macionis 521)

REVIEW 2: IDENTIFY THINKING PATTERNS For each of the following texts, complete these steps.

A. Highlight any signal word(s) and punctuation that indicate the pattern(s).
B. Predict, verify, and mark the text. (See activity 3, p. 316.)
C. In the margin, record the pattern(s) that are used: list, definition, sequence (chronological or process), classification, comparison and contrast, and cause and effect.
D. Outline, diagram, or chart the information on your own paper.

1. Sociologist Ira Reiss and his associates proposed a "wheel theory" of love that generated much research for several decades. Reiss describes four stages of love: rapport, self-revelation, mutual dependency, and personality need fulfillment. (Benokraitis 148)

2. Most crime is heavily, and in some cases overwhelmingly, male. This generalization applies to all major crimes except prostitution. Males constituted 99 percent of all rapists, 89 percent of all murders, and 90 percent of all robbers arrested in 2000. As with the tendency for criminals to be young, this overrepresentation of males is apparent worldwide. (Lindsey and Beach 188)

3. The situation in the former Yugoslavia remained dangerous and deadly. During 1997 and 1998, Serbia moved against ethnic Albanians living in its province of Kosovo. In 1999, NATO again undertook air strikes against Serbian forces, and forced Serbia to withdraw from Kosovo. In 2000, a popular revolution swept the non-democratic government of Yugoslavia. In 2003 the two remaining Yugoslav republics, Serbia and Montenegro, each became autonomous. (Craig et al. 750)

4. Some studies have found that female officers are often underutilized and that many departments are hesitant to assign women to patrol and to other potentially dangerous field activities. As a consequence, some women in police work experience frustration and a lack of satisfaction with their jobs. An analysis of the genderization of the criminal justice workplace by Susan Ehrlich Martin and Nancy Jurik, for example, point out that gender inequality is part of a historical pattern of entrenched forms of gender interaction relating to the division of labor, power, and culture. (Schmalleger 284)

5. The word "vaccine" comes from the word "cacca," which is Latin for "cow." What do cows have to do with vaccines? In 1796 an English country doctor, Edward Jenner, decided to test a bit of folk wisdom, which held that farm laborers who caught the mild

Notes

Notes

disease cowpox from cattle could never catch the dreaded disease smallpox from humans. Accordingly, Jenner took cowpox pus from a sore on the hand of a dairymaid and rubbed into scratches he made on the arms of an eight-year-old boy, James Phipps. The next step—a chilling one from a modern perspective—was that Jenner applied pus from smallpox sores onto Phipps. The boy sailed through this and several subsequent smallpox applications, however, and Jenner's belief was proved correct: A person could be made immune to smallpox by being exposed to cowpox.

With Jenner's demonstration, a revolution was launched—the vaccine revolution. Because of it, polio, diphtheria, whooping cough, and tetanus have been nearly eradicated from developed countries. (Krogh 591)

6. Interrogation has been defined by the U.S. Supreme Court as any behaviors by the police "that the police should know are reasonably likely to elicit an incriminating response from the suspect." Hence interrogation may involve activities which go well beyond mere verbal questioning, and the Court has held that interrogation may include "staged lineups, reverse lineups, positing guilt, minimizing the moral seriousness of crime, and casting blame on the victim or society." It is noteworthy that the Court has also held that "police words or actions normally attendant to arrest and custody do not constitute interrogation" unless they involve pointed or directed question. Hence an arresting officer may instruct a suspect on what to do and may chitchat with him or her without engaging in interrogation within the meaning of the law. Once police officers make inquiries intended to elicit information about the crime in question, however, interrogation has begun. (Schmalleger 223)

7. We are so dependent on our culture's symbols that we take them for granted. Sometimes, however, we become keenly aware of a symbol when someone uses it in an unconventional way, as when a person burns a U.S. flag during a political demonstration. Entering an unfamiliar culture also reminds us of the power of symbols; culture shock is really the inability to "read"

meaning in new surroundings. Not understanding the symbols of a culture leaves a person feeling lost and isolated, unsure of how to act, and sometimes frightened.

Because people attach different meanings to the word, culture shock is a two-way process. On the one hand, travelers *experience* culture shock when encountering people whose way of life is different. For example, North Americans who consider dogs beloved household pets might be put off by the Masai of eastern Africa, who ignore and never feed them. The same travelers might be horrified to find that, in parts of Indonesia and the northern regions of the People's Republic of China, people roast dogs for dinner.

On the other hand, a traveler *inflicts* culture shock on local people by acting in ways that offend them. A North American who asks for a cheeseburger in an Indian restaurant offends Hindus, who consider cows sacred and never to be eaten. (Macionis 62)

Notes

REVIEW 3: IDENTIFY WRITING PATTERNS Read each of the following texts and identify the writing pattern as you complete these steps.

A. Highlight any signal word(s) that indicate the pattern.
B. Predict, verify, and mark the text. (See Activity 3, p. 316.)
C. Identify which pattern is used: statement and clarification, spatial order, order of importance (or a hierarchy), and summary (of a discussion or another work).
D. Answer the questions that follow.

1. In conclusion, the important point in all three of these theories is that children grow and mature by learning to deal with new expectations and changes. The child who feels loved and secure has a good chance of developing as a reasonably happy and productive member of society, one of the family's major socialization functions. (Adapted from Benokraitis 331)

   Notes

   The pattern is: ______________________________.

   How does the pattern organize the information?

   ____

   ____

Notes

2. The durability of a gem depends on its hardness. That is, how long it lasts is a function of its resistance to abrasion by objects normally encountered in everyday living. For good durability, gems should be as hard or harder than quartz. One notable exception is opal, which is comparatively soft and brittle. Opal's esteem comes from its "fire," which is a display of a variety of brilliant colors, including greens, blues, and reds. (Adapted from Tarbuck and Lutgens 105)

   The pattern is: ______________________________.

   How does the pattern organize the information?

   ____

   ____

3. In the United States, more than 80 percent of pregnancies of girls under eighteen are unplanned and unwanted. All too often, they result in an abortion, a hasty and unhappy marriage, or an out-of-wedlock birth that forces the mother out of school and plunges her into poverty. To some extent, unwanted teenage pregnancies are part of a bigger problem: that adolescents are risk takers. (Adapted from Kassin 421)

   The pattern is: ______________________________.

   How does the pattern organize the information?

   ____

   ____

4. Richard Schulz and his colleagues (1994) analyzed the career records of major-league ball players and found that batters and pitchers peaked at the age of twenty-six. Football, basketball, and tennis players follow a similar age pattern. Yet world-class sprinters and swimmers peak in their teens and early twenties, while most professional bowlers and golfers reach the top of their game in their thirties. It all depends on whether a sport requires speed and agility, endurance, or power—which decline at different rates. (Adapted from Kassin 424)

   The pattern is: ______________________________.

   How does the pattern organize the information?

   ____

   ____

Notes

5. Although best known as gems, diamonds are used extensively as abrasives. Diamonds originate at depths of nearly 200 kilometers, where the confining pressure is great enough to generate this high-pressure form of carbon. Once crystallized, the diamonds are carried upward through pipe-shaped conduits that increase in diameter toward the surface. (Tarbuck and Lutgens 646)

   The pattern is: ____________________.

   How does the pattern organize the information?

   ____

   ____

6. One way to organize information for memory is to use a hierarchical arrangement as in an outline. Start with a few broad categories, then divide them into subcategories. This is how experts chunk new information, and it works. (Adapted from Kassin 240)

   The pattern is: ____________________.

   How does the pattern organize the information?

   ____

   ____

Check Your Motivation

1. Review your chapter goals. Did you achieve them? Explain.
2. Make a list of the new ideas and methods you've gained from this chapter. Think about how they will help you in the future.
3. Measure your motivation for this chapter topic. Think about each statement and how you will use it in the future. Mark it:

   A = never B = sometimes C = usually D = always

	A	B	C	D
To engage my interest, I plan to . . .				
1. think of details as interesting parts of the message.	___	___	___	___
2. view details as support for the main points.	___	___	___	___
3. look for the variety of details and what they add to the topic.	___	___	___	___
4. look for the various patterns and what they add to the topic.	___	___	___	___
To focus my efforts, I plan to . . .				
5. try to identify the type of details that authors use.	___	___	___	___
6. label the details that I find.	___	___	___	___

	A	B	C	D
7. think about how the details relate to the ideas.	___	___	___	___
8. look for major and minor details.	___	___	___	___
9. mark major and minor details in different ways.	___	___	___	___
10. look for thinking patterns as I read.	___	___	___	___
11. look for writing patterns as I read.	___	___	___	___
12. look for signal words to aid my comprehension.	___	___	___	___
To monitor my progress, I plan to . . .				
13. think about how the details are organized into a logical pattern as I recite.	___	___	___	___
To reflect on my gains, I plan to . . .				
14. think about the writing patterns authors use as I review.	___	___	___	___
15. use maps and charts for the thinking pattern as I take notes where appropriate.	___	___	___	___

SCORING: Write the number of answers you marked in each column in the following spaces. Compute the column scores, and then add them up to determine your total score.

# of A's ______ × 1 pt. = ______
# of B's ______ × 2 pt. = ______
# of C's ______ × 3 pt. = ______
# of D's ______ × 4 pt. = ______

Total points = ______

INTERPRETATION: 15–43 points = low motivation; 44–60 points = high motivation

SUGGESTION: Evaluate your scores. Reward yourself for your gains and empowered approaches. Make a plan to improve anything that needs more attention.

TABLE 20-2 Median Income by Sex and Educational Attainment*

Education	Men	Women
Professional degree	$100,000 (4.7)	$60,093 (3.7)
Doctorate	81,077 (3.8)	60,425 (3.7)
Master's	66,934 (3.2)	48,276 (3.0)
Bachelor's	53,108 (2.5)	39,818 (2.5)
1–3 years of college	40,159 (1.9)	28,839 (1.8)
4 years of high school	33,037 (1.6)	24,217 (1.5)
9–11 years of school	25,857 (1.2)	17,937 (1.1)
0–8 years of school	21,139 (1.0)	16,170 (1.0)

*Persons aged twenty-five years and over working full time, 2001. The earnings ratio, in parentheses, indicates how many times the lowest income level a person with additional schooling earns.

Source: U.S. Census Bureau (2002).

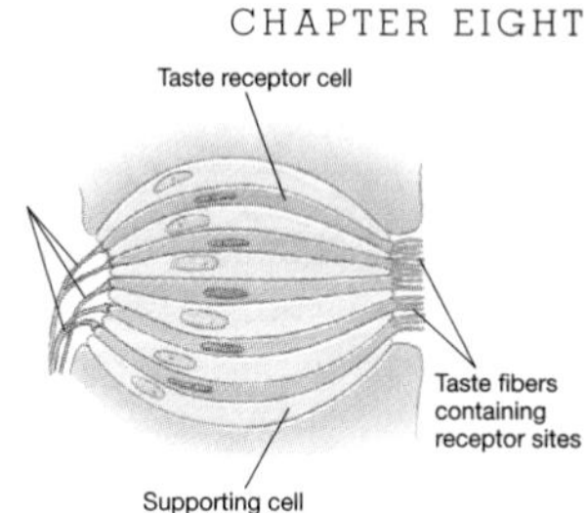

Graphic Aids

What do you do when you see graphics such as these? Do they make a clear point or overwhelm you with new information?

You've probably heard the saying that a picture is worth a thousand words. That idea is the single most important reason for the graphic aids that are included in every type of text, from newspapers and magazines to textbooks, reports, and reference materials. These aids condense multiple ideas, complex relationships, and many details into a one-look format. And, as the following quote suggests, with condensing comes a whole new level of understanding.

> Knowledge is a process of piling up facts; wisdom lies in their simplification.
>
> —Martin H. Fischer (1879–1962), German-born physician, author

Before you read . . .

Engage Your Interest: preread and divide

This chapter presents the methods for understanding graphic aids. Outline the chapter headings; start your outline with the Introduction.

After you preread and divide the chapter into reading tasks, set a goal for each one. Be specific about the task, topic, and reward(s).

1. I want to ________________ about ________________________________.
   My reward(s) will be ____
   ____.
2. I want to ________________ about ________________________________.
   My reward(s) will be ____
   ____.
3. I want to ________________ about ________________________________.
   My reward(s) will be ____
   ____.

As you read . . .

Focus Your Efforts: question and read

Graphics are a visual form of communication. Graphs, photographs, maps, diagrams, and charts are all graphics. A **graphic aid** is a visual designed to support the text, present details, illustrate relationships, and aid comprehension.

Authors include graphic aids to motivate and clarify. By their very nature, graphics presented within a text are inherently interesting, because they're colorful and eye-catching, they break up the sentences, and they highlight an intriguing point. They also assist comprehension. A diagram of the human ear can clarify the location of its many parts, simplify the complex information, and improve your understanding of the process of hearing. A table of salaries and education levels will show the value of a college education in a striking way. A line graph of average SAT scores over the past 50 years instantly displays a trend.

Comprehending graphics in reading for learning tasks requires the same kind of active thinking skills that you use with expository text. You undoubtedly already use this kind of approach when you look at photographs that interest you and maps you use to find your way somewhere. This chapter identifies the skills you need to understand graphic aids used in information texts. It focuses on:

- How to Read Graphic Aids
- Types of Graphic Aids

How to Read Graphic Aids

THINK ABOUT THIS . . .

1. Think about the graphic aids that you have found in your assigned readings. Then answer these questions.
   a. Exactly when do you look at the graphic aids?

   ____

   b. What methods do you use to comprehend graphic aids?

   ____

2. Reminder: Preread this section.

You may not think of looking at graphic aids as reading. But graphic aids are composed of titles, labels, and multiple pieces of information, all of which involve the processes of comprehension.

Gaining Comprehension

Graphic aids have some helpful similarities to body paragraphs in expository writing. They have topics and details that are presented to support ideas or other detailed statements. So looking for the topic, idea, and details is one good way to understand graphic aids. You'll generally find that the topic of a graphic is stated in a very visible caption, or title. The details are the obvious pieces of information in the graphic itself. They support a point that is located in one of the paragraphs.

Look at this example. The text presents an idea, refers the reader to a table for details, and then notes some, but not all, of the facts that appear in the table. As you read on, notice the topic, the idea, and what the details show.

EXAMPLE

Topic Sentence Industrial societies expand opportunities for schooling, but some people receive much more than others. Table 11-3 shows schooling for U.S. women and men aged twenty-five and older. In 2002, although 84 percent completed high school, only about 26 percent were college graduates. (Macionis 275)

Topic

TABLE 11-3 Schooling of U.S. Adults, 2002 (aged 25 and over)

Details that support the TS idea

	Women	Men
Not a high school graduate	15.6 %	16.2 %
8 years or less	6.7	7.1
9–11 years	8.9	9.1
High school graduate	84.4	83.8
High school only	33.1	31.0
1–3 years college	26.2	24.3
College graduate or more	25.1	28.5

Source: U.S. Census Bureau (2003).

(Macionis 275)

As you read the example, did you find yourself moving back and forth between the text and the table? If so, you're using one of the most essential methods for reading graphic aids: uniting the aid with the text. Both have partial information; they work together to cover the entire point. Thus, looking back and forth is necessary so that you can comprehend the topic, idea, and details as a unit. Like driving a car, this approach requires thoughtful skills and choices. But it's worth the effort because, as the cartoon illustrates, knowing you're headed in the right direction is like having a sign that tells you so.

ACTIVITY 1: COMPREHEND THE TEXT AND GRAPHIC TOGETHER

DIRECTIONS: Look at the following text and graphic. Then practice comprehending the topic, idea, and details by answering the questions.

Many people are pursuing college educations, preparing for jobs or careers, and spending more time in recreational or other activities before settling down. As a result, many of us are marrying later than our parents or grandparents. In 1970, the median age at first marriage was 21 for women and 23 for men. By 2000, these ages had risen to 25 for women and 27 for men (see Figure 9.3). (Benokraitis 237, 238)

1. The best topic for this graph is
   a. at what age do men and women first marry?
   b. when men and women marry.
   c. the median age of first marriage.
   d. the age of first marriage.
2. The idea that this graph supports is in
   a. sentence 1 of the paragraph.
   b. sentence 2 of the paragraph.
   c. sentence 3 of the paragraph.
   d. sentence 4 of the paragraph.
3. This graph supports the details in two sentences. Which two detail sentences does it support?
   a. sentence 1 of the paragraph
   b. sentence 2 of the paragraph
   c. sentence 3 of the paragraph
   d. sentence 4 of the paragraph

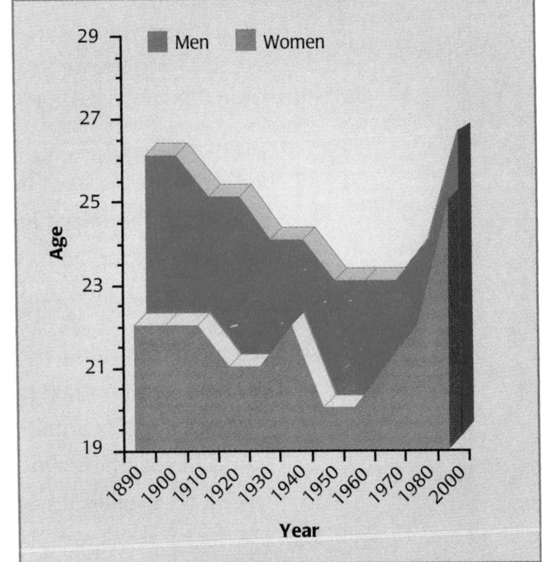

FIGURE 9.3 At What Age Do Men and Women First Marry? As the text points out, the median age of first marriage for men was almost the same in 2000 as in 1890, but the median for women has risen since 1960.

SOURCE: Based on data from Saluter, 1994, Table B; Saluter, 1996, Table A-33; and Fields and Casper, 2001.

4. Use the graph to answer these questions:
   a. True or false? The graph shows statistics for the year 2005.
   b. True or false? In 1930, men married at a median age of 26.
   c. True or false? In 1945, women married at a median age of 22½.
   d. True or false? The lowest median age for both sexes occurred in 1970.
   e. True or false? At all ages, women marry at a younger age than men.

> We only think when we are confronted with a problem.
> —John Dewey (1859–1952), American philosopher, educator

Of course, when you encounter graphic aids, you won't have a set of questions like these to guide your thinking. So, review the questions in Activity 1 and make a note to ask questions like them as you read graphics in the future. Posing these questions and answering them will be part of your PDQ3R question and read steps.

Gaining Insights

In addition to promoting comprehension, graphic aids can support reading for learning in two other ways. First, you can gain insights when you think about the information in a personal way. Second, you will achieve a deeper understanding of the topic when you work on the details and draw your own conclusions.

In brief, getting the most out of graphic aids involves comprehending the graphic with the text, applying the information to yourself, and analyzing the data. Approaching graphic aids in this way uses the levels of thinking (see Chapter 5) and these three steps:

1. *Comprehend* the graphic
   a. Identify the topic from the graphic's title or caption.
   b. Understand the information in the graphic.
   c. Connect the graphic to the ideas and details in the text.
2. *Apply* the information to yourself and those you know.
3. *Analyze* the information and draw conclusions.
   a. Compare and contrast pieces of data.
      What's large or small?
      Add or subtract related numbers to see the relationships.
      Look for similarities and differences between pieces of data.
   b. Look for patterns or trends.
   c. Make statements about what you figure out.

Here's an example of a reader thinking through these steps on the text and table about schooling in the United States (p. 358).

EXAMPLE

1. *Comprehend* the graphic
   a. The topic is the amount of schooling for U.S. adults in 2002 who were 25 years or older.
   b. The graph shows:
      Four major groups: men and women who are not high school graduates and men and women who are graduates.
      Overall about 16% have 11 years of school or less and about 84% have graduated high school or gone on to college.
   c. The graph supports the idea that some people get more education than others.

2. *Apply* the information to yourself and those you know:
   I am part of the 84.4% group of women (or 83.8% of men) who have graduated high school; I am also part of the group that has 1–3 years of college.
   Most of my friends are in these same groups.
3. *Analyze* the information and draw conclusions:
   a. The biggest difference between men and women is the college graduate group where more men graduate than women—28.5% versus 25.1%.
   b. About one-third of adults stop at the high school level, one-fourth get some college, and another one-fourth get a college degree or beyond.
   c. In the United States, a very large percentage graduate high school and about half of both men and women go on to college.

Record all of your calculations, useful insights, and conclusions on the graphic or as margin notes next to it.

> **You have to see the pattern, understand the order and experience the vision.**
>
> —Michael E. Gerber (contemporary), American businessman, author

---

ACTIVITY 2: APPLY AND ANALYZE GRAPHIC INFORMATION

DIRECTIONS: Use the text and graph in Activity 1 to answer the following questions.

1. Apply the information.
   Think of four people you know who were married before 2000. Try to have two men and two women in your list. List their names and wedding dates. Then look at the graph and see if they match the median marrying age.

PERSON	WEDDING YEAR	MATCH DATA? (Circle the answer)	
________________	______	yes	no
________________	______	yes	no
________________	______	yes	no
________________	______	yes	no

2. Analyze the information and draw conclusions. What conclusions can you draw from the graphic, your answers to questions 1–5 in activity 1, and your answers to question 1 in this activity?

   ____

   ____

   ____

Before you go on . . .

Monitor Your Progress: recite

As you read . . .

Focus Your Efforts: question and read

Types of Graphic Aids

THINK ABOUT THIS . . .

1. Think about graphics you have found in your assigned readings. Then answer these questions.
   a. What kinds of textbook graphics do you find particularly useful? How do they help your comprehension?

   ____

   ____

   ____

   b. What kinds of textbook graphics do you find confusing? What makes them difficult to understand?

   ____

   ____

   ____

2. Reminder: Preread this section.

Pictures and cartoons are generally the easiest graphics to use. Overall, they are interesting, engaging, and uncomplicated; so, it's easy to relate to them and to comprehend their message. Graphic aids that focus on facts and/or data present the most challenge, because facts and numbers are not immediately engaging to most of us and, when there are numerous pieces of information, the aid may look complex. Unless you can see an organizational scheme, the information simply does not have much meaning.

> **The medium is the message.**
> — Marshall McLuhan (1911–1980), Canadian communications theorist

The key, then, is to understand the format and how it organizes separate pieces of data into a related group. There are five common formats or types of graphic aids for facts and data. They are line graphs, bar graphs, pie charts, tables, and diagrams.

Line Graphs

You have probably seen line graphs in math classes, and you may have even created your own. **Line graphs** use a line on a graph to show how two sets of data relate to each other. A line graph is formed by perpendicular lines at the left and bottom of each graph that form an L. The vertical line is called the *y* axis, and the horizontal line is called the *x* axis. Each axis presents a different type of information, or *variable,* that has a numerical or chronological value. The line in the middle of the graph shows the points where the two variables occur together. Line graphs are often used to show changes over time. So they invite conclusions about trends.

One note about reading these graphs: careful "reading" is required to understand the details presented in line graphs. Line graphs are precisely drawn. Each point within the graph corresponds to a specific number on each axis, even if the number is not printed. To recognize that number, you may need to imagine where the midpoint or even the quarter-point marks would be on each axis. For example, in the first graph in Activity 3, the point at 1700 for European Americans should be read as "about 250,000" people.

ACTIVITY 3: READ LINE GRAPHS

DIRECTIONS: For each of the following tasks, read and mark the texts and the accompanying graphic. Then answer the questions that follow.

Most of the increase in the colonies' population came not from immigration or the slave trade but from natural increase, what Benjamin Franklin called "the great increase of offspring." The rate of population growth for both Europeans and Africans in the colonies was extraordinary (see Figure 5-3). (Boydston et al. 129)

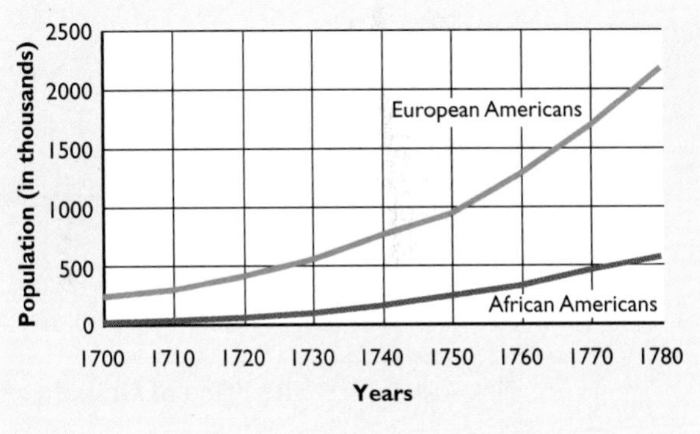

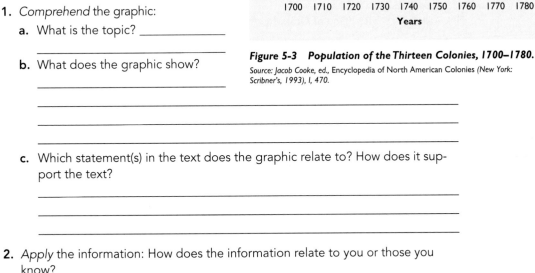

Figure 5-3* *Population of the Thirteen Colonies, 1700–1780.

Source: Jacob Cooke, ed., Encyclopedia of North American Colonies *(New York: Scribner's, 1993), I, 470.*

1. *Comprehend* the graphic:
   a. What is the topic? ____________

   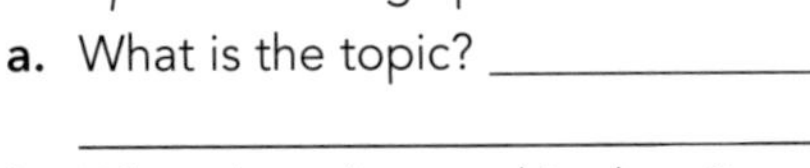

   b. What does the graphic show? ____________

   ____

   ____

   ____

   c. Which statement(s) in the text does the graphic relate to? How does it support the text?

   ____

   ____

   ____

2. *Apply* the information: How does the information relate to you or those you know?

   ____

   ____

   ____

3. *Analyze* the information: Compare and contrast pieces of data, look for patterns, and draw conclusions.

New technologies have made international communication and commerce much faster and cheaper. Figure 4.1 shows the decrease in the costs of two international business activities over the past several decades: the cost of a three-minute phone call from New York to London and the cost of transatlantic shipping per ton. (Adapted from Griffin and Ebert 96–97)

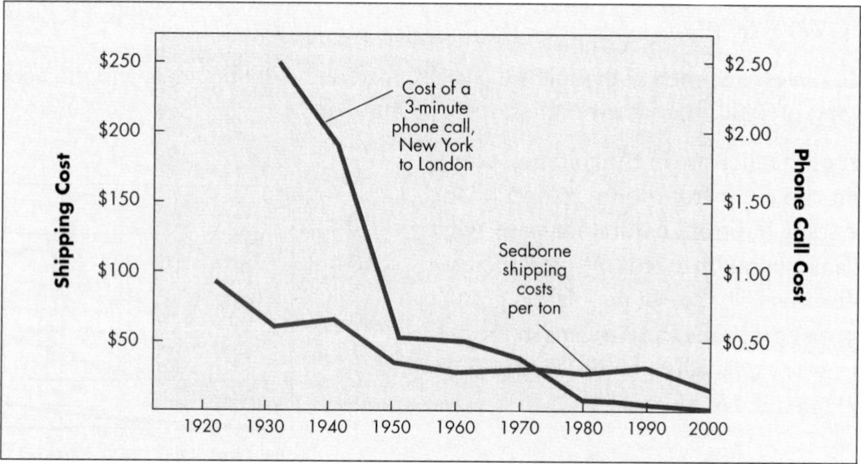

Figure 4.1 **The Price of Global Communication**

1. *Comprehend* the graphic:
   a. What is the topic?
   b. What does the graphic show?
   c. Which statement(s) in the text does the graphic relate to? How does it support the text?
2. *Apply* the information: How does the information relate to you or those you know?

3. *Analyze* the information: Compare and contrast pieces of data, look for patterns, and draw conclusions.

____

____

____

Bar Graphs

Bar graphs use bands or bars to show how two variables relate to each other. They have an *x*- and *y*-axis that presents the variables, and the height of each bar represents a precise number on the *y*-axis. Readers must take care in determining what that number is. While bar graphs can be used like line graphs to show changes over time, they are more often used to show differences between groups. This means that they invite comparison and contrast analysis.

Bar graphs can present single bars, like the first item in Activity 4, or stacked bars, as in item 2. A single bar shows one data point at the top of each bar. It invites comparisons between the major groups. A stacked bar shows two or more data points for the same group. Generally, the parts need to be added to get the total for the group. Stacked bars illustrate comparisons between the parts within each group, as well as comparisons of the totals from one group to another.

ACTIVITY 4: READ BAR GRAPHS

DIRECTIONS: For each of the following tasks, read and mark the texts and the accompanying graphic. Then answer the questions that follow.

Our culture celebrates romantic love—affection and sexual passion for another person—as the basis for marriage. However, as Figure 18-1 shows, in many countries romantic love plays a much smaller role in marriage. (Adapted from Macionis 470)

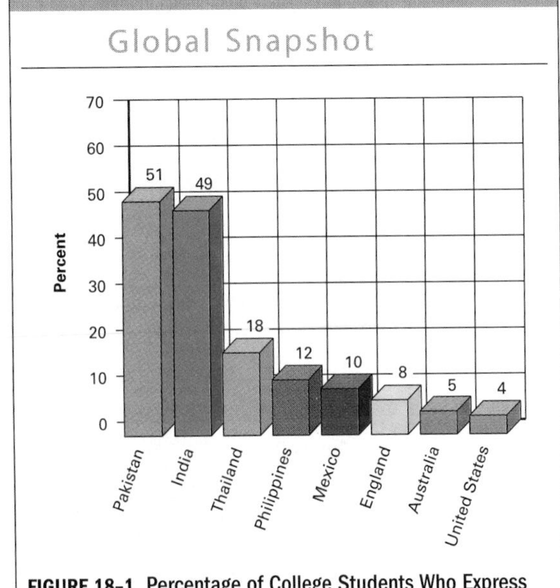

FIGURE 18-1 Percentage of College Students Who Express a Willingness to Marry without Romantic Love

Source: Levine (1993).

1. *Comprehend* the graphic:
   a. What is the topic? ______________________
   ____
   b. What does the graphic show?
   ____
   ____
   ____
   ____
   ____
   ____

c. Which statement(s) in the text does the graphic relate to? How does it support the text?

____
____
____

2. *Apply* the information: How does the information relate to you or those you know?

____
____
____

3. *Analyze* the information: Compare and contrast pieces of data, look for patterns, and draw conclusions.

____
____
____

To better understand the concept of structural mobility, look at Figure 8.9. Note that over the course of the last century there was a major shift in *the kinds of jobs* provided by the U.S. economy. In 1900, only 17.5 percent of all jobs were classified as white collar, whereas by 2000 that figure had risen to 59.4 percent. A shift like this means that many people will experience upward social mobility, simply because there are *more good jobs* and *fewer bad jobs* than there used to be. (Lindsey and Beach 320)

1. *Comprehend* the graphic:
   a. What is the topic? ______________________________
   b. What does the graphic show?

   ____
   ____
   ____

   c. Which statement(s) in the text does the graphic relate to? How does it support the text?

   ____
   ____
   ____

2. *Apply* the information: How does the information relate to you or those you know?

____
____
____

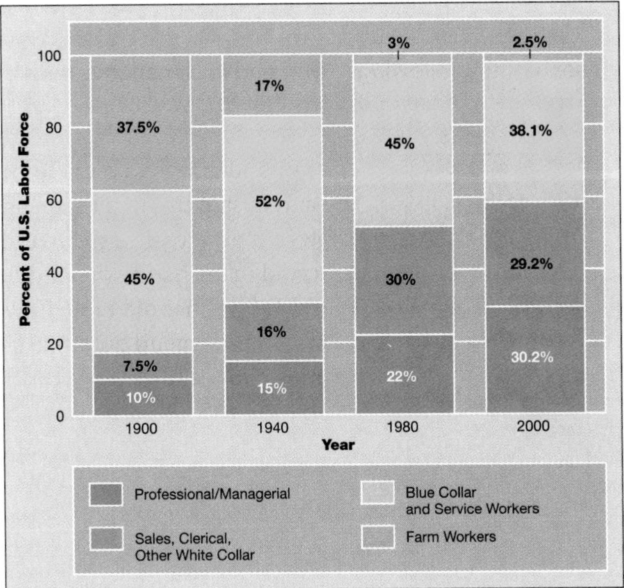

FIGURE 8.9 The Changing U.S. Occupational Structure, 1900–2000. Between 1900 and 2000, there was a major shift in the kinds of jobs available in the American economy.

Source: U.S. Bureau of the Census, *Historical Studies of the United States*, Vol. 1, 1975; U.S. Bureau of Labor Statistics, *Employment & Earnings*, 1993, Statistical Abstract, 2000.

3. *Analyze* the information: Compare and contrast pieces of data, look for patterns, and draw conclusions.

____

____

____

To think is to practice brain chemistry.

—Deepak Chopra (1946–), East Indian–American M.D., author

Pie Charts

Pie charts present numerical information in the form of a circle with wedges—like pie slices—to show proportions of various subgroups. When added together, the wedges or parts show the whole group and usually add up to 100 percent (although the actual number can range from 99 to 101 percent due to rounding-off errors). The primary purpose of a pie diagram is to show whole–part relationships and invite conclusions about the relative size of the pieces.

ACTIVITY 5: READ PIE CHARTS

DIRECTIONS: For each of the following tasks, read and mark the texts and the accompanying graphic. Then answer the questions that follow.

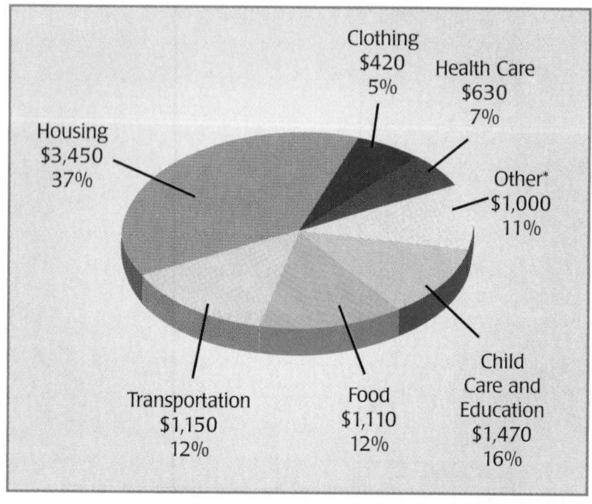

FIGURE 11.1 What a Middle-Income Family Spends during the First Two Years of a Child's Life In 2002, families earning $39,700 to $66,700 spent about $9,230 per year on each child under 2. This amount does not include the costs of prenatal care or delivery.

*Includes personal care items, entertainment, and reading materials.

SOURCE: Based on Lino, 2003.

Parenthood isn't paradise. To begin with, having and raising children is expensive. Figure 11.1 shows a typical year's expenses for a child 1 or 2 years old in husband-wife middle-income families. Middle-income ($39,700 to $66,700 per year) families spend about 25 percent of their earnings on a child every year from the child's birth to age 17. (Benokraitis 294–295)

1. *Comprehend* the graphic:
   a. What is the topic? ____________________
   ____
   ____
   b. What does the graphic show?
   ____
   ____
   ____
   ____
   ____
   c. Which statement(s) in the text does the graphic relate to? How does it support the text?
   ____
   ____
   ____

2. *Apply* the information: How does the information relate to you or those you know?
   ____
   ____
   ____

3. *Analyze* the information: Compare and contrast pieces of data, look for patterns, and draw conclusions.
   ____
   ____
   ____

A **psychologist** has no medical training, but has a doctorate degree. Psychologists undergo intense academic training, learning about many different areas of psychology before choosing an area in which to specialize. Because the focus of their careers can vary

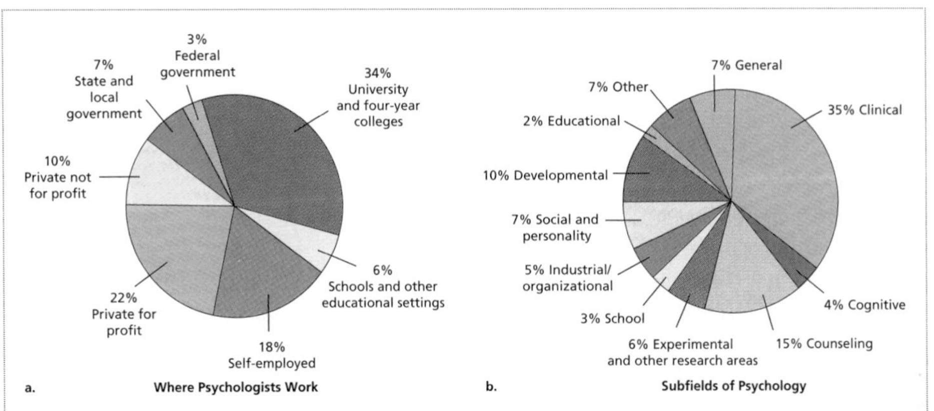

FIGURE 1.2 (a) There are many different work settings for psychologists. Although not obvious from the chart, many psychologists work in more than one setting. For example, a clinical psychologist may work in a hospital setting as well as teaching at a university or college. (b) This pie chart shows the specialty areas of psychologists who recently received their doctorates.

Note: Due to rounding, percentages may not total to 100 percent.

(a) National Science Foundation/Science Resources Statistics. 2001 Survey of Doctorate Recipients. http://www.nsf.gov/sbe/srs/nsf03310pdf/tabl4.pdf

(b) National Science Foundation, Division of Science Resource Statistics, Science & Engineering Doctorate Awards: 2003, NSF 05-300, Project Officer, Joan S. Burrelli (Arlington VA 2004). http://www.nsf.gov/sbe/srs/nsf05300/pdf/front.pdf

so widely, psychologists work in many different vocational settings. Figure 1.2a shows the types of settings in which psychologists work. Figure 1.2b shows the specialty areas for those who recently received doctorates. (Adapted from Ciccarelli and Meyer 17–18)

1. *Comprehend* the graphic:
   a. What is the topic? ______
   b. What does the graphic show? ______
   ______
   ______
   ______
   c. Which statement(s) in the text does the graphic relate to? How does it support the text?
   ______
   ______
   ______
2. *Apply* the information: How does the information relate to you or those you know?
   ______
   ______
   ______
3. *Analyze* the information: Compare and contrast pieces of data, look for patterns, and draw conclusions.
   ______
   ______
   ______

Tables

Some tables do not require analysis because they simply condense the text into a format that is easy to use for reference and learning. This textbook has a number of tables that follow this format; Table 7.1 (see p. 311) is a good example. **Numerical tables,** on the other hand, present data that's in the form of decimals, whole numbers, and percentages. The information is organized into columns and rows. The major categories or groups are generally listed as the column headings; the subcategories are usually presented in the row labels.

To understand numerical tables, you will need to analyze the data by adding and subtracting some of the numbers in order to see how they relate to each other. For example, in the first table in Activity 6, you will understand more if you see the differences between the numbers in the columns. Notice that in row 1 there's a 20% difference between the first two columns, a 4% difference between the second two, and 26% between the first and third. Once you see these differences, think about what they show and make statements about your conclusions.

ACTIVITY 6: READ TABLES

DIRECTIONS: For each of the following tasks, read and mark the texts and the accompanying graphic. Then answer the questions that follow.

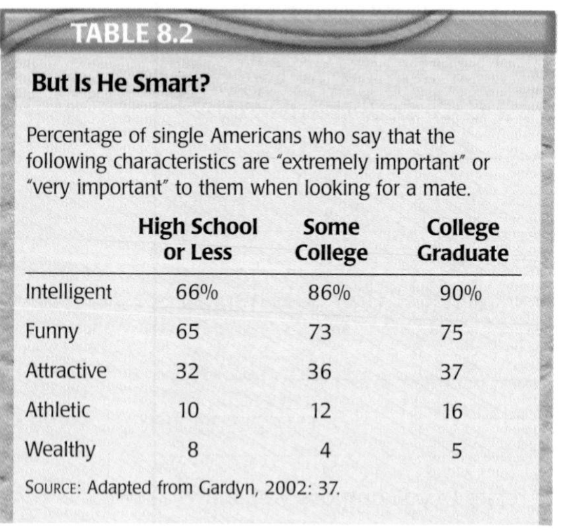

TABLE 8.2

But Is He Smart?

Percentage of single Americans who say that the following characteristics are "extremely important" or "very important" to them when looking for a mate.

	High School or Less	Some College	College Graduate
Intelligent	66%	86%	90%
Funny	65	73	75
Attractive	32	36	37
Athletic	10	12	16
Wealthy	8	4	5

SOURCE: Adapted from Gardyn, 2002: 37.

As Table 8.2 shows, 90 percent of the most highly educated singles say that finding a partner who is intelligent is extremely or very important, compared with only 66 percent of those with a high school degree. Intelligence and being a college graduate aren't synonymous, of course. Many singles, however, use formal education as a proxy for intelligence. Note also that wealth is much less important than intelligence. (Benokraitis 218–219)

1. *Comprehend* the graphic:
   a. What is the topic? ______________________
   ____
   ____
   b. What does the graphic show? ______________________
   ____
   ____
   ____
   ____

c. Which statement(s) in the text does the graphic relate to? How does it support the text?

____

____

____

2. *Apply* the information: How does the information relate to you or those you know?

____

____

____

3. *Analyze* the information: Compare and contrast pieces of data, look for patterns, and draw conclusions.

____

____

____

Over an individual's working lifetime, a college degree adds almost $500,000 to income. Table 20-2 shows why. In 2001, women with an eighth-grade education typically earned $16,170; high school graduates averaged $24,217, and college graduates $39,818. The ratios in parentheses show that a woman with a bachelor's degree earns two-and-one-half times as much as a woman with eight or fewer years of schooling. (Adapted from Macionis 527)

TABLE 20-2 Median Income by Sex and Educational Attainment*

Education	Men	Women
Professional degree	$100,000 (4.7)	$60,093 (3.7)
Doctorate	81,077 (3.8)	60,425 (3.7)
Master's	66,934 (3.2)	48,276 (3.0)
Bachelor's	53,108 (2.5)	39,818 (2.5)
1–3 years of college	40,159 (1.9)	28,839 (1.8)
4 years of high school	33,037 (1.6)	24,217 (1.5)
9–11 years of school	25,857 (1.2)	17,937 (1.1)
0–8 years of school	21,139 (1.0)	16,170 (1.0)

*Persons aged twenty-five years and over working full time, 2001. The earnings ratio, in parentheses, indicates how many times the lowest income level a person with additional schooling earns.

Source: U.S. Census Bureau (2002).

1. *Comprehend* the graphic:

a. What is the topic? ____

b. What does the graphic show? ____

____

____

____

c. Which statement(s) in the text does the graphic relate to? How does it support the text?

____

____

____

____

2. *Apply* the information: How does the information relate to you or those you know?

____

____

____

____

3. *Analyze* the information: Compare and contrast pieces of data, look for patterns, and draw conclusions.

____

____

____

____

Diagrams

A **diagram** is a drawing that shows what an object looks like or explains how a process or idea works. More than any other type of graphic, diagrams are used to simplify complex information and help readers visualize it. But because the concepts they illustrate can be very complex, reading a diagram can require a good deal of thought. Diagrams usually include both line drawings and labels, and they may also include arrows or lines that indicate the correct order for viewing the parts. When reading diagrams, focus on the sequence of steps that make up the process.

ACTIVITY 7: READ DIAGRAMS

DIRECTIONS: For each of the following tasks, read and mark the texts and the accompanying graphic. Then answer the questions that follow.

Taste, or *gustation,* occurs because chemicals stimulate thousands of receptors in the mouth. These receptors are located primarily on the tongue, but some are also found in the throat, inside the cheeks, and on the roof of the mouth. If you look at your tongue in a mirror, you will notice many tiny bumps: they are called **papillae** (from the Latin for "pimples"), and they come in several forms. In all but one of these forms, the side of each papilla are lined with **taste buds,** which up close look a little like segmented oranges (see Figure 6.9). The taste buds are commonly referred to, mistakenly, as the receptors for taste. The actual receptor cells, however, are *inside* the buds. These cells send tiny fibers out through an opening in the bud; the receptor sites are on these fibers. (Adapted from Wade and Tavris 196)

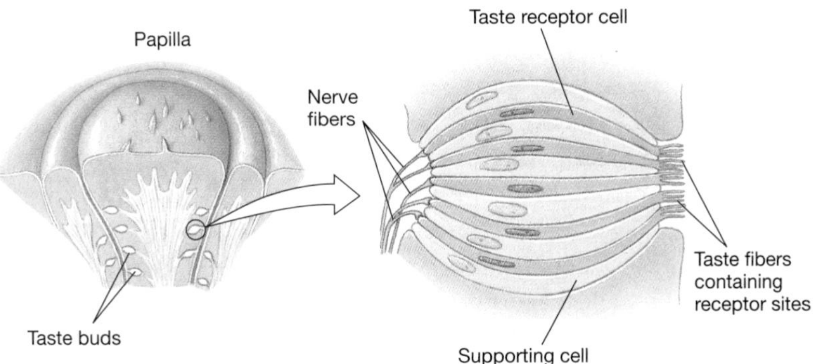

FIGURE 6.9 **Taste Receptors.** The illustration on the left shows taste buds lining the sides of a papilla on the tongue's surface. The illustration on the right shows an enlarged view of a single taste bud.

1. *Comprehend* the graphic:
   a. What is the topic? ____________________
   b. What does the graphic show?
   ____
   ____
   ____
   c. Which statement(s) in the text does the graphic relate to? How does it support the text?
   ____
   ____
   ____
2. *Apply* the information: How does the information relate to you or those you know?
   ____
   ____
   ____
3. *Analyze* the information: Compare and contrast pieces of data, look for patterns, and draw conclusions.
   ____
   ____
   ____

Solids can be changed to liquids, that is, they can be *melted.* The solid is heated, and the heat energy is absorbed by the particles of the solid. The energy causes the particles to vibrate in place with more and more vigor until, finally, the forces holding the particles in a particular arrangement are overcome. The solid has become a liquid. The temperature at which this happens is called the **melting point** of the solid. A high melting point is one indication that the forces holding a solid together are very strong.

A liquid can change to a gas or vapor in a process called **vaporization.** Again, one need only supply sufficient heat to achieve this change. Energy is absorbed by the liquid particles, which move faster and faster as a result. Finally, this increasingly violent motion overcomes the attractive forces holding the liquid particles in contact and the particles fly away from one another. The liquid has become a gas.

Removing energy from the sample and slowing down the particles can reverse the entire sequence of changes. Vapor changes to liquid in a process referred to as **condensation;** liquid changes to solid in a process called **freezing.** Figure 5.13 presents a diagram of the changes in state that occur as energy is added to or removed from a sample. (Hill and Kolb 145)

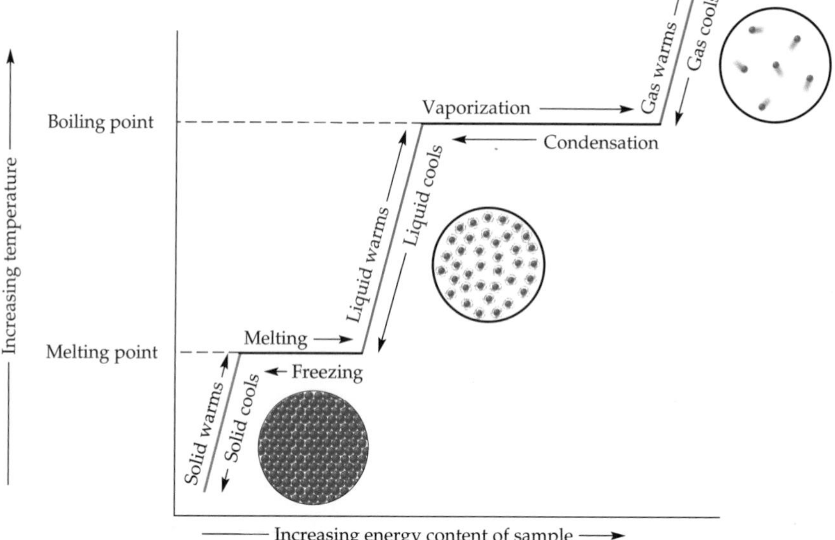

▲Figure 5.13 Diagram of changes in states of matter on heating or cooling.
Question: What factors determine the actual temperatures at which the changes of state occur?

1. *Comprehend* the graphic:
   a. What is the topic? ______________________________
   b. What does the graphic show? ______________________________
   ____
   ____
   ____
   c. Which statement(s) in the text does the graphic relate to? How does it support the text?
   ____
   ____
   ____
   ____

2. *Apply* the information: How does the information relate to you or those you know?

____

____

____

3. *Analyze* the information: Compare and contrast pieces of data, look for patterns, and draw conclusions.

____

____

____

Today knowledge has power.
It controls access to opportunity and advancement.

—Peter F. Drucker (1909–2005),
American management consultant, author

Before you go on . . .

Monitor Your Progress: recite

After you read . . .

Reflect on Your Gains: review

CHAPTER SUMMARY

Introduction

A **graphic aid** is a visual designed to support the text, present details, illustrate relationships, and aid comprehension. Authors use graphic aids because they motivate readers and clarify the information. Good comprehension of graphics uses the same approaches and skills that work with expository texts.

How to Read Graphic Aids

Graphic aids are similar to body paragraphs in that they have a topic and details that are presented to support an idea. Good comprehension begins by uniting the text to the graphic and looking for these three elements. Further insights can be gained after that by applying the information to yourself and/or those you know and then analyzing the information and drawing conclusions. This approach corresponds to the comprehension, application, and analysis levels of thinking.

Types of Graphic Aids

The format is what makes various graphic aids different. Understanding the format is critical because each one indicates relationships within the data and specific ways that they should be analyzed. Five common types of graphic aids are **line graphs, bar graphs, pie charts, tables,** and **diagrams.**

REVIEW ACTIVITIES

Use the following activities to check your understanding and aid your learning of the information in this chapter.

Expand Your Vocabulary

Match each term with the correct definition or characteristic.

______ **1.** graphic aids
______ **2.** line graph
______ **3.** bar graph
______ **4.** pie chart
______ **5.** numerical table
______ **6.** diagram

a. a drawing that helps readers visualize detailed information
b. an aid that presents data in rows and columns
c. a circle chart used to show proportions of subgroups
d. a graph with a line to show how two sets of data relate
e. a graph with bars to show comparisons and contrasts
f. a visual that supports the text and aids comprehension

Increase Your Knowledge

The following tasks will help you assess how well you understand the ideas presented in this chapter. They will also help you prepare for quizzes and exams on this material.

1. The following questions focus on the major chapter topics. Discuss them with others or form your own detailed answers.
   a. Why do authors use graphic aids?
   b. How is a graphic aid like a body paragraph?
   c. Explain the three steps for gaining in-depth comprehension of graphic aids.
   d. How does the approach for reading graphic aids use the levels of thinking? How does it work with PDQ3R?
   e. What are the five types of graphic aids? Describe the format and explain the kind of relationships readers should look for in each one.
2. Take notes on the information in this chapter.

Develop Your Skills

The following review tasks will give you an opportunity to practice the methods presented in this chapter.

REVIEW 1: READ A PIE CHART Read and mark the text and the accompanying graphic. Then answer the questions that follow.

Today probation is the most common form of criminal sentencing in the United States. Between 20% and 60% of those found guilty of crimes are sentenced to some form of probation. Figure 10-1 shows that 59% of all offenders under correctional supervision in the United States as of January 1, 2001, were on probation. Not shown is that the number of offenders supervised yearly on probation has increased from slightly over 1 million in 1980 to well over 3.9 million today—almost a 300% increase. (Schmalleger 446)

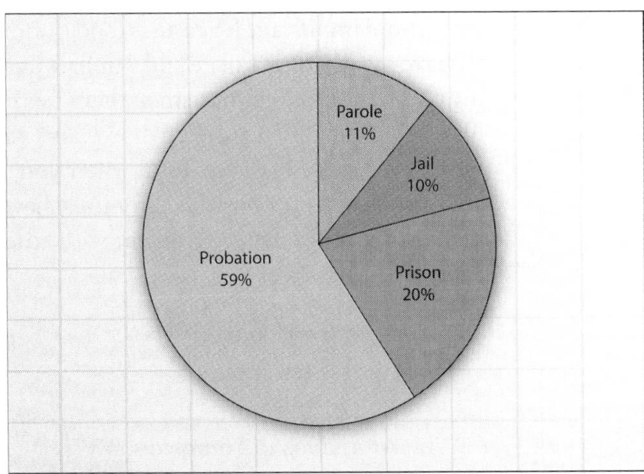

FIGURE 10–1
Offenders under Correctional Supervision in the United States, by Type of Supervision.
SOURCE: *National Correctional Population Reaches New High* (Washington, D.C.: Bureau of Justice Statistics, 2001).

1. *Comprehend* the graphic:
   a. What is the topic? ______________________________
   b. What does the graphic show?
   ____
   ____
   ____
   c. Which statement(s) in the text does the graphic relate to? How does it support the text?
   ____
   ____
   ____

2. *Apply* the information: How does the information relate to you or those you know?

3. *Analyze* the information: Compare and contrast pieces of data, look for patterns, and draw conclusions.

REVIEW 2: READ A BAR GRAPH Read and mark the text and the accompanying graphic. Then answer the questions below the graphic.

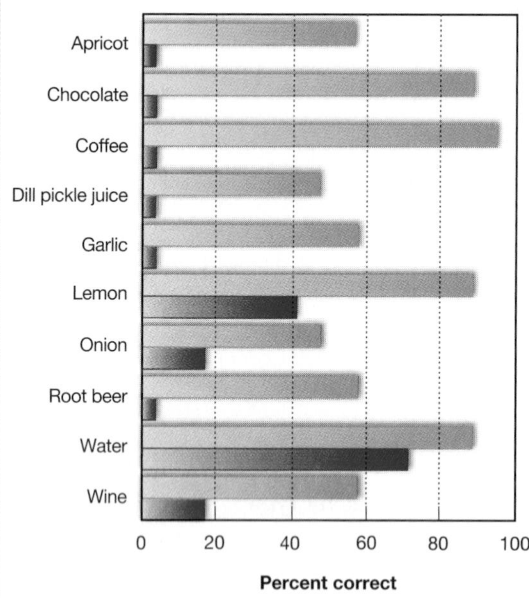

FIGURE 6.10
Taste Test
The orange bars show the percentages of people who could identify a substance dropped on the tongue when they were able to smell it. The blue bars show the percentages who could identify a substance when they were prevented from smelling it (Mozell et al., 1969).

Even more important for taste is food's odor. Subtle flavors such as chocolate and vanilla would have little taste if we could not smell them (see Figure 6.10). Smell's influence on flavor explains why you have trouble tasting your food when you have a stuffy nose. Most people who chronically have trouble tasting things have a problem with smell, not taste. (Wade and Tavris 197)

1. *Comprehend* the graphic:
   a. What is the topic?
   b. What does the graphic show?
   c. Which statement(s) in the text does the graphic relate to? How does it support the text?

2. *Apply* the information: How does the information relate to you or those you know?

3. *Analyze* the information: Compare and contrast pieces of data, look for patterns, and draw conclusions.

____

____

____

Check Your Motivation

1. Review your chapter goals. Did you achieve them? Explain.
2. Make a list of the new ideas and methods you've gained from this chapter. Think about how they will help you in the future.
3. Measure your motivation for this chapter topic. Think about each statement and how you will use it in the future. Mark it:

   A = never B = sometimes C = usually D = always

	A	B	C	D
To engage my interest, I plan to . . .				
1. look at graphics as a way to increase my interest in the topic.	___	___	___	___
To focus my efforts, I plan to . . .				
2. comprehend and analyze graphics.	___	___	___	___
3. identify the graphic topic.	___	___	___	___
4. think about what the graphic information shows.	___	___	___	___
5. connect the graphic to the ideas and details in the text.	___	___	___	___
6. estimate number points for line graphs.	___	___	___	___
7. look for similarities and differences in bar graphs.	___	___	___	___
8. figure out whole-part relationships in stacked bar graphs.	___	___	___	___
9. think about the relative sizes of pie chart sections.	___	___	___	___
10. do simple arithmetic on numerical tables.	___	___	___	___
11. compare and contrast the data in tables.	___	___	___	___
12. look for a process in diagrams.	___	___	___	___
To monitor my efforts, I plan to . . .				
13. apply the information to myself or those I know.	___	___	___	___
14. record anything I figure out and my insights in the margin.	___	___	___	___
To reflect on my gains, I plan to . . .				
15. draw my own conclusions about the information in graphics.	___	___	___	___

SCORING: Write the number of answers you marked in each column in the following spaces. Compute the column scores, and then add them up to determine your total score.

# of A's _____ × 1 pt. = _____
# of B's _____ × 2 pt. = _____
# of C's _____ × 3 pt. = _____
# of D's _____ × 4 pt. = _____
Total points = _____

INTERPRETATION: 15–43 points = low motivation; 44–60 points = high motivation

SUGGESTION: Evaluate your scores. Reward yourself for your gains and empowered approaches. Make a plan to improve anything that needs more attention.

Motivation Matters 3

Before you read . . .

Engage Your Interest: preread and divide

As a child, did you ask a lot of questions? Do you now have questions about a topic before you start reading? Do you think of questions as you read? Or after you've read a text?

After prereading, set a goal for your reading.

I want to ________________ about ________________________.
My reward(s) will be ______________________________________
____.

Right before you begin to read, record your START time in the Rate Box on page 387.

As you read . . .

Focus Your Efforts: question and read

A Flow of Questions

K. P. Baldridge, *Seven Reading Strategies*

> "always the more beautiful answer, who asked the more beautiful question." So said e.e. cummings.

It is with this spirit that the young child engages life. With questions—some stated, some not stated—he explores his world and learns. He learns words—literally thousands of them before he gets to school. He learns to use his language—to express tenses and moods—without ever knowing the difference between a noun and an adverb. He learns about money and mathematics, about the roles of men and women, about values, about identity. He learns a great deal without formal teaching. Psychology tells us that the preschool years are the richest ones for learning; that it's all down hill from there. These are the years rich in questioning. 1

What happens to this eager questioner when he gets to school? . . . In the formal learning of school, the process becomes more involved with answering the teacher's and the author's questions, rather than answering one's own questions. The flow of the student's questions lessens, in classroom discussions, as well as in reading; for some, questioning becomes a trickle; for others it virtually dries up. Only a few maintain the kind of pure curiosity which we find in the pre-school child. 2

What can the reader do? Seize every opportunity to raise questions. If curiosity isn't spontaneous, consciously create questions. 3

4 *When to question?* In general, question all of the time. More specifically, question before, during, and after reading.

Before Reading

5 Before Surveying, ask yourself what your *general purpose* is in reading this book. While surveying, and after surveying, ask yourself what is your *specific purpose* in reading the book. What do you want to learn? Purposive questions clarify your attitude so that you have a desire to cope rather than resist.

6 While surveying, develop questions from the title, subtitles, introductory and concluding paragraphs, etc. Surveying gives you enough information to ask well-directed questions—questions whose answers will fill in the gaps. Questions raised before thorough reading poise you for active participation during reading.

7 Study any questions at the end of the chapter or book. By reading them beforehand to get a good idea of what the author considers important, you will be more likely to take note of pertinent information when you encounter it in your thorough reading.

8 • Questions raised before thorough reading clarify the significance of the book to the reader and are aimed at anticipating the author's meaning—what is literally said.

During Reading

9 Turn topic sentences into specific questions. Questions raised throughout reading sustain interest and prolong the reader's efficiency. A subheading or the first sentence of a paragraph can be transformed into a question which will lead to clarification of what follows.

10 After you have a question, read for the answers. This process is most effective when you are reading something that is difficult or uninteresting for you.

11 Engage in a dialogue with the author. Imagine you are having a conversation with the author and aim your questions at him.

"What is your basis for making *that* statement?"

"Are you including the most relevant facts?"

"What is the practical application of your theory?"

"Why don't you come to the point?"

12 • Questions raised during reading sustain interest in discovering the literal meaning; they also probe beneath the surface; they lead to critical analysis.

After Reading

13 *Test yourself.* By raising comprehensive questions, you can discover whether you have understood; whether the structure is clear in your mind. Such questions prepare you for class discussions, examinations, quizzes and papers.

14 *Criticize.* Now that you have a reasonably full understanding of what you have read, you can raise comprehensive, critical questions about the internal consistency of the material, its value, its validity. And, you can raise questions about the ramifications of

what you have read, its importance, its application, and its relationship with other knowl- 15
edge.

- Questions raised after reading are a check on your understanding; they extend your understanding into practical applications; they generate criticism. (666 words)

As soon as you finish reading, record your END time in the Rate Box on page 387.

Before you go on . . .

Monitor Your Progress: recite

After you read . . .

Reflect on Your Gains: review

REVIEW ACTIVITIES

Use the following activities to check your understanding of this reading.

Expand Your Vocabulary

Define the underlined terms as they are used in the essay by circling the correct response. The numbers after each item indicate the paragraph where the term appears.

1. the young child <u>engages</u> life (1)
   - **a.** reserves
   - **b.** participates in
   - **c.** employs
   - **d.** marries
2. he learns words—<u>literally</u> thousands of them (1)
   - **a.** simply
   - **b.** approximately
   - **c.** actually
   - **d.** exactly
3. for others it <u>virtually</u> dries up (2)
   - **a.** almost completely
   - **b.** quickly
   - **c.** really
   - **d.** honestly
4. if curiosity isn't <u>spontaneous</u> (3)
   - **a.** impulsive
   - **b.** forced
   - **c.** created
   - **d.** automatic
5. <u>consciously</u> create questions (3)
   - **a.** carefully
   - **b.** with effort
   - **c.** without emotions
   - **d.** deliberately

6. purposive questions clarify your attitude (5)
   a. proposed
   b. focused on a purpose
   c. planned
   d. stated

7. poise you for active participation (6)
   a. prepare
   b. raise confidence
   c. get you started
   d. plan

8. take note of pertinent information (7)
   a. necessary
   b. detailed
   c. relevant
   d. potential

9. sustain interest (9)
   a. increase
   b. support
   c. maintain
   d. stand

10. prolong the reader's efficiency (9)
   a. lengthen
   b. shorten
   c. speed up
   d. intensify

Check Your Comprehension

Use the following questions to determine how well you understand the ideas, details, and inferences in this article. Circle the best response to each question.

1. The main idea of this essay is best stated as
   a. teachers destroy children's curiosity.
   b. effective readers think of questions all the time.
   c. reading curiosity should be spontaneous.
   d. reading questions create interest.

2. According to the author
   a. teachers do not teach well.
   b. schools should focus students' attention on the author's questions.
   c. only pre-school children are curious.
   d. when children focus on the questions of others, they stop focusing on their own.

3. The author implies that good readers
   a. are the students who respond to the teacher's questions.
   b. are curious and ask their own questions.
   c. lose their ability to question during classroom discussions.
   d. are the ones who asked a lot of questions as pre-school children.

4. Raising questions about your reading purpose
   a. makes it easier to identify what to skip as you read.
   b. should be done only during surveying.
   c. creates a desire to comprehend the text.
   d. has nothing to do with your attitude.

5. Looking at the end of chapter questions before reading
   a. alerts you to what's important as you read.
   b. is a short-cut reading technique.
   c. is a good technique only when you'll be tested on the information.
   d. helps you to find the essential details.

6. In this essay, the author presents
   a. cause and effect relationships.
   b. a comparison of different teaching methods.
   c. a process or steps for how to read well.
   d. a definition of good reading.

7. Forming questions and reading to find the answers is most useful when you are reading
   a. easy texts.
   b. topics you are very curious about.
   c. texts that have clear topic sentences.
   d. texts that are difficult or initially uninteresting.

8. What does it mean to engage in a dialogue with the author?
   a. Ask questions and expect the following text to answer them.
   b. Visualize the author as a real person while you read.
   c. Hear the author's voice as you read.
   d. Have a conversation with the author where you present your ideas.

9. Critical questions are asked
   a. as you read to understand the text.
   b. as they occur to you to generate interest.
   c. after reading to assess the consistency and value of the text.
   d. at any time as a way to test that you fully understand the text.

10. It is implied that after reading, you will
    a. form your own judgments about the topic.
    b. extend your understanding and evaluate the writing.
    c. remember the text if you have asked enough questions.
    d. benefit from a review of all of your questions.

Expand Your Thinking

Use these activities to expand your understanding of the ideas in this article.

1. The following discussion questions will help you comprehend the major text points and develop your own thoughts about the topic.
   a. How do pre-school children learn about their world?
   b. Why does the child's questioning approach change when s/he gets to school?
   c. Compare and contrast the before, during, and after reading question techniques. That is, what is the purpose of each type of question and how are the questions formed? Suggestion: Create a contrast chart.

d. Were you an "eager questioner" when you started school? Did that change? If so, when and why did it change?
e. Were you taught to ask questions during reading? Were you given questions to answer after reading? Why do you think many readers don't understand that questions are an important part of reading?
f. Do you agree with the author that formal school dries up questions and curiosity? What could teachers do to improve this situation?

2. Take notes on this reading.

Check Your Motivation

1. Review your reading goal. Did you achieve it? Explain.

2. Make a list of the new ideas that you've gained from this text. Think about how they will be useful to you in the future.

3. Measure your motivation for this chapter topic. Think about each statement and how you will use it in the future. Mark it:

A = never B = sometimes C = usually D = always

	A	B	C	D
To engage my interest, I . . .				
1. initiated an "I want to read about this" attitude.	___	___	___	___
2. preread the text.	___	___	___	___
3. identified the topic and/or thought about relevant or interesting points before reading.	___	___	___	___
4. looked for the author's organization before reading.	___	___	___	___
5. set a reading goal before reading.	___	___	___	___
To focus my efforts, I . . .				
6. chose my methods and had an "I know how to read this" attitude.	___	___	___	___
7. read where I was able to concentrate.	___	___	___	___
8. formed questions and read to find answers and other important points.	___	___	___	___
To monitor my progress, I . . .				
9. felt confident and had an "I believe I can read this well" attitude.	___	___	___	___
10. solved any reading problems during reading. (Mark D if there were none.)	___	___	___	___
11. marked the text as I read.	___	___	___	___
12. recited parts or all of the text.	___	___	___	___
To reflect on my gains, I . . .				
13. had an "I've accomplished something" attitude once I finished.	___	___	___	___
14. recognized the new or useful information I gained.	___	___	___	___
15. rewarded myself.	___	___	___	___

SCORING: Write the number of answers you marked in each column in the following spaces. Compute the column scores, and then add them up to determine your total score.

# of A's _____ × 1 pt. = _____
# of B's _____ × 2 pt. = _____
# of C's _____ × 3 pt. = _____
# of D's _____ × 4 pt. = _____
Total points = _____

INTERPRETATION: 15–43 points = low motivation; 44–60 points = high motivation

4. Compute your reading rate by following these steps:

Rate Box

1. **RECORD** your END time here: ___________
2. **RECORD** your START time here: ___________
3. **DETERMINE** your TOTAL reading time here: ___________
4. **ROUND OFF** the seconds to the nearest ¼ minute. For example, 4 minutes, 15 seconds would be 4.25. Write this on the **** line.
5. **DIVIDE** the number of words by your rounded off time:

666 words / _____ (****) = _____ WPM

5. Record your rate, comprehension, vocabulary, and motivation scores on the Progress Charts that are on the inside front and back covers of this text.

Motivation Matters 4

Before you read . . .

Engage Your Interest: preread and divide

What does the term "fantasy" make you think of? How have teachers and parents tried to motivate you? Have you ever had any work tasks that felt like play? Did they increase your concentration or motivation?

After prereading, set a goal for your reading.

I want to _________________ about ______________________________.
My reward(s) will be ____
____.

Right before you begin to read, record your START time in the Rate Box on page 394.

As you read . . .

Focus Your Efforts: question and read

Can Fantasy Increase Students' Motivation to Achieve?

Adapted from Saul Kassin, *Psychology*

1 Educators have long known that learning requires a student's active participation and that some children enter the classroom with a higher level of achievement motivation than others. The question is: What motivates students in their schoolwork?

2 Over the years, psychologists have approached the subject from different perspectives. Behavioral psychologists believe that motivation can be changed by using rewards (praise, grades, gold stars, smiley faces, pats on the back, and special privileges) and punishments (criticism, low grades, letters home, detention, suspension, and time in the principal's office). Most psychologists agree that reinforcements like these raise achievement in the classroom. But cognitive psychologists focus more on what students think about these reinforcements. As Dejorah Stipek (1996) put it, "What is important is not whether one has been rewarded in the past for the behavior but whether one *expects* to be rewarded in the future" (p. 85).

3 But there is another approach to the question of motivation. Try to recall your most memorable learning experiences from your elementary school days. Chances are that

what comes to mind are the kinds of activities that converted work into play. Examples include having students prepare a Renaissance banquet complete with food and music, perform rather than just read a Shakespearean play, and use logical reasoning to solve a crime. Anyone who has ever watched a child spend hours at a computer game knows the motivational power of fantasy play. But do these techniques promote better learning, or do they merely "sugarcoat" the work?

Guided by the assumption that children learn best when they are motivated by interest, **4**
not just by grades, Mark Lepper and his colleagues have sought, experimentally, to evaluate the effects of presenting standard academic tasks within the context of a rich fantasy. In one study, Parker and Lepper (1992) developed a lesson plan for teaching third- and fourth-graders computer-graphic commands. On one occasion, the children were presented with a standard lesson on how to draw simple lines, navigate mazes, and construct geometric shapes on the screen. On three other occasions, these same tasks were part of a fantasy or pretend games. In one, the students were encouraged to think of themselves as pirates in search of buried treasure. In another, they were detectives hunting down criminals. And in a third, they were astronauts exploring space for new planets.

So what were the effects? When the lessons were over, the experimenters asked the **5**
students to rank-order the motivational appeal of the different tasks. They preferred all the activities in the fantasy situation over those in the standard situation. In fact, when brought back two days later, they were more likely to choose the fantasy versions of the Logo tasks. Clearly, the children found the tasks more interesting in the game-like situation. But did this simple modification make for better education? The answer is *yes.* In a follow-up study, Parker and Lepper presented either the basic or a fantasy version of the same graphics lesson and then tested the children in writing to measure their knowledge of the material. Those who learned within a fantasy-rich context performed better—right after the lesson and again when retested two weeks later. Other studies also have confirmed the point (Cordova and Lepper, 1996): When instructional material makes work feel like play, students become more engaged, concentrate better, and are more likely to achieve. (554 words)

As soon as you finish reading, record your END time in the Rate Box on page 394.

Before you go on . . .

Monitor Your Progress: recite

After you read . . .

Reflect on Your Gains: review

REVIEW ACTIVITIES

Use the following activities to check your understanding of this reading.

Expand Your Vocabulary

Define the underlined terms as they are used in the essay by circling the correct response. The numbers after each item indicate the paragraph where the term appears.

1. from different perspectives (2)
   - a. points of view
   - b. depth perceptions
   - c. places
   - d. ideas of proportion
2. behavioral psychologists (2)
   - a. self-control
   - b. dealing with actions
   - c. counseling
   - d. therapy
3. cognitive psychologists (2)
   - a. counseling
   - b. culture focused
   - c. focused on mental problems
   - d. dealing with thinking
4. converted work into play (3)
   - a. exchanged
   - b. adopted
   - c. persuaded
   - d. changed
5. power of fantasy play (3)
   - a. day dreaming
   - b. fictitious
   - c. make-believe
   - d. fancy
6. "sugarcoat" the work (3)
   - a. to cover in sugar
   - b. to make it seem pleasant
   - c. to make it easier
   - d. to make it optional
7. have sought . . . to evaluate (4)
   - a. tried
   - b. pursued
   - c. worked
   - d. seen
8. navigate mazes (4)
   - a. sail
   - b. cross
   - c. plot a course
   - d. maneuver
9. within a fantasy-rich context (5)
   - a. lesson
   - b. text
   - c. computer program
   - d. situation
10. have confirmed the point (5)
    - a. agreed with
    - b. added to
    - c. made firm
    - d. proven

Check Your Comprehension

Use the following questions to determine how well you understand the ideas, details, and inferences in this article. Circle the best response to each question.

1. The main idea of this essay is best stated as
a. students learn more when they have fun.
b. fantasy play can increase students' motivation to achieve.
c. make-believe lessons make it easier for children to learn computer skills.
d. games increase motivation and learning.

2. The author implies that
a. active participation, motivation, and achievement are related.
b. the approach of behavioral psychologists is old-fashioned.
c. the approach of cognitive psychologists is impractical.
d. computer games will be the preferred educational method in the future.

3. Behavioral psychologists believe that motivation can be changed
a. with just praise, grades, and gold stars.
b. slowly and only over time.
c. with rewards and punishments.
d. with criticism and low grades.

4. To cognitive psychologists, motivation depends on
a. whether the student has been rewarded in the past.
b. the students' interest level in the topic.
c. what students think about.
d. the expectation of future rewards.

5. Memorable learning experiences
a. sugarcoat the work.
b. trick students into thinking they are playing rather than learning.
c. introduce aspects of play into the work.
d. must involve fantasy play.

6. Parker and Lepper
a. developed lesson plans for teaching computer skills.
b. studied the same children on three occasions.
c. believe that fantasy play is a good way to present standard lessons.
d. researched the effect of lessons that used fantasy on learning and motivation.

7. To determine interest, Parker and Lepper asked the students
a. to rank-order the different tasks.
b. to choose the tasks they wanted to work on.
c. how they liked to learn.
d. what they thought of the standard and fantasy lessons.

8. When the students in the study were tested on their knowledge and compared to those taught with standard lessons, those taught through fantasy
   a. learned slightly better.
   b. tested higher immediately and two weeks later.
   c. tested higher immediately but not two weeks later.
   d. tested higher after three weeks.

9. Other research studies
   a. used the same research methods.
   b. got the same results.
   c. demonstrated the same relationship between play and achievement.
   d. focused on play as a way to help students become more engaged.

10. The author implies that instructional materials
   a. should include more play.
   b. without the element of play in them are boring.
   c. determine a student's motivational level.
   d. that include play activities will raise motivation and achievement.

Expand Your Thinking

Use these activities to expand your understanding of the ideas in this article.

1. The following discussion questions will help you comprehend the major text points and develop your own thoughts about the topic.
   a. What do behavioral psychologists use to change motivation?
   b. What is the cognitive psychologist's approach?
   c. What is the fantasy approach presented by the author?
   d. Describe the Parker and Lepper studies. How were they conducted? What did they show?
   e. Why do you think children's concentration and learning improve when the material makes "work feel like play"?
   f. Do you think that fantasy can help adults learn? How could you use fantasy in your current courses?

2. Take notes on this reading.

Check Your Motivation

1. Review your reading goal. Did you achieve it? Explain.

2. Make a list of the new ideas that you've gained from this text. Think about how they will be useful to you in the future.

3. Measure your motivation for this chapter topic. Think about each statement and how you will use it in the future. Mark it:

   A = never B = sometimes C = usually D = always

	A	B	C	D
To engage my interest, I . . .				
1. initiated an "I want to read about this" attitude.	___	___	___	___
2. preread the text.	___	___	___	___
3. identified the topic and/or thought about relevant or interesting points before reading.	___	___	___	___
4. looked for the author's organization before reading.	___	___	___	___
5. set a reading goal before reading.	___	___	___	___
To focus my efforts, I . . .				
6. chose my methods and had an "I know how to read this" attitude.	___	___	___	___
7. read where I was able to concentrate.	___	___	___	___
8. formed questions and read to find answers and other important points.	___	___	___	___
To monitor my progress, I . . .				
9. felt confident and had an "I believe I can read this well" attitude.	___	___	___	___
10. solved any reading problems during reading. (Mark D if there were none.)	___	___	___	___
11. marked the text as I read.	___	___	___	___
12. recited parts or all of the text.	___	___	___	___
To reflect on my gains, I . . .				
13. had an "I've accomplished something" attitude once I finished.	___	___	___	___
14. recognized the new or useful information I gained.	___	___	___	___
15. rewarded myself.	___	___	___	___

SCORING: Write the number of answers you marked in each column in the following spaces. Compute the column scores, and then add them up to determine your total score.

# of A's ______ × 1 pt. = ______
# of B's ______ × 2 pt. = ______
# of C's ______ × 3 pt. = ______
# of D's ______ × 4 pt. = ______
Total points = ______

INTERPRETATION: 15–43 points = low motivation; 44–60 points = high motivation

4. Compute your reading rate by following these steps:

Rate Box

1. **RECORD** your END time here: ____________
2. **RECORD** your START time here: ____________
3. **DETERMINE** your TOTAL reading time here: ____________
4. **ROUND OFF** the seconds to the nearest ¼ minute. For example, 4 minutes, 15 seconds would be 4.25. Write this on the **** line.
5. **DIVIDE** the number of words by your rounded off time:

554 words / ______ = ______ WPM
****

5. Record your rate, comprehension, vocabulary, and motivation scores on the Progress Charts that are on the inside front and back covers of this text.

CHAPTER NINE

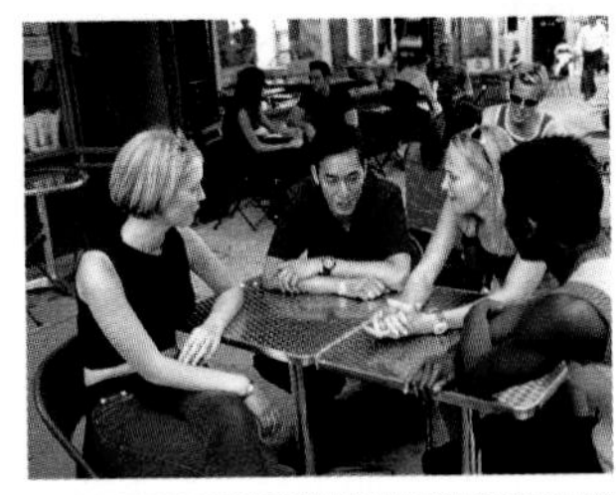

Drawing Conclusions

What can you determine about the speakers in these pictures? What do you think their purpose is? Can you tell anything about their attitude?

In face-to-face situations, listeners get a great deal of information about a speaker's message from what they see. Body language and setting can help you discover the true purpose and even the meaning of what a speaker says. Like listeners, skilled readers look at the author's style—or techniques—to draw conclusions that go beyond what the text states directly.

> Intuitively or not, an author chooses his techniques according to his meaning.
>
> —James Moffett (contemporary), College English professor and author

Before you read . . .

Engage Your Interest: preread and divide

This chapter focuses on how to draw conclusions by analyzing an author's indirect techniques. The diagram on the next page shows how it is organized.

After dividing the chapter into reading tasks, list at least one goal for each task.

1. I want to ________________ about ________________________________.
   My reward(s) will be ____
   ____
   ____.

2. I want to ________________ about ________________________________.
   My reward(s) will be ____
   ____
   ____.

3. I want to ________________ about ________________________________.
   My reward(s) will be ____
   ____
   ____.

4. I want to ________________ about ________________________________.
   My reward(s) will be ____
   ____
   ____.

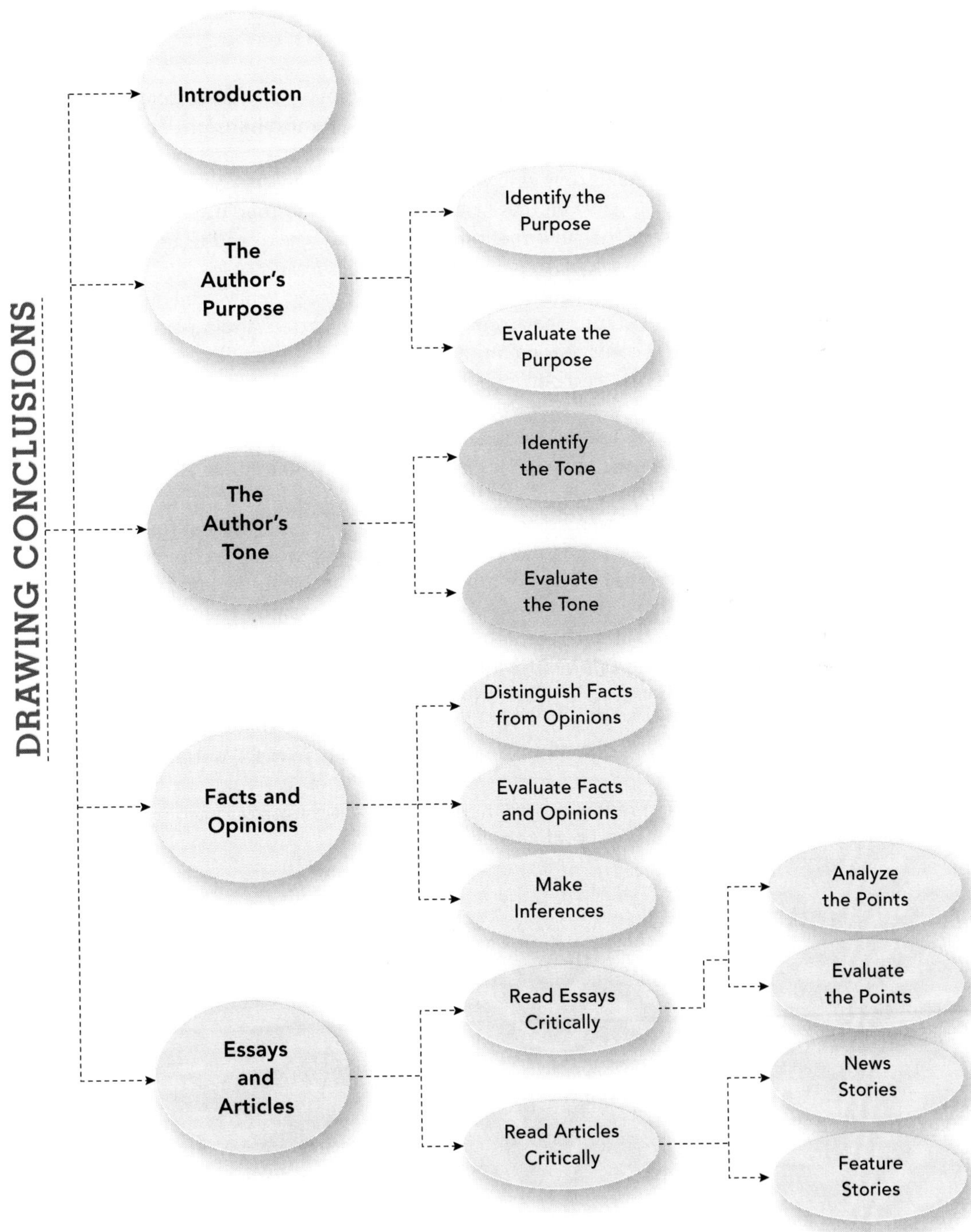
DRAWING CONCLUSIONS
Introduction
The Author's Purpose
Identify the Purpose
Evaluate the Purpose
The Author's Tone
Identify the Tone
Evaluate the Tone
Facts and Opinions
Distinguish Facts from Opinions
Evaluate Facts and Opinions
Make Inferences
Essays and Articles
Read Essays Critically
Analyze the Points
Evaluate the Points
Read Articles Critically
News Stories
Feature Stories

As you read . . .

Focus Your Efforts: question and read

Understanding the information that an author conveys—the ideas, details, and logical relationships—provides what is often called **literal comprehension.** As difficult as that can be at times, this level of understanding is considered basic or surface comprehension, because it deals only with what is directly stated. In many cases, such as textbook reading, this level is all that's needed. But, when reading essays and articles, where opinions rather than information are the focus, active readers use two additional approaches: inferential comprehension and critical reading.

In opinion pieces, authors do not completely or specifically spell out all the points. Instead, they convey some ideas by indirect means. Understanding on this higher level is called **inferential comprehension,** which means understanding what is implied. It's often referred to as "reading between the lines," because the reader has to infer or draw conclusions about parts of the message that are not stated.

Critical reading uses the understandings that comes from literal and inferential comprehension, but goes beyond them. It includes the reader's evaluation of the message. In general usage, the term *critical* means criticizing, faultfinding, or judging in a harsh manner. But critical reading is none of those. Instead, **critical reading** is a careful analysis and evaluation of the message based on appropriate criteria of excellence.

These approaches can be compared to viewing the surface and underwater levels of the ocean. A great deal happens on the surface of the sea, and good observation, which is akin to literal comprehension, will reveal activities such as fish jumping and people swimming or boating. Inferential comprehension goes below the surface, though, to why fish jump or how the people feel about what they're doing. Then, when critical reading is added, observers can analyze and draw conclusions about the value of the unseen interactions among the plants, animals, and chemicals underwater.

You employ inferential comprehension and critical reading processes whenever you draw conclusions and evaluate

- The Author's Purpose
- The Author's Tone
- Facts and Opinions
- Essays and Articles

Whatever you cannot understand, you cannot possess.

—Johann Wolfgang von Goethe (1749–1832),
German poet, dramatist, novelist

The Author's Purpose

THINK ABOUT THIS . . .

1. What do you think would be the author's purpose for writing each of the following texts? Who would be likely to read each text?
   a. A freshman biology discussion about the AIDS virus
      Purpose: ____________________
      Readers: ____________________
   b. A comic strip about miscommunications between teens and parents
      Purpose: ____________________
      Readers: ____________________
   c. A newspaper editorial on gun control
      Purpose: ____________________
      Readers: ____________________

2. Reminder: Preread this section.

Authors have a purpose when they write a text. They also have a particular group of readers in mind. Sometimes, the reason and intended audience are obvious: A freshman biology textbook helps first year college students learn the concepts of biology at the introductory level. In other situations, the purpose is less clear: A comic strip may have several potential audiences, and it may be created to promote a particular philosophy, to entertain, or to criticize. So, behind the text, there is always the author's **purpose,** or the objective the writer hopes to accomplish with an intended audience. Once you identify the purpose, you can evaluate whether the writer accomplished that goal.

Identify the Purpose

Writing purposes include both the general and specific effects that the author hopes to have on the readers. In general, writers write for three reasons: to inform, entertain, or persuade. But authors can have more than one purpose for writing a text. A lighthearted essay on couples' problems could be meant both to entertain and inform; a textbook chapter meant to inform readers about nutrition could include a persuasive insert about the dangers of eating disorders.

Within each general purpose, writers will have more specific goals that relate to the topic and the intended group of readers. For example, an author who wants to inform a general audience about a scientific discovery may describe, explain, discuss, introduce, and/or clarify it. An entertaining piece about teaching manners to children might be meant to amuse, excite, describe, surprise, or even disturb readers. And to persuade smokers not to smoke, a writer could attempt to convince, argue, condemn, or frighten readers.

Last, the purpose can be stated directly or it can be implied. In informative writing, such as textbooks, authors frequently use a phrase such as "the purpose of this text is to discuss (or review or examine)" followed by the topic. But in essays and articles, authors usually do not explain what they are trying to achieve or to whom they are writing. So as a critical reader, you will need to figure out the purpose. You can do this by paying attention to the following:

1. Signal words such as "this is the *most important part, key,* or *critical issue*"
2. Terms that are emphasized with capitals, bold, or italic font
3. Phrases or words that are repeated, particularly if they seem unusual
4. Details, such as facts, description, or emotions

Here are three sample texts that do not directly state their purpose. As you read each one, notice what is being emphasized: those parts have been underlined. Then try to determine the primary purpose (to inform, entertain, or persuade) and the intended audience before you read the analysis.

EXAMPLES

Text 1

No Turning Back: The Singer Named "Jewel"

Jewel Kilcher was just eighteen, fresh out of high school and completely unsure of what to do with her life. She had moved from Michigan to San Diego to be with her mother and was working a series of disappointing, low-paying jobs—waiting tables and punching cash registers. There was little time or money for exploring careers. In fact, she was barely scraping by. (Chazin)

Analysis: From the title, biographical facts, and descriptive words, the purpose of this writing is to entertain readers who are interested in Jewel by providing human-interest information about her.

Text 2

The 'un' game can be a subtle teaching tool

Parents spend a lot of time endeavoring to teach good principles and attitudes. Kids can find this boring, and unfortunately not memorable. So, let me suggest the "UN" game. The aim is to catch someone doing or saying an "UN" or the opposite of an "UN," called a FUN. What is an "UN"? It is anything that is negative, nasty, or naughty. Here is a simple example. Susie leaves her dirty dishes in the sink. That is certainly Unhelpful, since someone else has to clean up after her. The person who sees the dishes announces Unhelpful! So another family member does the opposite of the "Un" and handles the mess. That's a FUN. (Adapted from Krueger)

Analysis: The title indicates that the subject is a teaching tool. The unusual use of "UN," the quotation marks, the definition, and the example explain how this "game" works. The purpose of this piece is to inform parents about a technique for handling misbehavior.

Text 3

The Death of Reading

What's missing from these pictures?

- A couple of kids, waiting for bedtime, lie on the floor of a brightly painted room, busy manipulating the controls of a video game.
- Two hundred people sit in an airplane. Some have brought their own tapes, some doze, most stare up at a small movie screen.

What is missing from these pictures, and increasingly from our lives, is the activity through which most of us learned much of what we know of the wider world. What's missing is the force that, according to a growing consensus of historians, established our patterns of thought and, in an important sense, made our civilization. What's missing is the venerable, increasingly dated activity that you—what's the matter? Bored with all your CDs and videotapes?—are engaged in right now. (Stephens)

Analysis: The title indicates that the subject is reading. The word "death" and the repetition of the phrase "what is missing" develop a sense that this is a very serious problem. The intended audience is educated adults who read well, and the purpose is to persuade them that the lack of reading in our culture is a serious problem.

ACTIVITY 1: IDENTIFY THE AUTHOR'S PURPOSE

DIRECTIONS: Each of the following items presents the title and a short excerpt from a text. For each item, determine the author's primary purpose and intended audience.

For items 1–4, circle the best description of the purpose and audience.

1. **Field of Dreams: From Farm Work to Medical Work**

   My father used to tell me . . . "aunque no tengas buena punteria, si le tiras al cielo, a lo mejor le pegas a una estrella" (Even if you do not have good aim, if you shoot at the sky, you may hit a star). (Quinones-Hinjosa)

   Purpose: **a.** inform **b.** entertain **c.** persuade
   Audience: **a.** a general audience interested in success stories
   b. Hispanic adults **c.** farm workers **d.** medical students

2. **A SOARing Insult to Science**

   I find it annoying that members of the Student Organization for Animal Rights (SOAR) take advantage of the benefits of animal experimentation while protesting that scientists bash bunnies upside their heads with clubs. (McDonald)

   Purpose: **a.** inform **b.** entertain **c.** persuade
   Audience: **a.** members of SOAR **b.** college students
   c. those opposed to animal experimentation
   d. those in favor of animal experimentation
   e. both those in favor and those opposed to animal experimentation

3. In modern China, parents pushing for super tykes.

Four years ago, Zi fell out with his violin teacher. The artistic shakeup, which is how Zi's parents carefully describe it, led to his current love, the piano. Zi, who is now 7, spends every Saturday in a huge Beijing music studio with 45 private teaching rooms. (Marquand)

Purpose: **a.** inform **b.** entertain **c.** persuade
Audience: **a.** Chinese parents **b.** American parents of music students **c.** concertgoers **d.** music students who want to succeed

For items 4–6, identify whether the author's primary purpose is to inform, entertain, or persuade. Then describe a more specific purpose about the topic. You might use words such as describe, explain, amuse, disturb, argue, or criticize. Also, identify the intended audience.

1. What Do They Mean, "We"?

Should the phrase "In God We Trust" become part of our education system? Absolutely not. Should it even be our national motto? No. Federal endorsement of such a statement is a testimony to the degree that religious intolerance still pervades our government.

How many people are really included in that "we," after all? The phrase doesn't refer to any god; it refers to THE God. Capital "g." No Yahweh. No Allah. No Supreme Being.

I realize that a majority of the people in this country believe in a deity of some kind, and a majority of these believe in the Christian God. However, this type of "we" is not the same as that of the statement "we voted George Bush into office." It is immutable, eternal, and wrong. In matters of belief, popular opinion does not justify blanket statements.

Furthermore, having such a proclamation imposed upon our education system introduces new problems. Even if the Supreme Court has been unwilling to completely abolish religious influence in secular policy, it has been clear on the presence of religion in schools.

In considering this issue, let us weigh the influence of our heads, hearts, and Constitution. Hopefully they speak in unison. (Hall) (204 words)

Primary purpose: ______________________

Specific topic purpose: ______________________

____

Audience: ______________________

2. Sexuality

This chapter, written from a sociological point of view, presents some of what researchers have learned about human sexuality. (Macionis 221)

Primary purpose: ______________________

Specific topic purpose: ______________________

____

Audience: ______________________

3. Your Legacy

I had a philosophy professor who was the quintessential eccentric philosopher. His disheveled appearance was highlighted by a well-worn tweed sport coat and poor-fitting thick glasses, which often rested on the tip of his nose. Every now and then, as most philosophy professors do, he would go off on one of those esoteric and existential "what's the meaning of life" discussions. Many of those discussions went nowhere, but there were a few that really hit home. This was one of them:

"Respond to the following questions by a show of hands," my professor instructed.

"How many of you can tell me something about your parents?" Everyone's hand went up.

"How many of you can tell me something about your grandparents?" About three-fourths of the class raised their hands.

"How many of you can tell me something about your great-grandparents?" Two out of sixty students raised their hands.

"Look around the room," he said. "In just two short generations hardly any of us even know who our own great-grandparents were. Oh sure, maybe we have an old, tattered photograph tucked away in a musty cigar box or know the classic family story about how one of them walked five miles to school barefoot. But how many of us really know who they were, what they thought, what they were proud of, what they were afraid of, or what they dreamed about? Think about that. Within three generations our ancestors are all but forgotten. Will this happen to you?

"Here's a better question. Look ahead three generations. You are long gone. Instead of you sitting in this room, now it's your great-grandchildren. What will they have to say about you? Will they know about you? Or will you be forgotten, too?

"Is your life going to be a warning or an example? What legacy will you leave? The choice is yours. Class dismissed."

Nobody rose from their seat for a good five minutes. (D'Angelo) (325 words)

Primary purpose: ______________________________

Specific topic purpose: ______________________________

____

Audience: ______________________________

Above all be of single aim; have a legitimate and useful purpose, and devote yourself unreservedly to it.

— James Allen (1864–1912), British-born American essayist

Evaluate the Purpose

Critical readers recognize the author's purpose and measure the text against it. That means that the reader identifies strengths or weaknesses in the text that promote or hinder the purpose. For example, assume that an author wants to inform readers that illegal music downloading hurts recording artists. To accomplish that goal, the text would have to include clear explanations, facts, and relevant quotes showing that the costs of producing a song are not recovered when people get music for free. And enough information would need to be provided to indicate that this is a serious problem. Without sufficient information, you would rightly say that the text was weak and that the purpose was not achieved.

> **Read not to contradict and confute; nor to believe and discourse, but to weigh and consider.**
> —Sir Francis Bacon (1561–1626), English statesman, essayist, philosopher

Evaluating the purpose is a judgment, and so it is possible for two readers to draw different but equally valid conclusions. One reader of the Jewel text, for instance, might find it very entertaining, because it describes what the singer was doing at 18. Another reader might find it boring, because the facts are well known or because there's no information about her feelings and thoughts. Both readers could point to text elements to support their valid conclusions. But if a reader dismisses the article because she doesn't like Jewel's singing, she would be expressing her personal opinion, not making a valid conclusion about the text or the author's purpose.

ACTIVITY 2: EVALUATE THE AUTHOR'S PURPOSE

DIRECTIONS: Evaluate how well each author accomplished his/her purpose.

Task 1: Refer to items 4 and 6 in Activity 1. Note the primary purpose that you identified. Decide whether the author accomplished that purpose. Include specific examples from the text to back up your conclusion.

1. **What Do They Mean, "We"?**
   My evaluation: ____________________
   ____
   ____
   ____

2. **Your Legacy**
   My evaluation: ____________________
   ____
   ____
   ____

Task 2: Read the following text and identify the primary purpose, the specific topic purpose, and the audience. Then evaluate whether the author accomplished this purpose; cite text examples to back up your conclusion.

To the Editor

Re: "Winter Is Flu Season, but Maybe It Doesn't Have to Be"

You say "it would be nice to know for sure" that immunizing schoolchildren against influenza is the most effective route to prevent flu-related deaths among the vulnerable. There is no need for a new national study, nor do we need to await the analysis of Canadian data.

In Japan, from 1962 through 1987, influenza vaccination of schoolchildren was mandatory. Throughout the 1980's, the large majority of children in Japan were vaccinated, leading to adequate levels of community (formerly called "herd") immunity.

During those years, the death rate from influenza and flu-related pneumonia dropped by 70 percent among the elderly in Japan.

When the law was relaxed in 1987 and repealed in 1994 for political reasons, the death rate returned to its prior level.

Mass vaccination of schoolchildren in the United States would likely save thousands of lives here as well.

Gilbert Ross, M.D.

The writer is medical director, American Council on Science and Health. (179 words)

Primary purpose: ______________________________

Specific topic purpose: ______________________________

____

Audience: ______________________________

My evaluation: ______________________________

____

____

Before you go on . . .

Monitor Your Progress: recite

As you read . . .

Focus Your Efforts: question and read

The Author's Tone

THINK ABOUT THIS . . .

1. How would you describe the person's feelings in each of these situations?
   a. In a grocery store, a two-year-old is refusing to listen to his father, who has asked him repeatedly not to pull items off the shelves. The toddler reaches for a bottle, and it crashes and breaks, spilling soft drink all over the aisle.
   The father probably feels ______________________________
   ______________________________.

b. A woman has just received flowers from her boss. He comes out of his office to thank her for the extra time she spent helping him get a new client.
The employer probably feels ______________________________
____.

2. Reminder: Preread this section.

In our daily lives, we have feelings about our experiences, many of which go unspoken. You probably recognized the frustrated father and the grateful boss in the ***Think about this . . .*** scenes. The situations alone would lead you to expect those reactions, but you also could have recognized the emotions if you heard the tone of voice those people used as they spoke. Determining the feelings of others from context, wording, and tone of voice is a skill that we use without even thinking about it.

Similarly, critical readers try to determine the author's **tone,** or unstated attitude or feeling toward the subject. This information is important because it provides an additional mechanism for evaluating how well authors achieve their purpose.

Identify the Tone

Tone reflects the author's point of view about the subject. In general, the author's tone might be described as one of these:

1. Objective or subjective
2. Unfavorable or favorable
3. Serious, humorous, or emotional

These seven terms provide basic ways to label tone. As Table 9.1 illustrates, there are numerous words within each of these categories that can be used to describe the author's specific attitude. In addition to the variety of terms, you will also find that authors can have more than one point of view within the same text. So textbook authors are often objective and serious, while essay and article writers might have subjective, favorable, and even humorous attitudes.

To determine the author's tone, analyze the language, especially the descriptive phrases and words. Pay attention to the denotative and connotative meanings of the words the author chooses. **Denotation** is the accepted definition for a term, or the one you would find in a dictionary. **Connotation** is the implied or emotional meaning. It goes beyond the dictionary and suggests attitudes. To understand the connotative meaning, think about how the term is used. For example, *mother* is a formal and less emotional way of identifying a female parent than *mom,* which is informal and conveys positive feelings.

Connotation can suggest neutral as well as positive or negative attitudes. *Eat, walk,* and *talk* are good examples of neutral terms. An author using words like these would probably have an objective tone. But how does the tone change if the author says that a person *devoured their food, stumbled through the door,* or *droned on and*

TABLE 9.1 **Terms that Describe Tone**

GENERAL CATEGORY	SAMPLE TERMS: THE AUTHOR'S TONE IS . . .
Objective	Impersonal, analytical, direct, straightforward, informative, authoritative
Subjective	Personal, emotional, sentimental, romantic, passionate, concerned, involved
Unfavorable	Critical, condescending, cynical, disapproving, outraged, skeptical, ridiculing, exaggerated, satirical, self-righteous, sarcastic, judgmental, concerned, pessimistic, urgent, bitter
Favorable	Enthusiastic, praising, approving, positive, laudatory, passionate, enthusiastic, proud, arrogant, nostalgic, sentimental, hopeful, optimistic, enthusiastic, sympathetic, empathetic, respectful, admiring, intrigued, inspired, awe-struck
Serious	Insightful, observant, interested, thoughtful, speculative, respectful, realistic, curious
Humorous	Ridiculing, sarcastic, satirical, amused, joking, joyful, funny, playful, light-hearted, ironic
Emotional	Nostalgic, romantic, sentimental, empathetic, mysterious, enthusiastic, ominous, angry

on? These terms have negative connotations, and thus the writer's attitude is clearly disapproving, if not critical. Conversely, if the author described the person as *dining, strolling,* and *conversing,* the tone would be favorable.

As a case in point, look at these examples from a textbook author and a columnist. Before looking at the analysis, note the underlined terms and identify whether they are neutral, positive, or negative. Then determine what you think the tone is; use the general category labels from Table 9.1.

EXAMPLES

Textbook

<u>Many</u> federal and state <u>statutes</u> <u>regulate</u> <u>against</u> <u>deceptive pricing practices</u>. For example, the Automobile Information Disclosure <u>Act</u> <u>requires</u> automakers <u>to</u> <u>attach</u> a <u>statement</u> to new car window stating the manufacturer's suggested retail price, the prices of optional equipment, and the dealer's transportation charges. (Armstrong and Kotler 390)

Analysis: Except for *against* and *deceptive,* the words are neutral. The two negative terms become neutral because they are what is to be avoided. The overall tone is objective and serious.

Opinion Article

As a confessed car slob, my sole interest in the motor is that when I turn it on, it will go. Every 10 years or so, when I reluctantly enter a salesroom, I am more interested in cup holders and seat warmers than in anything remotely motor trendy. (Ellen Goodman)

Analysis: The words are predominantly negative (e.g., slob, sole interest, reluctantly, trendy), neutral (e.g., cup holders and seat warmers), and personal (e.g., I). Together they indicate a personal tone that is also humorous.

ACTIVITY 3: CONTRASTING CONNOTATION

DIRECTIONS: The following words are generally used as neutral terms. For each one, record two terms that are close to the original in meaning, but choose one that has negative connotations and one that has positive connotations.

	NEGATIVE	POSITIVE
1. teacher	__________	__________
2. drink	__________	__________
3. spectator	__________	__________
4. crowd	__________	__________
5. willing	__________	__________
6. group (the noun)	__________	__________
7. work	__________	__________
8. music	__________	__________

So to identify tone, pay attention to the feelings you have when you read the words and how these terms are usually used. *Noise,* for example, has a negative feeling, and *melodious* has a positive one. Even when you are unsure about the denotative meaning, you can often figure out the connotation by looking at the context, topic, and surrounding terms. In a discussion about making a speech, for example, if the author used the phrase "prattling about nothing," you might not know what *prattling* means. But you do know that *nothing* is negative. Combine that with the context, and you could guess that the phrase means "talking without saying anything important." It logically follows that the author's tone is negative and critical.

ACTIVITY 4: IDENTIFY THE CONNOTATION

DIRECTIONS: Look at the underlined terms in the following statements. Check off whether the connotation is neutral, negative, or positive. Then explain what the term means within the sentence.

1. When the law was relaxed in 1987 and repealed in 1994 <u>for political reasons</u>, the death rate returned to its prior level.

   The connotation is ______ neutral ______ negative ______ positive.
   The meaning is ____
   ____.

2. Mass vaccination of schoolchildren in the United States <u>would likely save</u> thousands of lives here as well.

   The connotation is ______ neutral ______ negative ______ positive.
   The meaning is ____
   ____.

3. Should the phrase "In God We Trust" become part of our education system? Absolutely not. Should it even be our national motto? No. Federal endorsement of such a statement is a testimony to the degree that <u>religious intolerance</u> still pervades our government.

   The connotation is ______ neutral ______ negative ______ positive.
   The meaning is ____
   ____.

4. I realize that a majority of the people in this country believe in a deity of some kind, and a majority of these believe in the Christian God. However, this type of "we" is not the same as that of the statement "we voted George Bush into office." It is immutable, eternal, and wrong. In matters of belief, popular opinion does not justify <u>blanket statements</u>.

   The connotation is ______ neutral ______ negative ______ positive.
   The meaning is ____
   ____.

5. I had a philosophy professor who was the quintessential eccentric philosopher. His <u>disheveled appearance</u> was highlighted by a well-worn tweed sport coat and poor-fitting thick glasses, which often rested on the tip of his nose.

   The connotation is ______ neutral ______ negative ______ positive.
   The meaning is ____
   ____.

6. Every now and then, as most philosophy professors do, he would go off on one of those esoteric and existential "what's the meaning of life" discussions. Many of those discussions went nowhere, but there were a few that <u>really hit home</u>.

   The connotation is ______ neutral ______ negative ______ positive.
   The meaning is ____
   ____.

Since an author can exhibit more than one tone about a subject, you will want to track the attitudes as you read a full-length text. To do this, you might circle the striking phrases or record plus and minus signs in the margin for the words with strong connotations. Then you can review your marks and recognize patterns and the tone(s) they imply.

ACTIVITY 5: IDENTIFY THE AUTHOR'S TONE

DIRECTIONS: Identify the author's tone in the following texts by completing these steps:

A. Highlight any striking descriptive phrases and terms.
B. Put positive or negative signs in the margin next to words with strong connotative meanings.
C. Answer the questions that follow each text. Use Table 9.1 to describe the author's tone.

1. **Cell Phones Destroy Solitude of Wilderness**

Notes

High above the trees and surrounded by sky, the Adirondack peaks can seem far removed from the everyday world.

Unless, of course, the guy next to you is jabbering on his cell phone. Such a surreal scene played out on Mount Marcy's summit in front of state forester Jim Papero. He remembers it well: "It was cold and windy. Beautiful. You could hear the wind whistling and everything, then this . . . he was talking to his stockbroker."

Cell-phone chatter, already common at restaurants and shopping malls, is heard more and more often in the wilderness. Hikers and campers are tapping into personal directories to ask directions and apologize for dinner delays, to bum rides and call in sick.

This is not amusing to many campers, hunters or others who appreciate nature's quiet. The problem has prodded New York environmental officials, who also worry about hikers using cell phones as lifelines, to promote phone etiquette in the wilderness.

Problem is, cell phones aren't reliable in the wild because cell towers tend to be far apart. Then there's the problem of getting a phone to work in gorges, gullies, and other pockets amid peaks. It's a Catch 22 because efforts to build cell towers in remote areas are often opposed by locals and conservationists concerned about rural eyesores.

Even when phones can hail a signal in the backwoods, rescuers complain about trivial "emergencies." Rangers in New York report picking up the phone to hear hikers asking directions or complaining about sprained wrists. (Adapted from the Associated Press) (256 words)

In general, the connotative words are
_____ negative _____ positive _____ both.
The overriding message is

____

____

____.

The author's tone is ____.

2. **Google attempting to digitize libraries—Internet company says books will be integrated into its overall search engine**

SAN JOSE—The Internet company that famously promised to "do no evil" is on a new mission to digitize the collections of some of the nation's leading research institutions and establish a massive online reading room.

But Google Inc.'s ambitious effort could herald the beginning of the commercialization of libraries, which have long been trusted as an independent resource for books and knowledge without the obvious trappings of marketing or goals of profit.

For the sake of wider public access, librarians and archivists are grateful and excited about Google's underwriting of the otherwise cost-prohibitive effort to scan millions of books and research materials.

Yet they also know that Mountain View–based Google, the world's leading Internet search engine, relies on revenues from advertisements that are often related to the search topic at hand.

And the agreements that Google worked out with the research institutions are non-exclusive, which means Google's rivals, such as Yahoo Inc. or Amazon.com, might try to get access to the same material Google digitizes and use it for their own purposes.

In other words, even if Google remains true to its word to "do no evil," another search engine without the same ethics might come along.

"There is anxiety about whether the student researcher, scholar or citizen will be guided into the free public access rather than being lured into a purchasing relationship with the publisher," said Duane Webster, the executive director of the Association of Research Libraries.

But Webster said those fears are tempered as long as free, open access remains an option, whether it involves guiding users to the actual digital versions online or the Web sites of the libraries that hold the material. (Adapted from Wong) (296 words)

In general, the connotative words are
_____ negative _____ positive _____ both.
The overriding message is

____

____

____.

The author's tone is ____

____.

Evaluate the Tone

When evaluating a text, critical readers assess whether the author's tone supports the purpose. We expect authors who wish to inform readers about scientific knowledge to be objective. Even if the topic is controversial, such as stem cell research, scientific writers are expected to be analytical and unbiased. Conversely, we expect a persuasive writer to be passionate about a particular view. And if the message is a warning about a danger, such as not having home fire alarms, we would expect the author to be very concerned or even alarmed about people's lack of preparation. In other words, the author should convey an appropriate attitude about the topic and an approach that gains the readers' respect.

For example, look back at the letter to the editor entitled "Winter Is Flu Season . . ." (p. 404). The author's purpose is to persuade readers to support mass vaccination of schoolchildren. He uses positive phrases such as *nice to know* and *most effective,* along with facts told in neutral terms. His tone is serious, respectful, objective, and informed. It makes the letter quite persuasive. In contrast, look at the text "What Do They Mean, 'We'?" (p. 402). Terms such as *absolutely not, no, THE God, wrong, does not justify,* and *imposed upon* clearly convey the author's unfavorable tone, but they also are a bit overwhelming and may not convince readers who have a different point of view.

ACTIVITY 6: EVALUATE THE AUTHOR'S TONE

DIRECTIONS: Use the texts in Activity 5. Evaluate the tone in each one by answering the following questions.

1. Cell Phones Destroy Solitude of Wilderness
   a. The general and specific purposes of this text are:

      ____

      ______________________________.

   b. Does the tone support the purpose? Does it gain the reader's respect? Explain.

      ____

      ____

      ____

2. Google attempting to digitize libraries . . .
   a. The general and specific purposes of this text are:

      ____

      ______________________________.

   b. Does the tone support the purpose? Does it gain the reader's respect? Explain.

      ____

      ____

      ____

Before you go on . . .

Monitor Your Progress: recite

As you read . . .

Focus Your Efforts: question and read

Facts and Opinions

THINK ABOUT THIS . . .

1. Label each of the following statements as a fact or an opinion by writing F or O on the line.
   _____ **a.** Ronald Reagan was the 50th President of the United States.
   _____ **b.** Working while going to college can produce enormous stress which, as research shows, can interfere with learning.
   _____ **c.** The primary colors are red, green, and blue.
   _____ **d.** The primary colors are red, yellow, and blue.
   _____ **e.** Most people enjoy warm, but not hot, weather.
2. Define the terms fact and opinion.
   A fact is ____.
   An opinion is ____.
3. Reminder: Preread this section.

Did you mark item *a* in the ***Think about this*** . . . activity as a fact or opinion? The item presents erroneous information: Ronald Reagan was the 40th president, not the 50th. Does that change your answer? Is wrong information a fact, an opinion, or neither? What about item *b*? It seems to have both an opinion and a fact in it. Can a statement be both? Last, can two contradictory statements, such as *c* and *d*, both be facts? As you will see, a fact has to do with the type of information, not the accuracy. In addition, a statement can contain both a fact and an opinion, and two contradictory statements can both be facts.

Every man has a right to be wrong in his opinions. But no man has a right to be wrong in his facts.
—Bernard M. Baruch (1870–1965), American financier

Separating facts from opinions is not always easy to do. But it is a very important part of critical reading, because facts and opinions are evaluated differently. In addition, identifying which is which will help you infer unstated points.

Distinguish Facts from Opinions

The definitions of facts and opinions are fairly straightforward. A **fact** is a piece of information that can be proven; it may be proven to be true or false. An **opinion** is a person's conclusion or judgment about people, places, ideas, or things; others may agree or disagree with it. For example, if I claim that the last sentence has five words in it, I am stating a fact. You could prove that statement by simply counting the number of words in the sentence, and you would find that the statement is false. If I claim that the same sentence is clear, concise, and well written, that is an opinion. You might agree or disagree with all or parts of that statement.

The key to identifying facts is to ask yourself this question: "If I wanted to, could I research this and find information that would prove it to be true or false?" If you can think of a source that you could use to verify the information, it's probably a fact. Sources don't just have to be books. They can also be reliable experts, Internet sites, or your own observations. Facts usually have other characteristics as well:

1. They are used to support another statement or idea.
2. They are narrow in scope.
3. They may include descriptions gathered from observation.
4. They are stated with specific, nonjudgmental words.
5. They include dictionary definitions or statements of meaning accepted by experts in the field.

Here is an example of an expert fact: "Teaching requires more than 40 hours of work every week." While this may sound like someone's opinion, it could be verified by observation, experts, and research. It is the kind of statement that would support an opinion about how demanding teaching is. It is narrow, concrete, specific, and stated in nonjudgmental terms.

Opinions, on the other hand, are judgmental and open to dispute. To identify opinions, ask yourself this question: "Could someone disagree with all or part of this statement?" If others, either non-experts or experts, might disagree with the point, it's probably an opinion. In addition, an opinion is

1. Someone's belief, judgment, or conclusion.
2. A statement that needs support, explanations, and examples.
3. Often introduced with terms, such as *believe, think, feel, propose, in my opinion, one interpretation*, or *the most important point*.
4. Often stated with qualifiers, such as *possibly, often, usually, could, might, suggest, it seems*, or *it appears*.
5. A statement presented about the future or actions that should, could, or might occur.
6. Stated with general, abstract, or judgment words that are open to personal interpretation.

An example of an opinion would be "In my opinion, teaching is emotionally rewarding." This statement is my personal conclusion. You would expect it to be followed by explanations and examples. It is introduced as an opinion, and the term rewarding is a judgment that people could define in a number of ways.

Two final points about facts and opinions need to be made. First, some statements contain both. If a writer says that "Seattle has more rainfall than any other U.S. city," that is a fact that could be checked out. But what if the writer ends that sentence with "and that explains the high rates of depression found there"? The addition is an opinion, because the extent to which rain affects depression is open to interpretation.

Second, distinguishing fact from opinion in course assignments is not always easy. Experts state their opinions forcefully and often in a way that sounds factual. When you don't know a lot about the field, a fact can sound like an opinion and vice versa. The best way to separate them is to use the criteria

Listen, everyone is entitled to my opinion.

—Madonna (1958–), American singer, actress

listed earlier and to look for general, abstract words that people could use in a variety of ways. Those terms signal opinions, not facts. And remember, much of the knowledge in your courses is made up of theories and explanations, which are opinions.

ACTIVITY 7: DISTINGUISH FACTS FROM OPINIONS

DIRECTIONS: Identify the facts and opinions in the following texts. Follow the directions for each task.

Task 1: Label each of the following items with F if it is primarily a fact and O if it is primarily an opinion.

1. These sentences are from the essay "When Patriotism Runs Amuck" (p. 425).
   ______a. In order to comply with a state law that requires a daily show of patriotism in public schools, the Madison school board decided to eliminate saying the Pledge of Allegiance as an option.
   ______b. They wanted to avoid making students of different backgrounds uncomfortable; also, some parents were concerned about the religious aspect of the line containing "one nation, under God."
   ______c. Their decision was met with outrage.
2. The following sentences are from a chapter in a business textbook.
   ______a. When an industry has only a handful of sellers, an **oligopoly** exists.
   ______b. The entry of new competitors is hard because large capital investment is needed.
   ______c. Thus, oligopolitic industries (the automobile, airline, and steel industries) tend to stay that way.
   ______d. Only two companies make large commercial aircraft: Boeing (a U.S. company) and Airbus (a European consortium).
   ______e. Furthermore, as the trend toward globalization continues, most experts believe that, as one forecaster puts its, "global oligopolies are an inevitable as the sunrise." (Griffin and Ebert 16)

Task 2: Read the following paragraphs. Put brackets ([..]) around each fact; highlight each opinion.

1. The following paragraph is from a sociology textbook in a section entitled "What Is Culture?"

   No way of life is "natural" to humanity, even though most people around the world view their own behavior that way. What comes naturally to members of our species is creating culture. Every other form of life—from ants to zebras—behaves in uniform, species-specific ways. This uniformity follows from the fact that most living creatures are guided by *instinct,* biological programming over which animals have no control. A few animals—notably chimpanzees and related primates—have the capacity for limited culture, as researchers have noted by observing them use tools and teach simple skills to their offspring. But the creative power of humans far exceeds that of any other form of life. In short, *only humans rely on culture rather than instinct to ensure the survival of their kind* (M. Harris, 1987). (Adapted from Macionis 59)

2. The following paragraph is from a *New York Times* article entitled "Hard-Wired for Prejudice? Experts Examine Human Response to Outsiders."

In a study that measured how emotional states affected views of outsiders, the researchers, from Northeastern University and the University of Massachusetts at Amherst, found that anger increased the likelihood of a negative reaction to members of a different group. The study will appear in the May issue of the journal *Psychological Science.* Taken together with other research, the findings suggest that prejudice may have evolutionary roots, having developed as a quick, crude way for early humans to protect themselves from danger. The new research on emotions and prejudice has been partly inspired by changing ideas about the nature of emotion itself. Social scientists once dismissed emotions as an illogical nuisance. But by the 1980s researchers had begun to consider emotions useful in their own right. In 1994, Dr. Bedenhausen at Northwestern University conducted one of the first studies to show that moods could affect whether people invoked hurtful stereotypes. For better or worse, he noted, stereotyping, arising as it does from the mind's tendency to make sense out of the world by categorizing and simplifying, provides a basis for rapid response. (Adapted from Wartik)

Evaluate Facts and Opinions

One reason to distinguish facts from opinions is to evaluate how well the writer uses them. What makes a fact good support is not the same as what makes an opinion insightful. So critical readers judge facts and opinions on the basis of different criteria.

To qualify as good support, facts must be true. But that's the minimum requirement. They must also be current, relevant, and reliable. Information is useless if it's outdated, off the issue, or from an untrustworthy source. So, for example, any "facts" presented in diet books that are not linked to research or expert knowledge about nutrition and human biology should not be accepted as good support, even if they are intriguing. How will you know if the information matches the criteria? Conscientious authors provide sources, quotes, and references to reassure readers that they are presenting true, current, and reliable data. Critical readers are on the lookout for writers who don't identify their sources.

Opinions are judged on a different scale. To be convincing, opinions must be relevant, useful, reasonable, and well supported with details. Opinions that aren't relevant to the issue are usually illogical or impractical; those that have few or no details to back them up are not convincing. Opinion letters in newspapers often fall into this category.

There are no eternal facts, as there are no absolute truths.

—Fredrich Nietzsche (1844–1900), Prussian philosopher

In the end, determining how much faith or trust to put in facts and opinions is a judgment call that critical readers must make on a case-by-case basis. Judging the quality and quantity of the sources and evidence will help you determine how valuable facts and opinions are. And, even more important, those judgments will provide the evidence to back up your conclusions.

ACTIVITY 8: EVALUATE FACTS AND OPINIONS

DIRECTIONS: Read the two passages below and do the following:

A. Label the most important facts and opinions in the margin.
B. Evaluate the quality of the facts and opinions by answering the questions.

Passage 1

Fluoridation and Question of Hip Fractures

Many United States communities have fluoridated their water supplies; this public health measure has resulted in significant decreases in dental cavities.

Concern about a possible connection between fluoride and hip fractures has been addressed in a study appearing in the January 22nd issue of *Lancet*, a leading British medical journal.

This study, which included in its research over 2,000 men and women age 50 and older, concluded that there was no evidence that fluoridation increased the risk of fractures. In fact, in an editorial in the same issue of *Lancet*, Dr. Clifford Rosen points out that fluoride has been used as a treatment for osteoporosis.

Fluoridation is safe and effective and has been consistently shown to lower the incidence of cavities, improve the health of our children, and save on health costs.

The American Dental Association, the Canadian Dental Association, and the American Academy of Pediatrics all support fluoridation. (Adapted from Littman) (148 words)

1. Evaluate the facts. Do they provide good support for the points? Explain.

____
____
____
____

2. Evaluate the opinions. Are they convincing? Explain.

____
____
____
____

Passage 2

Character Isn't What We've Built

As the cocaine train winds its way through the world of sports, and jails overflow with troubled athletes, one theme keeps coming up. "Athletes are just like other people," is what a lot of people say. "They have no more problems than people in other professions." I doubt that's true. I was in a locker room the other day and my guess is that drug use is up 50 percent. And there are those who have been involved in an arrest. Just last month a well-known baseball player was accused of leaving the scene of an accident.

The idea that sports make better people is the major reason—or so we say—that we push our children into sports. We've got them in organized games from the time they're old enough to mumble "baybaw" and "foobaw." But when you look at the results, you can come to only one conclusion. We are not creating leaders. Our professional athletes do not lead society; they reflect it. Sports programs produce nothing more than an expensive growing pain.

The system that was supposed to build character has made some of these guys weak and helpless. After being told how wonderful they were in high school by some idiot "win-at-all-costs" coaches, what do we expect? After being tutored through college, and sent out without being able to read or write, what do we expect? Then after having their noses wiped by money-hungry agents in the pros, what do we expect? Should we be surprised when they crumble at the sight of a problem they must face alone? (Imrem) (268 words)

1. Evaluate the facts. Do they provide good support for the points? Explain.

____

____

____

____

2. Evaluate the opinions. Are they convincing? Explain.

____

____

____

____

Till a man can judge whether they be truths or not, his understanding is but little improved.

—John Locke (1632–1704), British philosopher

Make Inferences

When you identify an author's purpose or tone, you are making inferences. In addition, you also make inferences about any points that are implied. When authors **imply,** they suggest or hint at a point rather than state it directly.

You might wonder why authors would ever imply a point; there are many reasons. In textbooks, for instance, authors might imply minor points that would be distracting if they were explained fully. In works meant to entertain, such as fiction or cartoons, indirectness produces humor, suspense, and interest. And in persuasive writing, authors may imply common values they assume the reader shares. Of course, indirectness can also be used to manipulate readers; this is a common method in political and sales texts where the goal is to gain something from the readers.

Critical readers **infer,** or figure out, unstated messages by drawing logical conclusions from what the author has stated and their own background knowledge. Look at this example from a sociology textbook about the way we present ourselves.

EXAMPLE

As we present ourselves in everyday situations, we convey information—consciously and unconsciously—to others. An individual's performance includes dress (costume) and objects carried along (props), and tone of voice and particular gestures (manner). In addition, people craft their performance according to the setting (stage). (Macionis 147)

You might infer from this paragraph that the author is saying

The way we present ourselves is a lot like being an actor in a play.

We all play roles, and we choose the appropriate costumes, props, and manners to fit an occasion, which is our stage.

Part of our performance is planned, like an actor following a script.

Notice how these inferences are ideas that are based on the text but that go beyond it. They are implied by the use of terms such as "performance," "costume," "props," and "stage."

Inferences, then, are logical extensions of the author's points or ideas, and in the end, they're guesses the reader makes about what it seems the author would agree with. Thus, an inference can't just restate or paraphrase the author; it also can't contradict the text. So, for the previous example, a statement like "individuals convey information by what they wear" simply paraphrases the author's idea. And a statement such as "what we wear is not important" would not be a valid inference, because that's the opposite of what the text says.

Inferencing goes hand in hand with finding facts and opinions. First, identify the author's facts and opinions. Then infer the implied points. That is, take the author's statement and expand on it, going one step further than the stated text. You might state assumptions the author seems to have, or supply information that is not included.

We can only reason from what is; we can reason on actualities, but not on possibilities.

—Henry Bolingbroke (1678–1751), British politician

ACTIVITY 9: MAKE INFERENCES

DIRECTIONS: Practice working with inferences by completing the following tasks.

Task 1: Read the following texts. Then label each statement that follows it with an O if it's the author's stated or implied opinion, an F if it's a fact presented in the text, and an I if it is an inference created by a reader.

1. We hybrid owners—a mere 50,000 in a sea of 17 million cars sold last year—are typecast as granola-crunching, tree-hugging enviro-snobs. Not only did a *New York Times* writer sneeringly call our vehicles "hip," another mocked us as "virtuous." A third suggested we drive with moral superiority, "the automotive equivalent of corrective shoes." Since Susan Sarandon eschewed the limo to pull up to the Oscars in her Prius, we've been tarnished with the Hollywood glitter. One professor declared that driving a hybrid was a way of saying, "I'm more intelligent than the next guy." (Ellen Goodman)

   ______ **a.** Some people criticize hybrid car owners.
   ______ **b.** Hybrid cars make up about two percent of the total car sales.
   ______ **c.** Some people assume that hybrid car owners must need those cars to overcome financial problems.
   ______ **d.** Susan Sarandon did not arrive at the Oscars in a limousine.
   ______ **e.** Even some people who are rich and famous buy hybrid cars.
   ______ **f.** The decision to buy a hybrid is generally made for intellectual, not emotional, reasons.

2. Africa is a continent of enormous diversity. Geographically, it ranges from vast deserts to tropical rain forests, from flat grasslands to spectacular mountains and dramatic rift valleys. Human diversity in Africa is equally impressive. More than 1,000 major languages have been identified, representing a seemingly infinite variety of cultures, each with its own history, customs, and art forms. (Stokstad 404)

   ______ **a.** In Africa, there are a great variety of human cultures.
   ______ **b.** There are more than 1,000 languages in Africa.
   ______ **c.** Human diversity may be the result of differences in geography.
   ______ **d.** Africa includes a wide variety of physical and cultural elements.

3. The patronage of the clergy and aristocratic families allied with the papacy dominated Italian art. But they were not the only patrons of the arts in the seventeenth century. Kings and nobles realized that impressive buildings and splendid portraits could secure and enhance their status by surrounding them with an aura of power. Patronage of the arts became expected of an absolute monarch. (Adapted from Stokstad 352 and 358)

   ______ **a.** Monarchs in the 17th century were expected to support the arts.
   ______ **b.** Artists in the 17th century sold their works to those in positions of power.
   ______ **c.** In the 17th century, church clergy and rulers supported the arts.
   ______ **d.** Art was a status symbol in the 17th century.
   ______ **e.** Only rulers, nobles, and the church leaders had enough money to support the arts in the 17th century.

Task 2: As you read and mark the following text, identify the major facts and opinions. Then, record one opinion, one fact, and one inference for each paragraph on the lines following the text.

Good News about the Environment

Notes

A sense of gloom about the environment may arise when one considers all of the environmental issues: global warming, nitrogen buildup, overuse of water resources, tropical rain-forest destruction. These are real problems, but their existence should not blind us to the fact that there has been a great deal of good news about the environment in the last 30 years, much of it showing how effective government can be when prodded into action by its citizens.

If there was a time for unrestrained gloom about the environment in the United States, it probably would have been in the late 1960s, when the country had plenty of endangered species but no Endangered Species Act; when levels of smog in Los Angeles were almost twice what they are now; when there was plenty of household trash to be recycled, but almost no recycling going on; when only a third of the bodies of water in the country were safe for fishing and swimming, whereas today two-thirds are.

Simply put, there has been a profound change with respect to the environment in the United States over the past 35 years. From pollution controls to species protection to personal recycling, environmentalism has entered not only our law books but, more important, our consciousness. When populations of Atlantic swordfish were observed to be declining in the late 1990s, a campaign titled "Give Swordfish a Break" was organized that quickly enlisted 27 top New York chefs. What could chefs do about swordfish populations? They pledged to take swordfish off their restaurants' menus. It was government action that brought the Atlantic swordfish population back to healthy levels, but initial public awareness of the swordfish campaign came about because of *personal* sensitivity to the environment—in this case, the sensitivity of a group of American chefs. And sensitivity to the environment has grown not just in America but in most developed countries. The cleanup of Lake Erie required the cooperation of the United States and Canada; the heartening trend in preservation of the Earth's ozone layer is the product of an international agreement. (Adapted from Krogh 736) (349 words)

1. Paragraph 1
   Opinion: ____________________
   ____
   Fact: ____________________
   ____
   Inference: ____________________
   ____

2. Paragraph 2
   Opinion: ____________________
   ____
   Fact: ____________________
   ____
   Inference: ____________________
   ____

3. Paragraph 3
   Opinion: ____________________
   ____
   Fact: ____________________
   ____
   Inference: ____________________
   ____

Before you go on . . .

Monitor Your Progress: recite

As you read . . .

Focus Your Efforts: question and read

Essays and Articles

THINK ABOUT THIS . . .

1. Think about the essays and articles you've read as class assignments.
   a. What classes were they assigned in?
   ____
   b. Why do you think the instructor assigned them?
   ____
   c. From your experience, what's the difference between essays and articles?
   ____
2. Reminder: Preread this section.

College professors generally assign essays and articles in addition to textbook chapters. These readings provide current information, alternative views, and controversial topics that go beyond the textbook assignments. Often students are not sure what they are supposed to do with them. Professors typically say "read or think about this," or "we'll discuss this next time," which sounds like "skim it and think about your own beliefs." But then in class, or on exams, you may find that the instructor expects in-depth comprehension and analysis of the text. In fact, when college professors say "think about this" or "read this for a discussion," they usually mean "read this text critically." That requires a process that goes beyond skimming and literal comprehension. It requires you to analyze the author's presentation of the content and evaluate its merits.

Read Essays Critically

Essays are a form of expository writing in which the author's general purpose is to present information. But the emphasis in an **essay** is on the author's personal ideas or experiences. Thus, essays are often a combination: they may contain a good deal of information, but that information is used as support for the author's opinions.

In Chapter 2, you learned to use PDQ3R as a way to promote motivated, essay reading. In this section, you will see how to add inferential comprehension and critical reading to that approach. To do this, you'll focus each step of PDQ3R on analyzing or evaluating the author's points.

Analyze the Points From prereading on, critical readers analyze essays by looking for the author's main idea and how it is developed. More specifically, they look for the structural elements that are common in essay writing. You are probably familiar with these elements. They are the title, introduction, thesis, body paragraphs, topic sentences, and conclusion. Look over Table 9.2; it briefly describes each part.

TABLE 9.2 **Essay Elements**

ELEMENT	PURPOSE	DESCRIPTION
Title	Attract the reader's attention	May state the essay topic directly or provide an intriguing phrase
Introduction	Draw readers into the essay subject	Usually includes: A *hook,* or attention getter, such as an interesting question, quote, story, or example *Background* information about the topic A *lead-in* to the body section, which may be the thesis Can be more than one paragraph long
Thesis	A statement of the author's dominant message or main idea for the essay	May come in the introduction, conclusion, or be unstated
Body Paragraph	A group of related sentences that support one part of the essay's main idea	Uses the same structure as those used in textbook chapters (see Chapter 6) May have a stated topic sentence anywhere in the paragraph or an implied main idea Is supported by the details in the other sentences
Conclusion	End the discussion by presenting the author's final points on the topic and the main idea	Often ends with a *clincher,* or decisive, final statement for the reader to think about

Look at the following sample essay. Notice the labeled elements.

EXAMPLE

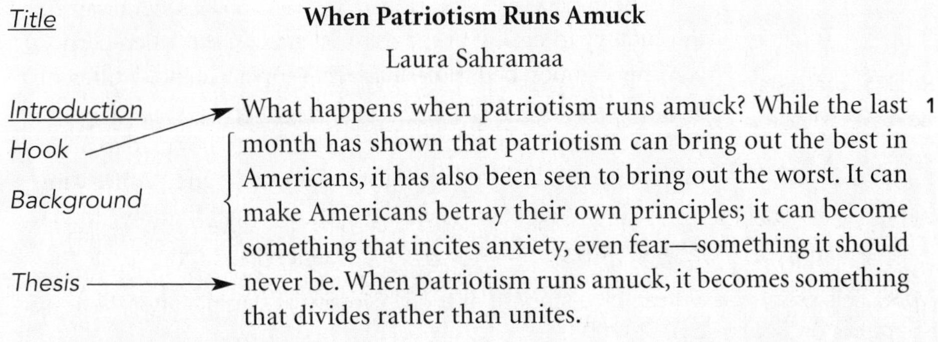

When Patriotism Runs Amuck

Laura Sahramaa

What happens when patriotism runs amuck? While the last month has shown that patriotism can bring out the best in Americans, it has also been seen to bring out the worst. It can make Americans betray their own principles; it can become something that incites anxiety, even fear—something it should never be. When patriotism runs amuck, it becomes something that divides rather than unites. 1

Body = Para 2-4
Topic Sentence
Details

Of all places, the most overt example of out-of-control 2
patriotism can be found in Wisconsin. In order to comply with a state law that requires a daily show of patriotism in public schools, the Madison School Board decided to eliminate saying the Pledge of Allegiance as an option. They wanted to avoid making students of different backgrounds uncomfortable; also, some parents were concerned about the religious aspect of the line containing "one nation, under God." Instead of having students recite the pledge, the board instead decided that schools would play an instrumental version of the Star-Spangled Banner every day. They felt it would be a more subtle form of patriotism and would ensure that students of all religions and backgrounds would feel comfortable in school.

Topic Sentence
Details

Their decision was met with outrage. The school board 3
received over 20,000 angry phone calls and e-mails, many from out of state. Some people suggested that the school board "move to Afghanistan"; others called the board's decision a "treasonous act." One woman wrote, "I am sick of weak individuals [like you] who are afraid to stand up to the minority voices in this country, and are afraid to tell them to 'get a life.' " "If you can't pledge allegiance to this flag, then go somewhere else," one Madison resident said. Sadly, the Madison School Board caved into the tremendous pressure and reversed its position.

Details
Topic Sentence
Details

Patriotism is out of control when normally reasonable peo- 4
ple become a shouting mob that throws around words like "treason," when an instrumental version of the Star-Spangled Banner just isn't patriotic enough. Wherever Americans are acting like this, they need to take a step back: They need to remember who they are and look at what they're doing. If they do not, things that previously have been valued greatly in this country—principles like tolerance and acceptance—will go out the window in the face of this new, almost rabid brand of patriotism.

Conclusion
Return to Thesis
Clincher →

The initial wave of patriotism was self-medicating, a way for 5
the country to deal with the terrorist attacks. But when patriotism runs amuck, bad things happen. People who hold different beliefs are divided when they should be feeling close to each other. Americans begin robbing themselves of things they used to pride themselves on, like multiculturalism and tolerance. Americans should love their country, but not to the extent that they forget what it stands for. (Adapted)

Note: This essay was written by a student at the University of Virginia after the terrorist attacks on September 11, 2001.

In Chapter 2, you learned how to combine the stages of motivation and the PDQ3R processes to read essays. Now you can perfect that method by paying more attention to the essay elements. More specifically, predict (or guess) what the topic and thesis are as you preread. Then verify (or check your guesses) as you read. (See Chapter 6 for more about predicting and verifying.) Here's a list of the reading processes and what to think about as you read essays:

***Engage:* preread and divide**

Preread and predict a likely topic and thesis.
Divide the essay; predict the number of body points. Set a goal.

***Focus:* question and read**

Form questions about the topic and thesis, as well as other key points.
Read to verify your predictions and find answers to your questions.
 Modify your predictions as needed.
 Mark the text with underlining and margin notes.

***Monitor and Reflect:* recite and review**

Recite what you marked; add insights and inferences to your margin notes.
Review the text; form your own opinions and evaluate the author's points.

ACTIVITY 10: IDENTIFY ESSAY ELEMENTS

DIRECTIONS: Read the following essay and answer the questions as soon as you can.

Essay 1

Engage: preread and divide

1. The predicted essay topic is: ______________________________.
2. The first few words of the predicted thesis are:

   ____
3. Look at the body. How many points does the author seem to present? ______
4. Set a goal.

   I want to ____________________ about ______________________.

   My reward(s) will be ______________________________________

   ____.

Focus: question and read

5. Question, read, and mark the essay.
   a. Form questions about the topic, thesis, and other key points as you read.
   b. Mark the important information and identify the essay elements (i.e., useful questions and answers, the introduction, hook, background information, thesis, body paragraphs, topic sentences, conclusion, and clincher).
   c. Modify and correct your predictions, if needed.

Notes

Champagne Taste, Beer Budget

Delia Cleveland

My name is Dee, and I'm a recovering junkie. Yeah, I was hooked on the strong stuff. Stuff that emptied my wallet and maxed out my credit card during a single trip to the mall. I was a fashion addict. I wore a designer emblem on my chest like a badge of honor and respect. But the unnatural high of sporting a pricey label distorted my understanding of what it really meant to have "arrived." 1

At first I just took pride in being the best-dressed female at my high school. Fellows adored my jiggy style; girls were insanely jealous. I became a fiend for the attention. In my mind, clothes made the woman and everything else was secondary. Who cared about geometry? Every Friday I spent all my paltry paycheck from my part-time job on designer clothes. Life as I knew it revolved around a classy façade. Then slowly my money started getting tight, so tight I even resorted to borrowing from my mother. Me, go out looking average? Hell no! I'd cut a class or wouldn't bother going to school at all, unable to bear the thought of friends saying that I had fallen off and was no longer in vogue. 2

Out of concern, my mother started snooping around my bedroom to see where my paycheck was going. She found a telltale receipt I'd carelessly left in a shopping bag. Worse, she had set up a savings account for me, and I secretly withdrew most of the money—$1,000—to satisfy my jones.* Then I feverishly charged $600 for yet another quick fashion fix. 3

"Delia, you're turning into a lunatic, giving all your hard-earned money to multimillionaires!" she screamed. 4

"Mama," I shrugged, "you're behind the times." I was looking fly,† and that was all that mattered. 5

Until I got left back in the tenth grade. 6

The fact that I was an A student before I discovered labels put fire under my mother's feet. In her eyes, I was letting brand names control my life, and 7

**Jones* is a craving for something.

†*Fly* is cool or fabulous.

I needed help. Feeling she had no other choice, she got me transferred to another school. I had screwed up so badly that a change did seem to be in order. Besides, I wanted to show her that labels couldn't control me. So even though everyone, including me, knew I was "smart" and an excellent student, I found myself at an alternative high school.

Meanwhile, I began looking at how other well dressed addicts lived to see where they were headed. The sobering reality: They weren't going anywhere. In fact, the farthest they'd venture was the neighborhood corner or a party—all dressed up, nowhere to go. I watched them bop around in $150 hiking boots—they'd never been hiking. They sported $300 ski jackets—never went near a slope. I saw parents take three-hour bus trips to buy their kids discount-price designer labels, yet these parents wouldn't take a trip to make a bank deposit in their child's name. Watching them, I was forced to look at myself, at my own financial and intellectual stagnation, at the soaring interest on my overused credit card. 8

That's when it all became clear. At my new high school I attended classes with adults—less emphasis on clothes, more emphasis on work. Although the alternative school gave me invaluable work experience, I never received the kind of high school education I should have had—no sports, no prom, no fun. I realized I had sacrificed an important part of my life for material stuff that wasn't benefiting me at all. 9

That was twelve years ago. Today I'm enjoying a clean-and-sober lifestyle. Armed with a new awareness, I've vowed to leave designer labels to people who can truly afford them. I refuse to tote a $500 baguette until I can fill it with an equal amount of cash. I'm not swaggering around in overpriced Italian shoes till I can book a trip to Italy. On my road to recovery, I have continued to purchase clothing—sensibly priced. And every now and then, the money I save goes toward a Broadway play or a vacation in the sun. I'm determined to seek the culture my designer clothes once implied I had. I no longer look the part—because I'm too busy living it. 10

(720 words)

Monitor and Reflect: recite and review

6. Add any insights and inferences you have about the author's points.

____

____

____

____

7. What are your opinions about this topic?

____

____

____

____

As noted above, the thesis is not always in the first paragraph. Sometimes the essay's main idea is located in the conclusion, and sometimes it's unstated. Why would an author construct an essay this way?

Expect a thesis in the conclusion when the essay narrates a story or presents an argument on a controversial subject. In narratives, readers lose interest if they're told the end or main point of the story before the details. In arguments, they might dismiss the idea or simply not read on if they disagree with it. So, in these cases, the author "works up to" the idea, and the essay is a process of discovery for the reader. You can often recognize the concluding thesis because it's a kind of "super idea" that all the other points lead up to. It may also be introduced by signals such as *in conclusion, finally, the most important point, so, thus, therefore,* or *in summary.*

When the thesis is implied, authors want the story or argument to stand on its own. They assume that readers will understand it and may even appreciate the main idea more if they have to reflect for a moment and figure out what it is. If you don't find a thesis anywhere in the essay, form a general main idea statement as part of the recite step. See Chapter 6, Implied Ideas for Sections (p. 266) for more about forming main ideas.

ACTIVITY 11: IDENTIFY A CONCLUDING THESIS OR IMPLIED MAIN IDEA

DIRECTIONS: Read the following essays and answer the questions as soon as you can. One of the essays does not have a stated thesis. For that essay, write your own main idea during the recite step as one of your inferences for Question 6.

Essay 1

Engage: preread and divide

1. The predicted essay topic is: _______________.
2. The first few words of the predicted thesis (if there is one) are:

____

3. Look at the body. How many points does the author seem to present? ______

4. Set a goal.
   I want to ____________________ about ____________________.
   My reward(s) will be ____
   ____.

Focus: question and read

5. Question, read, and mark the essay.
   a. Form questions about the topic, thesis, and other key points as you read.
   b. Mark the important information and identify essay elements (i.e., useful questions and answers, the introduction, hook, background information, thesis, body paragraphs, topic sentences, conclusion, and clincher).
   c. Modify and correct your predictions, if needed.

Cultural Identity vs. Ethnic Fashions

Sunita Puri

Notes

1 I live a hyphenated existence. South Asian–American. Indian-American. Punjabi-American. Physically, I am also a patchwork of different cultures: I wear jeans and T-shirts, I braid my hair in Punjabi *kudiya* style, have a nose ring, and wear a *bindi,* a small colored dot worn in between the eyebrows by South Asian women. Depending on who you talk to, though, I can be seen as an Indian trying to be "fashionably ethnic" in superficially "multicultural" American surroundings. While my extended family sympathizes with my efforts to reconcile my sense of belonging to both India and America, I do not meet with such understanding from those surrounding me who interpret my wearing *bindis* as a fashion statement rather than a statement of cultural belonging.

2 I recently had a conversation with an acquaintance who believed that I wear *bindis* because, in his words, "It's a, you know, convenient way to sort of like assert an identity. Like, you're making a statement, but it's not offensive or anything. It's actually fashionable." I was shocked, especially at his claim that many others agreed with him. I wear my *bindis* to demonstrate my adherence to and respect for my culture and religion and the large roles they occupy in my identity and everyday life—not to imitate a pop icon. My acquaintance then pulled out a picture

of Destiny's Child, taken at a recent awards program. Not only were the women clad in outfits made from sari material, but they all sported matching, colorfully flashy *bindis.*

This is cultural imperialism at its worst. Pop icons like Madonna perpetuate a faulty understanding of Indian culture by selecting exotic images from India, such as the *bindi,* taking them completely out of cultural context and popularizing them in the West. What people like Madonna don't realize, however, is that appropriating the *bindi* in such a way has devastating effects on the symbol's meaning in South Asia. For example, while in Delhi over the summer, I was hard pressed to find plain red *bindis,* finding instead very flashy, so-called "export quality" *bindis,* replete with sparkles and a variety of colors. The *bindi* is no longer what it once was—a symbol of being Hindu and of having a symbolic union with God. Now, it is not only a fashionable item to wear, but is also mass-produced specifically for export to other countries. The Madonnas and Gwen Stefanis of the world—along with those who have blindly followed their example—have successfully changed the meaning of the *bindi* in South Asia, for the worse. 3

And this new meaning obviously extends to South Asian–Americans, among them young women such as myself who are labeled as consumers of teenybopper culture rather than as heirs to the cultural legacy represented in small part by *bindis.* My stomach turns when I see non–South Asians wearing *bindis* to proms, social events, or simply "as part of their outfits." Without realizing it, they are transforming the meaning of the *bindi* from an inherently sacred entity to an accessory whose popularity will undoubtedly fade, as all trends do. And the popularization of this trend may suggest to our peers that those of us who wear *bindis* to bridge our hyphenated existences do so only to assert cultural identity in an acceptable, Americanized way. 4

While I do not mean to imply that all Americans think this way, even knowing a handful that do is insulting, both to me personally and to South Asian 5 culture. How am I, for example, supposed to react when I enter a bookstore and see *The Bindi Kit* lying on the shelf marked International Books? Am I supposed to be happy that *bindis* are now being sold along with body paint in kits that encourage girls to wear *bindis* as exotic belly button ring substitutes surrounded by colorful paint?

One could argue that the *bindi* phenomenon is a good thing because it could motivate interested Americans to examine diverse South Asian cultures and histories more closely. Even though this might be true, I resent the fact that a culture should be considered worthy of study or attention because of the fashion appeal of its symbols or traditions. Assigning new cultural meanings to symbols with very old traditions or deep personal significance is inappropriate and insensitive. It reduces the complexities of South Asian culture to mere physical items, rather than the continual process that culture is. 6

So please—don't wear *bindis,* and don't think of my homeland simply as the origin of yoga, incense, and exoticism if you are going to ignore the context and meanings of these cultural components as well as the reasons why we "ethnic folk" appreciate, treasure, and cling to them. (785 words) 7

Monitor and Reflect: recite and review

6. Add any insights and inferences about the author's points.

____

____

____

____

7. What are your opinions about this topic?

____

____

____

Essay 2

Engage: preread and divide

1. The predicted essay topic is: ______________________________.
2. The first few words of the predicted thesis (if there is one) are:

   ____
3. Look at the body. How many points does the author seem to present? _____
4. Set a goal.

   I want to ____________ about ______________.

   My reward(s) will be ______________________________

   ______________________________.

Focus: question and read

5. Question, read, and mark the essay.
   a. Form questions about the topic, thesis, and other key points as you read.
   b. Mark the important information and identify essay elements (i.e., useful questions and answers, the introduction, hook, background information, thesis, body paragraphs, topic sentences, conclusion, and clincher).
   c. Modify and correct your predictions, if needed.

What the Halloween Man Brought

Susan Messer

Notes

1 It's Halloween, a balmy, magical night for children. My husband took our daughter out trick-or-treating. And I'm alone at home—a nice two-story stucco house in an old tree-lined suburb, right on the edge of Chicago's west side. With half an hour of official trick-or-treat time left, I'm down to my last few Tootsie Rolls. I switch to spare change—nickels, pennies, a few dimes I find lying around. I've got them in a ceramic bowl near the door. I pick up a few coins, drop them in the waiting bags. The kids try to see what landed, but their bags have so much candy and I drop the coins so fast that they can't see them. One little boy says, "Hey, that lady's giving out quarters."

2 I'm not enjoying myself. I recognize few kids from the neighborhood, can't tell what any of the costumes are, and hate to guess, since I'm usually wrong. Vans park on my street and unload bunches of kids. Some don't have costumes at all, just a mask or a smudge of makeup on their little faces. They carry huge dingy pillowcases of candy, and some seem awfully big for trick-or-treating. They arrive on

my porch in large groups, nine, ten at a time, faces shadowed by their jacket hoods, real-life wraiths who make me afraid to open the door.

The bell rings again and I look out. It's a man. No kids. I wonder why he's there, whether I should open the door, but the spirit of Halloween presses me on. 3

"I don't mean any disrespect, ma'am," he says. He holds a mask in one hand, a credential. He stretches the other hand toward me, palm up, a soft brown bowl. "I heard you were giving out quarters." We both look at my bowl. "My wife and I, we wanted to take the children out for hot dogs after trick-or-treating." 4

The ceiling light in my front hall shines like a spotlight on the coins: six pennies and two nickels. I slide them around with the tip of my finger. I want this man to go away. I tip the bowl toward him, so he can see its contents. 5

I am at a loss. The simple Halloween script—rehearsed for ages, we all know it—no longer applies. I'm mad, confused, mistrustful, trapped in a blur of logistics. Should I close the door while I get my purse? It's in the other room, and I don't want to leave the door open. How much do I give him? How much are hot dogs? How many kids? 6

"Sorry," I say to him, "that's not what Halloween's about. It's for the children, a few coins, a few pieces of candy." I shut the door, hands trembling, real-life haunted. (Adapted) (466 words) 7

Monitor: recite

6. Add any insights and inferences about the author's points.

____

____

____

____

7. What are your opinions about this topic?

____

____

____

____

YEAH, GORG, I REALLY LIKE IT. BUT IT ISN'T ART.

Evaluate the Points As part of the final review step in PDQ3R, critical readers evaluate the merits of the essay message. This is an analysis and explanation of how well the author communicated the message. Unlike the thinking in the cartoon, it is not simply a statement of personal likes and dislikes or conclusions without reasons.

Critical readers evaluate the strengths and weakness in the main idea and whether or not the purpose was achieved. So, they think about the following elements and questions:

1. Consider the thesis or main idea: Is it worthy of consideration?
2. Consider the purpose:
   a. What is the author's purpose?
   b. Do the facts and opinions adequately support the purpose?
   c. Does the tone support the purpose?
   d. Did the author achieve his/her purpose?

The example shows how this thinking might be done with the essay in the example on p. 425.

EXAMPLE

1. Is the thesis worthy of consideration?

The thesis is certainly something we should think about. It promotes important questions such as what is patriotism? Can it go too far? What happens if it does go too far?

2. Consider the purpose:

a. What is the author's purpose?

The author wants to show that excessive patriotism jeopardizes our most cherished principles.

b. Do the facts and opinions adequately support the purpose?

The facts in the one example are relevant and current. But the source is not revealed. On the other hand, the example does support the purpose, because it is a good illustration of what the author means by patriotism that "runs amuck" and what is lost by such behavior.

The opinions are reasonable and useful. But they are supported by only one example, which does not prove that the problem is widespread.

c. Does the tone support the purpose?

The author's diction is clearly critical of the "normally reasonable people" who "become a shouting mob." Her tone is urgent, very concerned, and disapproving, which is appropriate for her message that people should not act this way.

d. Did the author achieve his/her purpose?
The author has demonstrated what can happen when patriotism goes too far and how such behaviors are the opposite of the principles we value. More examples would be useful to show that the problem is widespread and, thus, a threat to our principles.

ACTIVITY 12: ANALYZE AND EVALUATE ESSAYS

DIRECTIONS: Evaluate the essays in activities 10 and 11. Explain each of your answers in detail. Use your own paper.

1. Is the thesis or main idea worthy of consideration?
2. Consider the purpose:
   a. What is the author's purpose?
   b. Do the facts and opinions adequately support the purpose?
   c. Does the tone support the purpose?
   d. Did the author achieve his/her purpose?

Read Articles Critically

Newspapers and news magazines are a common source of texts for college courses. The writings in these sources include articles, opinion columns, and editorials. Opinion pieces and editorials tend to follow the format of essays. But articles written by reporters have a unique style.

What distinguishes articles from essays is that articles focus on recounting events or information rather than expressing and proving an opinion. The purpose of an **article** is to provide a report of an event, situation, or new discovery. Articles tend to have an objective style. Their format is similar to essays, because they have a title, introduction, body, and conclusion, but these elements are called the headline, lead, development, and conclusion. Articles typically do not have a thesis, because the author's personal opinion is not part of this type of writing. There are two major types of articles: news stories and feature articles.

> I still believe that if your aim is to change the world, journalism is a more immediate short-term weapon.
>
> —Tom Stoppard (1937–), Czech playwright

News Stories **News stories** report information about a current event. To be news, the story must be about an event that is reported as soon as it happens or as soon as it's discovered. The type of information in news stories is very specific. It focuses on what is often called "the 5 Ws": *what* the event was, *who* was involved, and *where, when,* and *why* it occurred. Other information, such as *how* the discovery or event affects people, quotes from appropriate people, and sources for the information may also be provided. But, generally, you will not find all of this information in a single article; only the most important and newsworthy details are given.

In news stories, the most important information is initially presented in the *headline* and first paragraph, or *lead,* as it's called. The *development,* or middle paragraphs, presents more details about what was introduced in the lead. This information is organized in short paragraphs, written in the order of most to least important. The *conclusion,* which is the last paragraph is simply a final point, example, or quote. Because it will be the first to be cut if the article is shortened, it is not an essential piece of information.

Look at the following sample news story. Notice the four structural elements. Also look at the circled points in the lead and how the development goes back and forth about them.

EXAMPLE

Headline

A City of Quitters? In Strict New York, 11% Fewer Smokers

Richard Pérez-Peña

Lead

In the wake of huge tobacco tax increases and a ban on smoking **1**
in bars, the number of adult smokers in New York City fell 11 percent from 2002 to 2003, one of the steepest short-term declines ever measured, according to surveys commissioned by the city.

Development

The surveys, to be released today, show that after holding **2**
steady for a decade, the number of regular smokers dropped more than 100,000 in a little more than a year, to 19.3 percent of adults from 21.6 percent. The decline occurred across all boroughs, ages and ethnic groups.

The surveys also found a 13 percent decline in cigarette con- **3**
sumption, suggesting that smokers who did not quit were smoking less. Like similar local and national polls, the surveys counted as smokers all people who said that they had smoked more than 100 cigarettes in their lives and that they now smoked every day or "some days."

City health officials and opponents of smoking said they be- **4**
lieved that the decline was caused primarily by sharply higher tobacco taxes that went into effect in 2002, including an increase to $1.50 from 8 cents a pack in New York City.

The drop also coincided with a new city law banning smok- **5**
ing in bars, a new state law prohibiting it in restaurants and bars, and the Bloomberg administration's aggressive anti-smoking campaign, which has included advertising and the distribution of free nicotine patches to thousands of people.

Administration officials said that the 2002 and 2003 telephone **6**
surveys were conducted for the Department of Health and Mental Hygiene by Baruch College researchers using identical methods and that the random dialing approach and questions were the

same as those used in annual surveys by the federal Centers for Disease Control and Prevention. They also point out that the city polls used very large samples, 10,000 people each time, which pollsters say makes the results more authoritative. The margin of sampling error is plus or minus 1 percentage point, officials said.

New York State raised its tax on cigarettes from 56 cents a pack 7
to $1.11 in March 2000, and on April 1, 2002, lifted it to $1.50, one of the highest tobacco taxes in the country. New York City raised its tax on July 1, 2002, from 8 cents to $1.50, by far the highest local levy in the country. The federal tax rose to 34 cents from 24 cents in January 2000, and to 39 cents on Jan. 1, 2002.

So the combined city, state and federal levies on a pack stood at 8
88 cents at the end of 1999, $1.53 at the end of 2001, and $3.39 by mid-2002.

A new city law took effect on April 1, 2003, prohibiting smok- 9
ing in bars and eliminating limited exceptions to the previous ban on smoking in restaurants. A statewide ban in restaurants and bars took effect on July 24.

The city conducted its 2002 survey from May to July, and the 10
2003 canvass from April to November.

Conclusion Health researchers say that smoking cuts short the lives of about 11
one-third of long-term smokers, by an average of about 14 years. Dr. Frieden, the city health commissioner, said reducing the smoking population by 100,000 people, if the change is permanent, "means that there will be at least 30,000 fewer premature deaths." (Adapted)

ACTIVITY 13: IDENTIFY THE TYPES OF INFORMATION

DIRECTIONS: The following pieces of information are from the sample news article. Refer to the article as needed to answer the following questions.

Task 1: Match the type of information to each item from the headline and lead.

a. what **b.** who **c.** where **d.** when **e.** why **f.** how **g.** quotes **h.** source

_____ **1.** A City of Quitters?

_____ **2.** Strict New York

_____ **3.** 11% Fewer Smokers

_____ **4.** In the wake of huge tobacco tax increases and a ban on smoking in bars

_____ **5.** the number of adult smokers in New York City fell 11 percent

_____ **6.** from 2002 to 2003

_____ **7.** according to surveys commissioned by the city

Task 2: Answer these questions about the development.

1. What type of information and topics are covered in the development?

TYPE	TOPICS
______________________	______________________________
______________________	______________________________
______________________	______________________________

2. Using the first topic covered in the development, make a list of all the information presented about it in this article. Use your own paper.

To analyze articles efficiently, use the essay reading approach on articles. But, since articles are so brief and the conclusions do not provide essential information, preread just the headline and lead. Then predict the news event rather than the topic. You won't need to divide the article into parts, although you will still want to focus your attention with a topic-related goal. Make sure to mark the topic of each body paragraph in the development as you read. This will help you keep track of the information as it shifts back and forth between the important points.

ACTIVITY 14: IDENTIFY NEWS ARTICLE ELEMENTS

DIRECTIONS: Read the following news article and answer the questions as soon as you can.

Engage: preread and divide

1. The predicted news event is: ____.

____

2. The newsworthy information includes:
Check off the type of information
_____ what _____ who _____ when _____ where
_____ why _____ how _____ source

3. Set a goal.
I want to ____________________ about ____________________________.
My reward(s) will be ____
____.

Focus: question and read

4. Question, read, and mark the article.

a. Form questions about the event and other key points as you read.

b. Mark the important information and identify the article elements (i.e., useful questions and answers, the 5 Ws, how and/or the source information, as well as the topic of each development paragraph).

c. Modify and correct your predictions, if needed.

New rules set on who can donate human tissue

Lauran Neergaard

Notes

1 WASHINGTON—Donors of sperm, cartilage and other commonly transplanted tissues and cells must be closely checked for infectious diseases, the government said Thursday in rules that aim to tighten safety in the burgeoning but loosely regulated industry.

2 Donated blood and organs have long been strictly regulated. But other donated tissue—such as skin for burn victims, ligaments for knee surgery, umbilical cord blood, and sperm and eggs—are subject to less oversight.

3 Human tissues can carry diseases, and the way cells are handled can make the difference between a therapy that works and one that is wasted or, worse, dangerous when the cells die or are contaminated. That risk made headlines in 2002, when a 23-year-old Minnesota man died after routine knee surgery that used bacteria-laden cartilage.

4 Thursday, the Food and Drug Administration announced rules that could cut risky donations: Tissue banks must test and screen potential donors for signs of infectious diseases that render them ineligible.

5 The FDA had first proposed those rules, and a list of others to strengthen tissue safety, in 1997. The death of Brian Lykins sped up the long-delayed proposals. Federal investigations of the death prompted the FDA to suspend some operations at the nation's largest tissue supplier and identified more than 60 other patients sickened from tainted tissue transplants.

6 With 1 million tissue transplants a year, problems are rare, Dr. Jesse Goodman, FDA's chief of biological products, said Thursday. Still, "we can do a better job," he said. The new rules require tissue banks to test donors and/or donated tissue for the AIDS virus, hepatitis B and C, syphilis and Creutzfeldt-Jakob disease, the human form of mad cow disease. There is no specific test for CJD, so banks instead must perform other checks such as examining the brain of a cadaver donor.

7 Additional testing is required for some tissue donations, such as ensuring that the donors of sperm and eggs don't have the sexually transmitted diseases chlamydia and gonorrhea.

The rules also allow the agency to order checks for new diseases, such as West Nile virus or SARS, as it deems necessary. 8

Tissue banks also must check donors' medical records, for such problems as recent bacterial or fungal infections. (373 words) 9

Monitor and Reflect: recite and review

5. Add any insights and inferences you have about the points in the article.

____

____

____

____

6. What are your opinions about this topic?

____

____

____

____

Since news articles do not have a main idea, you won't need to evaluate whether or not it's worthy of consideration. But you will want to determine whether or not the article achieves the reporter's purpose by considering the following questions:

1. What is the reporter's purpose?
2. Do the facts adequately support the purpose?
3. Does the tone support the purpose?
4. Did the reporter achieve his/her purpose?

The example illustrates this kind of evaluation of the news article on page 438.

EXAMPLE

1. What is the reporter's purpose?
The article has two purposes: to report the results of the surveys and to identify the causes for reduced smoking in New York City.

2. Do the facts adequately support the purpose?
While there are plenty of relevant and current facts, and the source (the surveys) appears to be reliable, it is not clear exactly what the 11 percent figure covers since it appears to contradict the 2 percent drop mentioned in the first development paragraph.

3. Does the tone support the purpose?
The tone is objective, serious, direct, informative, and authoritative. It supports the purpose very well.

4. Did the reporter achieve his purpose?

Except for the statistical issue, ample information is presented and the two purposes are achieved.

ACTIVITY 15: ANALYZE AND EVALUATE A NEWS ARTICLE

DIRECTIONS: Determine whether or not the article in Activity 14 achieves the reporter's purpose by answering the following questions. Use your own paper.

1. What is the reporter's purpose?

2. Do the facts adequately support the purpose?

3. Does the tone support the purpose?

4. Did the reporter achieve his/her purpose?

Feature Stories **Feature stories** are designed to interpret, give background information, or focus on the human-interest aspects of topics or events. They still use the headline, lead, development, and conclusion format, as well as the emphasis on the 5 Ws and the how. But because the focus is on interpretation and human interest, the type of information found in each part differs in the following ways from what is found in news articles:

1. *Headlines* are more indirect to increase the reader's curiosity.
2. The *lead* is still designed to attract the reader's attention, but it may not open with the 5 Ws. Instead, writers tend to use the kinds of hooks you find in essays, and they often write a lead that is more than one paragraph long.
3. The *development* presents the event and the newsworthy 5 Ws, how, quotes, and sources. Typically, it provides description and explanation, along with facts.

The following example of the beginning of a feature story illustrate these characteristics.

EXAMPLE

Headline	**When Students' Gains Help Teachers' Bottom Line**
Lead	As a teacher of emotionally disturbed children, Jeremy Abshire sets goals for each of his students. Geronimo, 14, an American Indian who knew only the letters for "Jerry," will read and write, and sign his true name. Shaneesa, a meek 12-year-old reading at a first-grade level, will catch up to her middle-school peers and attend regular classes in the fall.
what/who	Under a proposal approved by teachers here and to be considered by voters next year, if Mr. Abshire's students reach the goals he sets, his salary will grow. But if his classroom becomes a mere holding tank, his salary, too, will stagnate.

why	"The bottom line is, do you reward teachers for just sitting here and sticking it out, or for doing something?" said Mr. Abshire, who has been teaching for four years. "The free market doesn't handle things that way, so why should it be any different here?"
Development *when/where/who* *what*	In March, Denver's teachers became the first in a major city to approve, by a 59 percent majority, a full-scale overhaul of the salary structure to allow "pay for performance," a controversial approach that rewards teachers for the progress of their students. (Adapted from Schemo)

With slight adjustments, PDQ3R works well on feature stories. First, you will need to preread more: look at the headline, lead, and as many paragraphs as needed to find and predict the event. Second, look for both an event and a topic. The event will be a specific situation; the topic will be an issue of interest to many people. In the sample above, for example, the information about Jeremy Abshire is the event. The pay for performance issue is the topic.

ACTIVITY 16: READ FEATURE ARTICLES CRITICALLY

DIRECTIONS: Read the following feature article and answer the questions as soon as you can.

Engage: preread and divide

1. What is the article about?
   - **a.** The predicted event is: ____
     ____.
   - **b.** The predicted human-interest topic is: ______________________________
     ____.
2. Set a goal.
   I want to ______________________ about ______________________________.
   My reward(s) will be ____
   ____.

Focus: question and read

1. Question, read, and mark the article.
   - **a.** Form questions about the event, 5W information, and other key points as you read.
   - **b.** Mark the important information and identify the article elements (i.e., useful questions and answers, the 5 Ws, how and/or the source information, as well as the topic of each development paragraph).
   - **c.** Modify and correct your predictions, if needed.

Three days without a word becomes an eternity

May Wong, AP Technology Writer

Notes

Christina Rainie had been trying to reach her friend 1
for three days. For some reason, he wasn't responding to her wireless text messages, online instant messages, or cell phone calls.

When the pair of University of Georgia fresh- 2
men finally did make contact on the fourth day, they argued—heated cell phone exchanges interspersed with apologetic text messages.

A frustrated Rainie decided she no longer 3
wanted him to be her date for the upcoming sorority dance.

"Three days? It's like eternity!" she explained. 4

For a generation accustomed to near-instanta- 5
neous keeping in touch—primarily via instant messaging, cell phones and email—Rainie's complaint doesn't seem so far fetched, especially since she and her generational peers are perfectly comfortable roaming in a social sphere where real face-to-face encounters take a back seat to cyber contact.

Yet it's unclear whether the relative ease of digital 6
communication boosts or harms developing young adults. While it may widen social circles, it also raises questions about whether skills suffer for handling the vibrant, breathing real world.

"Sometimes I long for the days when kids went 7
outside and played and were not so wired," said Sid Royer, a Seattle lawyer with a daughter, 18, and a son, 21.

"To some extent, it affects their creativity and 8
their attention span and there's a desire to have everything immediately."

Then again, "were it not for cell phones and 9
emails, I'd have much less contact with both my children," who are away at school.

For better or worse, the new era is here. 10

"Digital devices are the social lubricant now," 11
said Derek White, an executive vice president at Alloy Inc., a youth marketing and research firm.

While their time spent in front of the computer 12
and on line has grown, teens are now spending less time on other social activities. In a 2004 survey of

youths 13 to 18, White said the number of teens going to the mall and on dates dropped by 5 percent, compared to 1997. Those going to dances decreased by 10 percent.

Chris Saribay, 17, of Hawaii, quit the regular school scene altogether for an all-online public high school, where he watches video lectures and frequently instant-messages or emails his teachers. But the junior is anything but lonely—he has friends from all over the world and has maxed out the allowed instant-messaging buddy list of 200. 13

"It's great—50 years ago this was impossible. Your friends ranged from those maybe five miles away to across the hall," Saribay said. "But this generation, we could communicate with whoever we want—time and place doesn't matter." 14

While experts agree that online communication can be as wonderful or painful as it is in the off-line world, they are only in the first stages of studying how faceless interactions affect a teen's social development. Initial observations are that, more than shaping one's personality, the use of online communication extends existing habits and traits. 15

"If they happen to not be physically active already in life, then I think the Internet just pushes them in the direction of not doing anything," said Kaveri Subrahmanyam, an associate professor of child development at CSU Los Angeles. "But if they're already active, the Internet doesn't pull them away; it just bolsters their activity." (Adapted) (553 words) 16

Monitor and Reflect: recite and review

4. Add any insights and inferences you have about the points in the article.

____

____

____

____

5. What are your opinions about this topic?

____

____

____

____

6. Consider the purpose:
   a. What is the reporter's purpose?

   b. Do the facts adequately support the purpose?

   c. Does the tone support the purpose?

   d. Did the reporter achieve his/her purpose?

Before you go on . . .

Monitor Your Progress: recite

After you read . . .

Reflect on Your Gains: review

CHAPTER SUMMARY

Introduction

There are three levels of comprehension: literal, inferential, and critical. **Literal,** or basic **comprehension,** deals with what's directly stated; **inferential comprehension** is focused on what is implied; **critical reading** involves analysis and evaluation of the message. Both inferential and critical comprehension are needed to draw conclusions about a text.

The Author's Purpose

The author's **purpose** is the objective that the writer wants to achieve. There are three general purposes: to inform, entertain, and persuade. In addition, writers have more specific purposes that relate to the topic and the readers of the text. To determine what the purpose is, readers need to identify what is emphasized and then draw conclusions about it. With that in mind, the critical reader can evaluate how well the writer achieved his or her goal.

The Author's Tone

Tone is the author's attitude toward the subject. To determine the tone, critical readers examine the language, looking not only for **denotation** but also for **connotation** to determine undertones of meanings. They also evaluate the writing to determine whether the tone supports the purpose and gains the reader's respect.

Facts and Opinions

Distinguishing facts from opinions is important because they are evaluated with different criteria. In addition, analyzing these two also allows the reader to make inferences. A **fact** is a piece of information that can be proven to be true or false. To be considered good support, facts must be true, current, relevant, and reliable. An **opinion** is a person's conclusions or judgments about people, places, or things. To be convincing, it must be relevant, useful, reasonable, and well supported with details. **Inferencing** means figuring out unstated messages. You infer the author's purpose and tone, as well as any points that are **implied,** or only hinted at, in the text.

Essays and Articles

To read essays and articles critically, readers analyze the structure of the content and then evaluate the merits of the message. An **essay** is an expository text designed to give the author's personal ideas or experiences. It has five structural elements: the title, introduction, thesis, body paragraphs, and conclusion. **Articles,** which include **news stories** and **feature articles,** provide a report of an event, situation, or new discovery. Articles have four structural elements: the headline, lead, development, and conclusion. Critical readers can use PDQ3R to analyze the structural elements in both essays and articles and evaluate the merits of the points.

REVIEW ACTIVITIES

Use the following activities to check your understanding and aid your learning of the information in this chapter.

Expand Your Vocabulary

Match each term with the correct definition or characteristic.

______ **1.** literal comprehension
______ **2.** inferential comprehension
______ **3.** critical reading
______ **4.** purpose
______ **5.** tone
______ **6.** denotation
______ **7.** connotation
______ **8.** fact
______ **9.** opinion
______ **10.** imply
______ **11.** infer
______ **12.** essay
______ **13.** article
______ **14.** news story
______ **15.** feature article

a. the writer's attitude about a subject
b. writing that presents the author's personal ideas or experiences
c. a provable piece of information
d. writing which reports on an event, situation, or discovery
e. to determine what the author is implying
f. understanding information that is directly stated
g. an article that reports information about a current event
h. an article about the human-interest aspects of a topic
i. to suggest a point
j. judgments about people, places, ideas, or things
k. understanding what an author implies
l. the objective a writer wants to achieve with readers
m. the dictionary definition of a word
n. analysis and evaluation based on appropriate criteria
o. the implied or emotional meaning of a word

Increase Your Knowledge

The following tasks will help you assess how well you understand the ideas presented in this chapter. They will also help you prepare for quizzes and exams on this material.

1. The following questions focus on the major chapter topics. Discuss them with others to form your own detailed answers.
  a. What is purpose? How do you figure out what an author's purpose is? How do you evaluate it?
  b. What is tone? Provide example terms from each of the seven general categories of tone. How do critical readers determine the author's tone? How do they evaluate it?

c. Define the terms *fact* and *opinion*. What are the characteristics of each one? How do critical readers evaluate facts? How do they assess opinions?
d. What is the difference between imply and infer? How do critical readers draw inferences?
e. What are essays? How do critical readers analyze and evaluate an essay?
f. What are articles, news stories, and feature articles? How do critical readers analyze and evaluate articles?

2. Take notes on the information in this chapter.

Develop Your Skills

The following review tasks will give you an opportunity to practice the methods presented in this chapter.

REVIEW 1: EVALUATE PURPOSE, TONE, FACTS AND OPINIONS Read and mark the following text. As you read, make notes in the margin about the author's tone and use of facts and opinions. Then answer the questions that follow.

Free Speech: A Balancing Act for Schools

Teri Figueroa

Notes

On one high school campus, a student wore a shirt with an anti-gay statement. He did it twice, once on a day other students planned to demonstrate in support of gay rights, and then again the next day. 1

On another campus, a student whose mother is in the military donned a shirt calling war "justifiable homicide." He wore it on a day when other students held a war protest. 2

Both kids found themselves suspended on the grounds that their messages could have caused problems or incited fights. 3

Both incidents happened on North County campuses [in San Diego] in the last few years, and in both cases, school administrators said they were forced to perform a balancing act between allowing free speech for students and avoiding disruption or even violence. 4

The question administrators face is a tough one, they said. They're charged with keeping kids safe. They're charged with state mandates to teach tolerance. And they have to allow students their First Amendment rights of free speech. 5

First Amendment advocates say the Constitution protects kids' speech and that students don't check their first amendment rights at the door of their schools. 6

"It's the government's duty to protect them from attack, not to shut them up," said Terry Francke, who heads up a public rights and open government group called Californians Aware. 7

The courts have made some rulings and given some guidelines, but some administrators said they often find themselves relying on their own judgment about when they should step in when it comes to free speech. 8

The issue of free speech at one Poway school found itself in a federal courtroom this week. 9

The case, filed in June, alleged that officials at Poway High School violated free speech rights of student Tyler Chase Harper in April when they suspended him for writing anti-gay statements such as "homosexuality is shameful" and biblical references on masking tape and placing the tape on his shirt. 10

The boy, who goes by Chase, wore a shirt with a similar homemade message the previous day when an on-campus group was participating in a day of acceptance of homosexuality. 11

The teenager's family is now suing the district for violating his rights to free speech, for "chilling" opposing viewpoints, his attorney argued this week in court. 12

Lawyers for the district responded that Chase's shirt attacked an entire class of people. It also could have led to disruption among students. 13

If only the boy had chosen a positive message for his dissent—maybe love the sinner, hate the sin—the school could have looked the other way, the district's attorney said. But the school is state-mandated to teach tolerance. 14

U.S. District Judge John Houston took the matter under advisement. 15

Whatever the outcome of the Poway situation, school administrators said they still face the possibility that political speech could cause a problem with students. 16

Politics does find its way to the campus. Take the case in March 2003 of El Camino High School in Oceanside when a student wore a shirt that read "War: Justifiable Homicide." At the time, his mother was a Marine stationed in Kuwait. 17

The school suspended the 15-year-old, then quickly reversed itself on the advice of its attorneys. 18

Ken Noonan, the superintendent of the 22,000-student Oceanside Unified School District, said students do have the right to express themselves on campus. 19

"Is it any different from a student who raises their hand in class and says war is justifiable homicide?" Noonan said. "If that statement can be made in the classroom, it can be worn. It's the same intellectual freedom." 20

Noonan also said he believes that school administrators have to make a judgment call on the intent of the person making the statement. The context of the situation, he said, matters. 21

The courts have given schools some guidance, said public rights advocate Francke. In the 1960s, the Supreme Court ruled that students have the right to express opinions through clothing—as long as the message doesn't lead to violence or cause physical disruption. 22

Essentially, the court said, students don't give up their rights when they reach the school grounds. 23

"The courts have said repeatedly that this is something beyond mere uneasiness of school administrators, more than just a kind of anxiety or dread," Francke said. "The standard is disruption, not hurt feelings." 24

The schools also cannot give what is known as a heckler's veto—that is, they cannot censor students at the first sign of complaint by others, he said. 25

The courts have built some wiggle room into the standards of what constitutes campus disruption, said Jordan Budd, the legal director of the American Civil Liberties Union in San Diego and Imperial counties. 26

Mostly, Budd said, the rules are fluid, based on the context of the statement and the situation in which it comes. 27

It's the administrators' responsibility, he said, to 28
conclude that the statement would in fact prevent the school from its mission of education. The disruption must rise to a higher level than simply "ruffling feathers," he said.

"If it's a tinderbox environment where there's a 29
reasonable and rational concern that a situation is at the breaking point . . . it may be acceptable to suppress," Budd said. But the starting point that campuses must have, he said, is that free speech is permissible. (886 words)

1. Purpose

a. Circle the author's primary purpose: inform entertain persuade

b. Who is the intended audience? ______________________________

____

c. Describe the specific purpose.

____

____

____

2. Connotation: Identify the connotative feelings and definitions for the following phrases.

a. It's the government's duty to protect them from attack, not to shut them up.

The connotation is ______ negative ______ positive.

The meaning is ______________________________.

b. The teenager's family is now suing the district for violating his rights to free speech, for "chilling" opposing viewpoints.

The connotation is ______ negative ______ positive.

The meaning is ______________________________.

c. The schools also cannot give what is known as a heckler's veto—that is, they cannot censor students at the first sign of complaint by others.

The connotation is ______ negative ______ positive.

The meaning is ______________________________.

d. The courts have built some wiggle room into the standards of what constitutes campus disruption.

The connotation is ______ negative ______ positive.

The meaning is ______________________________.

e. It's the administrators' responsibility to conclude that the statement would in fact prevent the school from its mission of education. The disruption must rise to a higher level than simply "ruffling feathers."

The connotation is ______ negative ______ positive.

The meaning is ______________________________.

3. Tone

a. In general, the connotative words are ______ negative ______ positive ______ both.

b. The author's tone is ______________________________.

c. Does the tone support the purpose? Does it gain the reader's respect? Explain.

____

____

____

4. Facts and opinions

a. Evaluate the facts. Do they seem to be true, complete, relevant, and trustworthy? Are there enough of them? Explain.

____

____

____

b. Evaluate the opinions. Are they relevant, useful, and reasonable? Explain.

____

____

____

REVIEW 2: IDENTIFY FACTS, OPINIONS, AND INFERENCES Follow the directions for each task.

Task 1: Read the following texts and accompanying statements. Then mark each statement with an O if it's the author's stated or implied opinion, an F if it's a fact presented in the text, and an I if it is an inference created by a reader.

1. Dozens of tests for genetic diseases are already available, and many more are under development. To administer these tests appropriately, the physician or genetic counselor must decide who should receive the tests, and then educate the patients about the disorder and assist them in making a series of difficult decisions about their own health or that of potential offspring. Questions include whether to conceive or adopt a child, whether to have prenatal testing, and whether to abort a fetus with a fatal or permanently debilitating disorder. Should insurance companies pay the lifelong costs to treat children with genetic diseases born to parents who know they carry the defective gene? Both the rapid acquisition of knowledge about genetics and the power to manipulate the genome of humans and other organisms threaten to outpace our ability to deal with the consequences. (Adapted from Audesirk et al. 264)

______ **a.** A great deal of research has been devoted to finding ways to detect genetic diseases.

______ **b.** Physicians and counselors decide who gets the tests.

______ **c.** The questions people must answer about genetic diseases are personal, moral, and even religious matters.

______ **d.** One difficulty with the decisions people must make is that they are based on what might happen in the future.

______ **e.** We know more about genetics than we do about how to deal with the results of genetic issues.

2. All of us are subject to **social control,** attempts by society to regulate people's thought and behavior. Often, this process is informal, as when parents praise or scold their children or friends make fun of someone's clothing or musical tastes. (Adapted from Macionis 190)

______ **a.** Sarcasm is a potentially hurtful kind of informal social control.

______ **b.** Social control happens to everyone.

______ **c.** Social control involves the attempt of others to direct a person's thinking or actions.

3. Japanese Americans faced their greatest challenge after December 7, 1941, when Japan bombed the U.S. naval fleet at Hawaii's Pearl Harbor. Rage toward Japanese living in the United States was made worse by fear that Japanese Americans might spy for Japan or commit acts of sabotage. Within a year, President Franklin Roosevelt signed Executive Order 9066, requiring 110,000 people of Japanese descent to be relocated to inland military camps. (Macionis 372)

______ **a.** President Roosevelt signed Executive Order 9066.

______ **b.** President Roosevelt signed the act in order to help safeguard Americans.

______ **c.** It was feared that some Japanese Americans were spies for Japan.

______ **d.** Many Americans believed that the large Japanese American population was a threat to America.

______ **e.** Many Americans felt intense anger and fear toward Japanese Americans.

Task 2: Read and mark the following text. Put brackets ([. . .]) around each fact; highlight each opinion. Then record two inferences that you could make about the paragraph.

What if you knew that legalizing assisted suicide meant that sick and disabled people who don't ask to die nonetheless would be killed? That's the central question that lawmakers in California will have to address as they consider a bill to legalize assisted suicide to be introduced by Assemblywoman Patty Berg, D–Eureka. Simple fact: After the Netherlands essentially decriminalized the practice of assisted suicide and euthanasia, a government report conducted by Jan Temmelink found that 1,000 patients were killed without requesting to die in 1990, and 900 in 1995. (Saunders)

It can be inferred that

1. ____
____.

2. ____
____.

REVIEW 3: READ ESSAYS CRITICALLY Read the following essays and answer the questions as soon as you can.

Essay 1

Engage: preread and divide

1. The predicted essay topic is: ______________________________.
2. The first few words of the predicted thesis (if there is one) are:
____
3. Look at the body. How many points does the author seem to present? _______
4. Set a goal.
I want to ____________________ about ____________________.
My reward(s) will be ______________________________
____.

Focus: question and read

5. Question, read, and mark the essay.
   a. Form questions about the topic, thesis, and other key points as you read.
   b. Mark the important information and identify the essay elements (i.e., useful questions and answers, the introduction, hook, background information, thesis, body paragraphs, topic sentences, conclusion, and clincher).
   c. Modify and correct your predictions, if needed.

Confessions of an Ex-smoker

Franklin Zimring

Notes

1 Americans can be divided into three groups—smokers, nonsmokers, and that expanding pack of us who have quit. Those who have never smoked don't know what they're missing, but former smokers, ex-smokers, reformed smokers can never forget. We are veterans of a personal war, linked by that watershed experience of ceasing to smoke and by the temptation to have just one more cigarette. For almost all of us ex-smokers, smoking continues to play an important part in our lives. And now that it is being restricted in restaurants around the country and will be banned in almost all indoor public places in New York State,

it is vital that everyone understand the different emotional states cessation of smoking can cause. I have observed four of them; and in the interest of science I have classified them as those of the zealot, the evangelist, the elect, and the serene. Each day, each category gains new recruits.

Not all antitobacco zealots are former smokers, 2
but a substantial number of fire-and-brimstone opponents do come from the ranks of the reformed. Zealots believe that those who continue to smoke are degenerates who deserve scorn, not pity, and the penalties that will deter offensive behavior in public as well. Relations between these people and those who continue to smoke are strained.

One explanation for the zealot's fervor in seek- 3
ing to outlaw tobacco consumption is his own tenuous hold on abstaining from smoking. But I think part of the emotional force arises from sheer envy as he watches and identifies with each lung-filling puff. By making smoking in public a crime, the zealot seeks reassurance that he will not revert to bad habits; give him strong social penalties, and he won't become a recidivist.

No systematic survey has been done yet, but 4
anecdotal evidence suggests that a disproportionate number of doctors who have quit smoking can be found among the fanatics. Just as the most enthusiastic revolutionary tends to make the most enthusiastic counterrevolutionary, many of today's vitriolic zealots include those who had been deeply committed to tobacco habits.

By contrast, the antismoking evangelist does not 5
condemn smokers. Unlike the zealot, he regards smoking as an easily curable condition, as a social disease, and not a sin. The evangelist spends an enormous amount of time seeking and preaching to the unconverted. He argues that kicking the habit is not *that* difficult. After all, *he* did it; moreover, as he describes it, the benefits of quitting are beyond measure and the disadvantages are nil.

The hallmark of the evangelist is his insistence 6
that he never misses tobacco. Though he is less hostile to smokers than the zealot, he is resented more.

Friends and loved ones who have been the targets of his preachments frequently greet the resumption of smoking by the evangelist as an occasion for unmitigated glee.

7 Among former smokers, the distinctions between the evangelist and the elect are much the same as the differences between proselytizing and nonproselytizing religious sects. While the evangelists preach the ease and desirability of abstinence, the elect do not attempt to convert their friends. They think that virtue is its own reward and subscribe to the Puritan theory of predestination. Since they have proved themselves capable of abstaining from tobacco, they are therefore different from friends and relatives who continue to smoke. They feel superior, secure that their salvation was foreordained. These ex-smokers rarely give personal testimony on their conversion. They rarely speak about their tobacco habits, while evangelists talk about little else, Of course, active smokers find such blue-nosed behavior far less offensive than that of the evangelist or the zealot, yet they resent the elect simply because they are smug. Their air of self-satisfaction rarely escapes the notice of those lighting up. For active smokers, life with a member of the ex-smoking elect is less stormy than with a zealot or evangelist, but it is subtly oppressive nonetheless.

8 I have labeled my final category of former smokers the serene. This classification is meant to encourage those who find the other psychic styles of ex-smokers disagreeable. Serenity is quieter than zealotry and evangelism, and those who qualify are not as self-righteous as the elect. The serene ex-smoker accepts himself and also accepts those around him who continue to smoke. This kind of serenity does not come easily nor does it seem to be an immediate option for those who have stopped. Rather it is a goal, an end stage in a process of development during which some former smokers progress through one or more of the less-than-positive psychological points en route. For former smokers, serenity is thus a positive possibility that exists at the end of rainbow. But all former smokers cannot reach that promised land.

What is it that permits some former smokers to become serene? I think the key is self-acceptance and gratitude. The fully mature former smoker knows he has the soul of an addict and is grateful for the knowledge. He doesn't regret that he quit smoking, nor any of his previous adventures with tobacco. As a former smoker, he is grateful for the experience and memory of craving a cigarette. 9

Serenity comes from accepting the lessons of one's life. And ex-smokers who have reached this point in their world view have much to be grateful for. They have learned about the potential and limits of change. In becoming the right kind of former smoker, they developed a healthy sense of self. This former smoker, for one, believes that it is better to crave (one hopes only occasionally) and not to smoke than never to have craved at all. And by accepting that fact, the reformed smoker does not need to excoriate, envy, or disassociate himself from those who continue to smoke. (943 words) 10

Monitor and Reflect: recite and review

6. Add any insights and inferences about the author's points.

____

____

____

____

7. What are your opinions about this topic?

____

____

____

____

8. Is the thesis or main idea an idea that is worthy of consideration?

____

____

9. Consider the purpose:

a. What is the author's purpose?

____

____

b. Do the facts and opinions adequately support the purpose?

____

____

c. Does the tone support the purpose?

____

____

____

d. Did the author achieve his/her purpose?

____

____

Essay 2

Engage: preread and divide

1. The essay topic is: ______________________________.
2. The first few words of the predicted thesis (if there is one) are:

   ____

3. Look at the body. How many points does the author seem to present? ________
4. Set a goal.

   I want to ____________________ about ____________________.

   My reward(s) will be ______________________________

   ____.

Focus: question and read

5. Question, read, and mark the essay.
   - **a.** Form questions about the topic, thesis, and other key points as you read.
   - **b.** Mark the important information and identify the essay elements (i.e., useful questions and answers, the introduction, hook, background information, thesis, body paragraphs, topic sentences, conclusion, and clincher).
   - **c.** Modify and correct your predictions, if needed.

A Not-so-random Act of Kindness

Will Keim

Notes

I have seen many astounding acts of kindness during my twelve years of speaking to over two million college students on more than one thousand college campuses. 1

Students pitching in to collect money to send a student home to see his mother who was dying of cancer. 2

A blood drive to aid automobile victims near campus. 3

Fraternity men who go once a year to the retirement home near their chapter to dance with the older ladies the day before Valentine's Day. 4

Who could doubt the generosity and goodness 5
of college students! Despite media reports to the contrary, college students care deeply about others and the world in which they live.

But one event, though small in national stature 6
or international importance, touched my heart. At Bethany College in West Virginia, I was speaking at a dinner for student leaders, with my five-year-old son, J. J., sitting next to me. After twelve years on the road, I now take one of my children—Christa, Samantha, J. J., or Hannah—with me on every trip. I have just gotten tired of being away from them.

We were eating dinner, when my son made a 7
strange reptile-like sound and deposited his dinner on the table at what could have been called, up to that point, a semiformal event. It is hard in life to always think of the other person when you are dealing with your own agenda and personal embarrassment. In this case, however, I was able to "get over myself" and realize that the little guy was in trouble. We caught the subsequent "blasts" in a bucket quickly provided by one of the students and actually finished the meal—though those with a view of my son's problem passed on dessert!

The big question I then encountered was what 8
to do with his clothes. Being a guy, I reached the conclusion they would be thrown away, justified by the reality that we were traveling and leaving for Cincinnati that night. Suddenly I heard a voice that I now realize belonged to an angel, or perhaps a saint, standing next to me.

She said, "Give me his clothes, and I will wash 9
them during your speech." She was a student at the dinner, she seemed sincere, and I immediately began to question her sanity. Who takes someone else's very dirty clothes and washes them, willingly? We all know it is bad enough doing your own clothes or those of someone you know and love.

"You don't have to do that. I couldn't ask that of 10
you," I said.

"You did not ask," she stated. "And that Tigger 11
sweatshirt is his favorite," she said.

"How do you know that?" 12

"Tigger is my favorite, too," she replied, "and he and I talked about it during dinner." 13

I realized then that I had been wrapped up in myself and missed their entire conversation. I knew, too, that I was dealing with an extraordinary young woman who wanted to reach out to someone in need, even though she had never met us before. As she left with the clothes in a trash bag, I turned to her mentor and said, "She is really something. What year is she?" He said, "A freshman, and what you have seen is a regular occurrence with her." 14

When something silly happens on a campus now, or even a bad thing takes place, I think of that young woman, armed with J. J.'s clothes in a bag, heading for her residence hall. She gives me hope because I know there are others like her. Students who are good and kind—persons who will be in charge of the world my children will grow up in. That night I was theoretically the teacher . . . but in reality, she was my teacher, and I was her humble student. 15

That is the beauty of being an educator. If you are open to the possibilities, there is a good chance that we will exchange roles at times and grow together. Dean Robert Schaffer of Indiana University once said, "I have to believe that the student's life will be better because we have met rather than if we had not, because I know how much richer my life has become because of my students." 16

One fall night in Bethany, West Virginia, my life became richer, my purpose empowered, my spirit lifted because of a not-so-random act of kindness by a wonderful college freshman. (743 words) 17

Monitor and Reflect: recite and review

6. Add any insights and inferences about the author's points.

____

____

____

____

7. What are your opinions about this topic?

____

____

____

8. Is the thesis or main idea an idea that is worthy of consideration?

____

____

9. Consider the purpose:

a. What is the author's purpose?

____

____

b. Do the facts and opinions adequately support the purpose?

____

____

____

c. Does the tone support the purpose?

____

____

____

d. Did the author achieve his/her purpose?

____

____

REVIEW 4: READ NEWS STORIES CRITICALLY Read the following news story and answer the questions as soon as you can.

Engage: preread and divide

1. The predicted news event is: ____.

2. The newsworthy information includes:

Check off the type of information here

______ what ______ who ______ when ______ where ______ why

______ how ______ source

3. Set a goal.

I want to ______________________ about ______________________.

My reward(s) will be ____

____.

Focus: question and read

4. Question, read, and mark the article.

a. Form questions about the event and other key points as you read.

b. Mark the important information and identify the article elements (i.e., useful questions and answers, the 5 Ws, how and/or the source information, as well as the topic of each development paragraph).

c. Modify and correct your predictions, if needed.

Most Travelers Want To Keep In-Flight Cell Phone Ban

Notes

Barbara De Lollis

People who fly at least occasionally are strongly opposed to lifting the ban on cell phone use during flights, according to a new *USA Today*/CNN/Gallup Poll. 1

Almost seven in 10 frequent or occasional fliers want the federal government to keep the ban. Women and fliers 50 or older are the most strongly inclined to keep airline cabins free of cell phone chatter. 2

Cell phone use is banned once the cabin doors are closed for takeoff. Some airlines allow calls once a flight has touched down and is taxiing to the gate. The Federal Communications Commission last month authorized a review of the ban, a first step toward letting fliers chat on phones during flights. 3

Also involved is the Federal Aviation Administration, which is concerned that wireless devices could hinder navigation and communications systems. Airlines, meanwhile, question whether cellular service could be provided profitably. Any policy change could be years away. 4

Many frequent fliers view their time in the sky as their only downtime on a hectic business trip. The absence of cell phones increases the odds that they'll be able to nap, read or think. Others chafe at the enforced downtime and yearn to put it to use with phone calls. 5

Michael Latkovich, 40, of Boynton Beach, Fla., is among those who cringe at the thought of a cacophony of chatter, ring tones and travelers out-talking seatmates. 6

"Such competition on a plane at 33,000 feet is begging for trouble," says Latkovich. "It could get ugly very quickly." 7

Some fliers say that most chats they overhear now upon landing don't warrant disturbing their peace. 8

"I don't want to have to hear someone else yell at their children or remind their spouse to take out the trash," says flier Stacie Edwards, 34, of Rogersville, Tenn. 9

But retired police officer Joe Sylvia of Warwick, R.I., 53, an occasional flier, says he wouldn't mind if cell phone chatter were allowed. "Whether it's a crying baby or somebody on a phone, it wouldn't bother me," he says. (359 words) 10

Monitor: recite

5. Add any insights and inferences you have about the points in the article.

____

____

____

6. What are your opinions about this topic?

____

____

____

7. Consider the purpose:
   a. What is the reporter's purpose?

   ____

   ____

   b. Do the facts adequately support the purpose?

   ____

   ____

   c. Does the tone support the purpose?

   ____

   ____

   d. Did the reporter achieve his/her purpose?

   ____

   ____

REVIEW 5: READ FEATURE STORIES CRITICALLY Use the feature story in Review 1 to answer the following questions.

1. What is the article about?
   a. The predicted event is: ____

   ____.

   b. The predicted human-interest topic is: ______________________.

2. For each type of newsworthy information, record a brief description of what was presented. If no information was presented, leave the item blank.
   a. What: ______________________________
   b. Who: ______________________________
   c. When: ______________________________
   d. Where: ______________________________
   e. Why: ______________________________
   f. How: ______________________________
   g. Source: ______________________________

3. List the major topics covered in the development paragraphs (4–28):

4. Look for implications; devise inferences and record them here.

5. What are your opinions about this topic?

6. Consider the purpose:

a. What is the reporter's purpose?

b. Do the facts adequately support the purpose?

c. Does the tone support the purpose?

d. Did the reporter achieve his/her purpose?

Check Your Motivation

1. Review your chapter goals. Did you achieve them? Explain.
2. Make a list of the new ideas and methods that you've gained from this chapter. Think about how they will help you in the future.
3. Measure your motivation for this chapter topic. Think about each statement and how you will use it in the future. Mark it:

   A = never B = sometimes C = usually D = always

	A	B	C	D
To engage my interest, I plan to . . .				
1. look at essays and articles with a critical reading approach.	___	___	___	___
To focus my efforts, I plan to . . .				
2. look for the author's purpose.	___	___	___	___
3. analyze the connotation of words to identify the author's tone.	___	___	___	___
4. distinguish facts from opinions.	___	___	___	___
5. look for the structural elements as I read essays.	___	___	___	___
6. look for the structural elements as I read articles.	___	___	___	___
7. use PDQ3R as I read essays and articles.	___	___	___	___
To monitor my progress, I plan to . . .				
8. look for implied points and form inferences.	___	___	___	___
9. recite essays and articles to gain more insights.	___	___	___	___
To reflect on my gains, I plan to . . .				
10. evaluate whether authors accomplish their purpose.	___	___	___	___
11. evaluate whether the tone supports the author's purpose.	___	___	___	___
12. evaluate whether the facts are good support.	___	___	___	___
13. evaluate whether the opinions are convincing.	___	___	___	___
14. evaluate the merits of the points in an essay.	___	___	___	___
15. evaluate the merits of the points in an article.	___	___	___	___

SCORING: Write the number of answers you marked in each column in the following spaces. Compute the column scores, and then add them up to determine your total score.

# of A's ______ × 1 pt. = ______
# of B's ______ × 2 pt. = ______
# of C's ______ × 3 pt. = ______
# of D's ______ × 4 pt. = ______

Total points = ______

INTERPRETATION: 15–43 points = low motivation; 44–60 points = high motivation

SUGGESTION: What do your scores show? Plan to change anything that needs improving. Praise yourself for every empowered approach!

Evaluating Arguments

Why do people argue? Do people in professional settings argue? What are the differences between personal and professional arguments?

Passion and determination often drive arguments. So do reasoning and good thinking, which are generally the most successful approaches. As Charlotte Bronte puts it,

CHAPTER 10 EVALUATING ARGUMENTS

> The passions may rage furiously, like true heathens, as they are; and the desires may imagine all sorts of vain things: but judgment shall still have the last word in every argument, and the casting vote in every decision.
>
> —Charlotte Bronte (1816–1855), British novelist

Before you read . . .

Engage Your Interest: preread and divide

This chapter is about evaluating arguments and using the skills of critical thinking to determine the strengths and weaknesses of an argument. On the next page, draw a tree diagram (like the one on p. 397 of Chapter 9) of the headings in this chapter; be sure to include the introduction.

After dividing the chapter into reading tasks, list at least one goal for each task.

1. I want to ________________ about ______________________________________.
   My reward(s) will be ____
   ____
   ____.

2. I want to ________________ about ______________________________________.
   My reward(s) will be ____
   ____
   ____.

3. I want to ________________ about ______________________________________.
   My reward(s) will be ____
   ____
   ____.

As you read . . .

Focus Your Efforts: question and read

When you think of the word "argue," what do you imagine? To most people, arguing refers to heated disagreements, fights, disputes, or quarrels. Interpersonal arguments like these are characterized by power struggles and each person's desire to get his or her way. But to **argue** also means to give reasons in support of a particular opinion or point of view. This kind of argument is a discussion or presentation in which good thinking and evidence are used to convince others that one view is the strongest or most reasonable. This rational form of argument is used in academic, scientific, and professional discussions.

Evaluating arguments requires critical thinking, which is an objective rather than personal way to consider the merits of an argument. Critical thinking can be used in many situations, including class discussions, essay reading, essay writing, personal disagreements, as well as problem solving on the job and in personal relationships. When readers apply critical thinking to argumentative texts, they combine the critical reading strategies presented in Chapter 9 with a questioning approach and an open-minded attitude.

A critic is a reader who ruminates.
—Friedrich Schlegel (1772–1829), German philosopher, critic, writer

This chapter focuses on the attitudes and skills needed to read and evaluate written arguments. It covers how to

- Be a Critical Thinker
- Understand Arguments
- Judge Arguments

Be a Critical Thinker

THINK ABOUT THIS . . .

1. Think of a friend or family member whom you spend a lot of time with. Then answer these questions about their thinking.
   - **1.1.** When a new idea is presented that's different from his or her way of thinking, does this person
     - **a.** Adopt it quickly if it's fashionable?
     - **b.** Reject it quickly?
     - **c.** Ask a lot of questions?
   - **1.2.** When a problem comes up, does this person
     - **a.** Quickly identify a solution?
     - **b.** Offer a lot of advice?
     - **c.** Gather information and think about it?
   - **1.3.** Does this person trust the recommendations of celebrities and sports stars?

     a. often **b.** sometimes **c.** not usually

1.4. Can this person provide good reasons and evidence to back up the ideas and recommendations s/he proposes?

a. not usually **b.** sometimes **c.** often

1.5. Does this person think that

a. there is usually one best approach?

b. the approach s/he uses is best?

c. there are often several different and effective approaches?

Would you say that this person is a good thinker? Explain.

____

____

2. Reminder: Preread this section before you go on.

Being a good thinker requires thinking. That may seem obvious or even ridiculous to say, but the truth is that it's not always easy to think or carefully consider what we hear about and read, especially when the ideas differ from our own. Many people respond to differing opinions either by believing them too easily or rejecting them too quickly. Often, these reactions are based on emotions rather than thoughtful deliberation, and both responses prevent people from completely understanding issues and situations.

Critical thinking, an alternative approach, is the ability to examine and evaluate events, issues, and problems objectively. It begins with a mindset of skepticism and fairness.

Thinking is not to agree or disagree. That is voting.
—Robert Frost (1875–1963), American poet

Be Skeptical

Accepting what others say without question is not good critical thinking. Whenever opinions, beliefs, or recommendations are presented, good thinkers are skeptical. **Skepticism** is an attitude of doubt; a skeptical person does not accept claims without adequate proof and support. Anyone can propose that something is wrong, good, or needed; that is not the same as proving it. The critical thinker looks for the backup before deciding that the idea has merit.

Advertisers and politicians often depend on a lack of skeptical thinking to succeed. They promise what many want in exchange for purchases and votes. Their emotional and manipulative appeals often succeed with those who fail to question unsupported claims. Look at the *Zits* cartoon on page 474; it's a perfect example of this tendency.

To be skeptical, carefully look at the presenter's qualifications, as well as the reasons and evidence she or he gives to support the ideas, prove the claims, or indicate that the promises will be kept. Ask questions such as these:

Who is the presenter?

Is the person an expert or very knowledgeable about the topic?

Does the presenter want something from me?

Does the person give proof?
Does the evidence come from respected sources?
How likely am I to get what's promised?

Here's an example of skeptical, critical thinking about a newspaper report.

EXAMPLE

Behavior: When "R" Stands for Risky for Teenagers

Eric Nagourney

The New York Times

A new study reports that teenagers whose parents place no restriction on their viewing R-rated movies appear much more likely to use tobacco or alcohol. The findings appear in the current issue of *Effective Clinical Practice.* The lead author, Dr. Madeline A. Dalton, and her colleagues at Dartmouth University based their report on a survey of 4,544 students in the fifth through eighth grades in New Hampshire. (Adapted from Nagourney)

Critical thinking: Initially, a reader should be skeptical of this news report since the reporter is unknown and the initial sentence could be about a study done by anyone. In the next two sentences, however, support is presented. The opinion is not the reporter's. It's the conclusion of a researcher, conducting research at a reputable university, on a sizeable number of students. In addition, the researcher's name and the publication where the study was first reported are presented so that a reader could verify the proof. All of this shows that the opinion is worthy of consideration.

With logical proof and good sources from reliable presenters, skepticism can be replaced with respect for the idea. Without them, maintain your doubt.

A wise skepticism is the first attribute of a good critic.

—James Russell Lowell (1819–1891), American poet, critic, editor

ACTIVITY 1: BE SKEPTICAL

DIRECTIONS: Read each of the following sentences skeptically. Then list the questions or proof that you would need before you could accept the claim.

1. Hybrid cars save their owners money and protect the environment.

2. The city government has installed cameras to catch drivers who go through red lights. They also shortened the yellow light so that more people would get caught and they could raise more money for the city.

3. The federal government is offering free computers to anyone who can't afford to buy one.

4. Stem cell research will lead to human cloning and attempts to create superbeings.

5. The draft should be reinstated. In addition, women and men should both have to serve their country. This one act would give us unequaled protection from our enemies.

Be Fair

While critical thinkers don't accept opinions without question, they also don't reject an idea or suggestion without considering it fairly. They recognize that a new or different idea is not automatically wrong or unworthy. In many situations, multiple points of view have merit; in other instances, the best ideas are a combination of several views. An attitude of fairness helps critical thinkers understand these situations. **Fairness** means being open-minded and willing to consider new or opposing ideas.

Some people have trouble being open-minded and evaluating arguments on controversial topics because they think that evaluation and agreement are the same thing. This is not so. Evaluating an argument means identifying how strong or weak it is. You can acknowledge a strong argument or good thinking without giving up your own beliefs. For example, in a discussion about how to spend family funds, one person could present good arguments for saving a large portion; another might have equally good arguments for paying off a credit card debt. Seeing the benefits of the other side does not mean giving in or agreeing.

It is the mark of an educated mind to be able to entertain a thought without accepting it.
—Aristotle (384–322 B.C.), Greek philosopher

Being fair also means considering ideas that you're initially opposed to. Here's an example. Suppose that your college is considering raising fees by $10.00 per unit to pay for a child development center. Assume that you don't have any children, you're putting yourself through college, and you don't have a lot of money. You're against this proposal, but in fairness you discuss the issue with a friend who is in favor of the proposal. This person has two small children, and since childcare costs are very high, she can only pay for enough babysitting to take one class per semester. A center would help her take more classes, and she points out that it could also provide classes to teach parenting skills. What you realize is that you're in favor of both those outcomes, but opposed to mandatory fees for all students. Fair-minded thinking like this often reveals that a proposal is complex and that it has a number of issues embedded in it.

ACTIVITY 2: BE FAIR

DIRECTIONS: Read each of the following opinions. In the margin, put a checkmark next to points that you agree with and an X next to those you don't agree with. Then list two of the points that you disagree with. Follow each of those with a fair-minded response about a part that you could accept or a situation in which the point makes sense to you.

Opinions about College Drinking

Opinion A

The problems associated with college drinking are overstated and misunderstood. Since college students have limited responsibilities, they can usually drink heavily without serious repercussions. Drunken college students do sometimes get into trouble, of course. But this is not a drinking problem; it is a drinking behavior problem. College students get into trouble not because they drink to get drunk but because they get drunk to be irresponsible. Drinking makes people lose control, and some may want to use alcohol as an excuse for their own behavior. (Adapted from Carson 602)

Opinion B

The results of a national survey of students at 140 campuses confirm that binge drinking is widespread on college campuses. Overall, almost half of all students were binge drinkers. Binge drinking was defined as the consumption of five or more drinks in a row for men and four or more for women. One-fifth of all students were frequent binge drinkers and were deeply involved in a lifestyle characterized by frequent and deliberate intoxication. Frequent binge drinkers were much more likely to experience serious health and other consequences of their drinking behavior than other students. One of three reported they were hurt or injured, and two in five engaged in unplanned sexual activity. Frequent binge drinkers also reported drinking and driving. Colleges need to be committed to large-scale and long-term behavior change strategies, including referral of alcohol abusers to appropriate treatment. (Adapted from Wechsler et al. 595)

1. I disagree with this point: ______________________________

____

To be fair, the point has these strengths or applies in these situations:

____

____

____

____

2. I disagree with this point: ______________________________

____

To be fair, the point has these strengths or applies in these situations:

____

____

____

____

When two texts, or two assertions, perhaps two ideas, are in contradiction, be ready to reconcile them rather than cancel one by the other.

—Marguerite Yourcenar (1903–1987), Belgian-born American writer

The Benefits of Critical Thinking

Critical thinkers are neither gullible nor close-minded. Gullibility and closed-mindedness lead to judgments based on emotions and limited experience. Critical thinkers avoid such errors and rely on intellect. They withhold judgment until they have sufficient information to make informed choices and develop knowledgeable opinions. They use rational rather than emotional approaches to evaluate the thinking of others.

You will find that the critical thinking approach has quite a few advantages. First, it will be easier to recognize unsupported claims, falsehoods, and propaganda. As a consequence, you will be less vulnerable to manipulation by others. Second, critical thinking will help you be intellectually independent. You will have thoughts and ideas of your own that you can support and explain to others. Those ideas will serve you well in every area of your life. Finally, when you think critically, you ask more questions. In a learning context, asking questions makes you an active thinker who understands more and remembers the information more easily. Within your daily life, you will find that questioning produces better understanding of people, situations, issues, and evidence. As a result, you will make better decisions and choices.

To read an argument well, you will need to use both critical reading (see Chapter 9) and critical thinking skills. In short, you will use skepticism and fairness to analyze and judge the value of the argument. The skills of analysis and evaluation are the focus of the rest of this chapter.

Before you go on . . .

Monitor Your Progress: recite

As you read . . .

Focus Your Efforts: question and read

Understand Arguments

THINK ABOUT THIS . . .

1. Read each of the following situations. Then briefly explain what the person could do that would (*a*) convince you or (*b*) make you reject the proposal.

Situation #1. A salesperson is trying to sell you a specific brand of TV.

a. I might be convinced if the person

____

______________________________.

b. I would reject this suggestion if the person

____

______________________________.

Situation 2. A friend wants you to join the student government organization on campus.

a. I might be convinced if the person

____

______________________________.

b. I would reject this suggestion if the person

____

______________________________.

Situation #3. A friend wants to convince you that airport security needs to be improved. You think it's fine just the way it is. Your friend wants you to sign a letter she is writing to your senator.

a. I might be convinced if the person

____

______________________________.

b. I would reject this suggestion if the person

____

____.

2. Reminder: Preread this section before you go on.

In each of the situations just described, acceptance is most likely when the person uses good thinking and backs up his or her opinions with convincing evidence. You would probably reject suggestions that do not meet your needs, do not seem relevant, or do not sound reasonable.

The same is true when judging or arguing in class. In a class discussion about a text, for example, some students drift off the topic and focus on their own experiences, beliefs, and personal opinions. The professor often ignores these opinions and calls on someone else. Why? Presenting personal opinions is not the same as discussing an issue or evaluating a text. To participate in a discussion and evaluate texts, critical thinkers begin by understanding the difference between persuasion and argument. Then, before judging, they locate the parts of an argument in the essay or article they're reading.

Persuasion Versus Argument

Persuasion and argument are terms that are often used interchangeably, but they are not the same. Persuasion is one of the three major writing purposes (see Chapter 9), along with informing and entertaining. Textbooks, reference materials, technical manuals, and news stories are generally written to inform, while novels, poems, and fiction are meant to entertain. What's left is persuasive writing, which includes essays, feature articles, editorials, magazine articles, advertisements, many Web sites, and political and sales mailers. Many of these texts are written to **persuade,** or convince readers to accept an idea and react, think, or act on it.

There are two basic categories of persuasion: promotion and argument. **Promotions** are created to convince readers to buy a product or support an organization or a cause. In promotions, authors appeal to the reader's emotions, desires, and needs. Sales brochures, mailers, and advertising, for example, are designed to convince readers that they need a specific product or brand and that it is superior to all others. Web sites and mailers that solicit political, charitable, or membership support frequently focus on readers' sympathy for the less fortunate or their desire to have a better world. Information that contradicts these promotions or supports an alternative is not presented.

The real persuaders are our appetites, our fears and above all our vanity. The skillful propagandist stirs and coaches these internal persuaders.

—Eric Hoffer (1902–1983), American author, philosopher

Arguments, on the other hand, are designed to convince readers that one point of view is best or, at least, is worthy of respect. The primary appeal is made to the reader's intellect. The author uses evidence, logic, and good thinking to convince readers of the merits of his or her ideas. Emotional appeals and other persuasive techniques may be used, but they are not the primary tools of successful arguments.

The most common place for arguments is a courtroom. There, attorneys try to prove their case by presenting evidence and explanations that will intellectually convince jurors. They can, of course, use persuasive techniques and emotional appeals, but juries are generally instructed to make decisions based on the evidence. A written argument works this way as well. The author presents a position and good evidence to back it up. Persuasive tactics may be used, but critical thinkers recognize that the intent is to convince, not sell, and they judge the text accordingly.

ACTIVITY 3: DISTINGUISH PROMOTIONS FROM ARGUMENTS

DIRECTIONS: Read the following examples of persuasive writing. Think about what each one says and what you would expect the author to present after these opening remarks. Mark each item P if it promotes a cause or product or A if it presents a point of view on a debatable topic.

______ **1.** Join the Peace Corps. You can make a difference in the world.

______ **2.** If you know the symptoms of drug abuse, you can help your teens avoid addiction.

______ **3.** Anyone will tell a lie if they are very stressed and feel overly pressured to please someone else.

______ **4.** You will experience better workouts and more stamina in our brand of shoes.

______ **5.** The American Diabetes Association needs your help to find a cure.

______ **6.** You can afford the car of your dreams with our financing terms.

______ **7.** You can afford the car of your dreams with good financial planning.

______ **8.** Automobiles are still a major contributor to serious respiratory illness for millions of people. Encourage members of Congress to vote for tougher antipollution standards on automobiles.

______ **9.** Automobiles are still a major contributor to serious respiratory illness for millions of people. But stricter standards won't be passed until people change their life style.

______ **10.** Most forest fires result from careless people who do not follow simple safety procedures.

The Parts of an Argument

Like courtroom cases, arguments focus on a matter of dispute or a controversial topic. For example, the question "Do most high schools start at 8 a.m.?" is not a controversial issue. Research could answer that question with statistics that could be proven. But if we change the question to "Should high schools start at 8 a.m.?" we have a disputable issue. The term "should" is the tip-off. In addition, a little thought would reveal that some people would be for it and some would be against it. Further, some people could even be at various midpoints, asserting that it would be acceptable in some cases but not others. Each person who has an opinion about this issue would also have his or her reasons or explanations as to why his or her point of view is best.

An argument, then, has three major parts: the issue, the claim, and the reasons. Written arguments have the following characteristics:

1. *The issue*

   The **issue** is the controversial or debatable subject. It differs from a topic in that it must be a matter people disagree about. As the following examples illustrate, it can be stated as a phrase or a question.

   EXAMPLES

   Campus binge drinking

   Is campus binge drinking a problem?

   To find the issue in an argument, ask "What is the issue or debatable topic?"

2. *The claim*

   The **claim** is the author's position or opinion. Argumentative claims offer a specific point of view about the issue or a solution to a problem. Here are some examples:

   EXAMPLES

   Binge drinking is a major problem on this campus.

   Campus binge drinking can be reduced by enforcing severe punishments.

   The campus should start an information program to educate people about the dangers of binge drinking.

   To find the claim, ask "What is the author's position on the issue?"

3. *The reasons*

   Reasons are the explanations and evidence that the author gives to support the claim and gain the readers' acceptance. They can be ideas, beliefs, evidence, expert opinions, research data, facts, examples, or personal experiences. Here are some examples based on two of the previous claims:

   EXAMPLES

   Claim: Binge drinking is a major problem on this campus.

   Reasons: To prove this claim, the author could quote the opinions of campus leaders, provide personal experiences about campus parties, or cite statistics from the campus police.

   Claim: The campus should start an information program to educate people about the dangers of binge drinking.

   Reasons: To prove this claim, the author could cite studies showing that knowledge can change behavior or give examples of effective programs at other campuses.

   To find the reasons, ask "Why does the author believe that the claim is true?"

In some writing, these three parts are clearly stated. But in other texts the issue and claim are implied, and the reasons are only briefly sketched. If this is the case, you will need to use what the author provides, your own background knowledge, and logical inferences to determine the three parts.

ACTIVITY 4: FIND THE PARTS OF AN ARGUMENT

DIRECTIONS: Find the parts of the following arguments by answering the questions.

Task 1

1. Label each of the following phrases with a T if it's a topic and an I if it's an issue.
   ______ **a.** food production
   ______ **b.** equitable salaries
   ______ **c.** teachers' pay
   ______ **d.** overcoming world hunger
   ______ **e.** patriotism
   ______ **f.** fighting for the freedom of others

2. Provide your own examples of the following:
   a. A topic: ______________________________
   b. An issue: ______________________________
   c. A claim about the issue in "b": ______________________________
   ____
   d. Two reasons to support your claim:
   ____
   ____
   ____
   ____

Task 2

Read each of these passages and then answer the questions that follow. If the author does not state the issue or claim, infer them and state them in your own words.

1. The following statements are from a sociology textbook.

   In 1996, the American Medical Association (AMA) issued the startling statement that violence in television and films had reached levels that were a health hazard to this country's people. More recently, a study found a strong link between the amount of time elementary school children spend watching television and using video games and aggressive behavior. Moreover, three-fourths of U.S. adults report walking out of a movie or tuning off a television show due to high levels of violence. (Adapted from Mancionis 129)

   a. What is the issue? ______________________________
   b. What is the author's position on this issue? ______________________________
   ____
   ____

c. Why does the author believe that the claim is true?

____

____

____

____

2. The following statements are from a geography textbook.

Looking at just the facts; Africa's future looks dismal. Population growth has been exceeding economic expansion for some years. The living standards of most of the region's inhabitants have steadily declined. Sub-Saharan cities are now growing rapidly, but few jobs await the rural migrants or the youngsters born and raised in the urban environment. (Adapted from Rowntree et al. 167)

a. What is the issue? ______________________________

b. What is the author's position on this issue?

____

____

c. Why does the author believe that the claim is true?

____

____

____

____

3. The following excerpt is from an essay written by a professional writer and mother about toy guns.

I hate guns. I do. But I've fired a gun, and I know that if I had to, I could fire one again. I am not afraid of guns, but I am afraid of what guns in the hands of ignorant thrill-seekers can do. That is why I am firmly in favor of toy gunplay for preschool-age children. I believe that you can bring guns down from their status as something illicit and desirable and turn them into just another thing from which children can learn.

Children should be free to experiment. Obviously, I am not saying that kids should be issued Colt revolvers and told to find out what happens when they pull the trigger. What I am saying is that by banning guns and gun play from preschool, we are squashing a natural impulse toward exploration. Kids are curious. They want to know why they are not allowed to have guns: This is the perfect opportunity to let them in on the idea that guns kill people.

If you forbid something, it becomes that much more attractive. You can't expect children to understand that gun play is "bad." They merely learn that it is something interesting that they are not allowed to do, so they do it when you're not around and get that sweet illicit thrill of having fun and being disobedient without really hurting anything. I do not believe that gun play in children creates violent adults; I have never read a study that claims anything close. If anything, I would wager that kids who work out their feelings about guns and power as children are healthier adolescents. (Adapted from Crane) (273 words)

a. What is the issue? ______________________________

b. What is the author's position on this issue?

____

____

c. Why does the author believe that the claim is true?

____

____

____

____

Arguments in Essays and Articles

You will undoubtedly be asked to read argumentative essays and articles in many of your courses. PDQ3R provides an efficient approach for analyzing and evaluating the arguments in those texts.

The Argumentative Essay The introduction, body, and conclusion format of an essay (see Chapter 9, p. 425) provides a useful framework for the parts of an argument. In an argumentative essay, the author usually presents the issue in the title or as part of the background information in the introduction. It may be stated as a phrase within a key sentence or a question. Even if it isn't precisely stated, however, the controversy should be clear to you after reading the text.

The claim will generally be stated as the thesis and placed in either the introduction or the conclusion. Successful authors usually make it very clear where they stand. Often they emphasize their position and the claim with phrases such as "in my opinion" or "I believe." But even when the claim is implied, it's usually obvious whether the author is for or against the issue, and so you can easily create a statement about that.

Finally, the reasons will be presented in the body paragraphs. Topic sentences are usually used to present reasons that are in the form of ideas and beliefs. Details will be used to present reasons that are evidence, facts, examples, research data, and expert knowledge.

You can find the parts of an argument efficiently by using PDQ3R and the predict and verify approach (see Chapter 6, p. 249). First, look for or predict what the issue and claim are as you preread and divide. Then question and read to verify your predictions and find the reasons. As you recite and review the text, pay particular attention to the author's reasons. You might even briefly list them so that later you can easily judge how well they cover the issue and the claim. You can also use that list to quickly determine your own opinions on the issue.

ACTIVITY 5: UNDERSTANDING ARGUMENTATIVE ESSAYS

DIRECTIONS: Read the following essays using PDQ3R. Answer the questions as soon as you can.

Essay 1

Engage: preread and divide

1. The predicted issue is: ______________________________.
2. Record the first few words of the predicted claim.

   ____

3. Look at the body. How many points does the author seem to present? ______
4. Set a goal.

   I want to ____________ about ______________________.

   My reward(s) will be ______________________________

   ______________________________.

Focus: Question and read

5. Question, read, and mark the essay.
   a. Form questions about the topic, claim, and other key points as you read.
   b. Mark the important information and argumentative parts (i.e., useful questions and answers, the issue, claim, and reasons).
   c. Modify and correct your predictions, if needed.

Mall Culture

Steven L. Shepherd

Notes

1 Some time ago I had one of those thoughts so simple as to be embarrassing. Still, though it has struck with me.

2 It occurred to me while driving through Los Angeles in summertime, through mile after mile of store after store. Sign after sign, mall after mall. I thought: "What if you could do magic? What if you could suddenly give everyone everything they wanted? What, that is, if you could do away with the wanting? With the wanting of new cars, new clothes, new CDs, new stereos, new appliances and amusements, new gadgets and gizmos; with the ceaseless, endless torrent of stuff. What if you could give everyone what they wanted?—make them content and end the wanting. What would happen?"

The answer, of course, is simple: Life as we know it would end. Without the wanting, there would be no malls, no factories or design studios working feverishly to replace one hot item with the next. None of the associated jobs. Except for the producers and purveyors of necessities—bulk flour and Soviet-style clothes—the economy would stop. Which means in turn that contemporary American culture is based on unsatisfied want. On unhappiness, really. People have to be unhappy for our way of life to continue. For if we didn't ceaselessly want new things, there would be little to sell or care about. 3

Depressing though it is, this is not an unfamiliar concept to some people. I first realized this on hearing the editor of a women's fashion magazine interviewed on the radio. "Why," she was asked, "don't your models look like your readers? Why not foster a definition of beauty that most women could meet? Wouldn't your readers be happier if they weren't encouraged to aspire to physiques they will never have?" 4

"Yes," she replied. "But then we would have no advertisers. Because our readers wouldn't need their help to be beautiful." 5

The true business of her magazine, the editor understood, was the manufacture of desire—of unending discontent with one's present circumstances. If the magazine's readers were to believe they could be beautiful without the advertisers' products, the readers would have no need for the advertisers, and the advertisers none for the magazine. Therefore, the readers must be kept unhappy, always in quest of a goal that must always he kept out of reach. 6

I was reminded of all this when my son, then twelve, was invited recently to "go to the mall." My immediate inclination to my son's request ("Dad, can I go to the mall?") was to say "no." But my wife said that she too had gone to the malls when she was young and that it had merely been a safe place she and her friends could go, a place to socialize without the tyranny of parental oversight. 7

I will grant that the mall is safe, that kids need time away from parents, that they need a place to be 8 together. So why then do I object to my son's "going to the mall"? Why does his request evoke in me such visceral opposition?

In part, because an activity that affords safety is not of itself innocuous. It can, for instance, displace more valuable activities. When I was growing up my father used to tell me and my siblings to turn off the TV and find something to entertain ourselves—read a book, play in the yard, play with a friend, daydream. Do anything, but do it of your own initiative, generate it from within. Because if you provide for yourself from within you will never be bored, never be lonely, never need rely on the amusements of others. But now, when I say these words to my son they sound as anachronistic as if I'd told him to hitch up the horse. For our culture today has no use for reflection, for solitude, for that which you can provide for yourself—for a rich inner life. These are things that cannot be sold and they are antithetical to a society that sees people primarily as customers or market share. 9

But as important, "going to the mall" is a part of a long and many-pronged courtship, a part of the relentless and powerful seduction of our children by that portion of our culture that accords human beings no more value than the contents of their wallet. It is a part of the initiation into a life of wanting that can never be sated, of material desires that will never be satisfied, of slaving to buy and to have, of a life predicated on unhappiness and discontent. 10

And why would I want that for anyone? Much less my son? (778 words; adapted) 11

Monitor and reflect: recite and review

6. *Recite*
   - **a.** Add any new insights and inferences to your margin notes.
   - **b.** List the reasons that support the claim.

____

____

____

____

____

7. *Review:* Do you agree or disagree with the points presented in this essay? Explain.

____

____

____

____

Essay 2

Engage: Preread and divide

1. The predicted issue is: _______________.
2. Record the first few words of the predicted claim.

   ____

3. Look at the body. How many points does the author present? ______
4. Set a goal.

   I want to _______________ about _______________.

   My reward(s) will be _______________

   _______________.

Focus: question and read

5. Question, read, and mark the essay.
   a. Form questions about the topic, claim, and other key points as you read.
   b. Mark the important information and argumentative parts (i.e., useful questions and answers, the issue, claim, and reasons).
   c. Modify and correct your predictions, if needed.

A Question of Ethics

Jane Goodall

Notes

David Greybeard first showed me how fuzzy the distinction between animals and humans can be. Forty years ago I befriended David, a chimpanzee, during my first field trip to Gombe in Tanzania. One day I offered him a nut in my open palm. He looked directly into my eyes, took the nut out of my hand, and dropped it. At the same moment he very gently squeezed my hand as if to say, I don't want it, but I understand your motives. 1

Since chimpanzees are thought to be physiologically close to humans, researchers use them as test subjects for new drugs and vaccines. In the labs, these very sociable creatures often live isolated from one 2 another in 5-by-5-foot cages, where they grow surly and sometimes violent. Dogs, cats, and rats are also kept in poor conditions and subjected to painful procedures. Many people would find it hard to sympathize with rats, but dogs and cats are part of our lives. Ten or fifteen years ago, when the use of animals in medical testing was first brought to my attention, I decided to visit the labs myself. Many people working there had forced themselves to believe that animal testing is the only way forward for medical research.

Once we accept that animals are sentient beings, is it ethical to use them in research? From the point of view of the animals, it is quite simply wrong. From our standpoint, it seems ridiculous to equate a rat with a human being. If we clearly and honestly believe that using animals in research will, in the end, reduce massive human suffering, it would be difficult to argue that doing so is unethical. How do we find a way out of this dilemma? 3

One thing we can do is change our mind-set. We can begin by questioning the assumption that animals are essential to medical research. Scientists have concluded that chimpanzees are not useful for AIDS research because, even though their genetic makeup differs from ours by about 1 percent, their immune systems deal much differently with the AIDS virus. Many scientists test drugs and vaccines on animals simply because they are required to by law rather than out of scientific merit. This is a shame, because our medical technology is beginning to provide alternatives. We can perform many tests on cells and tissue cultures without recourse to systemic testing on animals. Computer simulations can also cut down on the number of animal tests we need to run. We aren't exploring these alternatives vigorously enough. 4

Ten or fifteen years ago animal rights activists resorted to violence against humans in their efforts to break through the public's terrible apathy and lack of imagination on this issue. This extremism is counterproductive. I believe that more and more people are becoming aware that to use animals thoughtlessly, without any anguish or making an effort to find another way, diminishes us as human beings. (491 words) 5

Monitor and reflect: recite and review

6. Recite

a. Add any new insights and inferences to your margin notes.

b. List the reasons that support the claim.

____

____

____

____

____

7. Review: Do you agree or disagree with the points presented in this essay? Explain.

____

____

____

____

The Argumentative Article In addition to essays, newspaper, magazine, and Internet articles on controversial topics are often part of course reading assignments. These texts use the feature article format of headline, lead, development, and conclusion (see Chapter 9, p. 443).

In such articles, the issue is usually identified in the headline or lead, although the controversy or opposing sides may not be completely clear until you read about the event in the development. As mentioned in Chapter 9, articles are meant to report an event, situation, or discovery, rather than personal opinions. So, if the text follows the article format, the claim will not be directly stated. But feature articles do provide interpretation, and that allows the writer to present his/her own point of view. You can then infer the claim once you think about the writer's position. Other articles, particularly those from magazines and the Internet, may not be written in strict article form. In those, you may find a clearly stated claim.

The reasons will appear in the development. They may include the writer's ideas, the opinions of quoted experts, or researched facts. Whenever articles follow standard newspaper formatting, the paragraphs will be short. In those cases, you should expect each reason to be broken down into several paragraphs, which you may have to identify and combine in order to comprehend the entire reason. The conclusion of an argumentative article may provide a final piece of evidence or a clincher comment that underscores the author's attitude.

With these guidelines in mind, you can use the PDQ3R approach for argumentative articles.

ACTIVITY 6: UNDERSTAND ARGUMENTATIVE ARTICLES

DIRECTIONS: Read the following articles using PDQ3R. Answer the questions as soon as you can. One of the articles does not have a stated claim. For that article, write your own version during the recite step as one of your inferences for question 5a:

Article 1

Engage: preread and divide

1. The predicted issue is: ________________________.
2. Record the first few words of the predicted claim (if there is one).

   ____
3. Set a goal.

   I want to ____________ about ________________.

   My reward(s) will be ________________________

   ____________________________________.

Focus: question and read

4. Question, read, and mark the article.
   a. Form questions about the issue, event, and other key points as you read.
   b. Mark the important information and argumentative parts (i.e., useful questions and answers, the issue, claim, and reasons).
   c. Modify and correct your predictions, if needed.

Lip-synching Standard Practice

New York (AP)

Notes

1 It seems Ashlee Simpson will forever bear the scarlet "L"—for lip-synching. The 20-year-old singer has been lampooned and shamed, held up as an example of today's style-over-substance culture—all because of one lip-synch gone famously awry on *Saturday Night Live.*

2 Yet must Simpson bear the cross alone, while all the entertainment world goes free? Consider this:

- Now-classic footage from shows like *American Bandstand* featured artists lip-synching.
- Michael Jackson mouthed part of his superstar-making moment on the *Motown 25* TV show in 1983.
- Whitney Houston's spine-chilling rendition of "The Star-Spangled Banner" at the 1991 Super Bowl was prerecorded.

"It doesn't make the least bit of difference," Dick Clark, creator of "American Bandstand," told The Associated Press. 3

"Every motion picture you've seen, every 'American Bandstand' you saw, most of all MTV you see, it's all lip-synched," he said. 4

It never seemed to matter in the past. 5

We've all watched performances where singers dance, prance, and almost do back-flips while singing—but aren't a bit out of breath. Or when they sing earnestly to a prerecorded ballad during a TV show. 6

Producer Jimmy Jam, who's worked with artists ranging from Janet Jackson to Usher, said he too was surprised over the Simpson incident—surprised that it was such a big deal. 7

"I thought everybody knew that everybody lip-synched," he said. "I just thought when you went and saw Britney Spears, you knew that she lip-synched the whole concert.. . . They're seeing a show, and to them, that's what a show is." 8

Not for everyone. R&B veteran Patti LaBelle, known for her booming voice and creative improvisations, lamented that "the whole world is so phony today so people are accepting it. People are loving phonies." (AP) (289 words) 9

Monitor and Reflect: recite and review

5. Recite

a. Record any new insights and inferences, including a statement of the claim if it was not directly stated.

____

____

____

____

____

b. The author gives the following reasons to support the claim:

____

____

____

____

____

____

6. Review: Do you agree or disagree with the points presented in this essay? Explain.

____

____

____

Article 2

Engage: preread and divide

1. The predicted issue is: ______________________________.
2. Record the first few words of the predicted claim (if there is one).

____

3. Set a goal.
   I want to ______________ about ______________.
   My reward(s) will be ______________________________
   ____.

Focus: question and read

4. Question, read, and mark the article.
   a. Form questions about the issue, event, and other key points as you read.
   b. Mark the important information and argumentative parts (i.e., useful questions and answers, the issue, claim, and reasons).
   c. Modify and correct your predictions, if needed.

Voters key to election security

Notes

Jim Trageser

So this was progress: The punch card machines were too unreliable, the touch-screen voting machines too vulnerable, and so under congressional mandate and court order, those of us in San Diego County ended up voting with cutting-edge optical scanning equipment. 1

Of course, optical scanning equipment is cutting-edge 1960s technology. Admittedly, punch cards are even older—going back a couple centuries to when they were introduced in France to store patterns for rug weavers (true story). 2

Still, if you think hanging chads on a punch card has the potential for misrepresenting or confusing a voter's intent, try reading some of those Scantron forms. If an oval isn't properly marked, how do you determine what the voter's intent was? 3

4 We'll find out soon enough, because this week Ralph Nader's campaign asked for a recount in New Hampshire alleging that the scanning machines (the same model as used here in San Diego County) could have been manipulated to miscount ballots.

5 The plain fact is that the potential for voter error was much greater this go-round, because we ended up going backward in voting technology to a system that is less reliable at accurately capturing a voter's intent. Whatever problems may have existed with punch cards were only compounded by the optical scanning ballots.

6 I don't know about you all, but trying to fill in that oval just right was a lot tougher than jabbing a stylus through a hole. And don't get me started on the ease of use and intuitive interface of the now-banned touch-screen machines we used in the primary.

7 That's how voting *should* work.

8 Besides, while the optical scanning ballots do provide the paper trail that was not provided by the touch-screen machines the government ordered (although the government could have ordered touch-screen machines with printers if they'd chosen), the optical scanners still rely on computers to tabulate the results.

9 Rather than running punch cards through a tabulator this election, we ran optical scanning forms through a tabulator. The days of a mechanical tabulator are long gone—computers run everything—so the potential for hackers and other mischief was unchanged by the multi-million-dollar equipment changeover.

10 And all of this wrangling and ever more ridiculous conspiracy theories both miss the larger point: The technology has very little to do with the trustworthiness of our elections. Any system can be manipulated. A lack of computers never stopped the Tammany Hall or Daley machines from getting the results they wanted. Julius Caesar didn't need punch cards to strong-arm an election.

11 Today we have one of the most transparent election processes ever, with each party welcome to wit-

ness voting, tabulation and security and with various interest groups represented. This year, we even had international observers monitoring our elections—with the full blessing of the government.

12 Our elections are secure because most Americans believe in the sanctity of the ballot. It is this shared belief in the value of the vote that ultimately creates the kind of security that no technology will ever be able to provide. (502 words)

Monitor and Reflect: recite and review

5. Recite
   a. Record any new insights and inferences, including a statement of the claim if it was not directly stated.

      ____
      ____
      ____
      ____
      ____

   b. The author gives the following reasons to support the claim:

      ____
      ____
      ____
      ____
      ____

6. Review: Do you agree or disagree with the points presented in this essay? Explain.

   ____
   ____
   ____

Before you go on . . .

Monitor Your Progress: recite

As you read . . .

Focus Your Efforts: question and read

Judge Arguments

THINK ABOUT THIS . . .

1. Consider this situation: Your landlord has just notified you that your rent will be increased by 15 percent in two months and that he won't give leases any more. Your roommate wants to move; you haven't decided yet. Your roommate provides the following reasons for moving. Evaluate and check off each one as a good or poor reason.

	GOOD	POOR
a. All landlords want as much money as they can get.	______	______
b. The landlord is a money-hungry crook.	______	______
c. This is just the first increase; there'll be more in the future.	______	______
d. Let's look for a place where we can get more for our money.	______	______
e. We'll have to get extra jobs just to pay the increased rent.	______	______
f. Everyone in the complex is moving.	______	______
g. The landlord raised our rent because he doesn't like us and wants us to move out.	______	______
h. We've had complaints about this place before; paying more for a place we don't like doesn't make sense.	______	______
i. My father, a real estate agent, says we have very few rights if the landlord won't give us a lease.	______	______

2. Reminder: Preread this section before you go on.

Did you rate most of the previous reasons good or poor? Actually, although many of them might occur to people, only reasons *d*, *h*, and *i* qualify as good reasons. The others are emotional reactions and unsupported opinions, which are not good reasons on which to base an argument. In contrast, good reasons are reliable and logical.

Reliability

Since essays and articles are written to promote the opinions or research of the author, the reader must determine whether the writer is reliable. **Reliability** refers to how trustworthy the writer is and how confident the reader can be that the information is complete, true, and accurate. People who know little or nothing about a subject are not reliable sources for opinions about it. For example, a person who has never filled out loan papers for a new car would not be a good source of information about how difficult the loan process is. Likewise, those who are trying to influence others for personal gain or who have lied in the past are not reliable.

How will you judge an author's reliability? There are a number of ways. First, look at the author's credentials. College degrees, special training, and employment at respected institutions indicate reliability. Look for this kind of information in the footnotes or descriptions about the writer. Second, look for evidence of knowledge in the text itself. The author's experience and research or use of verifiable facts and quotes as support count for a lot. Third, consider the author's purpose. If the author's primary intent seems to be sharing opinions and information, reliability is generally high. In contrast, if the author may benefit by convincing you, reliability may be low. Finally, look at the publisher of the text. If you know that the source is reliable, you can put more faith in the author.

The highest compact we can make with our fellow is—"Let there be truth between us two forevermore."

—Ralph Waldo Emerson (1803–1882), American poet and essayist

Look at these three imaginary examples about authors reporting on a new drug to help AIDS patients. Decide which author is most reliable and why before you read the analysis that follows.

EXAMPLES

Author 1: This writer is a spokeswoman for the company. She has a master's degree in business and has talked extensively to the scientist responsible for developing the drug. She is writing a press release.

Author 2: The scientist who developed the drug is writing an article for a scientific journal. He has a Ph.D. in pharmacology and has been the head of the research team for this drug for 10 years.

Author 3: This writer is a reporter for *The Wall Street Journal* who has a bachelor's degree in biology. He has spent six months researching the drug, how it was developed, and how it will help patients. He is writing a feature article about the drug.

Author 1 could be a very fair person, but since her company will profit from positive reporting, and since her text is designed to promote sales, her reliability would be the least of all three. For very technical information about the drug, Author 2 would be the most reliable. For information that might influence drug sales, his views would be less reliable. For an unbiased and general description of the drug, Author 3 would probably be the most reliable of all, as long as the information is written to inform readers and not to promote the company.

This example brings up a final point about reliability. Reliability is not an all or nothing judgment. There are degrees. When you assess reliability, you come to a conclusion about the author that can range anywhere from very reliable to very unreliable.

ACTIVITY 7: JUDGE RELIABILITY

DIRECTIONS: Judge the reliability of each of the following authors. Use a 1 to 4 point rating scale, where 1 is totally unreliable and 4 is extremely reliable. Then briefly explain the reasons for your rating.

1. A reporter on your local TV station explaining the governor's new budget. He belongs to the same party as the governor.
   Rating: ______________________________
   Reasons: ______________________________
   ____

2. Your economics professor outlining the pros and cons of the governor's new budget. You don't know her political affiliation.
   Rating: ______________________________
   Reasons: ______________________________
   ____

3. A historian writing about Albert Einstein.
   Rating: ______________________________
   Reasons: ______________________________
   ____

4. A reporter writing a newspaper article about Einstein for a series of articles about famous scientists.
   Rating: ______________________________
   Reasons: ______________________________
   ____

5. Jane Goodall, as the author of the essay "A Questions of Ethics" (page 488). She is an anthropologist who has spent her life studying wild chimpanzees.
   Rating: ______________________________
   Reasons: ______________________________
   ____

6. Steven L. Shepherd, as the author of "Mall Culture" (page 485). He has been a writer and editor for *Executive Health Report.*
   Rating: ______________________________
   Reasons: ______________________________
   ____

7. Think of an important topic that you would like to get more information about. Then describe the kind of authors and sources that you would rate at each of the four levels of reliability.
   Topic: ______________________________
   Level 1 author: ______________________________

Level 2 author: ______________________________

Level 3 author: ______________________________

Level 4 author: ______________________________

Logic

Since arguments should be a reasoned presentation of a position, it is essential to evaluate the author's logic. Good arguments avoid bias and logical fallacies.

In thinking, if a person begins with certainties, they shall end in doubts, but if they can begin with doubts, they will end in certainties.

—Francis Bacon (1561–1626), British philosopher, essayist, statesman

Bias One expects authors of arguments to be critical thinkers and, thus, to be fair and open-minded in their discussions. They can and should present strong ideas, but they should do so without bias. A **bias** is a one-sided presentation. Bias weakens an argument because it prevents both the writer and the reader from thinking clearly about the issue.

Biased authors knowingly or unknowingly use a number of misleading techniques. First, they may leave out information. Advertisers do this all the time in promotions. An ad for one kind of truck, for example, is not going to present the strengths of other vehicles. While this tactic may effectively sell products, it's not good argumentative writing.

Biased authors also manipulate language to make their position appear stronger. One method, **sweeping generalizations,** suggests that events or members of a group all have the same characteristics. For example, statements such as "politicians are self-serving" means that every one of them is this way. It is rare that anything in this world includes all instances, so unqualified statements are almost always biased. This kind of thinking also reveals prejudice and a tendency to stereotype, dismiss, and diminish others. It is definitely not a good argument.

Reason transformed into prejudice is the worst form of prejudice, because reason is the only instrument for liberation from prejudice.

—Allan Bloom (1930–1992), American educator and author

Finally, a biased author often uses slanted or loaded language to manipulate the reader's emotions. **Slanted language** includes terms with strong negative connotations or descriptions designed to make readers feel rather than think about the issue. You can see this kind of bias whenever you read labels such as "bleeding-heart liberal," "callous conservative," or "greedy lawyers." Those phrases have nothing to do with the issue, but they do sway a lot of readers to quickly dismiss the statements made by a member of one of those groups. Slanted language may also be used to provoke reactions such as horror, anger, fear, worry, or pity. For example, the statement that "high schools are controlled by *gangs and thugs*" is designed to conjure up frightening images of crime rather than provide solid evidence about who is in control of the schools.

Look at this example of a biased letter to the editor. Try to find the biased techniques before you read the analysis that follows.

EXAMPLE

Red-light Cameras Are Un-American

You have to prove that you are innocent when a machine declares you guilty. It's taxation of the poorest, whose only possession is their car. . . . The city shortens the yellow light to ensure steady violations. There are over 1,000 citations a month, and the city wants to install more money-making devices. Money goes to the most affluent, who pretend to be taking care of public interest. . . . Bureaucrats spend a lot of time thinking how to extort more money from the public, and then they present themselves as protectors of the people. Red-light cameras are a way of stealing a lot from the general public. . . . (Cheleski E-3)

This letter is an extreme example of a biased argument. It uses all the devices of biased writing. First, the author fails to include any information about the income levels of those who are caught by the cameras. That information might disprove his point about the red-light cameras being a tax on the poor. Then, he characterizes bureaucrats as extortionists, a sweeping generalization that engages in stereotyping and name-calling. In addition, slanted language is used throughout: Phrases such as *money-making devices* and *a way of stealing* are designed to anger people. Finally, the entire letter and opening line are designed to make readers worry that they too will be caught by this unfair system.

Extremely biased writing like the previous example is rare in essays and articles. More often, you will find only a few biased sentences. Then you will have to determine whether the bias is minor—a weakness in an otherwise good argument—or serious evidence that the argument should be dismissed.

ACTIVITY 8: IDENTIFY AND JUDGE BIAS

DIRECTIONS: Read each of the following texts and look for bias. Then answer the questions that follow.

Text 1

To the Editor:

President Bush's immigration proposal has nothing to do with compassion; it is an outrageous effort to give business interest something they have been after for years—the ability to replace high-wage American workers with low-wage foreign workers, without the inconvenience of having to relocate their operations to another country. (Brock, *The New York Times* 12/29/04)

1. What is the issue? ______________________________
2. What is the claim? ______________________________

____

3. What are the reasons?

____

____

4. Evaluate the bias in this text:
   a. Has information been omitted? Are the reasons strong?

   ____

   ____

   b. Are there any sweeping generalizations?

   ____

   ____

   c. Is there any slanted language?

   ____

   ____

5. How serious is the bias in this argument?

____

____

Text 2

Car-pooling Is the Answer

Car-pooling is the answer to many of our existing problems. One extra person in your car would cut traffic in half, reduce pollution and reduce the need for oil. It would cut our travel expenses in half. It would give us more control over the price of oil. It would reduce the danger of travel.

Wider freeways are not the answer. That only creates more expense and danger. Park and Ride, I think, is a better solution.

The boss is important. I used to commute from Carlsbad to San Clemente, about a 300-mile round trip per week. Five of us lived in Carlsbad. The boss put us all on the same shift. Instead of 300 miles each, it was 60. We car-pooled. We saved money, and there were four fewer cars on the road. Smart boss. It feels good to be in control rather than being controlled.

Supply and demand is the basis by which every big corporation establishes its prices. Maybe we (America) produce enough oil to meet our needs. I guess we could tell OPEC we are in control. Which one do you want, to be in control or be controlled? Try car-pooling. (Martinez) (199 words)

1. What is the issue? ______________________________
2. What is the claim?

____

3. What are the reasons?

____

4. Evaluate the bias in this text.
   a. Has information been omitted? Are the reasons strong?

   ____

   ____

   b. Are there any sweeping generalizations?

   ____

   ____

   c. Is there any slanted language?

   ____

   ____

5. How serious is the bias in this argument?

   ____

   ____

Logical Fallacies **Logical fallacies** are mistakes in reasoning. They are statements that may initially appear reasonable but that are actually inaccurate, illogical, and invalid. Like bias, they weaken the argument. Logical fallacies are a problem because they come from faulty assumptions and they mislead the reader. The faulty assumption is generally drawn from insufficient knowledge about the topic. When that idea is put forth, it can mislead readers into believing ideas and facts that are untrue or illogical.

> Reason itself is fallible, and this fallibility must find a place in our logic.
>
> —Nicola Abbagnano (1901–1990), Italian philosopher

Look at these examples. These are each based on assumptions that are simply not true, and readers who accept them would be misled. As you read, try to identify the faulty assumption and what's misleading about each statement.

EXAMPLES

1. Everyone is staying out until 1 A.M.; I should be able to also.
2. If you skip a class, you'll end up failing and dropping out of school.
3. You're either for me or against me.
4. Pit bulls can't be trusted; my neighbor's dog bit three people.
5. Because my sister used my car yesterday, I had a flat tire and lost the hub cap today.
6. Mr. Jonathan was a great math teacher. He'll make a good senator.
7. Research shows that boys are inherently more active and aggressive than girls.

There are numerous logical fallacies, but these seven examples illustrate the most common ones. The following descriptions include the name of the fallacy and what's illogical about the thinking.

1. *Bandwagon—Everyone is staying out until 1 A.M.; I should be able to also.*

   The **bandwagon fallacy** proposes that since a large number of people are acting or thinking one way, it's the right approach. It is based on a number of faulty assumptions: We're all the same, what others do is right for everyone, the group known to the thinker represents everyone, and that the more people agree, the greater the truth. Bandwagon thinking is misleading because it is an exaggeration designed to pressure people into conformity.

   Hint: Look for statements that use words like "all," "everyone," "no one" or "people" as part of the reason for thinking or behaving a certain way.

2. *Slippery slope—If you skip a class, you'll end up failing and dropping out of school.*

   The **slippery slope fallacy** predicts that one step will automatically start a chain reaction that will end with one predetermined outcome. The outcome can be desirable, but more often it's a disaster. The erroneous assumption is that you can foretell the future by looking at one event. This kind of reasoning is misleading, because it implies that a chain of events cannot be changed or stopped once it begins.

   Hint: Look for a claim that one event leads to others, with only one possible outcome.

3. *Either-or thinking—You're either for me or against me.*

   The **either-or fallacy** reduces an issue to two and only two sides, which are presented as "my right way" and "all other wrong ways." The faulty assumption is that one view is completely correct and that all others are completely wrong. It's also based on the belief that issues and problems are simple matters with only pro and con options and one right solution. This kind of thinking is misleading because it ignores the reality of middle positions, compromises, and new ideas.

   Hint: Look for a simple, right-versus-wrong approach.

4. *Hasty generalization—Pit bulls can't be trusted; my neighbor's dog has bitten three people.*

   A **hasty generalization** is a conclusion drawn from too little evidence. It's based on the mistaken assumption that a limited experience will be repeated in all other cases. This error misleads others to accept something as true that has not been adequately proven.

   Hint: Look for the use of one example or a few experiences as proof about a whole group or all future situations.

5. *Questionable cause—Because my sister used my car yesterday, I had a flat tire and lost the hub cap today.*

   A **questionable cause** wrongly identifies what caused an event. In this fallacy, the person either assumes that he or she knows another person's motives or that whenever two events happen in a sequence, the first caused the second. A questionable cause misleads others, because it directs attention to superficial reasons or coincidences.

   Hint: Look for cause and effect explanations based on unknown motives or chronological sequence.

6. *Non sequitur—Mr. Jonathan was a great math teacher. He'll make a good senator.*

   A **non sequitur** is a statement that does not follow logically from the previous point. In this kind of reasoning, the thinker uses "off the topic" information to explain a result. It's misleading because it avoids an analysis of the factors that actually would produce the desirable outcome.

   Hint: Look for unrelated causes and effects or points that seem to be off the topic.

7. *Abstraction—Research shows that boys are inherently more active and aggressive than girls.*

   The **abstraction fallacy** treats a general category as if it were made up of people with a single idea. This kind of thinking is revealed by terms such as "*research*," "*sociologists*," or "*teachers*." These terms are used as if they name a group that has a single thought. The faulty assumption is that what some members have said represents what the entire group believes. This thinking misleads by implying that the author has done extensive research and knows what the group thinks. It also implies that there is consensus and agreement when, in fact, there is diversity and disagreement.

   Hint: Look for general labels and statements about what an entire group thinks.

Authors could avoid many fallacies by simply qualifying their statements or providing adequate evidence and explanations. For instance, example 7 that states "research shows" would not be a fallacy if it simply said "*some* research shows," and, the non sequitur example in 6 could be valid if the writer listed teaching skills such as informing and speaking to others that would actually make someone a good senator. When you are looking for logical fallacies, therefore, look for statements that are not restricted and that lack good supporting evidence.

ACTIVITY 9: IDENTIFY LOGICAL FALLACIES

DIRECTIONS: Read each of the following statements and match it to the fallacy that it illustrates. Each fallacy is used only once.

a. bandwagon
b. slippery slope
c. either-or
d. hasty generalization
e. questionable cause
f. non sequitur
g. abstraction

______ **1.** People in this state want their children to have good moral values. They want school prayer. So, we should all support the new law to have prayer in schools.

______ **2.** Professor Rochele is always late to class. He obviously doesn't care about teaching.

______ **3.** The attorneys for Jack Kevorkian, who is now in a Michigan prison for killing Thomas Youk as an act of supposed euthanasia, is asking for a full pardon. The attorney "cites Kevorkian's health problems—high blood pressure, arthritis, hernias, hepatitis C, cataracts, heart disease, adrenal insufficiency suggestive of Addison's disease and lung disease—as cause for (the Michigan governor) to release Kevorkian from the slammer." (Saunders)

______ **4.** My friend didn't do well in Dr. Thomas' history class. Obviously, Dr. Thomas is a poor teacher.

______ **5.** Car-pooling is the answer to many of our existing problems. One extra person in your car would cut traffic in half, reduce pollution and reduce the need for oil. It would cut our travel expenses in half. It would give us more control over the price of oil. It would reduce the danger of travel." (Martinez)

______ **6.** "Educators have reported a steady decline in the ability of Americans to spell, to speak properly, to write a job application letter, to think rationally, etc. In short, the dumbing down of America." (Waldman)

______ **7.** More freeways with more lines won't solve our traffic problems. Car pooling is the only answer.

Three more points about logical fallacies need to be made. First, in complex writing, a statement may actually have a number of fallacies in it. For example, consider this sentence: "We all must start eating differently or we will die at a very early age." There's a bandwagon fallacy here, as well as either-or reasoning and a hint of a slippery slope. Second, as with bias, a single logical fallacy will not invalidate an entire argument, although several might. Again, critical thinkers and readers need to decide how any fallacy affects the overall strength and quality of the argument. Finally, bias and logical fallacies often go together, so skilled critical readers look for both.

We like to test things . . . no matter how good an idea sounds, test it first.

—Henry Block (1926–2004), American businessman, founder of H&R Block

ACTIVITY 10: IDENTIFY BIAS AND LOGICAL FALLACIES

DIRECTIONS: The following statements come from the texts in this chapter. Each one may contain bias, a fallacy, or a combination of errors. Explain what the error or errors are. Then explain whether you think it's a serious or minor weakness in the thinking. Refer to the original text and notice the context before you make your judgment about the seriousness of the error(s).

1. The problems associated with college drinking are overstated and misunderstood. Since college students have limited responsibilities, they can usually drink heavily without serious repercussions. (p. 476, paragraph 1)

Error(s): ______________________________

____

____

Seriousness: ______________________________

____

____

2. If you forbid something, it becomes that much more attractive. You can't expect children to understand that gun play is "bad." (p. 483, paragraph 3)
Error(s): ______________________________

____

____

Seriousness: ______________________________

____

____

3. We can begin by questioning the assumption that animals are essential to medical research. Scientists have concluded that chimpanzees are not useful for AIDS research because, even though their genetic makeup differs from ours by about 1 percent, their immune systems deal much differently with the AIDS virus. (page 489, paragraph 4)
Error(s): ______________________________

____

____

Seriousness: ______________________________

____

____

4. . . . an activity that affords safety is not of itself innocuous. It can, for instance, displace more valuable activities. When I was growing up my father used to tell me and my siblings to turn off the TV and find something to entertain ourselves—read a book, play in the yard, play with a friend, daydream. Do anything, but do it of your own initiative, generate it from within. Because if you provide for yourself from within you will never be bored, never be lonely, never need rely on the amusements of others. (page 487, paragraph 9)
Error(s): ______________________________

____

____

Seriousness: ______________________________

____

____

5. . . . the whole world is so phony today so people are accepting it. People are loving phonies. (page 492, paragraph 9)
Error(s): ______________________________

____

____

Seriousness: ______________________________

____

____

Logic is the anatomy of thought.
—John Locke (1632–1704), British philosopher

Support Your Evaluations

When critical thinkers conclude that a part or the entire argument is weak or strong, they support their judgments with specific examples from the text. As you read, be on the alert for bias and logical fallacies and inadequate support. When you find these weaknesses, ask "am I convinced by this argument?" If not, point out why. But remember that you don't have to dismiss the entire argument even when it has weaknesses. It's perfectly appropriate to say that the ideas are very interesting, just not well supported or convincing.

Critical thinkers also look for excellence. They can point out strong reasoning, good evidence, and effective writing whenever it's used. They appreciate the insightful idea, the well-thought-out argument, the thorough presentation, and the memorable phrase that marks exceptional writing. And, as with weaknesses, critical thinkers support their opinions with text examples.

In conclusion, as a critical thinker and reader, you should expect good thinking from writers, judge texts with skepticism and fairness, and look for both weaknesses and strengths in their arguments. Record these assessments as you read, recite, and review a text.

Neither praise nor blame is the object of true criticism. Justly to discriminate, firmly to establish, wisely to prescribe, and honestly to award: These are the true aims and duties of criticism.
—William Gilmore Simms (1806–1870), American author

ACTIVITY 11: SUPPORT YOUR EVALUATIONS

DIRECTIONS: Read the following essay and find the parts of the argument. In addition, put brackets ([. . .]) around any biased statements or logical fallacies you find. Then note the type of error in the margin. Answer the questions as soon as you can.

Engage: preread and divide

1. The predicted issue is: ______________________________.
2. Record the first few words of the predicted claim (if it's stated).

   ____
3. Look at the body. How many points does the author seem to present? _____
4. Set a goal.

   I want to ____________ about ____________________.

   My reward(s) will be ______________________________

   ______________________________.

Focus: question and read

5. Question, read, and mark the essay.
   a. Form questions about the topic, claim, and other key points as you read.
   b. Mark the important information and argumentative parts (i.e., useful questions and answers, the issue, claim, reasons, and logical errors).
   c. Modify and correct your predictions, if needed.

No, It's a Moral Monstrosity

Eric Cohen and William Kristol

Notes

Dr. Michael West, the lead scientist on the team that recently cloned the first human embryos, believes his mission in life is "to end suffering and death." "For the sake of medicine," he informs us, "we need to set our fears aside." For the sake of health, in other words, we need to overcome our moral inhibitions against cloning and eugenics. . . . 1

But as the ethicist Paul Ramsey wrote, "The good things that men do can be complete only by the things they refuse to do." And cloning is one of those things we should refuse to do. 2

The debate is usually divided into two issues—reproductive cloning (creating cloned human beings) and therapeutic cloning (creating cloned human embryos for research and destruction). For now, there is near-universal consensus that we should shun the first. . . . Americans agree that human cloning should never happen—not merely because the procedure is not yet "safe," but because it is wrong. 3

Many research advocates say that they, too, are against "reproductive cloning." But to protect their research, they seek to restrict only the implantation of cloned embryos, not the creation of cloned embryos for research. This is untenable: Once we begin stockpiling cloned embryos for research, it will be virtually impossible to control how they are used. We would be creating a class of embryos that, by law, must be destroyed. And the only remedy for wrongfully implanting cloned embryos would be forced abortions, something neither pro-lifers nor reproductive rights advocates would tolerate, nor should. 4

But the cloning debate is not simply the latest act in the moral divide over abortion. It is the "opening skirmish" as Leon Kass, the president's bioethics czar, describes it—in deciding whether we wish to "put human nature itself on the operating table, ready for alteration, enhancement, and wholesale redesign." Lured by the seductive promise of medical science to "end" suffering and disease, we risk not seeing the dark side of the eugenic project. 5

Three horrors come to mind: First, the designing of our descendants, whether through cloning or germ-line engineering, is a form of generational despotism. Second, in trying to make human beings live indefinitely, our scientists have begun mixing *our* genes with those of cows, pigs, and jellyfish. And in trying to stamp out disease by any means necessary, we risk beginning the "compassionate" project of killing off the diseased themselves, something that has already begun with the selective abortion by parents of "undesirable" embryos. 6

Proponents of the biogenetic revolution will surely say that such warnings are nothing more than superstitions. Naive to the destructive power of man's inventions, they will say that freedom means leaving scientists to experiment as they see fit. They will say that those who wish to stop the unchecked advance of biotechnology are themselves "genetic fundamentalists," who see human beings as nothing more than their genetic make-ups. Banning human cloning, one advocate says, "would set a very dangerous precedent of bringing the police powers of the federal government into the laboratories." 7

But the fact is that society accepts the need to regulate behavior for moral reasons—from drug use to nuclear weapons research to dumping waste. And those who say that human identity is "more than a person's genetic make-up" are typically the ones who seek to crack man's genetic code, so that they might "improve" humans in the image they see fit. In promising biological utopia, they justify breaching fundamental moral boundaries. 8

C. S. Lewis saw this possibility long ago in *The Abolition of Man.* As he put it, "Each new power won by man is a power over man as well." In order to stop the dehumanization of man, and the creation of a post-human world of designer babies, man-animal chimeras, and "compassionate killing" of the disabled, we may have to forgo some research. We may have to say no to certain experiments before they begin. The ban on human cloning is an ideal opportunity to reassert democratic control over science, and to reconnect technological advance with human dignity and responsibility. (676 words) 9

About the authors: Eric Cohen has published articles in newspapers such as *The Wall Street Journal* and *Washington Times.* William Kristol is editor and publisher of the *Weekly Standard* and has appeared on ABC's *This Week* program. Together they co-edited the text *The Future Is Now: America Confronts the New Genetics* (2002).

Monitor and reflect: recite and review

6. Recite

a. Add any new insights and inferences to your margin notes.

b. The authors give the following reasons to support the claim:

____

____

____

____

____

7. Review

a. Are the authors reliable?

____

____

____

b. Is there evidence of bias or logical fallacies? If so, are they a serious weakness?

____

____

____

c. Are there instances of excellence? If so, identify them and explain what makes them so.

____

____

____

____

d. Do you agree or disagree with the points presented in this essay? Explain.

____

____

____

____

Before you go on . . .

Monitor Your Progress: recite

After you read . . .

Reflect on Your Gains: review

CHAPTER SUMMARY

Introduction

In academic and professional arenas, people are expected to **argue** by presenting reasons to support their opinions. They convince others by using rational methods. Engaging in and evaluating these arguments requires critical thinking.

Be a Critical Thinker

Critical thinking is an intellectual rather than emotional approach that is used to analyze and evaluate events, issues, and problems. It requires a mindset of **skepticism** and **fairness,** along with analysis and evaluation skills. Critical thinkers question what they hear and read, and they maintain doubt whenever claims are presented without support or proof. They are also fair-minded and open to new ideas and opinions even when they don't agree with them. Critical thinkers reap a number of rewards for their good thinking.

Understand Arguments

Persuasion, one of the three writing purposes, is designed to convince readers by presenting **promotions** or **arguments.** Promotions make appeals to the reader's emotions, desires, or needs, while arguments appeal to the reader's intellect. Critical thinkers analyze persuasive texts to separate promotions from arguments and locate the parts of an argument in essays and articles. Arguments have three main parts: the **issue,** the **claim,** and the **reasons.** PDQ3R is a useful method for identifying these parts in argumentative essays and articles.

Judge Arguments

Critical thinkers evaluate both the author's reliability and logic. **Reliability,** or trustworthiness, is determined by assessing the author's credentials, use of support, and purpose. To judge the logic or reasoning, critical thinkers look for weaknesses, including bias and logical fallacies, as well as strengths in the argument. **Bias,** a one-sided presentation, is revealed whenever authors omit important information, make **sweeping generalizations,** or use **slanted language. Logical fallacies,** or mistakes in reasoning, come from faulty assumptions and are a problem because they mislead the reader. Seven common fallacies are **band wagon, slippery slope, either-or thinking, hasty generalization, questionable cause, non sequitur,** and **abstraction.** As part of their evaluation, critical thinkers support their judgments with proof from the text.

REVIEW ACTIVITIES

Use the following activities to check your understanding and aid your learning of the information in this chapter.

Expand Your Vocabulary

Match each term with the correct definition or characteristic.

_____ **1.** argue
_____ **2.** critical thinking
_____ **3.** skepticism
_____ **4.** fairness
_____ **5.** persuasion
_____ **6.** promotion
_____ **7.** argument
_____ **8.** issue
_____ **9.** claim
_____ **10.** reasons
_____ **11.** reliability
_____ **12.** bias
_____ **13.** sweeping generalization
_____ **14.** slanted language
_____ **15.** logical fallacy
_____ **16.** band wagon
_____ **17.** slippery slope
_____ **18.** either-or thinking
_____ **19.** hasty generalization
_____ **20.** questionable cause
_____ **21.** non sequitur
_____ **22.** abstraction

a. an error that identifies an illogical cause for an event.
b. a claim that all situations or group members have the same characteristics.
c. a one-sided presentation
d. the author's position statement or opinion.
e. a mistake in reasoning.
f. strong, connotative terms that appeal to emotions.
g. predicts a chain of events and one outcome.
h. links a conclusion to evidence that doesn't lead to it.
i. treats a group as if all members think or behave the same way.
j. a general writing purpose that seeks to convince readers
k. a conclusion made on the basis of too little evidence.
l. to give reasons in support of a particular point of view.
m. an attitude of doubt when there is inadequate proof.
n. the author's trustworthiness.
o. the ability to examine and evaluate with objectivity.
p. the objective that seeks sales or support of a cause.
q. explanations and evidence given to support a claim.
r. a presentation that seeks to convince readers that one point of view is best or worthy of respect.
s. open-mindedness and willingness to consider opposing ideas.
t. the controversial or debatable topic.
u. reduces an issue to two and only two sides.
v. a claim that refers to the behavior of a large number of people as a valid reason.

Increase Your Knowledge

The following tasks will help you assess how well you understand the ideas presented in this chapter. They will also help you prepare for quizzes and exams on this material.

1. The following questions focus on the major chapter topics. Discuss them with others or form your own detailed answers.
   a. Explain the difference between interpersonal arguments and those used in academic and professional discussions.
   b. What does it mean to be a critical thinker? How do noncritical thinkers react to new ideas and issues? How do critical thinkers react?
   c. Define skepticism and fairness. How do critical thinkers use these attitudes?
   d. What's the difference between persuasion, promotions, and arguments?
   e. What are the parts of an argument? Where would you generally find each in argumentative essays and articles?
   f. What is reliability? How do you assess it?
   g. How do writers reveal bias?
   h. What are logical fallacies? Name and explain the seven fallacies mentioned in this chapter.
2. Take notes on the information in this chapter.

Develop Your Skills

The following review tasks will give you an opportunity to practice the methods presented in this chapter.

REVIEW 1: BE SKEPTICAL The following sentences all come from the same article. Read them skeptically: After each passage, note the information that you would need before you could accept the statement. Or, if enough proof has been given, write OK to indicate that the statement is acceptable.

1. Global warming, or climate change, as it's often now called, is a factless creation of environmental extremists and money-hungry attorneys. The specter of rising sea levels and upending of long-established climates by the emission of greenhouse gases such as carbon dioxide is just a scare story.

   ____
   ____
   ____

2. That is the message of author Michael Crichton's novel *State of Fear,* modestly blurbed by the publisher as a "superb blend of edge-of-your-seat suspense and thought-provoking commentary on how information is manipulated in the modern world."

3. A majority of the most eminent scientists in the field agree that global climate change is caused at least in part by human-caused greenhouse gases that trap heat in the atmosphere.

4. The respected Scripps Institution of Oceanography at U.C. San Diego has done a lot work on the subject. Visit *tinyurl.com/4c5tc* for details.

5. But Crichton doesn't trust the experts. Trained as a physician, Crichton took it upon himself to learn the science of climatology, and concluded that the experts had it wrong. For an amateur to say his study of an issue is enough to overturn a consensus based on decades of research is pretty arrogant.

6. At least Crichton's motivation for faking science is obvious: He is out to sell books and make money. Others are far more insidious and despicable. For decades, glib quote-ready people with scientific credentials have made a lot of money by saying what companies want to hear.

7. Tobacco industry companies such as Philip Morris used such paid prevaricators for decades to deny that smoking is a health hazard. Read more here: *tinyurl.com/6mjql.*

8. Moral: Never accept anything said by a think tank or academic expert at face value without first investigating who pays the bills. (Adapted from Fikes)

____

____

____

REVIEW 2: BE FAIR Use the statements in Review 1. Select two that you disagree with and briefly note them here. Then follow each of those with a fair-minded response about the merits of the point, a part of it that you could accept, or a situation where the point makes sense to you.

1. I disagree with:

   ____

   ____.

   To be fair, the point has these strengths or applies in these situations:

   ____

   ____

2. I disagree with:

   ____

   ____.

   To be fair, the point has these strengths or applies in these situations:

   ____

   ____

REVIEW 3: IDENTIFY LOGICAL FALLACIES Read each of the following statements and match it to the fallacy that it illustrates. Each fallacy is used only once.

a. bandwagon

b. slippery slope

c. either-or

d. hasty generalization

e. questionable cause

f. non sequitur

g. abstraction

_____ **1.** Until recently, Holland had a reputation for free speech, openness, tolerance, even licentiousness. But that all changed when they relaxed their immigration policies. (Adapted from Bell)

_____ **2.** If marijuana is legalized for those with terminal illnesses, physicians will soon prescribe it for anyone who has any kind of pain, including those with just a normal headache or upset stomach.

_____ **3.** The new psychology professor wears Hawaiian shirts and uses movies and PowerPoint in his lectures. He must be an easy grader.

______ 4. History clearly shows us that human beings are not trustworthy, especially when they acquire political power.

______ 5. Did you hear that another death row inmate was released because new evidence proved his innocence? Our judicial system simply does not work.

______ 6. You have to choose. Are you for us or against us?

______ 7. Everyone wants to get a degree as quickly as possible. So colleges should offer accelerated and short-term classes for every course.

REVIEW 4: EVALUATE THE ARGUMENTATIVE ESSAY. Use PDQ3R to analyze and evaluate the following essays. One of the essays does not have a stated claim. For that essay, write your own version during the recite step as one of your inferences for question 6a.

Essay 1

Engage: preread and divide

1. The predicted issue is: ______________________________

2. Record the first few words of the predicted claim (if it is stated).

   ____

3. Look at the body. How many points does the author seem to present? _____

4. Set a goal.

   I want to ______________ about ______________

   My reward(s) will be ______________________________

   ______________________________.

Focus: question and read

5. Question, read, and mark the essay.
   a. Form questions about the topic, claim, and other key points as you read.
   b. Mark the important information and argumentative parts (i.e., useful questions and answers, the issue, claim, reasons, and logical errors).
   c. Modify and correct your predictions, if needed.

A SOARing Insult to Science

Kristien McDonald

Notes

1 How much do you like those nice leather Doc Marten sandals? How important is your violin bow to you, or perhaps your mink coat? I suppose we could all get by without the furs and fancy accessories, but I wonder how important your mother is to you, or a sibling, or even a child.

2 I find it annoying that members of the Student Organization for Animal Rights (SOAR) take advantage of the benefits of animal experimentation while

protesting that scientists bash bunnies upside their heads with clubs. I find it annoying that there truly are people out there who have a problem with developing a vaccine for otherwise devastating sicknesses. I find it annoying that there are people out there who have a problem with granting a small child life because it may be at the expense of an earthworm.

However, I thought it worth fifty minutes of my 3
life to enlighten my mind a bit with the stimulating views of these social activists. I found that the experience stimulated my appetite far more than it did my intellect. In the end, I don't view such an idea as the ethical comparison of a human baby to swine very appealing or worthy of my signature on their petition.

A compelling theme of the activists' defense was 4
that every animal used for experimentation on campus can feel pain and that no scientist has the supreme right to inflict such pain on a creature that can experience it. I work in a radiobiology lab in Research Park, and the procedures we perform on our lab rats are far from painful. We study the effects of pregnancy and lactation on their bones, and not once from the day they're born to the day they die do we inflict any form of pain upon them. Yet, every time we have to endure an inspection, we are reprimanded by an inspector who has never performed a lab experiment for not "degassing" a rat's lungs after putting it under anesthesia or giving it aspirin through a stomach tube when it "appears" to be in pain. You tell me how to de-gas a rat's lung and perhaps we can work something out.

I found it fairly amusing to hear a group of hu- 5
manities students explain to me their ideologies concerning the advancement of research and how if scientists would simply abandon tests on animals, far better, kinder, and effective alternatives would just show up spontaneously. They tried to convince me that alternatives such as cell and organ cultures and population studies were sufficient for scientific study. Who wants to be the first to try a drug that has been approved by a chart of demographic statistics? Don't be afraid—it's just a drug.

Or we could just do the research on dead human 6
bodies. We'll disregard the fact there could not

possibly be enough available cadavers to supplement the constant demands of science. Perhaps it's not such a terrible idea to dig Grandma's bones back up—just try not to disturb the ephemeral glory of the pill bugs underneath. Unfortunately, as members of SOAR imply, it is not merely social or economic distress that causes medical problems. It is not simply due to increased stress or poor health habits that the human population is stricken with lung cancer. Why not try telling that to a five-year-old with leukemia? "Well, if you had just listened to your father and not swallowed your dinner so fast, this might not have happened." Many medical conditions are strictly just that—medical conditions. Some are purely genetic, and the only way to study preventive means is through animal experimentation.

I don't buy the idea that all animals are the 7
"cousins" of humanity, as SOAR tries to persuade us to believe. Comparing the worth of a human being to a Drosophila fly is demeaning and a disgrace to the intelligence of mankind. A leader of SOAR claims that it is arrogant of scientists and researchers like me to exercise prejudice against a creature because it is weaker and more helpless.

Animal experimentation is not prejudice; it's 8
progress. Perhaps the most radical idea proposed by SOAR is that if research were performed on rats for the benefit of rats, then it would be ethically acceptable. I suppose that after we discover a cure for AIDS, lung cancer, heart disease, multiple sclerosis, and arthritis (and all through studying only cell cultures, mind you), it might not be such a bad idea to research how to increase the life span of a rat from two years to three.

But maybe they have a point here. Lab rats 9
shouldn't be forced to be "martyrs" for the human race. So perhaps on your way to lunch you could volunteer yourself for cancer research. (795 words)

About the author: The author is a columnist at the *Daily Utah Chronicle* at the University of Utah.

Monitor and Reflect: recite and review

6. Recite

a. Record any new insights and inferences, including a statement of the claim if it was not directly stated.

b. The author gives the following reasons to support the claim:

7. Review

a. Is the author reliable?

b. Is there evidence of bias or logical fallacies? If so, are they a serious weakness?

c. Are there instances of excellence? If so, identify them and explain what makes them so.

d. Do you agree or disagree with the points presented in this essay? Explain.

Essay 2

Engage: preread and divide

1. The predicted issue is: ____.
2. Record the first few words of the predicted claim (if it is stated):

   ____

3. Look at the body. How many points does the author seem to present? _____
4. Set a goal.

   I want to ______________________ about ______________________________.

   My reward(s) will be ____

   ____.

Focus: question and read

5. Question, read, and mark the essay.
   a. Form questions about the topic, claim, and other key points as you read.
   b. Mark the important information and argumentative parts (i.e., useful questions and answers, the issue, claim, reasons, and logical errors).
   c. Modify and correct your predictions, if needed.

Thank Barbie for Britney

Kay Hymowitz

Notes

1 Ruth Handler, legendary founder of Mattel Toys and creator of Barbie, the company's most successful product, died last week, thereby prompting the most urgent cultural debate since Botox made the headlines. Was Barbie, as feminists said, poisonous for young girls' self-image and the cause of an epidemic of anorexia and bulimia? Or was she—as conservatives insisted, taking the view that "the enemy of my feminist enemy is my friend"—simply good childhood fun?

2 Actually, both sides are wrong. Barbie may not have prompted a national crisis in female self-esteem, but she's no innocent either. The vampy fashion doll helped to bring about the sexualization of childhood, evidence of which is everywhere today. In truth, Barbie is the not-so-spiritual godmother of Britney Spears.

3 Many parents were less than thrilled once Barbie hit American stores. In fact, marketing researchers found that mothers *hated* Barbie. They thought she

was too grown up for their four- to twelve-year-old daughters, the doll's target market. Before being redesigned with a sunnier California look, Barbie was sold in a sultry leopard-skin bathing suit, sunglasses, and with what looked like collagen-enhanced lips. Mothers had good reason to suspect she was meant to be a swinger—a kind of Playboy for little girls. After all, she had her own Playboy Mansion, called Barbie's Dream House. She had a flashy car and a sexy wardrobe. God knows what she was doing on those make-believe dates their daughters quickly began arranging for her.

Still, Mattel wasn't overly worried about *what* 4
mothers thought, because the company had just developed a brilliant new advertising strategy that all but bypassed parents. Previously, toy manufacturers, who rarely advertised anyway, never hawked their wares directly to kids. But in the late 1950s, Ruth and Eliot Handler gambled their company's entire net worth on an advertising slot during *The Mickey Mouse Club.* The risk paid off big time: The first product to be given its own TV ad, the Burp Gun (don't ask) was a phenomenal success. Barbie came next; little girls immediately grasped her faintly forbidden allure and went on a "Buy me!" rampage.

Between her sexy look and her TV appearances, 5
Barbie, then, marked a big turning point in American childhood. It's not that no one had ever tried to make a buck off kids before. But up until Barbie, manufacturers and advertisers generally respected the prevailing cultural view about both the vulnerability of children and their subordination to their parents. Ruth Handler helped to change all that. As those disapproving mothers well understood, Barbie invited girls to identify not with mom but with their hormonal and independent older teenaged sisters. Television further fueled the fantasy of teen sophistication and independence by speaking directly to kids, and sometimes trying to sell them things their parents might disapprove of. It didn't happen right away, but over time children's television increasingly hyped the teenager as the childhood ideal. By the 1980s, bewildered parents began to see the emergence

of the tween—eight- to twelve-year-olds who look (and in some cases act) like teenagers. Today's eight-year-old girls want their MTV, and demand their belly shirts and lip gloss. Even six-year-olds are Britney wannabes.

Thus her story makes moot the question of whether or not you should let your girls play with Barbie. When they were little, my own daughters had so many dolls that my living-room floor often looked like an Omaha Beach of half-naked Barbies (and Barbie heads and arms). But that phase doesn't last very long. The irony for Mattel is that, today, no self-respecting seven-year-old would be caught dead playing with a Barbie. Who needs a doll when you can play the teen vamp yourself? (Adapted) (618 words) 6

About the author: The author is a senior fellow at the Manhattan Institute and an affiliate scholar at the Institute for American Values. She authored the book *Ready or Not: Why Treating Our Children as Small Adults Endangers Their Future and Ours* (2000).

Monitor and Reflect: recite and review

6. Recite

a. Record any new insights and inferences, including a statement of the claim if it was not directly stated.

____

____

____

____

____

b. The author gives the following reasons to support the claim:

____

____

____

____

____

7. Review

a. Is the author reliable?

____

____

____

b. Is there evidence of bias or logical fallacies? If so, are they a serious weakness?

____

____

____

____

c. Are there instances of excellence? If so, identify them and explain what makes them so.

____

____

____

____

d. Do you agree or disagree with the points presented in this essay? Explain.

____

____

____

____

REVIEW 5: EVALUATE THE ARGUMENTATIVE ARTICLE Use PDQ3R to analyze and evaluate the following article. If there is no claim, create one as part of the recite step and record it under question 5a.

Engage: preread and divide

1. The predicted issue is: ______________________________.

2. Record the first few words of the predicted claim (if there is one):

____

3. Set a goal.
I want to ____________________ about ____________________.
My reward(s) will be ______________________________
____.

Focus: question and read

4. Question, read, and mark the article.

a. Form questions about the issue, event, and other key points as you read.

b. Mark the important information and argumentative parts (i.e., useful questions and answers, the issue, claim, and reasons).

c. Modify and correct your predictions, if needed.

The ABC's of Money

Wendy Cole

Notes

Never has a generation of young people spent so much money yet understood so little about how to manage it. Over the past decade, the average credit-card debt of Americans ages 18 to 24 doubled, to nearly $3,000. Among high school seniors, 4 out of 5 have never taken a personal-finance class, but nearly half have an ATM debit card, and more than a quarter have bounced a check, according to a survey of 5,775 teens, released in April by the nonprofit Jump-Start Coalition for Financial Literacy. If those trends continue, declaring bankruptcy could become as common as earning a bachelor's degree. 1

The scourge of financial illiteracy is worrisome not only for young debtors but also for their parents, many of whom are facing retirement and can't keep bailing out their kids forever. But at least one financial institution has found a way to capitalize on the problem. San Francisco–based Wells Fargo Bank has launched an online role-playing video game aimed at teaching teens and young adults the basics of financial management—with no strings attached, although Wells Fargo wouldn't object if users ended up opening accounts at the bank. The game can be found at *stagecoachisland.com* and works only on Windows® machines. 2

The biggest challenge, says Erik Hauser of Swivel Media, who developed the game, was to find a way to engage kids' attention. "They're used to instant messaging, instant gratification and instant pudding. We had to find an approach that wasn't dry or static': Players travel around a fantasy world, plunking down virtual cash at the mall or a car-rental agency, and earn spending money at any of the island's seven virtual ATMs by taking quizzes (after a brief tutorial) on such real-world fundamentals as credit, auto loans and online banking. Sample question: What does APR stand for? (*a*) account percentage rate, (*b*) average parcel rate, (*c*) American paper route or (*d*) annual percentage rate. For choosing *d*, you net $15 plus a shockingly generous 10% interest each day on your virtual savings account. 3

4 But no computer game alone can cure adolescent financial ignorance. Some curriculum experts wonder why high schools are still teaching algebra, trigonometry and calculus but not the financial skills their students will need to survive in the real world, such as how to fill out tax forms, compare interest rates or calculate the return on an investment. "More schools need to offer money-management classes:' says Lewis Mandell, a finance professor at the State University of New York at Buffalo who oversaw the JumpStart research. "The curriculum has to be made relevant to their lives." (448 words)

About the author: Wendy Cole is currently a *Time* magazine correspondent. She has worked for the magazine for decades, including as a New York reporter in 1986 and the magazine's Midwest Deputy Bureau Chief in 2000. She has been based in Chicago since 1994 and focuses on stories related to the American heartland.

Monitor and Reflect: recite and review

5. Recite

a. Record any new insights and inferences, including a statement of the claim if it was not directly stated:

____

____

____

____

____

b. The author gives the following reasons to support the claim:

____

____

____

____

____

6. Review

a. Is the author reliable?

____

____

____

b. Is there evidence of bias or logical fallacies? If so, are they a serious weakness?

____

____

____

____

c. Are there instances of excellence? If so, identify them and explain what makes them so.

____

____

____

____

d. Do you agree or disagree with the points presented in this essay? Explain.

____

____

____

____

Check Your Motivation

1. Review your chapter goals. Did you achieve them? Explain.

2. Make a list of the new ideas and methods you've gained from this chapter. Think about how they will help you in the future.

3. Measure your motivation for this chapter topic. Think about each statement and how you will use it in the future. Mark it:

A = never B = sometimes C = usually D = always

	A	B	C	D
To engage my interest, I plan to . . .				
1. value good thinking and strong reasons in arguments.	___	___	___	___
2. be skeptical about claims and ideas that aren't well supported.	___	___	___	___
3. consider ideas I disagree with fairly.	___	___	___	___
4. predict the issue and claim as I preread.	___	___	___	___
To focus my efforts, I plan to . . .				
5. separate promotions from arguments.	___	___	___	___
6. modify the predicted issue and claim if needed.	___	___	___	___
7. look for the author's reasons as I read.	___	___	___	___
8. look for bias in the form of omitted language.	___	___	___	___
9. look for sweeping generalizations and slanted language.	___	___	___	___
10. look for logical fallacies.	___	___	___	___
11. look for and identify examples of excellence.	___	___	___	___
To monitor my progress, I plan to . . .				
12. recite the reasons I find and consider or list them as a group.	___	___	___	___

	A	B	C	D
To reflect on my gains, I plan to . . .				
13. evaluate the reliability of authors who present arguments.	___	___	___	___
14. support my evaluations with text examples.	___	___	___	___
15. form my own opinions about the issue.	___	___	___	___

SCORING: Write the number of answers you marked in each column in the following spaces. Compute the column scores, and then add them up to determine your total score.

# of A's ______ × 1 pt. = ______
# of B's ______ × 2 pt. = ______
# of C's ______ × 3 pt. = ______
# of D's ______ × 4 pt. = ______
Total points = ______

INTERPRETATION: 15–43 points = low motivation; 44–60 points = high motivation

SUGGESTION: What do your scores show? Plan to change anything that needs improving. Praise yourself for every empowered approach!

Motivation Matters 5

Before you read . . .

Engage Your Interest: preread and divide

Are you surprised that a college education may not provide all that you need? What skills do you think you need to succeed in college? Do you feel that you are the "master of your destiny"?

After prereading, set a goal for your reading.

I want to ________________ about ______________________________.

My reward(s) will be ____

____.

Right before you begin to read, record your START time in the Rate Box on page 534.

As you read . . .

Focus Your Efforts: question and read

What You Don't Get Out of a College Education

Richard L. Weaver II

1 What I would like to do today is share with you some of those things that you don't get out of a college education—personal success skills necessary to exceed in school and in life. My purpose is more than just exposure to a list of items. My purpose is to help you realize that these are things over which you have some control, things that you can polish and perfect, things that will go with you when you leave college, and things that can make a major difference in your success or failure in life.

2 Now, I can't say that I was a model student, nor can I say that I possessed all of these traits myself—although I think I possessed most of them, albeit in some small measure in some cases. But I had a true "Aha" experience while traveling abroad with my parents just after a disastrous freshman year at the University of Michigan.

3 My "Aha" experience occurred when I went around the world with my family. Both my parents had Fulbright scholarships to teach in East Pakistan—now Bangladesh. When I told people I was attending the University of Michigan, the overwhelming response was always incredibly positive, like "Wow, the University of Michigan!" People not only knew of, but highly respected, the U of M and I continually wondered—to myself of course—why was I wasting such a valuable opportunity? After getting myself readmitted to the U of M I began to take college seriously and received mostly "As" in my

course work. Once I accepted the U of M's challenge, I made a serious effort to not just accept and anticipate it, but to appreciate, enjoy, and even prefer it.

What I learned first was control—that I control my life, my circumstances, my successes and failures. I was into blaming others; "My parents made me go to the U of M," "Teachers expect too much of their students," or "My father told me I wouldn't amount to anything." It was easy not to take control of my own life, because I found all the necessary recipients for blame. Blame is the easiest thing to do when you fail. I didn't realize that "When we blame," as Greg Anderson wisely pointed out, "we give away our power." 4

What I learned second was expectations—that you are likely to get out of your college career just about what you expect. If you expect to learn, it will affect your willingness to learn. If you expect a course to be tough, in general it will be. I found mastering course work incredibly easy, once I decided my expectation was growth, development, and change. But an amazing related discovery was that even weak instructors can teach, if learning is your main goal. There is no situation that is devoid of instruction. Admittedly, some situations are saturated, and some are more barren; but when the learner is in you, everything becomes a jungle of stimuli for potential growth. 5

What I learned third was self-discipline—that I did not have to rely on my instructors for the systematic training I needed to become an informed, knowledgeable person. If I was going to accomplish all that was expected of me and I held a job all the way through college as well as taking a full course load each semester, I had to regulate my own life. This is certainly part of control, but I found it more related to organizing and prioritizing than controlling. All time management begins with self-discipline. I discovered that my future was hidden in my daily routine. 6

What I learned fourth was responsibility—the power and ability to make decisions and act by myself and for myself. Again, this is an aspect of control. For me, this wasn't simply being responsible. It was a matter of coming to the conclusion that even though others cared about me and my life, like my parents, that I was the one who had to take action. When I switched from pre-medicine to speech, I consulted with my parents, but, ultimately I was responsible not just for making the decisions but—and this is the hard part—taking responsibility for the consequences of those decisions as well. My switch of majors cost me more course work and more time in school. But I discovered that taking responsibility for yourself creates a hunger to move forward, accomplish, and achieve. 7

What I learned fifth was transference—the need to apply what I was learning in textbooks and in the classroom to life beyond the ivy walls. Some instructors—even some textbooks—are very good at making this transference of material from the written or spoken word to everyday experiences that are significant, relevant, and interesting to me. As a teacher and as a textbook writer, I try to do this. As I a student, I learned to do this on my own—that if I was going to learn things I had to apply them to me. To understand, I had to see the practical side of ideas and theories. For the most part, I had to do this myself. 8

What I learned sixth was commitment—the value of sustained commitment, or what I sometimes like to call constancy—willingness to stay at the task until it is completed. 9

In our quick-fix society, I learned that success at anything takes practice and work. It is easy to be mediocre; that is why so many people are achieving it. Failures, disappointments, and blunders will occur. After all, we're human. But with sustained commitment to a task, achievement, success, and, finally, victory will occur and will suppress any problems or barriers encountered along the way. Pablo Picasso said, "I am always doing that which I can not do, in order that I may learn how to do it." Do you realize how hard it is to do that which you cannot do? That's commitment.

10 Today, you can say, I am the master of my destiny. It is my motivation, my inspiration, my interests, and my encouragement that will make the most difference in my life. Begin right now to use the system to get every bit of knowledge out of it that you can. Begin right now to reveal the emotional fortitude necessary to make a difference in your own life. (1042 words)

As soon as you finish reading, record your END time in the Rate Box on page 534.

Before you go on . . .

Monitor Your Progress: recite

After you read . . .

Reflect on Your Gains: review

REVIEW ACTIVITIES

Use the following activities to check your understanding of this reading.

Expand Your Vocabulary

Define the underlined terms as they are used in the essay by circling the correct response. The numbers after each item indicate the paragraph where the term appears.

1. <u>exceed</u> in school and in life (1)
   a. succeed **b.** excel **c.** survive **d.** function
2. <u>albeit</u> in some small measure (2)
   a. but **b.** and **c.** except **d.** almost
3. <u>recipients</u> for blame (4)
   a. reasons **b.** people **c.** receivers **d.** excuses
4. <u>incredibly</u> easy (5)
   a. unusually **b.** unbelievably **c.** hardly **d.** indeed

5. some situations are <u>saturated</u> (5)
   a. rich b. covered c. drenched d. filled
6. some are more <u>barren</u> (5)
   a. uninformative b. a waste c. unproductive d. boring
7. <u>systematic</u> training (6)
   a. traditional b. organized c. simple d. sensible
8. to be <u>mediocre</u> (9)
   a. indifferent b. unimportant c. ordinary d. uncommon
9. <u>suppress</u> any problems or barriers (9)
   a. take the place of b. smother c. conceal d. overcome
10. reveal the emotional <u>fortitude</u> (10)
   a. fortunate b. maturity c. strength d. passion

Check Your Comprehension

Use the following questions to determine how well you understand the ideas, details, and inferences in this article. Circle the best response to each question.

1. The main idea of this essay is best stated as
   a. You can promote your success with certain attitudes and skills.
   b. Focus on what you can control; ignore your failures.
   c. Take advantage of every opportunity.
   d. Take responsibility for your success; don't blame others.
2. The easiest thing to do when you fail in college is
   a. Ignore the problem.
   b. Recognize that teachers expect too much of their students.
   c. Realize your limitations.
   d. Blame others.
3. The author implies that
   a. Growth and development come from failure.
   b. Your expectations color and help create the experience you have.
   c. Weak instructors interfere with learning.
   d. Stimuli are necessary for growth.
4. The author discovered that time management and his future both depended on
   a. Responsibility.
   b. The skill of transference.
   c. Self-discipline.
   d. Commitment.
5. Responsibility
   a. Is a weight good students must accept.
   b. Means staying with a task until it's completed.
   c. Means making decisions on your own and accepting the consequences of them.
   d. Creates a hunger to achieve.

6. The author implies that
   a. Working and taking a full load of classes is not a good way to promote success.
   b. Self-discipline can be controlled.
   c. Your daily routine reveals whether you're self-disciplined.
   d. Time management begins with self-discipline.
7. According to the author, how important is it to apply course information to everyday experiences?
   a. It's useful, but not necessary.
   b. It's somewhat important.
   c. It's important, because it improves memory.
   d. It's a very important aid to learning.
8. Comprehension is improved by
   a. Recognizing practical uses for ideas and theories.
   b. Having a hunger to learn.
   c. Having good teachers and texts that make the information relevant.
   d. Finding interesting professors who teach in a systematic way.
9. Commitment and constancy
   a. Are the solution to our quick-fix society.
   b. Lead to success and overcoming problems.
   c. May not work when we fail, because we're human.
   d. Cannot help you do what you don't know how to do.
10. Inspiration
   a. Comes from great teachers.
   b. Comes from interesting books.
   c. That comes from within will have the greatest impact.
   d. Reveals how much emotional fortitude you have.

Expand Your Thinking

Use these activities to expand your understanding of the ideas in this article.

1. The following discussion questions will help you comprehend the major text points and develop your own thoughts about the topic.
   a. According to the author, what are the six attitudes and skills that promote success?
   b. What's the relationship between control and blaming others?
   c. What kind of expectations make coursework more difficult? What expectations make it easier to master course work?
   d. What does commitment mean? What can it do for you?
   e. Rank order Weaver's six insights. Which one do you think is the most important? Why?
   f. Explain the following quote: "When we blame, we give away our power."
   g. If you were to advise high school students about college, what would you recommend?
   h. How could you apply these six personal success skills to your life?
2. Take notes on this reading.

Check Your Motivation

1. Review your reading goal. Did you achieve it? Explain.
2. Make a list of the new ideas that you've gained from this text. Think about how they will be useful to you in the future.
3. Measure your motivation for this chapter topic. Think about each statement and how you will use it in the future. Mark it:

   A = never B = sometimes C = usually D = always

	A	B	C	D
To engage my interest, I . . .				
1. initiated an "I want to read about this" attitude.	___	___	___	___
2. preread the text.	___	___	___	___
3. identified the topic and/or thought about relevant or interesting points before reading.	___	___	___	___
4. looked for the author's organization before reading.	___	___	___	___
5. set a reading goal before reading.	___	___	___	___
To focus my efforts, I . . .				
6. chose my methods and had an "I know how to read this" attitude.	___	___	___	___
7. read where I was able to concentrate.	___	___	___	___
8. formed questions and read to find answers and other important points.	___	___	___	___
To monitor my progress, I . . .				
9. felt confident and had an "I believe I can read this well" attitude.	___	___	___	___
10. solved any reading problems during reading. (Mark D if there were none.)	___	___	___	___
11. marked the text as I read.	___	___	___	___
12. recited parts or all of the text.	___	___	___	___
To reflect on my gains, I . . .				
13. had an "I've accomplished something" attitude once I finished.	___	___	___	___
14. recognized the new or useful information I gained.	___	___	___	___
15. rewarded myself.	___	___	___	___

SCORING: Write the number of answers you marked in each column in the following spaces. Compute the column scores, and then add them up to determine your total score.

# of A's ______ × 1 pt. = ______

# of B's ______ × 2 pt. = ______

# of C's ______ × 3 pt. = ______

# of D's ______ × 4 pt. = ______

Total points = ______

INTERPRETATION: 15–43 points = low motivation; 44–60 points = high motivation

4. Compute your reading rate by following these steps:

Rate Box

1. **RECORD** your END time here: __________
2. **RECORD** your START time here: __________
3. **DETERMINE** your TOTAL reading time here: __________
4. **ROUND OFF** the seconds to the nearest ¼ minute. For example, 4 minutes, 15 seconds would be 4.25. Write this on the **** line.
5. **DIVIDE** the number of words by your rounded off time:

1042 words / ______ (****) = ______ WPM

5. Record your rate, comprehension, vocabulary, and motivation scores on the Progress Charts that are on the inside front and back covers of this text.

The Reader

The Reader includes the kind of textbook selections, essays, and articles that are assigned in freshman and sophomore courses. On these pages, you will find four paired readings; you will find additional readings and two complete chapters on the CD-ROM.

The Paired Readings

Each set of paired readings begins with a Reading for Learning page. On that page, you'll find information about the discipline, characteristics of writings in that field, and motivation and reading tips. This page will help make the texts personally relevant and indicate what to look for as you read.

The paired texts include either an opinion essay or an article reporting an event, plus a textbook section on a single issue of current concern. (See Chapter 9 for more about the differences between essays and articles.) All of these readings have the motivation and reading banners introduced in Chapter 2, and they end with a Check Your Motivation survey so that you can assess how well you applied the motivated reading processes to the material.

THE READER: READING FOR LEARNING

The essays and articles have four Review Activities:

1. Expand Your Vocabulary questions to practice thinking about the meaning of words in context.
2. Check Your Comprehension questions to assess the reading skills presented in this text.
3. Expand Your Thinking questions to provide opportunities for applying, analyzing, and/or evaluating the information in the readings.
4. A Rate Box to determine your words per minute reading speed.

The textbook sections have two Review Activities: Reading for Learning and Expand Your Thinking questions. The former will test your understanding of the information and are the kind of questions that you will see on course exams.

Unless instructed otherwise, when you answer the Review questions, you should feel free to look back at the texts to help you choose the best answers. In most cases, these questions require some thought or analysis of specific parts of the text and would not be easy to answer without prior study. On the other hand, you should have an initial idea about how to answer each question by just reading the text. So if you overlooked the information covered in the questions, make a note to read more carefully and thoroughly in the future.

The Complete Chapters

There are no banners or Review Activities with the full chapters on the CD-ROM. So, on those texts, you will need to use all of the skills and methods without the help of reminders and preset tasks. You do, of course, have the chapter aids that the author provides. But it will be up to you to engage, focus, monitor, and reflect as you read these chapters. As part of those stages, you will want to think about the kinds of questions presented in the Review Activities throughout the rest of The Reader. So, do the following during and after your reading: (1) define important terms; (2) think about the ideas, details, and implications; (3) identify and pay particular attention to the content you would need to know for tests.

The Progress Charts

On the inside of the covers of this book, you will find Progress Charts for recording your reading rate as well as your scores on the vocabulary, comprehension, Reading for Learning, and Motivation Checks. Fill these out as soon as you get the scores for each activity so that you can keep track of your progress and make mental notes about where you are improving and what, if anything, needs more attention.

Reading for Learning: Psychology Texts

Psychology is the science that studies behavior and the mind. Behavior, which includes both human beings and animals, covers the way the body physically responds to sensations as well as the ways individuals react to and cope with various situations. The study of the mind includes thinking, emotions, intelligence, and motivation. In addition to these areas, introductory psychology textbooks typically cover learning, memory, language, social influences, personality, psychological disorders, and the stages of development, including infancy, childhood, adolescence, and adulthood.

What to Look for As You Read

As a field, psychology is devoted to figuring out why and how individuals act. The writing provides theories, explanations, supporting details, and evidence.

Articles and essays about psychological topics may be written by experts or scientists in the field, journalists and writers reporting on what the experts have found, or even non-experts presenting their personal opinions. These texts usually use descriptions, examples, and anecdotes or stories to show that the ideas are reasonable and true. In the following essay entitled "Pop Culture is Destroying True Beauty," for example, the author, who is not an expert, uses descriptive details and personal examples to support her ideas. Psychology textbooks—which are written by experts in the field—focus heavily on research, often citing relevant studies as explanations and proof of the theories. As you will see in the chapter section entitled "Attraction" that follows, textbook writers provide descriptions of the studies and research findings throughout the paragraphs.

Motivation and Reading Tips

1. *Look for useful, personal insights.*

   Psychology texts will help you understand yourself, others, and all of your relationships, as well as how to maximize your individual potential. To increase your reading motivation, apply the information to yourself and those you know.

2. *Pay close attention to the theories.*

   Theories, or organized knowledge and explanations, are generally researched conclusions drawn by experts. Study them carefully to understand the context and any cause and effect relationships or processes that they present. When more than one theory is presented, compare and contrast them.

3. *Focus on the technical terms.*

   As a science, psychologists define words precisely. When a definition is presented, stop and learn it. You will need to think about that meaning in order to comprehend the sentences about that term.

4. *Create relationships among the supporting details.*

   Relate the examples and research details to yourself, those you know, the technical terms, and the theories.

Psychology Reading: Essay

Before you read . . .

Engage Your Interest: preread and divide

Do you pay attention to the images of beauty that are portrayed in the movies and magazines? Do they seem accurate to you? Do you think that they can be harmful?

After prereading, set a goal for your reading.

I want to ______________________ about ____________________________.

My reward(s) will be ____

____.

Right before you begin to read, record your START time in the Rate Box on page 543.

As you read . . .

Focus Your Efforts: question and read

Pop Culture is Destroying True Beauty

by Rachel Drevno

The Spectator Online, October 11, 2001

1 Our society affects us every day. In simple ways, it makes us aware of new products or calls our attention to new movies. Or it can affect us more deeply by suggesting we aren't good enough because we don't look a certain way. Billboards, magazine ads, and TV commercials portray ideal images of people as skinny, beautiful, and sexy, frequently playing on the general public's vulnerability about their bodies. These messages generally go unnoticed until people reach a point where they dislike everything about themselves.

2 Everywhere you look you will find images of women and men who typify what our society considers "beautiful." More often than not the women have visible ribs, hipbones that jut out, and emaciated faces. Men are portrayed as sculptures chiseled out of granite, with rock hard abs and broad shoulders. Rarely do advertisers use someone with a little meat on their bones to sell their product, unless of course they are pitching some newfangled weight-loss product. Open a magazine, closely watch a movie or TV show, and you can't help but be inundated with images of "perfect people."

3 In countless movies, characters who at first appear quiet, nerdy, or unfashionably dressed are overlooked until they receive a makeover and then suddenly to our surprise they become hot commodities. But such rapid makeovers (usually set to lively music)

do not yield the same results in real life. Every year men and women spend absurd amounts of money on products that promise to make them beautiful, skinny, or physically enhanced in some way. Slap a pretty face on a box, add a so-called "guarantee," and people will flock to buy it.

I have friends who starve themselves, or throw up everything they eat, because pop culture tells them they aren't worthy unless they look perfect. Somewhere along the way, movies, magazines, TV shows, and music videos have persuaded women to believe that they must be skinny to be accepted. Our popular culture has led women to hate their unideal bodies. It's an atrocity that our society continues to sanction such images, especially when it is quite evident that they damage the self-esteem of millions. 4

On occasion someone's self-hatred can be fatal. A good friend of mine lost a cousin to anorexia. Her cousin was 18 years old and she had a heart attack. How can we sit back and watch things like this happen? We need to live in a world where it is acceptable to be thin and equally acceptable not to be thin. 5

I am tired of reading magazines and seeing ads that display scantily clad, objectified women to sell products. I don't need to see a woman wearing a bra and underwear and a pair of wings, posing provocatively. That image certainly doesn't encourage me to run out and buy a bra. Instead it causes me to question my appearance. 6

I find it absurd that we live in a society that supposedly prides itself on "individuality" and "uniqueness" but then turns around and promotes a popular culture that relies heavily on uniformity and a set of ideal standards. I don't pretend to assume that one day people will be accepted for exactly who they are and not what society thinks they should be. I would, however, like to imagine that one day people won't feel so ashamed of who they are because they don't look like Brad Pitt or Julia Roberts. It should not be up to the movie industry or any other industry for that matter, to decide for us what is beautiful and what is not. Beauty is different for everyone. There should be no standards to follow. If we continue to see beauty as a carbon copy of our cultural ideal, the true meaning of beauty will die. (633 words) 7

As soon as you finish reading, record your END time in the Rate Box on page 543.

Before you go on . . .

Monitor Your Progress: recite

After you read . . .

Reflect on Your Gains: review

REVIEW ACTIVITIES

Use the following activities to check your understanding of this essay.

Expand Your Vocabulary

Define the underlined terms as they are used in the essay by circling the correct response. The numbers in parentheses indicate the paragraph where the term appears.

1. the general public's vulnerability about their bodies (1)
   a. weakness **b.** injury **c.** insecurity **d.** defenselessness
2. women and men who typify what our society considers "beautiful" (2)
   a. show **b.** pass for **c.** represent **d.** stand for
3. emaciated faces (2)
   a. sickly **b.** underfed **c.** masculine **d.** make-up
4. be inundated with images of "perfect people" (2)
   a. burdened **b.** overcome **c.** overwhelmed **d.** surrounded
5. they become hot commodities (3)
   a. sexy products
   b. expensive merchandise
   c. desirable people
   d. valuable resources
6. people will flock to buy it (3)
   a. ask **b.** fly **c.** swarm **d.** rush
7. it's an atrocity (4)
   a. outrageous act
   b. horrible scandal
   c. violent crime
   d. serious matter
8. society continues to sanction such images (4)
   a. allow **b.** authorize **c.** defend **d.** support
9. posing provocatively (6)
   a. seductively **b.** proudly **c.** forcefully **d.** passionately
10. I find it absurd (7)
    a. pointless **b.** silly **c.** humorous **d.** ridiculous

Check Your Comprehension

Use the following questions to determine how well you understand the ideas, details, and inferences in this essay. Circle the best response to each question.

1. The main idea of this essay is best stated as:
   a. Society affects us every day.
   b. The media is responsible for eating disorders.
   c. Pop culture makes women hate their bodies.
   d. Ideal images of beauty are unrealistic and damaging.

2. The author implies that
   a. people use media images to judge themselves.
   b. pop culture is destroying true beauty.
   c. many people do match society's view of beauty.
   d. advertisers often use skinny models.

3. According to the author, the image of a beautiful woman is
   a. one with "meat on her bones."
   b. someone who is underweight.
   c. a woman in a bra and underwear.
   d. a pretty face.

4. According to our society, a "beautiful" man is
   a. physically enhanced.
   b. strong and calm.
   c. quite fashionably dressed.
   d. very muscular and broad shouldered.

5. The author suggests that movie makeovers make people in the audience
   a. want to be hot commodities.
   b. happy with who they are.
   c. believe that beauty can be purchased.
   d. more popular than they were.

6. Pop culture gives people the message that being a worthwhile person
   a. can be created with good products.
   b. is not important.
   c. should be everyone's goal.
   d. means looking perfect.

7. To be accepted, the message to women is
   a. be skinny.
   b. have true inner beauty.
   c. live with your flaws.
   d. think about society's role models.

8. Our society
   a. is divided about what beauty is.
   b. approves of unrealistic images at any cost.
   c. has different standards for different body types.
   d. is to blame for deaths from anorexia.

9. According to the author, there's a serious contradiction between
   a. our cultural values and our ideas about beauty.
   b. our images of beauty for men and women.
   c. what we say beauty is and how we treat people.
   d. the way men and women react to the image of beauty.

10. The author predicts that if we continue to rely on the cultural ideas of beauty, we will
  a. have more deaths from eating disorders.
  b. lose our ideals about individuality.
  c. lose our understanding of what beauty is.
  d. give the movie industry too much power.

Expand Your Thinking

Use these activities to expand your understanding of the ideas in this essay.

1. The following questions will help you develop your own ideas about this topic.
  a. How would you define the terms society, media, and beauty?
  b. Has your idea of beauty been affected by the media?
  c. Do you think the media are at all responsible for eating disorders?
  d. Do you agree with the author that society should not promote ideal images that damage people's self-esteem?

2. Take notes on this text.

Check Your Motivation

1. Review your reading goal. Did you achieve it? Explain.

2. Make a list of the new ideas that you've gained from this text. Think about how they will be useful to you in the future.

3. Assess your current motivation. Think about how you read this text. Then mark each statement:

A = not at all B = a little C = fairly well D = very well

	A	B	C	D
To engage my interest, I . . .				
1. initiated an "I want to read about this" attitude.	___	___	___	___
2. preread the text.	___	___	___	___
3. identified the topic and/or thought about relevant or interesting points before reading.	___	___	___	___
4. looked for the author's organization before reading.	___	___	___	___
5. set a reading goal before reading.	___	___	___	___
To focus my efforts, I . . .				
6. chose my methods and had an "I know how to read this" attitude.	___	___	___	___
7. read where I was able to concentrate.	___	___	___	___
8. formed questions and read to find answers and other important points.	___	___	___	___

	A	B	C	D
To monitor my progress, I . . .				
9. felt confident and had an "I believe I can read this well" attitude.	___	___	___	___
10. solved any reading problems during reading. (Mark D if there were none.)	___	___	___	___
11. marked the text as I read.	___	___	___	___
12. recited parts or all of the text.	___	___	___	___
To reflect on my gains, I . . .				
13. had an "I've accomplished something" attitude once I finished.	___	___	___	___
14. recognized the new or useful information I gained.	___	___	___	___
15. rewarded myself.	___	___	___	___

SCORING: Write the number of answers you marked in each column in the following spaces. Compute the column scores, and then add them up to determine your total score.

# of A's ___ × 1 pt. = ___

# of B's ___ × 2 pt. = ___

# of C's ___ × 3 pt. = ___

# of D's ___ × 4 pt. = ___

Total points = ___

INTERPRETATION: 15–43 points = low motivation; 44–60 points = high motivation

Rate Box

Compute your reading rate by following these steps:

1. **RECORD** your END time here: ____________
2. **RECORD** your START time here: ____________
3. **DETERMINE** your TOTAL reading time here: ____________
4. **ROUND OFF** the seconds to the nearest ¼ minute. For example, 4 minutes, 15 seconds would be 4.25. Write this on the **** line.
5. **DIVIDE** the number of words by your rounded off time:

633 words / ______ = ______ WPM
****

Reminder: Record your rate, comprehension, vocabulary, and motivation scores on the Progress Charts.

Psychology Reading: Textbook Section

Before you read . . .

Engage Your Interest: preread and divide

What makes people physically attractive? Does attractiveness reveal anything about a person's personality? Does it reveal anything about his/her values?

After prereading, set a goal for your reading.

I want to ________________________ about ______________________________.
My reward(s) will be ____
____.

As you read . . .

Focus Your Efforts: question and read

Attraction

by Saul Kassin

Psychology, 4th edition

When you meet someone for the first time, what are you drawn to? Common sense is filled with contradiction: Does familiarity breed fondness or contempt? Do birds of a feather flock together, or do opposites attract? And is beauty the object of our desire, or do we think appearances are deceiving? Over the years, researchers have identified various determinants of attraction (Berscheid & Reis, 1998; Brehm et al., 2001). Two of the most powerful are similarity and physical attractiveness.

Similarity and Liking

Time and again, studies have revealed a basic principle of attraction: The more exposure we have to a stimulus, and the more familiar it becomes—whether it's a face, a foreign word, a melody, or a geometric form—the more we like it (Zajonc, 1968; Bornstein, 1989; Harmon-Jones & Allen, 2001). In Chapter 4, we saw that this **mere-exposure effect** occurs even when stimuli are presented subliminally, without a participant's awareness. Mere exposure can also influence our self-evaluations. Imagine, for example, that you had a photograph of yourself developed into two pictures—one that depicted your actual appearance, the other a mirror-image copy. Which picture would you prefer? Which would your friends prefer? Theodore Mita and others (1977) tried this experiment with female college students and found that most preferred their own mirror images, whereas their friends liked the actual photos. In both cases, the preference was for the view of the face that was most familiar.

Although exposure tends to increase liking, interactions provide us with additional information about others. Imagine that you meet someone for the first time and strike up a conversation about politics, sports, restaurants, or your favorite band—only to realize that the two of you have a lot in common. Now imagine the opposite experience, of meeting someone who is very different in his or her interests, values, and outlook on life. Which of these strangers would you want to see again: the one who is similar or the one who is different?

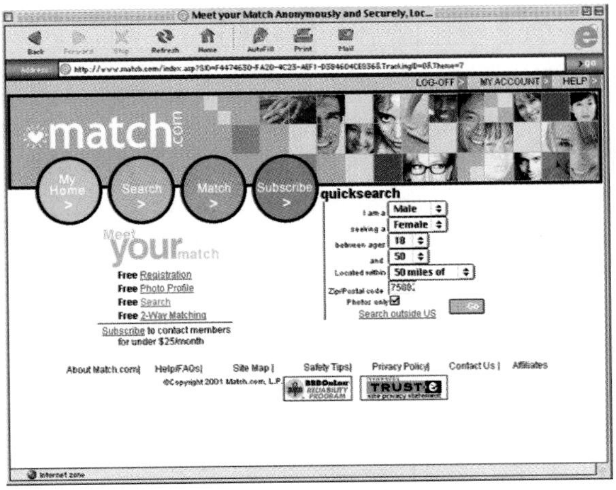

As a general rule, people prefer to associate with others who are similar to themselves. According to Donn Byrne and others (1986), this effect on attraction is a two-step process: (1) We avoid others who are very different; then (2) among those who are left, we seek out those people who are the most similar to us. As a result, friends and couples are more likely than are randomly paired persons to share common attitudes and interests. They are also more likely to be similar in their age, race, religion, education level, intelligence, height, and economic status. The more similar two individuals are, the better are the chances that the relationship will last (Byrne, 1971; 1997). Commenting on the magnetlike appeal of similarity, even in diverse multicultural societies, sociologist John Macionis (2001) notes, "Cupid's arrow is aimed by society more than we think." One unfortunate result, as we'll see in Chapter 14, is that by associating only with similar others, people form social niches that are homogeneous—and divided along the lines of race, ethnic background, age, religion, level of education, and occupation (McPherson et al., 2001).

In a survey of forty-five hundred single men and women, Internet dating service match.com asked, "What attribute do you find most attractive in a potential partner?" What do you predict would be most important? The top pick, as chosen by a third of all respondents: a good sense of humor.

Physical Attractiveness

When we first encounter people, our perceptions are influenced in subtle ways by their height, weight, skin color, hair color, clothing, and other aspects of outward appearance. Among North Americans, blonds are considered fun-loving and sociable, and obese people are seen as weak-willed and lazy. Whether these perceptions are accurate or not, people connect outward appearance and personality (Bruce & Young, 1998; Zebrowitz, 1997).

The most influential aspect of appearance is physical attractiveness. As children, we were told that "beauty is only skin deep." Yet as adults, we like others who are good looking. Inspiring Nancy Etcoff's (1999) book *Survival of the Prettiest,* studies have shown that in the affairs of our social world, attractive people fare better in the way they are treated by teachers, employers, judges, juries, and others (Langlois et al., 2000). Through interviews conducted in the United States and Canada, for example, economists discovered that across occupational groups, good-looking men and women earned more money than others who were comparable—except less attractive (Hamermesh & Biddle, 1994). But wait. What is meant by the term *attractiveness?* Is beauty an objective and measurable quality, like height and weight? Or is beauty subjective, existing in the eye of the beholder?

Some psychologists believe that some faces are inherently more attractive than others (Rhodes & Zebrowitz, 2001). This "objective" view of beauty has two sources of evidence. First, when people rate faces on a 10-point scale, there are typically high levels of agreement over which are more or less attractive (Langlois et al., 2000). It appears that people prefer faces with eyes, noses, lips, and other features that are not too different from the average. Judith Langlois and Lori Roggman (1990) showed actual yearbook photographs to college students as well as computerized facial composites that "averaged" the features in these photos. Time and again, participants preferred the averaged composites to the actual faces. Other studies have since confirmed this effect (Langlois et al., 1994; Rhodes et al., 1999). Still other studies have shown that people are attracted to faces that are symmetrical—in other words, faces in which the right and left sides closely mirror each other (Grammer & Thornhill, 1994; Mealey et al., 1999).

A second source of evidence comes from the infant research laboratory, which shows that even babies who are too young to have learned their culture's standards of beauty exhibit a measurable preference for faces seen as attractive by adults. Judging from their eye movements, young infants spend more time gazing at attractive faces than at unattractive ones—regardless of whether the faces are young or old, male or female, or black or white (Langlois et al., 1991). Other studies have similarly revealed that infants look longer at faces that are "averaged" in their features (Rubenstein et al., 1999). "These kids don't read *Vogue* or watch TV," notes Langlois, "yet they make the same judgments as adults" (Cowley, 1996, p. 66).

Other researchers argue that beauty is subjective and is influenced by culture, time, and the circumstances of our perception. People from different cultures enhance their appearance with face painting, makeup, plastic surgery, hairstyling, scarring, tattooing, the molding of bones, the filing of teeth, braces, and the piercing of body parts—all contributing to "the enigma of beauty" (Newman, 2000). Even within a culture, standards change from one generation to the next. Brett Silverstein and others (1986) examined measurements of female models appearing in women's magazines between 1901 and 1981, and they found that "curvaceousness" (as measured by the bust-to-waist ratio) varied over time, with a boyish slender look becoming most desirable in recent years. Finally, judgments of beauty can be inflated or deflated by various circumstances. For example, we evaluate others as more attractive after we have grown to like them (Gross & Crofton, 1977). In contrast, participants who viewed nude *Playboy* models later lowered their ratings of the attractiveness of average-looking women—the result of a contrast effect (Kenrick et al., 1989).

The bias for beauty seems so shallow, so superficial. Why, then, are we drawn to people who are physically attractive? One explanation is that it's rewarding to be in the company of others who are aesthetically appealing, that we derive pleasure from beautiful men and women the same way we enjoy breathtaking scenery. A second explanation is

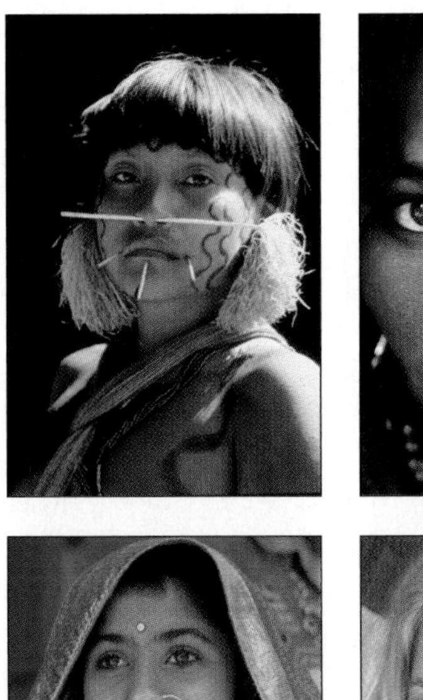

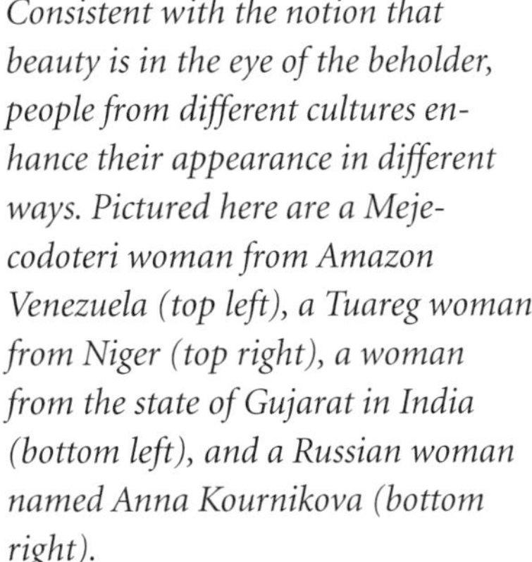

Consistent with the notion that beauty is in the eye of the beholder, people from different cultures enhance their appearance in different ways. Pictured here are a Mejecodoteri woman from Amazon Venezuela (top left), a Tuareg woman from Niger (top right), a woman from the state of Gujarat in India (bottom left), and a Russian woman named Anna Kournikova (bottom right).

that we associate beauty with other desirable qualities. Over the years, studies have shown that good-looking people are also assumed to be smart, successful, well adjusted, happy, confident, assertive, socially skilled, and popular (Dion et al., 1972; Eagly et al., 1991).

This perceived link between beauty and goodness is not hard to understand. Think about children's fairy tales, where Snow White and Cinderella are portrayed as beautiful *and* kind, and where the witch and stepsisters are depicted as ugly *and* cruel. This association between beauty and goodness can even be seen in Hollywood movies. Stephen Smith and others (1999) had people watch and rate the main characters appearing in the hundred top-grossing movies from the years 1940 to 1990. They found that the more attractive the characters were, the more they were portrayed as virtuous, romantically active, and successful. In a second study, these investigators showed college students a film that depicted either a strong or weak link between the beauty and goodness of the characters. In what was supposed to be an unrelated experiment, these students were then asked to evaluate graduate school applicants who had equivalent credentials but whose photographs differed in attractiveness. The result was both interesting and disturbing: students who watched a film that depicted the beautiful-is-good stereotype were more likely than those who watched a nonstereotypic film to favor the physically attractive student applicant in their evaluations (see Figure 13.7). This study suggests that the

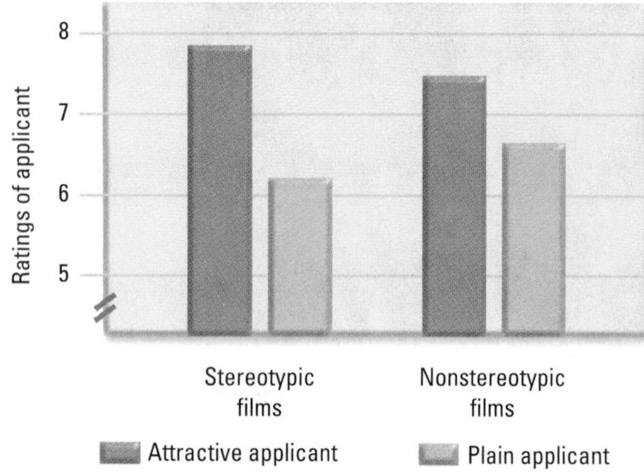

FIGURE 13.7 **Media influences on the attractiveness stereotype**
In this study, participants evaluated graduate school applicants who differed in their physical attractiveness. Indicating the power of the media to influence us, those who had first watched a stereotypic film in which beauty was associated with goodness were more likely to favor the attractive applicant than those who had first seen a nonstereotypical film (Smith et al., 1999).

entertainment industry unwittingly may help to foster and perpetuate our tendency to judge people by their physical appearance.

Is the physical-attractiveness stereotype accurate? Only to a limited extent. Research shows that good-looking people have more friends and a more active sex life, but that beauty is *not* related to measures of intelligence, personality, personal adjustment, or self-esteem. In these ways, it seems that popular perceptions exaggerate the reality (Feingold, 1992). It also seems that the specific nature of the stereotype depends on our cultural conceptions of what is "good." Ladd Wheeler and Youngmee Kim (1997) asked people in Korea to rate photos of various men and women and found that people seen as physically attractive were also assumed to have "integrity" and "a concern for others"—traits that are highly valued in that culture. In contrast to what is considered desirable in most Western cultures, attractive people in Korea were not assumed to be independent or assertive. What is beautiful is good, but what is good is culturally defined.

So why, you might wonder, does the physical-attractiveness stereotype endure? One possibility is that social perceivers create support for their biased impressions. Think about the three-step model of the *self-fulfilling prophecy* described earlier. Snyder and others (1977) demonstrated this phenomenon in a classic study of interpersonal attraction. The participants were unacquainted pairs of male and female college students. All were given a background sketch of their partners, with each man also receiving a photograph of an attractive or unattractive woman, supposedly his partner. At that point, the men rated their partners and then had a conversation with them over headphones. The result: Men who thought that their partner was physically attractive formed more positive impressions of her personality and were friendlier in their conversational behavior. And now for the clincher: Female participants whose partners had seen the attractive photograph were later rated by listeners to the conversation as warmer, more confident, and more animated. Fulfilling their own prophecies, men who expected an attractive partner actually created one. This finding calls to mind the Greek myth of Pygmalion, who fell in love with the statue he had carved—and brought it to life. (1743 words)

Review Questions

- Distinguish between personal and situational attributions. What three types of information do we consider when making attributions?
- What is the fundamental attribution error and why does it occur?

- What is the primacy effect in impression formation? Why does it occur?
- Describe the chain of events involved in behavioral confirmation.
- How do similarity and physical attractiveness influence liking?

The following parts are from the end of the chapter:

Summary
Attraction
There are several factors that spark a positive impression, or attraction. The first is familiarity. Through the mere-exposure effect, exposure to a person increases liking. A second factor is physical attractiveness. People like others who are physically attractive and behave more warmly toward them. Third, people like others who are similar in attitudes and interest.

Key Term
Mere-exposure effect

Before you go on . . .
Monitor Your Progress: recite

After you read . . .
Reflect on Your Gains: review

REVIEW ACTIVITIES

Use the following activities to check your understanding of this reading.

Reading-for-Learning Questions

The following questions are the type you might see on a course exam about this chapter section. Check your understanding of the information by circling the best response to each question.

1. Suppose you and your friends were shown two pictures of you: one that depicted your actual appearance, and one that showed how you look to yourself in a mirror. If everyone behaves in a manner consistent with the mere-exposure effect, when asked which picture is preferred,
   a. you and your friends will prefer the actual picture.
   b. you and your friends will prefer the mirror-image picture.
   c. you will prefer the actual picture and your friends will prefer the mirror-image picture.
   d. you will prefer the mirror-image picture and your friends will prefer the actual picture.

2. You know a number of people who have had the same "best friends" for several years. Based on attraction research, you can expect that long-lasting friendships are between two
   a. people who are very similar.
   b. people who are only somewhat similar, since being very similar is boring.
   c. people who are only similar in one area, since the need for independence makes people dislike those any more similar than that.
   d. women who are very similar, or between men who are not similar, since men need their independence.

3. According to Donn Byrne and his colleagues, which of the following best describes the process of attraction?
   a. We avoid people who are different, then seek people similar to us from the remainder.
   b. We actively seek people who are very different in interests, values, and outlook.
   c. We seek people randomly, then change ourselves to match those whom we find.
   d. We seek people randomly, then are attracted to those similar to us.

4. What have research studies shown with respect to the way that physically attractive people are treated by others?
   a. They tend to be treated unfavorably.
   b. They tend to receive better treatment.
   c. They tend to be treated similarly to others.
   d. How they are treated depends on how they treat others.

5. A researcher has a database of thousands of yearbook pictures and uses a computer program that can weight certain features and develop various facial composites. When subjects are shown these computer-generated faces, they are most likely to prefer those with
   a. overly large features.
   b. especially wide-set eyes.
   c. noses that are particularly small.
   d. an "averaged" set of features.

6. Research has shown that an infant who is given the opportunity to look at a variety of faces will look longest at
   a. faces judged most attractive by adults.
   b. all faces equally.
   c. female faces.
   d. young faces.

7. While at the museum, you notice that the women painted by Rubens appear markedly overweight and not particularly attractive to you. This most directly supports the idea that
   a. there is a "contrast effect" when it comes to beauty.
   b. standards of beauty for men and women differ.
   c. beauty is influenced by culture and time.
   d. individuals have different standards for what they see as attractive.

8. Your friend has a blind date and can choose where they go. If she wants to increase her chances of being seen as physically attractive, she should choose
   a. to dine at a Playboy-type club.
   b. go to a beauty pageant.
   c. go to a college party where both of them know other people.
   d. do whatever he wants to because the circumstances in which they interact will not affect how attractive he will see her as being.

9. All you know about a person is that he or she is good looking compared to others. Based on research findings, you can also assume that he or she will
   a. be more intelligent.
   b. have more friends.
   c. be better adjusted.
   d. have higher self-esteem.

10. In Mark Snyder's classic study of interpersonal attraction, men's beliefs about the physical attractiveness of their unknown female telephone partners affected
   a. only the men's behavior toward the women.
   b. only the women's behavior toward the men.
   c. both the men's and women's behavior.
   d. neither the men's nor the women's behavior. (Caruso 324–325)

Expand Your Thinking

Use these activities to expand your understanding of the ideas in this chapter section.

1. The following questions will help you develop your own ideas about the topic.
   a. What do you think the term "attractive" means?
   b. Have you had any experiences in which attractive people seem to be treated better by teachers? Employers? Others?
   c. Why do you think people often assume that those who are beautiful are also good, honest, intelligent, or nice?
   d. The last study mentioned in this chapter section talks about a "self-fulfilling prophecy" in which the "men who expected an attractive partner actually created one." How do you think that could that happen?

2. Take notes on this text.

Check Your Motivation

1. Review your reading goal. Did you achieve it? Explain.
2. Make a list of the new ideas that you've gained from this text. Think about how they will be useful to you in the future.
3. Assess your current motivation. Think about how you read this text. Then mark each statement:

   A = not at all   B = a little   C = fairly well   D = very well

	A	B	C	D
To engage my interest, I . . .				
1. initiated an "I want to read about this" attitude.	___	___	___	___
2. preread the text.	___	___	___	___
3. identified the topic and/or thought about relevant or interesting points before reading.	___	___	___	___
4. looked for the author's organization before reading.	___	___	___	___
5. set a reading goal before reading.	___	___	___	___
To focus my efforts, I . . .				
6. chose my methods and had an "I know how to read this" attitude.	___	___	___	___
7. read where I was able to concentrate.	___	___	___	___
8. formed questions and read to find answers and other important points.	___	___	___	___
To monitor my progress, I . . .				
9. felt confident and had an "I believe I can read this well" attitude.	___	___	___	___
10. solved any reading problems during reading. (Mark D if there were none.)	___	___	___	___
11. marked the text as I read.	___	___	___	___
12. recited parts or all of the text.	___	___	___	___
To reflect on my gains, I . . .				
13. had an "I've accomplished something" attitude once I finished.	___	___	___	___
14. recognized the new or useful information I gained.	___	___	___	___
15. rewarded myself.	___	___	___	___

SCORING: Write the number of answers you marked in each column in the following spaces. Compute the column scores, and then add them up to determine your total score.

# of A's ______ × 1 pt. = ______
# of B's ______ × 2 pt. = ______
# of C's ______ × 3 pt. = ______
# of D's ______ × 4 pt. = ______
Total points = ______

INTERPRETATION: 15–43 points = low motivation; 44–60 points = high motivation

Reminder: Record your Reading for Learning and motivation scores on the Progress Charts.

Reading for Learning: Business Communication Texts

The field of business communication focuses on how to create messages that effectively exchange information during interoffice communications, interactions with customers, and international dealings. All forms of communication, such as speaking, writing, and listening, are included in this field. Freshman courses in this area typically examine the elements of effective business writing, listening skills, nonverbal and intercultural communication, business etiquette, oral presentations, teamwork, and even preparation for job interviews.

What to Look for As You Read

Business communication texts focus on practical principles, or generalizations, about communication, as well as guidelines, or directions, for handling communication situations and creating presentations. Real-world examples are used to make the ideas clear and demonstrate how well the ideas work.

In the following article, entitled "Indian Companies Are Adding Western Flavor," the author describes the kind of training Indian software employees are receiving to "appear culturally seamless with Americans." Specific companies and examples of the American style are mentioned throughout the article to support the points.

In the textbook section, entitled "Improving Intercultural Sensitivity," the author focuses on principles of culture and the differences between low and high context groups. This section also presents a number of guidelines about how to handle intercultural differences, as well as numerous examples.

Motivation and Reading Tips

1. *Look for useful information.*

   Business communication information is very practical. It is used in virtually every type of work and in every position from entry level to top management and in professional positions. To become more motivated as you read, look for tips about how to improve your skills and interactions with others.

2. *Pay particular attention to the important principles.*

   Look for the generalizations that describe and explain how communication works. Use them as the foundation for understanding the practical guidelines and examples.

3. *Identify the parts within the guidelines.*

   The how-to guidelines tend to present steps or lists that describe a process. To get the complete message, you will need to identify the separate parts and then understand how they work together.

4. *Apply the examples.*

   Link each example to yourself, the principle, or the guideline it relates to. Think about what it shows or illustrates.

Business Communication Reading: Article

Before you read . . .

Engage Your Interest: preread and divide

If you were meeting people from other countries as part of your job, would it matter what you wore? Would it matter if you were traveling to meet those people in their country? Should you give your opinion or just do your job when dealing with customers from other nations?

After prereading, set a goal for your reading.

I want to ______________________ about ______________________.
My reward(s) will be ______________________
______________________.

Right before you begin to read, record your START time in the Rate Box on page 560.

As you read . . .

Focus Your Efforts: question and read

Indian Companies Are Adding Western Flavor

by Saritha Rai

The New York Times, August 19, 2003

Arun Kumar had never shaken hands with a foreigner nor needed to wear a necktie. He vaguely thought that raising a toast had something to do with eating bread. If it was dark outside, he greeted people with a "good night." 1

But Mr. Kumar, 27, and six other engineers graduating from the local university with master's degrees in computer applications, were recently recruited by the Hyderabad offices of Sierra Atlantic, a software company based in Fremont, California. And before they came face to face with one of Sierra's 200 or so American customers, the new employees went through a grueling four-week training session aimed at providing them with global-employee skills like learning how to speak on a conference call, how to address colleagues (as Mr. or Ms.) and how to sip wine properly. "Teetotalers practice by sipping Coke out of their wine glasses," Mr. Kumar said at the session in early July. 2

As more and more service- and knowledge-intensive jobs migrate to India, such training programs, covering some substance as well as style, are increasingly common at companies with large numbers of Indian employees. It is particularly imperative for employees of software companies to appear culturally seamless with Americans. 3

American clients account for more than two-thirds of India's software and services export revenues.

4 Sierra Atlantic, a midsize software services company, says that one-fourth of its 400 employees, all but a handful of them Indian and most of them working out of the Hyderabad offices, are constantly interacting with foreigners. For Sierra and others, the training in Western ways is intended not only to help employees perform daily business interactions with American or European colleagues and customers but to help the companies transcend their image as cheap labor.

5 Mr. Kumar is typical of the thousands of eager young engineering graduates. Though he and his peers are technologically adept and fluent in English, most lack the sophistication needed to flourish in a global business setting. "It is not always understood that speaking a common language, English, is rarely a guarantee of communicating the same way," said Partha Iyengar, vice president for research at Gartner India Research and Advisory Services.

6 "Your interaction with people of alien cultures will only increase," Col. Gowri Shankar, a 30-year veteran of the Indian Army and Sierra's trainer, told Mr. Kumar and half a dozen other young engineers that morning in July, "and you should be equally at ease whether in Hyderabad or Houston."

7 The Sierra programmers listened raptly as Colonel Shankar listed common complaints: speaking one of India's many languages in front of foreigners, questioning colleagues about their compensation and cracking ethnic jokes. Some things he covers are not acceptable in any corporate setting and some are particular sore points with foreigners. He is fiendish about punctuality and a stickler for protocol.

8 "Americans are friendly, but do not slap an American on his back or call him by his first name in the first meeting," said Colonel Shankar, whose training materials are fine-tuned by information from programmers returning from trips abroad.

9 Across the world, Global Savvy, a consulting company in Palo Alto, California, trains high-tech employees to work together in projects around the world. "The training in American culture is not to make Indian software professionals less Indian," said Lu Ellen Schafer, the executive director. "It is to make them more globally competent."

10 "As an aggregate, Indian software professionals have not changed in the way they present themselves," said Peter Nag, vice president and global program management officer for Lehman Brothers in New York, which is a client of Wipro. "We find that Indians hesitate to say no even though we ask them all the time to speak their minds. Then there are small things, like getting up from the seat when a senior colleague enters the room. This feels strange."

11 Still, some companies training their employees say they are already seeing the benefits. Sierra said that in February its Indian unit won a bid against a technically able Indian competitor because the Sierra employees were seen as a better fit. "It all adds up to better rates and bigger projects," said the project leader, Kalyani Manda.

12 Ms. Manda said she noticed a difference when she herself conformed, even in a seemingly minor way. On her first trip to the United States three years ago, she wore a salwar kameez, a loose-fitting Indian garment, and felt totally out of place. "On the next trip," she said, "I wore pants, fitted in better and delivered more." (750 words)

As soon as you finish reading, record your END time in the Rate Box on page 560.

Before you go on . . .

Monitor Your Progress: recite

After you read . . .

Reflect on Your Gains: review

REVIEW ACTIVITIES

Use the following activities to check your understanding of this article.

Expand Your Vocabulary

Define the underlined terms as they are used in the article by circling the correct response. The numbers in parentheses indicate the paragraph where the term appears.

1. grueling four-week training session (2)
   a. physically challenging **b.** mentally demanding **c.** emotionally draining **d.** energetic
2. It is particularly imperative (3)
   a. urgent **b.** demanding **c.** serious **d.** useful
3. to appear culturally seamless (3)
   a. without barriers **b.** within restrictions **c.** from the same country **d.** joined together
4. transcend their image (4)
   a. travel **b.** overcome **c.** think beyond **d.** exceed
5. he and his peers are technologically adept (5)
   a. adequate **b.** skilled **c.** knowledgeable **d.** quick
6. lack the sophistication needed (5)
   a. worldly knowledge **b.** well traveled **c.** education **d.** sensitivity
7. to flourish in a global setting (5)
   a. have a fancy style **b.** survive **c.** do well **d.** exist
8. he is fiendish about punctuality (7)
   a. devilish **b.** ruthless **c.** furious **d.** demanding
9. a stickler for protocol (7)
   a. disciplinarian **b.** purist **c.** fanatic **d.** champion

10. a stickler for protocol (7)
   a. professional behavior
   b. good work
   c. correct conduct
   d. polite speech

Check Your Comprehension

Use the following questions to determine how well you understand the ideas, details, and inferences in this article. Circle the best response to each question.

1. The main idea of this article is best stated as:
   a. Training is needed to change the style of Indian software professionals so that they're less Indian.
   b. Cultural training is helping the Indian software professionals.
   c. Training is overcoming the educational deficiencies of Indian software professionals.
   d. Training is helping Indian software professionals "transcend their image as cheap labor."

2. The training described in this article is for Indian professionals who
   a. work in the United States or for U.S. businesses.
   b. have American clients.
   c. travel in the United States.
   d. want to succeed with American and European colleagues and customers.

3. True or false? Only service jobs are being sent to countries such as India.

4. In companies such as Sierra Atlantic, employees interact with foreigners
   a. constantly.
   b. often.
   c. occasionally.
   d. at various times.

5. The author implies that some Americans and Europeans view Indian workers
   a. as highly qualified.
   b. as unqualified.
   c. as cheap labor that may not be completely qualified.
   d. as cheap labor that is very qualified.

6. According to the article, to succeed in global business, professionals need to be
   a. multi-lingual.
   b. technologically adept.
   c. fluent in English.
   d. sophisticated.

7. The author implies that speaking a common language
   a. does not ensure good communication.
   b. is the most important aspect of being culturally aware.
   c. helps people learn about other cultures.
   d. is required for global business people.

8. The author implies that speaking one of India's languages in front of foreigners
   a. is rude.
   b. will offend most people.
   c. is irritating to many foreign business people.
   d. is acceptable as long as the message is translated.

9. At the first meeting, Americans are
   a. very friendly and informal.
   b. friendly but very formal.
   c. not friendly.
   d. friendly but somewhat reserved.

10. It is implied that American and European business people
   a. are easily offended.
   b. want people to speak their mind.
   c. want honesty as long as it's phrased politely.
   d. prefer to make all the decisions.

Expand Your Thinking

Use these activities to expand your understanding of the ideas in this article.

1. The following questions will help you develop your own ideas about this topic.
   a. What behaviors or attitudes of people from cultures other than your own do you find hard to understand? What do those actions or attitudes signify to you?
   b. What American behaviors or attitudes do you think people from other cultures find hard to understand? How do you think people of other cultures interpret those actions or attitudes?
   c. What could people from different cultures do to lessen the tensions caused by cultural differences? Give some examples.
2. Take notes on this text.

Check Your Motivation

1. Review your reading goal. Did you achieve it? Explain.
2. Make a list of the new ideas that you've gained from this text. Think about how they will be useful to you in the future.
3. Assess your current motivation. Think about how you read this text. Then mark each statement:

   A = not at all   B = a little   C = fairly well   D = very well

	A	B	C	D
To engage my interest, I . . .				
1. initiated an "I want to read about this" attitude.	___	___	___	___
2. preread the text.	___	___	___	___
3. identified the topic and/or thought about relevant or interesting points before reading.	___	___	___	___
4. looked for the author's organization before reading.	___	___	___	___
5. set a reading goal before reading.	___	___	___	___
To focus my efforts, I . . .				
6. chose my methods and had an "I know how to read this" attitude.	___	___	___	___
7. read where I was able to concentrate.	___	___	___	___
8. formed questions and read to find answers and other important points.	___	___	___	___

	A	B	C	D
To monitor my progress, I . . .				
9. felt confident and had an "I believe I can read this well" attitude.	___	___	___	___
10. solved any reading problems during reading. (Mark D if there were none.)	___	___	___	___
11. marked the text as I read.	___	___	___	___
12. recited parts or all of the text.	___	___	___	___
To reflect on my gains, I . . .				
13. had an "I've accomplished something" attitude once I finished.	___	___	___	___
14. recognized the new or useful information I gained.	___	___	___	___
15. rewarded myself.	___	___	___	___

SCORING: Write the number of answers you marked in each column in the following spaces. Compute the column scores, and then add them up to determine your total score.

# of A's ______ × 1 pt. = ______
# of B's ______ × 2 pt. = ______
# of C's ______ × 3 pt. = ______
# of D's ______ × 4 pt. = ______
Total points = ______

INTERPRETATION: 15–43 points = low motivation; 44–60 points = high motivation

Rate Box

Compute your reading rate by following these steps:

1. **RECORD** your END time here: ____________
2. **RECORD** your START time here: ____________
3. **DETERMINE** your TOTAL reading time here: ____________
4. **ROUND OFF** the seconds to the nearest ¼ minute. For example, 4 minutes, 15 seconds would be 4.25. Write this on the **** line.
5. **DIVIDE** the number of words by your rounded off time:

750 words / ______ = ______ WPM
****

Reminder: Record your rate, comprehension, vocabulary, and motivation scores on the Progress Charts.

Business Communication Reading: Textbook Section

Before you read . . .

Engage Your Interest: preread and divide

Does culture affect the way we communicate with others? Could cultural knowledge affect our level of success at work and in our lives in general?

After prereading, set a goal for your reading.

I want to ____________________ about __________________________.
My reward(s) will be ___________________________________
____.

As you read . . .

Focus Your Efforts: question and read

Improving Cultural Sensitivity

John V. Thill and Courtland L. Bovee

Excellence in Business Communication, 6th ed.

Culture is a shared system of symbols, beliefs, attitudes, values, expectations, and norms for behavior. You belong to several cultures. The most obvious is the culture you share with all the people who influenced you as you grew up in your own family, community, and country. In addition, you belong to **subcultures,** other distinct groups that exist within a major culture—including an ethnic group, probably a religious group, and perhaps a profession that has its own special language and customs. In the United States subcultures include Mexican Americans, Mormons, wrestling fans, Russian immigrants, disabled individuals, Harvard graduates, and uncountable other groups.

As you can imagine, culture strongly affects communication. Members of a culture have similar assumptions about how people should think, behave, and communicate, and they tend to act on those assumptions in much the same way. You learn culture directly and indirectly from other members of your group. As you grow up in a culture, group members teach you who you are and how best to function in that culture. Sometimes you are explicitly told which behaviors are acceptable; at other times you learn by observing which values work best in a particular group. This multiple learning format ensures that culture is passed on from person to person and from generation to generation.[1]

Needless to say, the world does not fall into neat and tidy categories. Although some places tend to be fairly homogeneous, having few subcultural groups, other places are heterogeneous, having many subcultural groups. In the United States, for example, many

Putting more people of various ethnicities on the floor—and in executive positions—is commonplace for Wal-Mart, which was recently ranked by Fortune *magazine as one of America's 50 best companies for Asian, African, and Hispanic Americans. This diverse group of Wal-Mart managers clearly understand the importance of being sensitive to others' cultures.*

subcultural groups retain their own identity and integrity, adding to the complexity of the culture in general. Generalizing about values and behaviors in such heterogeneous societies is certainly difficult, but some generalization is possible.[2]

From group to group, cultures differ widely in more than just language and gestures. Cultures vary in how quickly or easily they change. They differ in their degree of complexity and in their tolerance toward outsiders. All these differences affect the level of trust and open communication that you can achieve with the people who belong to these various cultures.

To improve your ability to communicate effectively across cultures, first be able to recognize cultural differences and then make sure you can overcome your own **ethnocentrism**—your tendency to judge all other groups according to your own group's standards, behaviors, and customs. When making such comparisons, people too often decide that their own group is superior.[3]

Recognize Cultural Differences

When you write to or speak with someone from another culture, you encode your message using the assumptions of your own culture. However, members of your audience decode your message according to the assumptions of their culture, so your meaning may be misunderstood. The greater the difference between cultures, the greater the chance for misunderstanding. For example, exhibitors at a trade show couldn't understand why Chinese visitors were passing by their booth without stopping. The exhibitors were wearing green hats and giving them away as promotional items. They discovered, however, that many Chinese people associate green hats with infidelity; the Chinese expression "He wears a green hat" indicates that a man's wife has been cheating on him. As soon as the exhibitors discarded the green hats and began giving out T-shirts instead, the Chinese attendees started visiting the booth.[4]

Such problems arise when people assume, wrongly, that others' attitudes and lives are like their own. As a graduate of one intercultural training program said, "I used to think it was enough to treat people the way I wanted to be treated. But [after taking the course] . . . I realized you have to treat people the way they want to be treated."[5] You can increase your intercultural sensitivity by recognizing and accommodating four main types of cultural differences: contextual, ethical, social, and nonverbal.

Contextual Differences

One of the ways people assign meaning to a message is according to **cultural context,** the pattern of physical cues, environmental stimuli, and implicit understanding that convey meaning between two members of the same culture. However, from culture to culture, people convey contextual meaning differently. In fact, correct social behavior and effective communication can be defined by how much a culture depends on contextual cues (see Table 3–1).

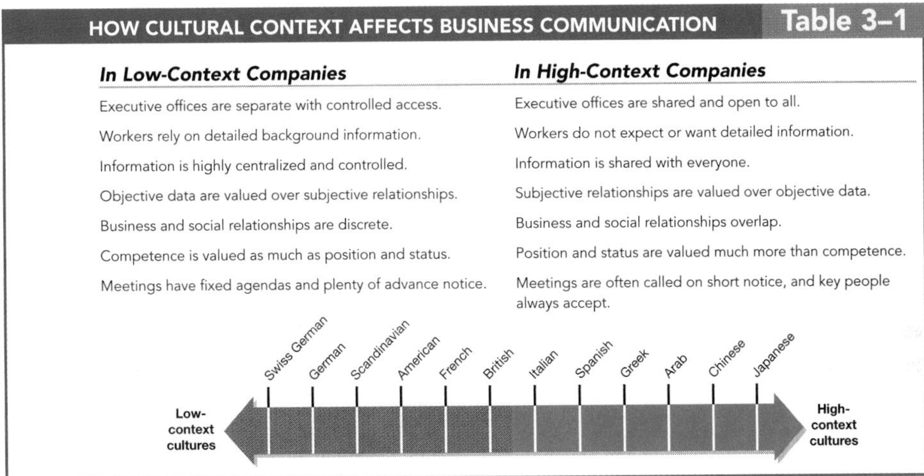

HOW CULTURAL CONTEXT AFFECTS BUSINESS COMMUNICATION — **Table 3–1**

In Low-Context Companies	*In High-Context Companies*
Executive offices are separate with controlled access.	Executive offices are shared and open to all.
Workers rely on detailed background information.	Workers do not expect or want detailed information.
Information is highly centralized and controlled.	Information is shared with everyone.
Objective data are valued over subjective relationships.	Subjective relationships are valued over objective data.
Business and social relationships are discrete.	Business and social relationships overlap.
Competence is valued as much as position and status.	Position and status are valued much more than competence.
Meetings have fixed agendas and plenty of advance notice.	Meetings are often called on short notice, and key people always accept.

In a **high-context culture** such as South Korea or Taiwan, people rely less on verbal communication and more on the context of nonverbal actions and environmental setting to convey meaning. A Chinese speaker expects the receiver to discover the essence of a message and uses indirectness and metaphor to provide a web of meaning.[6] In high-context cultures, the rules of everyday life are rarely explicit; instead, as individuals grow up, they learn how to recognize situational cues (such as gestures and tone of voice) and how to respond as expected.[7]

In a **low-context culture** such as the United States or Germany, people rely more on verbal communication and less on circumstances and cues to convey meaning. An English speaker feels responsible for transmitting the meaning of the message and often places sentences in chronological sequence to establish a cause-and-effect pattern.[8] In a low-context culture, rules and expectations are usually spelled out through explicit statements such as "Please wait until I'm finished" or "You're welcome to browse."[9]

Contextual differences affect the way cultures approach situations such as decision making, problem solving, and negotiating:

- **Decision making.** In lower-context cultures, businesspeople try to reach decisions quickly and efficiently. They are concerned with reaching an agreement on the main points, leaving the details to be worked out later by others. However, in a higher-context culture such as Greece, executives assume that anyone who ignores the details is being evasive and untrustworthy. They believe that spending time on each little point is a mark of good faith.
- **Problem solving.** Low-context U.S. executives typically enjoy confrontation and debate, unlike high-context Japanese executives who may use a third party to avoid

the unpleasant feelings that might result from open conflict. Chinese executives also try to prevent public conflict by avoiding proposal-counterproposal methods. Chinese team members cannot back down from a position without losing face, so trying to persuade them to do so will ruin the relationship.

- **Negotiating.** Low-context Canadian and German negotiators tend to view negotiations as impersonal, setting their goals in economic terms and trusting the other party, at least at the outset. However, high-context Japanese negotiators prefer a more sociable negotiating atmosphere, one conducive to forging personal ties as the basis for trust. They see immediate economic gains as secondary to establishing and maintaining a long-term relationship.[10]

Legal and Ethical Differences

Cultural context also influences legal and ethical behavior. For example, because people in low-context cultures value the written word, they consider written agreements binding and tend to adhere to laws strictly. But high-context cultures put less emphasis on the written word; they consider personal pledges more important than contracts and view laws as flexible.[11]

As you conduct business around the world, you'll find that legal systems differ from culture to culture. In the United Kingdom and the United States, someone is presumed innocent until proven guilty, a principle rooted in English common law. However, in Mexico and Turkey, someone is presumed guilty until proven innocent, a principle rooted in the Napoleonic code.[12] These distinctions can be particularly important if your firm must communicate about a legal dispute in another country.

Making ethical choices can be difficult enough within your own culture. But what does it mean for a business to do the right thing in Thailand? Africa? Norway? What happens when a certain behavior is unethical in the United States but an accepted practice in another culture? For example, in the United States, bribing officials is illegal, but Kenyans consider paying such bribes a part of life. To get something done right, they-pay *kitu kidogo* (or "something small"). In China, businesses pay *huilu,* in Russia they pay *vzyatha,* in the Middle East it's *baksheesh,* and in Mexico it's *una mordida* ("a small bite").[13] Making ethical choices across cultures can seem incredibly complicated, but doing so actually differs little from the way you choose the most ethical path in your own culture.

Keep your intercultural messages ethical by applying four basic principles:[14]

- **Actively seek mutual ground.** Both parties must be flexible and avoid insisting that an interaction take place strictly in terms of one culture or another.
- **Send and receive messages without judgment.** Both parties must recognize that values vary from culture to culture, and they must trust each other.
- **Send messages that are honest.** Both parties must see things as they are—not as they would like them to be—and must be fully aware of their personal and cultural biases.
- **Show respect for cultural differences.** Both parties must understand and acknowledge the other's needs and preserve each other's dignity.

Social Differences

In any culture, rules of social etiquette may be formal or informal. Formal rules are the specifically taught do's and don'ts of how to behave in common social situations, such as table manners at meals. When formal rules are violated, members of a culture can explain why they feel upset. In contrast, informal social rules are more difficult to identify and are usually learned by watching how people behave and then imitating that behavior. Informal rules govern how males and females are supposed to behave, when it is appropriate to use a person's first name, and so on. When informal rules are violated, members of a culture are likely to feel uncomfortable, although they may not be able to say exactly why.[15] Such informal rules are apparent in the way members value wealth, treat social roles, recognize status, define manners, and think about time.

- **Attitude toward materialism.** Although people in the United States have many different religions and values, the predominant U.S. view is that material comfort (earned by individual effort) is an important goal and that people who work hard are more admirable than those who don't. But other societies condemn such materialism, and some prize a more carefree lifestyle: Each year U.S. workers spend some 300 more hours on the job than many Germans and 60 more than their Japanese peers (see Figure 3–1).

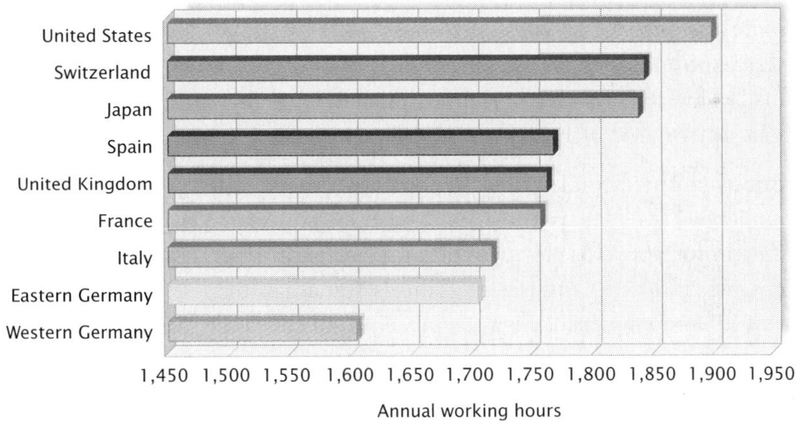

FIGURE 3–1
Working Hours Vary from Culture to Culture

- **Roles.** Culture dictates who communicates with whom, what they say, and in what way. For example, in some countries, women are not taken seriously as businesspeople. In modern western Europe, women can usually behave as they would in the United States. However, they should be more cautious in Latin America and eastern Europe, and they should be extremely cautious in the Middle East and East Asia.[16]

- **Status.** Culture also dictates how people show respect and signify rank. For example, people in the United States show respect by addressing top managers as "Mr. Roberts" or "Ms. Gutierrez." However, people in China show respect by using official titles, such as "President" or "Manager."[17] Also, a U.S. executive's rank may be reflected by a large corner office, deep carpets, and expensive accessories. But high-ranking French executives sit in an open area, surrounded by lower-level employees. And in the Middle East, business is conducted in cramped and modest quarters, while fine possessions are reserved for the home.
- **Manners.** Asking an employee "How was your weekend?" is a common way to make small talk in the United States, but the question is intrusive in cultures where business and private life are kept separate. In Arab countries taking gifts to a man's wife is impolite, but taking gifts to his children is acceptable. In Germany giving a woman a red rose is a romantic invitation. In India, if invited to visit someone's home "any time," you should make an unexpected visit without waiting for an invitation. Failure to do so would be an insult.
- **Time.** German and U.S. executives see time as a way to plan the business day efficiently; they focus on only one task during each scheduled period and view time as limited. However, executives from Latin America and Asia see time as more flexible. Meeting a deadline is less important than building a business relationship. So the workday is not expected to follow a rigid, preset schedule.[18]

Nonverbal Differences

Nonverbal communication is extremely reliable in ascertaining meaning. However, that reliability is valid only when communicators belong to the same culture. Nonverbal elements are apparent in attitudes toward personal space and in body language.

- **Concepts of personal space.** People in Canada and the United States usually stand about five feet apart during a business conversation. However, this distance is uncomfortably close for people from Germany or Japan and uncomfortably far for Arabs and Latin Americans. Thus, a Canadian manager may react negatively (without knowing exactly why) when an Arab colleague moves closer during their conversation. And the Arab colleague may react negatively (again, without knowing why) when the Canadian manager backs away.
- **Use of body language.** Don't assume that someone from another culture who speaks your language has mastered your culture's body language. For example, people in the United States and Canada say no by shaking their heads back and forth, people in Bulgaria nod up and down, and people in Japan move their right hand. People from another culture may misread an intentional nonverbal signal, overlook the signal entirely, or assume that a meaningless gesture is significant. For example, an Egyptian might mistakenly assume that a Westerner who exposes the sole of his or her shoe is offering a grave insult.[19]

Recognizing cultural differences is only the first step in improving your intercultural communication. To achieve intercultural sensitivity, be sure to balance cultural awareness with cultural flexibility. To accommodate cultural differences without judging them, do your best to overcome the human tendency toward ethnocentrism.

Overcome Ethnocentrism

When communicating across cultures, your effectiveness depends on maintaining an open mind. Unfortunately, many people lapse into ethnocentrism. They lose sight of the possibility that their words and actions can be misunderstood, and they forget that they are likely to misinterpret the actions of others.

When you first begin to investigate the culture of another group, you may attempt to understand the common tendencies of that group's members by **stereotyping**—predicting individuals' behaviors or character on the basis of their membership in a particular group or class. For example, Japanese visitors often stereotype people in the United States as walking fast, being wasteful in utilizing space, speaking directly, asking too many questions in the classroom, not respecting age and status, lacking discipline, and being extravagant.[20]

IBM's corporate workforce diversity staff is sensitive to cultural differences, both inside and outside the company. An important goal for staff members is to ensure effective communication among co-workers and with customers by helping fellow employees recognize and grow beyond their own ethnocentrism.

Although stereotyping may be useful in the beginning, the next step is to move beyond the stereotypes to relationships with real people. Unfortunately, when ethnocentric people stereotype, they tend to do so on the basis of limited, general, or inaccurate evidence. They frequently develop biased attitudes toward the group, and they fail to move beyond that initial step.[21] So instead of talking with Abdul Karhum, unique human being, ethnocentric people are talking to "an Arab." They may believe that all Arabs are, say, hagglers, so Abdul Karhum's personal qualities cannot alter such preconceptions. His every action is forced to fit the preconceived image, even if that image is wrong.

To overcome ethnocentrism, follow a few simple suggestions:

- **Acknowledge distinctions.** Don't ignore the differences between another person's culture and your own.
- **Avoid assumptions.** Don't assume that others will act the same way you do, that they will operate from the same assumptions, or that they will use language and symbols the same way you do.
- **Avoid judgments.** When people act differently, don't conclude that they are in error, that their way is invalid, or that their customs are inferior to your own. (2602 words)

Note: This chapter does not have a summary or a list of key terms. Instead, it has the following objectives at the beginning of the chapter that you can use to focus your reading.

Learning Objectives

1. Define culture and subculture, and summarize how culture is learned.
2. Explain the importance of recognizing cultural differences, and list four categories of cultural difference.
3. Define ethnocentrism and stereotyping. Then give three suggestions for overcoming these limiting mind-sets.

The following parts are from the end of the chapter:

References

1. Lillian H. Chaney and Jeanette S. Martin, *Intercultural Business Communication* (Upper Saddle River, NJ.: Prentice Hall, 2000), 6.
2. Gary P. Ferraro, *The Cultural Dimensions of International Business,* 4th ed. (Upper Saddle River, N.J.: Prentice Hall, 2002), 98.
3. Chancy and Martin, *Intercultural Business Communication,* 9.
4. Chaney and Martin, *Intercultural Business Communication,* 159.
5. Otto Kreisher, "Annapolis Has a New Attitude Toward Sexual Harassment," *San Diego Union,* 30 July 1990, A–b.
6. Linda Beamer, "Teaching English Business Writing to Chinese-Speaking Business Students," *Bulletin of the Association for Business Communication* 57, no. 1(1994): 12–18.
7. Edward T. Hall, "Context and Meaning," in *Intercultural Communication,* edited by Samovar and Porter, 46–55.
8. Beamer, "Teaching English Business Writing to Chinese-Speaking Business Students."
9. Chancy H. Dodd, *Dynamics of Intercultural Communication,* 3d ed. (Dubuque, la.: Brown, 1991), 69–70.
10. Chancy and Martin, *Intercultural Business Communication,* 206–211.
11. James Wilfong and Toni Seger, *Taking Your Business Global* (Franklin Lakes, N.J.: Career Press, 1997), 277–278.
12. Phillip R. Harris and Robert T. Moran, *Managing* Cultural *Differences,* 3rd ed. (Houston: Gulf, 1991), 260.
13. Skip Kaltenheuser, "Bribery Is Being Outlawed Virtually Worldwide," *Business Ethics,* May–June 1998, 11; Thomas Omestad, "Bye-bye to Bribes," *U.S. News & World Report,* 22 December 1997, 39, 42–44.
14. Guo-Ming Chen and William J. Starosta, *Foundations of Intercultural Communication* (Boston: Allyn & Bacon, 1998), 288–289.
15. Sharon Ruhly, *Intercultural Communication,* 2nd ed. MODCOM (Modules in Speech Communication) (Chicago: Science Research Associates, 1982), 14.
16. Mary A. DeVries, *Internationally Yours* (New York: Houghton Mifflin, 1994), 194.
17. Robert O. Joy, "Cultural and Procedural Differences That Influence Business Strategies and Operations in the People's Republic of China," *SAM Advanced Management Journal,* Summer 1989, 29–33.

18. Chancy and Martin, *Intercultural Business Communication,* 122–123.
19. Laray M. Bama, "Stumbling Blocks in Intercultural Communication," in *Intercultural Communication,* edited by Samovar and Porter, 345–352; Jean A. Mausehund, Susan A. Timm, and Albert S. King, "Diversity Training: Effects of an Intervention Treatment on Nonverbal Awareness," *Business Communication Quarterly* 38, no. 1 (1995): 27–30.
20. Chen and Starosta, *Foundations of Intercultural Communication,* 39–40.
21. Richard W. Brislin, "Prejudice in Intercultural Communication," in *Intercultural Communication,* edited by Samovar and Porter, 366–370.

Before you go on . . .

Monitor Your Progress: recite

After you read . . .

Reflect on Your Gains: review

REVIEW ACTIVITIES

Use the following activities to check your understanding of this chapter section.

Reading-for-Learning Questions

The following questions are the type that you might see on a course exam about this chapter section. Check your understanding of the information by circling the best response to each question.

1. Culture is defined as
   a. a distinct group that exists within a country.
   b. a shared system of symbols, beliefs, attitudes, values, expectations, and norms for behavior.
   c. the pattern of cues and stimuli that convey meaning between two or more people.
   d. "high" art forms such as classical music, painting, sculpture, drama, and poetry.

2. Which of the following is *not* an example of a subculture?
   a. Mormons
   b. Wrestling fans
   c. Television viewers
   d. Members of a fraternity

3. Culture is learned from
   a. family members.
   b. explicit teaching by others in the culture.
   c. observing the behavior of others in the culture.
   d. all of the above

4. In business, why is it important to recognize cultural differences?
   a. Doing so helps reduce the chances for misunderstanding.
   b. Someone from another culture may try to take advantage of your ignorance.
   c. If you don't, you'll be accused of being politically incorrect.
   d. Doing so helps you become more ethnocentric.
5. An example of low-context cultural communication would be:
   a. someone from China using metaphors to convey meaning.
   b. someone from Greece insisting on reaching agreement on every detail of a deal.
   c. someone from Canada vigorously arguing his point of view in a problem-solving situation.
   d. someone from Japan encouraging socializing before entering into official negotiations.
6. Bribing officials is
   a. outlawed in all Middle Eastern countries.
   b. avoided by most U.S. businesses, even though it is perfectly legal under U.S. statutes.
   c. considered legal but unethical in China.
   d. a natural part of doing business in African countries such as Kenya.
7. If you will be visiting an Arab business executive, you
   a. should take a gift for his wife.
   b. can expect his office to be cramped and modestly appointed.
   c. should maintain as large a physical distance as possible between the two of you.
   d. should do all of the above.
8. People who are ethnocentric
   a. tend to judge all other groups according to their own group's standards, behaviors, and customs.
   b. tend to strongly support affirmative action.
   c. are usually religious fanatics.
   d. are usually the best organizers of intercultural exchanges.
9. An example of stereotyping would be
   a. expecting a basketball player to be tall.
   b. assuming that a dog owner loves all types of animals.
   c. assuming that an Italian American knows or is related to someone in the mob.
   d. expecting someone with a Ph.D. in linguistics to be good at playing Scrabble.
10. One way to overcome ethnocentrism and stereotyping is to
    a. ignore the differences between another person's culture and your own.
    b. assume that others will use language and symbols the same way you do.
    c. avoid judging others when they act differently than you would.
    d. do all of the above. (Adapted from Thill and Bovee 86)

Expand Your Thinking

Use these activities to expand your understanding of the ideas in this text.

1. The following questions will help you develop your own ideas about this topic.
   a. What are some intercultural differences that U.S. business people might encounter in dealings with business people from other countries, such as China or Mexico?
   b. What are some intercultural issues to consider when deciding whether to accept an overseas job with a firm whose headquarters is in the United States? Explain.
   c. What are some intercultural issues to consider when deciding whether to accept a job in the United States with a local branch of a foreign-owned firm? (Adapted from Thill and Bovee 87)
2. Take notes on this text.

Check Your Motivation

1. Review your reading goal. Did you achieve it? Explain.
2. Make a list of the new ideas that you've gained from this text. Think about how they will be useful to you in the future.
3. Assess your current motivation. Think about how you read this text. Then mark each statement:

   A = not at all B = a little C = fairly well D = very well

	A	B	C	D
To engage my interest, I . . .				
1. initiated an "I want to read about this" attitude.	___	___	___	___
2. preread the text.	___	___	___	___
3. identified the topic and/or thought about relevant or interesting points before reading.	___	___	___	___
4. looked for the author's organization before reading.	___	___	___	___
5. set a reading goal before reading.	___	___	___	___
To focus my efforts, I . . .				
6. chose my methods and had an "I know how to read this" attitude.	___	___	___	___
7. read where I was able to concentrate.	___	___	___	___
8. formed questions and read to find answers and other important points.	___	___	___	___
To monitor my progress, I . . .				
9. felt confident and had an "I believe I can read this well" attitude.	___	___	___	___
10. solved any reading problems during reading. (Mark D if there were none.)	___	___	___	___

	A	B	C	D
11. marked the text as I read.	___	___	___	___
12. recited parts or all of the text.	___	___	___	___
To reflect on my gains, I . . .				
13. had an "I've accomplished something" attitude once I finished.	___	___	___	___
14. recognized the new or useful information I gained.	___	___	___	___
15. rewarded myself.	___	___	___	___

SCORING: Write the number of answers you marked in each column in the following spaces. Compute the column scores, and then add them up to determine your total score.

# of A's _____ × 1 pt. = _____
# of B's _____ × 2 pt. = _____
# of C's _____ × 3 pt. = _____
# of D's _____ × 4 pt. = _____
Total points = _____

INTERPRETATION: 15–43 points = low motivation; 44–60 points = high motivation

Reminder: Record your Reading for Learning and motivation scores on the Progress Charts.

Reading for Learning: History Texts

History courses generally cover extensive periods of human activity in a geographical area, such as the United States, a particular time period, such as the Middle Ages, or a specific group, such as African Americans. But no matter what the theme is, history courses emphasize the events, people, and trends that explain why the incidents occurred, what the consequences have been, and what is significant about them.

What to Look for As You Read

Historical information—which may be provided by non-experts as well as experts—provides facts, explanations, causes, effects, and trends. The *who, what, when,* and *where* of events are the facts that often take up much of history textbooks. But facts alone don't tell the historical story. So writers also present background information, explanations, and analyses to make the facts meaningful. To the discerning reader, much of this information provides the basis for cause and effect relationships. Finally, historical writings also examine issues, movements, and ideas that characterize and, in some cases, provoke actions and events.

In the following essay entitled "Melding in America," the writer uses historical facts and details about famous people, the Office of Management and Budget, and the U.S. census to provide the context for the issue of racial categories. In the textbook excerpt "Debating Diversity," the authors provide a historical view of the diversity issue, facts and descriptions about the makeup of the American family, conservative and liberal views about family structure, and why it has changed. The section as a whole deals with the trend toward greater diversity.

Motivation and Reading Tips

1. *Look for illuminating ideas about the world.*

   History will help you understand the world you live in. It provides explanations about the social, cultural, political forces, and human stories that have shaped the present. To increase your reading motivation, imagine the people and conversations of the time, how you would have reacted in those circumstances, and even what would have happened if different events and reactions had occurred.

2. *Put the facts together.*

   Group all the details about the events and who took part in them; learn the information as a unit.

3. *Look for causes and motives.*

   Identify the social, political and individual reasons, motives, and causes that created each situation or event.

4. *Emphasize significance.*

   Pay particular attention to the results of the events or issues. Ask yourself what makes the situation noteworthy. Why should it be remembered, understood, analyzed?

History Reading: Essay

Before you read . . .

Engage Your Interest: preread and divide

Do the racial or ethnic labels we use to define ourselves matter? When you're filling out a form and you have to check off the group you belong to, how do you feel? Does the label represent who you are?

After prereading, set a goal for your reading.

I want to ______________________ about ______________________.
My reward(s) will be ______________________________________
____.

Right before you begin to read, record your START time in the Rate Box on page 580.

As you read . . .

Focus Your Efforts: question and read

Melding in America

by George F. Will

The Washington Post, May 4, 1997

1 An enormous number of people—perhaps you—are descended, albeit very indirectly, from Charlemagne. And an enormous number are descended from Charlemagne's groom. Trace your pedigree back far enough, you may find that you are an omelet of surprising ingredients.

2 Booker T. Washington, Frederick Douglass, Jesse Owens and Roy Campanella each had a white parent. Martin Luther King Jr. (who had an Irish grandmother, and some Indian ancestry), W. E. B. Du Bois and Malcolm X had some Caucasian ancestry. The NAACP estimates that 70 percent of those who identify themselves as African American are of mixed racial heritage. And then there is Tiger Woods, who calls himself "Cablinasian"—Caucasian, black, Indian, Asian. Bear such things in mind as the Office of Management and Budget decides whether to make a small but consequential change in the census form. The 1790 census classified Americans in three categories—free white male, free white female, slave. In 1850 "free colored" was added. Then came mulatto, octoroon and quadroon (one-eighth and one-quarter black). In 1890 Chinese and Japanese were included as distinct races. Today there are five categories—white, black, Asian/Pacific Islander, American Indian/Native Alaskan and other.

Now there is a rapidly spreading belief that the "other" category is unsatisfactory, because it does not contribute to an accurate snapshot of the population, and it offends sensibilities: Why should a child of a white-black marriage be required to identify with one parent, or as an "other"? So OMB is considering adding a sixth category—"multiracial." 3

This would serve the accuracy of the census in a nation experiencing a rapid surge in interracial marriages, which increased about 550 percent between 1960 and 1990. The number of children in interracial families rose from 500,000 in 1970 to 2 million in 1990. Between 1960 and 1990 the percentage of African American marriages involving a white spouse more than tripled, from 1.7 percent to 6 percent. Sixty-five percent of Japanese-Americans marry someone of another race. 4

The multiracial category would serve civic health by undermining the obsession with race and ethnicity that fuels identity politics. Such politics proceed on the assumption that individuals are defined by their membership in this or that racial or ethnic group, often a group that cultivates its sense of solidarity by nurturing its grievances. The multiracial category is opposed by many who have a stake in today's racial spoils system, and thus favor maintaining the categories that help Balkanize America. 5

It is estimated—probably too conservatively—that 10 percent of blacks would check a "multiracial" box on the census form. As more and more people accurately identify themselves as "multiracial," the artificial clarity of identity politics will blur. The more blurring the better, because it will impede application of the principle of categorical representation—the principle that people of a particular group can only be understood, empathized with and represented by members of that group. 6

Today some native Hawaiians want out of the Asian/Pacific Islander category, and some Indian and native Alaskans do not want the native Hawaiians included in their category. Some Creoles, Americans of Middle Eastern descent (there are 2 million of them), and others want their own categories. Such elbow-throwing prickliness is one consequence of government making membership in distinct grievance-groups advantageous. 7

Race and ethnicity are not fixed, easily definable scientific categories. The law once regarded the Irish "race" as nonwhite. Today, ethnicity and race can be, to some degree, matters of choice. Many Hispanics regard "Hispanicity" as an attribute of race; others are more inclined to identify themselves as Hispanic when it is not presented as a racial category. 8

OMB's decision will follow last week's report from the Commission on Immigration Reform, which recommends a "new Americanization movement" emphasizing the melding of individuals rather than the accommodation of groups. It argues that national unity should be built upon a shared belief in constitutional values, and that the nation "admits immigrants as Individuals" and must "emphasize the rights of individuals over those of groups." 9

Today the government concocts "race-conscious remedies" such as racial preferences for conditions it disapproves. This encourages Americans to aggregate into groups jockeying for social space. Perhaps it would be best to promote the desegregation of Americans by abolishing the existing five census categories, rather than adding a sixth. 10

11 However, the "multiracial" category could speed the dilution of racial consciousness. One criticism of this category is that "multiracial" does not denote a protected class under the law and therefore gathering data about those who think of themselves as "multiracial" serves no statutory purpose. To which the sensible response is: good.

12 Take this writer. English by culture, British by passport; and beneath that in my veins courses a dollop of Irish, a drop of Jewish, a pinch of German, combined with a heap of Anglo-Saxon. Scratch the skin, and we're all multiracial. (808 words)

As soon as you finish reading, record your END time in the Rate Box on page 580.

Before you go on . . .

Monitor Your Progress: recite

After you read . . .

Reflect on Your Gains: review

REVIEW ACTIVITIES

Use the following activities to check your understanding of this essay.

Expand Your Vocabulary

Define the underlined terms as they are used in the essay by circling the correct response. The numbers in parentheses indicate the paragraph where the term appears.

1. <u>albeit</u> very indirectly (1)
   a. but b. although c. not d. all
2. trace your <u>pedigree</u> (1)
   a. genes b. history c. ancestry d. race
3. it offends <u>sensibilities</u> (3)
   a. senses b. reactions c. feelings d. common sense
4. <u>undermining</u> the obsession (5)
   a. weakening b. eliminating c. frustrating d. overcoming
5. sense of <u>solidarity</u> (5)
   a. solid b. strength c. unity d. membership
6. by <u>nurturing</u> its grievances (5)
   a. fixing b. promoting c. discussing d. noting

7. it will <u>impede</u> (6)
   a. block b. prevent c. aid d. slow down

8. such elbow-throwing <u>prickliness</u> (7)
   a. touchiness b. troubles c. objections d. arguments

9. the government <u>concocts</u> (10)
   a. cooks up b. makes up c. composes d. plans

10. no <u>statutory</u> purpose (11)
   a. important b. useful c. racial d. legal

Check Your Comprehension

Use the following questions to determine how well you understand the ideas, details, and inferences in this essay. Circle the best response to each question.

1. The main idea of this essay is best stated as:
   a. Using the "other" category on forms is unsatisfactory.
   b. Adding the multiracial category to the census will blur identity politics.
   c. Adding the multiracial category to the census is good for the American society.
   d. People are too concerned about race and the grievances of groups.

2. Well known black leaders in many fields
   a. have a mixed racial heritage.
   b. support the multiracial category.
   c. maintain that they are African Americans.
   d. promote continued desegregation efforts.

3. The main idea of paragraph 7 is best stated as:
   a. Hawaiians don't want to be in the Asian/Pacific Islander category.
   b. Sensitive attitudes about racial categories are caused, in part, by government policies.
   c. Racial groups are inherently bigoted.
   d. Groups encourage prejudice.

4. The proponents of the multiracial category believe that it would
   a. fuel identity politics.
   b. protect people of mixed races from prejudice.
   c. Balkanize America.
   d. improve our civic health.

5. Identity politics supports the principle that
   a. only a group member can represent the group needs.
   b. a racial or ethnic group defines an individual's identity.
   c. racial identity should promote the grievances of that race.
   d. anyone who is understanding can promote the needs of a group.

6. True or false? The article implies that identity politics has increased the tension between some racial groups.

7. According to the way people identify themselves, "Hispanicity" is an example of
   a. a racial group.
   b. an ethnic group.
   c. a racial label.
   d. how race and ethnicity can be matters of choice.

8. The author believes that one way to dilute racial consciousness would be to
   a. abolish the existing five census categories.
   b. continue using the "other" category.
   c. support identity politics.
   d. add the "multiracial" category to the last census.

9. According to the author, one positive effect of using the "multiracial" category would be that
   a. people could ignore it if they wanted to.
   b. we could become less conscious of race.
   c. some groups would lose the protected status that they now have.
   d. it would lead to needed reforms in our laws and policies.

10. The author believes that
    a. the term "multiracial" does not accurately apply to the American population.
    b. using the multiracial category will weaken some political groups.
    c. special preferences for racial groups are unfair.
    d. we are all multiracial.

Expand Your Thinking

Use these activities to expand your understanding of the ideas in this essay.

1. The following questions will help you develop your own ideas about this topic.
   a. Identify your racial makeup by listing the background of your parents and your grandparents. How do each of these groups contribute to your self-identity?
   b. How do you define the terms "race" and "ethnicity"?
   c. Think of a situation in which identifying yourself as a member of a particular group would be a benefit. It could be any kind of group—racial, ethnic, age, religious, or even sports-related. Explain how the group label could help you. Then think of a situation in which being a member of a group would not be beneficial. What would be the negative effects?
   d. Do you agree with the author that adding the multiracial category would be good for America? Why or why not?

2. Take notes on this text.

Check Your Motivation

1. Review your reading goal. Did you achieve it? Explain.

2. Make a list of the new ideas that you've gained from this text. Think about how they will be useful to you in the future.

3. Assess your current motivation. Think about how you read this text. Then mark each statement:

A = not at all B = a little C = fairly well D = very well

	A	B	C	D
To engage my interest, I . . .				
1. initiated an "I want to read about this" attitude.	___	___	___	___
2. preread the text.	___	___	___	___
3. identified the topic and/or thought about relevant or interesting points before reading.	___	___	___	___
4. looked for the author's organization before reading.	___	___	___	___
5. set a reading goal before reading.	___	___	___	___
To focus my efforts, I . . .				
6. chose my methods and had an "I know how to read this" attitude.	___	___	___	___
7. read where I was able to concentrate.	___	___	___	___
8. formed questions and read to find answers and other important points.	___	___	___	___
To monitor my progress, I . . .				
9. felt confident and had an "I believe I can read this well" attitude.	___	___	___	___
10. solved any reading problems during reading. (Mark D if there were none.)	___	___	___	___
11. marked the text as I read.	___	___	___	___
12. recited parts or all of the text.	___	___	___	___
To reflect on my gains, I . . .				
13. had an "I've accomplished something" attitude once I finished.	___	___	___	___
14. recognized the new or useful information I gained.	___	___	___	___
15. rewarded myself.	___	___	___	___

SCORING: Write the number of answers you marked in each column in the following spaces.

Compute the column scores, and then add them up to determine your total score.

# of A's ______ × 1 pt. = ______
# of B's ______ × 2 pt. = ______
# of C's ______ × 3 pt. = ______
# of D's ______ × 4 pt. = ______
Total points = ______

INTERPRETATION: 15–43 points = low motivation; 44–60 points = high motivation

Rate Box

Compute your reading rate by following these steps:

1. **RECORD** your END time here: ____________
2. **RECORD** your START time here: ____________
3. **DETERMINE** your TOTAL reading time here: ____________
4. **ROUND OFF** the seconds to the nearest ¼ minute. For example, 4 minutes, 15 seconds would be 4.25. Write this on the **** line.
5. **DIVIDE** the number of words by your rounded off time:

808 words / ______ = ______ WPM
****

Reminder: Record your rate, comprehension, vocabulary, and motivation scores on the Progress Charts.

History Reading: Textbook Section

Before you read . . .

Engage Your Interest: preread and divide

How would you describe the type of family you grew up in? Is it a "traditional" nuclear family made up of a father, mother, and children, all living together? Do you think that the artistic and cultural contributions of all the groups in our society are equally valued?

After prereading, set a goal for your reading.

I want to ______________________ about ____________________________.

My reward(s) will be ____

____.

As you read . . .

Focus Your Efforts: question and read

Debating Diversity

from Jeanne Boydston, and others

Making a Nation: The United States and Its People, combined edition.

Disagreements about diversity were at the heart of the immigration controversy. They also drove debates over two other charged issues: the status of the family and American culture. By the 1990s the ongoing transformation of the American family had become unmistakable. The supposedly "traditional" nuclear family of father, mother, and children no longer predominated in American households. Married couples with children, 40 percent of all households as late as 1970, made up only 25 percent by 1996 (see Table 31-1). There were proportionally fewer families because more Americans were living alone. The percentage of single-person households rose from 17 percent in 1970 to 25 percent in 1996. Families themselves were less likely to fit the traditional model, romanticized in the situation comedies of 1950s television. By 1996 27 percent of families with children contained one parent, usually a mother, rather than two.

A number of factors led to these changes in family structure. Americans were marrying later, having fewer children, and having them later in life. The divorce rate had doubled from 1960 to 1990. In the 1990s about half of all marriages were ending in divorce. As women's wages gradually rose, more women could afford to live alone or to head families by themselves.

Many conservatives and Republicans blamed these developments on the nation's moral decline. Allegedly, the counterculture of the 1960s, liberals, the media, feminists,

TABLE 31-1

The Changing American Family, 1960–1996*

Year	Households	Families	Married-Couple Families	Single-Parent Families	One-Person Households
1960	52,799	44,905	23,358	3,332	6,917
1970	63,401	51,456	25,541	3,271	10,851
1980	80,776	58,426	24,961	6,061	18,296
1990	93,347	66,090	24,537	7,752	22,999
1996	99,627	69,594	24,920	9,284	24,900

Source: U.S. Census Bureau, Web Site, http://www.census.gov/population/socdemo/hhfam/rep86/96hh4.txt, http://www.bls.census.gov/population/socdemoc/hhfam/rep96/96hh1.txt and /96fml.txt
**Numbers given in thousands.*

gays, and others had undermined the nation's "family values." In 1992, for instance, Bush's vice president, Dan Quayle, attacked the TV sit-com *Murphy Brown* for supposedly denigrating fatherhood through its positive portrayal of the title character's decision to have a child out of wedlock. Some defenders of the family suggested that single mothers should receive fewer welfare benefits and that divorce should be made more difficult.

Liberals fought back by denying that conservatives spoke for real "family values." The conservatives, they claimed, did not understand that the family was not dying but simply adapting to change as it always had. The different forms of the family, like diversity in general, were supposedly a good thing.

While liberals and conservatives quarreled over the family, they also fought over the state of culture in America. Since the 1960s, the authority of the western literary, artistic, and philosophical heritage had been under attack from several directions. Literary critics and other advocates of "deconstruction" had argued that cultural products possessed no inherent, objective value, that western culture was revered not because of any intrinsic merit but because it reflected the interests of powerful Europeans and Americans. Other people, these critics felt, should be free to place a lesser value on western culture.

Beginning in the 1960s, several groups did just that. As they demanded rights, feminists, African Americans, gays, and other groups maintained that white heterosexual European men had not produced all important ideas and art. Society in general and schools in particular needed to recognize the cultural contributions of the disadvantaged and the oppressed. Instead of worshiping one culture, America needed to practice multiculturalism. At Stanford University in 1987, the Reverend Jesse Jackson joined students to protest a western culture course that excluded the accomplishments of women and minorities. "Hey hey, ho ho," the crowd chanted, "Western culture's got to go!"

That cry horrified such conservatives as William Bennett, who headed the National Endowment for the Humanities (NEH) in the 1980s. Western cultural values were, activists like Bennett insisted, vitally important for the well-being of American society. The conservatives charged that the multiculturalists were destroying the western heritage.

Further, the multiculturalists were destroying free speech by making it impossible for anyone to question their positions. This coercive "political correctness" or "PC" was actually promoting conformity instead of diversity. On some college campuses, the conservatives noted, PC speech codes punished students for using language that might offend others. The conservatives also attacked the NEH and the National Endowment for the Arts (NEA). These federal agencies, they claimed, were displaying a liberal bias by funding politically correct academic and artistic projects that flouted western values.

Liberals, academics, artists, and others responded by defending the NEH, the NEA, campus speech codes, and multiculturalism. It was the conservatives, they asserted, who were trying to censor curricula and wipe out diversity.

In the end, the controversies over culture and the family did little to undermine the new diversity of American life. Although Congress cut the budgets of the NEH and the NEA, these agencies survived the conservative attack. States did virtually nothing to make divorce more difficult. More broadly, the trends toward diverse households and multiculturalism had not halted at the turn of the century, but the controversies revealed just how deeply Americans were divided over diversity. (779 words)

The following parts are from the end of the chapter:

Conclusion
There was little agreement about the rights of individuals and groups in an increasingly diverse society. American politics, caught somewhere between liberalism and conservatism, reflected all these uncertainties.

Review Question
Why was diversity such an important issue in the 1990s? (Adapted from Boydston 917)

Before you go on . . .

Monitor Your Progress: recite

After you read . . .

Reflect on Your Gains: Review

REVIEW ACTIVITIES

Use the following activities to check your understanding of this chapter section.

Reading-for-Learning Questions

The following questions are the type you might see on a course exam about this chapter section. Check your understanding of the information by circling the best response to each question.

1. The transformation of the American family was unmistakable by the
   a. 1950s. **b.** 1960s. **c.** 1980s. **d.** 1990s.
2. The changes in the "traditional" nuclear family included
   a. married couples without children.
   b. fewer families because more Americans lived alone.
   c. more single parents.
   d. all of the above.
3. One primary reason for the changes in the "traditional" nuclear family was
   a. Americans were marrying younger.
   b. the divorce rate tripled from 1960.
   c. women's wages increased.
   d. Americans were tired of the traditional values.
4. Many conservatives and Republicans blamed ______ for the changing family.
   a. the nation's moral decline
   b. TV programs like *Murphy Brown*
   c. the alliance of feminists and gays
   d. single mothers
5. Liberals believed that
   a. conservatives coined the term family values to suit their political needs.
   b. the family was adapting to change.
   c. conservatives attacked western heritage.
   d. cultural products possess no inherent value.
6. Advocates of deconstruction argued that
   a. western culture was the best and others should appreciate it more.
   b. western culture was revered because of the influence of powerful people.
   c. all educated people understand the value of western culture.
   d. people should construct their own artistic culture.

7. Feminists, African Americans, and gays promoted
   a. family values.
   b. deconstruction
   c. multiculturalism
   d. the National Endowment for the Humanities

8. True or false? According to the conservative point of view, political correctness promoted conformity instead of diversity.

9. True or false? Politically correct speech codes on some college campuses punished students for using language that might offend others.

10. True or false? The trends toward diversity and multiculturalism halted by the turn of the century.

Expand Your Thinking

Use these activities to expand your understanding of the ideas in this chapter section.

1. The following questions will help you develop your own ideas about this topic.
   a. What values do you think were promoted and taught by the "traditional" nuclear family? What values do you think are promoted by the modern family?
   b. In general, what positive values do the following groups promote?
      a. Married couples without children
      b. divorced men and women
      c. single mothers
   d. Why do you think disagreements over art and funding for NEH and NEA have been part of the diversity debate?

2. Take notes on this text.

Check Your Motivation

1. Review your reading goal. Did you achieve it? Explain.

2. Make a list of the new ideas that you've gained from this text. Think about how they will be useful to you in the future.

3. Assess your current motivation. Think about how you read this text. Then mark each statement:

   A = not at all B = a little C = fairly well D = very well

To engage my interest, I . . .	A	B	C	D
1. initiated an "I want to read about this" attitude.	___	___	___	___
2. preread the text.	___	___	___	___
3. identified the topic and/or thought about relevant or interesting points before reading.	___	___	___	___
4. looked for the author's organization before reading.	___	___	___	___
5. set a reading goal before reading.	___	___	___	___

	A	B	C	D
To focus my efforts, I . . .				
6. chose my methods and had an "I know how to read this" attitude.	___	___	___	___
7. read where I was able to concentrate.	___	___	___	___
8. formed questions and read to find answers and other important points.	___	___	___	___
To monitor my progress, I . . .				
9. felt confident and had an "I believe I can read this well" attitude.	___	___	___	___
10. solved any reading problems during reading. (Mark D if there were none.)	___	___	___	___
11. marked the text as I read.	___	___	___	___
12. recited parts or all of the text.	___	___	___	___
To reflect on my gains, I . . .				
13. had an "I've accomplished something" attitude once I finished.	___	___	___	___
14. recognized the new or useful information I gained.	___	___	___	___
15. rewarded myself.	___	___	___	___

SCORING: Write the number of answers you marked in each column in the following spaces. Compute the column scores, and then add them up to determine your total score.

# of A's ___ × 1 pt. = ___
# of B's ___ × 2 pt. = ___
# of C's ___ × 3 pt. = ___
# of D's ___ × 4 pt. = ___

Total points = ___

INTERPRETATION: 15–43 points = low motivation; 44–60 points = high motivation

Reminder: Record your Reading for Learning and motivation scores on the Progress Charts.

Reading for Learning: Biology Texts

Biology is the study of life, which encompasses the entire natural world. The scope of this discipline is incredibly far reaching, including the minute aspects of molecular biology such as atoms, cells, energy, and genetics; the organizing principles of evolution; physiology which involves structures and process within plants and animals; and ecology.

What to Look for As You Read

Articles and essays about biological topics report on current research or present opinions about controversial issues. As part of those discussions, scientific facts and descriptions are presented as supporting information. For example, in the following article entitled "Temperature Rising: Feeling a bit warm? You may just have to live with it," the writer presents a point of view about global warming, along with numerous facts about both a specific area in Washington state and the planet as a whole.

Biology textbooks, on the other hand, focus on scientifically proven information. Thus, they emphasize scientific terms, research methods, and research conclusions; detailed and factual descriptions; processes and cause and effect relationships, as well as the form and function of the parts within them. Since the processes tend to be quite complex and extremely detailed, numerous diagrams and figures are provided to link pieces in a visual format.

In the following chapter section, "The Greenhouse Effect," you will notice that the author begins with terms and information about global warming, provides very detailed descriptions and diagrams of the processes involved, and then gives descriptions of the effects in specific areas.

Motivation and Reading Tips

1. *Look for information to help you make informed decisions.*

   Biology texts will help you understand and, in some cases, improve your own health, as well as make choices about ethical issues such as cloning and ecology. To increase your reading motivation, consider how the information affects you, your world, and the environment in which you live.

2. *Emphasize the terminology.*

   Stop and review the terms and definitions as you come to them, so that the complex processes that follow will make the most sense.

3. *Look for processes, causes, and effects.*

   Biological processes include steps that often have cause and effect interactions. Identify each step; then think about what created it and what occurs as a result of it.

4. *Use the diagrams.*

   Carefully examine the figures and diagrams when they are first mentioned and as you read. They generally illustrate a number of points and will help simplify complex relationships.

Biology Reading: Article

Before you read . . .

Engage Your Interest: preread and divide

Have you noticed changes in the environment where you live that might be caused by global warming? What climate changes have you noticed?

After prereading, set a goal for your reading.

I want to ______________________ about ______________________.

My reward(s) will be ____

____.

Right before you begin to read, record your START time in the Rate Box on page 594.

As you read . . .

Focus Your Efforts: question and read

Temperature Rising: Feeling a bit warm? You may just have to live with it

by Bret Schulte

U.S. News & World Report, June 5, 2006

1 KING COUNTY, WASH.— From a chopper buzzing the forested foothills of the Cascade mountains just outside Seattle, County Executive Ron Sims describes this as "a good year." The craggy canvas below is a gorgeous bottle green. The lakelike reservoirs are nearly full. Crisp-white snow caps much of the Cascade Range. It's everything one would expect in this cool, water-rich corner of the world. But residents here worry that the "good years" are becoming increasingly rare. According to scientists at the University of Washington, the Pacific Northwest has gotten warmer by 1.5 degrees since 1900, about a half-degree higher than the global average. That might not seem like much, but the effects are being noticed here, particularly in the amount of snow in the Cascades. Since 1949, snowpack in the lower mountain range, a primary source of water for the area, has declined 50 percent, raising the odd specter of water shortages in the rainy Pacific Northwest. The culprit is unusually warm weather, which is melting snowpack and changing the precipitation cycle. More water is falling as rain—and being lost as runoff—and less is falling as mountain snow, a natural banking system that holds the precipitation until the spring, when it melts to fill reservoirs for the dry summer season. "Our water system is based on snowmelt," Sims says. "But we're continually losing huge volumes."

2 The problem snapped into focus over the past two years, when the state was hit by a severe drought—the kind of extreme weather fluctuation that scientists expect will

become more common as temperatures climb. The governor declared a statewide emergency. Ski resorts closed. Rivers and reservoirs fell to dangerous lows. For Sims, the water crisis was a worrisome sign of things to come. "How are we going to meet the needs of people and fish," he asks, "when the snowmelt is going away?"

It's a question haunting the 58-year-old Sims, who has made fighting the effects of climate change a central theme for much of his 10-year tenure as county executive. The quest puts him on the front line of what is shaping up to be the next battle in the climate-change wars: preparing for and adapting to a warmer climate. Even if people everywhere unplugged their appliances, left their cars home, and shuttered their factories today, enough fossil fuel emissions are already in the atmosphere to heat up the planet an additional 1 degree Fahrenheit this century, experts say. In reality, however, emissions are increasing—and scenarios put the likely temperature increases at 2.5 to 8 degrees over the same span. While politicians wrangle over mitigation, i.e., cutting emissions of gases like carbon dioxide and methane, some environmentalists and policymakers are increasingly focusing on the controversial concept of adaptation—preparing for changes increasingly seen as inevitable. Adaptation has long been the third rail of green politics for fear it would pull the focus away from fixing the problem. For many, however, the next debate in the climate-change debate is not why the planet is warming, or if we can stop it. It is this: How do we *live* with it? 3

Stormy Weather

The consequences of a warmer planet, potentially, are enormous. Thermal expansion of ocean waters and melting ice sheets could raise the ocean by 3 feet in the next 100 to 150 years, threatening valuable coastal property and the estimated 100 million to 200 million people worldwide who live within 3 feet of sea level. Higher oceans would damage wetlands, natural shock absorbers for big storms, as well as escalate storm surges like those produced by Hurricane Katrina—a frightening thought if global warming is producing stronger hurricanes, as some scientists contend. Climate change might also outpace the ability of ecosystems to adapt. Many of those systems are already stressed by pollutants and fragmented by highways, cities, and ever creeping suburban sprawl. Drier dry years and wetter wet years, with their accompanying severe droughts and flash floods, are expected to grow more frequent. 4

Adapting to climate change is not only necessary, experts say; it's unavoidable. Humans have always adapted to their environment, from donning warm clothes in cold weather to creating complex drainage systems for too much water and irrigation systems for too little. "If you can be resilient to what you know has already happened," says John Christy, director of the Earth System Science Center at the University of Alabama–Huntsville, "you're well on your way to adapting to any changes in the future." But our existing survival techniques will face a host of costly new stressors. Flash floods will require better drainage in cities. On the coasts, artificial wetlands and sea walls may become more common, and development could be restricted or require tougher building codes, with higher elevations. 5

Promoting common-sense adaptation as public policy, however, is no easy thing, even among those who agree on the dangers of global warming. The idea of adaptation 6 has been around for decades, but talk of living with global warming was deemed reckless by many environmentalists, who feared it would take pressure off polluters. This tussle over strategy spilled over into the highest reaches of climate-change science and analysis: the U.N.'s influential Intergovernmental Panel on Climate Change. The panel's reports, dating back to the early 1990s, emphasized cutting emissions to deal with global warming, while ideas for adaptation were muted. The cost of implementing adaptation strategies—ideas like higher bridges and stronger levees—was also widely viewed as prohibitive. Now, however, for a host of reasons, including the aftermath of Hurricane Katrina, the pendulum is swinging. "We've realized how difficult it is to cut emissions," says John M.R. Stone, a vice chair for the U.N.'s climate-change panel, "so adaptation no longer becomes a choice. It's essential." (967 words)

As soon as you finish reading, record your END time in the Rate Box on page 594.

Before you go on . . .

Monitor Your Progress: recite

After you read . . .

Reflect on Your Gains: review

REVIEW ACTIVITIES

Use the following activities to check your understanding of this essay.

Expand Your Vocabulary

Define the underlined terms as they are used in the essay by circling the correct response. The numbers in parentheses indicate the paragraph where the term appears.

1. the craggy canvas below (1)
   - **a.** cracked
   - **b.** steep and rocky
   - **c.** wooded
   - **d.** dense with brush
2. the odd specter of water shortages (1)
   - **a.** ghost
   - **b.** impressive sight
   - **c.** spectacle
   - **d.** disturbing prospect
3. a question haunting . . . Sims (3)
   - **a.** troubling
   - **b.** inhabiting
   - **c.** tormenting
   - **d.** possessing
4. The quest puts him on the front line (3)
   - **a.** voyage
   - **b.** conflict
   - **c.** search
   - **d.** question
5. fossil fuel emissions (3)
   - **a.** eruptions
   - **b.** discharges
   - **c.** oozing
   - **d.** secretions

6. politicians <u>wrangle</u> (3)
   a. debate b. discuss c. consider d. disagree
7. wrangle over <u>mitigation</u> (3)
   a. misuse b. negotiation c. reduction d. improvement
8. <u>thermal</u> expansion of ocean waters (4)
   a. heated b. temperate c. temporary d. serious
9. if you can be <u>resilient</u> (5)
   a. yielding b. carefree c. bendable d. responsive
10. widely viewed as <u>prohibitive</u> (6)
   a. promoting b. preventive c. confirming d. forbidden

Check Your Comprehension

Use the following questions to determine how well you understand the ideas, details, and inferences in this essay. Circle the best response to each question.

1. The main idea of this essay is best stated as:
   a. Politicians have argued about what to do about global warming.
   b. We must create adaptation strategies to cope with global warming.
   c. Global warming is a reality.
   d. The earth's temperature is rising.
2. According to the text, global warming
   a. affects only selected and small areas.
   b. can be stopped.
   c. can cause droughts and climate changes.
   d. is a political issue that needs national legislation.
3. The phrase "changing the precipitation cycle" (paragraph 1) refers to a situation where
   a. there is less rainfall.
   b. there is more rainfall throughout the entire year.
   c. reservoirs are filling up too quickly.
   d. there is less snowmelt.
4. The fossil fuel emissions created by people and businesses
   a. could be halted and global warming could be stopped.
   b. are currently enough to heat up the planet by 2.5 degrees in this century.
   c. are caused primarily by appliances and cars.
   d. are increasing and could raise the temperature by 8 degrees in this century.
5. In the past, adaptation proposals were
   a. dismissed because the focus has been on pressuring polluters to change.
   b. unpopular with people in the U.S. who don't want to change their lifestyle.
   c. promoted only by politicians.
   d. promoted primarily by environmentalists.

6. Thermal expansion of ocean waters and melting ice sheets could
   a. raise the ocean by 3 feet in less than 100 years.
   b. decrease the amount of wetlands.
   c. threaten 100–200 million people living within 3 feet of sea level.
   d. produce stronger but fewer hurricanes.

7. Ecosystems may not adapt well to increased global temperatures because they
   a. are already stressed by pollutants.
   b. are divided by highways and cities.
   c. will be subject to more frequent and more severe droughts and flash floods.
   d. all of the above.

8. The author stresses that adaptations will require
   a. cooperation among competing governmental agencies.
   b. costly solutions.
   c. a shift in the U.N. policies.
   d. world-wide cooperation.

9. The U.N.'s Intergovernmental Panel on Climate Change
   a. has promoted adaptation for decades.
   b. has ignored the warnings that adaptations are needed.
   c. ranks as one of the most important agencies dealing with this issue.
   d. has emphasized the need to identify the causes of global warming before taking any action.

10. The author implies that adaptation to global warming
   a. is a local problem that needs local solutions.
   b. will be the focus of future discussions and efforts.
   c. is a global problem that needs U.N. leadership.
   d. will be ignored until there are more crises like Katrina.

Expand Your Thinking

Use these activities to expand your understanding of the ideas in this essay.

1. The following questions will help you develop your own ideas about this topic.
   a. How could fossil fuel emissions be reduced? Who would have to be involved?
   b. What kind of adaptation strategies do you think the U.S. government should focus on? What should individual communities do?
   c. How could schools become more involved in the issues of global warming and adaptation?

2. Take notes on this text.

Check Your Motivation

1. Review your reading goal. Did you achieve it? Explain.
2. Make a list of the new ideas that you've gained from this text. Think about how they will be useful to you in the future.
3. Assess your current motivation. Think about how you read this text. Then mark each statement:

   A = not at all   B = a little   C = fairly well   D = very well

	A	B	C	D
To engage my interest, I . . .				
1. initiated an "I want to read about this" attitude.	___	___	___	___
2. preread the text.	___	___	___	___
3. identified the topic and/or thought about relevant or interesting points before reading.	___	___	___	___
4. looked for the author's organization before reading.	___	___	___	___
5. set a reading goal before reading.	___	___	___	___
To focus my efforts, I . . .				
6. chose my methods and had an "I know how to read this" attitude.	___	___	___	___
7. read where I was able to concentrate.	___	___	___	___
8. formed questions and read to find answers and other important points.	___	___	___	___
To monitor my progress, I . . .				
9. felt confident and had an "I believe I can read this well" attitude.	___	___	___	___
10. solved any reading problems during reading. (Mark D if there were none.)	___	___	___	___
11. marked the text as I read.	___	___	___	___
12. recited parts or all of the text.	___	___	___	___
To reflect on my gains, I . . .				
13. had an "I've accomplished something" attitude once I finished.	___	___	___	___
14. recognized the new or useful information I gained.	___	___	___	___
15. rewarded myself.	___	___	___	___

SCORING: Write the number of answers you marked in each column in the following spaces. Compute the column scores, and then add them up to determine your total score.

\# of A's ______ × 1 pt. = ______

\# of B's ______ × 2 pt. = ______

\# of C's ______ × 3 pt. = ______

\# of D's ______ × 4 pt. = ______

Total points = ______

INTERPRETATION: 15–43 points = low motivation; 44–60 points = high motivation

Rate Box

Compute your reading rate by following these steps:

1. **RECORD** your END time here: ____________
2. **RECORD** your START time here: ____________
3. **DETERMINE** your TOTAL reading time here: ____________
4. **ROUND OFF** the seconds to the nearest ¼ minute. For example, 4 minutes, 15 seconds would be 4.25. Write this on the **** line.
5. **DIVIDE** the number of words by your rounded off time:

967 words / ______ = ______ WPM
****

Reminder: Record your rate, comprehension, vocabulary, and motivation scores on the Progress Charts.

Biology Reading: Textbook Section

Before you read . . .

Engage Your Interest: preread and divide

What do you think contributes to the greenhouse effect? If it continues, how could it affect you and your children?

After prereading, set a goal for your reading.

I want to ____________________ about ____________________.
My reward(s) will be ____
____.

As you read . . .

Focus Your Efforts: question and read

The Greenhouse Effect

by Colleen Belk and Virginia Borden

Biology: Science for Life with Physiology, 2nd ed.

A nine-island chain in the South Pacific, located between Australia and Hawaii, comprises the nation of Tuvalu. Each of the tropical islands that is part of the chain is an atoll—a circular column of coral rising up from the sea floor and extending above sea level. The 10,000 or so people inhabiting these islands farm and fish in order to feed themselves and their families. Tuvaluans live peaceful lives in a nation where crime is virtually unheard of; in fact, most residents sleep with their doors open to allow in the cooling night breezes. The islands have no television service, and the lone bank closes at 1:00 p.m. each day; no one takes credit cards. Transportation is largely via bicycle or motor scooter.

But there is one big problem in this seemingly idyllic island paradise—the islands of Tuvalu are disappearing. The storm surges and high tides that have become more common in recent years are eroding protective offshore barriers and beaches, destroying roads, and flooding homes and plantations. Recently, a record high tide submerged much of the country, causing week-long telephone service outages and flooding Tuvalu's only airport. The flooding of plantations with salty seawater kills the crops, forcing citizens to grow crops in metal containers filled with compost.

What is causing the sudden rise in sea levels of the Tuvaluan islands? The prime minister of Tuvalu believes that global warming, which is causing the polar ice caps to melt and deposit water into the seas, is at fault. Concern that the tides will soon be high enough to submerge the nation and force the exodus of its remaining residents has led the prime minister to attempt to sue those he believes to be responsible—namely, the United States. Per capita, this country is producing more of the gasses associated with global warming than any other country.

Global warming is the progressive increase of Earth's average temperature that has been occurring over the past century. The prime minister of Tuvalu is not alone in his belief that global warming is caused by increased emissions of certain gases. Most scientists agree that global warming is caused by recent increases in the concentrations of particular atmospheric gases including methane, nitrous oxide, water vapor, and carbon dioxide. Because increases in carbon dioxide seem to be the major source of problems related to global warming, we will focus mainly on that gas for the rest of this discussion.

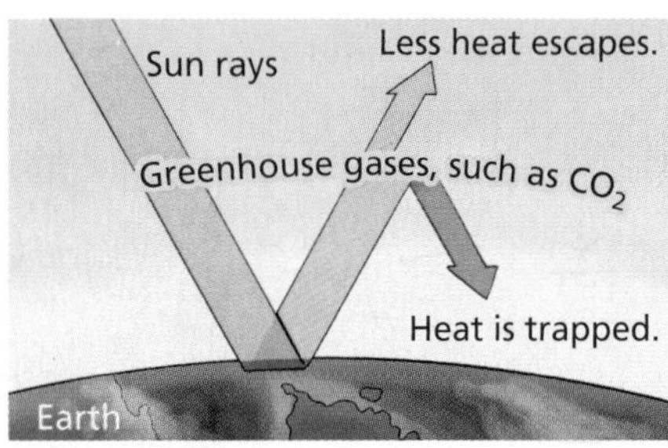

Figure 4.1 The greenhouse effect. Heat from the sun is trapped in the atmosphere by water vapor, carbon dioxide, and other greenhouse gases. Increased levels of carbon dioxide contribute to the greenhouse effect.

The presence of carbon dioxide in the atmosphere leads to a phenomenon called the **greenhouse effect.** The greenhouse effect works like this: Warmth from the sun heats Earth's surface, which then radiates the heat energy absorbed outward. Most of this heat is radiated back into space, but some of the heat is retained in the atmosphere. The retention of heat is facilitated by carbon dioxide molecules, which act like a blanket to trap the heat radiated by Earth's surface (Figure 4.1). When you sleep under a blanket at night, your body heat is trapped and helps keep you warm. When the levels of greenhouse gases in the atmosphere increase, the effect is similar to sleeping under too many blankets—the temperature increases. The trapping of this warmth radiating from Earth is known as the greenhouse effect.

This is not exactly how panes of glass in a greenhouse function, that is, by allowing radiation from the sun to penetrate into the greenhouse and then trapping the heat that radiates from the warmed-up surfaces inside the greenhouse. But the overall effect is the same—the air temperature increases.

The greenhouse effect is not in itself a dangerous or unhealthy phenomenon. If Earth's atmosphere did not have some greenhouse gases, too much heat would be lost to space, and Earth would be too cold to support life. It is the excess warming due to more and more carbon dioxide accumulating in the atmosphere as a result of coal, oil, and natural gas burning that is causing problems.

In the absence of excess greenhouse gases, water vapor and carbon dioxide work together to keep temperatures on Earth hospitable for life.

Water, Heat, and Temperature

Bodies of water absorb heat and help maintain stable temperatures on Earth. Heat and temperature are measures of energy. **Heat** is the total amount of energy associated with the movement of atoms and molecules in a substance. **Temperature** is a measure of the intensity of heat—for example, how fast the molecules in the substance are moving.

Water molecules are attracted to each other, resulting in the formation of weak chemical bonds, called hydrogen bonds, between neighboring molecules. When water is heated, the heat energy disrupts the hydrogen bonds. Only after the hydrogen bonds have been broken can heat cause individual water molecules to move faster, thus increasing the temperature. In other words, the initial input of heat used to break hydrogen bonds between water molecules does not immediately raise the temperature of water; instead, it breaks hydrogen bonds. Therefore, water can absorb and store a large amount of heat while warming up only a few degrees in temperature. When water cools, hydrogen bonds re-form between adjacent molecules, releasing heat into the atmosphere. Water can release a large amount of heat into the surroundings while not decreasing the temperature of the body of water very much (Figure 4.2).

Water's high heat-absorbing capacity has important effects on Earth's climate. The vast amount of water contained in Earth's oceans and lakes moderates temperatures by storing huge amounts of heat radiated by the sun and giving off heat that warms the air during cooler times. Therefore, the balance between releasing and maintaining heat energy is vital to the maintenance of climate conditions on Earth. This balance can be disrupted when increasing levels of carbon dioxide cause more heat to be trapped.

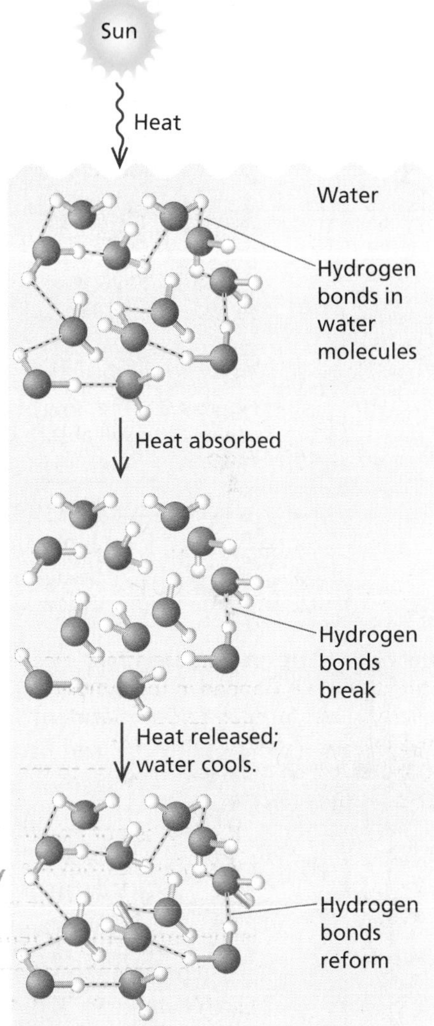

Figure 4.2 Hydrogen bonding in water. Hydrogen bonds break as they absorb heat and reform as water releases heat. Water remains in the liquid form because not all the hydrogen bonds are broken at any one time.

Carbon Dioxide

Many of the atoms found in complex molecules of living organisms are broken down into simpler molecules and recycled for use in different capacities. Carbon dioxide (CO_2) is no different. The carbon dioxide you exhale is released into the atmosphere, where it can absorb heat, diffuse into the oceans, or be absorbed by forests and soil. Volcanic eruptions return carbon dioxide trapped within Earth's surface to the atmosphere. As you can see in Figure 4.3, carbon dioxide naturally flows back and forth between living organisms, the atmosphere, bodies of water, and soil.

It is not just carbon that flows between plants and other organisms—energy does also. Plants use energy from the sun to produce sugars and other organic molecules that other organisms consume. The energy is stored in the bonds of these organic molecules and can be used to produce energy for the cell. When plants use energy from sunlight to produce organic molecules, by a process called **photosynthesis,** they also release oxygen (O_2) into the atmosphere. The metabolism of organic molecules by **cellular respiration** produces not only energy but also carbon dioxide and water (Figure 4.4).

The carbon dioxide produced by respiration is taken up by plants during the process of photosynthesis, is absorbed by both chemicals and organisms in the ocean, or accumulates in the atmosphere. The ocean has served as Earth's largest carbon dioxide and

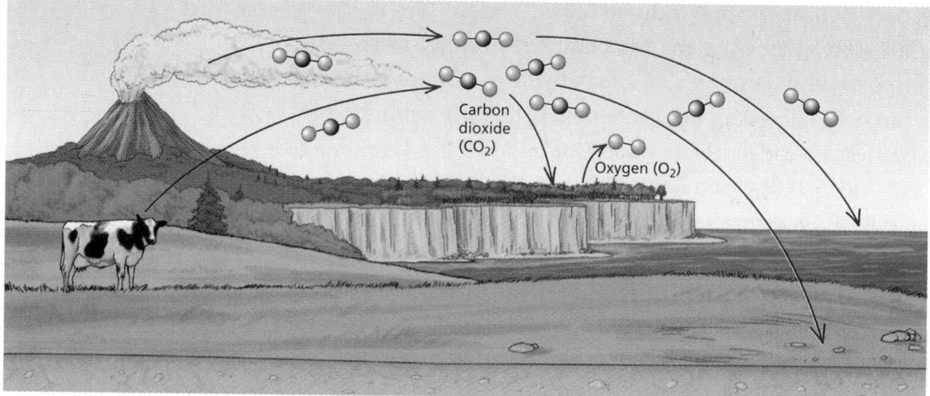

Figure 4.3 The flow of carbon. All living organisms and volcanoes produce CO_2. Forests, oceans, and soil absorb CO_2 from the air.

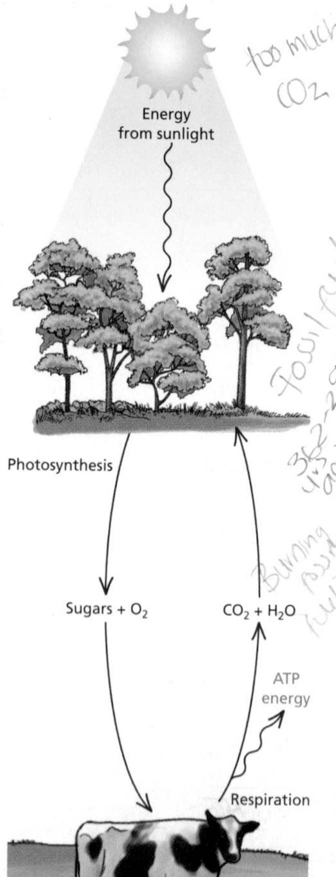

heat reservoir, but oceanic and atmospheric scientists are very concerned about the ocean's ability to absorb carbon dioxide at the rate that it is being emitted into the atmosphere. This is because human activities have rapidly increased the rate of carbon dioxide released into the atmosphere, largely by burning fossil fuels (Figure 4.5).

Fossil fuels are the buried remains of ancient plants and microorganisms that have been transformed by heat and pressure into coal, oil, and natural gas. These fuels are rich in carbon because plants remove carbon from the atmosphere during photosynthesis; consequently, plant structures are rich in organic carbon. Dead plant materials that are buried before they decompose, and thus before their carbon is released in the form of carbon dioxide, can produce fossil fuels. Humans combust this stored organic carbon to produce energy. The plants that made up the majority of fossil fuels lived from 362 to 290 million years ago, during a geological period called the Carboniferous period.

Burning these fossil fuels to generate electricity, power our cars, and heat our homes releases carbon dioxide into the atmosphere. Increases in carbon dioxide are well documented by direct measurements of the atmosphere over the past 50 years (Figure 4.6).

Scientists can also directly measure the amount of carbon dioxide that was present in the atmosphere in the past by examining cores of ice sheets that have existed for thousands of years. This is because snow near the surface of ice traps air. As more snow accumulates, the underlying

Figure 4.4 The flow of chemicals and energy. Energy enters biological systems in the form of sunlight, which is used to convert carbon dioxide and water into sugars during photosynthesis. The products of photosynthesis are broken down during cellular respiration to produce carbon dioxide and water and release energy.

snow is compressed into ice that contains air bubbles. Cores can be removed from long-lived ice sheets and analyzed to determine the concentration of carbon dioxide trapped in air bubbles. These bubbles are actual samples of the atmosphere from up to hundreds of thousands of years ago (Figure 4.7). In addition, certain characteristics of gases trapped in the bubbles of ice cores can provide indirect information about temperatures at the time the bubbles formed. Ice core data from Antarctica, shown in Figure 4.8, indicate that the concentration of carbon dioxide in the atmosphere is much higher now than at any time in the past 400,000 years and that increased levels of carbon dioxide are correlated with increased temperatures.

Although Earth has gone through temperature cycles many times in the past, the concerns regarding current warming trends are that human activities are inflating the rate of increase and that

Figure 4.5 Burning fossil fuels. The burning of fossil fuels by industrial plants and automobiles adds more carbon dioxide to the environment.

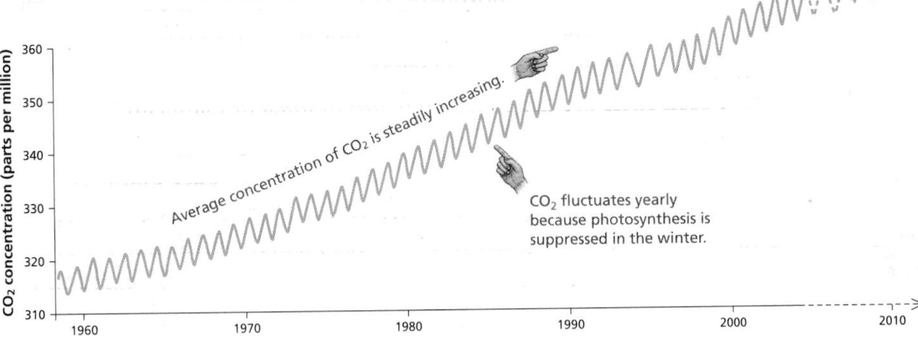

Figure 4.6 Increases in atmospheric carbon dioxide. Carbon dioxide levels have increased over the years.

these increases may persist for thousands of years. Many scientists believe that the effects of increased temperatures will be far reaching. Even now, the Tuvaluans and their Pacific islands are not the only organisms and environments being affected.

The Greenhouse Effect, Organisms, and Their Environments

Several million tourists visit Glacier National Park, located in the northwest corner of Montana, every year. With each passing year, the glaciers in this park decrease in size and number. As the glaciers shrink, they take with them natural habitat set aside for protection in this national park. Some of the park's glaciers have already shrunk to half their original size, and the total number of glaciers has decreased from approximately 150 in 1850 to around 35 today.

Figure 4.7 Ice core. By analyzing ice cores, scientists can measure the concentration of carbon dioxide that was present in early atmospheres.

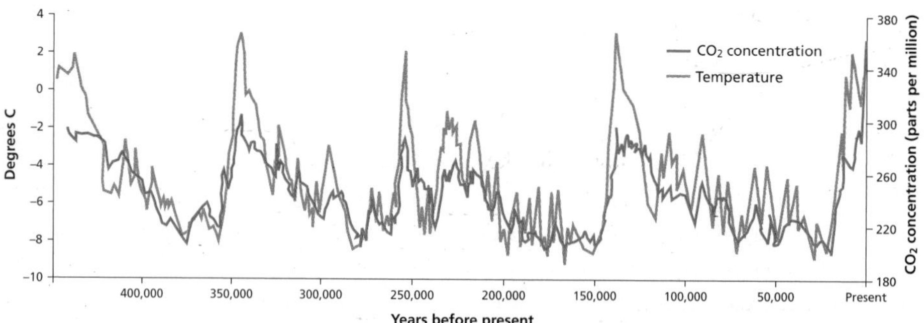

Figure 4.8 Records of temperature and atmospheric carbon dioxide concentration from Antarctic ice cores. These data indicate that increases in carbon dioxide levels are correlated with higher temperatures.

Like ice masses all over the world, these glaciers are slowly succumbing to warmer temperatures. According to the U.S. National Climate Data Center, the entire planet has warmed by 0.25°C (0.5°F) during the twentieth century. If this trend continues, scientists predict that by the year 2030, not a single glacier will be left in the park.

Melting glaciers are not confined to this park; in fact, they are melting worldwide. Mountain glaciers are receding from their peaks as far away as Tanzania, where Mount Kilimanjaro has lost 82% of its ice cap since 1912. The Greenland ice sheet is becoming thinner at its margins every year. Alpine glaciers contain half as much ice as they did in the mid-nineteenth century, when climbers first hiked to their peaks. In Antarctica, rising temperatures have led to the collapse of massive ice shelves. In the past 3 years, two massive chunks of ice, each about the size of Rhode Island, have fallen into the ocean.

The loss of ice has been a problem for the polar bear population in Hudson Bay. Seals, the bears' main food source, live on the ice of Hudson Bay, but this ice is breaking up earlier and earlier. The amount of time ice exists on western Hudson Bay has decreased by 3 weeks over the last 20 years. Rising temperatures thin the ice pack, making it too fragile to support seals and the bears that hunt them and driving the bears to shore in poor condition for hibernation. The average weight of polar bears in this region is declining, and fewer cubs are being born.

Sea levels have risen by 10 to 20 cm (4–8 inches) in the twentieth century. Increased ocean volumes due to the addition of water from melted ice can also lead to changes in climate. Worldwide rain and snowfall over land has increased by about 1%, and rain storms, as seen in Tuvalu, are expected to become more frequent and more severe. In addition to its impact on the humans who live there, flooding of tropical oceanic islands disturbs some of the most unique and diverse habitats on the planet.

A review published in the journal *Nature* in March 2002 described various species that have been affected by climate change. Many of these species are temperature sensitive, and they must move closer to the poles or to higher elevations to find regions with the proper climate. Arctic foxes are retreating northward and being replaced by the less cold-hardy red fox. Edith's checkerspot butterfly is now found 124 meters higher in elevation and 92 kilometers north of its range in 1900, and a wide variety of corals have experienced a dramatic increase in the frequency and extent of damage resulting from increased ocean temperatures.

It is not just animals that need to migrate along with changing temperatures. Plant species with specific temperature requirements will have to move as well. Those that cannot migrate quickly enough will likely become extinct. One example of a plant that will need to undergo this forced migration is the sugar maple, the source of maple syrup.

New England risks losing its profitable maple syrup industry along with its leaf-watching tourists as the cool-weather-adapted sugar maple population declines in a warming climate. Turning the maples' sugar into syrup requires nighttime temperatures that are below freezing and daytime temperatures in the mid-forties. Warmer temperatures overall have led to tapping seasons that start earlier, end sooner, and produce syrup of a lesser quality. A report by the U.S. Office of Science and Technology Policy indicates that the ideal range of the sugar maple is now close to 300 miles north of New England. The effects of warming temperatures on species of less commercial importance are not as well documented, and these species are less likely to receive human aid in making the transition.

The cost of global warming to Tuvaluans is even more dramatic. While migrating to drier climes would not mean extinction of the Tuvaluan people, it might well mean the extinction of their culture, since its members would likely disperse to many different countries. Reducing the biological, economic, and social losses caused by global warming will require not only slowing the rate of warming but also mediating the effects of increasing temperatures that are inevitable given current atmospheric carbon dioxide levels. Before they can effectively mediate these effects, scientists need to understand how warming temperatures affect not only climate factors such as average temperature, rainfall, and storm intensity and frequency but also biological processes. For the remainder of the chapter, we will focus on the effects of increased carbon dioxide and increased temperatures on the physiology of living organisms. (2174 words)

The following parts are from the end of the chapter:

Summary

- The planet is warming. This warming will lead to a rise in ocean levels, changes in weather patterns, and the disruption of biological communities.
- Greenhouse gases, particularly carbon dioxide, increase the amount of heat retained in Earth's atmosphere, which then leads to increased temperatures.
- Water can absorb large amounts of heat without undergoing rapid or drastic changes in temperature because heat must first be used to break hydrogen bonds between adjacent water molecules. A high heat-absorbing capacity is a characteristic of water.
- Carbon dioxide cycles between animals, plants, soil, oceans, and the atmosphere.
- Carbon dioxide levels in the atmosphere are increasing. This increase is caused by human activities such as the burning of fossil fuels and is leading to global warming.
- Glaciers are melting and causing sea levels to rise. This changes habitats for many organisms and forces migrations.

Before you go on . . .

Monitor Your Progress: recite

After you read . . .

Reflect on Your Gains: review

REVIEW ACTIVITIES

Use the following activities to check your understanding of this reading.

Reading-for-Learning Questions

The following questions are the type you might see on a course exam about this chapter section. Check your understanding of the information by circling the best response to each question.

1. Many scientists believe that the global warming observed over the past 100 years has been caused by elevated levels of gases in the atmosphere. Which of the following gases is primarily responsible for this problem?
   - **a.** carbon monoxide
   - **b.** carbon dioxide
   - **c.** nitrous oxide
   - **d.** oxygen
   - **e.** ozone
2. The greenhouse effect is most similar to
   - **a.** heating up the air inside a car by parking it in the sun.
   - **b.** warming the air for a hot-air balloon with a propane burner.
   - **c.** burning kerosene in a heater to warm up the air inside a cold house.
   - **d.** growing plants in your office to reduce indoor air pollution.
   - **e.** cooking food with a charcoal grill.
3. Each of the following statements about the greenhouse effect is true *except:*
   - **a.** Most life on Earth relies upon the hospitable temperatures resulting from the greenhouse effect.
   - **b.** The greenhouse effect is a dangerous phenomenon that should be stopped as soon as possible.
   - **c.** The greenhouse effect results from the presence of greenhouse gases in the atmosphere.
   - **d.** Global warming is likely the result of excess greenhouse gases, and is thus due to the greenhouse effect.
   - **e.** All of the above.
4. Temperature is a measure of
   - **a.** the potential energy in a substance.
   - **b.** how fast the molecules in a substance are moving.
   - **c.** the energy lost from a substance to its surroundings.
   - **d.** how much heat is being absorbed by a substance.
   - **e.** all of the above.

5. Why is water so important in controlling Earth's climate?
   a. Water vapor is one of the greenhouse gases that help trap heat.
   b. The water in oceans and lakes stores the energy radiated by the sun and releases it slowly.
   c. Water can absorb and store a lot of energy while only warming up a few degrees.
   d. All of the above.
   e. None of the above.

6. What are fossil fuels?
   a. carbon-rich remains of plants and microorganisms
   b. underground deposits of carbon dioxide
   c. accumulations of partially decomposed dinosaurs
   d. bubbles of gas that were trapped in ice thousands or millions of years ago
   e. timber from old-growth forests

7. Regarding global warming and the greenhouse effect, why is burning fossil fuels worse than burning wood?
   a. When burned, fossil fuels contain different, more dangerous forms of CO_2 than wood.
   b. Burning fossil fuels to generate a given amount of energy releases more CO_2 than does burning wood to generate the same amount of energy.
   c. The CO_2 released from burned wood was absorbed from the atmosphere recently by a photosynthetic plant, and thus does not contribute as much "new" CO_2 to the atmosphere as do burned fossil fuels.
   d. The CO_2 generated by burning fossil fuels cannot be used by plants during photosynthesis, whereas the CO_2 generated by burning wood can be used by plants.
   e. All of the above.

8. How do scientists "know" the atmospheric levels of carbon dioxide that existed on Earth hundreds or thousands of years ago?
   a. They deduce it from the carbon dioxide content of fossil fuels.
   b. They measure it from bubbles of gas trapped in Antarctic ice.
   c. They estimate it from the relative numbers of carbon-based life forms that existed over time.
   d. They measure it from erupting volcanoes, bubbling hot springs, and seeping hydrothermal vents.
   e. All of the above.

9. Which of the following is NOT evidence of global warming?
   a. There are fewer glaciers in Glacier National Park today than there were 150 years ago.
   b. Some cold-adapted animals are moving farther north (away from the equator) each year.
   c. Sea levels rose and ocean volumes grew in the 20th century.
   d. Mount Kilimanjaro lost the majority of its ice cap in the past 100 years.
   e. In New England, maple syrup season now occurs in the late fall rather than in the early spring.

10. According to the U.S. national Climate Data Center, how much did the Earth warm *overall* during the 20th century?

a. 0.005°F **b.** 9.5°F **c.** 1°F **d.** 5°F **e.** 10°F

(Belk and Borden, Test Item File, 48)

Expand Your Thinking

Use these activities to expand your understanding of the ideas in this chapter section.

1. The following questions will help you develop your own ideas about this topic.
  - **a.** What can individuals do to slow the effects of global warming?
  - **b.** Do you think it is okay for the individuals of one country to produce more greenhouse gases than do individuals of other countries? Why or why not? (Belk and Borden, Chapter 4, 99)

2. Take notes on this text.

Check Your Motivation

1. Review your reading goal. Did you achieve it? Explain.

2. Make a list of the new ideas that you've gained from this text. Think about how they will be useful to you in the future.

3. Assess your current motivation. Think about how you read this text. Then mark each statement:

A = not at all B = a little C = fairly well D = very well

	A	B	C	D
To engage my interest, I . . .				
1. initiated an "I want to read about this" attitude.	___	___	___	___
2. preread the text.	___	___	___	___
3. identified the topic and/or thought about relevant or interesting points before reading.	___	___	___	___
4. looked for the author's organization before reading.	___	___	___	___
5. set a reading goal before reading.	___	___	___	___
To focus my efforts, I . . .				
6. chose my methods and had an "I know how to read this" attitude.	___	___	___	___
7. read where I was able to concentrate.	___	___	___	___
8. formed questions and read to find answers and other important points.	___	___	___	___
To monitor my progress, I . . .				
9. felt confident and had an "I believe I can read this well" attitude.	___	___	___	___

	A	B	C	D
10. solved any reading problems during reading. (Mark D if there were none.)	___	___	___	___
11. marked the text as I read.	___	___	___	___
12. recited parts or all of the text.	___	___	___	___
To reflect on my gains, I . . .				
13. had an "I've accomplished something" attitude once I finished.	___	___	___	___
14. recognized the new or useful information I gained.	___	___	___	___
15. rewarded myself.	___	___	___	___

SCORING: Write the number of answers you marked in each column in the following spaces. Compute the column scores, and then add them up to determine your total score.

# of A's ______ × 1 pt. = ______
# of B's ______ × 2 pt. = ______
# of C's ______ × 3 pt. = ______
# of D's ______ × 4 pt. = ______
Total points = ______

INTERPRETATION: 15–43 points = low motivation; 44–60 points = high motivation

Reminder: Record your Reading for Learning and motivation sense on the Progress Charts.

Appendix

SUMMARY OF THE MOTIVATION STAGES

Stages	*Description*	*Reading Processes*	*Attitudes (Chapter Reference)*	*Techniques & Skills (Chapter Reference)*
Engage Interest	***The "I want to" stage*** This essential starting point is where you create the desire to participate, complete a task, or achieve more than you have. It depends on your curiosity and awareness of the personal relevance of the content, as well as your view of the achievement, rewards, and benefits you'll get from the task.	Preread Divide	▪ Recognize the power of self-motivation (1) ▪ Preview and divide tasks (1) ▪ Direct your self-talk to positive thinking (1) ▪ Think about what's useful, interesting, and intriguing (1)	▪ Assess your self-motivation (1) ▪ Create motivating goals (1)
			▪ Recognize the benefits of active reading (2) ▪ View texts as reading for learning opportunities (2)	▪ Preread essays (2) ▪ Preread textbook chapters (2, 5) ▪ Divide essays (2) ▪ Divide textbook chapters (2, 5)
			▪ Recognize the benefits of reading efficiently (3)	▪ Identify a reading purpose (3) ▪ Choose the best rate (3)
			▪ Recognize the benefits of expanding your vocabulary (4) ▪ Develop an interest in learning new words (4)	
			▪ Recognize the benefits of using reading for learning methods (5) ▪ Review and decide how to use textbook aids (5)	▪ Use textbook aids to increase interest in the topic (5)
			▪ Recognize the benefits of finding main ideas (6)	▪ Make predictions about topics and ideas (6)
			▪ Recognize the benefits of identifying and organizing details (7)	
			▪ Recognize the benefits of, reading graphic aids (8) ▪ Recognize the benefits of critical reading (9)	▪ Use graphic aids to increase interest and comprehension (8)
			▪ Recognize the benefits of drawing conclusions about the author's purpose, tone, facts and opinions (9)	
			▪ Recognize the benefits of evaluating arguments (10) ▪ Recognize the benefits of critical thinking (10)	▪ Separate persuasions from arguments (10) ▪ Make predictions about issues and claims (10)

SUMMARY OF THE MOTIVATION STAGES (*Continued*)

Stages	*Description*	*Reading Processes*	*Attitudes (Chapter Reference)*	*Techniques & Skills (Chapter Reference)*
Focus Efforts	***The "I know how" stage*** This is the working stage. It's the time to promote your own efforts by choosing to use the best techniques, methods, and skills to complete the task. It's also the time to plan your reading and learning tasks and to set the standards you want to achieve.	Question Read	▪ Think about how to create the best results (1)	▪ Take charge of your concentration (1) ▪ Manage your time (1) ▪ Set high standards (1)
			▪ Recognize the benefits of active reading (2)	▪ Use questions to direct your essay and chapter reading (2) ▪ Read to find answers and what's important (2) ▪ Underline and mark texts (2, 5)
			▪ Be alert for blocks to efficient reading (3)	▪ Eliminate psychological blocks to rate (3) ▪ Eliminate physical blocks to rate (3) ▪ Use skimming and scanning (3)
			▪ Seek out vocabulary learning opportunities (4)	▪ Use word parts, context clues, and the dictionary (4)
				▪ Use textbook aids to increase comprehension (5) ▪ Use the levels of thinking (5)
				▪ Verify topic and main idea predictions (6) ▪ Find stated main ideas (6)
				▪ Identify types of details and relate them to the ideas (7) ▪ Identify major and minor details (7) ▪ Identify logical patterns (7)
				▪ Use levels of thinking to read graphic aids (8)
				▪ Identify the author's purpose, tone, connotations, facts and opinions (9) ▪ Identify the parts of an essay (9) ▪ Identify the parts of an article (9)
				▪ Identify the parts of an argument (10) ▪ Verify issue and claim predictions (10) ▪ Identify bias and logical fallacies (10)

(*continued*)

SUMMARY OF THE MOTIVATION STAGES (*Continued*)

Stages	*Description*	*Reading Processes*	*Attitudes (Chapter Reference)*	*Techniques & Skills (Chapter Reference)*
Monitor Progress	***The "I believe I can do it" stage*** This is the self-guiding and feedback stage that occurs as you work. It depends on taking control, maintaining your self-confidence and reducing stress. It includes any methods you use to solve problems and keep yourself on track.	Recite	▪ Adopt an internal locus of control (1) ▪ Think positively about your own abilities (1) ▪ Identify stressors (1) ▪ Be alert for signals of reading problems (2) ▪ Be ready to change rate as needed (3)	▪ Use a positive self-fulfilling prophecy (1) ▪ Visualize success (1) ▪ Balance your life (1) ▪ Develop support groups (1) ▪ Analyze and solve reading problems as they occur (2) ▪ Recite what you've read and marked (2) ▪ Vary your rate as purpose and text difficulty change (3) ▪ Paraphrase new definitions to test comprehension (4) ▪ Paraphrase and summarize as you recite (5) ▪ Use review questions as you recite (5) ▪ State implied main ideas (6) ▪ Apply information from graphics to your life (8) ▪ Look for implications; make inferences (9)

SUMMARY OF THE MOTIVATION STAGES (*Continued*)

Stages	*Description*	*Reading Processes*	*Attitudes (Chapter Reference)*	*Techniques & Skills (Chapter Reference)*
Reflect on Gains	***The "I've achieved something" stage*** This is the stage where you think about what you've gained from your efforts and get the benefits of your work. It includes any thoughts or review activities that you engage in about the content, as well as all of the rewards that you get. It produces a sense of accomplishment and pride that increases your motivation for similar tasks in the future.	**Review**	▪ Appreciate new and useful information (1, 2) ▪ Recognize your intellectual gains (1, 2) ▪ Realize how new words expand your mind (4) ▪ Recognize the insights ideas provide (6) ▪ Realize how logical patterns organize and simplify details (7) ▪ Recognize how visual aids simplify information (8)	▪ Review text information (1) ▪ Create notes and learning tools (1, 2, 5, 7) ▪ Give yourself rewards (1, 2) ▪ Use vocabulary memory aids (4) ▪ Use new terms as you speak and write (4) ▪ Paraphrase and summarize as you review (5) ▪ Use review questions as you review (5) ▪ Create and use pattern diagrams for review (7) ▪ Draw conclusions about graphic aids (8) ▪ Evaluate the author's purpose, tone, and facts and opinions (9) ▪ Evaluate the merits of essays And articles (9) ▪ Evaluate the reliability of authors (10) ▪ Evaluate bias and logical fallacies (10) ▪ Evaluate the merits of an argument (10)

Credits

Text Credits

Chapter 2 *pp. 44–45:* Maggie Ford, "School, Girls, and Information Age." Copyright 1998 American Association of University Women Ed. Foundation. Permission given by AAUW Communications on behalf of the AAUW and the AAUW Educational Foundation.; *pp. 48–49:* © 1999, The Washington Post Writers Group, Reprinted with Permission.; *pp. 61–66:* Lindsey, Linda L., Beach, Stephen, *Essentials of Sociology,* © 2003. Reprinted by permission of Pearson Education, Inc., Upper Saddle River, NJ.; *pp. 75–76:* Jay Chiat, "Illusions are Forever." *Forbes ASAP,* October 2000. Reprinted by Permission of Forbes ASAP Magazine © 2005 Forbes Inc.; *pp. 79–83:* Solomon/Stuart, *Marketing: Real People, Real Choices,* 3rd Edition, © 2003, pp. 343–345, 365–368. Reprinted by permission of Pearson Education, Inc., Upper Saddle River, NJ.
Chapter 3 p. 91: Anahad O'Connor, "The Claim: You Can Treat a Snakebite by Sucking Out the Venom," *New York Times,* July 13, 2004. Copyright © 2004 by The New York Times Co. Reprinted with permission.; *p. 92:* Craig, Albert M.; Graham, William A.; Kagan, Donald M.; Ozment, Steven; Turner, Frank M., *Heritage of World Civilizations,* Combined Volume, 6th Edition, © 2003. Reprinted by permission of Pearson Education, Inc., Upper Saddle River, NJ.; *p. 93:* Scott Weaver, "The Power of Profanity," *The Depauw,* DePauw University, March 7, 2001. Reprinted by permission of DePauw University.; *pp. 108–109:* Erick Nagourney," Good Day, Sunshine: Why They Tan," *New York Times,* July 13, 2004.Copyright © 2004 by The New York Times Co. Reprinted with permission.; *pp. 112–113:* O'Connor, Anahad, "Dreams Ride on Freud's Royal Road, Study Finds." *New York Times,* March 23, 2004. Copyright © 2004 by The New York Times Co. Reprinted with permission.; *pp. 114–115:* Schmalleger, Frank, *Criminal Justice: A Brief Introduction,* 5th Edition, © 2004. Reprinted by permission of Pearson Education, Inc., Upper Saddle River, NJ.; *pp. 115–116:* Evans, Alan; Martin, Kendall; Poatsy, Mary Ann, *Technology In Action,* 3rd Edition, © 2007, pp. 354–355, 163, 139, 270–273. Reprinted by permission of Pearson Education, Inc., Upper Saddle River, NJ.; *pp. 117–118:* Anahad O'Connor, "The Claim: You Can Treat a Snakebite by Sucking Out the Venom," *New York Times,* July 13, 2004. Copyright © 2004 by The New York Times Co. Reprinted with permission.; *pp. 118–119:* Sherman, Mark. "Drug use by teenagers declines and continues its decline," Associated Press, December 19, 2003, p. A-3. Reprinted by permission.; p. 119: **I'm Sensitive**/Lyrics and Music by Jewel Kilcher/© 1994 EMI April Music Inc. and Wiggly Tooth Music/All Rights Controlled and Administered by EMI April Music Inc./All Rights Reserved. International Copyright Secured. Used by Permission.; *p. 121:* Dolphins Using Tools to Help in Hunting for Food, Associated Press, June 7, 2005. Reprinted by permission.; *pp. 122–123, 124, 125:* Thill, John V., *Excellence In Business Communication,* 6th Edition, © 2005. Reprinted by permission of Pearson Education, Inc., Upper Saddle River, NJ.; *pp. 126–127:* Evans, Alan; Martin, Kendall; Poatsy, Mary Ann, *Technology In Action,* 3rd Edition, © 2007, p. 139. Reprinted by permission of Pearson Education, Inc., Upper Saddle River, NJ.
Chapter 4 *p. 155:* Definition of "prepare" is from McKechnie/Webster's New Twentieth Century Dictionary of the English Language 2e. Copyright © 1983 by Simon & Schuster. Reprinted with permission of John Wiley & Sons, Inc.; *pp. 170–171:* Solomon, Andrew. "The Closing of the American Book," *New York Times,* July 10, 2004: © 2004, The New York Times. Reprinted by permission.; *p. 174:* Wade, Carole; Tavris, Carol, *Invitation To Psychology* 3rd Edition, © 2005. Reprinted by permission of Pearson Education, Inc., Upper Saddle River, NJ.
Motivation Matters 1 *pp. 177–178:* Excerpts from Saul Kassin, *Psychology*, 3rd edition, Prentice Hall. Reprinted by permission of the author.
Motivation Matters 2 *pp. 183–184:* Misconceptions About Reading from Joan Rasool, Caroline Banks, and Mary-Jane McCarthy, *Critical Thinking: Reading and Writing in a Diverse World,* Belmont, CA: Wadsworth Publishing Company, 1993, pp. 40–42. Reprinted by permission of the authors.
Chapter 5 *pp. 199–203:* Macionis, John J., *Sociology*, 10th Edition, © 2005. Reprinted by permission of Pearson Education, Inc., Upper Saddle River, NJ.; *pp. 212–213, 218:* Krogh, David, *Biology: Guide to the Natural World,* 3rd Edition, © 2005. Reprinted by permission of Pearson Education, Inc., Upper Saddle River, NJ.; *p. 225:* top left—Excerpts from *Prentice Hall Biology* by Kenneth R. Miller, Ph.D. and Joseph Levine, Ph.D. © 2002 by Pearson Education, Inc., publishing as Pearson Prentice Hall. Used by permission.; top right, bottom left—Saul Kassin, *Psychology*, 3rd edition, Prentice Hall. Reprinted by permission of the author; bottom right—Lindsey, Linda L., Beach, Stephen, *Essentials of Sociology,* © 2003. Reprinted by permission of Pearson Education, Inc., Upper Saddle River, NJ.; *p. 226:* Excerpts from *Prentice Hall Biology* by Kenneth R. Miller, Ph.D. and Joseph Levine, Ph.D. © 2002 by Pearson Education, Inc., publishing as Pearson Prentice Hall. Used by permission.; *pp. 230, 236–241:* Wade, Carole; Tavris, Carol, *Invitation to Psychology* 3rd Edition, © 2005. Reprinted by permission of Pearson Education, Inc., Upper Saddle River, NJ.; *pp. 231–232, 233–234:* Krogh, David, *Biology: Guide to the Natural World,* 3rd Edition, © 2005. Reprinted by permission of Pearson Education, Inc., Upper Saddle River, NJ.
Chapter 6 *pp. 252–253:* Boydston, Jeanne; Cullather, Nick; Lewis, Jan; McGerr, Michael; Oakes, James, *Making a Nation: The United States and its People,* Combined Edition, © 2002. Reprinted by permission of Pearson Education, Inc., Upper Saddle River, NJ.; *pp. 264–265, 266:* Benokraitis, Nijole V., *Marriages and Families: Changes, Choices, and Constraints,* 5th Edition, © 2005. Reprinted by permission of Pearson Education, Inc., Upper Saddle River, NJ.; *pp. 268, 300–301:* Krogh, David, *Biology: Guide to the Natural World,* 3rd Edition, © 2005. Reprinted by permission of Pearson Education, Inc., Upper Saddle River, NJ.; *pp. 290–291, 295–296:* Lindsey, Linda L., Beach, Stephen, *Essentials of Sociology,* © 2003. Reprinted by permission of Pearson Education, Inc., Upper Saddle River, NJ.; *pp. 291–292:* Hill, John W.; Kolb, Doris K., *Chemistry for Changing Times,* 10th Edition, © 2004, p. 145. Reprinted by permission of Pearson Education, Inc., Upper Saddle River, NJ.; *pp. 297–298:* Evans, Alan; Martin, Kendall; Poatsy, Mary Ann, *Technology in Action,* 3rd Edition, © 2007, p. 139. Reprinted by permission of Pearson Education, Inc., Upper Saddle River, NJ.; *pp. 302–303:* Benokraitis, Nijole V., *Marriages and Families: Changes, Choices, and Constraints,* 5th Edition, © 2005. Reprinted by permission of Pearson Education, Inc., Upper Saddle River, NJ.
Chapter 7 *pp. 308 ff.* : Boydston, Jeanne; Cullather, Nick; Lewis, Jan; McGerr, Michael; Oakes, James, *Making a Nation: The United States and its People,* Combined Edition, © 2002. Reprinted by permission of Pearson Education, Inc., Upper Saddle River, NJ.; *pp. 308 ff.*: Benokraitis, Nijole V., *Marriages and Families: Changes, Choices, and Constraints,* 5th Edition, © 2005. Reprinted by permission of Pearson Education, Inc., Upper Saddle River, NJ.; *pp. 309 ff.*: Excerpts from Saul Kassin, *Psychology*, 3rd edition, Prentice Hall. Reprinted by permission of the author.; *pp. 310 ff.*: Macionis, John J., *Sociology*, 10th Edition, © 2005. Reprinted by permission of Pearson Education, Inc., Upper Saddle River, NJ.; *pp. 312 ff.*: Schmalleger, Frank, *Criminal Justice: A Brief Introduction,* 5th Edition, © 2004. Reprinted by permission of Pearson Education, Inc., Upper Saddle River, NJ.; *pp. 313 ff.*: Krogh, David, *Biology: Guide to the Natural World,* 3rd Edition, © 2005. Reprinted by permission of Pearson Education, Inc., Upper Saddle River, NJ. ; *pp. 316–317 ff.*: Craig, Albert M.; Graham, William A.; Kagan, Donald M.; Ozment, Steven; Turner, Frank M., *Heritage of World Civilizations,* Combined Volume, 6th Edition, © 2003. Reprinted by permission of Pearson Education, Inc., Upper Saddle River, NJ.; *pp. 319 ff.*: Hill, John W.; Kolb, Doris K., *Chemistry for Changing Times,* 10th Edition, © 2004, p. 145. Reprinted by permission of Pearson Education, Inc., Upper Saddle River, NJ.; *pp. 321 ff.*: Lindsey, Linda L., Beach, Stephen, *Essentials of Sociology,* © 2003. Reprinted by permission of Pearson Education, Inc., Upper Saddle River, NJ.; *pp. 325 ff.*: Armstrong, Gary; Kotler, Philip, *Marketing: An Introduction,* 6th Edition, © 2003, pp. 300, 191–199. Reprinted by permission of Pearson Education, Inc., Upper Saddle River, NJ.; *pp. 333 ff.*: Excerpts from *Prentice Hall Biology* by Kenneth R. Miller, Ph.D. and Joseph Levine, Ph.D. © 2002 by Pearson Education, Inc., publishing as Pearson Prentice Hall. Used by permission.
Chapter 8 *pp. 359, 368, 370:* Benokraitis, Nijole V., *Marriages and Families: Changes, Choices, and Constraints,*5th Edition, © 2005. Reprinted

by permission of Pearson Education, Inc., Upper Saddle River, NJ.; *p. 363:* Boydston, Jeanne; Cullather, Nick; Lewis, Jan; McGerr, Michael; Oakes, James, *Making a Nation: The United States and its People,* Combined Edition, © 2002. Reprinted by permission of Pearson Education, Inc., Upper Saddle River, NJ.; Fig. 5-3 adapted from *Encyclopedia of North American Colonies* by Charles Scribner's Sons, © 1993, Charles Scribner's Sons. Reprinted by permission of The Gale Group.; *p. 364:* Griffin, Ricky W., Ebert, Ronald J., *Business,* 8th Edition, © 2006, pp. 58–66. Reprinted by permission of Pearson Education, Inc., Upper Saddle River, NJ.; *pp. 365, 371:* Macionis, John J., *Sociology,* 10th Edition, © 2005. Reprinted by permission of Pearson Education, Inc., Upper Saddle River, NJ.; *pp. 366, 367:* Lindsey, Linda L., Beach, Stephen, *Essentials of Sociology,* Reprinted by permission of Pearson Education, Inc., Upper Saddle River, NJ.; *pp. 372–373, 378:* Wade, Carole; Tavris, Carol, *Invitation to Psychology* 3rd Edition, © 2005. Reprinted by permission of Pearson Education, Inc., Upper Saddle River, NJ.; *pp. 373–374:* Hill, John W.; Kolb, Doris K., *Chemistry for Changing Times,* 10th Edition, © 2004, p. 145. Reprinted by permission of Pearson Education, Inc., Upper Saddle River, NJ.; *p. 377:* Schmalleger, Frank, *Criminal Justice: A Brief Introduction,* 5th Edition, © 2004. Reprinted by permission of Pearson Education, Inc., Upper Saddle River, NJ.

Motivation Matters 3 *pp. 381–383:* A Flow of Questions in *Seven Reading Strategies.* Greenwich, Conn: Baldridge Reading and Study Skills, Inc. 1974. Reprinted by permission.

Motivation Matters 4 *pp. 388–389:* Excerpts from Saul Kassin, *Psychology,* 3rd edition, Prentice Hall. Reprinted by permission of the author.

Chapter 9 *pp. 404–405:* Gilbert Ross, "Winter is Flu Season, but Maybe It Doesn't Have to Be," *New York Times,* December 27, 2004, Letter to the Ed. Reprinted by permission of The American Council on Science and Health.; *pp. 410–411:* Excerpt from "Cell Phones Destroy Solitude of Wilderness," The Associated Press, ÊJuly 5, 1999. ÊReprinted by permission.; *p. 419:* Imrem, Mike, "Character Isn't What We've Built," DAILY HERALD, August 10, 1985. Reprinted by permission.; *pp. 422–423:* Krogh, David, *Biology: Guide to the Natural World,* 3rd Edition, © 2005. Reprinted by permission of Pearson Education, Inc., Upper Saddle River, NJ.; *pp. 425–426:* Laura Sahramaa, "When Patriotism Runs Amuck," *The Cavalier Daily,* University of Virginia, October 23, 2001. Reprinted by permission of The Cavalier Daily.; *pp. 428–429:* Cleveland, Delia, "Champagne Taste, Beer Budget," originally published in *Essence* Magazine, March 2001. Reprinted by permission of the author. Delia Cleveland is a freelance writer and novelist. She speaks widely on young adult empowerment to public schools throughout New York City.; *pp. 431–433:* Suniti Puri, "Cultural Identity vs. Ethnic Fashions," *The Yale Herald,* February 2, 2001. Reprinted by permission of The Yale Herald.; *pp. 434–435:* Susan Messer, excerpt from "What You Give and What You Get." From *Chicago Reader,* October 15, 1999, copyright (c) 1999 by Susan Messer. All rights reserved. Reprinted by permission of author.; *pp. 438–439:* Perez-Pena, Richard, "A City of Quitters? In Strict New York, 11% Fewer Smokers," *New York Times,* May 12, 2004. Copyright © 2004 by the New York Times Co. Reprinted with permission.; *pp. 441–442:* Neergaard, Lauran, "Government Sets New Rules on Who Can Donate Sperm, Eggs, Skin, Other Tissue," Associated Press, May 20, 2004, p. A-3. Reprinted by permission.; *pp. 445–446:* Wong, May, "Three Days without a Word becomes an Eternity," Associated Press Technology Writer, as found in *North County Times,* 12/19/04. Reprinted by permission.; *pp. 450–453:* Figeroa, Teri, "Free Speech a Balancing Act for Schools," *North County Times,* September 20, 2004, A-1. Reprinted by permission.; *pp. 445–459:* Zimring, Franklin. "Confessions of an Ex-Smoker," *Newsweek,* 4/20/87. Reprinted by permission of the author.; *pp. 460–462:* Will Keim, "A Not-So-Random Act of Kindess" is reprinted by permission of the author.; *p. 464: USA Today,* 1/14/05. Reprinted with permission.

Chapter 10 *p. 483:* Elizabeth Crane, excerpt from "Do Toys Guns Teach Violence? No." First appeared in *Brain, Child* magazine, Spring 2001. Copyright © 2001 by Elizabeth Crane. Reprinted by permission of the author.; *pp. 485–487:* Excerpt from "Mall Culture" by Steven L. Shepherd, from the *Humanist,* 1998. Reprinted with permission of the *Humanist* magazine.; *pp. 488–489:* From *Newsweek,* May 7, 2001, © 2001 Newsweek, Inc. All rights reserved. Reprinted by permission.; *pp. 491–492:* Lip-synching Standard Practice, Associated Press, as found in *North County Times,* November 7, 2004. Reprinted by permission.; *pp. 493–495:* Jim Trageser, "Voters Key to Election Security," *North County Times,* Opinion, 11/9/04. Reprinted by permission of the *North County Times.*; *pp. 508–509:* Eric Cohen and William Kristol, "No, It's a Moral Monstrosity," *Wall Street Journal,* December 5, 2001. Copyright 2001 by Dow Jones & Company, Inc.. Reproduced with permission of Dow Jones & Company, Inc. in the format Textbook via Copyright Clearance Center.; *pp. 516–518:* Kristien McDonald, "A SOARing Insult to Science" from *The Daily Utah Chronicle,* 4/19/01. Reprinted by permission.; *pp. 520–522:* © 2002 by National Review Online, www.nationalreview.com. Reprinted by permission.; *pp. 524–525:* © 2006 Time Inc. Reprinted by permission.

Motivation Matters 5 *pp. 528–530:* "What You Don't Get Out of a College Education" by Richard L. Weaver, II from *Vital Speeches of the Day,* 7/15/03, Volume 69, Issue 19. Reprinted by permission of the author.

The Reader *pp. 538–539:* "Pop Culture is Destroying True Beauty," Rachel Drevno, *The Spectator Online,* Seattle University, October 11, 2001. Reprinted by permission of Rachel Drevno.; *pp. 544–549:* Excerpts from Saul Kassin, *Psychology,* 3rd edition, Prentice Hall. Reprinted by permission of the author.; *pp. 555–556:* Saritha Rai, "Indian Companies are Adding Western Flavor, *New York Times,* College Section, August 19, 2003.Copyright © 2003 by The New York Times Co. Reprinted with permission.; *pp. 561–569:* Thill, John V., *Excellence in Business Communication,* 6th Edition, © 2005. Reprinted by permission of Pearson Education, Inc., Upper Saddle River, NJ.; *pp. 574–576:* © 1997, The Washington Post Writers Group. Reprinted with permission.; *pp.581–583:* Boydston, Jeanne; Cullather, Nick; Lewis, Jan; McGerr, Michael; Oakes, James, *Making a Nation: The United States and its People,* Combined Edition, 1st Edition, © 2002. Reprinted by permission of Pearson Education, Inc., Upper Saddle River, NJ.; *pp. 588–590:* Copyright 2006 U.S. News & World Report, L.P. Reprinted with permission.; *pp. 595–601:* Belk, Colleen; Borden, Virginia, *Biology: Science for Life,* 2nd edition, © 2007, pp. 72–76. Reprinted by permission of Pearson Education, Inc., Upper Saddle River, NJ.

Photo Credits

Chapter 1 p. 1 (left): Vicky Kasala/Getty Images, Inc.—Photodisc; p. 1 (center): AP Wide World Photos; p. 1 (right) JIM CUMMINS/ Getty Images, Inc. – Taxi (right); p. 9 (top): Mike Kemp/ Getty Images Inc—Rubberball Royalty Free; p.9 (center top): Bruce Laurance/Getty Images – Photodisc; p. 9 (center bottom): Getty Images Inc—Rubberball Royalty Free; p. 9 (bottom): Kaoru Fujimoto/Taxi/Getty Images; p. 11: © Zits partnership. King Features Syndicate.

Chapter 2 p. 31 (left): Erik Dreyer/Stone/Getty Images; p. 31 (center): White Packert/Getty Images – Iconica; p. 31 (right): Photodisc/Getty Images; p. 36 (top left): Palmer/Kane; p. 36 (top right): SuperStock, Inc.; p. 36 (bottom): Peanuts: (c) United Feature Syndicate, Inc.; p. 64: Kevin Fleming/Corbis/Bettmann

Chapter 3 p. 87 (left): Tony Dizinno/Allsport Concepts/Getty Images; p. 87 (center): Esbin/Anderson/Omni-Photo Communications, Inc.; p. 87(right): FogStock LLC / Index Open; p. 94: © 1998 Randy Glasbergen

Chapter 4 p. 133 (left): www.indexopen.com; p. 133 (center): Jose L. Pelaez/Corbis/Stock Market; p. 133 (right): Michael Newman/ PhotoEdit Inc.; p.139: ScienceCartoonsPlus.com.

Chapter 5 p.189 (left): Gary Conner/PhotoEdit Inc; p. 189 (center): Will & Deni McIntyre/ Photo Researchers, Inc.; p. 189 (right): Skjold Photographs; p.200: Bill Bachmann/ The Image Works; p.210: Reproduced by Peaco Todd.; p. 237 (top left): Jessica T. Offir; p.237 (top right): Earl Roberge/ Photo Researchers, Inc.; p.237 (bottom): R. Hutchings/ PhotoEdit Inc.; p.239: Chandoha Photography

Chapter 6 p. 243 (top left): Gary Conner/PhotoEdit Inc.; p. 243 (center and right): Fabio Cardoso/ AGE Fotostock America, Inc.; p. 246 (left): www.CartoonStock.com; p. 246 (right): Don Addis, Creators Syndicate

Chapter 7 p. 305 (left): Upitis, Alvis/Getty Images Inc.—Image Bank; p. 305 (center): Frank La Bua/ Pearson Education/PH College; p. 305 (right): Jon Feingersh/ Corbis Zefa Col-

lection; p. 318: www.cartoonstock.com
Chapter 8 p. 355 (center): Shutterstock; p. 358: www.cartoonstock.com
Chapter 9 p. 395 (left): www.indexopen.com; p. 395 (center): Serge Krouglikoff/Corbis Zefa Collection; p. 395 (right): ImageState/International Stock Photography Ltd.; p.436: www.cartoonstock.com
Chapter 10 p. 469 (left): Annabella Bluesky/Photo Researchers, Inc.; p. 469 (center): Corbis Royalty Free; p. 469 (right): ImageState/International Stock Photography Ltd.; p. 474: (c) Zits Partnership. Reprinted with special permission of King Features Syndicate.
The Reader: p. 535: Photodisc/Getty Images; p. 545: Match.com; p. 547 (top left): Gerard Sioen; p. 547 (top right): George Steinmetz Photography; p. 547 (bottom left): Anthony Cassidy/Getty Images Inc.—Stone Allstock; p. 547 (bottom right): Mark Mainz/Getty Images, Inc—Liaison; p. 562: Brian Coats Photography; p. 567: John Abbott/John Abbott Photography

Index